Women's Political Voice

In the series

WOMEN IN THE POLITICAL ECONOMY

edited by RONNIE J. STEINBERG

Women's Political Voice

*How Women
Are Transforming
the Practice and Study
of Politics*

Janet A. Flammang

TEMPLE UNIVERSITY PRESS
Philadelphia

TEMPLE UNIVERSITY PRESS, PHILADELPHIA 19122

Printed in the United States of America

∞ The paper used in this book meets the requirements of the
American National Standard for Information Sciences—
Permanence of Paper for Printed Library Materials,
ANSI Z39.48-1984

Text design by Gary Gore

Library of Congress Cataloging-in-Publication Data

Flammang, Janet A.
    Women's political voice : how women are transforming the practice
and study of politics / Janet A. Flammang.
        p.   cm. — (Women in the political economy)
    Includes bibliographical references and index.
    ISBN 1-56639-533-X (cloth : alk. paper). — ISBN 1-56639-534-8
(pbk. : alk. paper)
    1. Women in politics—United States—History.   2. Political science—
Research—United States.   3. Feminist theory—United States.   I. Title.
II. Series.
HQ1236.5.U6F53   1997
320'.082—dc20   96-35873

To Lee, Alexander, and Jacob Friedman

Contents

Preface: The Puzzle of the Feminist Capital ix
Acknowledgments xiii

Part One: Women's Political Voice in the Academy and the Community

1 Women's Political Voice in Political Science 3
The Women's Movement Challenges Conventional Wisdom in the Academy

2 Women's Political Life in Santa Clara County 35
A Favorable Climate for Women's Political Activism

Part Two: Women and Mass Politics

3 Political Mobilization 57
Women's Shift from Individual to Group Consciousness and Activity

4 Political Participation 96
Women's Civic Activity in Communities and the State

Part Three: Women and Elite Politics

5 Political Recruitment 149
Women's Distinctive Path to Public Office

6 Policy Preferences and Political Style 196
Female Officials as Liberal Feminist Problem Solvers

Part Four: Women and Elite-Mass Interaction

7   Agenda Setting   253
    Women Bring New Issues to Public Attention

8   Political Coalitions   297
    The Hard Work of Sisterhood

    Notes   357
    Index   403

Preface

The Puzzle of the Feminist Capital

THIS BOOK is the result of a decade-long intellectual journey to answer a seemingly simple question posed by a student in 1982: Why is Santa Clara County called the feminist capital of the nation? As a professor of political science and women's studies, I was embarrassed that I did not have a quick answer to her question. In retrospect, I can see why I did not. Women's studies scholars had written extensively about feminist theory and the women's movement, but this scholarship had not been systematically brought to bear on many empirical case studies. Political scientists had conducted many empirical studies, but virtually none of them had focused on a feminist presence in local politics. Although I took these two bodies of scholarship with me as maps, I had the distinct impression that I was entering uncharted territory.

Why would local women see themselves as inhabiting a feminist capital? Did local women's self-understandings of feminism bear any relationship to the writings of feminist theory? Did women's politics look the same as the men's politics so well documented in mainstream political science? The logical place to begin was to talk with local female officials and activists.[1] What I learned from these interviews was that local women were both shaped by and shapers of the women's movement and feminist thought; that the women's movement was a political, not just a social, movement; and that the standard categories used in political science were only partially helpful in making sense of what I observed. Concepts from women's studies were useful correctives to conventional wisdom: consciousness-raising, the personal is political, group identity, women as the fundamental unit of analysis, and the like. Political science seemed resistant to group analysis, relying instead on surveying individual preferences in public opinion polls. So what began as a simple case study of local politics soon became an excursion into the limitations of political science as a field of study.

Along the way I discovered that theorists of the sociology of knowledge were correct: with very few exceptions, women, not men, thought women's politics was worthy of study. And although some women embraced the concepts and methods of political science uncritically, many found them to have limited utility. In the pages that follow, I place these scholars on a continuum: at one end are accommodationists, who believe the discipline needs only marginal adjustments to comprehend women's politics; at the other end are transformationalists, who maintain that the discipline needs to undergo fundamental changes.

I conclude that the discipline of political science needs to move in the transformational direction if it wants to capture the full picture of women's politics. This book is structured to provide evidence to support this claim. I engage the discipline on its own ground by focusing on standard political science concepts and demonstrating their deficiencies. There are six concept chapters: two describe "mass politics" (political mobilization and political participation); two deal with "elite politics" (political recruitment, and policy preferences and political style); and two involve "elite-mass interaction" (agenda setting and political coalitions). Each chapter demonstrates how women's politics and scholarship have transformed our understanding of a concept, using a three-part structure: what the discipline has had to say about it, how accommodationist and transformational feminists have challenged conventional wisdom, and how the need for a transformed concept is illustrated in the case of women's politics in Santa Clara County.

Of course, this book is addressed not just to those who care about transforming the discipline of political science. It is aimed at readers who want to understand contemporary women's politics in the United States—from increased awareness of domestic violence and sexual harassment, to growing numbers of women in public office and the gender gap, to calls for pay equity and an end to the feminization of poverty. The key is apprehending the political significance of the women's movement. First-wave feminists challenged the exclusion of women from male-dominated politics, and second-wave feminists changed the male-dominated nature of politics itself. In turn, the study of politics was modified by feminist scholarship about what these women were saying and doing. In both transformations, theory and practice developed alongside each other, crossing the artificial boundaries of academic disciplines. For example, in the women's movement, consciousness-raising groups developed the theoretical insight that the personal is political, and feminist scholars used this insight to shed light on the public-private split in Western political theory and to reclassify women's community activities as political.

It has been with great reluctance and resistance that the academic discipline of political science has come to terms with these transformations, well behind the other social sciences and the humanities. "Politics" referred to nation-state and electoral behavior, and "social movements" were left to sociologists. The only groups worthy of study were political parties and interest groups, because they were participants in electoral politics; women's behavior as a group was interesting only insofar as women voted, had opinions, joined parties, or formed a cohesive interest group. Insider decision making was more interesting than outsider change. Formal, measurable activity was more appropriately the stuff of politics than were the informal politics of everyday life. The keepers of conventional wisdom seemed oblivious or resistant to more than two decades of women's movement activity and ideas, a doubling of the number of women in elected office, a completely new women's policy agenda, and hundreds of publications about women and politics by feminist scholars. Scores of women, but only a handful of men, conducted feminist research, which appeared in specialized journals and was absent from the *American Political Science Review*. Women and politics courses were not routinely offered by tenured faculty in the major political science Ph.D.-granting departments, let alone required of newly minted graduates of these programs. The field of women and politics was regarded by many as a fad, with no epistemological, methodological, or empirical justification for its existence.

Most male political scientists did not familiarize themselves with the literature on women and politics, either because they thought such writings were intrinsically not worth knowing about or because it sufficed that their female colleagues had specialized knowledge in this area. Of course, not all women in the discipline were familiar with this literature either. And even among those female political scientists who conducted feminist research, feminist theorists and feminist empiricists rarely listened to each other. Although their work became increasingly informed by the other "camp" over the years, the two groups seldom appeared on the same professional panels or referred to each other in their publications.

In this book I argue that there are epistemological, methodological, and empirical justifications for feminist scholarship that must be recognized in order to discover important truths about the contemporary political world of women. I synthesize the arguments and findings of hundreds of writings that document how, since the 1960s, women have been transforming the practice and study of politics. These writings are interdisciplinary (although primarily from political science), theoretical, and empirical. I hope to demonstrate that an adequate answer to a question about women's feminist political identity in one locality entails a fascinating journey into the realm of socially constructed knowledge. The puzzle of the feminist capital was ultimately a puzzle about the political life of American women swept up in the second wave of a women's movement, which posed a new political question: Is this right and good for women? And the public, the media, the government, and the academy have been grappling with the consequences of this radical query ever since.

Acknowledgments

I AM extremely grateful to Joan Tronto for her thoughtful comments on an earlier draft of this book, and to Shirl Buss and Alma Garcia for their ideas about Chapter 8.

Dee Ann Dixon Hazani posed the question, "Professor Flammang, why is San Jose called the feminist capital of the nation?" My thoughts at the time were in the rarefied world of feminist theory, and I supposed that I could get back to her with an answer after a few months of research. Here is my answer more than a decade later. My thanks to her and to all the Santa Clara University students in my women and politics courses, whose interest, questions, and observations kept this project alive for me. Melissa Lehane's research was superb.

I am indebted to Santa Clara University, which generously supported my work with course releases and Presidential Research Grants.

Fanny Rinn was a mentor for me in this project from the outset: suggesting names of people to interview, reading drafts of manuscripts, and providing detailed editorial comments. I am grateful for her selfless dedication to young scholars and her excitement about delving into the complexity of women's politics at the local level. In her honor and memory, I hope to pass on to other scholars an enthusiasm for researching women's politics.

All those I interviewed gave generously of themselves in conversations that invariably went over the time requested. Each interview contributed in an important way to my understanding of women's politics. I am also grateful to the many scholars whose pathbreaking work has given voice to women's political concerns.

Finally, thanks to family, friends, colleagues, and Michael Ames at Temple University Press for their patience and encouragement.

Part One

*Women's Political Voice in the
Academy and the Community*

Part One

1 Women's Political Voice in Political Science

The Women's Movement Challenges Conventional Wisdom in the Academy

WHY DID political scientists fail to see the political significance of the women's movement? Possibly it was because until the 1970s, almost all political scientists were men who considered their politics more interesting and important than those of women. To take nineteenth-century politics as an example, men found nation-building, war, and diplomacy more interesting than the suffrage, temperance, and settlement house movements. Scholarly interest in women's politics grew as the number of women in the discipline increased. But the absence of women was only part of the explanation. Many female political scientists found that when they tried to understand the political significance of the women's movement, the discipline's tools were flawed in three important ways: epistemologically, methodologically, and empirically.

Conventional political science epistemology posits objective observers who study atomistic, autonomous individuals; feminists posit gendered observers of socially interdependent people. It uses neutral categories in value-free research to construct universal theories; feminists use socially constructed categories in value-encoded research to construct socially contingent theories. Conventional political scientists seek explanations; feminists, understanding and interpretation. The conventional approach tacitly assumes that the male is normative; feminists uncover this tacit assumption. Conventional political scientists think quantitative methods and survey research techniques that impose concepts and meanings on respondents are adequate to the task of cap-

3

turing the most important features of people's political lives; feminists prefer qualitative methods such as participant observation and intensive, open-ended interviews that do not impose concepts and meanings on people. And there are important differences in what the two camps find empirically interesting, or worth knowing about: state vs. community, government vs. politics, military state vs. welfare state, stability vs. change, powerful vs. powerless, insiders vs. outsiders, elite vs. mass, interest groups vs. social movements, electoral politics vs. family politics, political parties vs. voluntary associations, opinions vs. consciousness, power over vs. power to, force vs. empowerment, rights vs. responsibilities, public-private separation vs. public-private integration, and the separation of politics and morality vs. the integration of politics and morality.

The Invisibility of Women's Politics in Political Science

In the United States the academic discipline of political science began in 1880, when the first graduate program in the field was established at Columbia University by John W. Burgess, whose scholarly concern was improving state-building in the German mode. He opposed women's suffrage for fear it would turn middle-class women away from their voluntary, charitable work, which would then be taken over by the state. As a proponent of limited government, Burgess saw an expansion of the social welfare state as an incursion on individual liberty. In addition, he was alarmed by the Progressive claim that women would have a distinctive point of view in government, and he opted for the separate spheres argument, namely, that women should remain in "their sphere of communal action" while government and politics should be left to men. The discipline's professional association, the American Political Science Association (APSA), was founded in 1903. The two most important journals during this time were Burgess's *Political Science Quarterly,* published at Columbia beginning in 1886, and the APSA's *American Political Science Review,* first published in 1906. Both journals paid scant attention to women's suffrage or any other women's issues. Between their respective foundings and the mid-1920s, the *Political Science Quarterly* published 1,038 articles, only 10 of which dealt with women; and only 3 of the *American Political Science Review's* 406 articles dealt with women.[1]

Barbara Nelson notes the gender bias in the early days of the discipline. Its epistemology was a positivist dualism: "An omniscient, rational, neutral, separated observer recorded and analyzed political and historical events, discerning patterns that repeated over time"; the separation of the political tasks and places of women and men was "a positivist reconstruction of the dualism of the Enlightenment, a dualism that defined reason, rationality, severity, and action as male and emotion, irrationality, generosity, and dependency as female." Methodologically and empirically, early political scientists emphasized statutory governmental forms and official functions over individual or group actions: "A state-centered view of politics emphasized the offices and activities where men predominated. Women were often legally and customarily excluded from precisely the activities and positions that the authors defined as essentially political. The authors ignored women's efforts in social movements directed at their own enfranchisement just as they did not comment on the role of women in the creation of the welfare state."[2]

Political scientists seemed indifferent to the fact that there were no scholarly books devoted exclusively to women in American political life. That changed in 1968 with the publication of Martin Gruberg's *Women in American Politics*, which challenged the discipline by taking women's politics seriously enough to write a book about it, dethroning a state-centered view of politics, finding political significance in women's organizational activities, and letting women speak for themselves through the extensive use of quotations, a methodology deemed unrigorous by many in the discipline.[3] Gruberg located the roots of women's political subordination deep in the subconscious and in American culture. Things would change only by an act of women's will and organization. Women had to change sex-role socialization, provide girls with citizenship programs and role models, alter school curricula, and promote job and educational opportunities for women.

Gruberg could see such acts of women's will and organization looming on the horizon, as the nation began to reassess its attitude toward women. To support this claim, he cited three political events that we now know were emblematic of an emerging women's movement: President Kennedy's creation of the Commission on the Status of Women (1961), Betty Friedan's publication of *The Feminine Mystique* (1963), and Republican Senator Margaret Chase Smith's candidacy for the presidency (1964).[4] A closer look at these three events illustrates important themes of this book: that the academy reconsidered women's politics in response to the women's movement, that the women's movement was a dynamic relationship between political insiders and outsiders, and that political scientists' claims to understanding the political world were only partial until they paid attention to what female activists and officials were doing.

Journalist Betty Friedan wrote about the problem of women's vicarious identity through husband and children and recommended women's increased labor force participation. In 1966, she became a founding member of the National Organization for Women (NOW), an organization formed by women critical of the federal government's inattention to sex discrimination, which had recently been made illegal. President Kennedy, in need of the female vote in 1964 that had gone to Nixon in 1960, had established the Commission on the Status of Women in 1961 to identify discriminatory laws so that an Equal Rights Amendment would not be necessary. The pro-labor faction in the Democratic party had opposed the ERA for fear it would undo protective labor laws for women, and the Republican party gained points with business and professional women for its support of the amendment.[5] And in 1964, insider Senator Margaret Chase Smith (R-Maine) boldly challenged the sanctity of separate spheres in a speech announcing her candidacy for the presidency: "We often hear the comment that 'women are all right in their place.' But what is their place? The answer of practically all men and women is The Home. You never hear the comment that 'men are all right in their place,' because their place has never been restricted."[6]

Smith's relationship to women's groups reflected the historical transformations in such organizations that had occurred during her political lifetime, namely, the 1940s to the early 1970s. Smith credited Business and Professional Women (BPW) for her first political success, in a 1940 congressional race, since it gave her leadership opportunities and an apprenticeship in public service.[7] BPW had been formed during World War I, when the secretary of war was anxious to recruit the services of business and professional women in the war effort; by 1968, there were 174,000 members in 3,550 clubs nationwide. BPW sought to promote the interests of business and professional women and to encourage their political participation. It consistently supported the Equal Rights Amendment, along with equal pay and uniform social security retirement benefits.[8] In the Senate, Smith supported the ERA and prevented her colleagues from adding hostile amendments to the 1964 Civil Rights Act, which outlawed race and sex discrimination in employment. Smith warned her fellow Republicans that they could not afford to be seen as anti-woman. She also publicly expressed attitudes and supported policies at odds with the new women's movement, however. She rejected feminism for seeking special privileges for women. Smith saw herself as an exceptional woman, with no special affinity to women as a group, and she supported a strong military buildup. In her unsuccessful reelection bid for the Senate in 1972, the Maine NOW chapter actively worked against her.[9]

It would take two decades of feminist scholarship to unearth the complex relationship among the ERA, partisan concern about attracting the women's vote, the agendas of women's groups and elected female officials, the mobilization of female campaign workers, and the federal government's role in the creation of women's groups (BPW directly and NOW indirectly). Meanwhile, during the 1960s and 1970s, the women's movement proceeded apace while an oblivious discipline of political science went about business as usual. After Gruberg's pioneering book, the task shifted to female political scientists to alert the discipline to its shortcomings.

Earliest Feminist Critiques of Political Science: 1974

The first three salvos were fired in 1974. One was an accommodationist appeal to the discipline to add to its lexicon "gender roles" as an explanatory variable, based on an interdisciplinary literature review of more than two hundred works published over five years. The other two were full-blown transformational critiques of the discipline.

The cautious critique, by Wilma Rule Krauss, appeared in the prestigious *American Political Science Review,* a journal that never became an outlet for feminist revision of the discipline.[10] Krauss defended the sociological notion of gender roles as an explanatory variable for understanding "the complex of civic cultural relations," which both caused and were affected by political participation (e.g., voting, campaigning, and officeholding). She wanted to remove barriers to women's political participation; unlike later critics, she did not challenge the discipline's definition of political participation. In carving out "civic cultural relations" as an important part of political life, however, she called into question the standard political science practice of divorcing politics from culture, which was usually left to the anthropologists. Krauss was concerned with both explanation (determining causal variables for politics) and understanding (making sense of politics), emphasized both behavior (political science) and thought (political theory), and called attention to the women's protest movement as a subject worthy of study.[11] These concerns emerged even more centrally in two other critical essays published in the same year.

Susan C. Bourque and Jean Grossholtz catalogued male bias in the political science classics of the 1950s and 1960s.[12] Some authors were so quick to accept sex roles as natural or necessary that they made assertions without evidence; for example, that childrearing responsibilities led to permanent sex differences in political participation.[13] Expecting to find sex-role differentiation, one researcher distorted original sources, which had in fact found evidence of role sharing.[14] Some political scientists had assumed, without evidence, that just because a husband and wife voted the same way, the husband had influenced the wife's decision.[15] Women were described as "moralistic," without a clear definition of what was meant by that term but with the assumption that moralistic concerns were either irrelevant or unsophisticated.

Male political behavior was the norm. Evidence for boys' "natural enthusiasm" for politics came from a study in which most of the boys (9 of 12) and none of the girls (0 of 9) liked pictures of war; when a girl's response to how she would like to change the world was "get rid of all the criminals and bad guys," this response was labeled "distinctly nonpolitical."[16] When girls were more likely than boys to describe the rich and labor unions as powerful, political scientists saw yet "another expression of the tendency of girls to personalize the governmental process."[17] When men voiced higher levels of political efficacy than women, they were seen as more political, despite the fact that it could be argued that women were more realistic in their appraisal of the political influence any one individual could have.[18] It was assumed that women personalized politics. One political scientist said that in the 1952 presidential elections, women were more "candidate oriented" than men. Yet on the same page he cited a poll indicating that in the campaign, women were more concerned than men with the issues of the Korean war and allegations of government corruption.[19] The author did not comment on this seeming contradiction, which was especially odd since Eisenhower's candidacy was so focused on ending the Korean war. It was just assumed to be natural that women would be more swayed by the personal attractiveness of the candidate and that men would have issue reasons for their votes.

Even when women managed to make their way into top decision-making posts, male researchers often failed to see them or downplayed their significance. One political scientist described the "men" in a local power structure, even though five of the powerful were women.[20] Another described the "men" who were local subleaders, even though one-third were women.[21] Another researcher asserted that the presence of women as decision makers on a bond issue reinforced his judgment that these decision makers were relatively less powerful than other decision makers. Women leaders in this study were categorized as "specialists" rather than the more powerful "decision makers" or "influentials." "Specialists" were highly educated people with "an exceptional interest in community improvement of a welfare kind."[22]

Implicit assumptions about women's nature and proper sphere got in the way of doing good political science: females were emotional, domestic, moralistic, personalistic, invisible, or nonconsequential decision makers, and community minded do-gooders. Males were political, reasonable, influential decision makers. It was not part of the gestalt of these researchers to look at the political world from the point of view of women. If they had, they might have taken into account factors such as that suggested by Katie Loucheim, former Democratic Women's Division director, who said, "The discreet wife, if she is at all clever, will not say that it was she who influenced her husband, but rather will go around saying, 'I voted the way my husband did.' A great many women do this even though it is they who have influenced their husbands."[23] In the context of a woman's economic dependence on, and perceived need to appear subservient to, a husband, one might have to dig for the true meaning of political behavior by using qualitative methodologies to supplement quantitative approaches. One had to listen to women to do good political science.

Bourque and Grossholtz faulted political scientists for proffering explanations based on social norms while ignoring the government's role in maintaining such norms. On this point they quoted New York congressmember and women's movement leader Bella Abzug: "I suggest what is really ludicrous is a political structure that denies representation to a majority of its population and then winds up fingering the victims of this situation as somehow responsible for it because of personal inadequacies."[24] The women's movement critique of a "blame the victim" mentality had made its way into the discipline.

The third early salvo was fired by Mary Shanley and Victoria Schuck, who argued that the three most important clues to understanding why political science had ignored women were the discipline's definition of "political," the kinds of questions asked, and the methodologies used in the two approaches that had dominated thinking in the discipline since 1903: legalistic institutionalism and behaviorism.[25]

Early political scientists adopted an approach to the study of politics which saw Anglo-American democracy capping the evolution of political systems, fostering a complacency about maintaining the political system as it was. No wonder scant attention was paid to the thousands of women who organized to obtain the right to vote in an already perfected system. Early political scientists differed over the wisdom and justice of women's suffrage. The author of a popular 1916 textbook argued that women were "mentally inferior to men in those particular aptitudes required for the proper exercise of political rights," and that since women voted as their male relatives directed them, their vote "would unfairly duplicate the voting power of their male relatives." For many of these early political scientists, "the evolution of the state from the family was a natural one, and the division of political labor (or the division of social labor, assigning the domestic part of it to women and the political part to men) seemed perfectly 'natural' and unquestionable."[26] In scrutinizing formal governmental structures and processes (statutes, ordinances, charters, and written constitutions), scholars never stumbled on what women were doing politically.

The behavioral revolution, which began to dominate the discipline in the 1950s, pushed aside dusty legal documents and formal institutions and focused instead on the concrete behavior of the individuals and groups who carried out institutional functions. Description was replaced by explanation and prediction. Behaviorists sought to make the study of politics a science, discovering the rules and regularities of political behavior and specifying the variables that produced it. As empiricists they eschewed matters that were not observable, and as scientists they said they were not concerned with evaluating or passing judgment on the activities they observed. The discipline became bifurcated into "political scientists," who objectively studied facts, and "political theorists," who speculated about values, ethics, and the collective good, primarily through scrutiny of the classic texts of political philosophy. But the behavioral revolution was no revolution in the study of women's politics, as Shanley and Schuck pointed out: "One set of blinders was replaced by another. Just as the study of institutional procedures and processes injected a bias into the study of politics, so behaviorism shaped what political science would learn about women. Method is not neutral; it establishes the criteria by which one judges the validity of conclusions, and consequently carries with it not simply technical skills but deeper philosophical commitments and implications."[27]

Shanley and Schuck noted that behaviorism's concentration on the regularities of political behavior implicitly assumed that irregularities were not worth studying. For example, organizing and protesting to obtain the right to vote was irregular; what was regular was having the right to vote and studying whether or not one exercised that right (white male political experience in the twentieth century). Working as a volunteer in the League of Women Voters to educate women about political issues was irregular (women's political life); what was regular was having the personal ambition to be a candidate for public office (male political experience). Embedded in the notion of "regularity" were, of course, definitions of "political." Behaviorists did not challenge institutionalist definitions of political activity: running for office, holding public office, and voting. It was true that they introduced an emphasis on interest group behavior, but as women did not appear to be an interest group, they were also invisible in this literature. Behaviorists studied political elites, but women were so few in these ranks (only 2 percent in Congress and 5 percent of state legislators in 1964) that they were not worth studying.

Behaviorist blinders prevented researchers from looking at their own data in an "objective" fashion, even when using a standard definition of "political." As Shanley and Schuck remarked "The dismissal of women was all the more peculiar because repeated studies showed that women in the United States voted nearly as much as men, expressed the same degree of party loyalty, shared men's sense of civic responsibility, and discussed politics within the home as much as men."[28] If women were as political as men by these measures, why were they not found in public office in large numbers? That did not emerge as an important research question because it was not perceived as an anomaly. It was only "natural" that women did not venture into men's public sphere. Like the institutionalists before them, most behaviorists were content with the state of American democracy. This complacency, coupled with an emphasis on value-free description of regularities,

> gave existing social and political arrangements an aura of inevitability. The scientific description of activity purports to be value-free, but once a social scientist has said "this is the way things are now" there is a tendency to think "this is the way things are, inevitably." There is, in other words, a temptation to let the descriptive become the normative. . . . Political science not only accepted, but also reinforced, the stereotypes of appropriate male and female behavior, stereotypes which excluded women from meaningful political activity.[29]

The complacency of behaviorist regularity was shaken by the activity of "irregulars" in the 1960s: the antiwar and New Left movements depicted the United States as more imperialistic than democratic, the civil rights and black power movements saw white privilege instead of a neutral system of government, and the women's movement zeroed in on male privilege instead of natural spheres for the sexes, one apolitical, the other political. Caucuses reflecting these movements challenged mainstream political science's purported value neutrality. The New Caucus for Political Science insisted that political scientists take public stands against war, poverty, and racism. Articles appeared in the *American Political Science Review* addressing the growing demand for a more normative political science.

Women made inroads into the discipline as well. Between 1912 and 1969, women received only 6 to 9 percent of the doctorates awarded in political science. But in the 1970s, the percentage of women in the profession began to increase, along with doctoral dissertations about women. In the 65 years between 1901 and 1966, there were only eleven such dissertations; in the three years from 1969 to 1971, seven dissertations on women appeared.[30] The concerns of women were institutionalized within the American Political Science Association with the formation of the Committee on the Status of Women in 1969 and the Women's Caucus for Political Science in 1971. Shanley and Schuck were convinced that the discipline would never be the same again, thanks to the women's movement:

> Two of the obvious impacts of the contemporary women's movement on political science, then, have been the entry of more women into the discipline, and an increase in the amount of study done about women and the political dimensions of their lives. The blindness to women's activity during the first 65 years of the discipline is being superseded by a careful examination and evaluation of "political woman." It is a safe prediction that we will learn more about women and politics in the 1970s than in any other decade in the history of the discipline, indeed, than in all previous decades combined. Moreover, those interested in the study of women are not simply looking at new data and increasing the amount of material analyzed by political scientists, they are also seeking to change the parameters of what political scientists are willing to call "political activity," and thereby to change our conception of politics.[31]

Their prediction turned out to be true: the proportions of women in the discipline increased; these women came up with new definitions of and approaches to the study of politics, which opened the discipline's eyes to the activities of women; and the 1970s saw the outpouring of more scholarship on women than during the prior six decades of the discipline combined. The authors did not anticipate that political science would remain virtually impervious to these challenges for two decades, however. Women and politics research continued to be conducted by women, who made only a dent in the castle walls. The slow pace of change was the result not only of male resistance but also of academic women's ambivalence toward change.

Accommodationist and Transformational Feminist Approaches: 1975–1985

Feminist scholars ranged on a continuum, from those who were more inclined to accommodate the concepts and methods of behaviorism to those who were more inclined to transform the study of politics.[32] Typically, accommodationist feminists were political scientists, trained in the quantitative methods of behavioral research, and transformational feminists were political theorists, schooled in the classic texts of political philosophy. When women entered the discipline in increasing numbers during the 1970s, they had to "choose sides" in graduate school as an understandable response to a bifurcated profession. But the price of having to make this choice was that feminist "empiricists" and "theorists" did not really listen to each other. They did not routinely attend each other's panels at professional conferences and did not read each other's writings. By the late 1980s, however, some feminist scholars from both sides began to realize that this artificial bifurcation of the discipline was taking an unacceptable toll on the progress of feminist scholarship on women's politics, which needed both the empirical findings from political science and the conceptual insights from political theory. This realization sparked a gradual shift in the focus of review essays, from criticism to alternatives. But before such synthetic attempts could be made, feminists had to grapple with the pros and cons of accommodating and transforming behaviorism.

On the transformational end of the continuum, the concept of culture was introduced as a linchpin of feminist analysis. Culture focused on the meaning people gave their actions, and such meanings were assumed to vary by group depending on their life experiences. Before the women's movement, it was commonly understood that people inhabited different cultures by virtue of their nationality, language, race, ethnicity, class, religion, and the like. But with the advent of the women's movement, male and female cultures in the United States were identified. For example, in her national bestseller *You Just Don't Understand,* Deborah Tannen describes how inhabiting different cultures prevented men and women from understanding each other in the simple act of conversation. For women, conversation meant connection, intimacy, consensus, support, and confirmation of feelings; for men, it meant independence, status, contest, hierarchy, and problem solving.[33]

For feminists, meanings were best obtained through the use of ethnographic, qualitative methodologies. It did not occur to male political scientists to conduct domestic ethnographic studies of women's culture, because male culture was assumed by them to be all there was, to be "normal" for everyone, until feminists demonstrated that it was in fact male. Furthermore, cultural analysis produced understanding or inter-pretation, not explanation. From the outset, feminists in political sci-ence argued that a complete picture of political life had to include both forms of knowledge.

In an application of the concept of culture to women's politics, Thelma McCormack argued that conventional wisdom about women's supposed voter apathy, familism, and conservatism necessitated an ex-amination of women's political culture. As for voter apathy, women must have been more highly motivated than men to vote, given a political cul-ture that excluded them from all roles except that of voter. Yet women's lower turnout rates were conventionally taken to mean less interest, de-sire, and self-esteem on the part of women. As for familism and the vot-ing decision, the image of women desiring family solidarity and willingly sacrificing their independence was so entrenched in investigator as-sumptions that it was never tested: "As long as we do not have indepen-dent measures of family cohesion and decision-making, as long as we do not understand what voting means to women, and as long as no account is taken of the sex bias in the real world of politics, the studies are in-conclusive and the generalizations about female voting are mislead-ing."[34] And as for early voting studies' depiction of women as conserva-tive, various definitions were used: favoring candidates of conservative parties, a conservative motivation, support for the status quo, and indif-ference to politics generally:

> Failure to distinguish what is meant by conservative results in a composite picture of the working-class woman as someone with all the undesirable features of the "culture of poverty," "amoral familism," "ressentiment," and "false consciousness." When a woman is not being swayed by charismatic leaders like Hitler, it is because she adheres faithfully to her church or is drawn to-ward other leaders who are more charismatic. The fact is that when all these studies are examined closely, the only thing they show is that class variables are not as highly predictive for women as they are for men.[35]

McCormack underscored how women's conservatism was portrayed as irrational, in contrast to the rational basis for men's politics. The stan-dard procedure for ascertaining how men acquired their rationality was to look at their group memberships and network contacts and to note the presence or absence of countervailing subgroups or cross-pressures.

This procedure was not applied to women, however; researchers substituted a gender stereotype for careful empirical research. Even if cross-pressures affected men and women in the same way, it was inaccurate to assume that institutions affected the sexes in the same way. For example, it was wrong to assume that political parties were as busy wooing women as churches were. Church membership was a culturally sanctioned part of women's lives, whereas party activity reflected male culture: party meetings in saloons and pubs, coarse language, male imagery on posters, and the like.

Whereas an emphasis on culture was a transformational wedge into behaviorist concepts and methods, a common accommodationist tactic was pointing out how gender bias in behavioral studies had resulted in bad science. For example, Murray Goot and Elizabeth Reid, in response to the query in their title, *Women and Voting Studies: Mindless Matrons or Sexist Scientism?* came down on the side of sexist scientism.[36] They attributed political science's indifference toward women's electoral behavior to behaviorism's supposed neutrality, which in fact concealed gender bias about what was politically interesting. For instance, the first comparative examination of women's electoral behavior (in Europe) was Maurice Duverger's UNESCO study, *The Political Role of Women,* published in 1955. Duverger reported that his study encountered "a certain degree of indifference. The political scientist . . . often tended to regard its purpose as a secondary one of no intrinsic importance."[37] In another example, a chapter on political behavior in a 1969 handbook of social psychology devoted just over one page to the political behavior of women.[38] And a 1974 guide to electoral behavior did not include sex as a priority variable in comparative electoral research.[39]

According to Goot and Reid, in some ways ignoring women was preferable to behaviorists' treatment of them as naturally confined to their proper sphere. One political scientist castigated "working girls and career women, and women who insistently serve the community, and women with extra-curricular interests of an absorbing kind" for depriving their children of the time and attention they rightfully deserved, thus contributing to their children's juvenile delinquency and homosexuality; these developments could "partly be attributed to the feminist movement and what it did to the American mother."[40] And some political scientists said that a state could be a democracy even if it withheld the vote from women.[41]

Goot and Reid challenged survey research and other behaviorist findings that purported to show that children adopted the party preference of their father, that wives followed their husbands, and that women were more conservative and personalized politics more than men did. They also noted that even researchers sympathetic to the women's movement endorsed the findings of survey research when they should have questioned them. Behaviorists frequently assumed that questionnaires "spoke for themselves," when in fact they embodied the language, concerns, and concepts of male investigators. To the extent that women had different meanings in mind when they responded to questions, such meanings were not captured by structured questionnaires. Accordingly, Goot and Reid advocated a detailed study of the experiences of women and of the qualities of their political thought: "The pre-coded, superficially quantitative ('Do you get a little/a lot of political information from newspapers?' 'Do you work?') questionnaire items commonly employed merely reflect the weakness of the theory while ensuring that such data as might expose the theory cannot emerge."[42] Existing research was not value neutral; it reflected the values of male researchers operating in a male-dominated society in which they were beneficiaries.

Three Review Essays in Signs: Political Science Meets Women's Studies

Between 1975 and 1979, three political science review essays appeared in *Signs,* an interdisciplinary women's studies journal. For the first time, female political scientists were self-consciously positioning their discipline in an interdisciplinary women's studies setting. Each of these reviews described a mix of transformational and accommodationist feminist scholarship. In the first one, Kay Boals outlined three major functions of feminist scholarship in political science: one was accommodationist, the expansion of empirical knowledge within given frameworks, and two were transformational, a critique of theories of political socialization and political participation, and a reconceptualization of the concept of politics.[43]

Boals praised two books for expanding existing knowledge about women as political elites: *Political Woman,* by Jeane J. Kirkpatrick, and *Clout: Womanpower and Politics,* by Susan and Martin Tolchin.[44] These works focused on what kinds of women became legislators and what difference they made in politics. Kirkpatrick's study was based on in-depth interviews with forty-six female state legislators who attended a 1972 conference sponsored by Rutgers University's Center for the American Woman and Politics (CAWP). CAWP was to become a national clearinghouse for information on female elected officials. Although this first study found that female legislators differed little from their male colleagues, subsequent CAWP studies would find that women were more liberal and feminist than their male counterparts. Kirkpatrick's female state legislators for the most part accepted social and political structures. By contrast, some of the "new breed of political woman" portrayed in the Tolchins' book challenged politics as usual. Those without links to the women's movement were content to gain access to the male system of politics; those with links to the movement—Bella Abzug, Shirley Chisholm, Frances Farenthold, Patricia Schroeder, and Gloria Steinem—wanted to transform the system.

Boals also considered transformational works that critiqued behaviorist theories of socialization and participation, maintaining that research instruments used to measure political attitudes embodied gendered assumptions. The most flagrant was perhaps the 1936 Gallup poll question, "Would you vote for a woman for President if she was qualified in every other respect?" Questionnaires in studies of children's political attitudes reinforced a male-only view of politics by their use of pronouns, choice of pictures, and direction of questions to the father's, but not the mother's, relation to politics. Feminists encouraged researchers to ask children questions that dealt with the politics of their lives in home and at school, since they saw politics as part of human relationships at many levels, not solely as the distant activity of government. And they raised questions as to how change could be built into women's view of politics and of themselves within the political system. As Boals noted, research that did not raise change-oriented questions was just as political as change-oriented research; it merely functioned "to help perpetuate the status quo by default rather than contributing to its transformation."[45]

Studies of political participation treated the male as the norm and the female as deviant. A study of convention delegates found that a majority of men believed that a delegate should make decisions based on individual judgment, whereas a majority of women preferred to follow party leaders or public opinion. The authors evaluated the female preference negatively, saying it evidenced women's timidity, need for assurance from others, lack of personal independence, and inability to make one's own decisions. An alternative evaluation, not considered by the authors, was that women might legitimately view their function as representatives rather than as Burkean trustees. Similarly, findings that women were more idealistic, reformist, or candidate-oriented than men were negatively evaluated and explained as resulting from female naiveté. When women injected ethical considerations into politics, as Jane Jaquette argued, they were considered "hopelessly moralistic, unsophisticated, or at worst, a threat to the proper functioning of the system"; when they were found to participate in politics less than men, the problem was said to stem from women not being enough like men politically: "weak, unable to overcome outworn stereotypes, and lacking participatory élan."[46]

In the transformational view, the problem lay not with women but with the American political system. Mainstream politics was biased in favor of political participation by those who were satisfied with the status quo, and it tended to discourage the expression of alienation. Furthermore, issues central to women's everyday lives, such as housework, child care, and reproduction, were characterized as private, not public, and were thereby excluded from the political arena. To the extent that women were alienated from a male politics that did not address their everyday concerns, they would not be likely to participate in a system in which they sensed they had no real stake. A reconceptualization of politics was an important transformational task of feminist scholarship. Boals commented: "In writings by feminist political scientists that touch on conceptions of politics, two basic themes recur: one is the need to see as political substantive concerns that have conventionally been thought of as private and apolitical; the other is the need to move away from definitions of politics that center on competition for power toward conceptions that are oriented to shared values and interpersonal relationships."[47] This reconceptualization was informed by the insight from the women's movement that "the personal is political." Women's personal problems were not necessarily the result of individual weakness; they were frequently caused by social institutions that perpetuated male power: laws, ideologies, sex roles, and the like. Politicization meant consciousness-raising.

In the second review essay in *Signs,* Jaquette highlighted four critical contributions of feminist scholarship: how changing sex roles affected political participation, how the women's liberation movement affected policymaking, how the public and private spheres could be integrated, and how a feminist revisionist position could politicize the private sphere.[48]

Women's increased feminist consciousness and labor force participation meant that researchers could no longer take static sex roles as a given. Analysis of data from the University of Michigan Survey Research Center's National Election Studies (1952 through 1972), the 1972 Center for Political Studies Convention Delegate Study, and the 1972 Virginia Slims poll revealed the importance of the feminist movement for women's political attitudes. Feminist beliefs had a slight impact on female citizen participation and a significant impact on female elite (convention delegate) participation.[49] Employment outside the home was also a key factor in women's increased political participation, both as citizens and as elites (convention delegates). Two spurts in women's participation were caused by the spread of a new feminist consciousness, first among white-collar and professional women (1956–60) and then among blue-collar women (1968–72). From 1960 through 1972, working women participated at virtually the same rate as men, while homemakers' participation was significantly lower.[50]

The women's movement also had an effect on policymaking in Washington, D.C., where a "policy system" of pressure groups, sympathetic legislators, and "woodwork feminists" within the government used the "moral climate" of the women's movement and legal precedents from the civil rights movement to advance women's policy concerns, such as the inclusion of "sex" in the 1964 Civil Rights Act, and the 1972 congressional passage of the ERA and Title IX of the Education Amendments. Behaviorism's emphasis on interest groups had been at the expense of social movements, blinding the discipline of political science to the importance of this policy system.[51]

Another important theme for Jaquette was a feminist analysis of the separation of public and private spheres, which feminists sought to integrate. She discussed how Jean Bethke Elshtain had traced the historical origins of the conceptions of private moral woman and public immoral man. In this dualistic way of thinking, Elshtain said, women were morally superior because they were publicly inferior. Nineteenth-century women's suffragists accepted this dualism when they based their arguments on the need for women's superior private morality to clean up men's public immorality. Suffragists' failure to challenge this dichotomy meant accepting presuppositions that prevented full female participation and socioeconomic equality by concentrating on the legal trappings rather than the substance of male power: suffragists won the battle but lost the war. The public-private dichotomy had several negative implications for understanding women's politics, including the definitional exclusion of the private sphere from open political consideration, a narrow focus on political interest groups, a trivialization of moral concerns as they related to public political matters, and the justification of social inequality on grounds of political stability.[52]

For Jaquette, the integration of personal and political life would be on male terms unless women became conscious of their own needs and values and until men and women were seen as equally responsible for "women's work" and "productive work." She wanted to avoid two pitfalls: opting for total assimilation into a male-defined public world and allowing a "male romantic" definition of the private sphere to govern the terms by which "female values" become public values. To this end, Jaquette posited three elements of a "feminist revisionism" to study the politicization of the private sphere. The first point was that women's behavior should be viewed as self-interest maximizing within constraints. A focus on organizational constraints had the advantage of concentrating on adult behavior and the system rather than on childhood and the psyche; it did not portray women as helpless victims of their own oppression. Second, Jaquette's "private sphere" was not limited to family and the home; it also included the Western concept of individual freedom. Third, the politics of everyday life should be studied by political scientists as it had been by psychologists and sociologists, in, for example, small group studies on female and male behavior in coalitions, studies of female communication and leadership styles, and research on mixed-sex consciousness-raising groups. In a nod to one of the most influential early writers in the women's movement, Jaquette concluded, "Without this kind of research, the idea of personal interactions as a political arena, a brilliant concept brought most sharply into focus for feminists by Kate Millet's analysis of sexual politics, will be lost and the 'private sphere' will remain an ambiguous abstraction."[53]

The third *Signs* review essay was by Berenice A. Carroll.[54] She reported that between 1976 and 1978, few books but an impressive eighty-five journal articles on women and politics had appeared. Not one of these was published in the *American Political Science Review,* however, and her overall conclusion was that feminist scholarship had not yet made an impact on the discipline of political science. Most studies employed the traditional concepts of the discipline rather than reformulations from the women's movement. Researchers used theories developed by male analysts for male experience. Top textbooks still had inadequate treatments of women. There were no studies of women's unconventional forms of political action, and too few studies of non-elite women and of current policy issues. There were no new challenges to the traditional authorities and conventional stereotypes of women's political behavior. Researchers emphasized sex-role socialization "blame the victim" explanations, which placed the burden on women, not the system, to change. Above all, in Carroll's view, there was a reluctance to examine the system itself on a theoretical level.

The Sociology of Knowledge and Women's Interests

In 1979, Virginia Sapiro and Jean Bethke Elshtain contributed to a volume using a sociology of knowledge approach.[55] By this point it had become clear that the behavioral revolution in political science was holding its own in the face of the feminist revolution in knowledge in other disciplines. In her essay, Sapiro argued that political science had not embraced feminist revisions with open arms because scholarship on women confronted dominant values and attacked "standards" of the field. Alteration of an academic field of inquiry was an essentially political process, whereby the power and authority of influentials to designate the truth was challenged by newcomers, who changed the procedures by which members of the community judged the validity of research. Political science had gone through this experience with the behavioral revolution, but in the contemporary period, behaviorists were not anxious to relinquish their dominance. According to Sapiro, political conflict in the discipline centered on three issues: positivism, advocacy, and the definition of politics.

By adopting a positivist approach, behaviorists restricted their analysis to the clearly observable and assumed that they were not imposing their own beliefs on the people they studied. But this strategy contributed to the invisibility and biased interpretations of women's politics. Since psychological phenomena were not directly observable, the field of vision was narrowed to behavior itself and very specific political attitudes; researchers lost sight of the fact that in creating and conducting a study they necessarily imposed personal values on the subject of study; and political scientists became impressed with technique (computers and statistical models) at the expense of understanding politics. The advocacy debate was ironic, given the discipline's birth as part of the Progressive reform movement. Sapiro noted: "From the days of the civic reformers to the Kissingers and Brzezinskis, political scientists have always been involved in political advocacy. And this advocacy has not been restricted to extracurricular political activity. Advocacy—or at least expression of values—remains an intrinsic part of almost any political research."[56] The behaviorist definition of politics shifted focus from "the government" to "the public." But an emphasis on "the public" meant that "the private" was outside the domain of political science, and of course "the private" was a female realm of family, social relationships, sexuality, reproduction, and children. Even when women were observed to be involved in politics as conventionally understood, their motives, styles, and activities were construed as somehow less political (more personal) than those of men.

Sapiro discussed Robert Dahl's *Who Governs?* as an example of the invisibility and biased treatment of women's politics by behaviorists. Dahl was one of the major theorists of the behavioral movement in political science, declaring it in 1961 a "successful protest."[57] His book was considered by many to provide evidence that the United States was a pluralistic, relatively egalitarian political system. Sapiro said that although Dahl included important information about women, "sexist blinders" prevented him from drawing obvious conclusions about women's politics.[58] He investigated the extent to which local decision makers in New Haven were drawn from high-status groups (as elite theorists maintained) or, alternatively, represented the citizenry at large (as pluralist theorists maintained). Indicators of social status were occupation, religion, race, and ethnicity, but not sex. Educational policy was one of the three decision-making areas Dahl examined. Women entered the picture in his discussion of the PTA as an educational interest group. He asserted without evidence that for many women, "the PTA is obviously an outlet for social needs; PTA meetings furnish opportunities to escape from the home for a few hours, meet neighbors, make new friends, gossip, talk about children, partake of coffee and pastry, and achieve a fugitive sense of social purpose. Some female Machiavellians even look upon PTA activity as a way of assuring favorable treatment for their own children."[59] It was assumed that women had personal and social, but not political, motivations, and they were "Machiavellian" if they used an organization to protect their interests. By contrast, male motivation sounded rational, self-interested, and instrumental. Compare Dahl's description of three men who "all became involved in the politics of public schools via the PTA. To be sure, each of these men had already possessed a strong prior interest in education. But it was when the education of their own children was at stake that they became active in their PTA."[60] The same behavior on the part of men and women received stereotypical interpretations, not objective analysis: women were social butterflies and Machiavellians, men were informed and interested.[61]

Furthermore, even though women were more active in the PTA than men were, men, by their own account, were actively recruited because of their gender to become president of the organization. One man said that he was asked by the principal to be the president of the PTA and "was quite taken by surprise. I have never had anything to do with the PTA before. . . . My wife usually went to the meetings." When a woman was a PTA president, she was described as a "housewife who lacks the time, experience, interest and drive to move into the real centers of educational influence."[62] This focus on self-selection ignored the equally plausible explanation, based on his own data, that there was gender discrimination in the educational policy arena, where men were actively recruited, with less experience than women, into leadership positions. Such discrimination was not seen by Dahl as counterevidence to his pluralist argument, perhaps because leaders were "naturally" assumed to be male.

Sapiro noted that women trained in the techniques of empirical political science had little trouble pointing out the flaws of traditional behavioral work on women on its own terms, and she added that feminist scholars were also challenging assumptions about women's private nonpolitical world: "In doing so we reveal traditional political scientists as people who have not transcended the values, norms, and prejudices of their political cultures as well as they had thought." Women's studies research was thus "a radical political enterprise for most of us. . . . Accusations of sexism—whether leveled at a field as a whole or at an individual's work—are accusations of poor scholarship. Scholars cannot make assumptions about women or ignore gender where it is relevant without violating their own canons of research. Women's studies, when done well, is simply good research. At the same time, however, it is a powerful source of conflict and thus a means to real political change."[63]

Jean Bethke Elshtain's critique of behaviorism focused on the questions of values and meaning. Behaviorism had what Elshtain termed a crude verificationist theory of meaning whose goal was the construction of verifiable hypotheses instead of understanding or interpreting political life. In Elshtain's view, in order to understand political meaning, one had to include the social context and intersubjective meanings. In behaviorism, the social context was taken for granted and meanings of survey research terms were provided by the researcher. Values were reduced to "opinions, attitudes, and preferences" expressed in categories formulated by researchers. Individuals were presumed to calculate prudential self-interest, which could be measured by research categories; but since people's values and self-understandings did not fit neatly into the paradigm, they were bypassed.[64]

Elshtain said that questions about values and bias on the part of the researcher could not be resolved by pretending that one could bracket one's values for purposes of research. Every explanatory theory of politics implicitly adopted notions of human nature and human purposes, set the boundaries of phenomena to be investigated, and precluded seeing the political world under an alternative characterization. The task for feminist scholars was to develop a critical science of politics that brought predominant presumptions of the discipline to the surface, subjected these presumptions to rigorous scrutiny, incorporated interpretive self-criticism as a central feature, developed a more coherent, rational, lively, and critical account of political life through the use of a richer descriptive vocabulary, and broke down the artificial barriers between the study of politics and the study of morals.[65]

In their critique of conventional wisdom, feminists were ambivalent about the concept of women's interests. In a 1981 review essay in the *American Political Science Review,* Virginia Sapiro staked out a claim on the accommodationist end of the spectrum. She proffered the concept of women's interests as a way of folding feminist insights into the discipline, a "mix and stir" approach that left the basic epistemological and most of the conceptual structures of the discipline intact. She noted how the feminist movement had opened up a new question about political representation: women wanted representation not only as individuals but also as members of a group. She did not use the term "interest group" in the narrow political science sense, that is, an organized group of people interacting through conventional political channels in opposition to other organized interest groups. Indeed, part of the political relevance of women and other oppressed groups was that they had systematically been denied the means by which to form themselves into an interest organization: self-consciousness and identification. Thus, women's interest was based on both their distinctive objective situation and their subjective consciousness. Analysis of women's interests and how governments represented and responded to them necessitated a new look at the boundaries between public and private domains and a new vocabulary to describe women's politics. Sapiro asserted: "Political scientists have difficulty incorporating women into the political world because they lack or reject the appropriate language. 'Patriarchy,' 'sexism,' 'feminist,' and 'male-dominated' appear to be emotionally charged words, the tools of the polemicist rather than the scholar. But are these words necessarily more charged than 'monarchy,' 'democratic,' 'Democratic,' or 'authoritarian'?"[66]

In a rejoinder to Sapiro's article, Irene Diamond and Nancy Hartsock questioned the language of interest politics, in which the rational man of classical economics maximized his satisfactions, in which human emotions were reduced to interests and interests to rational gain, and in which human community was reduced to an instrumental, unstable alliance between isolated individuals. They noted that although this scheme might have been an accurate description of male experience, it did not capture women's experiences nurturing children, fostering interdependent relationships, and paying attention to human emotions. By adopting this view, Sapiro perpetuated the belief that women just wanted to catch up with men, when in fact much of what women wanted and needed was not the same as what men wanted and needed. For Diamond and Hartsock, the starting point for attributing common interests to women was an examination of the psychic and institutional consequences of the sexual division of labor. Taking women's lives seriously, as a point of departure for understanding women's politics, meant including questions of reproduction and sexuality as part of political analysis. When it came to issues of conventional political representation, men could "act for" women in most stages of the policy process, but only women could "act for" women "in identifying 'invisible' problems affecting the lives of large numbers of women. At the same time, women's ability to 'act for' women must be understood in the context of the survival strategies women have created in response to their powerlessness."[67]

In 1983, Marianne Githens summarized the state of the art of gender and politics research, describing both its accommodationist and its transformational features. On the accommodationist side, she saw the bulk of contemporary research as filling information gaps about the distinctive political behavior of women using traditional definitions of political participation. Githens said that this work was primarily descriptive rather than analytical; it focused on small, often unrepresentative subsets of women within a relatively short time span; and its results were frequently contradictory. Consequently, it was difficult to draw conclusions about women as a group. On the transformational side, Githens argued that "even a more systematic and less fragmentary study of women's political behavior would not resolve the basic problems encountered in gender related research. The fundamental problems . . . stem from the gestalt of the discipline of political science itself," which contained faulty assumptions about the nature and diversity of intragroup relations, the parameters of political activity, the prioritizing of political activity, and the definition of political elites. Githens said that to the extent that gender research had been analytical, it had focused on constraints on participation, such as socialization, rather than developing alternative theoretical frameworks. She concluded that as long as existing frameworks were used, women's political behavior would be more obfuscated than illuminated.[68]

From Feminist Criticism to Feminist Alternatives: 1986–1993

A decade after the first feminist calls to transform the discipline, it seemed as though little had changed, as reflected in the title of Gertrude Steuernagel and Laurel U. Quinn's 1986 APSA paper, "Is Anyone Listening? Political Science and the Response to the Feminist Challenge." The authors looked at six political science journals, representing the major subfields of the discipline, published between 1976 and 1985. In the 240 journal issues examined, there were only 43 articles on women (with none in *Foreign Policy*), most of them authored by women and few of them calling for conceptual or methodological revision. Like Berenice Carroll, Steuernagel and Quinn concluded that the impact of the feminist challenge on these journals was minimal.[69] By 1987, however, an important change was under way. Feminist critics of the discipline began to shift from criticism to developing alternatives. To be sure, these alternatives were based on critical assessments of political science as usual. But whereas earlier critics filled their pages with detailed accounts of the limitations of what researchers had done, later critics devoted as much energy to outlining where feminist researchers ought to go epistemologically, conceptually, and methodologically.

An Ethic of Care versus Behaviorist Studies

Many were influenced by Carol Gilligan's model of an ethic of care, which suggested that women framed moral dilemmas in terms of interpersonal relations and conflicting responsibilities, whereas men did so in terms of abstract categories and a hierarchy of rights.[70] Gertrude Steuernagel derived several possible political implications from Gilligan's work. Women might look at a policy's long-term impact on the preservation of the community, whereas men might look at its ability to balance rights. Women might think in terms of nonviolent problem solving, whereas men might be more likely to look to violent solutions to problems. Women might value connections with others as much as men value autonomy. Women might feel estranged from a public life based on artificial ties or contracts. In order to provide a meaningful response to a questionnaire, women might need to know the context of a question, where men might feel more comfortable responding to an abstract set of categories. Men and women inhabited the cultural world of genders that needed to be decoded by listening to women's voices.[71] Gilligan's model informed Steuernagel's critique of three behaviorist books about women's political participation: Virginia Sapiro's *Political Integration of Women*, Ethel Klein's *Gender Politics*, and Keith Poole and L. Harmon Zeigler's *Women, Public Opinion, and Politics*.[72] Each of these authors in turn responded to Steuernagel's observations.

Sapiro looked at women who came of age in a "post–women's movement" world to see whether changes in their private roles as workers, mothers, and wives had had an effect on their integration into the political system. She concluded that women were still only marginally connected to American political life. Steuernagel said that though Sapiro was sensitive to the problems involved in studying gender (a cultural variable with many levels of meaning) as opposed to sex (a dichotomous variable), she was forced by survey research methodology to look at sex rather than gender; she was precluded from hearing from women about why they responded as they did; and she assumed that women participated in politics for the same reasons men did.

In response to Steuernagel, Sapiro both cautioned against extracting Gilligan's findings out of the context of her developmental psychology theoretical framework and noted methodological weaknesses in Gilligan's analysis.[73] Nevertheless, she agreed that certain implications from Gilligan's work were worth pursuing: assessing the empirical relationship between moral and political development, distinguishing between modes of reasoning and the conclusions of the reasoning process, investigating gender-relevant contextual effects on reasoning, evaluating the impact of political institutions and processes on reasoning and its relationship to behavior, and exploring the causes and processes of gender differentiation. Sapiro said that her book explicitly did *not* compare men and women; rather, it studied the connections between different parts of women's lives: "Gender is involved when we look at women's understanding of their situation as women, or at their experiences that simply have no ready comparison in most male lives: being a homemaker, a wife, or mother; experiencing woman-to-woman friendships; or fearing violence directed at women as women." She agreed with Steuernagel that "dichotomous sex difference research will never be enough; it must be filled out by attending to gender identity and gender consciousness."[74] Sapiro defended survey research methodology by saying that it was useful when appropriate and that methods were traps only when one could not say enough or when one made more claims than the evidence warranted.

Steuernagel also looked at Ethel Klein's *Gender Politics*, which related women's changing roles as wives and mothers to their political participation. Klein noted that men came to feminism through an abstract commitment to equality, whereas the feminism of women was based on personal experience, a distinction that Steuernagel said reflected Gilligan's model. But, Steuernagel faulted Klein for depicting women as creatures determined by circumstances, not as political actors in their own right, in contrast to how men were portrayed as having the capacity to develop political views that transcended social determinants. The use of role theory made it difficult for Klein to respond to women's voices and lent itself to survey research, since the indicators of roles, such as marital and employment status, were readily available to the researcher. As Alison M. Jaggar pointed out, however, role theory was based on assumptions about human nature that did not reflect women's experiences. "On this conception of human nature, human beings are not necessarily constituted by society but instead are capable, in principle, of withdrawing from society to redefine their own identity. Thus, an individual is able to throw off the identity imposed by society and can consciously choose her or his own future destiny."[75] This abstract individualist belief that people are free to adopt roles and able to cast them off at will was more reflective of male than female experience. Steuernagel called for the development of ways to study politics that did not automatically assume that political attitudes and behaviors were functions of social forces. They were also functions of self-described political understandings, and feminist political scientists had to develop ways to hear these voices, much as Gilligan heard women's moral reasoning.

Klein's response to Steuernagel was much like Sapiro's: that her methods were appropriate to the research questions she posed. Klein wanted to know why the women's movement happened when it did and how women's political consciousness had changed over time. She drew on two kinds of literature, by theorists of social movements and by behaviorists on political consciousness, to trace the evolution of the sexual division of labor and its implications for political movements and consciousness. She defended the use of surveys to address questions of political participation, since they provided insights into how people decided their votes:

Multivariate analysis taking into account proximity measures, party identification, ideology, and retrospective judgments allows us to determine the different priorities the electorate places on issues for any given election. It allows us to establish whether men and women use a different decision calculus. Qualitative interviews can then be used to try to explain why men and women have different priorities for public policy. It would be good to lay out a series of testable hypotheses about differences in men's and women's approaches to politics.[76]

Klein was baffled by the argument that survey research methodology forced researchers to examine sex rather than gender. She said that demonstrating that women's life experiences (marital status, work experience, education) determined their political views was an analysis of gender and thus that political meaning could be ascertained through survey instruments.

When I was working with ways to measure support for feminism, I faced an interesting conundrum: There were a fair number of feminist men. Well, it was clear to me that these issues did not have the same meaning for men as they did for women, but how was I to prove it? How can you say that when men say that they believe women face discrimination it has a different meaning than when women give the same response? The fact that men and women come to this position from a different set of experiences and relate them to political commitments in different ways illustrates a difference in meaning.[77]

Klein argued that liberal ideology influenced both men's and women's orientation but had a greater role in shaping men's perspective because gender roles played a much stronger part in shaping women's orientation. Men came to understand gender discrimination through ideology, and women came to understand it through personal experience as well as ideology. In a similar fashion, abstract principles played equally critical, but different, roles in male and female support for feminist protest: liberalism played a greater role in male support, and feminism played a greater role in female support.

The final work Steuernagel analyzed was Poole and Zeigler's *Women, Public Opinion, and Politics.* Using conventional models and concepts of political participation, these authors found that "women do not appear to be a political group; there are no political attitudes and behaviors which are unique to them as *women.*"[78] Steuernagel faulted Poole and Zeigler for their lack of awareness of feminist critiques: they assumed that women participated in politics for the same reasons as men and in the same manner, and they described the struggle over women's issues as a battle among elites, with the mass of women showing little or no interest. Poole and Zeigler mentioned some differences between men and women: women were more sensitive to religious and discrimination issues, more antinuclear and pro-environmental, and more supportive of redistributive economic policies. Nevertheless, Poole and Zeigler predicted that increased political participation by women would not, for the most part, lead to a major restructuring of our political and social lives.

Steuernagel pointed out that although men and women might respond similarly on a survey questionnaire, the "why" of the response was significant, because so much empirical research made the implicit assumption that the importance of events was similar for men and for women. Poole and Zeigler agreed that the whys might differ, but they asked if it really mattered that men and women arrived at policy preferences by a different route, since politicians cared only about the end result. On another point, they said that survey research was not inherently unable to link public and private realms. In their book, for example, they looked at the effect of marriage and satisfaction with life on attitudes toward feminism.

If Steuernagel was charging that survey research was incompatible with "feminist sympathies," then Poole and Zeigler said that they agreed, adding that any mode of empirical research should be incompatible with any personal ideology. They feared that Steuernagel rejected their use of survey research methodology because their findings were at odds with her personal ideology and even suggested that Steuernagel believed that all empirical research undermined feminism. If so, they said, "then serious scholarship and feminism are incompatible. We cannot agree with this view; nor do we agree that survey research is incompatible. When people hear things they do not wish to hear, they can ignore them or they can examine them in order to refute them. We urge women's studies to take the latter course."[79]

It is interesting to compare the more measured responses of Sapiro and Klein with the less measured responses of Poole and Zeigler. Poole and Zeigler seemed to be unaware of a decade of feminist critique of behaviorist methodology in political science, acting as if they were being singled out because of their findings, not their method; Sapiro and Klein made reference to this larger critique in their more extended and substantive responses. Poole and Zeigler launched an ad hominem attack on Steuernagel as an ideologue, not a scholar; Sapiro and Klein engaged in a conversation with Steuernagel as a peer with whom they disagreed. In response to her earlier query—is anyone listening?—it must have seemed to her that the discipline was listening in a very uneven fashion to feminist scholarship.[80]

Communities and Calls for Transformations

The concept of different communities was another feminist alternative to conventional wisdom in political science. Instead of viewing society as composed of individuals who self-interestedly compete for power, feminists shifted the focus of research to dominant and subordinate groups in society and to how subordination affects people's sense of themselves. One could speak of experiences as members of a subordinate community. "Community" was different from "interest group": it referred to a broader range of people's experiences (e.g., taking care of members, common foods and language), and it included people's self-understandings (in modes of expression that frequently differed from that of the dominant group). In their review essay of the discipline, Martha Ackelsberg and Irene Diamond made the case for a focus on different communities:

> To fail to examine relationships of domination and subordination in society is to ignore the ways in which such structures affect people's sense of themselves. Feminist and black studies activists and scholars have spoken of the need for members of oppressed groups to find their "voice," to articulate and act on their own understanding of their experiences. . . . Significantly, both for white women and for people of color, community seems crucial to the development of such an alternative perspective. Methodologically, then, getting a sense of what differential experience is, or has been, for different women (or members of different groups) in a polity may mean looking much more carefully at the (communal) context of people's lives, rather than treating citizens as isolated individuals who come to "political" life with no prior ties.[81]

Ackelsberg and Diamond said that feminist scholars had used three approaches to understand women's distinctive experiences as a community. The first drew on object relations psychological theory to locate the source of women's distinctive experiences in prevailing patterns of mothering: the fact that women were the primary caregivers to young people of both sexes created a community of women who were attuned to caring, empathy, and nurturance and a community of men whose primary concerns were separation and individualism.[82] The second approach emphasized patterns of mutual support that many women had developed through social and political activities.[83] And the third focused on the relationships of domination and subordination which defined and constrained the expression of women's personal and political selves.[84] Research on women's community activities challenged the conventional notion of women as passive members of the polity, living their lives in the nonpolitical "private" sphere of the home. Women were active in neighborhoods, schools, churches and temples, and other voluntary associations in efforts to secure better schools, safe neighborhoods, adequate child and health care, and the like.[85]

Finally, there were calls for a comprehensive transformation of the discipline.[86] Barbara J. Nelson recommended a twofold strategy, "emphasizing that all political subjects are gendered while also giving special attention to those areas and concerns where women have traditionally put their political energy," such as families, communities, voluntary groups, social movements, and the welfare state.[87] In Nelson's view, this topic expansion was intimately bound to epistemology. The inclusion of women and other socially marginal groups raised issues about the knowing process itself, especially the conflict between humanistic/interpretive approaches and positivistic ones. Nelson said empiricism was necessary, as long as it meant the systematic study of events (broadly construed) through observation directed at attaining universal truths. It was the universalism of the findings and the disinterestedness of the observer that needed to be questioned. This issue was not a technical problem of reliability, that is, that other people would see the same things if they were the observers, but a matter of understanding the link between the see-er and the seen.

Nelson described the dilemma of "methodological individualism," an emphasis on the discrete actions of atomistic individuals. Methodological individualism emerged as an intellectual school in the 1950s and could be traced to three postwar developments: a scholarly interest in how individuals came to support antidemocratic regimes, the chilling effect of the McCarthy era on scholarly inquiry into controversial politics, and a typically American interest in the technology of statistical models. This emphasis on the technology of statistics led to a denigration of narrative as a creative, theoretical act in itself: "The epistemological consequences of methodological individualism were an exaggeration of the individual as both subject and object, and the denial of contexts in the search for explanations. The recognition of context, on the other hand, leads to an understanding that social theories are inherently socially contingent rather than inherently universalistic."[88]

Joan Tronto noted several limitations in the accommodationist approach. First, because male behavior had been studied first, any discrepancy in women's matching political behavior was viewed as the problematic to be explained. For instance, research on the gender gap in voting had for the most part focused on why women voted as they did and presumed that male voting was unproblematic and thus normative. Second, by opting for a specialized niche in the discipline's division of scholarly labor, accommodationists unwittingly reinforced the view of women as outside politics. And third, there was little in the accommodationist approach to prevent the study of gender and politics from becoming isolated from the discipline as a whole. Studies showing that women behaved differently from men were not enough to change how political scientists thought about men and women politically; women would remain an anomaly in the pursuit of science as usual. Finally, Tronto said that there was no motivation for political scientists to venture outside conventional boundaries of public and private. For example, if female recruitment for elective office followed a different life plan tied to different roles of men and women in the family, then political scientists would probably think they could stop there. There was no reason to study family roles as problematic.[89]

Transformationalists, in contrast, advocated a more profound alteration of the discipline's boundaries. First, Tronto said, political science needed to move in a radically democratic direction. It needed to overcome the elitism inherent in the discipline: its focus on the powerful and political stability, at the expense of the powerless and political change. Second, political science needed to look more closely at the context within which politics appeared, specifically the interrelationship between private and public life, the place of morality in politics, and a definition of power as empowerment. Tronto said that pushing the public-private boundary meant viewing family structure as affected by laws, social practices, and economic conditions, not as a natural given; looking at family support or opposition to political activity; and studying male authority in the family. Expanding the politics-morality boundary meant investigating the moral as well as institutional limits of political life. And pushing the power boundary meant adding to the conventional understanding of "power over" the equally valid notion of "power to." Conventional political scientists preferred to use the concept of "power over" because it was most congruent with the kinds of political behaviors and questions they were interested in, centering on how powerholders got their way. Feminists emphasized the concept of "power to," often designated as "empowerment," because it was most congruent with the kinds of political behaviors and questions they were interested in, centering on how people developed and expressed a political consciousness.[90]

Tronto argued that since empowerment was often a community act, a focus on empowerment shifted attention to communities, in addition to the more conventionally studied individuals and institutions. Indeed, one could even speak of the empowerment, as opposed to the power, of an entire polity. Inherent in conventional definitions of the state was the notion that there were no limits to its power insofar as it monopolized the legitimate use of physical force. But an alternative view of the polity was that it was empowered: its powers were bounded by what the community thought was the purpose of the community. When a government went beyond its purpose, it lost power, whether in the end it was able to compel people to act or not. To ask the question, "Are there some political acts (global destruction, for example) that simply go beyond the boundaries of what humans should have the power to do?" was nonsense from a power perspective but legitimate and central from an empowerment perspective. Tronto asserted, "If feminist political science can reintroduce such questions for political science, it will transform the study of politics and resuscitate political life within the context of the ultimate questions of the good of human existence."[91]

Not all feminists wanted to revise the discipline of political science in such a comprehensive way. Some saw more virtue in behaviorism than others did. They disagreed about survey research, the role of the researcher, and "interesting" questions. Although there was not unanimity of opinion about *what* was wrong with conventional wisdom, there was a consensus among scores of women in the discipline that *something* was wrong. As this intellectual history has made clear, people who try to understand politics wear gendered lenses, just as they wear lenses crafted by other significant life experiences. Behaviorism, with its methodological individualism, is an inadequate tool for apprehending interdependent group relations; with its imposed meanings it has silenced self-understandings; with its universalistic explanations it has concealed problematic contexts. It has deemed uninteresting major concerns of women's politics: communities, movements, families, sexuality, voluntary associations, non-elites, and empowerment. Now that we have our revised map, based on feminist correctives to conventional political science, we are ready to explore the terrain of women's politics.

2 Women's Political Life in Santa Clara County

A Favorable Climate for Women's Political Activism

F OR A time in the 1980s, Santa Clara County was known as the feminist capital of the nation. Why? San Jose, the county's largest city, did not have a national reputation for political or feminist activism. The moniker seemed more appropriate for New York, Chicago, or Boston, homes to early women's liberation groups and feminist writings. Certainly other California cities—San Francisco, Berkeley, or Los Angeles—had more distinguished records of political, and presumably feminist, activism. Before talking to local women about their understandings of politics, I wanted to know more about the area's history of political activism. So I pulled out my conventional political science map to use as a point of departure.

First, political science distinguishes between mass and elite politics. Mass politics is the politics of citizens generally—as voters, political letter writers, campaign contributors, demonstrators, interest group members, and the like. The world of elite politics is made up of elected officials, candidates, and political party officials, in short, people who spend a good part of their lives running government. Mass politics, often referred to as "outsider politics," attempts to influence the elite world of "insider politics." Of course, such distinctions are not always neat and clean; for example, a low-income community activist who runs for city council probably does not see herself as an elite. What is meant here is a governmental elite, not an economic elite.

This elite-mass distinction may not always be easy to draw, but it is nevertheless essential to analyses of political movements. Movement members

35

start as outsiders critical of insider politics, or politics as usual. If they remain outsiders, they run the risk of limited efficacy. If they become insiders, they run the risk of losing their critical élan. Most movement members make strategic decisions about whether and how to deal with people who run the government. And most movements are judged by their ability to achieve their goals, given the governments with which they must deal.

Second, political science has identified factors related to the amount of political activism in a given area: its economy, social groups, culture, and electoral structures. As a general rule, there will be more political activism the more prosperous the economy, the more educated and affluent the citizenry, the less traditional the culture, and the more there are at-large, as opposed to districtwide, local elections. In the case of Santa Clara County, each of these general rules held, with the exception of at-large electoral structures benefiting female candidates. Contrary to expectations, district elections were instrumental in getting female majorities on the San Jose City Council.

A Progressive Political Culture

Political culture consists of shared political values and appropriate guides to political activity. The political culture of Santa Clara County was conducive to women's political participation. Its Progressive legacy removed the barrier of male-dominated political machines, put a premium on "clean" politics, and valued neighborhood civic duty. And its ethos of can-do risk taking created a climate open to anyone who could get the job done, regardless of establishment credentials.

Daniel J. Elazar identified three political cultures in America—moralistic, individualistic, and traditional—and traced their development to class, ethnic, and religious differences. The moralistic political culture emerged in New England, where northern European, English, and German liberal Protestants established the town-meeting ideal of an active citizenry. Citizens had a moral obligation to participate in their own governance, and public officials were supposed to be honest, selfless, and committed to the public good. The individualistic political culture developed in the commercial centers of New York, Philadelphia, and Baltimore, where southern and eastern European and Irish Catholics viewed politics as a means by which individuals could improve their economic and social status. Corruption was accepted as natural, in contrast to the "clean politics" ideal of the moralistic culture, and participation was limited. The traditional culture emerged in the plantation economy of the Old South, where fundamentalist white Protestants viewed politics as an activity controlled by an elite, whose family and race privileges bestowed the "right" to govern. In traditional cultures, voting regulations were restrictive and voter turnout was low. Corruption was even more widespread and tolerated than in individualistic cultures.[1]

Political cultures also differed with respect to how citizens viewed government bureaucracies. Moralistic cultures were the most positively inclined toward them, and they were permitted to expand to provide the public a wide array of services. Individualistic cultures tended to see bureaucracies both as a means to advance the personal goals of public officials and as a way to provide a more limited range of government services than was the case in moralistic cultures. Bureaucracies were somewhat mistrusted for encroaching on private matters. Bureaucracies were least trusted in traditional cultures, where they were viewed as interfering with close personal ties between politicians.[2]

California has a mixed moralistic-individualistic political culture, illustrated by the battle between the Progressives and the Southern Pacific Railroad political machine. In 1900, the railroad, owned by "robber barons" Leland Stanford, Collis Huntington, Charles Crocker, and Mark Hopkins, controlled about 10 percent of California land, as well as the state legislature and political party conventions. At the 1908 Republican state convention, a group of Progressive reformers sent anti-railroad delegates to liberate their party and the legislature from the railroad. In order to bypass future railroad-controlled conventions, Progressives adopted the direct primary in 1909. In 1910, Progressive Republican Hiram Johnson was elected governor, and Progressives dominated the state legislature. By 1913, California had the slew of clean-government electoral reforms typically associated with Progressive antiparty fervor: the direct primary, initiative, referendum, recall, nonpartisan local elections, women's suffrage, and severe restrictions on party operations. This gutting of party power had a profound impact on California politics. To this day, parties are relatively weak: virtually all local political races were nonpartisan until quite recently, and popular initiatives bypassed the state legislature to create such significant policies as slashing property taxes, reforming insurance rates, and protecting the coastline.[3]

California's battle between Progressives and political machines was played out in Santa Clara County. San Jose became a commercial center during the gold rush of 1848, providing the valley's produce for the miners. By 1880, San Jose was dominated by a Southern Pacific Railroad political machine, "the gas house gang," which controlled the utility companies (hence its name), streetcars, and canneries. In the 1890s, a merchant and professional class had developed in San Jose, and its vision of expanded commercial development clashed with the machine's corrupt, amateurish, and inefficient operation of the city. The construction of streets, storm drains, and sewers was not keeping pace with middle-class demands for better urban services. In 1896, a group of business-men, orchardists, doctors, lawyers, and judges succeeded in revising the city charter to weaken the power of the mayor and to enhance the city commissions' control over schools, police, fire, and other city services. In 1902, reformers elected their own mayor. San Jose's Good Government League, New Charter Club, and Women's Civic Study League, made up of middle- and upper-class business and professional men and women, became part of the state and national Progressive movement. As Philip J. Trounstine and Terry Christensen put it: "Nationally known muckrakers passed through San Jose, speaking to frenzied middle-class audiences. They attacked the bosses, the railroad, the utilities, the monopolies, and the immigrants. They studied innovative governmental structures designed to lessen the influence of their enemies while bringing good government and enhancing their own power."[4]

By 1915, San Jose reformers had abolished the office of mayor, installed a city manager appointed by the city council as the city's chief executive, expanded the city council from five to seven members elected at-large to reduce the parochial influence of wards, established primary elections for city council, and instituted local initiative, referendum, and recall. Non-partisan elections for at-large posts benefited affluent candidates with access to newspaper support and campaign funds and disadvantaged the working class, which could no longer rely on party cues and ward connections. Although another short-lived political machine emerged in the 1920s, San Jose's Progressive legacy would eventually win the day.

Clean Government versus Machine Politics and Developers

During the heyday of urban machines in the late nineteenth and early twentieth centuries, American women spent much of their political energy trying to dismantle them or to deal with issues neglected by them. In the nineteenth century, middle-class urban women were energetic supporters of benevolent and moral reform societies bent on eradicating poverty, prostitution, gambling, drunkenness, profanity, and Sabbath breaking. Groups such as the New York Female Reform Association, Charity Organization Society, General Federation of Women's Clubs, and Women's Christian Temperance Union (WCTU) emphasized individual improvement and justified their activities on "social housekeeping" grounds. As WCTU leader Frances Willard wrote to suffragist Susan B. Anthony in 1898, "Men have made a dead failure of municipal government, just as they would have of housekeeping; and government is housekeeping on the broadest scale."[5] Urban machines were also criticized by women in the settlement house movement, such as Jane Addams and Florence Kelley of Hull House in Chicago.[6] Settlement workers were quick to see the political dimensions of social reform. In the late 1890s, Jane Addams campaigned against the local ward boss. Florence Kelley's efforts to secure child labor laws eventually led to the establishment of the Children's Bureau in 1912. And the first national conference on city planning, held in 1909, was organized by women from settlement houses.

Women's key role in the moral reform, settlement house, and Progressive movements made them no friend of the liquor industry, which spent huge sums of money to defeat state and local referenda for women's suffrage, for fear that women would use the vote to ban "demon rum." In California the 1896 suffrage campaign was highly organized and effective. Wealthy women such as Mrs. Leland Stanford and Mrs. William Randolph Hearst donated substantial sums of money to the cause, but most funds came from poorer women. Ten days before the election, the Liquor Dealers League met in San Francisco and drafted a letter that they sent to saloon keepers, hotel proprietors, druggists, and grocers throughout the state. The letter urged defeat of the proposed women's suffrage amendment, which subsequently lost by a narrow margin, carrying every county in California except San Francisco and nearby Alameda counties.[7]

The last political machine to dominate San Jose politics was the Bigley machine of the 1920s. Charlie Bigley was a beer distributor and an ambulance operator who, through his control of the police and fire departments, kept the liquor and gambling interests loyal.[8] His power base was eventually eroded by reformers. Thus there were no political machines in sight in San Jose in the early 1970s, when women figured prominently as activists and newcomers to public office as part of the slow-growth movement.

In addition to sealing the fate of machine politics, the Progressive legacy in Santa Clara County benefited women by putting a premium on "clean" politicians who were beyond the potentially corrupting reach of developers. By the early 1970s, the consequences of a growth-at-any-cost policy were beginning to be challenged by environmentally conscious citizens who questioned the propriety of land deals approved by City Hall. Between 1950 and 1970, San Jose officials had approved nearly fourteen hundred annexations, adding 132 square miles to the city.

Annexations came under the jurisdiction of city manager Anthony P. "Dutch" Hamann, an oil company representative who was well connected to the city's business leaders, including Mayor Albert J. Ruffo. In Troutstine and Christensen's words: "The city did not accomplish [these annexations] by awaiting humble petitions from landowners and residents eager for its services. Annexations were hustled, and sometimes even coerced. . . . Growth came so fast the local mapmakers issued monthly packets of stickers to add to their master maps."[9] San Jose practiced leapfrog annexation, securing strategic strips of land to block the expansion of adjacent cities, most of which were powerless in the face of this unabashed land grab. The strongest resistance came from rural school districts adjacent to San Jose, which lost their tax bases and schools. Annexation left a legacy of two dozen school districts in San Jose, a factor that contributed to the city's fragmented politics, lack of identity, and racial segregation. This rapid and unplanned growth also came at the expense of downtown San Jose. Downtown department stores closed their doors as shoppers flocked to new suburban shopping malls; parking was inadequately developed; and City Hall moved out of downtown, taking hundreds of workers with it. As San Jose mushroomed in size, city officials benefited enormously, and many questionable deals were legal under the city's minimal conflict-of-interest laws.[10] As the city grew, newcomers began to outnumber old-timers, and eventually, the newcomers began to question the old-timers' priorities. The affluent aerospace engineers and electronics technicians who had thronged to Silicon Valley expecting good municipal services found instead a host of problems. In the sprawling city, dependence on the automobile meant air pollution. The sewage treatment plant's inability to keep up with the rate of growth meant polluted water. Police and fire departments had to protect large areas. Many schools were on double sessions, open spaces disappeared with no parks to replace them, and taxpayers had to foot the bill for growth-inducing capital improvements. In 1962, a watershed year, the growth machine faced an electoral challenge from the grass roots, and City Hall audiences became unruly for the first time in city history. Running on a strong anti-incumbent platform backed by emerging homeowners' organizations, Councilwoman Virginia Shaffer and two other new council members were elected.[11]

Councilwoman Shaffer, her allies on the city council, and the homeowners' organizations went on the offensive. They condemned shoddy developments, opposed a "new town" on the edge of San Jose, accused city officials of improper involvement in land-use deals, criticized the *San Jose Mercury News* for suppressing scandals, and launched a recall of councilmembers who supported city manager Dutch Hamann. Although Hamann's allies on the city council survived the recall, their share of the vote was far below their once-typical landslides.

In 1970, another environmentalist, future mayor Janet Gray Hayes, was elected to the city council. And in 1972, future county supervisor Susanne Wilson decided to be a candidate for the city council after she received a phone call from a woman who was looking for an environmentalist to run. Shaffer, Hayes, and Wilson all benefited from voters' perception of women as "clean" and unbeholden to developers. Their biographies illustrated the impulses of a moralistic and Progressive political culture.

Virginia Shaffer was a homemaker married to a Lockheed engineer. They had moved to San Jose five years before her historic 1962 election as the first woman on the San Jose City Council. She grew up in progressive Wisconsin and attended the University of Wisconsin. After getting into politics as the result of a zoning battle in her neighborhood, she ran for city council on a platform of city charter reform, district elections to make councilmembers more responsible to the voters, and ample city parks.[12] Janet Gray Hayes was a homemaker who had moved to San Jose in 1956 with her physician husband and four children. She was from Indiana and received her bachelor's degree from Indiana University and master's degree in social services administration from the University of Chicago. Before running for office, she had worked as a volunteer for parks, conservation, housing, and the arts and was active in the PTA and League of Women Voters, her neighborhood association, various council-appointed citizen committees, and open-space and environmental causes.[13] And Susanne Wilson grew up in Texas and moved to San Jose in 1960, when her husband, who was working for IBM, was transferred there from San Antonio. Wilson had been a church youth counselor, an active member of the YWCA, and president of a parent-teachers association, when she received the phone call from the group looking for a "hard-line conservationist and environmentalist." Although she was more interested in "opening up the system for women and minorities," she ran for the council anyway.[14]

Polls conducted by female candidates found that being a woman gave them a boost in a county that valued clean government and honesty. In her 1980 campaign, County Supervisor Zoe Lofgren snagged voters who fell into the category "I don't know who she is but I'll vote for her because she's a woman and will at least be honest."[15] A local poll conducted in 1982 found that being a female candidate was an asset in San Jose races.[16] These findings were in keeping with nationwide poll results that gave female officials the edge of being more honest and trustworthy than male officials.[17] It was not surprising to find that in 1980, the Pacific region of the nation, with its strong Progressive reform tradition, had a higher proportion of female elected officials in city government (18 percent) than the national average (13 percent).[18]

In addition to valuing clean government and destroying machine politics, the Progressive political culture benefited women in Santa Clara County through its emphasis on neighborhood civic duty. Since Progressives severely weakened political parties in California, civic-minded people had to work through other kinds of organizations to achieve their political goals. In the tradition of nineteenth-century female activism in urban moral reform associations and settlement houses, neighborhood associations were a point of entry into politics for many middle- and upper-middle-class women in the county, whether as activists, political appointees, or elected officials. As for the first women on the San Jose City Council, Janet Gray Hayes first appeared before the council as a mother protesting the lack of traffic signals near neighborhood schools, Susanne Wilson had been a PTA president, Iola Williams had been on the local school board, Pat Sausedo had worked for her neighborhood homeowners' group, and Nancy Ianni had been president of her neighborhood association. Female officials in other cities in the county had also been active in neighborhood concerns before seeking public office. Palo Alto city councilmember Betsy Bechtel had presided over the Committee for Green Foothills, a conservation organization; her colleague Ellen Fletcher got involved in city politics to establish a safer bicycling system near her children's schools. And Cupertino mayor Barbara Rogers's entry into politics began with a development controversy in her neighborhood.

The Can-Do Sunbelt

If the Progressive clean government ethos was the bedrock of Santa Clara County's political culture, the next stratum was a can-do boosterism and risk taking that characterized many Sunbelt cities. The term "Sunbelt" refers to the southern and western rim of the United States, from Virginia to California, in contrast to the "Frostbelt" of the northern and eastern parts of the country. After World War II, the Sunbelt experienced rapid increases in population, income, employment, and productivity. This boom was attributed to several factors: low costs for land and labor, low taxes, mild climate, and the growth of key industries such as oil and gas, aerospace and defense, computers, cameras, business machines, real estate, drugs, fast foods, and tourism. In addition, the Sunbelt was not saddled with outdated industrial facilities and obsolete management practices; thus, new industries had fewer startup problems.[19]

The Sunbelt and Frostbelt were homes to two contrasting social types and political cultures. Sunbelt "cowboys" were new-money industrialists, whereas Frostbelt "Establishment Yankees" were East Coast corporate types: "the traditional, staid, old-time, button-down Ivy League, tight-lipped patrician, New England–rooted WASP culture on the one hand, and the aggressive, flamboyant, restless, swaggering, newfangled, open-collar, can-do, Southern-rooted, Baptist culture of the Southern Rim on the other," as Kirkpatrick Sale puts it.[20] "Cowboys" were frequently "self-made" financial successes whose competitive struggle shaped their outlook on political life. They were typically individualists, upwardly mobile, deeply anti-Communist, suspicious of government intrusion, and anti-union. "Yankees" inherited wealth or achieved it through connections from elite institutions. They were taught to "do good" to improve the lives of others and were more tolerant of government and unions.

San Jose's post–World War II development exemplified many features of the Sunbelt political culture. In 1944, a new generation of business leaders wanted to bolster San Jose's economic development faster than city government was prepared to move. They formed the Progress Committee, consisting of one hundred merchants, attorneys, industrialists, and major property owners, and began thirty years of pro-growth boosterism. The Chamber of Commerce launched a national advertising campaign, and industrial development followed. Food Machinery and Chemical (FMC) Corporation, a local manufacturer of farm and cannery equipment, had shifted to building armaments during the Second World War and expanded its defense production afterward. International Business Machines (IBM) established its Pacific headquarters in San Jose, and other corporate giants soon built facilities in or near the city: General Electric, Pittsburgh Steel, Owens-Corning, and Kaiser.[21]

As was the case elsewhere in the Sunbelt, defense and aerospace production fueled industrial development. In 1985, Santa Clara County received $4.6 billion in defense contracts, or $3,272 for every resident in the county. The top contractor was Lockheed, at nearly $2 billion. Five firms received more than $100 million in defense contracts, and eleven others had contracts of over $30 million.[22] Twenty thousand to thirty thousand Silicon Valley scientists and engineers were working on elaborate defense projects of all kinds.[23] The engineers and entrepreneurs of Silicon Valley were the quintessence of Sunbelt culture, "the last American cowboys," possessing a "Silicon Valley Easy Rider mentality."[24] Driven by a fundamental urge to create and to take risks, they set up new forms of corporate structures and management styles that were looser than those back East in order to create new products.

Santa Clara County's ethos of can-do risk taking meant less resistance to women's adopting nontraditional, political roles. This ethos was part of the culture of Silicon Valley, with its venture capitalists, free-wheeling corporate structures and styles, and engineering outlook, namely, that there was always a better way to solve a problem, from audio oscillators to microprocessors. Talent was seen as something to be fostered, not stifled because of an outmoded sense of hierarchy. It did not matter what one's background was, as long as one got the job done. Silicon Valley was a land of uprooted and transplanted mavericks who flaunted their independence from old shackles. Journalists who interviewed local female officials noted how this political culture aided women's political careers:

> Many of the officeholders we talked to . . . credit the pioneering, open-minded atmosphere in Silicon Valley. People here are more open to change, they say, and less threatened by women in powerful positions than in other parts of the country. In fact, nearly all of the women interviewed moved here from other states. "We wouldn't be here in the first place," says County Supervisor Susanne Wilson, "if we weren't risk takers and entrepreneurs and gamblers. To be a Californian is to be an agent of change." Janet Gray Hayes, a native of Indiana, doubts that she could have become mayor of Indianapolis . . . [and] Sunnyvale city councilmember Lynn Briody described Sunnyvale as "very liberated" in its treatment of women in politics, compared to some other parts of the country where "to be an outspoken woman with ideas . . . is a novel experience."[25]

Affluence and Education Bode Well for Women's Political Activism

Support for nontraditional roles for women stemmed not only from the particular cultures of Silicon Valley and California but also from the culture of an affluent, educated citizenry. National polls show that affluent, highly educated men and women are more supportive of nontraditional roles for women and feminism than are the less affluent and less educated.[26] In 1980, Santa Clara County's median income and median buying power were the highest in the nation, and its per capita buying power was second in the nation. There were six thousand Ph.D.'s (one out of every six in California) and three universities.[27]

The county had high rates of voter registration, turnout, and partisanship. In the 1980 general election, 71 percent of the voting-age population was registered to vote and 79 percent of registered voters turned out to vote, well above the national figures of 66 percent and 59 percent, respectively. In the 1980 primary election, there was a 67 percent registration rate and a 64 percent turnout rate, both of which are high for such elections.[28] Partisan identification was also higher in Santa Clara County than in the nation as a whole. In 1982, when about 30 percent of U.S. voters considered themselves independent, 88 percent of county voters identified with a political party. The county weighed in 51 percent Democratic and 34 percent Republican, as compared to 45 percent Democratic and 25 percent Republican nationwide.[29]

The political economy of Santa Clara County was dominated by the economics of Silicon Valley, a swath of electronics firms along the southwest edge of San Francisco Bay, extending from Palo Alto in the north to San Jose in the south. In the 1970s and 1980s, the spectacular growth of the microprocessor industry and the corresponding surge in capital investment transformed the region. Santa Clara County ranked first in the nation in providing high-technology jobs, far outpacing second-ranked Los Angeles County.[30] Every job for a high-technology engineer or manager brought with it the need for four clerical and skilled manual workers and twelve additional jobs in support service industries.[31] This high-technology economy meant a rags-to-riches, life-in-the-fast-lane existence for a few and supporting jobs for many.

Class, Race, and Groups in Silicon Valley

Economically and geographically, Silicon Valley was divided into two classes. The upper-class, highly paid engineers and managers lived in the north county, while the skilled manual workers (half the county's workforce) resided in the south county, concentrated in San Jose, Milpitas, and Gilroy. In 1980, median family income in the south county was about $20,000, compared to the north's $48,000. And about 7 percent of south county residents lived in poverty, typically families headed by single mothers. The geographical division resulted from the growth of Silicon Valley from its Stanford conception in the north. As Everett Rogers and Judith Larsen describe it:

> Historically Silicon Valley began in the Stanford Industrial Park
> and gradually spread south toward San Jose. The North Coun-
> ty communities of Palo Alto, Mountain View, Sunnyvale and

Cupertino got first choice of the microelectronics firms. It was like an industrial development smorgasbord, with each city filling up its plate. Gilroy and San Jose were at the end of the line and what was left was to house the manual workers. From the viewpoint of a city's property tax base, providing housing for the poor was a losing proposition; costs of government services like education, welfare, police and fire protection are high relative to taxes paid per person. In short, North County profits at the expense of South County due to the segregation of Silicon Valley.[32]

Race and gender divided the valley's workforce as well. White males held engineering and management positions with the highest incomes and greatest power. Nonwhite men and white women fell lower in the socioeconomic hierarchy, and women of color were at the bottom of the occupational structure. Assembly-line jobs paid the minimum wage and experienced a 50 percent turnover because of a cheap pool of largely immigrant labor in the county. As of 1984, no Silicon Valley firm was unionized. The American Electronics Association argued that union wages would drive many firms out of business, and they provided training courses on how to prevent unionization. Union organizers complained of harassment against them. For example, at a 1982 hearing conducted by the Santa Clara County Commission on Human Relations, a Filipino employee stated that she had been fired by Fairchild for reading a union leaflet, printed in English, to a Tagalog-speaking fellow worker, who was also fired.[33]

As a rule, the most recent ethnic group to arrive in Silicon Valley started at the bottom of the occupational ladder. In the mid-1980s, the Vietnamese were the latest arrivals, making the south county second only to San Diego in concentration of Vietnamese in the United States. About four thousand Vietnamese worked at Hewlett-Packard, and two thousand Filipino immigrants worked at National Semiconductor. At the very bottom of the ladder were the thousands of undocumented workers, mostly from Mexico and Vietnam, who toiled in the valley's estimated two hundred sweatshops assembling circuit boards.[34]

The county's interest groups reflected its political economy. Economically based interest groups, such as the American Electronics Association, Santa Clara County Manufacturing Group, Semiconductor Industry Association, Chamber of Commerce, and Black Chamber of Commerce, promoted local business and commerce. Even though there were no unions in Silicon Valley's electronics firms, there were unions in some other industries and in the public sector. The most politically active were the Amalgamated Transit Union Local 265, the American Federation of State, County and Municipal Employees (AFSCME) Local 101, the American Federation of Teachers Local 957, the Santa Clara County Central Labor Council, the Santa Clara County Coalition of Labor Union Women (CLUW), the Service Employees International Union (SEIU) Locals 535 and 715, and the Warehouse Union Local 6.

Given Silicon Valley's economic dependence on government defense contracts, it was not surprising to find a wide array of peace groups, such as the Women's International League for Peace and Freedom, San Jose Peace Center, Computer Professionals for Social Responsibility, Los Gatos Peace Forum, and Campaign against Lockheed D-5/Trident II. Many religious groups were active in social justice causes. Reflecting the area's racial and ethnic diversity, there were numerous active ethnic and civil right groups, including the Mexican American Community Association, Mexican American Political Association (MAPA), League of United Latin American Citizens (LULAC), National Association for the Advancement of Colored People (NAACP) of Santa Clara County, Urban League of Santa Clara Valley, Asian-Americans for Community Involvement, Japanese-American Resource Center, Alliance for Philippine Concerns, and Bay Area Network of Gay and Lesbian Educators.

Many groups organized to oppose U.S. policy toward Central America, such as the Central American Refugee Committee, Committee in Solidarity with the People of El Salvador (CISPES), Nicaragua Work Brigades of San Jose, and Honduras Response Network. Groups concerned with U.S. policy in other parts of the world included the South Bay Middle East Peace Network, New Jewish Agenda of Santa Clara Valley, League of Arab American Women, General Union of Palestinian Students of San Jose, and South Bay Free South Africa Movement.

Advocates for the elderly included such groups as the American Association of Retired People, Older Women's League of Santa Clara County, and Gray Panthers of Santa Clara County. Environmental and housing concerns were represented by the Silicon Valley Toxics Coalition, Sierra Club, Audubon Society, People for Affordable Housing, and Emergency Housing Consortium. Civic groups that were active in local politics included various Rotary, Lions, and Kiwanis clubs.

Many women's organizations played an important role in local politics, among them the National Organization for Women, National Women's Political Caucus, League of Women Voters, American Association of University Women, Business and Professional Women, Chicana Coalition, and Women in Electronics, as well as three battered-women's shelters.

Although many of these groups had a liberal-left orientation, the county was not without its conservative-right groups, including the Los Gatos Christian Church, Christian Businessmen's Association, John Birch Society, and Ku Klux Klan. Many parts of the county had a strong tradition of neighborhood associations, particularly in San Jose. Often women began their political lives in these associations, focusing on neighborhood concerns and frequently attending local government meetings.

Political Structure: Types of Elections

In addition to an area's political economy and political culture, its political structure often had a bearing on the level of women's political involvement. Many political scientists found that in national legislatures, female candidates benefited from multimember electoral districts, where more than one candidate was elected to office, as opposed to single-member districts.[35] It was generally believed that voters were more likely to support women in a multimember race, because it was not a zero-sum choice for the voter (i.e., voting for a woman was not perceived as voting against a man).[36] Polls showed that voter sex discrimination was significant in the 1950s and 1960s, when only about half of Americans said they would vote for a woman for president. This proportion grew to three-quarters in the 1970s and 80 percent in the 1980s. There was less bias against women in Congress: in each decade Americans were about 10 percent more willing to vote for a woman for Congress as compared to the presidency. By the 1990s, pollsters had ceased asking the question about willingness to vote for a woman for Congress.[37]

Most studies of state legislatures in the United States also concluded that multimember districts benefited female candidates. A survey of legislative elections in states using both single- and multimember districts found that a greater proportion of women ran and were elected in multimember districts than in single-member districts. When states increased the number of multimember districts, there was an increase in the number of women among candidates and elected officials, and this increase was greater than the national trend of increasing numbers of elected women. And the obverse was also the case: when states shifted to fewer multimember districts, the number of female candidates and officials decreased.[38]

A more qualified conclusion was reached by Wilma Rule in her comparative study of women in state legislatures in 1974 and 1984. In accounting for the 100 percent increase in women's election to state legislative seats during this time, she determined that electoral structure was not as important as political culture and the effect of the women's movement. Rule said that the two most powerful predictors of women's greater recruitment were increased gains in moralistic states' assemblies and the presence of women in a state's congressional delegation: women in Congress served as models for women's eligibility and nomination, working with party influentials to recruit and support female candidates. In turn, women professionals and organizations such as NOW provided womanpower to assist in making women's candidacies succeed at the polls. A moralistic culture continued to have a positive effect on women's recruitment, and a traditional culture in the South remained an impediment (except in Florida and North Carolina). Rule found that multi-member districts were favorable to women's legislative recruitment beginning in the 1980s, but she cautioned that such districts were not a cure-all for women's low representation but rather one way to provide greater political opportunity for women. Indeed, a shift to single-member districts was followed by increasing proportions of female state legislators in Illinois, Oregon, and Colorado. Rule speculated that these exceptions might be explained by a strong women's political network in all three states, a weak competitive party system in Oregon, and the part-time nature of the Oregon and Colorado legislatures.[39]

Though the evidence at the national and state legislative levels seemed to lead to the conclusion that multimember electoral structures benefited women, findings were less compelling for local offices. A 1978 national study of city councils showed that women were slightly more likely to be elected in cities with multimember, at-large elections (as opposed to single-member, district elections), but by 1988, the difference was negligible: women constituted 24 percent of at-large councilmembers and 21 percent of district councilmembers.[40] There was overwhelming evidence, however, that district elections advantaged men of color.[41] When a minority population constituted at least 30 percent of a city's population and was geographically concentrated, a single-member district plan resulted in increased minority male representation.[42] Where there were district elections, blacks were represented in office almost proportionately to their numbers in the electorate.[43] Women of color, however, did not necessarily increase their numbers in office with district elections. Black women did almost the same in district as in citywide elections.[44] This evidence about electoral structure and race was used in Voting Rights Act litigation to secure a shift to district elections in many cities.

Analysts concerned with increased representation for both women and men of color suggested two solutions. One was to adopt district elections at the local level and at-large elections at the state level, since women were only slightly advantaged by at-large elections in municipal races, and men of color were greatly helped by district elections at the local level. At the state level, women were advantaged by at-large, multi-member arrangements, and blacks were not helped by single-member districts, largely because of the smaller proportion of blacks statewide as compared to large urban areas. A second solution was to switch to mixed electoral systems at the local level. In a mixed electoral system, some councilmembers were elected at-large and others (usually a larger number) were elected by districts. This plan was attractive to civil rights groups since it did not dilute minority vote the way at-large arrangements did. And it provided for simultaneous attention to both neighborhood and citywide issues. Numerous studies showed that district-based councilmembers got more calls from constituents regarding day-to-day problems than did city-based councilmembers. Compared to at-large arrangements, a mixed system caused a wider range of policy issues to be discussed at council meetings, greater citizen participation at council meetings and at the polls, and increased policy responsiveness through council coalition-building, especially in cities where minority voters cast the swing vote in the at-large mayoral contests.[45]

Why District Elections Benefited Women in San Jose

Even though women's constituency in San Jose was not geographically concentrated, female candidates benefited from district elections' relatively low cost, easier candidate visibility, and rewarding of grassroots organizing.[46] Throughout the 1970s, a coalition of minority, feminist, and labor groups tried to convince voters that the high cost of citywide campaigns had resulted in the two most affluent neighborhoods producing 78 percent of all councilmembers between 1950 and 1975. Some neighborhoods, such as the Hispanic east side, had never had a councilmember reside in their area. By 1978, many of the city's 118 neighborhood and homeowner groups had joined the coalition's efforts, and in that year voters approved district elections beginning in 1980.[47] In 1978, it cost more than $100,000 to run for a citywide council seat. Dividing San Jose into ten districts of 63,000 people each was expected to reduce this cost considerably. In 1980, primary campaigns were run for $5,000 and less, and the general races were in the range of $20,000 to $40,000. Three incumbent councilmembers—Jerry Estruth, Tom McEnery, and Iola Williams—won sizable majorities in the primaries and were returned to office. There were runoffs in the remaining seven districts, each of which featured a woman running against a man.[48]

Each of the five women who joined the San Jose City Council for the first time in 1980 said she would not have run in citywide elections, which were seen as too costly and time-consuming. District elections enabled neighborhoods to be heard, and most neighborhoods chose women to represent them. Several officials noted that if voters had been presented with a list of all the council candidates, odds are that they would not have elected a majority of women to the council. But with each district voting on a separate pair of candidates, electors did not express a preference for a desired composition of the overall council. The neighborhoods electing women included those with two of the highest median incomes (Lu Ryden's and Shirley Lewis's); a record for producing more city councilmembers than any other (Nancy Ianni's); the highest ethnic concentration in the city—43 percent Hispanic and 12 percent black (Blanca Alvarado's); and the city's biggest proportion of open space (Pat Sausedo's). For each of these women, districting dovetailed with her perception of representing her neighborhood, in such a way that she was encouraged to make her first bid for elective office.

For Councilmember Pat Sausedo, the key neighborhood concern was planning the remaining open space:

> District elections had a considerable effect on my decision to run this early. I was president of the homeowners' association when the planning commission seat opened up, and I went through the trauma of public interviews and got the appointment. I was on the commission two and one-half years. Without districting I would not have run so soon. I knew the district, and I knew increasingly more about the city from being on the planning commission. But I might not have run at all without districting.

Councilmember Blanca Alvarado was proud to represent the Chicano community. She was the first Hispanic woman and second Hispanic to be elected to a council seat in San Jose. While acknowledging the contributions of the feminist movement, she saw her victory as an extension of the political goals of the Chicano community. She had been active in community politics since 1948, beginning with voter registration drives and including eight years in the Mexican American Political Association (MAPA). "I was a member of the Charter Review Committee, which spent two years studying districting. I would not be here if it weren't for district elections. I would not have run at-large because it is too intimidating and too costly." She took particular pride in educating young Chicanas about local politics. And she pointed out how her campaign for the council was conducted by Hispanic women volunteers and aided by the Chicana Coalition, a group of local Chicana activists (with some Anglo members).

Both Lu Ryden and Nancy Ianni decided to run for office after reading in their newspapers about who was running in their districts. Ryden was upset at the thought of a young leftist representing her district, and Ianni was put off by the idea of "developer pawns" representing her neighborhood. Councilmember Ryden commented:

> The Republican party was trying for two months to convince me to run and I was hesitant. Finally in January 1980 I read in the newspaper who was running in my district and I said, "I don't feel represented by these people." One was a college kid about the age of my son. The other was a young Jane Fonda type. My opponents got all the group endorsements and they had been running for over a year. I owe my election victory to the power of prayer, a slick brochure I put out, the postcards I sent out to constituents the day before the election, and getting out and talking.

And Councilmember Ianni's noted: "Name recognition and money determine who gets elected. You can't get name recognition in a city this big. I decided to run when I realized that districting would wipe out all I had worked for because the other two candidates were pawns of the developers. One had been on the council for years and was pro-growth, and the other candidate got $30,000 from the developers in the primary. I ran on $15,000."

Finally, Councilmember Shirley Lewis saw crime and traffic as the major concerns of her neighborhood. She had worked as an aide to the city council, where she gained specific knowledge, skills, and awareness. She said she had always loved city government but was too intimidated to run until districting reduced the venture to a more accessible scale: "District elections played a big role. I would not have run in citywide elections. I wasn't ready for that. The district has 63,000, and the city has 630,000 residents. Citywide elections are too costly, take too much time, and campaigning is difficult."

In short, there would not have been a female majority of the San Jose City Council in 1980 if it had not been for district elections. Contrary to previous research findings, female candidates were enormously advantaged by single-member district electoral arrangements. And they did not suffer from the zero-sum choice by the voters between a woman and a man. The San Jose case supports an interpretation of electoral structure that distinguishes among levels of government: at-large, multi-member electoral structures benefit women in national legislatures, benefit them somewhat in state legislatures, and do not necessarily benefit them at the local level.

In the 1970s and 1980s, conditions in Santa Clara County were favorable for women's mass and elite political involvement. Indeed, it was a combination of activity at both levels that gave rise to the moniker "feminist capital of the nation." This self-designation was first coined at a 1974 meeting of the San Jose chapter of the National Women's Political Caucus (NWPC),[49] in response to the election of Janet Gray Hayes as the first woman mayor of a city as large as San Jose,[50] the election of Leona Egeland (D-San Jose) to the California Assembly, and the appointment of Geraldine Steinberg to the Santa Clara County Board of Supervisors. In 1978, Mayor Hayes was reelected, Susanne Wilson joined Steinberg on the county board, and a black woman, Iola Williams, was appointed to fill Wilson's vacant seat on the San Jose City Council. Until 1980, the phrase "feminist capital of the nation" was used primarily for local consumption. But the area received national attention after the 1980 elections resulted in female majorities on both the San Jose City Council (7–4) and the county board of supervisors (3–2). These gains were striking at a time when, nationwide, women constituted only 6 percent of county officials and 13 percent of municipal officials. At their 1981 inauguration, Mayor Hayes welcomed the city council to "an auspicious, historic and exciting occasion" of taking over "the fastest growing city in the country and the feminist capital of the country."[51]

Conventional political scientists might have ended the story here: Santa Clara County was called the feminist capital of the nation because in the 1970s and early 1980s conditions were favorable for the election of women, and women were elected in record numbers. But of course, not all elected women were feminists, and there was more to feminism than the election of women to public office. Many political puzzles remained. Why was Mayor Hayes inclined to use the word "feminist" with such pride the same year that an antifeminist Reagan administration was inaugurated at the national political level? What was the relationship among the local NWPC chapter that coined the expression, the electorate, and the female officials elected between 1974 and 1980? How many of these officials were feminists, and what kind of feminists were they? Was there anything feminist about the county besides its election of women to public office? To solve these puzzles we need to apply the insights of women's studies to six conventional political science concepts, beginning with political mobilization.

Part Two

Women and Mass Politics

3 Political Mobilization

Women's Shift from Individual to
Group Consciousness and Activity

THE CONCEPT of political mobilization is a good point of departure for our inquiry. It refers to the process whereby a group develops awareness of and acts on its distinctive political concerns. Initially, it takes the form of a movement, composed of people who are outside the centers of power. Over time, a movement typically "becomes institutionalized" or "goes mainstream" in the form of political parties and interest groups. Political parties seek to advance a platform by electing people to public office; interest groups try to influence government policy. Unlike its European counterparts, the U.S. women's movement was quickly institutionalized in the form of interest groups but had a belated and weak institutionalized relationship with political parties. In this book, women's interest groups are treated as part of women's political mobilization because of women's recent entrance into mainstream politics. Throughout the 1970s and 1980s, established women's groups in Washington, D.C., were still relatively new arrivals compared with their more powerful counterparts, especially economic interest groups, whose efforts were more a part of politics as usual. By contrast, groups representing the political movements of the 1960s, for the most part, were not as entrenched, did not have as many resources, and had to spend relatively more energy mobilizing their constituencies. Accordingly, this chapter focuses on women as part of the women's movement and interest groups.

Mainstream political scientists have done a poor job of understanding women's political mobilization. They had no trouble "seeing" this

57

mobilization in the form of interest groups, but they did not "see" either the women's suffrage or the women's liberation movement. Why did it take feminists to see the movement aspect of women's political mobilization?

Movements Did Not Fit the Paradigm

Conventional political scientists were unable to see the political mobilization of women because the prevailing political science paradigms in place during the first and second waves of the U.S. women's movement, institutionalism and behaviorism, operated as blinders to the extent that they described the relationship between the knower and the known in terms of objectivity and subjectivity. The researcher's personal characteristics, interests, or biases were downplayed or deemed irrelevant to the pursuit of knowledge, and research with a point of view was suspect. But as we have seen, purported objectivity about women's politics turned out to be androcentric bias, which went undetected until feminist researchers discovered it. Feminist researchers saw women's politics as a problematic to be explained, even if it did not conveniently fit into the puzzle of normal science. Their stance was neither "distanced" nor "aperspectival": they were interested in studying women's political life and wanted women to have more say in political life. Thus, feminists operated from an epistemology at odds with the dominant paradigm.

Feminists met with little success in transforming the discipline of political science precisely because they called for the adoption of a new paradigm. Each paradigm used its own evaluative criteria drawn from its own community life. Most male political scientists were satisfied, based on their experiences in their scientific communities, that behaviorist objectivity could get at all the important research questions about political life; most feminist political scientists were convinced, based on their experiences as scholars in the feminist community, that a perspectival, engaged approach was needed to get at some extremely important research questions about political life.

Androcentric science produced bad science. Feminist researchers produced more complete and less distorted research results because they paid attention to the women's movement and took seriously its claims about culturewide prejudice. Women (or feminists, male and female) as a group were more likely than men (nonfeminists) as a group to produce claims unbiased by androcentrism.

One way they did this was by focusing on "meaning," both "action meaning" (to the scientist) and "act meaning" (to the actor). In positivist social science, there was an incompatibility between disciplinary concepts and action meanings on the one hand and the realities lived by the subjects studied on the other. Action meaning called for scientific explanation, and act meaning called for semantic explanation. Both efforts involved interpretation, and if the interpretation of the act meaning was wrong, then it was impossible for the explanation offered by the disciplinary action meaning to be right. Meaning could not be imposed from without. For example, before feminist scholarship, social scientists looked at gender as a dichotomous variable: women were contrasted to men. There was no interest in or ability to elicit what gender meant to subjects. Or women and men were studied in terms of their complementary "sex roles," in functionalist accounts of social and political life. The meaning of these roles was seen one-sidedly in terms of system stability, ignoring what sex roles meant to subjects. With the advent of feminist scholarship, attention was shifted from sex to gender, social relations between the sexes and cultural meanings attached to those relations. In order to expand the empirical assessments of consciousness and meaning to the subject, political scientists had to go beyond survey research methodology, which imposed action meaning on subjects instead of eliciting act meaning from them. To carry out a true "social" science, scholars had to know what subjects thought of social acts and institutions, since every social act and institution was mediated through the categories of the mind.[1]

Knowledge was based on experience, and women's experiences, informed by feminist theory, were the grounds for more complete and less distorted knowledge claims. "Ruling activities" prevented rulers from seeing the whole picture, and knowledge on the part of the ruled emerged from the struggle against domination. One's "perspective" came with experience, and a "feminist standpoint" was achieved through an intellectual and political struggle against the partial and perverse perspective available from the ruling gender experience of men. The sexual division of labor (specifically, women's contributions to subsistence and childrearing) enabled women to see social relations more accurately than men insofar as men benefited from the exploitation of women in this division of labor. The vision of the ruling gender structured the relations in which all parties were forced to participate. The vision of the ruled gender was achieved through science, which saw beneath the surface of the social relations in which all were forced to participate, and through education, which grew from the struggle to change those relations. The adoption of a standpoint by women exposed the real relations among human beings as inhuman.[2]

In contrast to the Enlightenment insistence that only a distanced, "objective" observer could produce good science, feminists maintained that political activism against oppressive social relations was necessary for scientific reasons. It was only through struggle against male domination that one could understand the extent to which it permeated social and political life. If male domination was so obvious that any "objective" social scientist could see it, then why didn't male social scientists see it? Why did it take women (in the movement and in the academy) to unearth its existence? And why did feminist social scientists have to face such an uphill battle in transforming their disciplines in order to understand gender relations, which from their standpoint were an obvious and compelling aspect of social and political life?

Since gender relations were characterized by domination, feminist theory needed to be compensatory and critical, in addition to being truth-seeking. When women's experiences were made intelligible in the consciousness-raising process, women recognized that men's stories did not make sense. Consciousness-raising revealed women as authoritative pattern perceivers. Although there was no one story of women, there were detectable "fault lines": the fact that women did more work but controlled less wealth than men; the fact that men did far more violence to women than women did to men; and the fact that men's stories marginalized, reduced and erased women. Feminists discovered these and other patterns of common oppression as the grounds for an epistemic community.[3]

Feminists in the academy also created a methodological community. Feminists gathered evidence differently from men. In the social sciences, all evidence gathering fell into three categories: listening to informants, observing behavior, and examining historical traces and records. Feminists sought all three types of evidence; compared to men, they listened more carefully to how female informants thought about their lives and men's lives, they observed behaviors of women and men that traditional social scientists had not thought significant, and they sought examples of newly recognized patterns in historical data. Their first attempts to rectify the androcentrism of traditional analyses were to "add women": to discover "lost" female social scientists, to study women who contributed to the public life that social scientists were already examining, and to document women's victimization by male dominance. But there were limits to these additive efforts. The work of early female social scientists was constrained by immense pressures to make their research conform; consequently, one could not expect it to produce the kind of powerful analyses that emerged as part of the social revolution of the women's movement. Simply looking at women's contribution to public life did not question androcentric standards of that public life; it left out social practices of reproduction, sexuality, and motherhood; and it did not ask about the meanings for women of women's contributions to public life. And a focus on women as victims created the false impression that women are only victims.[4]

Going beyond the additive approach, women wanted their problematic experiences explained. Prior research had asked only those questions about social life that appeared problematic from within the social experiences of (white, Western, bourgeois) men. A problem was always a problem *for* someone. The questions an oppressed group wanted answered were rarely requests for pure truth; rather, they were queries about how to change its conditions. It was women who should be expected to be able to reveal for the first time what women's experiences were. There was a new purpose of social science: for women. In feminist scholarship, the researcher appeared not as an invisible, anonymous voice of authority but as a real, historical individual with concrete, specific desires and interests. The cultural beliefs and behaviors of feminist researchers shaped the results of their analysis no less than did those of sexist and androcentric researchers. These beliefs and behaviors were part of the empirical evidence for or against the claims advanced in the results of the research. As Sandra Harding asserted: "*This* evidence too must be open to critical scrutiny no less than what is traditionally defined as relevant evidence. Introducing this 'subjective' element into the analysis in fact increases the objectivity of the research and decreases the 'objectivism' which hides this kind of evidence from the public."[5]

Feminists might have been content to "add women" to existing paradigms if those paradigms had proved capable of providing satisfactory explanations of women's political mobilization. But existing paradigms were found to be lacking, and the normal science in which they were embedded became suspect. Political scientists were fond of studying political mobilization, but usually not in the case of the United States, which was assumed to be a stable, fully evolved democracy, and virtually never in the case of U.S. women. For example, a citation search for articles and book reviews published between 1989 and 1992 with the words "political" and "mobilization" in their titles resulted in forty-two citations. Thirty were cases outside the United States, such as the working class in Mexico and Venezuela, National Socialists in Germany, and North Africans in France. The twelve citations of U.S. cases covered such topics as the political mobilization of religious beliefs, of blacks, of Texas farmworkers, and of environmentalists. None was about women.

In addition to the limits of the dominant paradigm, there were other possible explanations for the lack of scholarly attention to the political mobilization of women. One might argue that by the 1990s women were already mobilized, so why bother studying a dead issue? But this line of argument was weakened by scholarly attention to the historical cases of "men's politics" listed above. Conversely, one might argue that women's political mobilization was too recent for scholarly distance on the subject. Nevertheless, it was contemporaneous with the environmental and farmworker movements found in the citation search.

A more plausible explanation was that the mobilization of women was seen as social, not political. Political scientists relegated the women's movement to sociology (the study of groups) and considered women's political mobilization only insofar as it took the form of interest groups influencing the government (the conventional definition of the study of politics). But, the truth was that the women's movement had always considered itself political. Its rallying slogan was "the personal is political." *Its* definition of the political, however, included gender power relations, not merely governmental power relations. Political scientists could not understand the political mobilization of women until they adopted a new definition of the political and listened to the definitions of reality provided by the subjects.

The Articulation of Women's Group Consciousness

Group consciousness is a necessary precondition for political mobilization. Members of a group have to realize that they have a common identity and distinctive political concerns. Coming to this realization is typically called consciousness-raising, a term implying that part of one's identity had been submerged—as unimportant, irrelevant, repressed, or unknown—and eventually emerged—as important, relevant, realized, or known. The second precondition for political mobilization is that a group act on its distinctive political concerns. In a totalitarian or authoritarian regime, or other conditions of close supervision, a group may not be able to act politically in spite of its consciousness. Members of a group may engage in isolated acts of resistance, but a group is generally not thought to be mobilized until it can and does act in a visible way as a group, articulating an identity and voicing distinctive political concerns.

The group consciousness of American women in the contemporary period began to develop in the 1960s, initially outside the academy but quickly entering into the writings of feminist political scientists. In fact, some of the political scientists whose writings are discussed in this book were movement activists. For example, Jo Freeman, who wrote the first, and still definitive, social science analysis of the women's movement, *The Politics of Women's Liberation,* organized the nation's first independent women's liberation group, in Chicago in 1967. She also founded and edited the first national feminist newsletter, *Voice of the Women's Liberation Movement.* In the early 1970s, she wrote three influential movement articles: "The Bitch Manifesto," "The Building of the Gilded Cage," and "The Tyranny of Structurelessness." [6] Feminist political scientists in the American Political Science Association formed the Women's Caucus for Political Science in 1969.

Outside the academy, women's political consciousness developed in settings that were not the places where male political scientists traditionally looked for politics, such as consciousness-raising groups, where women got together to discuss their lives, their feelings, and "male chauvinism." At first these women were hesitant to exclude men or to say that men oppressed women. But the more women met as a group, the more they endorsed such "radical" processes and ideas.[7] The widespread use of consciousness-raising as both an organizing and an educational tool for the new movement is usually credited to the Redstockings, a group founded in New York in 1969 by Ellen Willis and Shulamith Firestone, after they were humiliated by antiwar men during a counter-inaugural demonstration. The Redstockings became nationally known in the women's movement for disrupting a public abortion hearing in New York City and holding their own abortion hearings. As Judith Hole and Ellen Levine noted, "the group is also to be credited with the first articulation of what has become known as the 'pro-woman' line—the idea that women are in no way responsible for their oppression, and that men, not women, must change their behavior."[8] The Redstockings described women as a class engaged in political conflict with men as a class, necessitating a collective solution on the part of women:

> Because we live so intimately with our oppressors, in isolation from each other, we have been kept from seeing our personal suffering as a political condition. This creates the illusion that a woman's relationship with her man is a matter of interplay between two unique personalities, and can be worked out individually. In reality, every such relationship is a *class* relationship, and the conflicts between individual men and women are *political* conflicts that can only be solved collectively.[9]

As was the case for Firestone and Willis, the group consciousness of many women was raised when their views on women's condition were dismissed by their male comrades in civil rights and antiwar organizations. The phrase "women's liberation," for example, came from activists in the Student Non-violent Coordinating Committee (SNCC) in 1964 at a workshop in Mississippi where women challenged the position of women in the organization.[10] Many radical women insisted on operating as a collective, eschewing hierarchy and the cult of the leader. The Redstockings adopted a collective name as a revolutionary act to challenge the names given to them by fathers and husbands, just as many blacks had challenged the names of former slave masters. The name represented a synthesis of two traditions: that of nineteenth-century feminist theoreticians and writers who were insultingly called "Bluestockings," and the militant political tradition of radicals—the red of revolutions.[11] The small group was the basic unit of participation. For example, in Boston's socialist-feminist Bread and Roses, women formed "collectives" to share and analyze their life stories and to counter male cultural domination with an energized sense of solidarity with other women, as expressed in the slogan, "Sisterhood is powerful." Counting on other women to act as sisters defied the dominant culture's idea that individuals had to make it on their own: "We quite consciously provoked the surprise and dismay of straight liberal groups who would ask for one speaker on Women's Liberation and get three; they would ask, 'Who is *the* speaker?' and the Bread and Roses group would respond, 'We are.' "[12]

Bread and Roses members engaged in "zap actions" to raise the consciousness of people in the community. In these theatrical events with costumes and leaflets, women would go to some public place to expose the sexism of an institution or activity. The point was to reach new people, women and men, in new ways and to jolt spectators' normal way of seeing things. In a 1970 "Ogle-In," for example, men in a busy shopping area were subjected to stares, whistles, catcalls, and pinches.

Radical and Liberal Feminist Ideas about Women as a Group

Of course, not all women in the 1960s who developed a group consciousness saw themselves as radicals or revolutionaries. But the radicals articulated a new identity for women. For the most part, first-wave feminists had defined women either in conventional gender terms, that is, more moral and civilizing than immoral and selfish men, or in conventionally liberal terms, that is, equally capable of reasoning as men and deserving educational, economic, and political opportunities and rights. Radical feminists in the second wave developed unconventional concepts and ways to describe who women were.[13]

Both leftist and liberal women became more feminist because of the radicals' ideas, which they eventually adopted. Betty Friedan's 1963 best-seller, *The Feminine Mystique,* drew from liberal discourse about individual self-development and argued that, just like men, women needed to self-actualize, which they could not do as long as their identity was derived from being someone else's wife and mother.[14] Like their first-wave counterparts, liberal feminists emphasized the concepts of reason, education, economic autonomy, civil rights, political opportunity, and male prejudice. Unlike their earlier counterparts, they did not see "femininity" as grounds for "cleaning up male politics." Rather, they saw it as a problematic sex role that needed to be transformed in a more androgynous direction, so that both men and women could combine the best of the two sex-role worlds. Men should be able to express emotions, and women should be able to be assertive without feeling the weight of cultural sanctions. Men and women should be partners, sharing household responsibilities, working together in a nondiscriminatory market economy, and participating equally in electoral politics.[15]

Compared with the radicals, liberal feminists adopted a more traditional discourse and sought their goals through more conventional forms of organization, such as the National Organization for Women, university women's studies courses, the courts, and the commercial media. Liberal feminists did not work to abolish capitalism; instead, they sought positions of power for women within it. And liberals rejected the pro-woman line. Men could not be blamed for all of women's problems; women had to accept some individual responsibility for their lives. But as Zillah Eisenstein pointed out, all feminism was both liberal and radical, "liberal at its root in that the universal feminist claim that woman is an independent being (from man) is premised on the eighteenth-century liberal conception of the independent and autonomous self. All feminism is also radically feminist in that woman's identity as a sexual class underlies this claim."[16] Liberalism gave women the language for an individual identity; radical feminism gave women the language for a collective identity.

It is important to underscore the radical origins of women's group consciousness because the liberal formulation, greatly influenced by the radicals, became the dominant feminist discourse by 1975. But before their demise as a movement, radical feminists succeeded in pushing liberal feminists to the left and leftists toward feminism. After 1975, radical feminism was eclipsed by cultural feminism—an emphasis on personal rather than social transformation and on creating a female counterculture rather than opposing male supremacy.[17]

Radical feminist ideas also made their way into the academy. Catharine
A. MacKinnon argued that the women's liberation movement as she
knew it had been killed by liberalism. What the movement had meant
was a critique, from the standpoint of women's material existence, of
such ideas as consent, choice, equality, and freedom. It had always asked
the question, Is it good for women? It was informed by the insight that
the personal is political, namely, that what women did every day mattered, that women became part of what they did not resist, and that
women had a responsibility to all women. MacKinnon said the movement
thus conceived had been destroyed by the theory and actions of liberal
feminists: for example, by the ERA's emphasis on equality, by privacy-
based abortion arguments, and by opposition to antipornography ordinances. For MacKinnon, as long as liberals emphasized gender neutrality, they could not take gender into account and could not recognize
that neutrality enforced a non-neutral status quo. The liberal definition
of consent meant that whatever you were forced to do was attributed to
your free will. Liberal "privacy" protected a sphere of women's intimate
oppression. And liberal "protected speech" protected sexual violence
against women and the sexual use of women.[18]

Although not all women in the academy drew from radical feminist
analysis in such a pure form, radical feminist formulations had a profound effect on academic feminists. Feminist political scientists opened
up new ways of looking at women's group consciousness, explicitly acknowledging their intellectual debt to radicals in the movement and increasingly convinced that radical formulations necessitated the creation
of a new paradigm to understand women's politics.

Academic Analyses of Women's Group Consciousness: Twelve Key Concepts

Beginning in the mid-1970s, feminist political scientists began to construct the pieces of the puzzle of women's group consciousness. Though
there was no consensus on the final contours of the puzzle, there was
agreement that certain pieces were fundamental, had originated in the
women's movement, and challenged political science as usual.

1. Consciousness-raising groups. Consciousness-raising groups enabled
women to overcome their isolation from one another and to realize the
extent to which they had internalized the general social degradation of
women. The choice of small groups reflected women's greater familiarity with locality and other small units of organization and was both therapeutic and politicizing. It also enabled women to avoid negative features of other forms of organization and communication: hierarchy and

domination. The supportive, nonauthoritarian style of movement communication and organization was thought to form a uniquely feminine style of doing politics. Consciousness-raising groups provided women with both a new identity and a new form of organization.[19]

2. *Politics begin with feelings.* In consciousness-raising groups, feelings were a gateway to knowledge. As the San Francisco Redstockings put it in their manifesto breaking away from the male-dominated New Left, "our politics begin with our feelings," which were a response to humiliation, pain, and oppression. Women's knowledge had been rendered meaningless or empty by men, and there was no point jumping into "superficial pseudo-activities" until women analyzed their feelings and took themselves seriously enough to devise appropriate political strategies.[20]

Though early radical feminists were careful to make the point that their politics *began*, but did not end, with their feelings, some later cultural feminists valorized women's emotional experiences and rejected reason as male.[21] This approach led to a countercultural politics that was criticized by most feminist political scholars, who cautioned that feminists should not reject reason as male and not use "women's experiences" as a basis of epistemology. Such a stance invited a stereotypical treatment of the essential female; further, it was difficult to operationalize women's experiences across variations in culture, class, race, and sexual orientation, and there was no way to choose among competing claims. Feminist knowledge was in danger of degenerating into ontological arguments, judging people not by what they did or said but by who they were. It was not necessarily true that the more experiences of oppression one had, the more knowledge one had and the more universally applicable one's views were. Unless theories were based on reflection and on an evaluation of the interpretation of experience, such things as analogy, axiom, and assertion would pass for argument. Indeed, there could be no political discourse without reason.[22]

3. *The personal is political.* The personal became political when women had an opportunity to compare notes on personal unhappiness, to discover the social basis of that unhappiness, and to look for political solutions for women as a group. Movement women saw the conversion of the personal into the political in their respective causes. In the civil rights movement, as Nancy McWilliams observed, "where one sat on a bus, whom one married, in whose company one ate, where one swam, slept, and urinated, became questions of public policy. Women in SNCC and other radical organizations were expected to see the political nature of private things in relation to blacks but not in relation to themselves."[23]

The other side of the coin was personalizing the political, or more specifically, seeing gendered persons in politics. Male liberal theorists such as Locke and Hobbes had reduced politics to a power struggle among neuter individuals, all the while having men in mind. Feminists agreed that part of politics was a power struggle, and they added the idea that one type of power struggle was that between the sexes. But they insisted that politics was about more than power. It was about defining the good life, the common good, community values, in short, the ends to which power was rightfully used. They added the removal of sexism to the definition of the common good. And they reexamined in political terms what the male political world had dismissed as women's "do-good-ism," "moralism," and "community activity." McWilliams noted: "Thus, for instance, what Jane Addams did in Chicago was not politics but 'social work,' and Margaret Sanger's crusade was not political but 'educational.' That contemporary women should describe their condition in explicitly political terms still seems highly peculiar to many."[24] The "political" was more than the state or the government. It included relations between the sexes, previously deemed personal and private.

  4. Public/private interdependence. As we have seen, the dichotomy of private moral woman and public immoral man prevented political scientists from seeing women's politics and trivialized moral concerns in politics. The women's movement challenged this dichotomy, but feminists had not agreed on an understanding of the relationship between the two concepts. Radical feminists called for utopias, liberal feminists accepted the devaluation of the private in their rush to be like men, Marxist feminists were too quick to recast the two spheres as "production" and "reproduction," and psychoanalytic feminists lost sight of political history with their emphasis on domestic dynamics and family history. Some called for a reconstruction of the public and private by redeeming everyday life, affirming the value of the private-familial sphere, and envisioning an "ethical polity," with a public discourse based on concern for others, responsibility, care, obligation, and a nonsentimental "maternal thinking."[25]

  Ambivalence toward children was expressed by some radical feminists and in Simone de Beauvoir's pathbreaking *The Second Sex,* which saw childrearing as a burden on women. One feminist's first experience in a consciousness-raising group was neither mother- nor infant-friendly. In the late 1960s, she and a friend were struggling with their identities as mothers and graduate students and decided to attend a meeting of a feminist group. When her friend spoke of her conflict over public and private commitments, she was cut off abruptly by "the group's 'facilitator': 'We will have no diaper talk here. We're here to talk about women's liberation.' My friend and I left, for we could not treat our children as abstractions, as nuisances to be overcome, or as evidence of our sad capitulation to the terms of patriarchy."[26] It was not until the movement had gone more mainstream, and younger feminists themselves began to have children, that feminist theorists developed more complex formulations of the relationship between women's private and public lives.

5. *Meaning to the subject.* Feminist scholars agreed that women's group identity had to be articulated by women themselves. Jean Bethke Elshtain asserted: "We need an account of women's liberation which can incorporate the self-understanding of the female subject as an essential feature of its overall logic of explanation. We need to be able, cogently, to articulate the bases and steps in the creation of female identity, public and private. . . . We need to create a mode of political thinking that helps women redescribe social reality from a vantage point that allows for, and sustains, critical reflection."[27]

For many, the best way to ascertain the self-understandings of women was an ethnographic approach, with fieldwork and participant observation. Judith Stacey described the process through which she both adopted and saw the limitations of this approach. In an earlier research project, *Patriarchy and Socialist Revolution in China,* she had used a macrostructural, abstract approach based almost exclusively on library research, leaving out stories of actual women and patriarchs. Dissatisfaction with the methods she used caused her to "privilege methodological considerations over substantive interests" when she selected her next research project, a fieldwork study of family and gender relationships in Silicon Valley. "I was eager for a 'hands-on,' face-to-face research experience, which I also believed was more compatible with feminist principles," namely, an emphasis on the experiential, contextual, interpersonal, concrete realm of everyday reality and human agency, empathy, connection, concern, and respect for and power to one's research "subjects" as collaborators in the research project.[28]

After more than two years of fieldwork, however, Stacey saw problems in both the process and the product of her research. She was put in situations where she inevitably manipulated or betrayed one of her subjects. "Conflicts of interest and emotion between the ethnographer as authentic, related person (i.e., participant) and as exploiting researcher (i.e., observer) are also an inescapable feature of ethnographic method. . . . For no matter how welcome, even enjoyable the fieldworker's presence may appear to 'natives,' fieldwork represents an intrusion and intervention into a system of relationships . . . that the researcher is far freer than the researched to leave. The inequality and potential treacherousness of this relationship seems inescapable."[29] Ethnography did not eliminate the problem of authority. Ultimately, it was the researcher's project, in her voice, reflecting her judgments, and based on an unequal relationship in spite of the apparent mutuality during the research process. Stacey concluded that there could only be partially feminist ethnographies.

6. *Community*. Women's group consciousness often developed in their communities, through physical proximity at markets, churches and temples, laundries, beauty parlors, and neighborhood networks. "Female consciousness" reflected the gender division of labor by sex, whereby women were assigned the responsibility to preserve life. As such, it was a conservative consciousness, but it had a radical feminist potential if it led to political claims that challenged male power.[30]

Women's group consciousness could also be found at the workplace, where sex-segregated settings and family commitments and responsibilities fostered a female-centered consciousness regarding their working conditions.[31] Women's experiences as community members revealed the artificiality of the public-private split. Their multiple responsibilities across these two realms created distinctive forms of group consciousness and activism. For example, women's responsibility for nurturance of children and adult males in their households meant that they were the ones who negotiated with landlords, markets, welfare offices, healthcare providers, and the like. In joining their friends and neighbors to meet their needs, women often demanded that public institutions fulfill their obligations to citizens.[32]

Because of women's community involvement, they often entered the public world as members of networks, not necessarily as isolated individuals.[33] Women's community networks were often crucial to the development of their political consciousness, "a process of making connections—between their own lives and those of others, between issues that affect them and their families in the neighborhood or community and those that affect them in the workplace, between the so-called differing spheres of their lives. . . . Women's coming to political consciousness . . . may be more a phenomenon of *relationship* and *connection*, than one of recognizing *interests* in the traditional, individualistic sense."[34]

Some accommodationist scholars were not so willing to call women's community networks political, preferring instead the term "protopolitics" to describe collective appeals to authorities in organizations outside the political arena. In women's protopolitics, women acquired organizational skills, built networks, and developed consciousness in family and community organizations. Protopolitics were seen as an important addition to conventional understandings of politics as movements and as claiming politics (interest groups, elections, etc.).[35]

Of course, one problem with communities was that they divided those with common experiences from those who did not share such experiences. Women's multiple community identities could not be prematurely collapsed into *a* women's community. Women of color frequently criticized white women for their "cultural imperialism," in failing to understand diverse communities. Understanding the communities of women of color would come through friendship, not through scientific observation. As Maria Lugones and Elizabeth Spelman pointed out, "It demands recognition that you do not have the authority of knowledge; it requires coming to the task without ready-made theories to frame our lives. . . . Only then can we engage in a mutual dialogue that does not reduce each one of us to instances of the abstraction called 'woman.' "[36]

7. Family. Feminist scholars saw the family as an important locus of women's group consciousness, especially in light of trends that began in the 1970s: increases in women's labor force participation, the divorce rate, female-headed households, and the number of "working mothers."[37] As "the family" changed, so too did the kinds of questions feminists raised about what was fair for women or in the best interests of women as a group. Until there was justice in the family, women would not be able to gain equality in politics or at the workplace. In spite of all the rhetoric about equality between the sexes, the traditional division of family labor prevailed, leaving women and children socially and economically vulnerable.[38] Feminists argued that it was in the best interest of women to reorganize society so that wage-earning men and women had the time to be parents and members of communities. They maintained that women were better off when men and women parented together.[39] And feminist scholars looked to the state to pass laws allowing for greater workplace flexibility, better child-care options, and more extended parental leave policies.

Early radical feminists often dismissed the family as a patriarchal institution with little to recommend it, but feminists in the academy were more inclined to analyze the political implications of gendered experiences in the family. Women's family experiences gave them a distinctive identity vis-à-vis the state: in defiance of "state interests" women could bring a familistic identity to politics that rejected amoral statecraft and affirmed human dignity. In their day-to-day nurturance and protection of human life, women experienced a social world different from that of men, and women were ill-advised to rush into men's political world of hierarchy, bureaucracy, wars, and realpolitik.[40]

Feminist analyses of household labor revealed that wives did most of the work around the house, even when they were employed more hours than their husbands were. Consequently, the family was frequently the locus of a struggle over inequities in the division of labor in the family. Family historians had tended to assume that there was a unity of interests among family members. Feminist analysis recast "family interest" as a problematic notion once women's family experiences were taken seriously.[41]

8. Care. Feminist analysts took seriously women's experiences as caretakers and investigated how these experiences contributed to women's group consciousness. As we have seen, Carol Gilligan's work about an ethic of care was the point of departure for much of this analysis. Joan Tronto thought it was important to develop a theory of care but argued that rather than celebrating an ethic of care as a factor of gender difference that pointed to women's superiority, feminists should construct a moral theory of care. She said there was not sufficient evidence to link gender difference with a different moral perspective. Furthermore, it was strategically dangerous to assert gender difference in a social context that identified male as normal. Instead of defending women's morality, it was more important to look critically at the philosophical promises and problems of an ethic of care in order to understand the balance between caring for self and caring for others.[42]

Another important concept in this line of thought was "maternal thinking," derived from the practice of mothering and transformed by feminist consciousness. Women had cultures, traditions, and inquiries to bring to the public world. Maternal thinking arose from social practices aimed at the preservation, growth, and acceptability of the child. Interest in producing an acceptable child provided special opportunities for mothers to insist on their own values. But for these opportunities to be realized, maternal thinking had to be transformed by feminist consciousness. A transformed maternal thought in the public realm would make the preservation and growth of all children a work of public conscience and legislation and would encourage men to share equally and actively in transformed maternal practices.[43]

Both the powers and pitfalls of maternalism were illustrated in women's peace protests. On the one hand, previously apolitical women became politicized, and mothers lent respectability to the cause. A maternalistic approach sometimes led women to adopt a political economic analysis of war and peace, providing a collective education for women who might not otherwise have joined a political party and often developing into a feminist consciousness. On the other hand, women's maternalism often remained within the proscribed boundaries of patriarchy: heterosexist, antifeminist, and conservative, easily rallied for fatherland and war.[44]

9. *Sexuality*. Women's understanding of their sexuality was an important determinant of their group consciousness. Many feminists initially embraced the sexual revolution of the 1960s, only to discover that it too was characterized by male supremacy.[45] Some women in the civil rights and antiwar movements were treated more as sexual objects than as comrades and were told that they were "up tight" if they refused men's sexual advances.[46]

Some lesbian feminists defined their politics in terms of a critique of heterosexuality as the cornerstone of male supremacy. Lesbianism was not simply a personal decision, a civil rights concern, or a cultural phenomenon; it was an extension of the analysis of sexual politics to an analysis of sexuality itself as an institution. Lesbian feminist politics was a commitment to women as a group. It was not lesbianism (women's ties to women) but rather heterosexuality (women's ties to men) that divided women personally and politically. Heterosexual privilege was the way that women were given a stake in their own oppression. Lesbian feminism was not a political analysis for lesbians only; they were just the most likely to argue it given their materially different reality.[47]

Alternative understandings of sexuality characterized the debate between sexual liberals and radical feminists over pornography and free speech. Sexual liberals assumed that sexual expression was inherently liberating and must be permitted to flourish unchecked, even when it entailed the exploitation or brutalization of others. Radical feminists saw sexuality as a construct of culture that reflected and reinforced a culture's values, including its denigration of women.[48]

Some feminists shifted attention from sexuality to the erotic, a life force that was a source of information and power. It was a measure of the beginnings of women's sense of self, emphasizing the importance of internal rather than external directives. The erotic challenged self-negation, resignation, and self-effacement. Recognizing the power of the erotic in their lives gave women the energy to pursue genuine change in their worlds. Empowered women were dangerous, because they insisted on loving their lives and their work. Women needed to realize that the erotic had been misnamed by men as pornography and used against women.[49] Others argued that the erotic was a source of power for the powerless, because it was a longing for completeness and wholeness and a challenge to hierarchy and domination.[50] The erotic enabled the weak to break the cycle of domination in three stages: disbelief, bonding, and joint action. To begin to disbelieve the myths perpetuated by the powerful, the powerless had to experience an internal creative energy, life force, and sense of wholeness. Only then could they bond with their group and take joint action.[51]

10. Power. There were two views of power: the traditional view, offered by the powerful, of power as domination, control, and an object to be hoarded for its own sake, like money, and the feminist view of power as ability, energy, accomplishment, strength, and effective interaction.[52] Many feminist theorists refocused attention away from "power over" and toward "power to."[53] An emphasis on "power to" was linked to the idea of creating a community that was not based on violence and domination.[54] It was also connected to the idea of "empowerment," actions that challenged existing power relations.[55]

Some scholars saw problems with such feminist theories of power, saying that they bordered on an essentialism that made women's identity independent of their social situation, and were ahistorical insofar as some nonfeminist thinkers had also promoted a power-to model. In replacing "power over" with "power to," feminists would be in the contradictory position of using "power over" in order to make the world safe for "power to." Moreover, women would not necessarily use power better or differently than men.[56]

11. Equality/difference. Both the first and second waves of the women's movement confronted the equality-difference debate, and neither wave resolved it. Do, or should, women as a group think of themselves as equal with men or different from them?

Equality was a contested political concept, viewed differently by radical, liberal, and socialist feminists. It could mean a statement of fact or description of shared characteristics. Since factual descriptions of "natural inequality" had commonly been used to justify inegalitarian social arrangements,—about women and slaves, for instance—it was not surprising that some radical feminists wanted natural differences to be eliminated as much as possible (e.g., artificial reproduction). Liberal feminists tended to adopt a view of naturalistic equality, namely, that people were equal in most important respects, as sentient beings with common emotions and moral sensibilities, and that social constraints undermined this natural equality. Second, equality could mean possession of rights or equality under the law, the dominant focus in the first wave of the women's movement. Although suffragists were able to repudiate ascriptive bases for legal inequality, they were unable to achieve equal treatment under the law, which became the focus of many second-wave liberal feminists. Liberal feminists were also concerned with achieving equality of opportunity for women, a third meaning of equality and the dominant usage of the term in the United States. The fourth meaning of equality, equality of treatment and respect, was more commonly found in socialist feminist writings, which emphasized baselines below which no one fell, irrespective of capacity or merit. Equality based on need went beyond liberal market considerations. The goal of this equality was not "things" or "status" but rather the power of people to determine the conditions of their labor.[57]

The concept of difference was also contested. Initially, second-wave feminists looked at differences between men and women and made a distinction between biological sex and cultural gender, arguing that most social differences between the sexes were a function of culture, not chromosomes. By the late 1970s, however, feminists increasingly emphasized the interdependence of social and biological forces, for example, how cultural practices influenced the evolution of physiological differences and how those differences structured social relations. But some feminists were still not anxious to jettison the distinction between sex and gender, given the historical tradition of using biological determinism to women's disadvantage.

There were three feminist responses to this dilemma. One was to deny the essential nature of differences between men and women. In this view, gender bias in conventional paradigms gave cultural meaning to physiology, whether through sex-role socialization, the sex-based division of labor, or the devaluation of nonmarket work. This approach downplayed how nature and nurture were interrelated, and it tended to validate male norms. A second response was to celebrate differences between men and women. It stressed the importance of caretaking relationships in explaining attributes historically linked to women, provided an important counterweight to the dominant culture, enhanced women's sense of solidarity and self-respect, and identified directions for social change. But it homogenized women's experiences; downplayed the importance of other cultural institutions, ideologies, and ideals; oversimplified and overclaimed; and ignored the "downside of difference." A third response challenged dualisms that flattened analysis (for instance, that turned statistical frequencies into rigid dichotomies) and deflected attention from gender as a social relation. It focused on understanding how sex-linked attributes acquired social meaning.[58]

Just as the question of differences between men and women had become more problematic over time, so too had the issue of differences *among* women, along the lines of class, race, ethnicity, age, and sexual orientation.[59] The equality/difference debate as it affected women's group consciousness was as much about intragroup differences as it was about intergroup differences.

   12. Democracy/citizenship. Sexual difference and subordination were central to the construction of modern democratic theory. The "social contracts" of Locke and Rousseau were based on the "sexual contract," men's patriarchal right over women. Contracts were purportedly the paradigm of free agreement among individuals. But women were not naturally free, and they were historically excluded from the central category of the "individual" with social and legal standing. In contract theory, universal freedom was always a political fiction. Contract always generated political right in the form of relations of domination and subordination, whether one considered the contracts of marriage, employment, prostitution, or surrogate motherhood.[60]

   Feminism provided democracy—whether in its existing liberal guise or in the form of future participatory or self-managing democracies—with its most important challenge and comprehensive critique. Namely, democratic ideals and politics had to be put into practice in the kitchen, the nursery, and the bedroom. Women could not win an equal place in democratic productive life and citizenship if they were deemed to be destined for one ascribed task, nor could fathers take an equal share in reproductive activities without transformations in the concept of work and in the structures of economic life.[61]

   Citizenship was also redefined in light of women's knowledge of and expertise in welfare. In order for this knowledge to become part of women's contribution as citizens, as women had demanded during the twentieth century, the opposition between men's independence and women's dependence had to be broken down and new concepts of citizenship developed. The patriarchal dichotomy between dependent women, on the one hand, and independence-work-citizenship, on the other, was under challenge. There was a historic opportunity to move to real democracy, from the welfare state to a welfare society without involuntary social exiles, in which women and men could enjoy full social membership.[62]

   Feminist questions about the nature of "the good life" and political community provided alternatives to the liberal conception of citizenship. Democracy was a form of politics that brought people together as citizens, as speakers of words and doers of deeds in the public realm, as civic peers with mutual respect and positive liberty of self-government (as opposed to negative liberty of noninterference). Feminism as a political movement was informed by democratic organization and practice: spontaneous gatherings, marches, face-to-face assemblies, consensus decision making, nonhierarchical groups, and open speech and debate (its liberal interest group side notwithstanding). In its organizational and decentralized practices, the women's movement had been the most consistently democratic movement in the recent U.S. past. Feminists needed to transform their own democratic practices into a more comprehensive theory of citizenship in order to develop an alternative to nondemocratic liberal theory.[63]

For feminist political scientists, democracy was one of the twelve pieces of the puzzle of women's group consciousness. Taken together, these pieces constituted a new way of looking at women's group consciousness: incorporating a self-understanding in the group's own terminology, looking for politics in new places, and conducting scientific inquiry from an engaged perspective. But group consciousness was only half the story of women's political mobilization. The other half was how women as a group acted on their distinctive political concerns.

Acting as a Group: Origins, Organizations, and Tactics of the Women's Movement

Female scholars wanted to know why women became politically mobilized at certain historical junctures and not at others. What accounted for the emergence of the first wave (1830s–1920) and second wave (1960s–present) of women's group consciousness as expressed in a political movement? Most explanations centered on four factors: (1) economic conditions (urbanization, industrialization and employment), (2) group consciousness of gender deprivation, (3) an organizational base and communication network, and (4) mobilizing events.

Around the world, women's movements tended to emerge in response to industrialization and urbanization.[64] These early movements adopted ameliorative, reformist ideologies that supported rather than challenged traditional gender roles, because the socioeconomic conditions that might have bolstered a more radical feminist ideology were absent in the early stages of industrialization. Women's unfinished revolution had to await the postindustrial entrance of middle-class, and especially married, women into the full-time labor force. Under these conditions in the 1960s, radical feminist ideology gained more adherents than in the first wave.

Industrialization was an important factor in first-wave feminism because it intensified the sexual division of labor and separated the spheres of middle-class men and women. In nineteenth-century America, white middle-class men entered the "public sphere" of wage labor, business, the professions, and politics, while most white middle-class women remained at home as domestic and spiritual caretakers of the family and neighborhoods. Such women advanced their political claims from this sphere because few of them could realistically imagine themselves in the other sphere, given their economic dependence on their husbands. Urbanization was also critical to the development of first-wave feminism. Many white women's sense of their oppression as a group originated in American cities, where upper- and middle-class women became intensely involved with destitute women through their activities in voluntary associations. The broader their contacts with different classes of women, the more white middle-class women clarified their thinking about women's position in society. Given the rigid limits on acceptable feminine behavior, economically secure women sought fulfillment through their work with impoverished women. What began as charity was soon transformed into deeply felt sympathy and concern and developed a momentum and rationale of its own: women as a community were mistreated by society.[65] Most women in the first wave were not full-time members of the paid workforce, especially if they were mothers, but most women in the second wave were, even if they were mothers. Thus, employment status had an important, albeit different, effect on first- and second-wave women. Middle-class women could not successfully push for more radical group demands until more of them became economically autonomous from men in postindustrial economies. In both waves, it was predominantly middle-class women who were most active in the movement.

A second factor associated with the emergence of women's movements was a group consciousness of gender deprivation, which tended to develop either when women were involved in other movements, whose ideas they applied to women as a group, or when they were living nonconventional lifestyles, for which feminism provided an alternative to conventional norms.

First-wave women's group consciousness was forged in the cauldrons of several movements. Early feminists such as Sarah and Angelina Grimké, Sojourner Truth, Lucy Stone, Lucretia Mott, Elizabeth Cady Stanton, and Susan B. Anthony were active in the abolition movement. They compared the social, legal, and economic deprivation of women to that of slaves, and the notions of equality and natural rights were central in their writings.[66] The temperance movement was another training ground for first-wave feminists. The Women's Christian Temperance Union was founded in 1874 and endorsed women's suffrage in 1879. It was especially important in the South, where there were few women's organizations and the radical idea of suffrage could be presented in the conservative cloak of temperance.[67] Women wrote about the indignities and economic privations suffered by the wives and children of alcoholics. Women needed more property rights, education, and legal protection, and they had to venture into men's sphere to obtain these things.[68] First-wave women were also influenced by the Progressive, settlement house, consumer, and labor movements.[69] They began their movement activity from their "proper sphere," as caretakers for the home and community, only to realize that they needed to take action in the "public sphere." For second-wave feminists, the most important movements were civil rights, antiwar and New Left, which promoted the ideals of freedom, justice, equality, self-determination, participatory democracy, liberation, and revolution. Women applied these ideals to their own condition and found that these movements' analyses and practices failed to take women's condition seriously.[70]

Collective consciousness also emerged when women lived nonconventional lives. First-wave feminist Fanny Wright advocated free love and Susan B. Anthony turned down many marriage proposals to remain autonomous, but unconventionality was more common among second-wave feminists. Most did not get married right after high school but sought a college education instead. It was on college campuses that many of them became exposed to the civil rights, antiwar and New Left movements, launching pads to their feminist convictions. Compared to earlier generations, young women in the 1960s were more likely to enter the paid labor force, have fewer children, and get divorced. These three changes led to new lifestyles more centered on work and less centered on home. Feminism provided alternative norms that allowed women to integrate their nontraditional experiences.[71] Once married women entered the labor force on a long-term basis, the women's movement could not be reversed.[72]

The third factor necessary for the emergence of a women's movement was an organizational base and communication network, drawn from other movements and from women's organizations. From other movements, women gained not only provocative and useful ideas but also skills in public speaking, running meetings, raising funds, debating issues, building organizations, writing newsletters, and using the commercial media. First-wave women developed these skills in the organizations of the abolition, temperance, settlement house, Progressive, consumer, and trade union movements and used their existing communication networks.

First-wave women also gained organizational skills and tapped into preexisting networks in a vast array of female voluntary associations that predated abolitionist organizations.[73] A major strength of American feminism before 1920 was a separate female community that helped sustain women's participation in social reform and political activism. After 1920, many such institutions disintegrated, as "new women" attempted to assimilate into male-dominated institutions in work, social life, and politics, rejecting women's culture in favor of male promises of equality. This assimilation precluded the development of a women's bloc that might have protected and expanded earlier gains for women. Instead, the feminist movement became dormant until the 1960s.[74]

Second-wave women relied on the organizational bases and communication networks of both other movement organizations and existing women's organizations. Younger, radical women were associated with other movement organizations, whereas older, more conventional women were more likely to be connected with women's organizations, such as Business and Professional Women, the American Association of University Women, or the League of Women Voters. These two branches of the women's movement differed in their sources of leadership, types of organization, and forms of communication. The older strand consisted of professional women who worked in formal organizations with hierarchical operations and who used traditional channels to achieve political goals. The younger strand was made up of women from the New Left and civil rights movements, whose organizations and communications networks were more informal and less hierarchical, and who used nonconventional methods to achieve political goals.[75]

Finally, the fourth factor associated with the emergence of women's movements was mobilizing events, often discriminatory treatment from men in the movements in which women were involved. For first-wave women, discriminatory treatment at the 1840 World Anti-slavery Convention in London propelled Lucretia Mott and Elizabeth Cady Stanton to convene the first U.S. women's rights convention in Seneca Falls, New York, in 1848. In the second wave, mobilizing events also came from government and the media. President Kennedy's establishment of a national Commission on the Status of Women in 1961 was followed by the formation of a citizen's advisory council and fifty state commissions. Many of the people involved in these commissions became dissatisfied with the lack of progress made by the government on their recommendations. In 1966, they joined Betty Friedan to found the National Organization for Women.[76]

The women's liberation movement "took off" in 1970, when it became the latest fad of the national news media. Within the space of a few months, the media had legitimated the movement, which went from a struggling new idea to a national phenomenon. The birthday of women's liberation as a mass movement is often cited as August 26, 1970, the fiftieth anniversary of the passage of the Nineteenth Amendment and the day that the National Organization for Women called on women all over the country to support the Women's Strike for Equality. The magnitude of support for the strike surprised not only the mass media and the general public but also the event's organizers.[77]

Having accounted for the two waves of the women's movement, feminist scholars also explained the trough period between them beginning in the 1920s. Many women felt that with suffrage secured, the need for a movement was over. They could join the Democratic and Republican parties or the nonpartisan League of Women Voters. A small group of women remained active in the National Woman's Party, a suffrage organization that turned its attention to adoption of an equal rights amendment. This group remained isolated, small, exclusive, often highly conservative, and remote from blacks, labor, and socialists. The social climate was hostile to feminists, who had limited goals so as not to offend wealthy patrons. Organizational problems prevented feminists from expanding their base of support to other organized constituencies such as labor, socialists, or blacks.[78]

Support from presidential administrations contributed to the survival of feminism, even in the absence of a mass-based movement. Presidents from Franklin Roosevelt through Eisenhower courted the support of organized women's groups by appointing women to executive-level positions. President Kennedy broke this pattern of symbolic appointments by creating a substantive agenda of women's concerns, with equality playing a central role in his New Frontier. His Commission on the Status of Women provided the structural and psychological preconditions for a new women's movement. Under the auspices of the commission, national data on the status of women became available to women for the first time. Women were outraged at women's inferior social and economic status and frustrated with the government's failure to address this inequality.[79]

Second-Wave Feminist Organizations

When the mass-based movement emerged in the 1960s, it was led by new organizations, the most important of which were the National Organization for Women, formed in 1966; the Women's Equity Action

League (WEAL), created in 1968; and the National Women's Political Caucus, founded in 1971.

Each organization had a distinctive niche in the movement. NOW came into being when Betty Friedan and others attending the Third National Conference of Commissions on the Status of Women became convinced that the Equal Employment Opportunity Commission was not taking seriously the sex discrimination provision in Title VII of the 1964 Civil Rights Act. They felt it would be taken more seriously if there were "some sort of NAACP for women," as Friedan put it, to exert pressure on the government. The women wanted to form an action organization "to bring women into full participation in the mainstream of American society now, assuming all the privileges and responsibilities thereof in true partnership with men." The time for conferences was over; it was time to fight. The name NOW was coined by Friedan.[80]

Early NOW members were high-powered women who lacked the time and patience to put together a mass organization. They substituted media experience for organizational experience, often creating the appearance of activity more than organizing the substance of it. National media attention drew women to form local chapters, which were quite autonomous. Initially, NOW was the only action organization concerned with women's rights, so it attracted women with quite diverse agendas. By its second conference in 1967, it had grown to twelve hundred members, and diverse concerns came to a head when the conference proposed a Bill of Rights for Women to be presented to candidates and parties in the 1968 election. There was consensus on items dealing with sex discrimination in employment, maternity leave, child care, education, job training, and housing and family allowances. But when it came to support for the Equal Rights Amendment and repeal of all abortion laws, several members walked out.

Some union women withdrew over NOW's support of the ERA. Some conservative women thought abortion was too divisive an issue and left to form the Women's Equity Action League, which concentrated on legal and economic issues, especially in the areas of employment and education. At first, WEAL was centered in Ohio and consisted mostly of friends of its founder, Elizabeth Boyer, who had organized the Ohio NOW chapters. Some New York radical women left NOW because of its elitist structure. And some young lawyers withdrew after they became impatient with NOW's inability to form a tax-exempt organization to handle legal cases modeled after the NAACP Legal Defense and Education Fund. They founded Human Rights for Women, a nonprofit, tax-exempt corporation, to work on sex discrimination cases.

The 1970 strike swelled the ranks of NOW with a new stratum of women who helped relieve the tension between the older and younger branches of the women's movement. Many of these new members were white-collar and clerical workers with less education and professional training than members of the original two branches. And many of them were homemakers who had formed suburban discussion groups and wanted to make connections with a national movement. These new women brought different concerns to the organization. They were less interested in job discrimination than in media images of women and sex-role stereotyping in children's books. They also wanted to start consciousness-raising groups. Such activity was contrary to NOW's image of itself as an action organization, and many original members feared that energies would be diverted to solving personal problems rather than attacking political ones. Before long, however, NOW chapters became convinced of the value of consciousness-raising groups, institutionalizing them into ten- and fifteen-week courses with specific discussion topics.

NOW went through various organizational crises in its early years. It had a geographical distribution of functions that was chaotic: a legislative office in Washington, a public information office in New York, and an administrative office in Chicago. And there was tension between the more bureaucratic national organization and the more egalitarian local chapters, which resented paying part of their dues to the national organization, over which they had little control.

In its earliest years, NOW consistently moved in a more radical direction. The strike compelled the movement to define its goals nationally for the first time. It focused on three demands: abortion on demand, twenty-four-hour child-care centers, and equal opportunity in employment and education. In subsequent years, it expanded its concerns to antimilitarism, decriminalization of prostitution, a critique of capitalism's profit motive and competition, older women, sports, and rape.

Jo Freeman gave three reasons for the radicalization of NOW. First, once one adopted a feminist perspective on the world, it was easily applied to many aspects of society. The relevant questions then became where to begin and what to do first—strategic, not ideological, questions. Second, NOW's leaders always thought of themselves as being in the forefront of social change. Like members in other feminist organizations, they shared liberal and humanitarian values, lack of religious commitment, general nonconventionality, and openness to change. As old issues such as the ERA and abortion became socially acceptable, NOW looked for new ground to break. And third, the younger branch of the movement operated as an ideological vanguard. What began as a debate within the radical underground feminist media ultimately emerged as a NOW resolution. The transference was facilitated by a common middle-class background, a common education, and personal relationships that linked participants in both branches. An example of this radicalization was NOW's position on lesbianism. In 1969 and 1970, Betty Friedan alleged that lesbians were trying to take over the organization, and she used scare tactics to "purge" NOW of what she called the "lavender menace." Although she succeeded in driving many lesbians out of NOW and others back into the closet, NOW's 1971 convention passed a resolution acknowledging lesbianism as a feminist issue, because it had been defined as a civil rights issue and a women's issue and because support was the liberal, humanistic thing to do.[81]

As NOW became increasingly radicalized, WEAL kept a more conventional focus on equality in education and employment through legislation and lobbying. It was carefully organized from the top down to keep out radicals. Members made requests, not demands; they supported "feminine" behavior; they sympathized with their opponents and with homemakers; and they sought reform and compromise. Many of them were lawyers with little time to recruit new members. They formed a loose-knit organization, with top offices limited to women who had the time and money to pay for their own travel. Officers came from an inner circle around founder Elizabeth Boyer, who controlled nominations and elections. Unlike NOW, there was little input from the rank and file, and there were no demonstrations and pickets.[82]

If WEAL created a conventional niche for itself, NWPC carved out an electoral one. It was formed in 1971 to oppose racism, sexism, ageism, institutionalized violence, and poverty through the election and appointment of women to public office, party reform, and the support of women's issues and feminist candidates. Its original leadership was eastern, liberal, and Democratic. Some of its founding celebrities backed out in 1973 in a wave of anti-elitism. It avoided factionalism by establishing permanent caucuses for any interest that could garner at least 10 percent of members' support. By 1977, it had money to give to candidates and developed endorsement guidelines: any man or woman who was a feminist and supported the ERA, abortion rights, and child care. NWPC justifiably claimed credit for the creation of women as a political interest group. At the time of its formation, the issue of how many women served in public leadership roles had not scratched public consciousness. Rona Feit noted: "The representation of women at national party conventions was of interest only to a small group of reformers, and the concept of women's issues as a sub-group of political issues did not exist. There were no national campaign funds for women candidates and no one was lobbying for the appointment of women to public office. The Caucus was the leader in changing all of this."[83]

NWPC soon developed a reputation for professionalism and effectiveness in the two major political parties and in Washington and state capitals. Part of its success came from the legitimacy of political organizing as a relief from the more radical "sexual politics" of the women's liberation movement. Indeed, NWPC was criticized by radicals for its piecemeal change, selling out to mainstream politics, incrementalism, masculine power politics, and lack of a feminist vision in playing politics as usual. It depended on other feminist organizations, such as NOW, to frame social issues that it could then pursue through electoral politics. In many ways, the caucus functioned as a national political party: representing diverse members who wanted to effect social change through the existing political system; supporting candidates; and relying on volunteer labor, organizing, and fundraising.[84] And like a political party, NWPC was a political mobilizer, drawing women into the arena of electoral politics for the first time.[85]

The nonpartisan League of Women Voters also functioned as a political mobilizer, increasing women's knowledge of issues and encouraging them to run for public office. Initially, both the league and Business and Professional Women disdained any activity that might be labeled "feminist." But by the mid-1970s, the league supported many feminist policy initiatives, and BPW lobbied actively for women's legislation in Congress. The niche carved out by these two organizations was political education, which for many soon evolved into feminist education, in substance if not in name.[86]

When NOW, NWPC, and WEAL came to Washington in 1972–73, they received crucial support from BPW, the League of Women Voters, and the American Association of University Women. These more established women's groups were interested in attracting younger members, they knew the ropes in Washington, and they helped the feminist organizations break down their resistance to lobbying.[87] In the early 1970s, fourteen women's organizations formed ad hoc coalitions to pursue common legislative goals. Their strength derived from their diversity of interests in coalition. The need to maintain organizational autonomy, however, meant that group rivalry inhibited the development of more permanent umbrella organizations.[88]

By the mid-1980s, there were eighty-nine Washington-based women's groups. Women's rights organizations played a central role in mobilizing issue-specific alliances. Although they were relatively new organizations, they had sufficiently experienced staffs. Their strategies did not differ from those of other pressure groups, but they reported that women had a distinctive style: more sensitive, humane, issue-oriented, less comfortable with power, less willing to be bribed, forced by the old boys' network to be more careful, and having to work harder and to have all their facts in order. Most groups experienced internal dissension over issues, tactics, and organizational matters. Additional problems were limited financial resources, hostility to women's issues on the part of the Reagan administration, and sex discrimination against them.[89]

In an attempt to balance the conflicting needs of mobilizing a constituency and securing favorable policies, movement activists grappled with questions of leadership, hierarchy, and bureaucracy, vacillating between the extremes of avoidance of stars and the tyranny of structurelessness.[90] NWPC purged its founding "stars," for example, and Gloria Steinem and others came under fire from some radical feminists for being media favorites. At the other extreme was what Jo Freeman termed "the tyranny of structurelessness." After observing "unstructured," nonhierarchical movement groups, she concluded that formal structure was simply replaced by informal elites who achieved that status because of friendships or communication skills. Since the unstructured movement did not designate spokespeople, the media did, and whomever they designated was then attacked by her sisters. In addition, unstructured groups were usually politically inefficacious: they were better at getting women to talk about their lives than getting things done.[91] Nonhierarchical organizations seemed to work better in nongovernmental settings, such as consciousness-raising groups, feminist peace groups, and women's health collectives.[92] But many radical and anarchist feminists held out for the ideal of nonhierarchical, nonbureaucratic forms of organization, even when it came to government.[93] They described the feminist movement as divided between those who wanted access to established institutions and those who aimed to transform those institutions. Liberal feminists, through their interest in achieving equality with white men, appealed to the bureaucratic apparatus of the state and corporate world to integrate women into public life but failed to acknowledge the power of bureaucracy in modern life.[94]

Movement women hoped to bring to government the kind of leadership women were developing in grassroots settings. A distinction was made between women's leadership, based on social relations of reproduction (i.e., roles for home and neighborhood), which provided skills for successful grassroots mobilization, and men's leadership, based on social relations of production (i.e., roles for career and workplace), which provided skills for dealing with government and bureaucracies.

Movements needed both sets of skills in order to thrive at the grassroots level and to be effective in bureaucratic settings.[95] Women's leadership was often transforming leadership (i.e., responding to higher purposes that otherwise would not be realized), as opposed to transactional leadership (i.e., enabling everyday transactions to occur that otherwise might not take place). It needed to be documented from the bottom up, as women were often "invisible decision makers" working quietly behind the scenes for political transformation.[96]

Feminism, Antifeminism, Gender Consciousness, and Postfeminism

As the women's movement progressed throughout the 1980s, activists developed a more sophisticated understanding of strategies and tactics, triggered largely by the antifeminist Reagan administration and the defeat of the ERA in state legislatures. The movement went on the defensive amid charges from the popular media that it was dead. Betty Friedan offered advice on how to get things moving again: end a bitter internal power struggle in NOW's leadership, begin a new round of consciousness-raising for the new generation, mobilize new professional networks and old established volunteer organizations to save women's rights, focus less on pornography and more on the obscenity of poverty, confront the illusion of equality in divorce, return the issue of abortion to a matter of a woman's own responsible choice, affirm the differences between men and women, make breakthroughs for older women, bring in the men, continue the fight for political power, and move beyond single-issue thinking.[97]

Scholars took stock of lessons learned from the ten-year ERA campaign. They observed that although there was a strong feminist organizational presence at the national and local levels, the movement was weak at the state level, where final ratification decisions were made. Coalitional disunity was another factor. The various groups involved had widely differing kinds of organizations and tactics. NOW offered moral incentives and made moral appeals through demonstrations and the media. ERAmerica comprised religious, professional, civic, and labor groups, each of which had priorities different from those of the ERA coalition. BPW and the League of Women Voters wanted to avoid conflict and used educational tactics. Lesbians came out of the closet at high personal cost and wanted to display banners, which NOW banned. And feminist lawyers in Washington, D.C., were more committed to larger feminist or public interest issues than to the ERA per se.[98]

Feminist scholars also studied the fate of the women's movement dur-

ing the first explicitly antifeminist presidential administration, that of
Ronald Reagan. His administration spurred feminist interest groups into
unprecedented action, with a rapid increase in members and money to
NOW and NWPC. During 1982 (the year the ERA was lost), NOW's membership grew by 30,000 to reach 250,000 members, and NWPC's rose by
13,000 to total 73,000 members. NOW's budget nearly tripled between
1977 and 1982. (In contrast, Eagle Forum, the largest group organized
specifically to combat feminism, reported 50,000 members in 1982.) In
the 1980s, feminist organizations became increasingly active in electoral
campaigns and more professionalized: raising funds, recruiting candidates, and offering candidate training programs. Both NWPC and the
Women's Campaign Fund defined themselves as aiding women in a bipartisan effort, although their biases tended toward Democrats. The
NWPC president during the Reagan years was Kathy Wilson, a longtime
Republican activist. Across the country, women's organizations transcended party loyalty, even more so because of Reagan. And in 1982,
NOW changed its policy and began to endorse feminist men. While the
feminist movement matured and professionalized during the Reagan
years, the New Right became more visible at the state and local levels,
draining the women's movement of precious time and resources.[99]

Unlike the popular media, many scholars thought the women's
movement was alive and well in the 1980s.[100] Mary Fainsod Katzenstein
argued that its vital signs had to be measured by standards different from
those traditionally used to assess the health of other movements, such as
membership (unions) and protests (blacks). Instead the women's movement consisted of less visible networks, consciousness-raising groups, local organizations, professional caucuses, and women's studies programs.
The 1980s were characterized by the "unobtrusive mobilization" of feminism inside institutions, where women's groups and networks re-
invented feminism to make sense of their daily lives. Katzenstein studied
the unobtrusive mobilization of feminism in the Catholic Church and
the U.S. military. Church women linked their cause to social justice concerns, and military women tied their concerns to a narrow career focus.
Since many of them eschewed the term "feminist," Katzenstein used the
term "gender consciousness"—awareness of and opposition to gender
inequality—to describe the consciousness of these women. Consciousness of gender inequality was context-bound, often reflecting a mix of
values, and conditioned by a woman's institutional affiliations as much
as by her race or class background.[101]

Judith Stacey was less sanguine about the continuation of feminist
consciousness in the 1980s. In her ethnographic study of two kinship net-

works in Silicon Valley, she found a "postfeminist consciousness," namely, the simultaneous incorporation, revision, and depoliticization of many of the goals of second-wave feminism. What began as sympathy toward feminism on the part of these women ended up not so much as a retreat from feminism but as a selective blending and adopting of certain feminist ideas. In a setting with a high degree of family turbulence, an inequitable occupational structure, and a fast-track culture, women found it hard to form stable relationships and turned to evangelical groups for support, intimacy, and survival. They incorporated feminist criticism within fundamentalist thought to support patriarchal profamilialism.[102]

Stacey and Deborah Rosenfelt felt that feminist scholars were too quick to dismiss the importance of postfeminist consciousness, as if use of the term meant complicity in the death of the movement, or a new sexism, or a backlash. It was important to see how it differed from antifeminism as a mode of thought. The term was first used by journalists in 1982 to describe the views of relatively affluent and ambitious young women who voiced concern over the difficulties of combining work and family life. When worries about intimacy and loneliness were expressed in the popular culture, feminist scholars tended to disregard them as part of a right-wing backlash, but loneliness was a legitimate problem for many women, whose old feminist communities had become fragile and fragmented. Changes in gender relations of power had proved to be more difficult than anyone had anticipated, and feminists needed to address women's emotional needs with the same attention they had given women's economic agenda.[103]

Feminist consciousness and its spinoffs (antifeminism, postfeminism, and gender consciousness) proved difficult to specify, whether one used the ethnographic techniques of Stacey, the open-ended interviews of Katzenstein, or the survey research questionnaires of accommodationists. Survey researchers who measured the extent to which women were politically mobilized found that results differed depending on the referent in the question: equal roles, the women's liberation movement, women as a group, feminists, or women's issues. In general, they found that over time, women increasingly agreed with the issues and goals of the women's movement but never warmed to the term "feminist."

The American National Election Studies (ANES), conducted by the Center for Political Studies of the Institute for Social Research at the University of Michigan, used "feeling thermometers," measures in which respondents were asked to rate a person or group on a scale from 0 to 100 depending on how cool (negative) or warm (positive) they felt toward that person or group. Studying the 1972–84 ANES data, Elizabeth

Cook saw problems with the "close to women" feeling thermometer and said that the "women's liberation movement" feeling thermometer and the "equal role" item were better measures of women's group consciousness.[104]

Between 1972 and 1984, the ANES surveys had included the "women's liberation movement" feeling thermometer. In 1988 the survey changed the wording of the thermometer to "feminists," and in 1990 it was again changed to the "women's movement." Cook and Clyde Wilcox found that both men and women were cooler to "feminists" than to the "women's movement." These symbols tapped two distinct components of public attitudes: the women's movement was associated with gender equality and government aid to women, whereas feminists were associated with abortion.[105]

Using ANES data, Cook studied support for feminism between 1972 and 1984. She discussed three types of consciousness: nonfeminist (not in favor of equality for women), potential feminist (in favor of equality for women but cool to the women's movement), and politicized feminist (supporting both equality and the movement). She found that the cohort of women who came of age (turned 18) between 1978 and 1984, what she termed the "complacent/Reagan" cohort, did not support the women's liberation movement but was almost as supportive of feminist issues as were the "sixties" and "women's liberation movement" cohorts. And since 1972, there was no decline in the absolute level of politicized feminist consciousness: it characterized 13 percent of women in 1972 and about 20 percent of women in 1976, 1980, and 1984.[106]

Another study, using the same ANES data covering roughly the same time period, however, concluded that women had a weak gender consciousness. Patricia Gurin was interested in comparing women's group consciousness to that of blacks, the elderly, and workers. She found that women's gender consciousness was not as pronounced as the group consciousness of other subordinate groups; and it was not distinctly subordinate, since men expressed similar views (men were more supportive of gender equality than whites were of racial equality, for instance). She attributed women's comparatively weak group consciousness in part to the fact that women's emotional ties to and status association with men was the opposite of what made for group solidarity and recognition of relative deprivation in other groups.[107]

Commercial polling firms also charted the fate of women's group consciousness. For example, in 1989 *Time* magazine reported data from a Yankelovich poll of adult women that indicated widespread support for feminist issues and the women's movement. More than 80 percent described the following issues as very important to women: equal pay, day care, rape, maternity leave at work, and job discrimination. And 74 percent described abortion in this way. More than 80 percent said the women's movement had helped women become more independent, had given women more control over their lives, and was still improving the lives of women. Between half and two-thirds said the movement accurately reflected the views of most women, did not look down on women who did not have jobs, was not antifamily, and was not out of date in its goals. As in other surveys, use of the word "feminist" brought a mixed response. Although only one-third considered themselves feminists, two-thirds said feminists had been helpful to women (only 18 percent said feminists had been harmful to women).[108]

Throughout the 1980s, survey researchers tinkered with their measures of women's group consciousness, recognizing that it made a difference whether one asked about gender roles, the women's movement, feminist issues, or feminism. And they realized that gender was more than a dichotomous variable for describing differences between men and women, what was commonly called "gender cleavage." Rather, it was a continuous cultural variable that took on different meanings at different times. One study analyzing ANES data between 1972 and 1984 coined the term "gender politicization" to describe the increasing politicization of women's gender identification, which occurred primarily among younger, better-educated women. But, it had not uniformly moved women in a more liberal, profeminist direction, since there was a growing polarization among women on certain policy areas.[109]

The Political Mobilization of Women in Santa Clara County

Earlier we posed the question, Was there anything more to Santa Clara County's feminism than the election of record numbers of women to public office? We are now in a position to look for feminist mass political mobilization: the articulation of group concerns and the pieces of the puzzle of group consciousness, a puzzle that did not fit into the "normal science" of conventional wisdom. Throughout the 1970s, many women in Santa Clara County articulated group concerns and acted on those concerns through preexisting women's organizations, such as the League of Women Voters, Business and Professional Women, the Girl Scouts, and the Junior League, and through new organizations, such as the county's Commission on the Status of Women, local NOW chapters, the Chicana Coalition, and battered women's shelters. The group concerns were those of the women's movement: domestic violence, health care, employment discrimination, sexual harassment, pension denial, and the ERA. In the description of the cases that follow, one sees the pieces of group consciousness coming together to form a coherent picture. Women's consciousness was raised in small group settings, where political understandings began with feelings, personal problems were seen as group problems necessitating a political solution, and the public and private worlds were interdependent. Women gave meaning to their activities in communities, sought justice in the family, articulated an ethic of care, challenged male definitions of women's sexuality and power, fought for equality while recognizing differences, and acted as citizens in ways that broadened liberal, contractual definitions of citizenship.

Most of these themes were illustrated in the case of a local battered women's shelter, an unconventional setting for political mobilization.[110] San Jose's Woman's Alliance (WOMA) had its origins in 1974, when a group of women from a service agency for low-income people, Economic and Social Opportunities (ESO), decided to open a women's center to provide services to low-income and minority women in Santa Clara County. WOMA deputy director Anne McCormac described what precipitated the creation of a battered women's shelter: "We put in a phone, and 99 percent of the people who called us were being beaten up. They needed help, and there was really nothing available for them. And so our services developed along those lines." In 1977, using donations, a state grant, and United Way funds, WOMA opened its shelter facility, the second shelter in the state of California.

WOMA served as many as nine hundred women and children a year, both by housing them at its thirty-bed shelter and by helping women obtain temporary restraining orders against their batterers. Once assisted by the shelter, women helped one another directly, through support groups, and indirectly, through contributions. WOMA received assistance from just about every women's group in the area, from the San Jose Junior Women's Club, to women's church auxiliaries, to the local chapter of NOW, which completely furnished the shelter when it first opened. Even the Girl Scouts pitched in, providing child care at the WOMA-sponsored Women's Unity Day at a local park in July 1983.

Women's political mobilization can also be illustrated in the case of the Santa Clara County Commission on the Status of Women, created by county ordinance in 1973. It had indirect subpoena power (through a supervisor) and the power to conduct investigations and hearings with testimony taken under oath. The commission's charge was to eliminate sex discrimination in housing, employment, education, and community services. Throughout the 1970s, the commission mediated an average of five hundred sex discrimination complaints a year. To meet the needs of low-income women, who could not afford to take time off from work, come to the office, fill out a form, and wait a week for a response, the commission resolved complaints over the telephone. Commissioner Ann Bender knew this method was a rather expensive way to meet women's needs, but she said it was worth it. "Perhaps there were other ways to reach larger numbers of people more directly. But we got all these calls from women . . . that simply touched the heart. What were we to do? I have attended two conventions of the National Association of Commissions on the Status of Women where there were roundtable discussions of what other commissions were doing. I discovered that no one else was doing this kind of complaint resolution."

In addition to complaint resolution, Bender said the commission secured policy changes at the workplace.

> Somebody in a position to change policy learned what sex discrimination was, what they were doing, and how it needed to be corrected. In particular, there was a local hiring person at a national fast-food chain. He thought women should not be cooks in hot kitchens lifting heavy pans, which of course gave women a great laugh! We reminded the franchise that women had been engaging in such work for quite a while! In a number of companies, once an individual complaint had been resolved, the manager would ask someone from the commission to come out to the company to give a presentation on sex discrimination. Then this company passed information along to the personnel division or vice-presidents of other companies. And it got to the point where, when our calls first came through, instead of the first response being, "What's the commission and why should I talk to you?" it was, "Just a moment, let me close the door. Now what do you want?"

Frequently, the complaints of local women caused the commission to turn to higher levels of government to seek redress. As explained by Commissioner Pat Miller: "Take the ex-wives of military men who were dumped with nothing and got no pensions. They were destitute, mostly older women without careers because of constant moving. They were divorced and left with nothing. We did not know about this issue until they came to us. We pressured Congressmember Pete McCloskey and wrote to Congress to change laws on pensions for military wives. We have both a local and national focus."

Attorneys who had served on the commission remained on a referral list for women calling in with legal questions. Bender said commission members were pleased when problems with employers were resolved internally, without having to go to court. "That's really exciting because first of all that person has gotten the whole thing resolved in probably a week or two; and second, they are all excited about their power and they have learned to use the process. And then they can pass that on to other people. That's part of the network which I think really makes this the feminist capital of the nation." These networks were also called into action when the community mobilized to support congressional extension of the deadline for state ratification of the ERA.

Local women's groups were engaged in a constant process of educating and mobilizing their own members, other groups, neighbors, coworkers, and the community at large. Membership education was difficult when it came to controversial issues. A case in point was the consideration of abortion by the Chicana Coalition, established by Chicana feminists in 1979 to advocate the interests of Chicanas in educational, political, economic, health, social, and cultural areas. The group invited speakers from Planned Parenthood and a right-to-life group to debate the issue. Members heard both sides and decided to support a woman's right to choose regarding abortion.

In addition to educating their own ranks, women tried to raise the consciousness of other groups about women's issues. Ann Bender said staffers from the Commission on the Status of Women went into the community and attended meeting of groups that were not specifically directed at women's issues: "For instance, there was an Asian-American Concerns group, and other ones like that. When staffers went out to these groups, they simply monitored women's issues as they came up. Or perhaps even pointed them out as they came up when other people did not notice them. . . . They raised people's consciousness about what were women's issues."

Community consciousness-raising also resulted from the efforts of Stanford University's Center for Research on Women (CROW). CROW director Myra Strober described how the center had ripple effects on local corporate and individual donors. Corporate donors were invited to annual Corporate Associates Seminars, where the center's research relevant to the business community was presented. The center's hope was to influence corporate policies toward women regarding matters such as child care, stress, dual-career couples, and occupational segregation. The corporations typically sent women to these seminars, many of whom wrote to CROW detailing how their views had been affected, how they had created support groups at work, or how they had obtained larger contributions for CROW from their firms.

Community education also took place at conferences, in marches, and on the picket lines. CROW sponsored public conferences on topics ranging from careers for corporate women, to women writers, to divorce and midlife crisis. In March 1980, the National Hispanic Feminist Conference was held in San Jose to educate both the community and feminists. Conference organizer Sylvia Gonzales described these two goals: "Anglo women have been included from the start and in leadership roles with Latinos. . . . We are reaching out to non-Hispanic feminists. It is not enough to talk to ourselves. . . . It is unique in that it is dealing with theory and research, but we will also include community women."[111] Some two thousand women attended more than one hundred workshops. Gonzales said the conference provided "an opportunity for Hispanic feminist leaders to form a much-needed national network,"[112] but she added that "the community women were the ones who benefited most. They were the ones who were so excited. They were the ones who for the first time were hearing things they had never heard before. They were the ones attending the workshops where the majority of work was going on."[113]

Finally, community mobilization occurred during public demonstrations and rallies. The local NOW chapter was often at the forefront of such events. For example, in July 1983, NOW, the San Jose State University Women's Center, and the San Jose Peace Center cosponsored a protest at the third annual Ms. Nude America contest held at the San Jose Center for the Performing Arts.

Public rallies are commonly used as indicators of the magnitude of a group's political mobilization. The popular media gauge the strength of a movement by turnout at such events and assume its demise by a lull in protest politics. Conventional political analysts chart the ups and downs of feminist attitudes in public opinion polls and of membership in feminist organizations. But, as we have seen in this chapter, other indicators provide a more complete picture of women's political mobilization: leaving a batterer and talking to a support group at a shelter, negotiating joint parenting and household responsibilities, challenging sex-role stereotyping in children's books, resolving sex discrimination complaints over the telephone, and debating issues at seminars and conferences. Women's shift from individual to group consciousness and activity was detected by feminist scholars using new ways of looking at women's politics.

4 Political Participation

Women's Civic Activity in
Communities and the State

POLITICAL PARTICIPATION refers to actions taken by citizens to express political views, affiliate with political parties, select leaders, and influence government policies. Since colonial times, the political participation of women has differed from that of men. These dissimilarities were seen quite differently by accommodationist and transformational scholars. Accommodationists were more willing to accept conventional political science definitions of political participation, which focused on electoral activity, and to use survey research methodology in their studies. They detected bias in past studies, constructed better measures to capture women's participation, and provided new interpretations of existing data. When they found that women participated less than men, they developed models to explain why. They investigated the causes of the gender gap in opinions and voting in the 1980s. And they looked into how women were faring in political parties. By contrast, transformational feminists contended that political science definitions of citizenship were gender-biased to such an extent that researchers had overlooked what citizenship meant to women. In order to understand women's political participation, conceptual lenses needed to be refocused in three ways: from the military state to the social welfare state, from the state to the community, and from interest groups to voluntary associations. In addition, survey research methods had to be supplemented with qualitative ones, especially in-depth interviews and historical analyses.

Gender Bias in the Concept of Citizenship

Since political science was created to study political institutions, particularly the nation-state, its understanding of citizenship emphasized national identity and loyalty to the state. Political science also inherited understandings of citizenship from classic texts of political philosophy. Feminist scholars exposed bias in the concept, both in the canon of political philosophy and in empirical studies of nation-states. Major political theorists had excluded women from political participation on the grounds of their presumed disruptive sexuality, lack of justice, incapacity for reason, and "natural function" in the family, all of which made them unfit for public life. Feminists argued that what a theorist said about women was not irrelevant to, but rather constitutive of, his conceptualization of citizenship. Concepts of citizenship, justice, rights, and consent were given meaning through the absence of women as political actors.[1] Empirical studies of citizens in nation-states suffered from androcentric bias as well. In the institutional approach, citizen activities were male activities, from which women were excluded by law or custom, such as fighting in wars, voting, serving on juries, speaking in public places, or attending party caucuses. With the behavioral revolution in political science in the 1950s, attention shifted from institutions and formal rights to the behavior and attitudes of citizens. But the conception of citizenship remained focused on behaviors and attitudes directed toward government institutions and policies (not power relations more generally), and male behaviors and attitudes were construed as "normal."

Whether institutionalists or behaviorists, male political scientists assumed that women's public activities were social, cultural, or religious but not political, so there were no "interesting" research questions to investigate. It was not until women entered the academy that two "interesting" findings emerged: the first was that since colonial times, women had behaved as citizens in the ways men had, insofar as they were legally and culturally able to do so; the second was that women had developed distinctive citizenship organizations and activities that reflected the cultures in which they found themselves and responded to the legal and cultural constraints on their activities.

For the most part, these findings emerged more from historical and qualitative analyses than from survey research. Louise M. Young used a conventional definition of political participation from the *International Encyclopedia of the Social Sciences* and showed that women had been active citizens in male arenas from colonial times through the 1920s. In the country's early years, women's religious associations and salons were the equivalent of contemporary consciousness-raising groups, where women were exposed to radical political ideas (e.g., defiance of religious authorities, abolitionism, utopian socialism, and transcendentalism). Women could be counted on to deliver persuasive abolition speeches and petitions filled with signatures to state legislators and to lead scores of slaves to freedom on the Underground Railroad, only to have their credentials go unrecognized at antislavery conventions, to see the word "male" added to the Constitution for the first time by victorious Republicans in the post–Civil War Fourteenth Amendment, and to watch as both the Democratic and Republican parties opposed women's suffrage in a Kansas referendum in 1867.[2]

Women helped create some important U.S. political institutions. According to Young, women were involved in the origins of modern political campaigns, which evolved out of events resembling religious revivals, with tents, parades, long speeches, handshaking and baby kissing. Fanny Wright, who lectured in the 1820s in support of equal education for women and utopian socialism, is often described, along with Martin Van Buren, as the country's first "professional politician." Women's skill at securing petition signatures translated into the Progressive institutions of initiative, referendum, and recall. Suzanne Lebsock argued that Progressivism was essentially a women's movement and that women contributed to the turn-of-the-century shift from party to interest group politics. Women had no tradition of voting, good reason to be suspicious of political parties, and decades of experience organizing on the basis of interest groups.[3]

Feminist historical analysis took as its point of departure citizenship as women themselves defined it. It is interesting to compare conventional and feminist interpretations of women's citizenship activities in the 1920s. In the conventional view, when women got the vote, their organized political activity came to an end; when women failed to vote as a bloc, political parties ignored them; and when women turned out to vote in low numbers, they precipitated a decline in electoral participation among eligible voters. Things looked different from the viewpoint of female citizens and women in the academy, however. Postsuffrage women defined themselves as citizens in an era when political parties played a crucial role, and many accepted the Progressive critique of parties as self-serving rather than public-serving organizations. As Winifred Starr Dobyns, the first chair of the Republican Women's Committee in Illinois, put it in 1927, "Let us be frank. With some possible exceptions, the aim of the political organization is not good government, patriotic service, public welfare. These are but phrases used for campaign purposes. Political organizations are, for the most part, designed to fill the pockets of politicians at public expense, to give jobs to thousands who find politics an easy way to make a living, to maintain men in office who can do favors for business."[4]

In the context of corrupt, male-dominated parties, it was not surprising that many postsuffrage women took a nonpartisan route to citizenship through the League of Women Voters. These women felt an obligation to produce informed voters, not simply partisan ones. During the 1928 campaign between "wet" Democrat Al Smith and "dry" Republican Herbert Hoover, the league sponsored weekly radio broadcasts on politics, which increased women's interest in the campaign, especially in remote areas. Hoover's moralistic campaign thrust was aimed at the female "dry" vote, whereas Catholic Al Smith sought the vote of immigrant women. Indeed, the 1928 campaign mobilized both Republican and Democratic women. But organizationally, most women were not found in political parties; they were members of the league, the Women's Christian Temperance Union, and the General Federation of Women's Clubs.

Some women chose the partisan route. In the 1920s, women were granted formal equality on the national committees of the Democratic and Republican parties. In 1922, the director of the Women's Division of the Democratic National Committee started to organize the women of her party. She sent a questionnaire to three thousand county chairmen asking for the names of women on their county committees and received only seven replies. One said, "None, thank God," and another replied, "We haven't any, and don't propose to have." By 1947, women had become firmly established as auxiliary workers at the bottom level of political parties. As for the top levels, in a survey of national committeewomen of both political parties about two-thirds of them said they had a genuine influence as far as participation in policymaking was concerned, with one-third expressing a contrary opinion in rather vigorous terms.[5]

Organizational expressions of women's citizenship remained largely nonpartisan throughout the 1950s. Well-educated and well-off white women tended to join the League of Women Voters. A study of local league members in the late 1950s belied the image of bored suburban housewives portrayed in Betty Friedan's *Feminine Mystique*. These women were very involved in their communities, studying issues, training for leadership, and stimulating and legitimating women's political aspirations at a time when political parties were uninterested in these matters.[6]

Male bias in gauging the opinions of citizens can be seen from the earliest days of polling public opinion, in the 1930s. A review of poll data

from 1936 to 1970 provides a fascinating glimpse into what men thought
it was important to know about women's political views in pre–women's
movement America. One intriguing finding was that pollsters typically did
not even poll women until the late 1960s. In the 1930s, a couple of polls
asked women what they thought about women in public positions and
women's taking scarce jobs in the depression. In the 1940s and 1950s,
there were few polls of women's opinions, with the exception of one extensive Roper survey conducted for *Fortune* magazine in 1946. A second
finding was that there was increasing agreement between the sexes over
time: before 1945, men and women agreed on only 12 percent of the questions, but by the post-1950 era, there was 43 percent agreement. That was
still not much agreement during a period when wives were thought to
agree with their husbands about politics (and presumably the economic
issues raised in some of these questions). As a testament to the effect of the
women's movement, in 1968 pollsters began to ask respondents whether
they thought women had equal opportunities with men.[7]

Women's Self-understandings of Political Participation

Dissatisfied with a discipline that attempted to fit women's citizenship into a male mold, feminists in the academy used various qualitative
methods to try to understand women's citizenship. One thing they discovered was the gendered nature of "political spaces" and "life spaces."
One study looked at biographical data of thirty-six political women
(elected women, revolutionaries/terrorists, and wives of famous political men) in terms of four factors of political socialization: (1) a modern
sex-role ideology that enabled a girl to conceive of the possibility for herself of adult roles other than wife and mother, (2) a sense of personal
control over the day-to-day existence of her life space, (3) a view that politics was salient to her control over her life space, and (4) a reasonably
successful history of political participation at critical points in her life. The
authors used this scheme to challenge conventional assumptions about
supposedly gender-neutral political spaces—"community," "regime," and
"government"—which children learned about while being socialized
into citizens.[8]

The theme of a woman's life space was also central to a 1979 study of
black and white girls and women in a small Texas community. Women's
descriptions of their life space (defined as the objective and perceived
physical and social reality of their day-to-day existence around home and
family) indicated that they participated in political activity when their
home life and personal well-being were likely to be directly (usually neg-

atively) affected by political decisions, regarding issues such as government subsidies, police maltreatment of their children, schools, and streets. The life spaces of many women precluded their political participation in the conventional sense: they were too tired for electoral politics; they could not afford to feed their families, so campaign donations were out of the question; their low-paying jobs did not encourage political activism; their children came first; and they were more cynical than men about corrupt local sheriffs, police, and judges. If one adopted a more comprehensive definition of politics, however, then these women were very active politically: negotiating with school, police, or welfare officials; signing petitions to save neighborhood streets; or discussing child care, housing, or police treatment of teenagers.[9]

Women's self-understandings of political participation were predicated on conceptions of power and politics. One study of the relationship between power orientations and political participation used a variety of tests to measure power orientation in activities that were both formal (government, party) and informal (attempting to influence organizations). In the aggregate, there were no gender differences in participation or power orientation. For both sexes, increased participation was associated with low power anxiety and a more assertive power style. But there were some gender differences: males were more interested in influencing the spheres of job, country, and world (they were as interested as females in the realm of family, religion, and community), females were more ambivalent about seeking and exercising power, and formally participative females had higher power drives and enjoyment than their male counterparts.[10] These findings were consistent with the transformational approach of including the politics of family and community, not just the nation-state. Another study of self-understandings assessed subjective differences in political meanings among male and female delegates to national political party conventions in 1984. Respondents were given stimulus words followed by blank lines and had one minute to provide verbal associations with each word. Both Republican men and Democratic women comprehended a politics of connectedness, but there were both party and gender differences in the nature, purposes, and types of connectedness. In their conceptions of community, Republican men emphasized duty and global commitments; Republican women, the family; and Democratic men, abstract masses. For "representation," Democratic women stressed diversity, Republican women were vague, Republican men spoke of people and the public, and Democratic men mentioned demographics and interest groups. And as for "power," Democratic women were excited about it, frequently mentioning the political process and the grassroots and domestic arenas of politics. Republican women were not very interested in power and spoke of it as residing in leaders, authority, international relations, strength, and physical dimensions. Democratic men were disillusioned by power, with a narrow focus on issues and candidates and no mention of the international arena. And Republican men focused on national and international relations, family and friends, with no mention of groups or the grass roots. Clearly, political words were loaded with different meanings for women and men in a way that had a bearing on how these delegates thought about their political participation.[11]

Meanings of "the political" were the focus of Diane L. Fowlkes's interviews with white female activists in Atlanta. Some saw it as political scientists did: referring to candidates, holding office, governing, and advocating issues; others had a broader view: linking public and private concerns, developing power to bring about change, and changing people's daily lives. The themes of educating and consciousness-raising cut across all the women's conceptions of politics.[12]

Women provided alternative understandings of citizenship. Some proposed developing transitional representative mechanisms that acknowledged gender difference and inequality and ensured proportionality between the sexes in areas where political decisions were made. These mechanisms would guarantee a voice to the previously silenced and would be needed until the distinction between public and private spheres had lost its gendered quality: when men and women moved equally between the responsibilities of household and employment and shared in the care of dependents.[13]

Others emphasized how feminist politicization of the body and everyday life had increased the range, intensity, and scope of political action. The slogan "the personal is political" had opened up new public spaces, and new depths of political community were formulated using the language of kinship, duties, and obligations. An important theme was "the body politic." Feminists were not the first, of course, to politicize the body, especially the female body. The ancient Greek and early Christian political philosophers feared that the body (nature, passions, the flesh) would disrupt politics (the state, the city of God). For subsequent theorists, passions were often gender coded, whether as Machiavelli's Fortune as a woman who needed to be beaten, or as Rousseau's domestication of female sexuality and segregation of the sexes to ensure political order. Early liberal feminists such as Mill and Wollstonecraft seemed to have solved the problem with the creation of disembodied, abstract individuals as citizens. But feminists eventually realized that this formulation erased from the political slate too many important issues, such as sexuality, reproduction, gender relations, and the nature of the political roles for which women as individuals were to become liberated (e.g., warriors). The rights and obligations of citizenship had to be "reembodied" with women's bodies. In a woman-friendly polity, citizens would feel an obligation to create a public space free from sexual harassment and degrading images of women, and citizens would balance a "right to one's body" with an obligation not to participate in the creation of images of women as passive objects of male desire. The women's movement located women in significant places that were political but had little to do with their relationship to the state: gaining a sense of political efficacy from community organizing in the civil rights movement and developing a feminist consciousness from treatment by movement men. Political spaces were anywhere that previously defined personal problems became politicized issues. Kathleen Jones gave an example: "For instance, women's experiences of threat and danger have focused attention on certain features of the political geography of sexuality and personal freedom. 'Take-Back-The-Night' marches against sexual harassment, rape and pornography on college campuses are examples of a definition of participation that is focused not on government action but on the reclamation of public space itself."[14]

A woman-friendly polity would consist of "politics among friends." Jones said: "In this analysis, affective ties replace functional ones as the cement of a social order, the creative development of personality substitutes for the pursuit of instrumental goals, and a shared sense of community takes the place of competitive norms of capitalist culture. Similarly, trust supplants suspicion as the motivating political impulse."[15] While feminists raised the problem of the conflicting needs for personal autonomy and for community and differed about whether to model a political community on familial or friendship obligations, they attempted to suffuse the concept of citizenship with intimacy and community, in contrast to the traditional concept's combative, oppositional perspective on political action, which had been associated with a masculinist process.

From the Military State to the Social Welfare State

In addition to shedding light on gender-specific experiences of citizenship, transformational feminists called for a shift of focus from the military state to the social welfare state. Some argued that the cornerstone of masculinist citizenship was military prowess. Homeric epics set the stage for the Athenian all-male political community, or polis, so greatly admired (by men) in the Western political tradition. For the warrior-hero in the *Iliad,* the purpose on the battlefield was less to win battles than to achieve fame through the demonstration of masculine virtue (almost a redundant phrase, since the Latin root of *virtue* refers to manliness). The political community as community existed only on the battlefield, where the collective good was the primary concern of the hero. Later, in the Athenian political community, the warrior-hero was replaced by the good citizen, who engaged in rhetorical competition. In both cases, competition for dominance of others, the denial of the importance of the body, and a struggle to cancel death were presented as ideals for which the political actor, or citizen, should strive.[16]

Feminists discussed the implications of a militaristic conception of citizenship, from the ancient Greeks through nineteenth-century theorists of the nation-state (e.g., Hegel and Clausewitz) and anticapitalistic revolutions (Marx and Engels), to the twentieth-century science of international relations. They agreed that militaristic citizenship was engendered but were not of one mind concerning what to do about it. Those who traced military-based citizenship to male conceptions of rationality, power, and domination were more inclined to propose feminist alternatives: a feminist standpoint (Hartsock) or a feminist maternal peace politics (Ruddick). Others suggested that the point was not to feminize a masculinized discourse on war and citizenship but rather to produce citizens who were skeptical about state activity (Elshtain) and no longer in need of protection (Stiehm).[17]

Another line of thought emphasized that male preoccupation with a military state ignored the extent to which women defined their citizenship in relation to a welfare state. Women did not retire from public life in 1920 but pursued the interdependent aims of women's complete citizenship and the creation of a feminist welfare state. They sought equality in jury duty, naturalization law, and family law, and they recognized differences in the health needs of women and infants. A hostile political climate fractured the women's movement and put feminists on the defensive, with some supporting differences in presuffrage sex-based labor laws and others advocating equality in postsuffrage equal rights amendment efforts. Yet a core of feminist reformers held onto a comprehensive vision, a feminist synthesis of women's citizenship, which was an ideological motor for the development of a feminist welfare state: uncovering the negative aspects of gender difference as substantive gender inequality, proposing public policy remedies that embodied new relationships between equality and difference, and drawing out the emancipatory potential of gender difference within a new context of greater substantive and formal gender equality.[18]

From the outset, the United States developed gender-specific systems of welfare, with veterans' benefits being the most obvious example. Less obvious were mother's aid, for a woman in a home that had lost its primary wage earner, and workmen's compensation, for employed men who had lost wages because of work-related disability. By the 1980s, the United States had developed a two-tiered system of citizenship: relatively powerless predominantly female client citizens and more powerful predominantly male electoral citizens, a reflection of a dichotomous labor market. Men received benefits based on their individual work records and regarded as "legitimate" insurance regardless of household income. They faced the state as individuals. By contrast, women received benefits based on household income and seen as "illegitimate" means-tested programs. They faced the state as clients making group claims, with responsibilities for families. Women were the predominant beneficiaries of most federal social programs: Medicare, housing, Social Security, Aid to Families with Dependent Children, Medicaid, food stamps, and Supplemental Security Income (the only important exceptions were unemployment and veterans' benefits). The state was hostile to women's claims and experiences. There was an elitist strain in liberal democratic theory which maintained that nonparticipation was acceptable, either because it reflected popular satisfaction or because increased participation would mobilize the politically incompetent and subject the political system to instability. Early liberal theories of the state emphasized that an individual's productive capacity in the market was the only legitimate method by which citizen-based claims for social benefits could be made. In the masculinist social welfare state, the ideal of the (male) citizen soldier had been replaced by the ideal of the (male) citizen worker. The combination of women's poverty and the "illegitimacy" of their claims to public benefits doubly disadvantaged them in the political world. Not surprisingly, in the 1980 election, poor women did not engage in much electoral activity, but benefit claiming was an important political act for them (half of all income to the poor came from public benefits).[19]

From State to Community

The nation-state is, of course, only one organizational form of civic life. The term "civil" refers to laws and rights but also to the courteous, benevolent behavior that makes a common, public life possible. In civil society, citizens are members of and loyal to states and communities. In communities, people share common interests, geography, and interactions. At the time of the creation of American political science, "the state" was associated with the government's monopoly on the legitimate use of force, and "the community" was associated with the benevolence that made law and force unnecessary. The two realms were gendered, as John Burgess noted: women had "*their* sphere of communal action [as] the makers of the home, the builders of the church and the ministrants of charity, while politics and government have been left for the men. . . . With this general division of function and activity, the wide realm of voluntary socialism has been administered and preserved, and benevolence and beneficence have made law and force unnecessary in many directions."[20] And women's realm was devalued. According to Manuel Castells, "men took on the state," and deemed that significant, "and left the care of civil society to women."[21] This devaluation led to the political silencing of women's lives in their communities, as men moved onto more important things, to "real" politics. When feminists entered the academy, they gave voice to women's community activity and viewed it as political, resurrecting "doing good" and "taking care" from male ridicule and condescension.

Most historical accounts of women's community activism described middle-class women's organizations beginning in the 1820s and working-class women's organizations beginning in the 1960s (union women, of course, were active in their unions throughout this entire time).[22] In the 1820s and 1830s, middle-class women formed benevolent and moral reform societies to target gambling, prostitution, profanity, and Sabbath breaking; by the end of the nineteenth century, many women's organizations had shifted their focus to providing services to people in need. The Women's Christian Temperance Union (WCTU), formed in 1874, was the first truly national women's organization, with hundreds of thousands of members by the end of the century. In 1893, Jewish women, frustrated at attempts by male Jewish leaders to exclude them from national organizational work, formed the National Council of Jewish Women. They met immigrant women at Ellis Island, helped them find food and lodging, and assisted them with vocational training and social and medical services. The National Association of Colored Women, formed in 1896, provided college scholarship loans to women, helped thousands of southern black women who migrated north to find jobs, and raised funds for playgrounds, kindergartens, day nurseries, and health care centers.[23] The General Federation of Women's Clubs, founded in 1890 and claiming a membership of one million in 1911, saw the mission of its clubs as urban service and reform.

The settlement house movement shifted the focus of public attention from individual cases of poverty to the social and economic conditions that produced it. The women leaders of the settlement houses were transformed by their experiences and became the champions of reform in the Progressive movement. Many middle-class women entered the growing profession of social work, while working-class women participated in socialist or trade-union movements.[24] During the New Deal, female social workers took positions in government agencies and the Democratic party, partly because of the influence of Eleanor Roosevelt. Local power bases for women did not develop, however, and New Deal political and community activity, like that of the Progressive years, primarily involved middle-class women.

Beginning in the 1960s, working-class and poor women became much more active in community organizations. Nationally, there was an increase in membership in voluntary organizations between 1955 and 1962, especially among the poor and blacks.[25] Poor and working-class people organized in their communities in a supportive political climate of President Kennedy's New Frontier and President Johnson's Great Society and War on Poverty. The civil rights movement involved thousands of women of color in community organizing and in government-sponsored projects. In many grassroots voluntary community organizations, women outnumbered men, even in leadership positions.[26]

The daily maintenance of the civil rights movement at the local level was in women's hands. As Andrew Young of the Southern Christian Leadership Conference put it, "It was women going door to door, speaking with their neighbors, meeting in voter registration classes together, organizing through their churches that gave the vital momentum and energy to the movement, that made it a mass movement."[27] A case study of participation in the early years of the movement in Greenwood, Mississippi, found that middle-aged black women were much more likely to be active than similar men, a difference attributed to the greater sense of personal investment women had in kin and community networks and to women's greater sense of personal efficacy because of their religious beliefs. Neither personal and privatistic commitments nor religion had a conservative effect here, as was usually supposed.[28]

Women were also the mainstay of the National Welfare Rights Organization. Even though the organization was established primarily by black male activists from the civil rights movement, the majority of its active membership came from grassroots welfare recipients and from welfare mothers' organizations formed before the national organization. AFDC mothers staged hundreds of demonstrations at welfare offices and demanded a reform of the welfare system, which saw them as powerless clients, thus overturning the relationship between administrator and

client that had been established by middle-class reformers in the Progressive era.[29]

In one of the most extensive treatments of working-class women's activism, Kathleen McCourt studied forty white women in direct action
community organizations in Chicago in 1972. These women had not
been part of the civil rights or feminist movements but were drawn to
community organizations by their concern with issues of racial change,
housing, overcrowded schools, and pollution. Their activism increased
their political consciousness, their sense of political efficacy, their cynicism about machine politics, and the frequency of their political conversations. They legitimated their activity with the argument that neighborhood issues were the traditional concerns of women: the safety of
children and the quality of neighborhood life.[30]

Throughout the 1970s, community activism on the part of working-
class women and women of color grew along with changes in the labor
market, the unresponsiveness of local government, and the inadequacy
of social services. No longer was reform the exclusive province of the
urban middle class. As the number of stable, male-oriented union jobs
declined, families increased their dependence on the state for caretaking activities. Women built on their traditional concerns to demand
collective goods and services from the state.[31] For their part, middle-class
women, formerly associated with volunteerism in charitable, philan-
thropic, and service organizations, devoted less time to nonpolitical volunteer activity and more time to professional work and political organizations. The League of Women Voters suffered a significant decline
in membership in the 1970s. In 1973, the National Organization for
Women took a position against volunteering on the grounds that it was
an extension of women's unpaid housework, that it reinforced a woman's
low self-image by offering unpaid work with little status, and that it was
society's solution for those for whom there was little real employment
choice.[32]

An analytical focus on community participation revealed that working-
class women were more participative than standard indicators would suggest. Working-class women were less likely to be involved in neighborhood
voluntary organizations than were middle-class women; they were involved in church and school organizations, however, complementing
their roles as wives and mothers. Part-time paid work was the favored alternative to both full-time housekeeping and full-time paid work. Paid
work served the function of role expansion for working-class women,
whereas education performed this function for middle-class women.[33]

A focus on the community also pointed to the connection between women's networks and democratic policymaking "from below." Feminist scholars unearthed a history of feminist designs for American homes, neighborhoods, parks, and cities;[34] discussed the relationship between women's collaborative activities and urban policy;[35] examined women's community networks and local school policies;[36] and analyzed the development of women's political consciousness in coalition efforts to secure better health care.[37] Many of these studies had a common theme: how women's political involvement led to a redefinition of policymaking from below, as women transcended a single-issue concern to discover a world of political power shaped by gender, class, and race. A study of the grassroots activities of blue-collar women organized around toxic waste issues challenged traditional assumptions about the policymaking process that focused on dominant interest groups and institutions. This conventional view left little room for avenues of participation by blue-collar women, whose protests were usually trivialized, ignored, or viewed as self-interested, particularistic, parochial, and single-issue. Through the toxics issue, these women saw everyday experiences as the beginning point for a critical analysis of power in the family, society, economy, and polity.[38]

Feminist scholars of women's politicization in communities grappled with theoretical dilemmas concerning "family," "friends," and "women's interests." Some expressed concern at the portrayal of women's community life as a unidimensional projection of "family role" onto "community role," saying this bordered on essentialism and calling for a historical-social constructionist theory of women's political consciousness and activity in which women's female consciousness or maternalism was never abstracted from the particular race and class of the mothers involved.[39] Others noted that women conducted many of their community activities as friends and that a friendship model of comrades or companions was a viable alternative to a nuclear family model of motherhood and sisterhood.[40] Some argued that women had a group interest based on their objective situation and subjective consciousness which ought to be represented in government, while others critiqued the male language of interest politics, which devalued emotions and community. Anna G. Jonasdottir sought to transcend this either/or dilemma with a new theory of interests. She noted that the term "interest" was derived from Latin words meaning "to be among." The revolutionary middle class wanted to be among those who defined the public interest. This formal aspect of interests, the claim to active participation, tended to get lost in the liberal, utilitarian usage of the term to refer to content—what (values) people needed, wished for, or demanded in order to be satisfied. In the systems theory of political science, for instance, needs became articulated as demands on the political system. Feminists who rejected the theory of interests did so on the grounds that issues of reproduction, love, care, and nurturing did not lend themselves to utilitarian arguments. Yet these activities, say between parents and children, involved constant power struggles and conflicts; they embodied both utility and care, both control and commitment, and the promotion of children's own interests. Jonasdottir called for a theory of interests that was partisan and particularistic: each party as a member of a community or an association strove to ensure autonomy in community and to have a voice in the policy process that developed the community as a whole. Needs were mediated by interests. A simple focus on "needs" was not inclusive enough to cover the dynamic essence of feminist political claims.[41]

From Interest Groups to Voluntary Associations

The third transformational theme was a shift in focus from interest groups to voluntary associations, the locus of much of women's invisible political participation. Voluntary organizations were typically defined as organizations that people belonged to "part-time and without pay, such as clubs, lodges, good-will agencies, and the like"; they were "spare-time, participatory associations" that individuals joined by choice. Excluded were such groups as family, church, temple, military, unions; professional, business, and trade associations; and political parties and clubs.[42] Voluntary associations were described in functional terms: they had latent functions (those that participants did not intend or recognize but that could be observed by an outside analyst) and manifest functions (those that participants intended and recognized); and they performed functions for the individual (e.g., combating loneliness, providing organizational skills) and for society (e.g., learning social norms). In addition, voluntary associations mediated between primary groups and the state; they integrated minority groups into the larger society; they offered a "legitimate locus for the affirmation and expression of values"; they governed "in the sense of making decisions on policy and providing services to citizens"; they initiated social change; and they distributed power.[43]

Pluralist theories of American politics maintained that democracies required a multitude of independent, voluntary, nongovernmental associations to serve as buffers between the individual and the state, to prevent the arbitrary exercise of government power, to socialize the polity, to provide a sense of community, and to allow people to make the rules by which they lived.[44] Comparative studies of democracies found that voluntary organizations played a major role in democratic political cultures, increasing citizens' sense of competence and their political participation.[45] Indeed, in some cases organizational involvement had a stronger impact on political participation than social status did, leading some scholars to conclude that "organizational involvement may represent an alternative channel for political participation for socially disadvantaged groups."[46]

Between 1930 and the early 1970s, local case studies from around the country showed that participation in voluntary organizations was associated with voting and other forms of political participation.[47] Apart from churches and labor unions, most people did not belong to organizations, and those who did tended to be high-income, educated homeowners.[48] If one included unions, other job-related associations, and recreational groups, however, then most people were members of voluntary associations.[49] The more broadly one defined a voluntary association, the more likely one was to find membership and activity on the part of the working class, women, and people of color. For example, a study of Austin, Texas, found that black women participated more in voluntary groups of all kinds than did black men or whites.[50]

During the 1950s and 1960s, national surveys found that membership in voluntary associations was directly related to high socioeconomic status, as measured by level of income, occupation, homeownership, and education, and that middle-aged women out-volunteered their male counterparts.[51] Upper-class women placed a high value on membership in organizations, whereas working-class wives saw themselves in domestic housekeeping roles and did not value participation in voluntary associations as highly.[52]

In the 1970s, feminist social scientists began to take a look at women's participation in voluntary associations. The new theme they emphasized was the invisibility of women's volunteerism—to the economy, to the polity, and to women themselves. Doris Gold argued that volunteerism was "a vast but hidden subculture of women's lives, often not understood by the participants themselves," who opted to perform valuable work behind the scenes without pay. She noted how in 1971 the Nixon administration launched a $7 million media campaign to encourage voluntarism, while the national budget was spending more and more money on arms. Given the dual system of public and private social welfare services in this country, the more free labor the government could get for social services, the less it had to spend in that area and could redirect to the military. Government studies documented the money saved by using women volunteers instead of government employees, and economists estimated the monetary worth of volunteer work in the billions of dollars. In light of the political and economic contributions of women's voluntarism, Gold recommended concrete benefits for "women who had served," comparable to those of veterans who had also served their country.[53]

There were economic reasons for the invisibility of women's voluntarism to the economy—free labor saved money—but there were cultural reasons for the invisibility of women's voluntarism to the polity and to the participants themselves: women had internalized the norms of community self-sacrifice and anonymity. One study of seventy civic leaders conducted an occupational analysis of these women's volunteering as a lifelong, professional activity, indentifying initial attraction, recruitment, skills, job satisfaction, and working conditions. The women's main activities were identifying social needs, fundraising, public relations, and advocacy. Their "work" was invisible to them because of the ethos of community self-sacrifice, which perpetuated class values invisibly under the cloak of traditional gender roles.[54]

Norms of community self-sacrifice and anonymity contributed to women's invisibility in the polity as well. In a 1947 article, Florence E. Allen, the nation's first woman to serve on a state supreme court and at the time a U.S. appellate judge, described how prominent men kept asking her, "What have women done for the country with the vote?" There was widespread disappointment in women as a political force. In order to investigate the matter, Allen sent questionnaires to thirty-four state presidents of the League of Women Voters. She was overwhelmed by the range of responses she received. League members took credit for the following measures in their states and localities: toppling the Huey Long political machine in Louisiana, defeating machine candidates in St. Louis, correcting erroneous and misleading information on a San Francisco proposed charter amendment, revising state constitutions to recognize the rights of women to serve on juries and of collective bargaining between employer and employee, securing permanent voter registration to reduce machine power, attacking abuse in the pardon system, obtaining limitations of hours of work for women, securing funds for aid to dependent children, amending adoption laws, passing city-manager and civil service enabling laws, establishing local health units and housing authorities, passing state school attendance laws, securing ordinances for industrial smoke abatement, adopting safe milk codes, establishing workmen's compensation for domestic workers, and instituting equal pay for equal work. Her respondents often stated that there were many similar instances of effective political action too numerous to record.

Allen concluded that women were actively working to solve the nation's public problems and had failed only in publicity: "Public spirited women, when they face a corrupt political machine, an official faithless to his trust, or a reactionary senator, are not seeking credit for themselves. They are trying to do the job, and when it is done they are content to be forgotten. Fine women are like that naturally—and they have had long training in developing the gift of anonymity. But now it is time to speak."[55]

Decades of female disenfranchisement had resulted in an immense complex of alternative organizational structures and coalitions among diverse women. Since most women could not vote until 1910–20, were not welcome in political parties, and could not hold public office, the institutional form of their politics was the voluntary association. Most of these organizations were single-sex or female-dominated groups that insisted on promoting the interests of women (and often children as well) and looked to government to solve problems. Women's associations were nonpartisan and highly programmatic. They had a civics-book trust in government and wanted government to do things.[56] There was also a women's political culture in spite of some conflict among organized women's groups. This political culture stood in stark contrast to the political culture of men, for whom voting and party loyalty were most important. As Suzanne Lebsock commented, "Loyalty to the party was the primary virtue—'friendship,' it was called. Candidates were evaluated mainly according to character and how hard they worked for their friends; issues and programs counted for relatively little."[57] Women's public activity was not dignified with the name "politics"; it was "philanthropy," "service," or, in the case of radical women, "disorderly conduct."

Some termed the political culture of women's organizations—the values and experiences identified with women—"social feminism," a view of women as valuable because they were different. In the League of Women Voters and in women's organizations in Great Britain and France, women derived their public role from their private role and were assisted in going from home to the public sphere, eroding the conceptual and practical boundaries between the two spheres. The social feminism of these organizations had a radical impact on society, changing the basis for participation in policy formulation and expanding the agenda for social change.[58]

One study of the political culture of women's organizations compared their incentive systems and internal policies with those of professional societies and recreational groups. Women's associations were able to motivate intense loyalty and resource contribution among the mass membership. They closely resembled social movement organizations, uniformly emphasizing public-goods objectives among their major goals. Women's groups relied on normative incentives, in stressing the organization's main principles and goals, in enhancing their public stature and prestige, and in providing information to the larger community about the organization. The only utilitarian incentives were friendship and sociable interaction. Democratic decision making was important for building commitment to the collectivity: the larger the power gap between leaders and rank-and-file members, the greater the apathy about organizational issues and the lower the member involvement.[59]

While transformational feminists focused on voluntary associations, community, and the social welfare state, accommodationist feminists adopted a more conventional definition of political participation as government participation, along with a survey research methodology. In conventional political science, political participation was cast in four general areas: opinions, voting, party activity, and contacting public officials. (Running for public office, another form of political participation, is discussed in Chapter 5). Under the general rubric of opinions, political scientists wanted to know about citizens' knowledge about issues, liberalism or conservativism, and political efficacy or alienation. Voting included questions of registration, following campaigns, working for and donating money to campaigns, turnout, and reasons for making voting choices. Party activities included identifying with a political party, party volunteer work, and serving as a convention delegate or party official. And contacting public officials took the form of letters, phone calls, telegrams, and town hall meetings and covered particularistic needs and larger causes. A few studies of political participation treated more areas, such as protest activities and working to solve community problems.

When accommodationist feminists looked at the survey research data on women's political participation, they asked three main questions: What factors affected women's political participation? What accounted for the gender gap in opinions and voting in the 1980s? How were women faring in political parties?

Accommodationist Analyses of Women's Political Participation

The first thing feminist political scientists did was point out the bias in studies of political participation from the 1950s and 1960s. Two examples of how political scientists constructed conventional wisdom based more on stereotype than on fact were the assertions that wives followed their husbands' lead in politics and that women personalized candidates more than men did. In his 1966 book *Political Participation*, Lester

W. Milbrath summarized existing research about political participation. His claim that wives followed husbands was repeatedly cited in subsequent literature. A closer look at his assertion, however, revealed that it was unsupported. Milbrath said "A good deal of solid evidence still suggests that wives follow their husbands' lead in politics (sometimes vice versa), or at least that *husband and wife tend to support the same parties and candidates*" (his emphasis).[60] Note that these were three different statements. The "sometimes vice versa" statement got completely lost both in his emphasis and in subsequent citations of his work. The possibility that wives could influence husbands was unthinkable, or uninteresting, or in any event not worth noting or pursuing in a scholarly fashion. As for the "solid evidence" for the other two assertions, Milbrath cited four sources, three of which provided absolutely no evidence for the assertions that wives followed husbands and that husbands and wives supported the same candidates and parties. One source cited admittedly unreliable voting data from the 1920s indicating that men voted at a higher rate than women; one source found that women were 10 percent less likely than men to vote in the elections of 1952 and 1956 and speculated, without evidence, that a wife left the sifting of political information up to her husband and abided by his ultimate decision about the direction of her vote; and one source found that in 1956 voting turnout (and non-turnout) was a joint action between husband and wife.[61] In sum, these sources provided evidence about voter *turnout,* not about support for parties or candidates, and not about who influenced whom in making political decisions.

A second piece of conventional wisdom was that women personalized candidates more than men did. In most voting studies, anything other than issue stand and party identification was seen as an irrational basis for voter choice. In this case, the stereotype of women's irrationality was substituted for empirical fact. Goldie Shabad and Kristi Andersen traced the origin of the view that women personalized politics to a single table in the 1954 book *The Voter Decides,* which tallied "candidate attribute" statements by respondents in a 1952 election survey.[62] Shabad and Andersen found little sex difference in either "candidate" or "issue" responses in this survey. Looking at data from elections between 1952 and 1976, Shabad and Andersen found that men and women personalized candidates to the same extent (about 60 percent of their statements), more so than they provided "party" or "issue" reasons for their voting decision. An analysis of the 1960 data showing that women were influenced by John Kennedy's personal attributes found that women saw him as competent, trustworthy, and reliable. Even when such explicitly political characteristics (e.g., competence, leadership, reliability, trust) were separated from candidate attributes with little or no political content (e.g., personality, religion, attractiveness, background), there were no sex differences in the tendency to personalize candidates.[63]

Such second looks at the classics convinced accommodationist feminists of the need to develop better measures of political participation. In some cases, however, classic studies had used valid measures and discovered that women were less participative than men in certain important ways. Unlike their male behaviorist colleagues, whose aim was to describe how the system worked, feminists wanted to change what they saw. They developed and tested hypotheses to explain, and ultimately to make recommendations in order to change, women's lower rates of participation. Feminists developed three different explanatory models, based on sex-role socialization, situational factors, and structural factors. According to the socialization model, adopting the traditional belief that politics was for men suppressed women's participation, whereas adopting an egalitarian or feminist view of women's roles facilitated participation. In the situational model, family responsibilities caused women to be less participative than men. And in the structural model, the higher one's socioeconomic status, the more participative one was.

The Socialization Model of Women's Political Participation

Early studies using a sex-role socialization model speculated that sex roles caused women to participate less than men[64] and that girls' childhood political passivity would carry over into adulthood.[65] It was not until the 1970s that such speculation was actually tested. One study that drew on national survey data gathered during the mid-1970s in eight nations attributed males' greater political participation to the fact that participation was seen more as a male than as a female gender role within the family. Reports from sixteen-to-twenty-year-olds revealed that fathers dominated in political discussions (mothers were just as dominant in the areas of religion, sex, study, and work), fathers interacted with sons more than with daughters regarding politics, and fathers showed more frequent displays of overt political activity than mothers. The socialization explanation for women's low participation was defended on grounds that studies emphasizing structural and situational constraints on adults could not readily employ suitable indicators about the pre-adult socialization of those subjects.[66]

Another socialization study of parents and children in Wisconsin a year after the 1980 general election found significant gender differences between boys and girls and their parents on a variety of measures of politicization: cognitive (national politics, party ideology, political leaders, issues), affective (interest, attention to presidential policymaking, interest in election, candidate affect, partisan support), normative (efficacy, informed, duty to vote), and behavioral (campaign activity, watched television debate, child's prospective involvement). Girls were influenced by mothers, and boys equally by mothers and fathers. Women consistently scored lower than men on measures of political cognition, affect, and behavior (but not on normative measures). The biggest sex difference among pre-adults was affective: compared to boys, girls were less strongly oriented toward the political process and political leaders, had lower political knowledge, and were less likely to watch the televised debate. Girls participated more than boys in electoral campaigns, however, which the authors attributed to girls' volunteerism orientation. The authors admitted that this emphasis on electoral politics might not reflect the way girls developed politically, especially insofar as it ignored organizational and communal politics and emphasized national instead of state and local politics.[67]

Further support for the socialization model came from studies showing that in the 1980s, socialization by same-sex parents accounted for much of girls' continuing greater political passivity than boys',[68] that high school girls expected that the traditional roles of wife and mother would be impediments to their future political participation,[69] and that middle-aged and older women were more likely to hold traditional views of women's proper place and hence be more politically apathetic.[70]

Some thought that with the rise of feminism, gender-role political socialization in the United States might be ending. One study of Illinois children found no significant sex differences in views of presidential benevolence, governmental benevolence, political cynicism, or partisanship. Boys were more knowledgeable than girls among whites only, and there were no sex differences in campaign activity, demonstrations, or political discussions with friends, teachers, and parents.[71] It was thought that the feminist movement would send a new message to the young about women's role in politics. Indeed, younger generations appeared to embrace feminism to a greater extent than did their mothers.[72]

Claire Knoche Fulenwider looked at 1972 and 1976 American National Election Studies (ANES) data and found a strong causal relationship between feminism and political participation, more so among black women than white women. Her definition of participation included campaigning, voting, writing letters, protesting, and activity in local politics and with interest groups. The relationship among feminism, political participation, and political efficacy was different for black and white women. White feminists maintained a belief in the political system but mistrusted political officials and did not support nontraditional forms of participation. Black feminists had a low evaluation of the political system, of traditional forms of participation, of the federal government, and of the presidency; they were more alienated and more likely to support political protest. Black women who scored high in feminism scored low in political efficacy. Black women of all ages were feminists, and lower-class blacks were the most feminist. Fulenwider linked black feminism to black women's absolute deprivation. By contrast, white feminists tended to be women who were unmarried, young, childless, well educated, and members of families with high incomes. She said white feminism was "fraternal," linked to deprivation relative to middle-class males.[73]

Susan Ann Kay conducted a reanalysis of the 1976 ANES data and extended it to an analysis of 1980 ANES data. She came up with conclusions that differed from Fulenwider's: in Kay's view, the stronger relationship among black women Fulenwider had found was an artifact of cases that were abnormally high on both variables (feminism and political participation). Kay also found a stronger relationship between feminism and participation among white women. An analysis of 1980 data confirmed that black women's participation was not more affected by feminism than was white women's participation and suggested to Kay a weaker effect of feminism on participation. Kay argued, however, that methodological problems prevented one from concluding that feminism had less impact on women's participation in 1980 than in 1976. The first problem was the measurement of participation. The 1980 survey used a narrower range than the 1976 survey of items of participation, primarily partisan and electoral. The second problem was the measurement of feminism. Different scales of feminism were used in the two surveys. To the extent that the 1980 scale represented a more limited range of feminism, extremely profeminist or antifeminist women could have been misclassified, increasing the error and reducing the correlation between feminism and participation over that found in 1976.[74]

Both feminist consciousness and group consciousness seemed to increase women's political participation. One analysis of 1972 and 1976 ANES data revealed that disadvantaged groups (based on race, class, age, and gender) participated in politics at a higher rate than would be predicted by their socioeconomic resources. The authors attributed this participation to members' group consciousness, which they measured by four items: group identification, group affect, power discontent, and system blaming. These four items were strongly correlated with electoral turnout and slightly less correlated with nonelectoral activities. The authors concluded that group consciousness accounted for a large share of increased participation by blacks and women since the 1960s. Even though overall turnout had declined since that time, those more likely to continue voting were people who perceived a high degree of group polarization in society.[75]

The Situational Model of Women's Political Participation

Whereas socialization theorists emphasized that children learned that politics was male and unlearned that view with a feminist or group consciousness, situational theorists stressed the importance of women's adult family roles in influencing their political participation. Virginia Sapiro studied the impact of marriage and motherhood on 676 women interviewed in 1965, when they were in high school, and again in 1973, when they were "new women" in their twenties, the first generation to come of age during the women's movement. She determined that these women were not fully integrated into the political system because their adult roles had privatized them. Compared to unmarried women, married women were less favorable to the women's movement, more trusting of political leaders, less likely to participate in protest, and more conservative. Marriage seemed to foster women's faith in authority, dependency, and acquiescence. In contrast, motherhood had a mixed effect on women's political participation. On the one hand, it inhibited political efficacy and, among married women, political knowledge, and it restricted single mothers' political communication, voting turnout, and campaign activity. On the other hand, motherhood promoted community activism for less educated women and for homemakers, it increased an interest in politics beyond the state and local levels, and it expanded the communications networks in which mothers exerted political influence. Thus, it was important to separate homemaking from motherhood in understanding women's political participation.[76]

Sapiro's findings differed from prior research on women insofar as employment was not a powerful predictor in explaining women's political roles. Rather, privatization, or political femininity, was the factor most consistently related to political integration. Privatization was measured by self-placement along a continuum, with the statement "Woman's place is in the home" at one end and the statement "Men and women should have an equal role in business, industry, and government" at the other. Education and homemaking were significantly related to privatization. Less educated homemakers were more privatized and less participative than more educated employed or single women. Privatized women were more likely to see citizenship as support and less likely to see it as involving activism beyond voting.[77]

Sapiro's emphasis on adult gender roles stemmed from her dissatisfaction with conventional studies of political socialization, which had looked at sex differences, using male behavior as the standard, and which were more concerned with system stability than people's needs and the dynamics of change.[78] Instead of looking at dichotomous sex, she focused on meaning and the structure of gender. Sex-difference research asked only whether men and women did the same thing or thought the same thing;[79] gender-meaning research sought to understand the historically flexible and context-specific meanings of both politics and gender. For example, women could enter new political roles without challenging gender ideology if those roles were seen as mere extensions of their private roles; and, conversely, as the social welfare state became more nurturant, men could enter those areas of government without a challenge to their political masculinity. The relevance of gender to politics was not simply whether women did what men did; experimental evidence showed that women and men could do the same things but be perceived differently.[80]

Sapiro also took issue with survey researchers' measurement of "constraint" in belief systems, that is, the intercorrelation of closed-ended questions to measure the degree of connection between the attitudes of an individual. Such an approach typically found that women's belief systems were less sophisticated than men's.[81] Sapiro's research showed that the conceptual frameworks thus measured depended in part on women's gender roles and gender ideology. Conventional studies looked for interconnections among a narrow range of ideas that may have been of greater significance in men's political world than in women's. When it came to belief systems more central to women's political lives, such as gender ideology, researchers found more constraint among elements of women's views than of men's.[82] Research on abortion attitudes, for example, suggested that constraint for men was abstract sophistication about conventional norms, whereas for women it was sophistication in integrating public and private questions (i.e., the value of children in their life plans and their views on life and the right to life).[83]

Sapiro also questioned gendered definitions of politics and life cycles. Women's politics was seen as "social" or "personal" because it was not in the institutional forms that men associated with politics, it had no obvious power rewards, and it stemmed from "nonpolitical" values of nurturance or social commitment. Life cycle studies assumed a male model by presuming that women "delayed" labor force participation and by ignoring two important stages for women: when children left home and widowhood. Gender research on the subjective and ideological nature of social roles and their timing necessitated a shift from "life cycle" (which sounded natural but was in fact socially constructed) to "social clocks," the social and cultural definitions of roles being "on time" according to a normative schedule for both men and women.[84]

Other situational studies confirmed that motherhood had an effect on women's political participation. Cornelia B. Flora and Naomi B. Lynn looked at 1968 ANES data and conducted in-depth interviews with thirty-two new mothers. For women aged twenty to forty, mothers were less politically efficacious than nonmothers, with the greatest difference being among high-status women. These women were most likely to engage in political activity through voluntary organizational networks, with local issues interesting them the most. Their political interest had a child-centeredness, particularly among nonemployed wives. Working mothers also saw their children as a basis for political activity but were additionally (to a lesser extent) mobilized by issues around their professions. New mothers were socialized into politics by different mechanisms and at different stages in their lives than was the case for men, and their politics tended to be personalistic and practical.[85] Another study of motherhood found that it had an effect on the political participation of female delegates to the 1972 national Republican and Democratic party conventions. Societal punishment for these women's "deviance" from the mother role contributed to their tendency to be political amateurs and to justify their behavior in terms of self-sacrifice for higher causes.[86] In a 1976 study, college-educated women without children participated more than college-educated men; but there was a big drop in college-educated women's activities when they had preschool children, especially if they were working, because of lack of time. They dropped modes of participation that were time-consuming and disruptive and retained local community activities, which were dominated by women and oriented to the schedules of mothers.[87] Indeed, there was some evidence that parenthood had a salutary impact on participation in school politics. This pattern held across age groups and was more pronounced for women than for men, especially younger women.[88]

Although most situational theorists focused on how the adult roles of wife and mother influenced political participation, others noted the effects of specific adult experiences. For example, consciousness-raising in a formal training setting moved women from traditional sex-role attitudes to a more feminist perspective, a "resocialization" of an adult's political self. Not only was a resocialization focus a corrective to political socialization studies that were preoccupied with how system support developed early in the life cycle; it also was necessary insofar as the political ideas of the women's movement were more likely to be accepted by females as adults than as children.[89] A similar notion was "countersocialization," adopting values and norms that conflicted with dominant ones, either in childhood or as an adult. The source of countersocialization in childhood was a family that encouraged both masculine and feminine behaviors, and adult sources were childrearing, supportive spouses, employment in "brokerage occupations" (involving bargaining or conflict resolution), and a stake in politics regarding women's issues.[90]

Adult experiences figured prominently in a panel analysis of delegates to the first national women's conference in Houston in 1977. A survey of their views before and after the conference found that attendance had depressed women's political aspirations for holding office in either mainstream or movement politics. Perhaps exposure to the charismatic and extremely competent "stars" of the women's movement heightened the insecurity of some delegates. The more active a woman was at the conference, the more her sense of political competence increased. The reverse was true as well: inactive women came home feeling less competent. The event polarized women for and against a plan of action, which had controversial provisions concerning reproductive rights and sexual preference. But it was also the occasion for pro- and antiplan women to realize that they shared many important life experiences regarding personal and family matters.[91]

The Structural Model of Women's Political Participation

The third model of women's political participation focused on socioeconomic status as measured by income, employment, and education. Since these were the factors that best explained men's political participation, it was assumed, and often found to be the case, that once women's income, education, and employment levels matched those of men, their participation rates would as well. At each educational level, working women were more involved and participative than nonemployed women.[92] The participation rate of working women was the same as men's, whereas homemakers' was significantly lower. Working women's participation grew in two periods: between 1956 and 1960 for white-collar women and between 1968 and 1970 for blue-collar women.[93] In 1972, rates of voting, campaign activism, and political letter writing among college-educated or working women were equal to or greater than those of men of similar socioeconomic status.[94] A study comparing female and male sibling pairs differentiated only by college attendance found that the sibling with college exposure was consistently more politically interested, informed, and participatory than the one without college exposure.[95] And a review of ANES data from 1952 through 1982 concluded that women's improving socioeconomic status led to their increased political participation during this period.[96]

Even as structural theorists used an explanatory model drawn from male experience, they made refinements in the model to fit female experience. There were two tracks for women's increased participation based on status: one was derived through a husband's social class, and the other was achieved through education and occupation.[97] It was important to look at the number of years of full-time continuous work. Employed women participated more than homemakers did, and there were mixed findings for new entrants: going to work did not increase their political participation or change their beliefs about sex roles, but it did increase their support for equal rights for women.[98]

Karen Beckwith found that differences in political participation were greater among women than they were between men and women. In her examination of 1952–76 ANES data, she found few differences between the sexes in participation, except for women's lower political efficacy. The one combination of women's life experiences that appeared to have a positive impact on women's participation was a college education and support for feminist issues. College-educated feminists reported higher levels for some kinds of political activism than their male peers and than other women. On the other hand, there were great differences among women. Certain life experiences, such as having large numbers of children at home and blue-collar employment, reduced women's participation. Black women and working-class women were the least politically active women, particularly among the poorly educated, in each sample year. Professionally employed women and female clericals, middle-class women, and white women consistently reported higher levels of voting and electoral activism than did other groups of women. Overall, Beckwith was surprised to find how little women's employment or feminism explained women's political participation. She questioned whether the ANES data base was adequate to the task of understanding the relationship between feminism and politics, whether the variable used to represent political efficacy measured something altogether different for women than for men, and whether a feeling of political efficacy really mattered if women were as participative as men without it.[99]

Given the extensive literature in support of each of the three models of women's political participation, most overview essays emphasized how women's political activities were determined by some combination of socialization, situational, and structural factors.[100] Some analysts explicitly compared the relative effects of each model. A consideration of the three explanations using 1952, 1964, and 1972 ANES data found no systematic difference in levels of male and female participation once situational and structural variables were controlled. Marriage and children had little influence on women's overall participation. Employment had a dramatic impact on female voting and political activity, with a positive effect increasing over time. College-educated women were more politically active than college-educated men in almost all activities. Women were more likely than men to belong to political clubs and to do party work. Only unemployed, low-educated females participated less than similar males.[101] An analysis of 1967 national data found some support for all three models, with adult socialization and socioeconomic status providing a more sophisticated elaboration of childhood socialization theory by specifying the conditions that modified the strength of socialization into traditional female roles. Women differed by generation: those under thirty participated less than men under thirty; there were no differences in participation rates between women and men aged thirty to forty-four; and women over forty-five participated less than their male counterparts, except for particularized contacting (contacting an official about personal or family matters). Marriage had the same effect on men's and women's participation, but participation for women dropped off when they had preschool children (except voting). Traditional women participated less than women who adopted egalitarian sex roles. Highly educated professional men and women participated at the same rate. College-educated women who belonged to three or more voluntary associations participated more than did college-educated men. There were no gender differences in participation between blue-collar men and women, but there was a big gap in participation between (nonprofessional) white-collar men and women.[102]

Reasons for the Gender Gap

In addition to enhancing women's political participation, accommodationist feminists wanted to account for the gender gap in opinions and voting. After the 1980 election of Ronald Reagan, NOW activists searched for some hopeful sign to bolster their attempt to secure ratification of the Equal Rights Amendment before the June 1982 deadline. NOW president Eleanor Smeal, trained as a political scientist, immediately recognized the significance of the 8 percent difference in men's and women's vote for Reagan. She wrote op-ed pieces for Chicago newspapers to influence Illinois legislators, who were divided on the ratification issue. Disseminating the gender gap in polling data was launched as an explicit political strategy by NOW.[103] Over the next two years, feminists worked one on one, reporter by reporter, to demonstrate how specific races—gubernatorial elections in Virginia in 1981 and in Michigan, Texas, and New York in 1982—had been won with a margin of victory secured by women's vote.

With the defeat of the ERA in 1982, NOW mounted an all-out effort to get more women registered to vote and more feminists elected to office. Women's voluntary associations worked in coalition to register nearly two million new women to vote.[104] NOW turned its attention to getting a woman on the Democratic ticket in 1984 and to placing women at the core of party decision making. At the 1983 NOW convention, Democratic front-runners met with NOW and agreed to consider a female running mate. As Kathleen Frankovic noted, "Women were being addressed as a *constituency,* in the tradition of a pressure group in American party politics. Leaders talked about their 'political credibility,' and the potential value of the women's vote to the prospective Democratic nominee."[105] Women had majority status in the electorate, credible organizations, contacts with leaders in the party, and a track record of tipping races toward Democratic candidates. NOW's endorsement of Walter Mondale in 1983 was the first presidential endorsement in its seventeen-year history. In spite of Mondale's defeat in 1984, NOW emerged from the election as an interest group to be reckoned with by the Democratic party, having scored a historic first in pressing for and obtaining the nomination of Geraldine Ferraro, the first woman vice-presidential nominee of a major political party.

In the 1984 presidential election, gender differences in voting persisted at the same level as in 1980, even though a majority of women voted for Reagan. In subsequent elections, male and female voters made significantly different voting choices. For example, in 1992, such differences appeared in five U.S. senatorial and two gubernatorial races.[106] There was also a gender gap in party identification. Since the mid-1960s, women have been about 5 percent more likely than men to say they were Democrats. There was a turnout gap as well: beginning in 1980, women turned out to vote at a higher rate than men in presidential elections (they had outvoted men in sheer numbers since 1964, largely because there were more voting-age women than men). And there was a gender gap in presidential evaluations, with women more critical of President Reagan's performance than men.[107]

Having brought the gender gap to the attention of the media, politicians, the public, and political scientists, feminists in the movement and in the academy attempted to understand what caused it. The obvious starting place was political attitudes: women probably voted differently from men because they held different views. After all, an attitudinal gender gap had preceded the 1980 election. A review of Gallup and ANES data between 1936 and 1984 demonstrated that, since the advent of public opinion polling, women had had a distinctive set of political views. But, since these views did not fit neatly into the boxes of male politics—liberal vs. conservative or Democratic vs. Republican platforms—they did not figure prominently in male politics or male political science. Women had distinctive views in three areas: political corruption, war and peace, and sumptuary legislation (prohibiting alcohol and drugs). Between the 1930s and the 1980s, political parties had shifted their stands on these issues. Political reform and peace moved from Republicans to Democrats, and sumptuary laws shifted from Democrats to Republicans. Women's votes were not as explainable by socioeconomic status as men's votes were; for example, high-status men were more Republican than high-status women.[108]

Since the 1930s, there have been consistent gender differences in attitudes toward violence: 285 data points from six polling organizations revealed a 10 percent gender difference in a wide range of questions regarding violence: law enforcement, criminal punishment, the death penalty, television violence, the use of the military in international relations, and support for U.S. involvement in wars. The largest gender differences appeared in questions directly linked to gender socialization: gun ownership, hunting, gun control, and boxing. There were somewhat smaller differences were regarding defense spending, and the smallest differences on issues of interpersonal violence, such as hitting and spanking children. These gender differences were not mitigated by feminist ideology, age, or education.[109]

Before 1980, most conventional political science studies of public opinion found few issue differences between men and women, with the exception of questions of violence and, to a lesser extent, "moral issues" such as drug use, divorce laws, obscenity, and the like.[110] Some researchers noted women's domestic humanitarianism: compared to men, women had greater support for egalitarian race relations and relief programs such as aid to dependent children, unemployment assistance, old-age benefits, and antipoverty programs. But women were not seen as consistently more liberal than men, because of their "contradictory views," which placed them somewhat to the right of men on fiscal policy, the national debt, progressive taxation, labor unions, the minimum wage, and self-identification as a conservative.[111] With the advent of the gender gap in the 1980s, however, both conventional and feminist analysts delved more deeply into women's belief systems. Perhaps not surprisingly, conventional studies found little "constraint" among women's views and hence little to distinguish them as a group.[112] By contrast, feminist scholars were more likely to find group explanations for women's views and behavior. Some traced the gender gap to women's distinctive views about war and peace issues[113] and the ERA.[114] And others came up with explanatory models that were not necessarily those that had explained male behavior.

Ethel Klein looked at data about the gender gaps in 1980, 1982, and 1984 and argued that there were clear and persistent contrasts between women's and men's priorities and preferences, especially regarding New Deal values about fairness and the poor, defense, the environment, the Equal Rights Amendment, and the arms race. Women's vote reflected not so much policy assessments in terms of conscious group interests as women's increased confidence in their ability to assess public policy and their expectations for a governmental role that drew from their experiences and values as women. Women were more liberal than men, but there were class differences among them: middle-class women were more concerned about peace, women's rights, the economy, and educational opportunity, whereas lower-class women emphasized social services, employment, and economic security.[115]

Klein's analysis centered on the concept of group consciousness. The rise of political consciousness was a three-part process: a realization of group membership and shared interests, a rejection of traditional definitions of a group's status in society, and a realization that social institutions rather than personal failure were to blame for one's situation. Women's political consciousness emerged from their increased labor force participation, declining fertility patterns, and rising marital instability. People's support for feminism stemmed from self-interest, ideology, or group consciousness. Nontraditional women had a self-interest in supporting feminism, since it legitimized their way of life. Some men had an ideological commitment to feminism based on abstract notions of justice and equality. For women who had experienced discrimination, feminist activism was a matter of group survival, justified in terms of equality, justice, and liberty. Men's feminist sympathy was abstract and short-term; women's feminist consciousness was personally experienced and long-term.[116]

Feminism meant something different for men and for women. It was one thing to tell a survey researcher that one supported equal pay for women, the Equal Rights Amendment, and abortion. Indeed, many surveys showed no sex differences in support for these issues. It was quite another thing, however, to be on the barricades: initiating discussions of women's rights, demanding political solutions to problems, working to change the political agenda, feeling threatened by the status quo, and confronting issues on a day-to-day basis, not as an abstract matter. Conventional analysts tended to collapse the meaning of feminism into responses to survey items, and once men became just as feminist as women by these measures, women's group consciousness became less interesting.

Klein applied a women's group consciousness analysis to the presidential elections of 1972, 1976, and 1980. In 1972, there was a feminist vote but no women's vote. In 1976, men did not give feminism as high a priority as women did. In 1980, women's rights was a campaign issue: both women and men favored the ERA, but women voted for Carter because he lent women his support, while men did not (issues such as inflation and the hostage crisis were more important to men). In all three elections, party loyalty had more of an influence on men's votes than it did on women's. Over time, there was a diffusion of group consciousness from women who were single or divorced, college-educated, young, and urban to include women who were married, widowed, less educated, and elderly.[117]

A Feminist Alternative to the Liberal-Conservative Continuum

Scholars who looked for an overall logic to women's views as a group tended to emphasize some mix of pacifism, compassion, self-interest, and feminism. And they agreed that the liberal-conservative continuum did not necessarily apply to women as a group. Robert Y. Shapiro and Harpeet Mahajan reviewed national opinion surveys from the 1960s to the 1980s and found moderately large gender differences regarding the use of force and about half as much difference when it came to regulation and public protection, compassion issues, and traditional values. In the last three areas, the gender gap had increased over time. The salience of issues had increased greatly for women (that is, there was a decline in their "don't know" response rate), and preference differences had increased in ways consistent with the interests of women and the intentions of the women's movement. Before the 1960s, men were more likely than women to say that women's economic and political life should be expanded; by the 1960s, such differences had diminished or even reversed.[118]

Shapiro and Mahajan maintained that women's views did not fall neatly along a liberal-conservative dimension. Their stands on force and compassion put women in the liberal camp: lower defense spending and troop levels; opposition to capital punishment and support for gun control; and support for jobs, income redistribution, and health, education, and welfare issues. Willingness to support government measures for public protection put women in the liberal camp for the most part (support for environmental regulation and opposition to nuclear power plants) but could be construed as conservative "tough on crime" or anti–civil libertarian stances (favoring speed limits, seatbelts, jail for drunk drivers, and bans on cigarette advertisements and sales). And women's support of traditional values, measured by questions about home, family, children, religion, the neighborhood, and order, earned them a "social conservative" label. In Klein's terminology, these were the survival issues in women's day-to-day lives, an important source of their group consciousness. Women more than men struggled on a daily basis to provide a secure home, neighborhood, and school environment for their children. They were more personally threatened by pornography and more likely to be held accountable for their children's use of drugs and sexual behavior. And they were more likely than men to see religion as an important source of moral order in their lives. One could also use Klein's model to explain Shapiro and Mahajan's finding that women were more conservative than men on women's rights issues. Women's group consciousness had diffused to men and/or men's sympathy was genuine but did not have the same consequences for political behavior as did women's group consciousness, based on their personal experiences with survival issues. Men's support for abortion was based on self-interest insofar as men were not willing to assume the responsibilities of fatherhood, a tendency borne out by the fact that most single mothers received little child support from their children's father. And women's support for abortion was mediated by the importance of religion in their lives.

Further evidence that a female core belief system of a reduced military, fewer criminal penalties, more environmental protection, and a greater government role in securing social and economic equality undergirded the gender gap was provided in an analysis of the 1988 ANES survey. The authors attributed the gender gap to four factors: women's countersocialization experiences (especially education, which led to an increase in their support for women's rights, social compassion, and pacifism); self-interest (exemplified in women's support for issues such as child care); compassion for the poor on the part of wealthier women; and a gap among people with traditional values—men held such values out of ideological conservatism, women out of a concern for hearth and home. Two-thirds of both men and women supported equality for women, with men somewhat more likely to support abortion rights. The women's rights gap was closing as men increased their support for the issues of the women's movement.[119]

There were different interpretations of how women's economic self-interest figured into the gender gap. Some saw it in terms of jobs and government benefits, linking women's lower levels of support for Reagan to the fact that welfare state retrenchment threatened the economic fortunes of working-age women. Women constituted 70 percent of the more than twenty million participants in the social welfare state: four million as welfare family heads, and seventeen million as human service workers in health, education, and welfare jobs.[120]

Susan J. Carroll saw women's self-interest in terms of autonomy, arguing that the gender gap in 1980 and 1982 was best explained by women's economic and psychological independence from men. Economically independent women were professional and unmarried; economically dependent women were married homemakers or married "vulnerables" (i.e., employed in low-salary jobs and having a high school education or less). Psychological independence was measured by agreement with the statement "Women should have an equal role with men in running business, industry, and government." The autonomy thesis combined both economic and gender explanations of the gender gap. Economic explanations focused on women's self-interest (poverty, the wage gap, social welfare jobs and benefits) and on their economic vulnerability. Gender explanations emphasized nurturance (humanitarianism and preservation of life) and the feminist movement. The autonomy explanation accounted for the gender gap across class lines; it showed how economic independence enhanced receptivity to feminism; and it accounted for the strong relationship between marital status and the gender gap (unmarried women were much less supportive of Reagan).[121]

Other researchers cautioned that women's economic self-interest should not be construed in the same way as that of classical economics' "economic man," that is, primarily in terms of one's individual financial situation. Arthur Miller said women's economic views were less self-interested than those of men. Men voted their pocketbooks, but women did not, evidencing a "sociotropic economic orientation," in which the economy in general was of more concern to them than was their individual financial situation.[122] Other research agreed with this finding.[123]

Finally, feminism played a role in the belief system associated with the gender gap. As we have seen, support for feminism was hard to quantify. Most analysts of survey research data measured feminism by using opinions about women's issues and the women's movement. Somewhat ironically, the year the gender gap emerged, 1980, there were virtually no gender differences in support for major women's issues. Among both sexes, 60 percent supported the ERA, 55 percent agreed that society discriminated against women, and only 10 percent said that abortion should never be permitted.[124] Support for "women's issues" had obviously increased among both men and women, with less support expressed for either the movement or feminism per se.[125] Feminism had to be viewed historically, as providing a changed ideological climate that helped women—whether or not they called themselves feminists—to define their interests, feel confident articulating them, and seek public attention about them.

While feminism, self-interest, compassion, and pacifism constituted the female side of the gender gap, there was a male side as well, of course. During the 1980s, men defected in greater numbers than women from liberalism, Democratic party identification, and voting for Democratic presidential candidates.[126] Although no single explanatory model emerged to everyone's satisfaction, feminists brought the gender gap to the attention of the press and the public as a conscious political strategy, and they worked at specifying its components from the point of view of women's experiences.

Women and Political Parties

A third important question for accommodationist feminists was how women were faring in political parties. Much of women's politics in the nineteenth century was antiparty, and after even securing suffrage in 1920, women did not flock to political parties, preferring to accomplish public service through nonpartisan, community organizations. Women were divided on the Equal Rights Amendment, and the parties were as well. The Democratic party and pro-union women opposed the ERA for fear it would invalidate protective labor laws for women. The Republican party and entrepreneurial women supported the ERA as part of a world view endorsing individual achievement in the marketplace. As the 1964 Civil Rights Act dismantled state protective labor laws, the Democratic party shifted its position and endorsed the amendment in 1972. And as its right wing gained ascendancy, the Republican party reversed its position as well and opposed the amendment in 1980.

Of course, the women's movement had a role in the parties' respective stances on the ERA. Initially, activists had eschewed political parties. But 1972 was an important turning point. The National Women's Political Caucus, which had been formed in 1971, was a prominent force at the two major party conventions in 1972. This was the first large-scale effort by an organization of women to function within the conventions as a pressure group articulating women's interests.

Although the NWPC wanted very much to be bipartisan, from the beginning it played a greater role in the Democratic than in the Republican party. There were more Democrats than Republicans in the original NWPC, and the Democrats had just adopted new rules on delegate selection, making the party more permeable to newcomers. Both parties saw an increase in female convention delegates in 1972. In the previous two decades, their numbers had never topped 20 percent; in 1972, women constituted about 40 percent of Democratic delegates and 30 percent of Republican delegates. Most NWPC proposals, including support of the ERA, were added to both parties' platforms (neither party supported reproductive rights). At the 1976 conventions, Democratic feminists fought for power independently of other struggles going on in the party, and Republican feminists fought for the ERA as part of the contest between Gerald Ford and Ronald Reagan. At the 1980 conventions, feminists had poor relations with the campaigns of the dominant candidates (Carter and Reagan), resulting in the virtual exclusion of feminists at the Republican convention and the search for alternative routes of influence by Democratic feminists. Anti-ERA forces prevailed at the Republican convention. The Carter campaign was lukewarm to feminists, whom it saw as Ted Kennedy supporters. The 1984 conventions solidified the directions in which both parties had been moving for a decade; as Jo Freeman put it, "The Democrats adopted the feminist perspective on all public policy issues directly affecting women and made it clear that women, under feminist leadership, were an important part of the Democratic coalition. The Republican party adopted antifeminist positions on almost every issue."[127]

Freeman contrasted the experiences of feminists at the 1972 and 1984 conventions to illustrate how far women had come. In 1972, they had beseeched party leaders to listen to them. Leaders were polite but disdainful, offering token support by putting the ERA, recently passed by Congress, back in their platforms. By 1984, party leaders were listening to feminists but responding in opposite ways, with Democratic leaders taking feminist organizations and issues seriously and Republican leaders dismissing them. She attributed this differential treatment to the parties' respective political cultures: for the Democrats, it was "whom you represent" (organized constituencies), whereas for the Republicans, it was "whom you know" (personal connections). These cultures were reflected in the parties' structures: in the Democratic party, power flowed up; in the Republican party, power flowed down. Democratic groups were "constituencies," who communicated their group concerns to the party and for whom winning was often of secondary importance; Republican groups were "auxiliaries," whose purpose was to elect Republicans, not communicate group concerns. The Democratic party was pluralistic, with multiple power centers; the Republican party rewarded deference to leadership and being a good foot soldier. Republicans saw themselves at the center; Democrats saw themselves on the periphery. Republicans stood for the national interest; Democrats for special interests. Republicans maneuvered within the system; Democrats challenged the system. The unitary structure of the Republican party made it impossible to develop an independent feminist power base; Republican feminists needed to find Republican leaders who supported feminist positions. Democratic feminists had to continue to take their case to the American public and organize their supporters to participate in local politics in order to prevent the Republican party from making feminism an electoral liability as "just another special interest."[128]

Why didn't the women's movement work in a sustained way with parties until the 1980s? And why has the relationship between the movement and parties remained relatively weak in comparison to women's movements in Europe? Anne N. Costain and W. Douglas Costain answered these questions in terms of three strategic and tactical periods in the contemporary women's movement: the formative period of the 1960s, when protest was combined with working through political elites; the routinizing period of the 1970s, when all political tactics were tried; and the institutionalizing period of the 1980s, with a combined focus on legislative lobbying, electoral politics, and political parties. During the 1960s, radicals saw parties as a barrier and moderates bypassed parties to work directly with elites in the executive branch. Both the limited success of this strategy and the vanishing barriers between radicals and moderates led to new strategies of organizing and multiple points of access in the political system during the 1970s: parties, Congress, the courts, the executive branch, a constitutional amendment, lobbying, and protesting. By the 1980s, women's groups began to specialize in their functions. The creation of the Congressional Caucus for Women's Issues in 1977 cut down on duplication of effort and created a climate of concern for women's issues in Congress and the media. Fueled by the gender gap data in the 1980 election, the growth in the number of women's PACs, and evidence that women's vote was crucial in some races, women's groups made more political endorsements and raised more money for female candidates. These activities brought attention to the issue of groups' relations to political parties. Most women's groups started out bipartisan and remained so throughout the 1980s. But in 1980 NOW aligned itself with the Democratic party, in 1982 only 15 percent of its PAC money went to Republicans, and in 1984 it endorsed Walter Mondale, which limited the effectiveness of its bipartisan lobbying role. The dilemma for women's groups became how to balance the conflicting demands of policy influence and electoral politics and lobbying.[129]

The relationship of the women's movement with parties remained relatively weak for several reasons, according to Costain and Costain. It came up against policy "subgovernments," or iron triangles of congressional subcommittee members, executive branch agency officials, and interest groups, which dominated decision making in each policy area. Subgovernments rewarded those with expertise and experience, and parties were usually limited in their ability to reach these decision makers. In addition, parties were not consistently programmatic regarding policies and had lost their ability to provide a cue to voters in the age of individualized media campaigns. In short, parties were not confident, powerful political actors when the women's movement emerged, so the movement turned instead to interest groups. But women's groups had to avoid becoming so caught up in the policy game of insiders that they lost their grassroots support and hence their bargaining leverage and financial base.[130]

Not all scholars saw such a marginal relationship between parties and the women's movement. Indeed, Denise L. Baer argued that women had made great gains in the post-1972 reformed parties as convention delegates and national committee members. Since feminist researchers had failed to study the significance of these increased numbers, however, research on political parties was left largely in the hands of antireform analysts. She criticized feminist researchers for conveying two images of women and parties that were inconsistent with contemporary scholarship on parties: (1) that parties were weak and unable to recruit women even as scholars heralded the increased strength of parties in recruiting, training, and supporting candidates, and (2) that parties were strong and hostile to the recruitment of women, at a time when parties were more permeable than ever before to women. Baer also pointed out that feminists, given their greater sympathy with the Democratic party, were particularly ignorant of the role of women in the Republican party.[131]

Convention Delegate Studies: 1972 as a Watershed Year

Most studies of political parties focused on delegates to national nominating conventions. The 1972 conventions, with their high percentage of female delegates, captured the attention of political scientists, who produced a flurry of studies about women's political participation and the differences between male and female delegates. Until the women's movement was in the air in 1972 (indeed, the press had dubbed it "The Year of the Woman," and the McGovern campaign saw the "Nylon Revolution" as an important new resource),[132] there were virtually no studies comparing male and female convention delegates. Two notable exceptions were a study of Michigan delegates to the 1964 party conventions[133] and a 1965 study of California party leaders.[134] The Michigan study found that male delegates had more resources in terms of social background and political careers. Women and men had similar careers within parties, with women slightly more active in contacting voters and distributing literature and men giving more speeches and managing more campaigns. Women were slightly more active in party service, especially Republican women, and men held most of the powerful party posts. The California study found similar sex differences in background resources but more differences in party careers and personal motivations. Men were public office–oriented, and women were intraparty-oriented. Although the women were not newcomers to party politics, they were underrepresented at the national and state levels but as likely to hold local office. Women's interests were more local than cosmopolitan. Women's intraparty career style reflected a public-serving motivation whereas men's public office career style reflected a self-serving motivation, and women were less power-oriented than men.

Jeane J. Kirkpatrick's study of the 1972 convention delegates found that women's backgrounds were very similar to those of men, with women having somewhat less income and education. Most of the Democratic women but only about half the Republican women were employed. Both sexes were joiners: four-fifths belonged to at least one voluntary organization. Men and women had similar self-concepts regarding efficacy, influence on others, self-confidence, egostrength, and autonomy. Both sexes said men were more influential than women, with women being somewhat more likely than men to perceive other women as influential. It appeared that the mere increase in numbers of women at these conventions did not increase their influence. In both parties, across all candidate groups, and in all age cohorts, female delegates were significantly less ambitious for public office and had lower expectations of political achievement than men. Male delegates were much more likely than female delegates to say they participated in party politics to enhance their political careers.[135]

Kirkpatrick measured delegates' focus of attention by their responses to open-ended questions about the most important problems facing government and people like themselves. Virtually no woman in either party identified women's status as a salient public or personal issue. There were no sex differences on most issue positions, the most important exception being the use of military force. Women's disagreement among themselves over issues, especially abortion, busing, day care, foreign policy, welfare, and the women's movement, weakened their political influence at both conventions. Delegates indicated that in general male discrimination in political parties was a real problem for women. A majority of delegates in both parties agreed that men prevented women from seeking political careers. Most Democrats (but not most Republicans) agreed that most men in party organizations tried to keep women out of leadership roles. Many women reported that they were encouraged to run for office by local or county party leaders, however, and a majority of women said they had never been personally discriminated against. Male delegates were much more likely than female delegates to hold conventional views about women's role in politics, that is, to believe that women were less emotionally suited for politics, that politics meant sacrificing femininity, and that women were less logical and rational than men; men's views were reflected in the same proportions among the public at large. A 1972 Harris poll conducted for Virginia Slims found that 63 percent of adults agreed that men were better suited emotionally for politics than were most women, and half thought it was impossible to be a politician and a good mother at the same time.[136]

A study of delegates to the 1972 Democratic national convention documented the importance of the women's movement for female delegates. Only 14 percent of them said that they had not been affected by the movement; one-third were active in the movement in some way; and 72 percent identified a prominent movement spokeswoman. Most said that women in politics faced discrimination, that they had personally experienced discrimination, and that their status as female delegates made them less effective than male delegates. Experiences of sex discrimination and support for the women's movement cut across socioeconomic lines. When it came to women's issues, with the exception of willingness to vote for a woman for president, female delegates were much more supportive than male delegates. Women were more likely to believe that women in politics faced discrimination, that women could run businesses as well as men could, that most women were oppressed, and that the goals of the women's movement were agreeable to them. Given a list of ten controversial issues, women were more liberal than men on each.[137]

Another study of convention delegates noted how women's traditional roles and gender ideology may have channeled them into positions of political influence congruent with norms of women's service and civic responsibility. Their volunteerism could be translated into political ambition without a radical change in values. Women were less interested than men in holding office but as interested in a party career. Democratic women were more likely than Republican women to pursue officeholding, and Republican women were more committed to the party sphere. Homemakers preferred party office to public office; employed Democratic women were as likely to want party and public office.[138]

One of the most cited findings of the 1972 convention studies was that female delegates were amateur rather than professional in style. Amateur delegates were volunteers committed more to issues than to winning the general election. Professional delegates worked year after year for the party, were more concerned with winning, avoided controversial issues, and supported vague platforms. There was evidence that women's amateurism in political parties diminished over time, however. A study comparing Michigan delegates to the two party conventions in 1964 and in 1976 found that female delegates had changed from being articulators of issues (amateurs) to brokers of opposing views (professionals).[139] A 1980 study using a sample of convention delegates, states and county chairs, and members of national committees found no gender differences in amateurism.[140] Somewhat surprisingly, the Michigan study found that female delegates had not become more politically ambitious about public or party office over time, in spite of the fact that differences between the sexes had dwindled with respect to social background, political status, political careers, and perceptions of the political process. A comprehensive review of studies of convention delegates from 1972 to 1984, however, detected an increase in the proportion of women who held or had ambition to hold public office. Over time political parties had been altered by the sizable presence of women, who had introduced different voluntary group interests. Whereas male delegates were associated with veterans', fraternal, labor, service, and occupational groups, female delegates were affiliated with women's, abortion, school, teachers', public interest, and environmental groups. Women had not yet affected the public policy preferences of the parties, but they had introduced new attitudes about gender roles and they were more likely than men to see obstacles for women in politics.[141]

The Gender Division of Labor in Local Party Politics

Perhaps triggered by all the attention to national party activity in 1972, academic studies of women's local political activity began to be conducted in earnest in 1974. Ellen Boneparth looked at 103 female party functionaries and volunteers in Santa Clara County during the 1974 general election. They had a high socioeconomic status, only 30 percent of them worked full time, most were white and long-time residents, they were married with children, and they had prior campaign or volunteer experience. Their campaign activities were not restricted to support roles. Female party activists were more likely to hold top leadership posts in the campaigns of female candidates, and women who worked for female candidates were more likely to engage in a variety of activities, from the most to the least desirable, lessening the divisions between professionals and volunteers. Half these women felt excluded from party decision making on the basis of sex, reporting that men were patronizing and insensitive and did not take women seriously. Men in the party were said to treat "liberated" staffers equally and to be more sexist toward "conventional" women. Women noted that they experienced the least discrimination from the candidates themselves. Some women said female candidates attracted more competent women workers, more sympathetic and aware people, and people who made decisions by consensus. Compared to moderate party activists, feminists were more likely to be Democratic, working for female candidates, employed, and interested in running for office, but not actively pursuing feminist issues.[142]

Most comparisons of male and female local party activists found a division of labor between the sexes. Diane Margolis studied this division of labor in party organizations in a small Connecticut town in 1974. Different styles of performance made the men stand out more than the women, who operated in settings where they could not be seen, in roles without titles or acknowledgment, whereas the men held highly visible leadership positions. Women spent twice as much time on political activity and logged three times as many separate political interactions as men. There were similarities between family sex roles and the parts played out in the political arena. Women were task-oriented and measured political performance by completed projects; men were more concerned with enhancing their self-esteem through their inclusion in the decision-making process. Men sought positions; women waited to be wooed. Women who were service-oriented "drudges" (i.e., those who arranged fundraisers) were welcome; idealists who wanted to change things were not. "Women's work" was the day-to-day maintenance of the committee, regular tasks performed on a monthly or yearly basis. "Men's work" was what was assigned to them by their official role; they held the special, nonrecurring, and public posts.[143]

A similar division of labor was found in a 1977 study of party officials in Atlanta. In a test of instrumental-expressive gender-role theories, the authors looked at four aspects of party life and found that two of them differed by gender and two of them by party context. Party activities and electoral ambition differed by gender. Women had less electoral ambition, attended more meetings, did more telephoning and less canvassing, were less motivated to work for the party in order to get business contacts, and were more likely to define their electoral role as routine. Incentives for participation and party role definition differed by party context. Given the history of long-term Democratic dominance in Georgia, it was not surprising to find that Republicans were less ambitious but played more innovative party roles, whereas Democrats were more ambitious but played more routine party roles.[144]

In a study comparing local male and female party officials in the United States and Canada, the authors found that men had more elite social backgrounds but that men and women had equally politicized childhoods. Men were more likely to have had political careers, with the ratio of men to women increasing the higher the rank of the position. Women had a higher commitment to party work and invested more time in party activity and were only slightly less likely than men to have had continuous party careers. Compared to men, women devoted more time to party activity, enjoyed it more, and ranked it as important as other salient concerns, yet they were less likely to entertain expectations of future higher public or private office.[145]

Another angle on local party activists involved ideological differences between men and women. A study of party precinct committeepersons in Florida, where state law required equal representation of men and women at every level of party organization, found that although women were active at the local level, few of them ran for office, except widows. Party affiliation explained most of the ideological differences between those surveyed, with Democrats more liberal and Republicans more conservative. Democratic women were more liberal than Democratic men, but there was not a corresponding conservative gender gap among Republicans. On women's issues, female party activists were more supportive than men in both parties.[146]

Finally, researchers probed the political motivations of local party activists. In a comparison of the motivations of California party elites in 1964 and in 1981, respondents were asked why they initially became involved in partisan politics and why they wanted to be convention delegates. Their motives were divided into five types: self-enhancement, sociality, purposive (issue-based), personalist, and party allegiance. Republican and Democratic men and women had the same rank order of motivations, with purposive the highest and self-enhancement the lowest. In both parties women scored higher than men on all scales except self-enhancement. Women were noticeably more purposive, expressing an interest in issues and public service. Although women were less ambitious than men about holding public office, there was an increase in women's self-enhancement motivation over time, especially among Democratic women. Women in feminist organizations were more ambitious, as were ERA supporters and younger women. In 1981, just as in 1964, women engaged in internal party activity while men did the external work.[147]

These studies found a pattern of women working behind the scenes, expending more effort than men to hold the organization together yet not seeking public office for themselves. Depending on one's approach, one could easily miss women's partisan activity. If one simply counted those interested in or running for public office (the behaviorist emphasis on the male mode of political participation), then women were not active in partisan politics. If one focused on who did what work for political parties (the feminist emphasis on taking women's experiences seriously), then women were active in partisan politics but not necessarily in the male mode. They were less visible and careerist, but their efforts kept party organizations going. Parties rewarded service-oriented women and ambitious men, but there was evidence that the women's movement had begun to erode this gender division of labor.

Political Participation by Women in Santa Clara County

To the extent that women were organized into groups in Santa Clara County, they promoted the social welfare state as opposed to the military state. Silicon Valley was the recipient of lucrative governmental defense contracts, and it was not in the narrow economic self-interest of valley residents to lose jobs to bidders elsewhere. But local women's groups opposed weapons contracts at local firms, argued that such firms could be reconverted to produce socially useful products, and tried to convince the community that federal dollars were better spent for social welfare purposes. The most visible and active local antimilitaristic women's group was the San Jose branch of the Women's International League for Peace and Freedom (WILPF). WILPF was founded in 1915 when women from twelve countries, including a delegation from the United States led by Jane Addams, met in The Hague. They proposed continuous mediation to end World War I and visited heads of state in an effort to stop the war.[148] The San Jose branch of WILPF was founded in 1951. It worked for universal disarmament and a strong United Nations, an end to U.S. intervention abroad, peace education in schools and communities, civil rights for all, full rights for all women, an economy that put people before profits, and an end to government spying.[149]

Women were active in their communities to secure the benefits of the social welfare state. An example of women's citizenship on the health care front was the effort of the Chicana Coalition, which worked with local Gray Panthers and Chicana nurses to pressure local hospitals to improve services for Hispanic patients. As Kathy Espinoza-Howard, then president of the coalition, described it:

> We have had an ongoing struggle with the sixteen or seventeen local hospitals in the area. We have been addressing the lack of bilingual services, sliding-scale fees, and access. We have very convincingly used the government watchdog—the Health Services Administration's certificate-of-need process—to address these issues every time a hospital comes up to ask permission to grow or add equipment. They have to hold a public meeting, and our expert members come with their statistics. I look at their affirmative action plans and bilingual staffing.

Another health care example was how abortion rights advocates worked behind the scenes to influence county supervisors. According to Pat Miller, then director of Family Planning Associates and former member and chair of the Santa Clara County Commission on the Status of Women, there were no restrictive abortion practices (such as parental consent or prohibitive zoning) in the county. Although the county did not directly fund abortions, if someone had an abortion at the county hospital and could not pay for it, the county reimbursed the hospital for unpaid bills with general funds to the hospital. County supervisors passed a motion of support for *Roe v. Wade.* Miller attributed supervisor support to women's one-on-one efforts: "Women have learned the importance of telling candidates where we stand behind the scenes. You have to take the time and effort to talk about the issues. And then be there to support them."

Several informal women's networks were geared toward electoral politics. For example, Supervisor Susanne Wilson had served as president of

California Elected Women, a statewide organization of female state, county, and local elected officials. In this capacity, she had compiled a list of Santa Clara County women called GOG, or "Good Old Gals." As her aide Sarah Janigian described it:

> It is the equivalent of the old boys' network. If someone comes into town, at a moment's notice we can pull together a luncheon to hold in two weeks. About a hundred women usually come. Everyone pays for her own meal. It is mainly informational and a good networking tool. And it is all different kinds of women: different levels of government, business, and industry. It is very informal. Of course, every now and then some fundraising is done informally. You are sitting around a room and someone says, "Hey, this person is going to run for office and needs some money." And they all pull out their checkbooks.

Local women's groups made explicit efforts to recruit their members for elective and appointive posts.[150] The most active groups in this regard were local chapters of NWPC, NOW, and the League of Women Voters. Local chapters published newsletters announcing openings for appointive offices, offered members important personal contacts, and provided members with organizational skills and experience in public speaking. The League of Women Voters supplied mentors for women who later became local elected officials. For example, San Jose city councilmember Nancy Ianni credited the league for giving her organizational experience and a mentor.

The local NWPC chapter scouted new talent. Most of the time women came to it for endorsement, but occasionally it reached out to women who had never heard of the group. NWPC member Sarah Janigian told how she struck up a conversation with a woman in the parking lot of a local community college. The woman turned out to be a candidate in a local school board race. "She had never heard about us. This was her first time running. She was a Republican with very definite ideas about what she wanted to do on the school board. We endorsed her, and she won out of a field of eight candidates. She is one of our bright shining stars in recent years! She was very thankful for our endorsement and funds."

Local talent was pooled at the annual Women of Achievement Awards Dinner, sponsored by the League of Friends (a support group for the Commission on the Status of Women) and the *San Jose Mercury News*. Any individual or organization could submit names of outstanding women in five areas: government, business/professions, arts, education, and volunteerism. The first awards dinner was held in 1978. In 1980, there were forty-two nominees; by 1983, there were close to one hundred. The dinner raised funds for the commission and provided the occasion for activist women to meet one another and local influentials as well.

In addition to recruiting and grooming women for public office in informal ways, local women's groups such as NWPC, NOW, and the Chicana Coalition had formal candidate endorsement procedures.[151] NWPC sent out questionnaires to all candidates, who were screened with respect to five bottom-line issues: right to abortion, public funding for abortion, child-care funding, the ERA, and opposition to sex and race discrimination. After this screening, candidates were interviewed by teams of three or four NWPC members, who asked questions designed for each office: city council, county supervisor, school board, and so on. Interviewers' recommendations were published in the newsletter before the chapter meeting. Endorsement meetings were the best attended of the year, especially when there were contested races. Sometimes men were endorsed over women; sometimes two competing candidates were both endorsed. And incumbents' records were scrutinized before re-election support was granted. In Santa Clara County, the NWPC endorsement was sought by both radical and mainstream candidates, who liked to include it in their advertisements. Archconservative candidates from the county's Bible Belt did not seek the NWPC support, however, and school board candidates were not as likely as others to seek it. Chapter president Susan Charles speculated that this may have been because school races were associated with the family, which many voters feared was threatened by the women's movement.

Like NWPC, NOW had bottom-line issues for endorsement: the ERA, reproductive rights, lesbian rights, and antiracism. In fact, some San Jose chapter members had fought unsuccessfully to get state and national NOW endorsement committees to adhere to all four criteria before backing any candidate. According to Joyce Sogg, "We felt that those were four basic issues and that no matter how good a politician was on three of them, if they were not at least consonant with us on the fourth, we should not endorse or give money to that person." Other NOW members of the San Jose chapter were more inclined to support Democratic candidates, even if they did not meet all four criteria. Given this division in the local chapter, Democratic candidates could not assume that they had NOW's endorsement in their pocket.

Local candidates also sought the endorsement of the Chicana Coalition. Candidates were invited to come before a political involvement committee, which made recommendations to the general membership.

Members were polled both to develop questions for candidates and to make the final endorsement vote. Unlike NWPC and NOW, the coalition had no bottom-line checklist; rather, questions were different for each office. The coalition endorsed in several ways: with the use of its name, with financial support, and with volunteers.

All three women's groups had their share of difficult cases. When two Latinas were running for the same San Jose City Council seat, the Chicana Coalition endorsed only one of them. The woman who was not supported (a former coalition officer) did not return to the group. In a race for county supervisor, NWPC endorsed a man who had been very active in NWPC over a woman who did not yet have a track record on women's issues but who subsequently won the election and proved to be generally supportive of NWPC positions. The next time both a male and a female were popular with the group, NWPC decided to endorse both but give money to neither. NOW's experience in the 1980 election served as a reminder that feminist support was not a necessary condition for a woman's victory: in the primaries, NOW endorsed only one of the nine women who made it to the fall ballot for city council or county supervisor.

Funds from these women's groups were helpful to local candidates, and so was the "people power" of women who went door-to-door for candidates. Local activist Pat Miller illustrated this power with the case of Congressmember Pete McCloskey's first race for Congress, in a 1967 special election. McCloskey ran as an environmentalist against former movie star Shirley Temple Black. On learning that Black was ahead, McCloskey got together a group of mostly women to do last-minute campaign work for him. He told Miller that the areas leafleted by women were the areas where he won, so he attributed his victory to women's efforts. Miller added that women were more effective precinct walkers than men because people were often afraid to open their doors to men.

Finally, women's groups had a reputation for loyalty. They did not always have the resources to monitor the votes of all the candidates they had endorsed, but they rallied to the aid of their best allies when they came under fire. A case in point was support for public officials who had voted for local gay rights ordinances. In 1979, both the Santa Clara County Board of Supervisors and the San Jose City Council had passed ordinances protecting the rights of gay and lesbian citizens. In the 1980 election, the Los Gatos Christian Church and Concerned Citizens (a fundamentalist religious group) spearheaded a voter repeal of these measures by a three-to-one margin and mounted a drive to recall Supervisor Rod Diridon, who supported gay rights and tough environmental restrictions in county building permits. Local women's groups came to the defense of Diridon against an evangelical-developer coalition. He had been a strong advocate of women's issues, holding annual meetings to assess the policy needs of women in the county. He held local women's groups in high esteem, saying, "The League of Women Voters is one of the most powerful groups around, and I owe my reelection to them and other women's groups." Pat Miller summed up the relation between women's groups and the county board of supervisors: "The board is kept on their toes by us. We walk the precincts for them and support them when they are attacked. Diridon may annoy me sometimes, but he is a solid feminist. He goes to women's meetings. Concerned Citizens attacked him for his stand on gay rights and feminism. He is the most visible proponent of these issues in the county."[152]

Part Three

Women and Elite Politics

5 Political Recruitment

Women's Distinctive Path to Public Office

POLITICAL RECRUITMENT is the process whereby citizens seek public office. Until the advent of the women's movement, the academy was indifferent to research questions about the political recruitment of women. Beginning in the 1970s, however, feminist scholars discovered that female candidates had distinctive recruitment patterns, which presented both obstacles and advantages.

Indifference of Political Science to Women's Political Recruitment

Before the 1970s, only two political scientists looked at women's political recruitment in a systematic way: Sophonisba P. Breckinridge and Martin Gruberg. Breckinridge, the first woman to receive a doctorate in political science from the University of Chicago, catalogued women who had been congressmembers, congressional candidates, federal appointees, state appointees, governors and other statewide elected officials, state legislators, and county and local officials. In an attempt to learn more about the qualifications and successes of female state legislators, she sent letters to 320 of them and received 124 replies. No special types or common qualifying experiences were found. Forty percent of the respondents were employed, most as schoolteachers and a few as lawyers, businesswomen, social workers, doctors, and nurses. Half had advocated women's suffrage; nineteen were indifferent or hostile to it. Sixty percent had been identified with women's organizations in their communities. Twenty percent had held prior public office, as "members of boards

149

of education or school committees, members of city councils, county superintendents of schools, members of library boards, justices of the peace, town clerks, treasurers, city prosecutors, state's attorneys, city or county treasurers" and the like. Thirty percent had been active in party work, but for half the women, their legislative service was their first political office and they had had little party experience. A few reported that party leaders had asked them to put their names on the ticket. Only three mentioned that they had run at the solicitation of women's organizations (the Women's Christian Temperance Union and the League of Women Voters). Some reported that they were motivated to run by specific issues: to get a law passed to protect against forest fires, to secure adequate funding for a detention hospital for women in the city jail, to obtain Sheppard-Towner funds for maternity and infancy programs, and to pass public welfare legislation to meet human needs. Through their membership on committees and authorship of legislation, all but 26 of the 124 women demonstrated concern for social welfare questions, especially child welfare, education, state institutions, public health, and problems affecting the legal and political status of women.[1]

Breckinridge observed that only a few female state legislators were prevented from continuing their legislative duties because of home responsibilities, and a negligible number failed to be renominated. Most of them retired for unknown reasons. The smallest number of all used the state legislature as a stepping-stone to other political office. Although most respondents viewed their legislative experiences positively, many noted that men were better at extending courtesies than equality. They wrote that soon after the franchise was attained, political parties began to pay less attention to women, in spite of the fact that women had done 50 percent of the party work. Women felt that they were not getting their fair share of nominations, that the men wanted women to help only on election day, and that the men did not support female candidates of their own party to the same extent they supported male candidates.[2]

When it came to women in local office, the only systematic data Breckinridge could find were surveys conducted in 1925, 1927, 1929, and 1930 by the League of Women Voters in Minnesota, Wisconsin, Connecticut, and Michigan. During the first decade of their enfranchisement, women steadily increased their numbers in local government. Many more were serving at the local than at the state level of government. Breckinridge observed that "the woman in politics goes ahead more rapidly at home than in larger political units. It is of interest that women superintendents of schools, and women city, town, and county treasurers appear most frequently. The schools have long been considered the special responsibility of women. Their concern with fiscal responsibilities is more surprising."[3]

In his 1968 book *Women in American Politics,* Martin Gruberg provided a biographical paragraph on each of the women who had served in Congress and background information about women in other posts as well: federal executives, ambassadors, judges, governors, statewide officials, and local government officials. Although this work was an important sourcebook, it did not attempt to find patterns in women's recruitment to public office.[4]

One of the most frequently cited works on political recruitment was Kenneth Prewitt's 1970 book *The Recruitment of Political Leaders: A Study of Citizen-Politicians,* which studied city council members in the San Francisco metropolitan region, including Santa Clara County. It was based on interviews conducted in 1966–67 with what Prewitt referred to throughout the book as four hundred councilmen in eighty-two cities. Five percent of his sample, however, were women. The only way one could discern this fact was from a table listing the demographic characteristics of his "councilmen," which noted that 95 percent of them were male.[5] Women were otherwise invisible in his discussion of "councilmen." He never discussed anything about women as a group, in spite of the fact that in his chapter on the social bias in leadership selection, he noted that sex was "the most consistently pervasive ascriptive criterion determining who becomes a political leader: Politics is a man's world."[6] The social bias Prewitt was interested in studying was socioeconomic, as measured by occupation, education, and income. The most "consistently pervasive" form of bias in political recruitment was not yet an interesting research question.

Things began to change in the 1970s as a result of the women's movement, the increasing number of women in public office, and feminist scholarship in political science. Beginning in the 1970s, women sought and attained public office in record numbers, particularly at the state and local levels. Between 1975 and 1989, the proportion of female members of Congress remained stable at around 5 percent. By contrast, during this time the number of women in state legislatures doubled (from 8 to 17 percent), on county boards tripled (from 3 to 9 percent), and in local office tripled (from 4 to 14 percent). In 1978, only 6 percent of cities had female mayors; by 1989, that number had doubled to 12 percent.[7]

Feminist scholars picked up where Breckinridge had left off, and the systematic collection of data about women in public office began in earnest. The most comprehensive collection of such data was undertaken by the Center for the American Woman and Politics (CAWP), which was established in 1971 as part of the Eagleton Institute of Politics at Rutgers University. In 1972, CAWP sponsored the first national conference of female state legislators, to which fifty female state senators and representatives from twenty-six states were invited. CAWP commissioned Jeane J. Kirkpatrick to study the backgrounds and views of the women at the conference; the findings from her interviews were published in her 1974 book *Political Woman*.[8] Beginning 1975, CAWP collected data on elected women serving in municipal, county, state legislative, statewide, and federal offices. Information from this computerized data bank was used to publish directories and fact sheets on women in elective and appointive office. Fact sheets listed the number and percentage of female officials serving at each level, state-by-state rankings, and party identification and included historical information about women in public office. CAWP's newsletter, *News & Notes about Women Public Officials,* contained timely analyses about recent elections, gender gaps in voting, women's PACs, and the like.

Analysts came up with patterns similar to those observed by Breckinridge in the 1930s, the most obvious of which was the higher the level of political office, the fewer the women. That was a puzzle to those who viewed the United States from an international perspective. Compared to other nations, the United States was in the vanguard of female political emancipation at the mass level but lacking in the presence of women at the national level of government.[9] Some looked at this puzzle historically, to see if the proportions of women in public office had changed as a result of systemic forces, such as wars, the economy, or the political party in power in Washington.

Although the Great Depression had a negative impact on women's political recruitment, the effect of other factors differed by level of government. At the federal level, the proportion of women in the U.S. House of Representatives increased in the 1920s, fell during the depression, rose in the 1950s, declined in the 1960s, and rose again in the 1970s. The proportion of female federal appointees fluctuated by party, with Democratic presidents appointing more women, and by type of executive department, with women very likely to be appointed to social welfare posts and virtually absent in the Departments of Justice, Commerce, and Agriculture. The presence of mentors, such as Eleanor Roosevelt, and affirmative action programs, introduced under President Johnson, had a positive effect on women's federal appointments.[10]

In state legislatures, the number of women increased with suffrage, decreased with the Great Depression, rose during World War II, declined in the postwar period, grew again in the 1950s, fell in the 1960s (owing to legislative redistricting, contraction in the sizes of lower houses, and better salaries and benefits), and boomed in the 1970s with the women's movement. Appointments to state executive posts mirrored those at the federal level. Before suffrage, women were appointed to social welfare agencies (e.g., factory inspection, charities, corrections), and the trend continued after suffrage (especially in positions involving health care, children, and the elderly). Some states had "female slots," such as superintendent of public instruction, secretary of state, treasurer, or auditor. By 1970, women began to be appointed to more diverse posts. Women were rarely governors: the first three were selected to fill their husbands' shoes (Nellie Taloe Ross of Wyoming in 1925, Miriam "Ma" Ferguson of Texas in 1925, and Lurleen Wallace of Alabama in 1967). It was not until the 1970s that women were serious gubernatorial candidates in their own right, with the election of Ella Grasso of Connecticut in 1974 and Dixy Lee Ray of Washington in 1976.[11]

Carol Nechemias compared the numbers of women in state legislatures at three points in time—1963–64, 1971–71, and 1983–84—to test five variables thought to be related to the presence of women in state legislatures.[12] Prior research had suggested that a historical legacy of women in an office paved the way for more women.[13] This variable proved to have decreasing predictive power over time. A second factor was Democratic party dominance in the state, which was a barrier for women, even controlling for the traditional political culture of the South.[14] Democratic party dominance was less and less of a barrier for women over time. A third variable was the prestige of the office, as measured by salary and turnover in office. Women were most successful in states where the office of state legislator was viewed as less desirable by men and was poorly paid and less professional.[15] There was a weakening in the positive relationship between the presence of women and low salary but a growing positive relationship between the presence of women and high turnover. A fourth factor was the level of socioeconomic development in the state: a highly educated and materially well off district was thought to benefit women's election chances.[16] Indeed, women were more likely to be found representing such areas. The last variable was political culture. In keeping with findings that women were benefited by a moralistic political culture and disadvantaged by a traditional one,[17] a traditional political culture was a big obstacle for women into the 1980s.

In addition to looking for historical changes in women's recruitment patterns, analysts studied obstacles to women's recruitment, the most obvious of which was self-concept and social bias.

Self-concept, Social Bias, and Women's Political Recruitment

For centuries, women were socialized to believe that politics was a man's world, in which women's participation was unnatural and degrading to the "fairer sex." Jean Bethke Elshtain termed the philosophical underpinnings of this view the "Aristotelian–power politics paradigm," which bifurcated the public, political realm of immoral man from the private, apolitical realm of moral woman. In Aristotle's view, politics was the pursuit of the morally good life. Public persons (male property owners) were responsible, rational, and capable of achieving the highest good— participation in political life. Private persons (women and slaves) were not fully rational, were confined to lesser spheres of activity necessary to the operation of public life, and were capable of achieving goodness only in their inferior spheres and associations. Jean Bodin and Machiavelli divorced politics from moral considerations, equated it with force, and set up two standards of morality: public and private. The state was the ultimate political authority, and the good citizen was one who obeyed its laws. Women were not part of politics; rather, they provided a refuge from it in the home. Men's public power was judged by two standards: a "bad" man could be a "good" politician. According to Elshtain, the Aristotelian–power politics paradigm cut off the private sphere from the definition of the political, blamed the victim for settling for less than full participation, and trivialized moral concerns. She criticized the suffragists who accepted this bifurcation in their arguments about using women's moral superiority to reform corrupt politics. It was not until the feminism of the 1960s and 1970s that this public-private, immoral-moral dichotomous thinking was systematically undermined.[18]

Nevertheless, the effects of this paradigm on people's thinking did not disappear overnight. Although female suffrage had made a dent with its expanded definition of female citizenship, even voting was perceived by many as upsetting the "natural" division of politics and morality. In 1878, a Missouri senator warned that female suffrage "will unsex our mothers, wives and sisters, who are to-day influencing by their gentle caress the action of their husbands toward the good and pure. It will turn our blessed country's domestic peace into ward assemblyrooms."[19] Those who defended female suffrage often did so on grounds of enhancing women's role as moral educator in the home, especially insofar as women raised their sons to be good citizens. One scholar defended the expanded political role of mothers as voters in 1914 by saying, "The ballot will give her prestige equal to that of the father in her boy's mind; and so it will actually lighten her task as chief family teacher."[20]

The Aristotelian–power politics paradigm created a dilemma for women in the early twentieth century: counterpoised against the notion of civic duty was the idea of upsetting the natural order of things and being unfeminine. This dilemma partially explained why only about one-quarter of eligible women voted in the 1920 presidential election. Voting meant doing something masculine in a male space, literally as well as figuratively: one result of women's suffrage was that saloons and barbershops were replaced by schools and firehouses as places for balloting.[21] Cultural sanctions against the venturing of women outside their appropriate sphere were especially strong when it came to women in public office. Gallup poll data from the 1930s and 1940s indicated that the higher the public office, the less Americans thought a woman should be there. Only 30 to 40 percent said they would vote for a woman for president; 60 percent said we did not need more women in politics; and a majority said President Franklin Roosevelt should not appoint any more women to his cabinet and that they did not want a woman on the Supreme Court. There was less public resistance to having women hold the posts of governor, Red Cross chapter head, and PTA president.[22]

Elected women were a direct threat to the view that a woman's place was in the home, as illustrated in the case of Representative Coya Knutson. During the 1958 congressional elections, her husband made a national appeal to his wife to "come home" and give up her seat in the House. She was the only Democrat to lose her seat to a Republican in an election in which Democrats made a net gain of forty-seven House seats.[23] In the same vein, when a group of Wisconsin voters were asked whether being a female would make a difference in their support for a candidate for judge or school board, 65 percent said it would not. But if the candidate had young children, only 45 percent said being a female would not make a difference in their vote. Thus, having children counted against women running for school boards, even though members of school boards were disproportionately those with small children. Mothers of young children seeking judicial positions encountered even more opposition than those seeking school board posts.[24]

The contemporary women's movement began to erode the separate-spheres paradigm. The proportion of the American public willing to vote for a woman for president held constant from 1958 to 1969 (from 55 to 58 percent) but rose dramatically to 70 percent in 1972. This increase was more pronounced among women than among men, who before 1969 had been more supportive than women were of a female president. The sudden surge in women's support was due to the women's movement and to the recognition that women were a disadvantaged

group. The abruptness of the change ruled out a demographic explanation. Women's views fit the model of education leading to tolerance, but
men's views did not, as high-school-educated men were more supportive
of a woman for president than college-educated men were.[25]

A 1971 study illustrated how the women's movement was beginning
to erode the bias against women in public office. A comparison of Pennsylvania party committeewomen and registered female voters found
that there was little difference between the two groups in their levels of
support for women in politics, with much more support voiced for
women as councilmembers (90 percent) than as president (44 percent). Although 20 percent of the respondents did not support women
in politics, 60 percent said men and women were equally capable in office. And 20 percent were "female boosters," who saw women as more
qualified and capable than men in public office or who wanted to compensate for past discrimination by electing women. Consciousness
about women's outgroup status in society correlated more strongly with
support for women in public office than did any of the standard variables: religion, age, income, marital status, participation level, or party
identification.[26]

Analysis of survey research data from the 1970s revealed modest increases in support for female political activity. One study looked at three
questions from national surveys in 1972, 1974, and 1978: whether the respondent would vote for a woman for president, believed that women
should run their homes and leave the running of the country to men,
and felt that men were better suited emotionally for politics than women
were. Core supporters of greater female political activity were the young,
better-educated, and less frequent church attenders.[27] And a look at similar questions in the early 1980s found that economically independent
women were much more likely than women economically dependent on
men to think that women should have equal roles with men in running
the government.[28]

Social bias against women in public office had a dual effect on the
political recruitment of women: they faced external barriers from voters and political parties, and they faced the internalized norm that
politics was not for women. To the extent that women had internalized this norm, they did not think of themselves as potential candidates, so the number of women in public office remained small. Overcoming this internalized norm was often discussed in terms of
women's political ambition: an ambitious woman had the motivation
to confront internal and external obstacles to her pursuit of public office. Scholarship on women and political ambition took two tracks: ac-

commodationist research accepted the male model of political ambition and encouraged women to be as ambitious as men; transformational research took women's experiences as its point of departure and explained how ambition meant different things for men and women.

Women's Political Ambition

The model of political ambition most frequently used by political scientists was that of Joseph A. Schlesinger.[29] He defined politically ambitious people as those who tailored their political behavior in accordance with their goals for public office, who had a broad rather than a narrow policy perspective, who had policy perspectives associated with the higher posts to which they aspired ("anticipatory socialization"), and who were sensitive to the constituency of the aspired-to office. The desire of the politically ambitious for reelection became the electorate's restraint on its public officials. Using this model, studies found that the political ambitions of men varied by level of public office: the higher the level, the more the ambition.[30] An even more consistent finding was that women had less political ambition than men. In the last chapter, we saw that this was the case even among convention delegates, where one would most expect to find a pool of women with aspirations for public office. A study of U.S. congressmembers from 1789 to 1989 found that congresswomen were more likely than congressmen not to seek reelection.[31]

Scholars who adopted the conventional model of political ambition attempted to find out what factors were correlated with an increase in women's political ambition and argued that the time was right for women to become as ambitious as men. A 1977 study of Atlanta party activists discovered that the political ambition of white women was linked to nontraditional sex-role beliefs, whereas the ambition of black women was linked to current activities and parental interest in politics.[32] A 1975 survey of 774 municipalities found virtually no independent effect of any ecological variable on the presence of women on city councils: city size, southern location, the education and income levels of the constituency, nonpartisanship, or at-large elections. The chief obstacle to women's presence on city councils was a shortfall of female candidates: 70 percent of the variance between cities with and without female councilmembers was explained by the presence or absence of female candidates. The authors did not blame women for failing to run; rather, they faulted social bias and cultural expectations. But the upshot of their findings was that increased political ambition on the part of women would result in the election of more women to city councils.[33]

The same argument was made to get more women elected to the U.S. House of Representatives. During the 1960s and 1970s, there was no change in the number of women in the House, despite a tripling in the number of women nominated for House seats by the two major political parties. When incumbency and party strength were controlled, women won as often as men in the general elections for House seats between 1974 and 1984. Where women had difficulty was in winning primaries for open-seat nominations. Because of weaker party control over nominations and increased media emphasis during campaigns, primaries enabled ambitious young men to compete more successfully than women. Perhaps because of traditional career and family patterns, women tended to delay their entry into politics, thus dimming their drive for personal advancement. By contrast, young men seeking personal advancement or status through political office put more effort into campaigning, generated more media coverage, and met with greater electoral success in the primaries. Women would not increase their numbers in the House until they showed the same drive for personal advancement.[34]

Transformational feminist scholars critiqued the model of political ambition that had been constructed on male experiences, and they provided an alternative model based on women's experiences. Women had been socialized to serve others rather than to advance their own goals. They had a tradition of seeing politics as nonpartisan public service instead of partisan career advancement. Thus, the decision calculus women used to run for public office was different from that of men.

The literature on political ambition adopted a utilitarian perspective of rational men who weighed the material and psychological costs and benefits of running for public office, involving matters such as career, social prestige, civic duty, and service to party or interest group. Women had additional costs to add to their calculus: overcoming the feminine gender-role, battling perceived opposition, and enduring expected punishment for gender-role violations. Ambitious women had to undergo a gender countersocialization that men did not experience. This countersocialization was likely to take place in a childhood with politically involved parents who encouraged their daughter's nonconventional behavior, or in adulthood as a consequence of childrearing, a supportive spouse, employment in a brokerage occupation, or the emergence of a salient issue that gave a woman a stake in politics, such as the ERA.[35]

From the point of view of women's experiences and decision calculus, gender differences in ambition and aspirations might have been less a function of socialization to a passive sex role and more a result of a rational assessment by women about how their energies could best be used to achieve political goals. The political system did not appear as receptive to women as it was to men. Women experienced role strain from conflicting demands on them as politicians and as wives and mothers and from treatment by their male peers in public office.[36] Running for office did not raise the specter of compromising men's masculinity, but it did raise a "presentation" problem for women: how "masculine" or "feminine" they wanted to present themselves to the voters. Female congressional candidates in 1984 adjusted their gender characteristics when running for office, mostly in a masculine direction but sometimes in such feminine directions as loyalty and compassion. Unexpectedly, candidates did not make gender-role adjustments as a function of political culture or campaign experience. In competitive electoral positions, such as challenging an incumbent or competing for an open seat, women did not suppress feminine characteristics in individualistic states or emphasize them in traditional states, and more campaign experience did not elicit a greater response to political culture.[37] The male model of political ambition was also taken to task for its individualistic, Horatio Alger assumptions, which ignored the extensive system of political, professional, and social connections that accompanied political success.[38]

Feminist scholars sought to lay to rest popular stereotypes about widows succeeding their husbands in Congress. According to conventional wisdom, a bereaved widow was prevailed on by a political party official to accept a courtesy appointment in order to avoid party squabbling and to exploit voter sympathy until a real male candidate could be groomed; the widow reluctantly accepted a benchwarmer role and left Congress as soon as possible. A look at the historical record, however, revealed that widow succession was neither frequent (only 3 percent of widows in the Senate and 9 percent of widows in the House succeeded their incumbent husbands) nor easy (the Constitution mandated elections for House vacancies). Most widows in the House faced electoral opposition for seats that were increasingly contested over time. Some widows who sought their husbands' seats were denied the nomination by the party. The idea that a widow could actively seek congressional office so challenged the stereotype of passivity and diffidence that researchers ignored the evidence and assumed the stereotype. Although it was hard to measure the ambition of these widows, it appeared to increase over time. Only 27 percent of the pre-1950 elected widows sought reelection, but 69 percent of the post-1950 widows did.[39]

Whether one adopted a conventional or a nonconventional model of political ambition, it was clear that social bias about women's proper place had an effect on the political recruitment of women, adding more points to the negative side of women's decision calculus.

Self-concepts and Social Norms for Female Officials in Santa Clara County

During the time of the Santa Clara County case study, the popular lexicon of politics was gendered: candidates were supposed to be hard, not soft; they were supposed to play hardball and not be a wimp. Female candidates had to prove that they were "hard" and tough, whereas male candidates were assumed to be so until proved a wimp. Obviously, some women had no problem proving that they could be as "hard" as men. For example, in the 1990 gubernatorial races in California and Texas, where popular support for the death penalty was strong, Democratic candidates Dianne Feinstein and Ann Richards made their support for public executions centerpieces of their campaign strategies. But for other women, deciding how "hard" they want to be required some soul-searching. Two examples from Santa Clara County illustrated how some women did not necessarily accept male definitions of hardball politics.

For many of her ten years on the San Jose City Council (1980–90), Lu Ryden was the only conservative Republican voice. On the eve of her election to office in what was to constitute a female majority on the council, she said that her victory was based on her image as an individual—"as a family person, a conservative and a Christian, not necessarily that I am a woman"—and that she opposed the Equal Rights Amendment as "more federal government intervention" that was not necessary to provide equal opportunity for women.[40] For Ryden, the dilemma was to steer a course between the rock of "strident feminists" and the hard place of "male competition," neither of which was acceptable to her self-concept as a woman: "Women are softer, more compassionate, yet still firm. We can be firm without going overboard by being strident and hard. Soft does not mean weak; it means we can make things more palatable. Men always feel they have to compete with each other. Some women are just as masculine and competitive. Men relate to men on a different level. I don't compete like them."[41] Ryden not only rejected feminist and masculinist stances of being "hard" but also rescued from this fray a sense of being "soft" that was worth preserving as women entered public office: being firm, making things palatable, avoiding competition. She was not a feminist; indeed, she defined feminist as being feminine and believed that women should work only after their obligations in the home were over. Yet neither was she prepared to accept masculinist politics as usual. She was articulating a female style of politics and reaching some feminist conclusions from nonfeminist premises. Her dilemma exemplified how what was taken for granted by male candidates was problematic for female candidates.

The second example was Santa Clara County executive Sally Reed. Although her post was appointive, not elective, she nonetheless demonstrated an interesting alternative to male hardball politics. According to many observers, Reed held the most powerful political position in the county, which she obtained in part because of support from the female majority on the board of supervisors that appointed her.[42] The power of the county executive was based largely on information about how all the parts of the county's billion-dollar budget fit together. As county government became more complex, the five elected board members tended to specialize and to understand the budget in bits and pieces. By contrast, the county executive saw the big picture, frequently leaving supervisors at the mercy of her analysis of the numbers. This budget power was especially significant in the era of fiscal austerity of the 1980s, when the county budget was being squeezed from all sides. County executive Reed oversaw millions of dollars of cutbacks and hundreds of layoffs of county employees, doing the board's dirty work of making cuts. Yet she managed to do so in a way that even most of her toughest critics said was honest and evenhanded. People tended to have short-term disagreements with Reed but retained respect for her over the long term. What "hard" politics meant for Reed was not masculinist war, with winners gloating over losers, but rather an agreement in a difficult situation where both sides felt they got a fair deal.

In addition to resolving how "hard" or "soft" they wanted to be and deciding whose definitions of these terms they wanted to use, female candidates had to make the quantum leap from supporter to decision maker. Women were socialized to be *supportive of* "real" decision makers, whereas men were socialized to *be* the "real" decision makers, as illustrated in the genders of these pairs: nurse/doctor, secretary/boss, homemaker/breadwinner, and teacher/principal. The case of Councilmember Blanca Alvarado illustrated the difference between support and starring roles. Alvarado described her "political environment" in the Mexican American Political Association (MAPA), a group she worked with for eight years, including serving as northern California coordinator for Jimmy Carter's presidential campaign: "I was a state officer for MAPA, where I was happy and felt I both contributed and gained. But I did resent the fact that I was the secretary, and I have advised other women not to run for that. They should set their sights on something else. . . . Women have been the persons behind the scenes. They do the day-to-day work to make the man successful." And Councilmember Shirley Lewis described the transition from supporter to decision maker in these terms: "At one point I loved being the person behind the person, until I decided that I wanted to decide."

National studies found that two other dimensions of women's self-concept played a role in political recruitment: lack of self-confidence and fear of sex discrimination.[43] In Santa Clara County, where the political climate was perceived to be progressive and open-minded, fear of sex discrimination did not seem to be an obstacle to women's pursuit of public office. Lack of self-confidence appeared to play a part in women's hesitation to seek elective office, however. For example, Councilmember Pat Sausedo mentioned the "trauma" of public interviews: "I was president of the homeowners' association when the planning commission seat opened up, and I went through the trauma of public interviews and got the appointment."

An intriguing pattern that emerged in Santa Clara County was that many women's "Aha! I'm just as qualified as these elected officials" stemmed from the value they placed on their homemaking, parenting, and volunteer skills. In their minds, these were bona fide political skills. It was ironic that the women's movement had been faulted for supposedly denigrating homemaker and volunteer women, when in fact feminists' recognition of the value of women's nonpaid work empowered such women to affirm that the value of what they did was not solely determined by the marketplace. Monetary calculations of the value of women's nonpaid work were conducted by judges who compensated homemakers in divorce cases, by economists who figured the value of housework into the gross national product, and by divorced men who realized the market value of their former wives' services. In a capitalist economy with a high divorce rate, it was not surprising to find that such calculations gave new value to women's nonpaid work. In addition to this quantitative sense of value, however, the women's movement placed a qualitative value on women's nonpaid work.

The political value of homemaking skills was described in various ways. Councilmember Pat Sausedo related women's homemaking responsibilities to an enhanced understanding of the daily lives of one's constituency. Councilmember Lu Ryden saw homemaking as a springboard to neighborhood politics. In response to a local influential who referred to female officials as "housewives who got the political bug,"[44] Ryden said, "I don't agree with that characterization, which makes it sound like women went straight from the apron in front of the stove into politics. These women were first activists in their neighborhoods who got frustrated and said, 'Somebody has to do something and I will.' Being a concerned housewife enabled them to get into neighborhood groups in the first place."

Parenting was seen by some councilmembers as providing bona fide management and problem-solving skills useful in politics. Councilmember Shirley Lewis, a former adult education teacher, applied for a job as a neighborhood center superintendent in 1972 and was told that a woman with six children couldn't handle a job and family too. "Was I mad! I was one of two finalists and at the interview they raised my having six kids. I figured that if I managed six children then I had certain management skills. Plus I was already working full time!" Councilmember Iola Williams had seven children. In her case, her husband did most of the cooking and housework. But she said raising seven children gave her a keen sense of distinguishing political manipulation from legitimate demands: "I know when political maneuvering is going on. Any mother of seven will recognize that."[45]

One official spoke (not for attribution) of how a few years earlier Mayor Janet Gray Hayes was quoted in the *San Jose Mercury News* as saying that of course she could handle the job as mayor because she had experience with nine-year-olds at birthday parties. "She got criticized for that. People said she was implying that voters were like children. But I knew exactly what she meant. I understood that grown men are not that different. Women are good at solving constituent problems because they are good problem solvers at home." Hayes added that men did not understand what she meant by the statement and that she was very much taken to task for it.

> What I meant was that there are certain management skills in having a successful party for twenty-four nine-year-olds and juggling twelve balls at the same time successfully. I used to call myself a "domestic engineer" rather than a housewife because I got so tired of hearing "I'm just a housewife." And then I thought about that and I think that the managerial skills that are required to be a successful housewife and mother are enormous. I didn't want to see that role denigrated because I think it's such an important role and society does not pay enough attention to how valuable housewives and mothers are.

Finally, women spoke of the value of volunteering. Councilmember Nancy Ianni responded to the "housewives bitten by the political bug" charge by saying: "It's not that I'm bitten, it's that I have conviction for the projects I spent forty hours a week volunteering for. People tend to underrate volunteers, but we are professionals. I am proud of my associations. They have tremendous women. People who think we are so naive should see how we raise money. That takes organizational, political and managerial skills."

Family Obligations and the Political Recruitment of Women

A second obstacle faced by women on the male-defined office-seeking track was family obligations, which either discouraged women from seeking public office altogether or caused them to delay it until their children were grown. Although it was not uncommon for a man to run for public office in his thirties, most women waited until their forties. A 1981 study found that majorities of women at every level of office had no children or grown children but that this was not the case for men at all levels of government. Though the median ages of men and women in elective office were very similar, women were more often than men concentrated between the ages of forty and fifty-nine.[46]

Feminist scholars investigated how the presence of young children deterred women from seeking public office. One factor was the unpredictability of hours. A 1972 survey of three hundred politically active women and men in suburban New York found that even though women devoted more time to local politics than men did, they were less likely than men to seek public office for three reasons: the presence of young children in the home, views of women's proper place, and fear of sex discrimination. Having children at home was not a hindrance for men. And having young children did not limit the time women devoted to party activities in general, because meetings could be planned ahead and a babysitter secured. By contrast, running for office involved unpredictable hours.[47]

Another problem was press scrutiny. A 1973 comparison of female and male state legislators revealed that the women were older, had older children, were less likely to be married, and placed less emphasis on their families in their campaign literature, partly in order to avoid guilt-producing questions. When women campaigned for office, members of the press typically queried them on juggling family and official responsibilities but rarely put the same sorts of questions to men. Certainly in the 1970s and even into the 1980s, it was commonly assumed that women's family obligations were greater than those of men.[48]

And another factor was the difficulty of obtaining child care. Take the case of Pat Schroeder. In 1972, a few weeks after she was elected,

Congressmember Bella Abzug phoned to congratulate Schroeder on becoming the fourteenth woman to serve in the U.S. House of Representatives. "But no sooner had she welcomed me than she asked how in the world I thought I could manage being a congresswoman and a mother with a two-year-old and a six-year-old. I told her I really wasn't sure and hoped she would give the answer, not ask the question!" Schroeder was sworn into office with diapers in her purse and told reporters that her greatest fear as a freshman in Congress was losing her housekeeper: "I figured I could cope with almost anything, but that my life would go into free fall if she left. It was an answer that reporters did not often get. . . . I found learning the ropes in Congress a snap compared with arranging child care for two young children."[49]

As feminist researchers looked into the question of family responsibilities, they came to two important realizations: that men's careers were also affected by family responsibilities, a fact that previous researchers had paid little attention to, and that women and men handled family responsibilities differently. One study of state legislators found that family problems were the major factor leading to retirement from office for men as well as for women, although conventional wisdom had attributed legislative turnover primarily to low salaries.[50] Prior research had not even looked at men's private life costs and benefits of running for public office because it had been assumed that men had no such conflict. In the 1972 ANES convention delegate survey, in response to the question "To what extent do political activities conflict with your family life?" men expressed more conflict than women did, with the conflict increasing the greater the commitment to officeholding. Both sexes expressed a high degree of conflict when they had children under the age of five and little conflict when their children were over the age of eighteen. Women appeared to avoid this conflict by delaying the pursuit of public office, whereas men created conflict for themselves by pursuing public office when they had young children at home. Women accommodated both roles by sacrificing leisure time; men coped by withdrawing from the family.[51]

In a similar vein, a 1981 comparison of the family responsibilities of male and female federal appointees and state legislators found that men's political choices were more influenced by private concerns than had been commonly believed but that family matters were of greater significance to women than men. Among state legislators, women were more likely to state that childrearing had influenced the timing of their bid for public office. In all posts, women were less likely to be married and more likely to say their spouses were very supportive of their political careers. Among appointees, women were less likely to have young children, with half of them having no children at all.[52]

Family Responsibilities and Political Careers in Santa Clara County

The relationship between family responsibilities and the political careers of female officials in Santa Clara County mirrored those found in national surveys. Twelve of the fifteen women who served on the San Jose City Council and the Santa Clara County Board of Supervisors between 1970 and 1990 were in their forties when they were first elected to office. Councilmember Zoe Lofgren, elected in 1980 at age thirty-two, was the only one who gave birth to her children after her election, a daughter in 1982 and a son in 1985. Lofgren was an attorney whose recruitment path most closely resembled the male model of all the women in this study. A graduate of Stanford University and Santa Clara University Law School, she had been active in Democratic party politics, had worked for ten years as an aide to Representative Don Edwards (D-San Jose), and had been elected trustee of the San Jose Community College Board before her election to the board of supervisors. But there were differences from the male model when it came to her two children: she brought her newborn daughter to work and decided not to run for mayor in 1990 so she could spend more time with her five-year-old son.

In addition to influencing the timing of women's pursuit of public office, family obligations affected the level of office women pursued. There were, of course, several reasons why the numbers of women in public office were so much greater the lower the level of government. But one reason that loomed large for many women was a desire to stay near home, as opposed to the state capital or Washington, D.C. As San Jose councilmember Shirley Lewis put it: "People have talked about grooming me for statewide elections. But I like San Jose and would like to see a whole lot more happen here. I don't want to move to Sacramento or Washington, D.C. At this point I see no need to go on. I am a native, addicted to San Jose and family and I like that accessibility." Lewis had nine children, and family size may have been a contributing factor in her decision to stay local. Iola Williams was on the council from 1978 to 1990, when she decided not to seek reelection in order to spend more time with her seven children and many grandchildren. And Blanca Alvarado, elected to the council in 1980 and reelected through 1990, had a large family. A 1968 divorce left her with five young children, no high school education, and dependent on welfare to survive each month. It was not until 1987 that her salary as vice-mayor enabled her to make ends meet without a struggle. In 1989, she shared a home with her youngest daughter and said she was content to stay on the San Jose City Council: "I don't want to retire. There's too much work to do. I want to stay right here; I still have goals to accomplish. And I like where I am."[53] By contrast, family size did not seem to prevent men on the board of supervisors from moving to Sacramento. Dominic Cortese had five children when he was elected to the California Assembly in 1980, and Dan McCorquodale had three children when he went off to the California Senate in 1982.

A final dimension of family obligation that was more important to women's than to men's political recruitment was spousal support. In her 1968 description of three congresswomen, Martha Griffiths, Patsy Mink, and Margaret Heckler, Peggy Lamson noted that they had more in common than their law degrees: "Each of their husbands has been the moving factor in shaping the course of their public service. Hicks Griffiths, John Mink, and John Heckler have all served as their wives' campaign managers; they remain actively involved as advisers, strategists, and sounding boards."[54] A 1981 national survey found that, though large majorities of both men and women said spousal support was important in their decision to run for their current office, more women than men had spouses who were very supportive of their officeholding.[55]

With the exception of Blanca Alvarado, the fifteen women who served on the San Jose City Council and Santa Clara County Board of Supervisors between 1970 and 1990 were married to husbands who supported their officeholding. When Janet Gray Hayes was elected as the first woman mayor of San Jose, she thanked "all of those who helped her win, singling out her husband, Dr. Kenneth Hayes, and the neighbors who did her marketing and cooking during the hectic windup of the campaign."[56] She described her husband's support as returning the favor for her putting him through medical school at the University of Chicago.[57] Councilmember Shirley Lewis said her husband was the one who most influenced her to run for office. When the Republican party was trying to recruit Lu Ryden to run in 1980, she talked it over with her husband, who said it was fine with him if it made her happy. And Councilmember Iola Williams referred to her husband as "a doll" who kept the household running, doing the cooking and cleaning, so she could pursue political office.[58]

Occupational Background and Political Recruitment

A third obstacle to women's political recruitment was occupational background. Not surprisingly, women were more likely than men to have worked in female-dominated occupations and were less likely to have had law and business backgrounds. And, of course, women were much more likely than men to have been homemakers and, in Congress, to have succeeded a deceased spouse.

Before World War II, widow succession was the most common route women took to Congress.[59] As of 1970, 41 percent of women who had been in Congress came to fill vacancies created by the deaths of their husbands. These widows had different backgrounds from "regularly elected" congresswomen. Regularly elected congresswomen were more similar to congressmen with respect to education, occupation, and political activities. Indeed, they had more officeholding and party work than their first-term male counterparts. Thirty-seven percent of regularly elected congresswomen were educators, and 20 percent were attorneys; half the widows were homemakers, and none was an attorney. Compared to congresswomen, congressmen were five times more likely to be attorneys and three times more likely to be in business occupations. Party activity and election success were more important in the recruitment of women, with men more able to move laterally to Congress after achieving success in nonpolitical careers.[60]

A study of women who served in the House of Representatives through 1975 found a convergence in the career backgrounds of female and male members. Over time, fewer men and more women were attorneys, and occupational backgrounds were roughly the same for both sexes. An important exception was homemaking, the background of 42 percent of women in the House during the depression, falling to 16 percent during the period 1968–75. Since the 1950s, public service backgrounds were increasingly found among men and decreasingly found among women, who were less likely to be community volunteers and more likely to be a politician's staff member. Gender trends in prior state legislative experience converged in the 1940s and 1950s and then declined for women in the 1960s, as extensive party activity replaced state legislative experience. By 1975, half the men and one-third the women had been elected to state office before entering the House. Women increasingly came from "enterprising" professional backgrounds, such as law, public service, and business.[61]

Historically, lack of law and business backgrounds had hindered women's appointments to the president's "inner cabinet" (State, Treasury, Justice, and Defense). With more women entering these professions, increasing numbers were appointed to a widening range of departmental posts. Interest groups provided women with a career route different from men's legal and business route, but such groups limited the range of departments to which women were appointed to "outer cabinet" or client departments such as Health, Education and Welfare.[62]

The importance of male credentials was cast by Susan J. Carroll in terms of a social psychological theory of social control: that elites admitted members of new social groups who minimized social conflict. She found that women who played by the existing rules, with credentials and experiences similar to the norm, were appointed to state cabinet posts. Most women and men said that a combination of credentials and experience was the most important factor leading to their appointment. When it came to credentials, except among top gubernatorial staff, women were better educated than men, with younger women being much more educated and much more likely to have law careers than older women. Younger women were also held to higher qualifications than the group as a whole. Women were less likely to have held prior local or state office but as likely to have held federal office, and younger women had held more prior government posts than older women. And women were more likely than men to have been from the same party as the governor; party activism played a greater role in older women's appointments, as did their campaign activity for the governor, as compared to younger women.[63]

According to a 1981 CAWP survey of state and local elected officials, although most officials of both sexes had white-collar occupations, women were more likely to have professional and technical occupations but were less likely to have managerial and administrative jobs. About one-fourth of female county and local officials, compared with almost no men, listed their occupation as clerical or secretarial. Lawyers showed up in great numbers only among state legislators: about one in seven men, but only about one in twenty women. At every level of government, women were much more likely than men to be elementary or secondary schoolteachers (13 to 20 percent of female officials, compared to 1 to 9 percent of male officials).[64]

At the local level, women's civic volunteerism was the functional equivalent of men's business connections, and party activity was less important in these typically nonpartisan settings, as compared to the more partisan state and national political arenas. A 1973 study of nonpartisan races in Cook County, Illinois, by Sharyne Merritt found that candidates got their politically relevant skills from different sources. Female electoral success was related to women's nonelective political involvement as civic volunteers; male electoral success was related to men's social and occupational ties with local politicians. Merritt observed, "Through volunteer activities women become knowledgeable about issues and acquainted with problem-solving strategies; they sharpen their verbal and interpersonal skills; and they become known in the community, making connections with influentials and 'proving themselves' as competent and serious both to their potential constituents and to themselves."[65] Professional women were less likely to succeed in local races than were nonprofessional women, perhaps because professional women were perceived as more threatening than were churchgoing homemakers. Appointive office was especially helpful for women, substituting for men's social contacts with local politicians. A related study of city councilmembers in Cook County found that, compared to councilmen, councilwomen had lower educational levels and occupational status but were very active in the League of Women Voters and the PTA.[66]

Women's civic volunteerism loomed large in a study of sex differences in the political recruitment and electoral success of municipal candidates in nine states in 1980. Female candidates had lower incomes but the same educational attainment. One-third of the women were homemakers, and many were teachers. Education enhanced women's electability but not men's, and younger women did better at the polls than younger men did. The two parties were equally successful in getting women elected to municipal office. Neither sex benefited by running for causes; a feminine "civic responsibility" role helped women get elected more than a "cause" role did. Participation in civic organizations was significantly more important for women. Overall, men had higher income and occupational status; women, more civic group connections and less ambition. Men's connections were through business, and women's were through civic activity. Women's volunteerism lessened the "threat" of their candidacies. And women in male occupations did not have much success in municipal races.[67]

It is important to remember that generalizations about women's recruitment at the local level had to take into account whether local races were partisan or nonpartisan. Civic volunteerism was often used as a compensatory political resource in lieu of a male profession in the two-thirds of municipal elections in the United States that were nonpartisan. In the one-third that were partisan, women often used party activity as a compensatory political resource. For example, in Connecticut, a state with strong party control, local female officials used party activity to compensate for less education and lower-status occupations, as compared to their male counterparts.[68] It should also be noted that there are class differences between the two types of elections: compared to partisan municipalities, nonpartisan municipalities elected candidates with higher socioeconomic status.[69]

Although most female candidates came from female occupations, some had more typically male backgrounds in business and law. The importance of having a male occupation varied by level of government (the higher the level of government, the more important), by level of partisanship (the more partisan the arena, the more party activity could substitute for a male occupation), and by generation (the younger the candidate, the greater the likelihood of a male occupational background). It was not until the 1980s that women entered law and business schools in sufficient numbers to create a pool of potential female candidates with credentials from these previously male-dominated professions. Between 1975 and 1985, women's percentage of law degrees rose from 11 to 40, and of MBA degrees from 7 to 31.[70]

Thus it was not surprising to find that during the early 1970s, the female candidate pool was populated with women from female-dominated occupations, or indeed, occupation homemaker. For example, Jeane Kirkpatrick's 1972 study of forty-six powerful female state legislators found that, regardless of their educational background, almost all of them moved to the legislature from the role of full-time homemaker.[71] And Susan J. Carroll's 1976 study of a representative sample of all female state legislative candidates found that though virtually none of the women listed homemaker as her occupation, they were clustered in female-dominated occupations: less than 5 percent were lawyers, about 20 percent were elementary and secondary schoolteachers, and another 20 percent had clerical and secretarial jobs. Female candidates were relatively disadvantaged "to the extent that voters believe that certain types of professional credentials (e.g., law) equip one for officeholding while other types (e.g., teaching) do not."[72]

Each of the three occupational routes for female candidates—male occupation, female occupation, and volunteer/homemaker—had interesting consequences. The male occupational route accorded automatic credibility in a male-defined culture. As one of Kirkpatrick's female legislators put it, "If you are a woman and a lawyer, you have instant credibility that most women do not have."[73] Furthermore, some argued that male occupations did a better job of preparing women for the conflict and controversy of politics, in contrast to female occupations (which tended to be service oriented) and volunteer/homemaking (which did not expose women to the dog-eat-dog corporate world of high finance or the combative world of contracts, torts, and liability).

In the case of Santa Clara County, Supervisor Rod Diridon connected women's competence problem to their lack of business experience.

The industrial community feels it can "run the housewives." They feel they can play on the housewife elected official's lack of experience in the business world. They can dominate and impose their wills, through both sweet-talking and through coercion and veiled threats. I have seen it happen. The women are impressed and intimidated by wealthy individuals. But this is due more to their lack of exposure to the world of commerce and business than to their being women. Women with business backgrounds are less intimidated. Men in the business world have more opportunities for policy experience prior to office-holding than do women who are housewives with little organizational experience.

On the other hand, in many ways the volunteer/homemaker and female occupational routes provided the functional equivalents of the male occupational route. Women's civic organizations fostered women's self-confidence, offered public contacts, opened up leadership opportunities, and provided practice in running meetings, developing agendas, recruiting officers, and speaking in public. For their part, female occupations, like male occupations, supplied the occasion for proving oneself on a job, gaining the esteem of co-workers, and making public contacts. Transformational feminists argued that women's occupational routes did not simply clone those of men, nor should they be judged by male standards, according to which they would invariably be found deficient. Rather, women's backgrounds enabled women to bring something of value to the political world on their own terms.

Occupational Backgrounds of Santa Clara County Officials

Female officials in San Jose city and Santa Clara County government took all three occupational routes, with the male route in a distinct minority. The three female officials who had followed the male route were on the board of supervisors: Geraldine Steinberg and Zoe Lofgren were attorneys, and Rebecca Morgan was a bank vice-president. Six women on the San Jose City Council had worked in female-dominated jobs: Nancy Ianni had a teaching credential and had worked as a secretary to the director of Stanford Electronics Products; Shirley Lewis had been an adult education teacher; Pat Sausedo had worked on a Lockheed assembly line; Iola Williams had been a high school consultant; Blanca Alvarado had been an eligibility worker, employment counselor, real estate agent, tax consultant, and radio co-host; and Lu Ryden had hosted a television interview show and owned a modeling agency. The volunteer/home-maker route was traveled by Supervisors Susanne Wilson and Dianne McKenna; by Councilmembers Virginia Shaffer, Susan Hammer, and Judy Stabile; and by Mayor Janet Gray Hayes (who had worked in a wel-fare agency to put her husband through medical school but had no sub-sequent paid employment).

To what extent were these occupational backgrounds assets or liabil-ities? In light of Silicon Valley's open political culture, it was not surpris-ing to find that voters were willing to give candidates a try even if they lacked the credentials of male occupations. An ability to get the job done was more important than the right connections. Most of these women relied on networks they had built up through volunteer and neighbor-hood organizations. And it was in these organizations that they devel-oped leadership skills, overcoming any self-doubt they might have had about lacking a male occupational background.

For example, Nancy Ianni described her preparation for public of-fice as a "classic woman volunteer—some would say woman do-gooder—and community leader." Ianni said three kinds of organizational experi-ence prepared her for the city council: the local chapter of the League of Women Voters, whose president helped train women for public office and which organized the Willow Glen Homeowners Association in Ianni's neighborhood; her homeowners' association, which was con-cerned with overall planning issues and was where she "got her organi-zational and political skills"; and her job as secretary at Stanford Elec-tronics Products, where she learned "managerial skills dealing with professors who see themselves as little emperors." Between this job and the neighborhood association, she "learned to deal with all kinds of peo-ple and personalities."

Councilmember Pat Sausedo described her preparation for public office in her homeowners' group dealing with development issues:

> My philosophy in the homeowners' group was the same as it is now: listen to both sides and make up your mind. The devel-oper, staff, and politician each has a different perspective. It is insulting to give only one side. I have faith in the public. They are not stupid. They are survivors, and they make mistakes and are flexible. Most of the public does not trust politicians to give them more than one side. I will take controversial issues out into the community and present both the developer's view and that of their critics. Development is the big issue in my district, and critics can improve the quality of development projects.

Political Parties as Barriers to Women's Political Recruitment

A fourth hazard for female candidates was hostility or lukewarm support from political parties. Party resistance had historically been a problem in congressional and state races, but it decreased over time and was somewhat less of a problem in local, nonpartisan contests. After women got the vote in 1920, suffrage leaders sought to secure female representation on party committees. As we saw in the last chapter, however, local political parties were often hostile or patronizing to women trying to work their way up the ranks. Things looked brighter at the national level, where beginning in the 1920s, political parties adopted a fifty-fifty rule, whereby women constituted half the members of the Republican and Democratic National Committees. A 1944 study sought to determine how much influence these women exerted. A majority of national committeewomen said they were encouraged by the policymaking progress of women on national committees, but one-third of them expressed the view that women had little influence.[74] Eleanor Roosevelt wrote in 1954 that the fifty-fifty rule looked better on paper than it worked in practice. She said men tended to pick women who would not give them any trouble (were "mere stooges") and that too often a woman was selected for "her bank account, social prestige, or party service rendered by a deceased husband."[75] Edward J. Flynn, Democratic national chairman under President Franklin Roosevelt, listed his specifications for the ideal committeewoman: "She must be handsome, a lady, able to introduce the President gracefully, and wear orchids well; she must have an acceptable bank account—and she must never, never interfere with party policy."[76] By the 1950s, fewer than half the states had a fifty-fifty rule for party committees. And there were fewer than one hundred female county chairpersons in the nation's 3,072 counties. As one county official articulated the prevailing view, "Well, I don't see how she can be a county chairman. She won't be able to go into the saloons with the boys."[77]

Given the hostility of party machines toward the League of Women Voters and other female reform associations, it was hardly surprising that male-dominated parties took their time welcoming women into their ranks. To the extent that women were included in party activities, they were expected to serve the party by advancing male candidates. Over half the female state legislators interviewed as part of Kirkpatrick's 1972 study believed that the men in party organizations tried to keep women out of leadership positions.[78] Debra W. Stewart concluded her anthology on women in local elective office by noting that men had kept women from party leadership roles. The better women were at party work, the less likely they were to be tapped for elective office. The PTA and League of Women Voters were better launching pads than parties were for women's electoral bids.[79] Political parties did not initially recruit many congresswomen, including Bella Abzug, Pat Schroeder, Leonor Sullivan, Martha Griffiths, and Margaret Heckler. Heckler's experience was typical. Before deciding to run for office, she was a young attorney with three small children. She and other women devoted more time and energy campaigning for Republican party candidates than the candidates themselves did: "I'd have a whole team of women taking all the abuse that one receives at a railway station with commuters, about three days before the election, when all the worst things come out, right at the end, and report back to my candidate, and he would have been at home with his feet up by the fire sipping a cocktail. And that really annoyed me, and it happened repeatedly. So I decided that I would run."[80]

Until fairly recently, parties slated female candidates as sacrificial lambs, in races where they had the least chance of winning. In Pennsylvania congressional elections between 1920 and 1964, women were targeted to hopeless races about 60 percent of the time. The more winnable the seat, the more difficult it was for women to get the party's nomination. Parties showed more sexism than the general public did: women did as well as men in the general elections. And women in hopeless seats did slightly better than previous male throwaway candidates from their party had done.[81] Further evidence of women as sacrificial lambs was found in studies of nomination patterns to the House of Representatives between 1916 and 1978, female candidates for state office in three states between 1950 and 1978, female candidates for state and national office in 1972 from New York City and Long Island, and women who were candidates for state races in 1976.[82]

The sentiment that women were sacrificial lambs was borne out in a 1981 CAWP survey, which found that party leaders were most active in recruiting those women who ran in the most adverse circumstances.[83] But there was also evidence from the CAWP studies that parties were important to women's candidacies. The 1981 CAWP survey revealed that half or more of all female officeholders across all levels of government were specifically sought out by party leaders and encouraged to run, and that, except for mayors, female officials were more likely than male officials to have worked in others' political campaigns before being elected to office. Campaign work appeared to provide a training ground for women more so than for men who were considering running for office.[84] The importance of party activity differed by state and by level of government. In California, for example, party activity was not very important to candidates in local nonpartisan races, but it was at the state level. The women in the CAWP study agreed that working within political parties was an absolute necessity for the pursuit of higher office.

There was some evidence that the 1972 national party reforms were felt at the local level. Even though women constituted only 10 percent of county party leaders, a 1974 nationwide survey of these women found that parties were becoming more woman-friendly. The typical female county leader was middle-aged, with an above-average education, employed, married, with few children at home, and a longtime community resident. She had spent many years working for the party but had only recently had been named county chair, a promotion attributed to the women's movement and to Democratic party reforms. Three-quarters of the women said they were the first woman to serve as county chair in their county. A majority of them said that women in politics faced discrimination but that they had not personally experienced it; that male co-workers had a favorable reaction to their being chair; and that local party leaders encouraged women to become candidates.[85]

Along the same lines, other researchers found no evidence of party hostility to women's candidacies at the congressional, state legislative, or local levels of government. Between 1970 and 1984, female candidates were not recruited for hopeless congressional races; the problem for both men and women in such races was incumbency. Nor were women sacrificial lambs in state legislative races in six states between 1974 and 1980. And a 1983 national study of city councilmembers showed that parties were not a barrier to women running for city council.[86]

Barbara Burrell argued that by the 1980s, party leaders had moved from hostility to advocacy of women's candidacies. National party organizations responded favorably to women because of political expediency, a change in party leadership, and women's organizing. Parties paid attention to the gender gap in opinions and voting beginning with the 1980 election, and there were increasing numbers of female party leaders at all levels. Between 1980 and 1984, parties gave the same amount of money to female and male candidates. In the 1980s, the Democratic party set up the Eleanor Roosevelt Fund to assist female Democratic candidates, the National Federation of Republican Women recruited and trained Republican women seeking office, and for the first time both parties adopted platform planks advocating women's access to elective office.[87]

Political Parties in Santa Clara County

As a general rule, in California party support was crucial in state-level races and less critical in nonpartisan local contests. But even some women in the California legislature got there in spite of their party. For example, State Senator Marian Bergeson, the fourth woman to serve in the California Senate (where there were no women until 1976), explained the paucity of women in that chamber as a result of "the old boy warehousing system," whereby the party had a man in the pipeline anytime a winnable seat became available. Parties slated men from the Assembly to the Senate.[88] Assemblymember Jackie Speier overcame a male opponent in the primaries, who was backed by her party, which had decided that only a "Rambo type" Democrat could win in her district, to which she deadpanned, "I don't think I come off as a Rambo."[89] Gloria Molina, the first Latina in the California Assembly, won her office in 1982 in spite of the fact that local power brokers (the Hispanic Democratic leadership of Los Angeles) supported her male opponent in the primary.[90] And by the mid-1980s, local contests were becoming increasingly partisan, because they were seen as stepping-stones to the California state legislature. When County Supervisor Rebecca Morgan left the board to join the California Senate in 1984, partisan dust was raised in the campaign battle between Betsy Bechtel and Dianne McKenna—both Democrats—to fill the post. Bechtel supporters complained that McKenna openly courted Democratic support in the supposedly nonpartisan race.[91]

But for the most part, political parties played a minor role in the recruitment of women for local posts in Santa Clara County. In cases where parties were involved, their effects were similar to patterns found elsewhere, with the exception of offering up sacrificial lambs. Sacrificial lambs in Santa Clara County were Republicans in this predominantly Democratic area. In the 1980 elections, when the San Jose City Council switched to district elections and expanded from seven to ten members, Republicans managed to capture two seats, Claude Fletcher's and Lu Ryden's. Fletcher's seat went to a Democrat in 1988, but Ryden stayed in office ten years before voluntarily retiring in 1990. Ryden described her recruitment:

> The Republican party approached me. They saw that districting was coming up and wanted someone conservative to run. I had only done PR work for the party. I worked with the press in the campaigns of Ronald Reagan and [lieutenant gubernatorial candidate] Mike Curb. I was president of the Republican Women's

Club, but really in name only as I did not do all that much. I was
recruited by the Republican party as someone who had the right
philosophy, combined with poise from my TV background.

Three women had been very active in Democratic party politics, but
they were not recruited by the party to run. Supervisor Zoe Lofgren had
served on the county and state central committees, had been a delegate
to a national party convention, and had served as president of the Century Club, a local Democratic group. Although the party provided important contacts for her, party officials were not the ones who encouraged her to run for the open supervisorial seat. As Lofgren described it:
"Running for the board was an afterthought for me. I used the fund list
left over from my race for the Community College Board. When Dom
Cortese retired to run for Leona Egeland's Assembly seat, I called [San
Jose City Councilmember] Tom McEnery and told him to run, and he
told me to run. Several people convinced me to run very late in the
game." San Jose City Councilmember Blanca Alvarado's involvement
with the Democratic party went back to voter registration drives in 1948.
But it was her colleagues at the Mexican American Political Association
who first suggested that she was ready for a leadership position in the
community. "At first it was scary. I said, 'Me?' I never thought about running for anything. But then I decided to bite the bullet. I'd been com-
plaining about no Hispanic representation on the council. I said, 'OK, I'll
do it.' "[92] And San Jose City Councilmember Susan Hammer had been active in Democratic politics since 1962, when she and her husband went to
Washington, D.C., "as a couple of idealistic young liberal Democrats" to
work for the Kennedy administration. Her husband's family had been involved in the party and in San Jose civic affairs for a couple of generations.[93] Hammer also cochaired Mayor Janet Gray Hayes's reelection
campaign in 1978. Two other city councilmembers got their political feet
wet working for others' campaigns. Shirley Lewis was office manager and
volunteer coordinator for Congressmember Norman Mineta's campaign
in 1976 and for San Jose City Councilmember Jerry Estruth's campaign
in 1978. And Judy Stabile was an aide to Estruth, who urged her to run
for his seat in 1984, when he retired to spend more time with his family.

Resources: Opportunity Structure, Money, and Connections

A final obstacle for women's recruitment to public office was resources. Female candidates were disadvantaged when it came to political
opportunity structure (the extent to which incumbency, political cul-

ture, or type of election inhibited entry into public office), money (ability to raise campaign funds), and connections (inclusion in informal "old boys' networks").

Incumbency was a major barrier to the political opportunity structure of women, who sought public office in record numbers beginning in the 1970s. Although it was a problem for male challengers as well, men as a group were already overrepresented in public office. In congressional and state legislative races, incumbency was a significant barrier to female electoral success.[94] Throughout the 1980s, about 95 percent of House members and state legislators who ran were reelected. The fact that there was higher voluntary turnover in state legislatures helped explain why women entered state legislatures faster than the House. The relatively large gains women made in the House in 1992 were due in large part to the unusually high incumbent retirement rate. The cumulative impact of incumbency and low turnover played a big role in keeping women out of office. Once in office, however, female incumbents had about the same rate of reelection as male incumbents.[95]

Political culture often blocked women's access to public office. In the 1970s, states with moralistic political cultures were much more likely than those with traditional or individualistic political cultures to have female state legislators and judges.[96] One study found that the strongest predictor of the presence of women in a state's legislature in the 1970s was the presence of women there in the 1930s and that traditional states were moderately less likely than moralistic states to have female state legislators.[97] And a 1981 study of women in the lower houses of sixteen state legislatures found that distance from the state capital was one constraint on women but that it was overridden by the cultural milieu of a moralistic state and by the more progressive sex-role attitudes found in larger cities.[98] During the 1980s, most of the states with the lowest proportions of women in their legislatures were found in the traditionalistic South.[99]

The type of election also had a bearing on women's political opportunity structure. As we saw in Chapter 2, women typically benefited from at-large, as opposed to district, elections at the state and national levels but not necessarily at the local level. When it came to partisan versus nonpartisan elections, researchers were surprised to find that women did not fare better than men in nonpartisan settings, at either the local or the state level.[100] And as for primaries and general elections, though most studies found that women did equally well in both settings,[101] some research revealed that primaries were a weak link in the electoral chain for female candidates.[102]

State population and party dominance affected women's pursuit of public office. The best opportunity structure for women wanting to be judges was a large state with a political (as opposed to a professional) structure of judicial selection, strong party organizations, weak interest groups, and Democratic party hegemony.[103] Party dominance and state population size were also critical factors for female state legislators who were congressional aspirants. In states with a large pool of female state legislators (Republican, low population), there were few opportunities for congressional seats because of the small size of the state's congressional delegation. States with a small pool of female state legislators (Democratic, high population) elected few women to Congress because there were fewer women in the pool and because the party machinery supported male candidates.[104]

The women's movement was a positive feature for women in a state's opportunity structure. By 1984, women's political mobility from state legislatures to Congress had opened up. The 100 percent increase in the number of female state legislators between 1974 and 1984 was the result of two trends: a building on previous gains in Republican-moralistic states' assemblies, with an accompanying increase in women moving from assemblies to state senates, and the positive impact of the women's movement in "new wave" states (i.e., states with increases over 100 percent in the number of female state legislators, just over one-third of all states). The effect of the women's movement, measured by the number of NOW chapters in a state, was felt regardless of a state's party control, party competition, or political culture. Additional favorable factors between 1974 and 1984 were Republican party dominance, a moralistic political culture, high AFDC payments, and no second primaries in the state. Unfavorable factors were Democratic party dominance, especially in the states of the former Confederacy, and a traditional political culture. Factors no longer unfavorable to the recruitment of women were small-sized assemblies in highly populated states and low-income states. And there were new conditions that aided women's recruitment: an individualistic political culture, a high proportion of women in the state's labor force, the presence of NOW chapters, a high proportion of women in Congress and of professional women, and the prevalence of multi-member districts, which began to favor women's recruitment to state legislatures in the 1980s.[105]

In sum, scholars carefully dissected women's political opportunity structure, noting the importance of incumbency, political culture, type of elections, party dominance, state population size, and the women's movement. They found that the effects of these factors varied over time and across levels of government.

Most scholars and practitioners agreed that although female candidates had difficulty raising money in the 1970s and 1980s, this had become less of a problem by the 1990s. Since parties often did not take women's candidacies very seriously, it was not surprising that in the 1970s individual contributors were not forthcoming, especially given the fact that working women at the time made 60 percent of what men earned. Both Ruth Mandel's qualitative study of 102 female candidates and Susan Carroll's quantitative study of 1,200 female candidates emphasized the difficulty these women had raising money.[106] Fundraising was also difficult for many male candidates, but it was especially problematic for women. First, they faced a greater psychological barrier in asking for money for themselves. Women who ran for office in the 1970s grew to adulthood in a society with rigid sex roles, where breadwinners (men) were socialized to request money for what they did and homemakers (women) were socialized to raise money not for themselves but rather for charitable causes. Second, women were less likely to belong to the occupational and social networks that often served as a major source of campaign funds: golf and tennis clubs, male-only social clubs, dinner with "the guys," and so on. Third, even when women obtained funds from big donors and political action committees, they often received less money from those sources than men did. As Carroll noted, "Perhaps in part because few women are incumbents or occupy positions where they can wield political clout, even liberal PACs like the American Federation of State, County and Municipal Employees (AFSCME) and the National Abortion Rights Action League (NARAL) have in the past given smaller average contributions to women candidates than to men." And fourth, women were not as accustomed to donating money to political causes, and when they did contribute, they generally gave in small amounts. Carroll concluded, "Responses by candidates in this study highlight the overriding importance of fund raising as a problem for women who seek public office. Money was mentioned far more frequently than any other problem by women who ran in contested primaries for all four types of office [Congress, statewide, state house, state senate]."[107]

Other research confirmed these patterns. A study of campaign financing in Charlotte, North Carolina, between 1975 and 1980 discovered that compared to men, women relied less on their own money and received more funds from small contributions, their own neighborhoods, other women, blacks, Democrats, and sources outside the county in which they were running. Female contributors were more likely to give to female candidates, but women were much less likely than men to give money to a campaign.[108] Men received more campaign contributions than women did in state legislative races in Massachusetts from 1980 to 1988.[109] Some researchers, however, found that women were not inferior fundraisers in the 1970s and 1980s: in campaigns for the House of Representatives between 1972 and 1982, in Oklahoma state legislative races between 1968 and 1980, in 1980 congressional races, and during the 1984 general election for the House.[110]

By the 1990s, things looked better. In the 1990 elections, women's PACs gave $2.7 million to women's campaigns. In 1992, female congressional candidates raised about $80 million, as compared to their opponents' $99 million, a difference largely explained by the fact that more female challengers than incumbents were running. Women's PACs quadrupled their donations, giving $11.6 million to women's campaigns. EMILY's List's contribution of $6.2 million made it the largest funder of U.S. House and Senate candidacies in the 1992 election.[111]

Much more difficult to measure than campaign funds was acceptance by the "old boys' network." Some version of this phrase was used by most female candidates. It covered everything from the obvious (all-male clubs, golf games, and the like) to the subtle (patronizing attitudes, rendering women invisible in group conversations, sexist jokes, and so forth). Ruth Mandel noted that "aspiring officeholders know that without the endorsement and material support that come from access to established political networks, life as a candidate is lonely and defeating. It is simply a fact of history that established political networks are dominated by men." She quoted Congressmember Pat Schroeder of Colorado, who saw no significant change during recent years in women's acceptance as serious candidates within male circles, even when women were incumbents: "We're not in the same networks, men don't have women as friends and vice versa."[112]

Women's Access to Campaign Resources in Santa Clara County

Several female officials in Santa Clara County described female candidates' problems with fundraising and old boys' networks. Supervisor Susanne Wilson observed that raising money was a problem for female candidates, partly because of social conditioning that said it was unladylike for women to ask for money: "Men still control most of the companies and pocketbooks, even in this valley. But men also like aggressive women who ask for the money." Santa Clara City Councilmember Judy Nadler said the two main obstacles she saw for women who sought political power were difficulty in raising campaign money and having less well established networks than men. Palo Alto City Councilmember Betsy Bechtel seconded that notion, saying that raising money "can be more difficult for women if they don't have business connections. Far too frequently, men may be more willing to spend money. They have money available and can draw on those connections." Bechtel founded the Los Altos Women in Business Forum, an offshoot of the Los Altos Chamber of Commerce, "because there are existing organizations for men that presently women are excluded from joining. One is Kiwanis, and one is Rotary." The University Club was another important all-male bastion of social connections. Supervisor Rod Diridon described the valley's exclusive male clubs, some of which were "as old as the hills," as "the basic networking mechanisms for power." In a testament to their importance, Diridon, a Rotarian, encouraged San Jose's Downtown Rotary Club and other all-male groups to admit women: "You've got to invite women to be members. Otherwise the traditional power of the Rotary as a leadership organization in this valley is going to be eroded because many of the leaders are not going to be able to be members."[113]

The relatively lower cost of mounting local campaigns was one reason why some female officials chose not to pursue state or federal office. San Jose City Councilmember Susan Hammer put it this way: "Running for statewide office is just a big expensive media event. You don't have precinct walkers and coffees" or the other relatively inexpensive things that help individual voters get to know a candidate in a local campaign. Politics at the state and federal levels is "still an old boys' network," requiring lots of money that women have a hard time raising.[114]

In small districts, female candidates in Santa Clara County could substitute neighborhood "people power" for economic resources. For example, in Nancy Ianni's 1980 bid to represent the Willow Glen District on the San Jose City Council, she ran on $15,000, while her pro-growth opponent received $30,000 from developers in the primary. The Willow Glen District historically had the highest voter turnout rate in San Jose. Ianni attributed her victory to the district's "grassroots efforts— I had a network in a mature and stable community, unlike other districts with transient populations." And in the 1984 race for the West Side District on the San Jose City Council, Judy Stabile, who collected $16,000, was the leading vote-getter in the June primary, while Gene Amato, one of her opponents with a $50,000 war chest, finished third and did not make the runoff. As a journalist reported on this race, "'All the campaign pros thought his money would buy the election,' Stabile recalled. But she had a strong organization, and enough money to send one powerful, last-minute campaign mailer. It noted that Stabile had lived twelve years in the district, Amato, just two days. 'I had enough money to make that point, and it killed him,' Stabile said."[115]

As the costs of local campaigns skyrocketed in the late 1980s, substituting people power for economic power became increasingly difficult. For example, in the 1984 race for Rebecca Morgan's county supervisorial seat, Betsy Bechtel raised $115,000, mostly from friends, and a victorious Dianne McKenna received $240,000 in contributions, primarily from developers and industry (including a $94,700 personal loan to herself), in the most expensive supervisorial campaign in county history.[116] And the costs of San Jose mayoral campaigns had also grown considerably. In the 1986 campaign, incumbent Tom McEnery amassed a $290,000 war chest, and in the primary for the 1990 race for McEnery's post (San Jose's mayor has a two-term limit), top vote-getters Susan Hammer and Frank Fiscalini each spent about $500,000, in the most expensive race in city history.[117] Although San Jose City Council races were still a relative bargain, in 1986 incumbents raised four to five times more than challengers, with Susan Hammer packing away $46,000 for her reelection bid. And in the 1982 and 1984 elections, no San Jose City Council candidate who raised less than $15,000 won an election or was advanced to a runoff.[118]

Although female candidates in Santa Clara County and nationwide often faced obstacles when it came to resources, party resistance, occupational background, family obligations, and self-concept, they frequently enjoyed three advantages not shared by male candidates: women's networks, support from women's organizations, and voter perception of women's trustworthiness.

Women's Networks

Having been excluded from old boys' networks, many women formed connections of their own to advance women's candidacies. These networks took various forms, from lists of eligible women for appointments to female officials' sense of obligation to get other women into elective and appointive posts. Appointments were more crucial to women's recruitment to public office than they were to men's. A 1981 CAWP survey found that except for mayors, women elected to state, county, and municipal offices held more government appointments than their male colleagues. By contrast, men were more likely to have held elective office before to their current elected position.[119] Women were more likely to be selected as mayors of cities when the mayor was chosen by the city council (appointed) than when the mayor was elected directly by the people. Likewise, in countries with upper legislative chambers whose members were appointed, there were larger proportions of women members than in the lower, elected chambers.[120]

There were several reasons why appointments benefited women. First, they implied accountability, and the exclusion of women became increasingly difficult for officials to justify. By contrast, the mass electorate was not held accountable in this way. Second, authorities often sought to "balance" their appointments among relevant social groupings: religious, ethnic, racial, sex, and so forth. Third, elites often reduced conflict by establishing rules for appointment in their decision-making bodies, such as rotating chairs by seniority, so that a woman's turn came up automatically. Finally, elites sometimes selected women for appointed positions because they were typically less politically important than elective ones. To the extent that these jobs were honorary and symbolic, elites got credit for including women at little cost.[121]

Honorific or not, appointed posts were important stepping-stones for women's political careers. And women made it their business to have lists of women available when officials sought to fill appointive slots. In 1976, the NWPC created the Coalition for Women's Appointments (CWA), which pushed for the appointments of women to federal cabinet and subcabinet posts and to federal judgeships. In 1976, CWA brought together more than fifty women's organizations to press for high-level appointments to the Carter administration. CWA screened and compiled hundreds of women's names, responding directly to the claim by Carter and some of his top aides that they were having difficulty finding qualified women to appoint. This lobbying effort, combined with responsiveness from the Carter White House, resulted in record-breaking numbers of women's appointments, constituting about 22 percent of all appointments and 14 percent of Carter's top policy positions; the fourth, fifth, and sixth women ever to serve as U.S. cabinet secretaries; three of the five women who had ever served as undersecretaries; and 42 percent of the female judges on the federal bench.[122]

Similar organizations were set up in various states. The Women's Register for Leadership in Missouri, founded in 1979, included among its resources a computer talent bank with names and qualifications of women interested in appointment; a computer file of existing boards, commissions, and councils; appointment requirements; and conferences to teach women about all aspects of the appointment process. The Texas Foundation for Women's Resources set up Leadership Texas, a program that brought together Texan women to strengthen their leadership skills and facilitate their appointment to government posts. In 1981, the New Jersey Bipartisan Coalition for Women's Appointments (NJBCWA) was formed to influence the gubernatorial appointments process. Republican Governor Thomas Kean appointed several of the women the coalition had actively promoted, many of whom acknowledged the NJBCWA for its assistance. The NJBCWA also stimulated public awareness about the importance of women's appointments. And in 1982, Massachusetts women organized a coalition to press for the appointment of women to state government posts, based partly on the New Jersey model.[123]

In 1990, the California Elected Women's Association for Education and Research (CEWAER), after finding that only about one-third of state, county, and municipal board and commission seats were held by women, embarked on the California Board and Commission Outreach Project to encourage more women to apply for appointive posts. It established a California Appointments Coalition to achieve gender balance on the state's more than three hundred boards and commissions and to set up local projects. For example, in Los Angeles County, twenty-five women's organizations set up the Los Angeles Women's Appointments Collaboration.[124]

In addition to these organized efforts, many female officials expressed a sense of obligation to open doors for other women. In a 1981 CAWP study, a majority of female legislators said that they actively recruited women when hiring staff, that they encouraged individual women to become involved in politics, and that they spoke to various groups of women to urge them to participate in politics. Many of the female officeholders had female mentors or had worked on a woman's campaign.[125] Most female officials were "sisters," women who felt an obligation to other women, in contrast to "queen bees," who felt neither gratitude toward women who paved the way for them nor a duty to lower the ladder for other women.[126]

In the case of female officials in Santa Clara County, even nonfeminist Lu Ryden was a sister insofar as she felt a sense of obligation to women who opened doors for her. "I do feel indebted to those women who forged ahead of me. They took abuse, showed nerve, and weren't afraid. I admire anyone who forges new trails. People like Betty Friedan and Gloria Steinem. While I don't agree with anything they say, I do admire them for coming out." Nancy Ianni did not identify herself with women's issues at the time of her election. Nevertheless, she recognized that other women had paved the way for her, particularly her mentor in the League of Women Voters. As she put it: "I owe a lot to women who came before me. They did a good job and made it easier for me. . . . A former president of the League of Women Voters was my mentor. She never ran for office herself, but she helped many other women. To this day I ask myself, 'Now what would Margie do in this situation?' She died of cancer two months after I won the primary."

Janet Gray Hayes had a history of being the "first woman" in many posts. Before her election as the first female mayor of a large American city, Hayes had been the first woman to serve on the San Jose Metropolitan YMCA Board of Directors in that organization's 102-year history and the first woman member and chairperson of the San Jose Redevelopment Agency. Her guiding principle was to leave as many or more women on a board when she left:

> I felt an especially heavy responsibility when I was the only woman on board to do a good job so that they would appreciate what I was trying to do for the organization so that I could leave that organization with at least as many women or more than when I started on the board. And I always did, too. I left two on the YMCA board or helped them get on the board. And when I left the Redevelopment Agency to run for public office, I got Leona Egeland on. [Egeland went on to serve in the California Assembly from 1974 to 1980.] So I helped women get on the ladder to political leadership.

Hayes was the second woman to be elected to the San Jose City Council. Virginia Shaffer had served from 1962 to 1971, the year Hayes joined the council. Susanne Wilson arrived in 1973. After Hayes won the mayoral race, she was instrumental in securing the appointments of two women to vacancies that opened on the city council: Iola Williams in 1978 and Susan Hammer in 1982. Hayes's support for Williams was somewhat of a surprise, since Williams had publicly said she did not support Hayes's 1978 reelection bid. But the support for Hammer was not a surprise, since Hammer was a close friend, neighbor, and cochair of Hayes's reelection campaign.

The networker extraordinaire for women in Santa Clara County politics was Susanne Wilson. In her 1973 race for the San Jose City Council, the fact that she would be the second woman on the council was definitely an issue: "Ever since Virginia Shaffer, there had been a seat for the token woman on the council. With Hayes already on the council, bets were placed on whether San Jose was ready for two women. Seventeen men and three women ran, with two women in the runoffs. When I won, I inquired why it was never asked why the board should continue with the six men. The real issue was whether I could get the job done, and I proved to them I could." Wilson was the strongest feminist of all the women interviewed for this study. As early as 1973, she challenged the assumption that men's politics was the norm and that women's politics was the problem that needed to be explained. She managed to combine her feminism with a can-do pragmatism that was typical of county residents. Wilson was the "second woman" on both the San Jose City Council and the Santa Clara County Board of Supervisors. Geraldine Steinberg was on the board when Wilson came in 1976. Wilson had been instrumental in getting Steinberg appointed in 1973, and then Steinberg was elected in her own right in 1976.

As a supervisor, Wilson played a key role in securing board approval for the appointment of Sally Reed as county executive in 1981. When Zoe Lofgren and Rebecca Morgan joined Wilson on the board in 1980, they constituted a majority on the five-member body. The April 2, 1981, *San Jose Mercury News* ran an editorial entitled, "Finding the Best Man for County Executive," but these women had other ideas. While applications poured in from around the country, Wilson and Lofgren looked locally to Sally Reed, one of San Jose's three assistant managers.

> While the idea of bringing a city person in to run the county was tantamount to treason, Zoe Lofgren knew that Sally Reed was a brilliant administrator. So did Susie Wilson. They also knew that Reed knew how to write and decipher budgets—a prize aptitude, given the county's dire fiscal straits. They got the board to interview her, introducing her to Rebecca Morgan. The three supervisors eventually formed the one-vote majority Reed needed. "We plucked her out of the bureaucracy," Lofgren recalls. "The women got her in."[127]

Wilson self-consciously networked for women. "Networking has always been important for me. I admire women's competence. I am not jealous of other women. There is a lot of room at the top. I've worked with women from the start—church, Cancer Society, YWCA—and they networked me into office." Wilson was president of CEWAER, and under its auspices she established the Santa Clara County network called GOG, or Good Old Gals, described earlier. According to Sarah Janigian, Wilson's aide, other local city and county officials were also good at bringing women into office and onto their staffs, especially Rebecca Morgan, Shirley Lewis, and Iola Williams.

Support from Women's Organizations

A second advantage for female candidates was support from women's organizations. As we have seen, initially the women's movement did not focus on getting more women elected to office, because many radicals saw such an effort as tantamount to complicity in an oppressive, male-dominated system. Electing women was not an explicit aim in the early years of the National Organization for Women, for instance. To fill this void, several organizations emerged in the early 1970s. The National Women's Political Caucus was formed in 1971 to increase women's access to political power in the major parties and to encourage and support women committed to women's rights who sought elective and appointive office. In 1973, the nonpartisan National Women's Education Fund (NWEF) was founded to offer training programs in campaign techniques and to provide technical assistance and public information in order to increase the numbers and influence of women in politics. And the Women's Campaign Fund (WCF) was established in 1974 to elect qualified progressive women of both parties to national, state, and local offices. It was the first national political action committee established exclusively to provide financial contributions and technical consultation to female candidates.[128]

During the 1970s, most female candidates had an ambivalent relationship to feminist organizations and the women's movement. A 1974 survey conducted by NWPC of all female candidates for state and congressional office found that most of them had had no previous contact with NWPC and only 3 percent of them saw women's rights issues as crucial in their campaign. Most of them had never run for public office before, but they had held party offices in local communities. And they saw as many advantages as disadvantages to being a female candidate.[129]

Carol Mueller looked at the relationship between female candidates and the women's movement from a different angle, arguing that during the 1970s the primary effect of the movement on female candidates was legitimating their political ambitions. Female candidates initially were not directly aided by feminist organizations or funds but rather were assisted by traditional women's organizations. Only a small percentage of female candidates saw themselves as feminists or campaigned on women's issues. Mueller described three stages in the development of feminist consciousness among female candidates. Ambitious women developed a "career feminism" when a concern with their individual career was legitimated by the women's movement. Career feminism transformed into "structural feminism" when women confronted obstacles blocking their political opportunity structure. These obstacles were perceived as illegitimate forms of discrimination, leading women to join organizations and caucuses and to adopt feminist policy goals. "Group feminism" was a group identification with women and with the women's movement and a support for feminist policies. At all three levels of consciousness, the women's movement provided a legitimating set of ideas that had been lacking before 1970.[130]

Female candidates' ambivalence toward the women's movement and feminism also cropped up in Susan J. Carroll's 1976 nationwide survey of women who ran for state and congressional offices. Carroll found a mixture of feminist and nonfeminist tendencies that divided along attitudinal and behavioral lines. Attitudinal feminists favored the elimination of socially prescribed sex roles and the removal of legal constraints on women's potential. Behavioral feminists engaged in feminist acts, such as joining feminist organizations and publicly advocating feminist beliefs, measures, or legislation. About one-quarter of the women surveyed were both attitudinal and behavioral feminists; an equal proportion was attitudinally feminist but behaviorally nonfeminist, what Carroll termed "closet feminists." She cited two reasons for closet feminism on the part of female candidates: a fear of being stereotyped as narrowly concerned with women's issues, and a lack of conscious recognition and acceptance of feminism.[131]

By the 1980s, women's organizations had begun to play a significant role in the political recruitment of women. There was a high positive correlation between the proportion of women in a state's legislature in 1981–83 and that state's NOW membership.[132] In 1987, former NOW president Eleanor Smeal founded the Fund for the Feminist Majority, a nonprofit organization that worked to promote equality for women and a redirection of the nation's priorities. In October 1987, the fund launched a nationwide "feminization of power campaign" to flood tickets with feminist candidates and to promote a national feminist agenda. The number of women's political action committees mushroomed: from 1 in 1974, to 35 in 1988, to 42 in 1992. EMILY's List, whose philosophy was reflected in its title, which stood for Early Money Is Like Yeast (It Helps the Dough Rise), helped women early in their campaigns to make them viable from the outset. Other major women's PACs were the Women's Campaign Fund, Hollywood Women's Political Committee, NOW, NWPC, and WISH List. All these PACs supported only pro-choice candidates, and all were bipartisan except two (EMILY's List was Democratic and WISH List was Republican). Interestingly, in 1992 the greatest concentration of women's PACs was not in Washington, D.C., but in California, home to fourteen.[133]

The importance of women's organizations was borne out in CAWP's 1981 survey of elected officials.[134] Women more than men reported that an organization played an important role in getting them to run for the first time for their current offices. And this difference was largely due to women's organizations. With the exception of councilmembers, female officials cited women's groups more often than any other type of organization as having played an important role in getting them to run for their current posts. Nearly four-fifths of state legislators, over half of county commissioners, and more than one-third of local officeholders belonged to at least one of the following: the American Association of University Women, the National Federation of Business and Professional Women's Clubs, the League of Women Voters, the National Organization for Women, and the National Women's Political Caucus. Membership in explicitly feminist organizations was more common at the state than at the local level.

In addition to encouraging women to run for public office, women's organizations formally and informally supported women after they decided to run. The higher the level of office, the more likely that an elected woman had received the support of a woman's organization: half of state legislators, 18 percent of county officials, and 8 percent of local officeholders. By way of comparison, the proportions of male state legislators who received support from all types of organizations were smaller than the proportions of female state legislators receiving support from women's organizations alone.

There were partisan differences in organizational support for women's candidacies. Twice as many Democratic as Republican women in the state senates received support from women's groups when running for office. These partisan differences decreased with level of office, to the point where roughly equal proportions of Democratic and Republican mayors and local councilmembers received support from women's groups. Partisan differences showed up when it came to feminist organizations as well. Among state legislators, Democratic women were more than twice as likely as Republican women to have received support from NOW, NWPC, and other explicitly feminist groups.

Organizational support was more important for black female officials than it was for female officials overall. Black women were more likely than women overall to report that an organization had played an important role in getting them to run for the first time for their current office; that they belonged to women's and feminist organizations; and that they received formal or informal support from women's organizations when they ran for their current office.

The CAWP survey showed that the League of Women Voters and the National Women's Political Caucus were the women's organizations that played the biggest roles in helping women who sought public office. The league had the largest membership among female officeholders, but because of its nonprofit status, it was prohibited by law from direct involvement in partisan races. In keeping with the CAWP findings, the league and the caucus were the two most important women's organizations for female candidates in Santa Clara County. And the division of labor between them was along the same lines as in the CAWP survey. The league was instrumental in providing leadership skills and contacts for Janet Gray Hayes, Nancy Ianni, and Judy Stabile, all of whom had been presidents of local chapters. By contrast, the NWPC played an important role in the campaigns of the three most explicit feminists who ran for office: Susanne Wilson, Zoe Lofgren, and Shirley Lewis. The local NWPC chapter, which with about two hundred members was tied with the neighboring Contra Costa County chapter for being the largest in the nation, dispensed between three thousand and five thousand dollars to candidates, depending on the race. Zoe Lofgren described the timing of NWPC's help as crucial to her first supervisorial race in 1980: "Several people convinced me to run very late in the game. The NWPC gave me one of my biggest contributions, $2,000. Their help made a difference. They were one of the many groups which walked precincts for me. I did not run as a feminist in that race. It simply was not an election issue. But I did discuss my feminism with the NWPC." She added that the Democratic party was not too helpful, given the nonpartisan nature of the race. Shirley Lewis noted that although the NWPC was supportive, it did not encourage her to run. According to Sarah Janigian, former president of the local NWPC chapter, the caucus gave Lewis money once she decided to run, but seeking out candidates was not a well-developed function of the group.

Unlike the League of Women Voters and the National Women's Political Caucus, the local chapter of the National Organization for Women did not seem too interested in helping the careers of local female officials in Santa Clara County. It was a fairly radical group, and many of the members felt that these officials did not do enough for women. The NOW chapter was more involved in issues than in candidates during the time of this study, particularly the drive to ratify the Equal Rights Amendment.

Voter Perception of Women's Trustworthiness

Finally, female candidates benefited from a voter perception of women's trustworthiness. In a 1972 Louis Harris poll, women had a 15 percent advantage in the public's image of whether men or women could better maintain honesty and integrity in government.[135] And a

1990 survey by Republican pollster Linda DiVall confirmed that voters perceived female candidates as more trustworthy and less ambitious for personal power than their male counterparts.[136] Women's newcomer status was a plus insofar as citizens felt that the men who had been in charge had made a mess of things, whether Watergate, the Vietnam war, ecological suicide, corruption, or unbridled growth. Several female candidates sensed this "throw the boys out" sentiment. As a state legislator from a small midwestern city put it, "Actually, I think women have some advantages campaigning in some areas. I think people are apt to trust you more. They are apt to think you more honest—that's the image there is—and in my state where corruption is a problem, that's very important. Voters also think a woman will be more conscientious than a man—that she will do her homework. They know a woman isn't running for office just because of personal ambition."[137]

During the 1970s and 1980s, several studies indicated that voter bias against female candidates was eroding and that indeed a voter preference for women in office was increasing. In contested House races in 1970, 1972, and 1974, there was little sex difference in electoral success once candidate party and incumbency status were controlled; in six New Mexico elections between 1968 and 1978 for county, state, and national offices, the number of female candidates for nontraditional posts (state, legislature, county commissions, U.S. House and Senate) increased faster than for traditional posts (secretary of state, county treasurers and clerks, state board of education); and in gubernatorial and senatorial races in 1982, sex was not related to voting for a female candidate.[138] Female and male officeholders in Hawaii thought that women had special assets in campaigning, with women citing trustworthiness, sincerity, charm, compassion, and sensitivity and men noting more leisure time as housewives to devote to campaigning and voter preference for "clean" candidates in the post-Watergate morality. Both sexes believed that women had a greater concern for people and willingness to work for and listen to constituents. Only 24 percent noted voter hostility to female candidates.[139]

Voters' positive sense of women helped California assemblymember Maxine Waters in the 1976 Democratic primary. She was running in the district that included the Watts ghetto, scene of the 1965 riots. Not much had improved since the riots, and Waters's campaign centered on a new approach to old inner-city problems. Since she was a black woman and divorced mother, she thought she had an advantage in a district where many women were on their own. Out of thirty-five thousand Democratic households, seventeen thousand had only women registered as voters.

She put the bulk of her campaign money into three mailers with a positive stress on women's issues and the motto, "Isn't it about time? Now let's get together and show what a woman can do." According to Waters's campaign manager, "We got a lot of feedback from people, not only in the district but in other areas as well. Women were saying, 'If there's a woman running, I'll just vote for her because men have been running it long enough and it's a mess.' Even people I know who are not that liberal and who would say that they are anti-women's lib—they would say to me, 'I'll vote for the woman now, just to see what we can do.'"[140]

In a survey conducted by the National Women's Political Caucus during the week following the 1984 election, women in public office were rated higher than men on being caring and effective, having strong opinions and new ideas, understanding the needs of the voters, and speaking directly to the point. Women and men were rated equally on having leadership qualities and on inspiring confidence. The only characteristic for which women ranked lower than men was the ability to handle a crisis.[141]

Female candidates in Santa Clara County linked the "throw-the-old-boys-out-and-give-women-a-try" sentiment to voter dissatisfaction with Watergate, corruption, and unchecked local growth. According to Supervisor Zoe Lofgren:

> Overall, being a woman candidate in the county is an asset because people see women as more honest, and clean government has a lot of mileage around here. Remember, with the exception of Rosemary Woods, there were no women involved in Watergate. There have been no local scandals or bribes involving women. . . . In walking the precincts, I found two patterns that are worth investigating. One was the secret women's vote: old ladies who would whisper, "Don't tell my husband, honey, but I'm voting for you." The second was when all the candidates were unknown, the person would vote for the woman—both men and women would do this. Was this simply a "throw the rascals out" mentality? Clean government? The idea that women work harder than men?

San Jose City Councilmember Shirley Lewis noticed the same patterns in her 1980 race. "When I was running, I heard people say, 'I trust women more.' Being a woman is an asset for a candidate. She is seen as clean, and many women vote. Men trust women too." Her colleague, Councilmember Blanca Alvarado, shared this sense. "Women candidates are associated with morality, being refreshing and trusted. . . . This is a progressive city. In the eyes of the public, the political element is male-dominated, unethical, and—irresponsible is not quite the word—well, men are screwed up! Women are more independent and able to make decisions outside of the special interest relationship." Supervisor Susanne Wilson claimed that being a woman candidate gave female candidates an edge in local races. "Over the last twelve years, being a woman candidate has gone from being a liability, to being neutral, to the point where it is now an edge in this county. People trust women." This perception was backed up by polls conducted by local politicians, which showed that being a woman gave female candidates an advantage.[142]

6 Policy Preferences and Political Style

*Female Officials as Liberal
Feminist Problem Solvers*

POLICY PREFERENCES and political style refer to what
politicians do once they are in office. What kind of issues do they take on? How effectively? How do they view their relationship to the people who elected them? How do they relate to their
peers in the legislature? Until fairly recently, there were not enough
women at one time in a governing body to study them as a group. As of
1972, only 85 women had occupied congressional seats, with no more
than two in the Senate at one time and 5 percent females in Congress
overall. In 1969, there were only 305 women in all the nation's state
legislatures. Most female officials served at the local level of government, especially on school boards. In 1959, there were an estimated
twenty thousand women in county positions and another ten thousand
in city posts, out of the roughly half a million elective offices in the
United States.[1]

Information about what these women did in office was of little interest to political scientists and the press. Especially at the congressional
level, the popular press was more interested in their personal characteristics than in their legislative potential or accomplishments. When Jeannette Rankin, the nation's first congresswoman, arrived in Washington
in 1917, the reporters sent to interview her were instructed to ask her if
she could make pie.[2] The *Nation* gave an account of her appearance for
the opening day of the sixty-fifth Congress, describing her as the typical
woman from top to toe and paying special attention to her hair color
and style, nose, chin, cheeks, jaw, small figure, and well-fitting garments

with a V-shaped opening at the neck, sporting lace where a man would use flat linen stiff with starch.[3]

It was not until the 1960s that journalists and political scientists began to compile biographical data about female officials, primarily at the national and state levels, and to interview them about what they did in office. As the number of women in public office increased in the 1970s and early 1980s, several important works about women in Congress, state legislatures, and local offices were published.

Accommodationists were primarily concerned with how well women fit into male-defined offices and conventional political categories. One of the most important things they discovered was a historical track record of female officials' greater liberalism. Transformationalists challenged conventional concepts and methods, which had been devised to explain male experiences in public office. They focused on the distinction between "male careerism" and "female public service," female and male cultural differences regarding power and legislative success, and female versus feminist consciousness and behavior. The overall portrait of women in public office was of liberal feminist problem solvers.

Female Officials' Liberalism

It is somewhat ironic that although the liberal-conservative distinction did not adequately capture the political views of women in the mass electorate, it did so among female public officials, who were consistently shown to be more liberal than their male counterparts. In the early 1970s, congresswomen scored higher on liberal scales and lower on conservative ones.[4] In a study of four New England legislatures in the early 1970s, women had slightly more liberal policy views. For example, concerning the best means to discourage riots and disorders, women were more likely to emphasize solving problems of poverty while men more often stressed using all available force. Women tended to be more generous in providing day-care services, and on the question of abortion, the majority of women said the abortion law in their state should be repealed, while the majority of men took more moderate positions.[5] In a national study of the personality characteristics of female state legislators in 1970–71, compared to women as a whole, they were more assertive, venturesome, imaginative, unconventional, and liberal in their attitudes. Compared to male officials, they were more assertive, imaginative, and liberal in their attitudes, regardless of party affiliation.[6]

In 1977, two studies of the voting records of congresswomen showed a pattern of their greater liberalism as compared to congressmen. Once party was controlled for, congresswomen were more supportive of social welfare legislation and less supportive of defense spending and interventionist foreign policies.[7] Women in Congress were more cohesive and liberal than could be accounted for by party affiliation alone. Before 1970, congresswomen could be identified more readily by party identification than by gender, even on women's issues; but after 1970, they voted more as a bloc and could be identified by their degree of support for feminist issues.[8] A 1977 CAWP study found that female officials at all levels of government were more liberal than male officials.[9] An analysis of congressional voting records between 1972 and 1980 showed that congresswomen were more liberal than congressmen, with the gender gap diminishing over time as congresswomen's votes became less liberal and as differences became negligible among northern Democrats. Congresswomen's greater liberalism was attributed to the fact that female candidates were more likely to be elected from urban than from rural districts; that women in general were more liberal than men on many issues; that women were more likely to be Democrats than Republicans; and that female officials were typically not as careerist as male officials were. Congresswomen were somewhat more likely than congressmen to be elected from districts that were urban, northern, and populated by many foreign-born and black constituents.[10]

Female appointees in the Carter administration expressed more liberal views than their male counterparts on issues such as U.S. military strength, nuclear power, and the ability of the private sector to solve economic problems.[11] The liberalism of female officials in appointive federal posts could be expected to decline in conservative administrations. Indeed, that was the case for women in top posts in the Departments of State and Defense during the Reagan administration. They were few in number, segregated into stereotyped positions, and had no military experience. Given the ideological views of the Reagan administration, it was reasonable to expect that its female appointees would be very conservative.[12]

Legislative Roles: Male Careerism versus Female Public Service

Legislative roles are legislators' expectations of the kind of behavior they ought to exhibit in the course of their duties. Before the advent of the women's movement, political scientists had devised role typologies drawn from male experiences and based on the assumption that careerism was normal. Transformational female-based typologies were based on the assumption that public service was normal. One male-based typology was the broker-ritualist-inventor scheme. The broker enjoyed the give-and-take of conflict and compromise, the ritualist emphasized procedure and routine over the content of bills, and the inventor wanted to solve problems.[13] When Jeane Kirkpatrick applied this typology to the forty-six female state legislators she studied in 1972, she found that the categories were not useful: there were no ritualists and few brokers. Two-thirds of the women were inventors: pragmatic problem solvers. She linked this role to other "public service" orientations of these women: "The 'inventor' role has an obvious and close association with policy interests and with the idea that government is an agency for achievement of the public good. And just as most women in the sample conceive government as a means to achieve the public good, most conceive their roles as a search for new solutions to problems and new paths to progress."[14]

These women's backgrounds and experiences made them less likely to become brokers and more likely to become inventors. Although they had worked in a variety of occupations, few were lawyers, most did not have a strong vocational commitment other than politics, and the financial support of their husbands left most of them free not to work outside the home. By contrast, a survey conducted in the same year of a comparable sample of male legislators showed that most had professional degrees, most were lawyers, and all had been continuously employed. Before they were officeholders, most of the female state legislators had been volunteers, and half of them still belonged to three or more nonpartisan voluntary organizations. Such activity nourished their inventor orientation. In Kirkpatrick's words: "Membership in civic and other 'do-good' organizations rests on two predispositions: a tendency to identify public problems as private concerns, and a tendency to seek solutions through cooperative action."[15] Just as brokerage occupations had prepared men for a broker role in public office, so had volunteerism prepared women for an inventor role in public office.

The absence of women among the ranks of ritualists was likewise linked to women's public service orientation. Knowledge of legislative ritual and rules was an important skill to develop if one sought to become a legislative leader. Though few legislators of either sex desired to become legislative leaders, women were more likely than men to put their time and energy into becoming subject matter experts rather than formal legislative leaders. Women's legislative goals were specific to policy areas: becoming a recognized expert in the field or becoming committee chair. Adopting the role of expert was both a realistic response to male-dominated folkways in the legislative chamber and a genuine reflection of women's problem-solving orientation. Expertise could be attained by personal effort, hard work, and persistence and exercised independently of seniority, the power structure, and the buddy system. And it was a role from which, as Kirkpatrick noted, it was "possible to achieve a limited area of influence on legislative policy without long tenure or broad alliances, and many of these women are interested in having an impact on policy sooner rather than later."[16]

Another typology distinguished between delegate and trustee legislative roles. Delegates, or representatives, relied on the wishes of their constituency or party leadership to instruct them how to vote; trustees, or tribunes, made decisions based on principle and specialized knowledge. Kirkpatrick suggested that this model should be reviewed in light of the experiences of female legislators. About one-third of her sample described their roles chiefly in terms of representation of their district, getting things done for the people back home. Another quarter were tribunes, who saw themselves as representing higher causes and were quite unconcerned about the preferences of their districts, except insofar as they might prevent their reelection. And about half the women saw no conflict between representing their districts and following their consciences:

> To most of these women, the dichotomy between their district's opinion and their personal opinion is unreal. It is, after all, derived from a model that postulates conflict between a gross, short-sighted, self-interested majority and a wise, far-seeing, public-spirited representative. The model assumes that the majority and the representative will have different values or at least significant differences in perspective. Such differences are probably not the rule in democracies, especially at the lower levels of government.[17]

There was a symbiosis between constituency and conscience. According to one legislator, constituents trusted her judgment, and she had a responsibility to explain her behavior to them.

> The first job of a legislator is to represent her constituents. You are there because they chose you and trusted you. It's interesting, everyone who runs for office does a lot of talking about listening and never gets around to doing it. I sincerely believe that a legislator has a moral duty and a political responsibility to reflect the interests and opinions of the people in her district. But that's not as simple as it sounds. I quickly came to see that the

legislature deals with many problems about which my constituents have no opinions, some of which do not pertain to the district at all. And there are some times when I feel the people in my district would have different opinions than they do, if only they knew more about the subject. Being a legislator is tough because you have to balance different considerations. Sometimes they conflict. You have to represent your constituents, and be prepared to explain your behavior to them and answer for it, you have to keep in mind the whole state, and you have to look ahead all the time—because you have a kind of responsibility for the future. Anyway, a representative's first duty is to her district, but that is no problem to me. You have to remember that there are sensible people in my district and I am a lot like them. I don't mean to say that there aren't people with cockeyed ideas and selfish interests in my district, but there aren't too many of them, and they sort of balance each other off.[18]

This legislator's assumptions about the people in her district—that most were sensible and only a few were selfish—was consistent with a public service orientation toward politics, a belief that reasonable people could put aside selfish gain and work for the public good.

Like Kirkpatrick, Marianne Githens tried to fit female legislators into the trustee, delegate, politico model (politicos took on the other two roles simultaneously). In the conventional view, the trustee orientation was seen as the most realistic, sophisticated, and functional from the point of view of effective representation, given the complexity of governmental problems and the difficulty of finding out what constituencies wanted. In Githen's study, Maryland female legislators indicated some preference for trustee and politico roles and perceived these roles as more effective, but they were undoubtedly more difficult and conflicting for women to adopt. Women's backgrounds cast them in the feeling, responsive, and reactive roles of the delegate rather than in the thoughtful, detached, rational ones associated with the trustee specialists with male occupational backgrounds. The delegate category did not fully or adequately convey the role perceptions of the women interviewed, however. They did not exhibit an overwhelming concern to consult with their constituents in order to take action on legislation. Their commitments to legislation for the aged, against child abuse, and the like were too strong to fit the delegate model.[19]

Women in Congress had the same problem-solving orientation that Kirkpatrick detected among female state legislators. In 1976, Joan Hulse

Thompson interviewed congresswomen and found that although their backgrounds increasingly resembled those of congressmen in education, occupation, and political experience, they had different role perceptions. The most common role for both sexes was tribune, but the second most common role for men was ritualist and for women was inventor. Men's increased careerism in the House was expressed through the ritualist role, associated with male use of the party route to power in the chamber; women's increased careerism in the House was expressed through the inventor role, associated with female use of an expertise-based route to power in the chamber. Among the possible reasons for congresswomen's insider role of inventor were that the House climate which closed women off from leadership positions channeled them into the other insider role of inventor; that women had a prior preference for the problem-solving role based on socialization; that liberal, urban districts were more inclined to elect women; or that unconventional, liberal women were more willing to pursue political careers. Thompson said her findings were consistent with those of Kirkpatrick, two-thirds of whose female state legislators were inventors and none of whom were ritualists.[20]

A third typology was used by James D. Barber in his study of the Connecticut legislature: spectators, advertisers, reluctants, and lawmakers. Spectators participate at the margins in the substantive legislative process, advertisers are interested in career self-advancement, reluctants are the most withdrawn from legislative activity, and lawmakers take an active role in passing legislation. Connecticut had a large number of legislators and one of the highest proportions of women among them, about 15 percent, at the time of Barber's study in 1963–64. Most women were spectators: typically middle-aged, low-status homemakers of modest achievements, limited skills, and restricted ambitions, who had little sense of individuality, were other-directed, and were especially sensitive to approval and disapproval.[21] A 1970 study of one-third of all female state legislators nationwide, however, found that they more closely resembled Barber's lawmaker, who was active and had a strong and realistic sense of personal identity and personal and moral standards, self-confidence, high achievement motivation, and a fundamental respect for and empathy with people unlike oneself. Many of the legislatures in this study were in large, industrialized, urban states, where it was much harder to compete for a legislative seat than in Connecticut, because the number of available seats and proportion of women elected were much smaller (less than 5 percent).[22]

In her study of Maryland legislators, Githens also considered Barber's spectator role. Spectators enjoyed watching the spectacle of politics, had modest achievements, and harbored little ambition. Though some of these descriptions applied to the women she studied, the category of spectator was too passive to capture the issue and community interests of women, which Githens described as "their concern with the passage of legislation in the general area of social welfare, their generally positive orientation to equal rights for women and to at least some aspects of women's liberation, their perceptions of sex discrimination, and their view of their role within the legislature and in their own communities which they defined as serving as a role model and as sensitizing others to social concerns."[23]

Alternative Typologies of Women's Legislative Roles

Skeptical about the applicability of male-based typologies, feminist researchers developed alternative schemes to describe women's legislative behavior. Jeane Kirkpatrick developed a new four-fold typology based on the value preferences, goals, and interpersonal styles of the women she interviewed: leader, moralizer, personalizer, and problem solver. The leader valued power, sought an impact on the total process, and had an eclectic style. The personalizer valued affection, sought acceptance and approval, and had an ingratiating style. The moralizer valued rectitude, sought increased righteousness of the political process and output, and had an interpersonal style of ideological affirmation. The problem solver had a "multivalue personality," combining all three of the aforementioned values: power, affection, and rectitude. The problem solver had a goal of community service and a purposive socializing style. Kirkpatrick's personalizer differed from Barber's spectator by a greater commitment to politics as an arena in which satisfactions were sought. The spectator was unwilling to run for reelection, as though preoccupation with interpersonal relations were incompatible with long-range political participation. But the personalizers in Kirkpatrick's sample demonstrated that "just as power can be sought in the family or the church, the search for approval can be carried on in the legislature."[24]

For Kirkpatrick's problem solvers, legislative roles and personalities were linked. Their commitments to family and policy-oriented public service coexisted peacefully. Problem solvers were oriented toward affection, rectitude, and power, but affection was sought in the family, not in the legislature. Rectitude took the form of an internalized demand on the self to serve the community, not the form of a conception of politics as a battleground between the forces of good and evil. Their quest for power was for the purpose of accomplishing legislative goals. Problem solvers focused on the substance of legislation, and the committee was the center of their legislative world. They wanted to become substantive experts and committee chairs. Their interpersonal style was one of purposive socializing, that is, they were friendly, open, reasonably empathetic in relations with others, but their egos were not deeply involved in their reactions to others. Problem solvers aimed at harmonious working relationships that would expedite the achievement of legislative goals.

Kirkpatrick linked women's problem-solving legislative roles to their family and community experiences before entering public office. Men were socialized with the expectation that they would hold remunerative jobs throughout their adult lives. They tended to make a career out of elective office, using the state legislature as a stepping-stone to a more exalted political position, or they tended to be alert to opportunities for enhancing their occupational status or earnings. By contrast, Kirkpatrick's sample of women entered the legislature supported by their husbands, without further career ambitions or hope of financial gain, and untainted by association with special interests. As one legislator put it, "We women supported by our husbands are free to be virtuous."[25] Traditional roles encouraged men to exploit legislative office for careerist goals and predisposed women to take a disinterested view of the clash of economic interests, to see politics as public service.

Another important study that developed a typology of female state legislators was Irene Diamond's *Sex Roles in the State House*. In 1971, Diamond sent questionnaires to all female and selected male state legislators in Connecticut, Maine, New Hampshire, and Vermont, states where there was little competition for seats and a high proportion of female members. At that time, female legislators were most numerous in states where the office was viewed as less desirable by men, was poorly paid, and was less professional. The more competitive the offices were, the more similar the state legislative career patterns of men and women.

Diamond's typology was derived from the interaction of self-image and attitude toward women's role in society: housewife-benchwarmer, traditional civic worker, women's rights advocate, and passive women's rights advocate. Each type had a distinctive pattern of recruitment, commitment to politics, mode of legislative activity, and perception of sex-role salience. The housewife-benchwarmer was typically plagued by self-doubt and comfortable with women's role in society. She was recruited for the legislature only where competition for legislative seats was practically nonexistent. Once in the legislature she did not become involved in the center of the legislative process, nor did she experience a conflict between being a woman and a legislator. The housewife-benchwarmer acted in much the same way as Barber's spectator.

The traditional civic worker had a positive self-image and a favorable view of women's role in society but was receptive to some of the moderate ideas of the women's movement. Compared to the housewife-benchwarmer, she was better educated and more affluent, a background likely to expose her to contemporary ideas. She did not question her basic lifestyle, which in terms of commitment to children and family did not differ appreciably from that of the housewife-benchwarmer. The traditional civic worker was enthusiastic about running for the legislature because she was confident about her abilities and saw the legislative job as an opportunity to continue her involvement in substantive issues in her community. Her commitment was not to the game of politics but to the broader issues of government. She had progressive political ambitions only if she felt that she could be more effective in higher office and that her family situation allowed for such ambitions. Once she entered the legislature, the traditional civic worker became involved in the substantive legislative process. Like Barber's lawmaker, the traditional civic worker was especially concerned with producing laws and acting constructively. She spoke out, bargained, negotiated, and wanted to be treated as a competent individual, not with any special courtesies because she was a woman. Although the traditional civic worker did not feel any particular responsibility to represent the interests of women, rarely did she work in opposition to feminist issues (the abortion issue was an exception). She was particularly interested in seeing more women enter public office: women were thought to be higher-caliber politicians, less self-interested, more conscientious and hardworking, much harder for political machines to push around, and more likely to have already proved themselves than men.

The women's rights advocate had a positive self-image and wanted considerable change in women's role in society. She was willing to assert herself in matters she deemed important; the word "fight" was used more frequently by her than by any of the other types. The motivation to wage battles stemmed not from love of the fray but from a deep concern with public issues. Like the traditional civic worker, she had a basic concern for issues derived from community involvement and wanted to extend this involvement to the governmental realm. Unlike the civic worker, however, the advocate was devoted to a professional career. The civic worker, if she was financially advantaged, might have expended considerable time and energy on her volunteer role, but her basic identity was not derived from it and at no time did she make any long-term psychic commitment to politics. The advocate, in contrast, derived a basic part of her identity from her public affairs activities and was willing to make such long-term commitments. She always listed as her occupation the professional job she held before entering the legislature.

Because of her less exclusive commitment to family roles, the advocate typically entered elective office at an earlier age than the civic worker. Thus age was not a limiting factor for the advocate's political ambitions. Similarly, the advocate was not likely to be deterred by the lack of opportunity afforded women seeking public office: she would try to change the opportunity structure in politics, as she probably had done in her professional career already. And she was likely to have links to women's activist groups outside the legislature, which provided the emotional and organizational support to effect such changes.

As with the traditional civic worker, the women's rights advocate's positive self-image and concern with issues translated into active participation in the substantive legislative process. Unlike the civic worker, however, the advocate developed interests in women's issues and made different sorts of demands on her male colleagues: she felt a responsibility to represent the interests of women, took a leadership role in generating feminist issues in the legislature, worked with feminist groups in developing legislation to improve the status of women, and led organizational efforts within the legislature to enhance the power of female legislators. When it came to disparities between the sexes, she was likely to react with righteous indignation and to attempt collective solutions. The advocate took considerable pride in awakening the consciousness of both her female and male colleagues, and she experienced the most conflict between traditional feminine role expectations and professional expectations.

Diamond's fourth type of female legislator was the passive women's rights advocate, who had a negative self-image and a negative attitude toward women's role in society. She became a candidate at the urging of others. Although she did not approach political office with the trepidation of the housewife-benchwarmer, she did not share the self-confidence of the traditional civic worker and the women's rights advocate. She neither continually pointed to her legislative accomplishments nor reacted passively to the legislative environment, for, like the advocate, she was concerned about legislative practices that reflected society's valuation of women. Lacking the advocate's self-confidence, she did not exercise leadership in women's issues, even though she was intensely interested in them.

Diamond linked these four types of female legislators to the question of the representation of the interests of women in state legislatures. She determined that the political consequences of having women in legislatures depended not so much on the numbers of women as on the types of women. Each role type was associated with a particular conception of what the interests of women were. Diamond drew on Hanna Pitkin's distinction between descriptive representation (the extent to which representatives reflected the social characteristics of those they formally represented) and substantive representation (the activity of representatives on behalf of or in the interests of others).[26] New Hampshire had, since the 1930s, led the nation in the numbers of women in its state legislature, thus constituting the best case study to date of a state legislature's descriptive representation of women. Yet there appeared to be little substantive representation of women's interests in the New Hampshire legislature, where the typical female legislator did not see herself as acting for women. The two types that predominated were the housewife-benchwarmer and the traditional civic worker. The housewife-benchwarmer, so common because of the nonselectivity of the recruitment process, was by and large incapable of acting for any interest. The traditional civic worker could achieve some degree of influence, but her values did not lead to an orientation conducive to acting for women. The impetus for innovations, such as the idea of an informal women's caucus in the legislature, came from outside the state. In both Connecticut and New York, there was considerably more activity with regard to the representation of women's interests. This similarity existed despite the fact that Connecticut had a high percentage of female legislators and New York had only a handful. In both states, the activity of the women's rights advocates in the legislature, in conjunction with the activity of women's activist groups outside the legislature, seemed to have had some impact on the orientation of all legislators, female and male.

Female Officials and the Male Culture of Public Office

For many female officials, entering public office meant confronting a distinctive, and often alien and hostile, male culture. Many women subscribed to the moralist, as opposed to a marketplace, conception of the political world. In marketplace theory, the polity is comprised of self-interested competing individuals, politics is an arena of competition, and government is both the prize and the regulator of politics. Political parties are alliances of interests, whose goal is to control offices and remain in power. Politics is the arena in which conflicts of interest are compromised, where "problems" are a matter of who got what, when, and how.

Politicians are professionals, specializing in the representation of interests and expecting to benefit their personal interests in the process.
Compromise is the key political skill, and the broker is the chief political role. By contrast, the moralist conception of the political world rests
on the assumption that politics is a means for coming to grips with the
issues and concerns of civil society, a matter of concern to every citizen,
not just professionals. Political parties are associations of people united
in the pursuit of a common vision of the public good. Politics is a means
of communicating to others one's serious purposes, and politicians are
moved by a sense of civic duty and readiness to serve.[27]

The women in Kirkpatrick's study were overwhelmingly inclined to
the moralist conception of politics, where conflict was not an important
dimension. Politics was not a jungle in which each was pitted against all,
nor was it a zero sum game in which one person's advantage was another's disadvantage.

> In fact, there is almost nothing of the "game" model of politics
> with its teams, alliances, strategies, victories and losses. Almost
> completely missing, too, is that tamer "marketplace" or "plural-
> ist" version of conflict-based politics in which government serves
> as broker among competing and conflicting interests. None of
> these women thinks of government as principally concerned
> with compromising or policing. All describe government in
> terms of solving problems and achieving progress. . . . They dis-
> play a tendency to conceive problems as technical rather than as
> political or moral, and to conceive their solutions more as a mat-
> ter of fact-gathering and consultation than of moral or partisan
> struggle. Government, for most, is one instrument among oth-
> ers through which good citizens can seek to improve the quality
> of life. Their conception of government is the public service
> conception; it is consistent with civic work, with shared pur-
> poses, with common needs rather than individual goals. The
> pursuit of the public good is its central purpose.[28]

Women's political culture was often at odds with the male political
culture of legislatures, which resembled, in Kirkpatrick's words, "the ma-
cho culture of the locker room, the smoker, the barracks. . . . Among the
folkways of state legislatures none appears to be more widely shared than
the tradition of the masculine legislature." There was a pervasive initial
reluctance in many male legislators to take women seriously as colleagues. Female state legislators experienced four types of symbolic put-

downs: excluded by linguistic conventions ("men of the house") and "male only" jokes and profanity; killed with kindness (exaggerated courtesy, public flirtation, terms such as "sweetheart" or "darling of the house"); treated as having limited and specialized interests (excluding them from much of the business and discussion in the house); and put in "their place" by insulting remarks.[29]

Congresswomen also experienced these four forms of put-downs. When men got together in a predominantly male legislative setting, a friendship or camaraderie developed based on common purposes, as well as on other shared "male interests." If and when women entered the environment, they were considered intruders or outsiders, to be ignored, treated with dismissive courtesy, or treated with contempt and derision. Women were not and could never really be "one of the boys." As one male member put it: "Friendships bind men together in a way that women do not experience. There is a bonding, a male bonding that does it. The language we use, the drinking we do, make it very difficult for women to enter this world." One female member described a line between getting accepted by men and being one of the boys, a line she had no interest in crossing, even though it meant not being part of the process in the House.[30]

Some congressmembers and staffers attributed the maleness of the House to the behavior of female members which called attention to their minority status as women, thereby reinforcing the belief that "maleness" was the norm. Some of these respondents said women overcompensated for what they perceived to be weaknesses associated with gender, lest constituents see them as soft, unassertive, and politically ineffectual. Some women defined themselves as mavericks who were ideologically inflexible, indifferent to House norms, and unwilling to compromise. And a few male respondents, but no female members, noted that some of the women demonstrated an "unfortunate tendency" to identify themselves as "women" and to become too intimately associated with "so-called women's issues." This propensity diminished their standing in the eyes of some male members and jeopardized the potential influence of other women who became too closely linked to these feminists. As one congressman put it: "You don't see men defining themselves consciously as men. And this permits us to concentrate on other, more important, things."[31]

Congresswomen and female staff agreed that congresswomen were much better off than their female predecessors and that they were working with a new and more sensitive breed of congressmen. Before World War II, according to Irwin Gertzog, women in Congress "were seen as amateurs and curiosities, rather than as authentic public figures, by reporters, male colleagues, and government officials. The press was probably the principal purveyor of this unfortunate image, . . . [using] different criteria to explain and evaluate both the presence and the performance of females in a field for which women were expected to have little competence."[32]

Stories were legion about the treatment of women during their early years in Congress. Congresswomen were denied access to the House floor or to elevators because they were "reserved for members." Women who were not members were often inadvertently permitted onto the floor because men guarding the doors were so uncertain about who the congresswomen were. In 1925, House leaders permitted a woman to preside over the chamber for the first time. They selected a woman who had been a strong opponent of the Nineteenth Amendment and chose a time when a roll call vote on a trivial matter was under way, so the temporary "Speaker" was unable to exercise any of the powers accompanying that position. In 1938, President Franklin Roosevelt held a three day retreat for congressional Democrats at a Maryland island club that barred women, and six female Democrats were unable to attend the gathering, in spite of their voting record in support of New Deal legislation. In a 1947 speech on the House floor, Representative Charles Gifford expressed anxiety about the future of Congress, lest it had too many women, who talked "with their eyes" and presented men "an apple it is most difficult to refuse. Even old Adam could not resist." He said he admired women so much that he could not resist supporting any measure a woman proposed, "especially if she looked at me as such a woman can."[33]

The first scholar to take a systematic look at the policy preferences and political styles of women in Congress was Frieda L. Gehlen. In 1962, she interviewed all eleven women and twenty of the men serving in the House. Congresswomen were excluded from informal men's groups. Although they tended to deny the importance of such ties, congressmen did not. One woman who had served in Congress for twenty years had never even heard of the Board of Education, an informal daily gathering where the Speaker and his chosen associates went over the day's session and planned future strategy. The title came from the Speaker's interest in inviting new (male) members to teach them House lore and to learn from their reactions and attitudes. Many congressmen felt that congresswomen probably enjoyed advantages that offset the disadvantages of being excluded from informal men's groups. They thought that women could form, or had already formed, their own group. In fact, women seemed to Gehlen deliberately to shun the idea of being considered a bloc. As a general rule, the congresswomen who were most accepted by congressmen were rational, intelligent, articulate, and not too prudish. As for formal positions in the House, women automatically became chairs by seniority, and their effectiveness as chairs was a function of their individual personalities. They seemed to be categorically eliminated from consideration as party floor leaders, however, chiefly for lack of informal relationships, without which one could not be an effective party leader, and also because some congressmen saw women as too subjective and emotional and too tenacious and idealistic.[34]

Gehlen observed that cultural norms served to women's advantage when it came to casework and reelection. Women were more apt than men to spend a great deal of time solving problems individual constituents had with government bureaucracies. Perhaps congresswomen found the time because they were less included in informal and leadership groups. It was also a culturally legitimate female role to show concern for people and their problems. "More than half the women made some reference to the satisfaction they got from their case work as one of the basic rewards for staying in the position. Not one of the twenty men queried about the rewards of the job even hinted that case work would be one of them."[35]

Beginning in the mid-1960s, self-proclaimed feminists began to appear in the House: Patsy Mink (1965), Margaret Heckler (1967), Shirley Chisholm (1969), Bella Abzug (1971), Yvonne Brathwaite Burke, Elizabeth Holtzman, and Pat Schroeder (1973), Martha Keys and Gladys Spellman (1975), and Barbara Mikulski and Mary Rose Okar (1977). By the late 1970s, open male condescension had diminished, fewer congressmen consciously attempted to patronize female members, and the legislative achievements of several women made it impossible for women to be collectively ignored or dismissed.

The mid-1970s marked an important time of transition for women in Congress. Formally, they were receiving better treatment, but informally, they were increasingly feared and resented. The more they articulated the concerns of women as a group, the less they were seen as individual oddities who could be patronized and excluded and the more they posed a threat as a bloc. Recognized as representatives of their sex, congresswomen said they had an impact out of proportion to their numbers. The Congresswomen's Caucus, formed in 1977, provided a vehicle for unity among women, enabling them to maximize their power in the House. The tiny proportion of women in Congress (5 percent) contributed to their sense of responsibility to represent women. When congresswomen were asked whether they "have a special responsibility to represent not only their constituents, but also the women of the nation as a whole," three-quarters of the replies were positive, with most expressing strong agreement. Several staff members said the extent to which women were able to fit into the informal, personal networks of the Hill was a function of their age and personality. Younger women entered Congress with painful awareness of sex discrimination, and many men in Congress felt that these women's "bitterness" threatened informal relations. Male stereotypes about women's emotional, irrational reactions to problems jeopardized relationships within congressional work groups. Congresswomen had to prove that they were logical, practical decision makers in order to be trusted by their male colleagues. An inventor role was congruent both with a perceived need to prove oneself as a problem solver and with a desire to solve problems related to sex discrimination. Thus, the small number of women in Congress in 1976 had a special impact on the House because congresswomen tended to identify their role as representatives of women and as liberal policy innovators.[36]

As for women in state legislatures, during the 1960s and 1970s they reported negative stereotypes and various forms of exclusion: women were seen as incompetent, frivolous, unseemly, helpless, and muddled; politics was considered a man's domain, and woman's place was in the home; women who were different were resented; women were not fully accepted by men's political organizations; men wanted women to campaign for them but not compete with them for public office; and women were excluded from party policy decisions. Because of social customs, it was hard to drop in at the local tavern to catch up on political gossip or to join poker games and stag parties, where a great deal of informal political discussion occurred. Women had to be exceptionally worthy and work harder than men.[37] They felt marginalized: tracked onto committees more on the basis of their sex than on the basis of prior expertise, disproportionately consulted by public service and voluntary groups and not by powerful lobbies, and holding fewer leadership positions than their tenure would warrant.[38]

Male and Female Definitions of Legislative Success

Given the "men's club" atmosphere of most governing bodies and the token status of most women, how should one measure their success in public office? According to male models, success was typically measured by effectiveness in passing desired legislation. This was certainly an important indicator of success for women as well. One study of congresswomen's legislative effectiveness found that it was greater than congressmen's. Though congresswomen introduced fewer bills, a larger proportion of their bills were reported out of committee and eventually passed by the House. Sex differences in the rate of passage of bills were greater than differences by party or tenure in office. And there was no sex difference in the amount of federal funds spent in congressional districts.[39]

But success from the point of view of women's experiences also included a diminution of problematic male attitudes, behavior, and norms and an increase in colleagues' sensitivity to the needs and interests of women. Male officials entered what for them was a "normal" (all-male) environment, and many of them resented attempts by women to render it problematic. Men did not need to define themselves as men in institutions that prescribed orientations and patterns of behavior that men had already internalized. Female officials did not feel "normal" in male-dominated public offices, because there were so few of them, because of the way they were treated by men, or because of the informal "men's club" norms of the institution.

Consider the case of women who constituted about 10 percent of the Arkansas and Texas state legislatures, which were male-dominated, low in professionalism, and rife with powerful lobbyists, personal relationships, and an old boys' network. According to legislators and lobbyists, female legislators were not as effective as male legislators. Female legislators' effectiveness increased as they obtained more staff, which was more important to them than to men because they were more issue-oriented and less likely to be in leadership positions with alternative resources. In addition, informal bonds developed among female staff, female lobbyists, and female legislators, largely in response to the inhospitable environment in which they found themselves. Female legislators in both states avoided formal caucuses, for different reasons. Arkansas women did not form a formal caucus because of the suspicions of their male colleagues. They took pains to avoid denigrating one another, however, and often rallied around a female colleague whom they felt was unfairly treated. They even voted down a measure because its sponsor repeatedly used sexist language on the floor. The formation of a bipartisan caucus in Texas was inhibited by a growing Republican party, which actively recruited and generously funded women who toed the party line, and by the legislature's ideological conservatism. Texas women engaged in informal networking and tacitly agreed to avoid "cutting each other up" on the floor. As commonly found elsewhere, women in both legislatures said they had to work harder, be more prepared, and do more homework than their male counterparts. Men tended to pass a lot of bills crafted by others (especially business interests), whereas women often

came up with bills for friends or constituents or to change an unjust situation. Women opted out of the traditional power circles of the "big
money guys" and "the bond daddies." Although women in the Texas and
Arkansas legislatures were not seen as effective by male criteria, they
brought about change in some issues, but not in the "power issues." And
effectiveness had to be measured in the traditional context in which
these women found themselves.[40]

One problem with using a male model to measure women's legislative success was that it presupposed that politics was a bargaining process
or a strategic game in which individuals participated in coalitions and
had clout to enforce agreed on bargains. As Marianne Githens pointed
out, in this model the support of female officials was generally not seen
as critical to the success of an overall legislative program. Their numbers
were too few; they were not represented in legislative and party leadership positions; and they were viewed by men as less than serious, hard-
nosed, professional politicians and as representing a distinctive but pe-
ripheral set of concerns, such as women's rights and social welfare.
"Given the absence of these preconditions for successful pragmatic bargaining, it is no wonder that the application of existing measures for determining power and evaluations of their performance based on such
measures have found women wanting."[41]

In Maryland, male legislators, using their own experiences to judge
the effectiveness of female legislators, saw lawyers and businessmen as
the most competent and well-qualified members of the legislature. Since
women entered the legislature later in life and with less specialized training, they needed longer apprenticeships to prove their worth. Their low
status often forced them into the dysfunctional role of the charismatic
agitator, who spoke out for justice for the aged, women, and children.
Women's compensatory efforts to gain expertise in the legislature, coupled with their community outreach and education, were seen by men
as indicators of women's ineffectiveness and inefficiency. Max Weber's
distinction between charismatic and bureaucratic authority was relevant
here. Charismatic political leaders, like political priests, exhort follow-
ers, whereas bureaucratic political leaders base their authority on expertise. The bureaucratic role model was virtually foreclosed to women
in the Maryland legislature because of skill differential problems, but
women adopted a charismatic role in the form of an inspired cry for justice for at least the aged, women, and children. It was important to these
women to agitate for these issues and to go back to their communities to
educate them and to serve as role models.[42]

The criteria used by female officials to measure their success and in-

fluence formed an alternative model for judging legislative performance. For example, many female state legislators saw themselves as
both influential and successful for having made it into the political elite
rather than because of traditional notions of effectiveness and power,
such as legislative and party leadership positions. In addition, there was
evidence that men and women had different power styles. The male
power style was task-oriented, analytical, direct, action-oriented, and
based on abstracting common elements out of changing situations. The
female power style was generalist, contextual, self- and people-oriented,
indirect, and based on resolving many types of demands at the same
time. Male power styles may have been deemed "successful" more because men did them than because they produced results.[43]

And, of course, feminists often sought results that were not important to their male colleagues. For Bella Abzug, for example, an important legislative result was changing her colleagues' resistance to taking
women and their concerns seriously. By conventional measures, she did
not rank very high in legislative effectiveness. Although most of the time
she was a diligent, intelligent House member who did her homework,
had a good attendance record, and showed skill in getting anti–sex discrimination provisions added to House bills, she had strained relations
with House leaders and potential allies; she was seen as a "showhorse"
who appealed to a national constituency instead of a workhorse who respected House norms; and she was ridiculed and condemned by those
who objected to her outspoken feminism. As Irwin Gertzog said: "For
those who believed in her causes she was a dynamic, courageous, ora-
torically gifted and effective leader. For those who did not, she gained a
reputation in Washington as an abrasive, uncompromising, irresponsible, unpleasant, and fanatical woman whose support could be the kiss of
death, whose behavior was subversive, and whose image was a source of
ridicule." How should one measure the effectiveness of a legislator who
pushed the boundaries of the feminist agenda so that the views of other
feminists appeared tame and acceptable by comparison? Gertzog continued, "Abzug's forceful advocacy of women's rights and women's needs,
and the frames of reference she imposed on them paved the way for
House acceptance of the very same perspectives when offered in a manner that House members found less offensive."[44] This form of effectiveness was missing in male-based models of legislative performance.

At the other extreme, for those female officials who were not interested in claiming credit for their work, it was misleading to use legislative output as a measure of effectiveness. In many state legislatures, ag-
gressiveness and exhibitionism were unacceptable in both women and

men, but in women such behaviors were judged with special harshness. Kirkpatrick commented: "Several of the most influential women refer to their practice of not claiming credit for all the bills they in fact work out and introduce. 'I care not,' said one, 'who, in the house, gets credit for the passage of legislation in which I am interested,' and added, 'I feel that as a woman I don't have to be out on the front line. Credit can go to others. What matters is getting the legislation through.' "[45] Gender roles prescribed men to take credit and women to enable men to take credit. And women's preparation for elective office in civic organizations involved a track record of studying issues behind the scenes to reach consensus rather than calling attention to oneself as a partisan ready to do battle on a controversial issue.[46]

Irene Diamond cautioned that interpretations of self-report data on influencing committee deliberations had to take into account sex-role socialization. Despite female state legislators' greater participation in committee deliberations, they did not say they influenced committee deliberations as frequently as men did. The disparity between speaking and influence may well have been accurate reporting: men held more positions of legislative authority and had somewhat greater policy expertise, both of which were sources of influence. Moreover, conventional sex roles led females to accede and males to dominate in verbal interactions. But it was also possible that women's self-effacing attitudes engendered by traditional sex-role socialization distorted the actual situation.[47]

Female officials consistently reported that they were better prepared and had done their homework before meetings, spent more time doing their jobs, and had to work harder to prove themselves.[48] Given their public service experiences and legislative role orientation, female officials were more likely than male officials to evaluate their power and success in terms of changing a hostile male culture, getting results instead of credit, and doing homework. By contrast, male models of legislative power and success emphasized legislative output and leadership posts.

Transformational Feminist Analyses of Women's Political Culture

In order to understand the subtle differences between what men and women did in public office, transformational feminists argued that political science had to expand its methodological net. As Lyn Kathlene put it, conventional methods were unsuitable for capturing subtle differences in the thinking of public officials, such as which issues should or should not be addressed by public policy, whose opinions and expertise should be sought, and how one balanced protection of personal privacy and public concern for social welfare. She called for a contextual gender analysis of differential reasoning processes and attitudinal orientations arising from sex-role socialization. Political science needed a careful study of language to reveal the cultural differences between the sexes.[49]

Accordingly, Kathlene used an unconventional method to study the attitudes of members of the Colorado House of Representatives in 1985. She conducted a linguistic analysis to determine the extent to which legislators adhered to two attitudinal constructs: male instrumentalism and female contextualism. These constructs described different policy approaches related to gender, derived from the theories of Nancy Chodorow, Carol Gilligan, and Nel Noddings,[50] and they were operationalized through a variant of discourse analysis used in sociolinguistics. Kathlene asked respondents various questions about integrating their personal and professional experiences, about their current interests and activities in the legislature, and about a local policy problem on underweight newborn babies. She subjected responses to two types of analysis: a textual interpretation of the policy problem and a concordance analysis, which determined the number of times words were used, words in context, and words by speaker. These analyses revealed that the same words had different meanings for male and female legislators, depending on the context. Men were less likely to see underweight babies as a policy problem; women compared new problems to their personal experiences, whereas men saw new problems in terms of stereotypes; women used more nouns, whereas men used more political terms, to describe people; men were more likely to adopt a business viewpoint; women used more sources for legislation; and women were more likely to see themselves as part of a process and still learning.[51]

Female Colorado state legislators were more likely to think contextually, and male legislators were more likely to think instrumentally. In the instrumentalist world view, society was composed of autonomous individuals, separated and different from others. Human interactions were contractual arrangements of individuals who sought positions on a ladder of hierarchy. Problems were approached through logical systems of reasoning, applying rules and laws to make order out of the world. "Objective" sources of information were more highly valued than "subjective" ones. Universal principles created fairness, and all individuals were treated equally. Political elites with instrumental orientations defined their public role as protectors of constituents' rights, bounded by a duty to be fair. Problems were often framed in terms of rights, especially privacy rights, and of avoiding government infringement of individual liberties. By contrast, in the contextualist world view, people were

part of a community, affiliated with and related to one another, helping
and pleasing others. Problems were addressed by anticipating, interpreting, and responding to people's needs, while considering the consequences of one's actions or inaction. There were no obvious boundaries between the public and private spheres of one's existence. Problems
were as likely to be attributed to social failing as to individual fault, and
there was an attempt to address a problem at the root rather than respond to its symptoms. The use of "subjective" knowledge reflected unrecognized or underrepresented views of reality; "objective" knowledge,
which was not impersonal or value free, was useful but not superior to
personal or individuals' experiences. Solutions to problems were often
tentative, concrete, and open to revision.[52]

Using another nonconventional approach, transcript analysis, Kathlene examined the conversational dynamics of six legislative committee
hearings on women's issues in the Colorado legislature. She found highly
significant sex differences and no major differences based on party, age,
or length of time in office. Women's voices were notably muted even when
the bill's sponsor or the committee's chair was a woman, but male dominance of discussions declined in relation to the proportion of female legislators at the hearing. When women constituted more than half the committee, there was no sex difference in the amount of time people spoke.
Kathlene argued that until women made up a majority on a decision-
making body, rather than the oft-cited "critical mass" of 35 percent,
women's power and influence might be undermined or at least relegated
to behind-the-scenes negotiations. In any case, Kathlene maintained that
the assumption that women in elective office would be able effectively to
speak for women ignored the social dynamics that subordinated women's
words and actions in male-female interactions.[53]

In another nonconventional study of Colorado legislators, the authors interviewed House members and followed bills through the legislative process, audiotaping hearings and floor debates. They found that
gender had more of an impact on policymaking than did party, age, or
tenure (there were too few people of color to test for the effects of race).
Men were somewhat more likely to sponsor business legislation and
women somewhat more likely to sponsor health care measures. Women
and men were equally successful in getting laws passed. Measures introduced by women were treated differently in committee: they were assigned to more committees, subjected to longer discussion, and received
more hostile testimony. Women's bills were treated differently because
they were more innovative, had a greater fiscal impact, and used less conventional and politically acceptable problem-solving methods. Women's

innovative bills were more likely than those of men to address issues of education or the family and children. If their innovative ideas were not readily accepted, women pursued them for several years. Women were more likely than men to reintroduce bills, which was seen by women not as representing failure but rather as necessary to acquaint people with new ideas and to build coalitions. Women "believed in an issue"; men did not feel "married to a bill," but "had an interest" in a bill. For men, being emotionally involved in legislation was seen as likely to harm political judgment, and they adopted a more detached stance from their work. Other gender differences reflected differences between the instrumental and contextual models of the role of government. For example, women more often proposed spending money for direct services to help people rather than for government commissions and regulatory bodies, and women designed bills using government agencies directly, whereas men were more apt to use government indirectly.[54]

Susan E. Clarke and Lyn Kathlene summarized the various gender differences they had observed among Colorado legislators. In gathering information, women were connected to a wider range of people and groups; men were less active and used traditional sources. In framing crime policy problems, gender differences were greater than party differences: women adopted a social, relational, long-term, nonincremental view, whereas men emphasized individual responsibility and discrete events to be punished. Women sponsored as many bills as men, with the rate of sponsorship a function of term. First-term women sponsored fewer bills than first-term men did, but seasoned women sponsored more bills than did seasoned men, who had moved on to leadership positions, a process that was assumed to be typical but was in fact male. Women had to spend more time in office than men did to attain leadership posts. There were differences in political style: female committee chairs used their position to facilitate committee interaction, whereas male chairs controlled and directed debate. Women's bills were more likely to be innovative, long-term, and comprehensive; men's, modifications and updates. Women were more likely to assume a willing target population, whereas men tended to assume the need for incentives to coerce the target population. Clarke and Kathlene argued that they were able to notice such differences because they conducted an engendered policy analysis. They rejected essentialist assumptions about women's interests, values, or agenda. Rather, they argued that women's life experiences made them more likely to be contextualists than instrumentalists. Women's distinctive political and policymaking styles meant that their effectiveness was often blunted by instrumental institutional features in legislatures and overlooked by conventional policy analysts insensitive to gender concerns.[55]

Female versus Feminist Consciousness and Behavior

Feminist scholarship also altered the study of public officials by systematically asking, for the first time, whether female officials exhibited a female or feminist consciousness. Most women did not run for or serve in public office as self-described feminists. Especially in the early 1970s, many female officials sought to distance themselves from the women's liberation movement. At the same time, however, they expressed a female consciousness, a sense that being a woman had political import, whether in the form of coping with discrimination from voters and colleagues, feeling a special obligation to represent women, recognizing women's interests in legislation, advocating women's rights and interests, expanding the agenda to include women's issues, hiring and appointing women, or meeting informally with women to discuss common concerns. All these things were done by female officials who had no intention of calling themselves feminists. Although there were some antifeminist women in public office, the vast majority dwelt in that ambiguous land somewhere between the fixed poles of female and feminist consciousness, a terrain populated by "closet feminists."

Margaret Chase Smith, the first woman to be elected to both chambers of Congress and to seek a major party nomination for the presidency, is an interesting case in point. In the speech announcing her candidacy, she challenged the notion that women's place was in the home. In the pre–World War II period, no female House member had publicly identified with the Equal Rights Amendment. In 1945, Smith and her colleague Edith Nourse Rogers became the first female House members to cosponsor the Equal Rights Amendment. While in the Senate, Smith supported the Equal Pay Act of 1963 and the Civil Rights Act of 1964. She wanted to be regarded as a neutral professional and actively sought influence in policy areas traditionally viewed as beyond the competence of women. She fashioned an image as a frugal, defense-minded member of the Naval Affairs and Armed Services Committees. And she rejected the label of feminist.[56] How should one evaluate Smith's legislative record along antifeminist, female consciousness and feminist consciousness lines? Her actions made her a role model for other women whether she consciously sought this effect or not: Smith was a self-proclaimed antifeminist who did feminist things.

An example of a woman in Congress at this time whose female consciousness translated into feminist behavior was Edith Green, a Democrat from Oregon who served in the House from 1955 to 1975. She never explicitly identified herself as a feminist; rather, she came to Congress as an expert in education, a traditionally female field. Few women had served longer in Congress or played a more influential role in committee. For years, she chaired Education and Labor's subcommittee on higher education, serving as sponsor and floor manager of many important education laws. In spite of these accomplishments, she said women were not welcome in top leadership posts.[57]

Green cited as one of her three most important legislative accomplishments the Equal Pay Act of 1963, saying, "To get it passed took eight years, . . . eight years to persuade Congress that a woman doing identical work with a man ought to be paid the same salary!"[58] She also helped Martha Griffiths, a Michigan Democrat, get the Equal Rights Amendment out of the House Judiciary Committee. And she worked on the groundbreaking Title IX of the 1972 Educational Amendments to the Higher Education Act, a provision that outlawed sex discrimination in education. Despite the fact that her legislative behavior was responsive to inequities women experienced and that she believed her House career had suffered because of discrimination by male colleagues, Green had no desire to join a women's caucus in the House. She felt that a women's group in the House would do more to call attention to social and political divisions within the country than it would to ameliorate those divisions.[59] Given her reading of male opposition in the House, she had good reason to believe that it was strategically a mistake to call attention to women as a group. For example, the passage of Title IX came about not because of pressure from feminist groups but because of her efforts in the House. When she introduced the measure, she requested that women's groups *not* testify on behalf of it, "because she believed that if members of Congress were not aware of what was included in Title IX, they would simply vote for it without paying too much attention to its contents or its ultimate implications. Women's organizations complied with Representative Green's request and they stayed away from the hearings."[60]

The case of Edith Green illustrates how a female consciousness (recognizing and acting to counter discrimination against women) translated into some forms of feminist legislative activity (the ERA, Equal Pay Act, and Title IX) but not others (calling attention to women as a group in the House). Her behavior was an understandable response to the male-dominated institutional setting in which she operated quite effectively. As a nonfeminist, she accomplished many important feminist goals. In the early 1970s, the institutional and role orientations of senior women in Congress, such as Edith Green, Leonor Sullivan, and Julia Butler Hansen, contrasted sharply with the orientations of younger women, especially Bella Abzug. The establishment of the Congressional Women's Caucus was delayed until after these three senior women had left the House. And, ironically, the formation of a viable Women's Caucus had to wait until after feminist Bella Abzug had left the House as well.

There were three reasons why it took congresswomen so long to create a specialized caucus to draw attention to women's concerns: resistance from a few veteran congresswomen, questions about the legitimacy of such a group in the House, and the belief that association with a group whose most visible member was Bella Abzug would be a political liability, both in the House and at reelection time.[61] When Congresswoman Pat Schroeder came to the House in 1973, she was surprised to find that female members did not meet regularly to discuss the status of women, given the ease with which other caucuses in the House had been formed and the extent to which women's caucuses had been thriving in state and local government. Republican Margaret Heckler and Democrat Abzug had tried unsuccessfully to organize a women's caucus. It was not until 1977 that Heckler and Democrats Elizabeth Holtzman and Shirley Chisholm of New York and Barbara Mikulski of Maryland were able to get the caucus off the ground. These women were more pragmatic "insiders" than Abzug was. Yet, as noted earlier, Abzug played an important role raising issues that seemed tame and acceptable by the time other women raised them; she expanded the congressional agenda but delayed the formation of a Women's Caucus with which to advance that agenda. Thus, an assessment of Abzug's feminist legacy in Congress must take both effects into account.

The early days of the women's movement was a time of what Jo Freeman called "woodwork feminists" on Capitol Hill. Before the establishment of a formal Women's Caucus, congresswomen had formed an "incipient policy network" around the ERA and education legislation. This network made it easier to know who to approach for what kinds of support and for information on other women's bills. When Congress passed the ERA in 1972, women's rights legislation had already achieved its greatest success in the area of education. This success was due in part to the widely accepted value of equal educational opportunities in the United States and in part to the presence of both woodwork and self-described feminists on the House Education and Labor Committee: Edith Green, Shirley Chisholm, Patsy Mink (D-Hawaii), and Ella Grasso (D-Conn.). A symbiotic relationship developed between women interested in education and those interested in women's rights. Green acted as a broker, providing information to feminist organizations and individuals who could afford to testify publicly. She relied heavily on WEAL's numerous contacts with academic women for data and testimony for her education bills. And leaders of BPW, who in 1966 had disdained activity that might be labeled "feminist," found themselves lobbying actively for all the women's legislation in the Ninety-second Congress (1971–72) and urging their members to apply pressure in their home districts. The acceptability of NOW and WEAL was increased by media coverage of other women's groups seen as radical or revolutionary. As Freeman noted: "The latter groups provided a 'radical flank' against which other feminist organizations and individuals could appear respectable. Without the more flamboyant and/or extremist groups, organizations like NOW and WEAL would have been open to being dismissed as too far out."[62]

In the early 1970s, there were closet or woodwork feminists in state legislatures as well, women who took a dim view of the women's liberation movement but supported the Equal Rights Amendment and other measures to improve the status of women. Most of the female state legislators in Kirkpatrick's 1972 study opposed the women's movement, saying that it made exaggerated claims about the exploitation of women, that it was hostile to marriage and the family, that it was extremist in its criticisms and proposals, and that it was partisan and sectarian (Democratic and pro–George McGovern). Some said the women's movement had made it harder for women to be elected to office. The extremism and irresponsibility of some feminist organizations and individuals created a guilt by association, whereby all women seeking to do traditional men's jobs were lumped as "extremist nuts and bra-burners." These criticisms of the movement were encountered by some of the female legislators during their campaigns. About 20 percent said the movement was too strident and far out but was fundamentally useful to the cause of broader opportunities and equal rights for women. And another 20 percent explicitly supported and identified with the movement, attributing its poor image to distorted coverage by the media. Although there were partisan differences between these women when it came to particular child-care, health, and welfare bills, the Equal Rights Amendment was perceived by almost all these legislators as a true "women's issue."[63]

As these examples from Congress and state legislatures illustrate, assessing the feminism and feminist impact of women in public office was no easy matter. To capture the truth about the feminism of women in public office, one had to conduct a contextual and historical analysis, and look behind the scenes rather than at superficial responses to a reporter's question or researcher's questionnaire. "Feminism" and "the women's movement" were loaded terms for female officials, especially in the 1970s. Even into the 1980s, with electoral "gender gap" advantages accruing to many female candidates, these terms remained charged with multiple meanings. A respondent's self-understanding of "feminism" and "the women's movement" was a necessary component of research into the question of what women thought and did in public office.

Congresswomen's Increasing Willingness to Represent Women as a Group

When Frieda Gehlen described congresswomen as "quite feminist in attitude," she never defined what she meant by this term nor did she elicit meanings of the term from her interviewees. She was writing in 1969, before the advent of the contemporary women's movement, and what she meant by "stereotypic feminists" were "those who agitated for female suffrage a few generations ago." Gehlen found that neither congressmen nor congresswomen felt that women were pressured to specialize in traditional women's concerns (for instance, child care, education, health, beautification, culture, and consumers' rights). Although women were hesitant to state that they gravitated toward social issues any more than men did, they disproportionately sponsored bills related to the expected cultural concerns of women. Congresswomen seemed to have modified the role of a congressional representative to include the cultural concerns of women.[64]

In a comparison of the Eighty-eighth (1963–64) and the Ninety-first (1969–70) sessions of Congress, Gehlen found that Congresswomen were more concerned than Congressmen were with the inclusion of sex in the 1964 Civil Rights Act and with the Equal Rights Amendment. Although women were more likely to introduce bills in traditionally feminine areas, some of the men, but none of the women, thought that congresswomen specialized in female areas of legislation. When asked whether congresswomen had a feminine viewpoint on some problems, both sexes agreed in large numbers. Women said they brought distinctive experiences and expertise to their congressional work, and they expressed somewhat more interest in constituent problems. But there was no difference between the sexes when it came to private relief bills, political style, hiring female staff, attendance at roll call votes, and voting party line.[65]

During the Ninety-first (1969–70) and the Ninety-third (1973–74) sessions of Congress, when there were only ten to sixteen women in the House, the most significant sex differences were found in subject matter specialization, as measured by committee assignments, percentage of legislation sponsored related to one's committee, and the content of legislation one introduced. In the past, congresswomen had typically been assigned to low-status committees, in large part because of the high proportion of widows serving out the terms of their husbands. In time, new female members who were lawyers and/or professional politicians received prestigious committee assignments, whereas new women who were good citizen-amateur politicians were relegated to low-status committees. There were no sex differences, party differences, or tenure differences in percentage of committee-related legislation that representatives sponsored: those who were on the committee the longest sponsored the most such legislation. When it came to content, women were less likely than men to introduce business legislation and more likely to introduce legislation regarding health, education, and welfare. About one-fourth of the bills congresswomen introduced were in these traditionally female areas.[66]

Over time, congresswomen became increasingly willing to represent women as a group. Before World War II, most bills they introduced either ignored women as a class or spoke to a narrow range of their problems. According to Gertzog:

> Reasons for this lukewarm approach included a lack of interest in women's issues, a determination that a public display of interest would be politically damaging, a conviction that the problems women faced should be resolved at the state level or without benefit of government intervention, and a belief that a congresswoman associating herself with such issues would weaken her effectiveness among House colleagues. In fact, most legislative proposals directly affecting women were introduced by male lawmakers.[67]

During the mid-1960s, however, female representatives became much more likely than their predecessors to sponsor legislation designed to help women, with changes in the nature of such legislation: from traditional to equalitarian to affirmative. Traditional legislative measures addressed women's needs as mothers, wives, homemakers, and dependents; equalitarian bills sought equality with men in the public consciousness, marketplace, government, and academy; and affirmative measures facilitated women's claims to resources and recognition normally offered men as a matter of course. Before World War II, most bills introduced by congresswomen reinforced women's traditional roles (e.g., pensions for widows of military veterans). After the war, they turned their attention to measures that eliminated barriers to women's vocational, financial, and academic achievement (e.g., the 1963 Equal Pay Act and Title IX of the 1972 Education Amendments). And beginning in the early 1970s, congresswomen increasingly championed proposals to enable women to take advantage of equal opportunities (e.g., federally funded day-care centers and support for displaced homemakers).[68]

Congresswomen also changed the way they defined their roles as representatives. Before the 1960s, most of them rejected the claim that they were in Washington to represent American women. Jeannette Rankin was an important exception, and several others maintained that they could make a contribution to legislative deliberations by injecting a woman's point of view. Then, beginning in the 1960s, some congresswomen made it clear that they planned to represent women as a group. Bella Abzug was the most vocal and visible of these representatives, but six years before she took her House seat, Patsy Mink said, "With so few women in Congress, I feel an obligation to respond to the needs and problems of women in the nation."[69] In 1976, while campaigning for her first term, Barbara Mikulski told a group of garment workers that she would give special attention to women, adding, "If I don't, who will?"[70] Geraldine Ferraro thought that congresswomen had a special responsibility to speak with a single voice for the cause of women's issues, adding that even though American women were a diverse population, women in Congress reflected that diversity and there were enough areas of mutual agreement that congresswomen could formulate a common legislative agenda.[71]

Of course, not all congresswomen during this time adopted a feminist role orientation. For instance, Barbara Vucanovich (R-Nev.) was generally unsympathetic to feminist goals, and Marilyn Lloyd (D-Tenn.) rejected the political efficacy of such a stance. For some women, the political risks of such an orientation were substantial, and they expressed feminist inclinations on only a few, carefully selected items. The rise in the number of women prepared to invest their resources in women's issues was a product of several factors, including an increase in the number of such women who sought House seats and the emergence of a sympathetic electorate. But both these circumstances probably would not have produced the torrent of affirmative women's legislation had it not been for the formation of the Congresswomen's Caucus in 1977. Gertzog noted:

> The activities and goals of the Caucus did not necessarily encourage all of its members to adopt a feminist orientation. But they did serve as a magnet for female representatives interested in at least one women's issue, and as a source of positive reinforcement for those who were inclined to politicize incipient women's issues

which had not yet become part of the national agenda. Thus, the ascendancy of affirmative legislation and the tendency toward a feminist representational orientation were intimately linked with the activities of the Congresswomen's Caucus.[72]

In large part, scholarly interest in the feminism of female officials was sparked by the results of a national survey conducted in 1977 by the Center for American Woman and Politics. CAWP surveyed women, and a comparison sample of men, who held elective and appointive office in the federal executive branch, U.S. Congress, state executive cabinet level, state legislatures, state appellate and trial courts, mayoralties, and local councils. Female officials were more feminist than male officials regardless of ideology, party affiliation, education, district size, or age. Furthermore, across all categories of positions, between half and three-fourths of female officials named one or more forms of discrimination they had experienced as women in public office.[73]

Female appointees in the Carter administration were more feminist than their male counterparts. They showed greater intensity in their beliefs that women lacked equal opportunity to become political leaders, that the managerial capabilities of women were equal to those of men, and that women in office devoted as much or more time to the job than men did. They were more feminist on issues associated with the women's movement, including the ERA and abortion, and they voiced support for feminist positions with greater intensity. They reported high levels of membership in feminist organizations and high levels of activity to encourage the political involvement of other women. Almost half the women (but none of the men) who reported receiving assistance from organizations cited women's organizations. Several female appointees claimed that other women within the administration were the most influential in helping them obtain appointments. And in keeping with the public service orientation of women in public office, they more often cited policy-related reasons for accepting appointments, whereas men more often gave career-related reasons.[74]

Female and Feminist Concerns at the State Level

Studies of women serving in state legislatures revealed many of the same patterns that were observed in Congress. Not surprisingly, given the disproportionate power of southern men in Congress in the 1950s and 1960s, this was especially true in southern state legislatures. About 25 percent of women in southern legislatures between 1946 and 1968 were "fill-ins" for their predecessors; the remaining 75 percent were business and professional women, local officeholders, political party activists, or officials of women's organizations. Like the pre-1960s women in Congress, women in southern legislatures concentrated on traditional women's concerns, such as education, health, children and the aged, alcohol and drug abuse, and consumer and environmental protection. A few focused on women's rights' issues, especially jury service for women. They were split on the Equal Rights Amendment, civil rights, and school desegregation. They tended to be conciliatory peacemakers who avoided controversial stances and divisive issues. When it came to their treatment by the press and by their legislative colleagues, there were similarities to women in Congress as well. The press stressed the women's personal looks and lives, especially their children and husbands. And as long as they conformed to the stereotype of the southern woman, female state legislators were seen as nonthreatening.[75]

In the early 1960s, female state legislators nationwide specialized in women's traditional concerns: social welfare, education, urban life, and health and safety. They most frequently chaired education committees. Only a few had worked on legislation concerned with the status of women. They entered public office to clean up politics, to help rather than criticize, to bring a woman's viewpoint to the legislative process, to represent the average citizen instead of interest groups, and to take positive action to meet human needs. They commended women's social conscience: a personal and legislative concern for home, family, and children, and an understanding of community needs such as welfare, education, recreation, and mental health. They noted women's relative freedom from outside moral, political, and financial pressures: women were described as less likely than men to succumb to the pressures of special interest groups and the party organization; more service-oriented than career-oriented, so their vote was based on an issue's merit rather than on popularity at the polls; and free from having their business future tied to political decisions.[76]

In Irene Diamond's 1971 study of New England legislatures, traditional sex roles influenced the niches men and women developed, but otherwise the behavioral and attitudinal differences were not substantial. Women specialized most frequently in education and health and welfare, men in fiscal affairs and education. Party leadership positions were commonly held by men. In view of the fact that there was no difference between the sexes in length of tenure, sex was clearly a factor in the allocation of leadership positions. Men were more likely to speak on the floor, question witnesses, and take an active part in major negotiations, activities consistent with their leadership positions, which required such assertive behavior. Women, however, more frequently introduced bills and spoke in executive sessions of committees, activities consistent with sex-role socialization of nonassertive behavior. Compared to male legislators, female legislators were more negatively disposed toward bargaining, more likely to agree that lobbyists and special interests had too much influence in the legislature, and more likely to concur that a legislator, with better sources of information, should vote for what is best even when constituents disagree. Although women complained about being channeled into traditionally female areas of specialization and having to prove basic competence, they noted positive features: greater maneuverability in the legislature, ability to seek information more directly, less likelihood of being undercut by colleagues, receiving fewer sanctions for breaking the rules of the game, and being subject to less arm-twisting by lobbyists.[77]

In the early 1970s, most black female state legislators agreed that they brought to political office special expertise and competence. They were more optimistic about the future of women in politics than they were about the future of blacks in politics. Most felt that the women's movement had some merit, but they tended to accord it low status among their policy priorities: 53 percent gave it low priority, 19 percent were neutral, 16 percent gave it high priority, and 13 percent were opposed to it. Opponents saw the movement as liberating white women so that black women could take care of their children; others saw room for coalitions regarding issues such as equal pay and child care.[78]

Female State Legislators' Support for the ERA

One important indicator of female state legislators' feminism was support for the ratification of the Equal Rights Amendment, which passed in Congress in 1972 and was sent to the states for ratification by three-quarters of them by 1982. A 1976 study found that female state legislators were more likely than their male counterparts to vote for the ERA in both ratified and unratified states. But political party was an important variable—there was no difference in support for the amendment between Democratic men and Republican women.[79] In the 1977 CAWP survey, 96 percent of female state senators and 82 percent of female state house members strongly or moderately agreed that the ERA should be ratified, with only 4 and 14 percent of the women in the respective chambers moderately or strongly opposing the amendment. Across all offices, 67 percent of the women, but only 48 percent of the men, supported ratification of the ERA. In each ideological group (conservative, middle-of-the-road, and liberal), in each party affiliation group (Republican, Democrat, and Independent), in each educational group (not college graduate, college graduate, and postgraduate degree), and in every age group, female officials were more supportive of the ERA than were male officials.[80]

Another 1977 study found that overall female state legislators were very supportive of the ERA. Not surprisingly, opposition was higher among female state legislators with low education, less legislative seniority, Republican party affiliation, and living in states with legislative party leadership opposed to the ERA. Surprisingly, opposition was also higher in states with large proportions of female representatives. There were two possible explanations for this. The first was that offered by Diamond, namely, that in state legislatures with high percentages of women, most of the women were housewife-benchwarmers, who avoided issues, and traditional civic workers, who were not necessarily in the vanguard on women's issues. A second possible explanation was that a besieged mentality on the part of women in state legislatures with few women heightened their support for it. Another surprising finding, that there was greater opposition to the ERA by female legislators in moralistic states, might be explained by the fact that a traditional political culture increased the salience of the ERA for those female state legislators relative to those in moralistic states. Consistent with this "uphill battle" line of thinking, the level of support for the ERA was higher among female state legislators in nonratified states than among those in ratified states.[81]

In the 1970s, most female state legislators responded to party cues in their ERA votes as often as their male colleagues did, about 70 percent of the time. When the party strongly opposed the ERA, about 90 percent of both men and women voted party line. When the party weakly opposed the ERA, defections were more likely among women than among men. Republican women were more likely than Democratic women to reject party instruction. Republican women were more liberal than Republican men and more likely to be influenced by a women's caucus. One-third of female state legislators had a conflict between party and caucus cues, and this conflicted group had a low level of party voting. Republican women with no caucus conflict voted party line 90 percent of the time, whereas those with caucus conflict voted along party lines only about 40 percent of the time.[82]

It was at a 1982 CAWP conference for female state legislators that the importance of women's caucuses became clear. In most states, female legislators had both formal and informal organizational strategies. The type of organization varied, depending on three factors: the perception of male colleagues, which influenced how visible the women wanted to be; the strength of partisanship in the legislature, since bipartisan caucuses were harder to form where there was strong party loyalty; and the legacy of divisions from previous battles, especially over the ERA and abortion, which made it harder for women to unite on other matters, especially in conservative states. Most female legislators joined together for moral support, relaxation, personal development, exchange of information, and the pursuit of common political goals. Membership was usually automatic, although not all female state legislators joined. The most common organizational strategy was the formation of coalitions on an issue-by-issue basis. Once issues were selected, women used three time-honored legislative strategies: covering the major committees, handling bills on the floor, and building a base of support in the community.[83]

Female state legislators had two different ways of viewing the success of their organizational strategies. The first was an assessment of the amount and type of legislation that a caucus or coalition was instrumental in passing. The second, limited to formal caucuses, was the credibility issue: whether the caucus had become a presence recognized by the legislative leadership, male colleagues, lobbyists, and outside organizations as a source of power and influence in state government. The dilemmas inherent in each approach were illustrated by the comments of a male legislator at the CAWP conference. He had not been aware of the activities of the women's caucus in his legislature, but he interviewed some of its members before coming to the conference. He reported that the caucus had been really quite successful in a low-key, bipartisan manner in passing legislation of major importance for women. He then itemized the caucus's legislative achievements and said he knew of no major legislation supported by the caucus that had been defeated. Nonetheless, he felt the caucus had failed by not becoming a visible political force. This, he argued, was essential if women were to win positions of legislative leadership, because "that's where the action is."[84] Once again, female officials' substantive, public service approach can be contrasted with male public officials' procedural, careerist approach, leading to alternative definitions of legislative success.

The Proportion of Female State Legislators and Policy Impact

Another key to female state legislators' ability to advance a women's or feminist policy agenda was the proportion of women in a governing body. It was not possible to examine the question whether increasing the proportion of women in a legislature had a policy impact at the congressional level until 1993, following the elections of 1992, the so-called Year of the Woman. The previous all-time high of two women in the U.S. Senate tripled to six, and forty-seven women won seats in the House, up from the previous high of twenty-eight in 1992, giving women 11 percent of House seats. The number of feminists in Congress reached an all-time high, and for the first time since Jimmy Carter's presidency, feminists had an ally in the White House with Bill Clinton. Between 1975 and 1990, the percentage of women in Congress was negligible and barely changed, inching from 4 to 6 percent. By contrast, during this time the proportion of female state legislators jumped from 8 to 17 percent, with nine state legislatures having between one-quarter and one-third female members.[85] Thus it was possible at the state legislative level to investigate whether a change in numbers in itself made any difference in women's legislative output.

Michelle A. Saint-Germain picked an appropriate laboratory, the Arizona legislature, to test Rosabeth M. Kanter's theory on token women. Kanter had conducted a field study of a large industrial corporation's sales force in a division where women were entering for the first time. She found that proportions (that is, relative numbers of socially and culturally different people in a group) were critical in shaping group dynamics. A "skewed group," up to the ratio of 85:15, contained numerical "dominants" and rare "tokens." Above 15 percent, a group began to lose its token status. Tokens' visibility generated performance pressure, their polarization led dominants to heighten group boundaries, and their assimilation led to role entrapment as "queen bees." Kanter said that tokens under*lined,* rather than under*mined,* majority culture: in the presence of token women, men exaggerated their displays of aggression and potency. There were too few of a token's kind to generate a counterculture. Tokens were given loyalty tests and were viewed as exceptions who patrolled in a "gate-keeping" function on behalf of the dominant group. For example, laughing with others was seen as a sign of a common definition of a situation. Tokens felt pressured to work twice as hard as dominants, to remain less visible, to spend more time resolving problematic interactions, to turn against others of one's kind, and to join with dominants in their assaults on tokens through humor. In these ways, tokens were under more stress than were dominants.[86]

Saint-Germain studied bills introduced in the Arizona legislature between 1969 and 1986, comparing women's legislative output both under token conditions (less than 15 percent) and approaching a more favorable "tilted" condition (about 35 percent). As the proportion of women grew beyond 15 percent, female legislators introduced more traditional women's interest and feminist bills; they authored more proposals in nontraditional areas, such as commerce, state and local government, and transportation; they stepped up their bill-making activity; they scaled back on making honorary proposals; and they achieved greater success in enacting all types of bills. Overall, female legislators were more successful than their male counterparts in passing their bills. Women's rates of enactment were 27 percent for general bills, 23 percent for traditional women's interest bills, and 17 percent for feminist bills. Both traditional women's interest and feminist measures had a better chance of passing if women introduced them.[87]

Saint-Germain concluded that female state legislators had a decisive impact on legislative output in Arizona and that the nature of this impact changed as women increased their numbers. She called for comparative studies to consider rival explanations for her findings. Such studies might take into account characteristics of the state legislature, such as its professional versus amateur nature (Arizona's was amateur), its partisan composition (Arizona's was Republican-dominated), and its women's caucus (Arizona did not have one); characteristics of the female legislators (such as age, occupational background, and education); and environmental factors (such as the impact of the women's movement and the effects of perceived public opinion on policy).

Just such a comparative study was undertaken by Beth Ann Reingold, who compared the views and activities of men and women in the California and Arizona legislatures during 1989–90. In contrast to Arizona, California's legislature was professional, Democratic-dominated, and had a women's caucus. Comparisons could also be made with respect to women's token status, as 30 percent of Arizona's state legislature was female, whereas only 16 percent of California's was. Arizona legislators worked in a more conservative institution and served a more conservative state constituency than did California legislators. Reingold was particularly interested in the question of representation, the extent to which legislators were attitudinally predisposed to represent women and engaged in representational legislative behavior. In both states, female officials were attitudinally more predisposed to represent women's concerns than were their male colleagues. Women were more likely to perceive strong support from their female constituents and to consider such women a very important—if not their most important—reelection constituency. Female officials believed that they were uniquely qualified to handle the concerns of their female constituents, and they held this belief to a greater extent than male officials refuted it.[88]

The patterns of gender differences were not the same in the two states. California women were more likely than Arizona women to mention women as a group they represented, to perceive strong support from their female constituents, and to feel that female legislators were more capable of representing women's concerns. And, compared to their Arizona counterparts, California men were less likely to perceive strong support from their female constituents and more likely to reject the notion that women best represented women's concerns. The more liberal and Democratic nature of California politics may have set a political and policy agenda more attuned to the issues of gender. Although prior research, such as that of Saint-Germain, suggested that increasing the proportion of women in a legislature increased the likelihood that women would mobilize around women's issues, Reingold said her study raised the possibility that exactly the opposite may occur, especially when one considered attitudes rather than behavior: "It is possible that when women comprise 30 percent of a legislature—as they do in Arizona—they are too numerous to be considered a cohesive group that has common interests or common traits (positive or negative). Being a woman may become less important to both female and male legislators. Having many other female colleagues may make it easier for a female legislator to *act* for women as a woman, but it may make it less likely for a female legislator to *want* to or feel the need to act for women."[89]

Although female state legislators in both states were more predisposed than male legislators to the idea of representing women, there were few significant gender differences in representational legislative behavior outside the realm of agenda setting. Reingold considered policy priorities (stated priorities and bills introduced), policy preferences (roll call votes), legislative strategies (self-reported "feminine" or "masculine" strategies for getting bills passed), and representational priorities (paying attention to constituents). The most significant gender differences in both states were in policy priorities, with respect to both stated priorities and bills introduced. Significant differences in legislators' roll call votes were found only among Arizona Democrats, where the votes of female legislators corresponded more closely with positions women tended to favor in public opinion polls. Male and female legislators in both states endorsed a similar legislative strategy involving honesty, building personal relationships with colleagues, and a willingness to compromise (a "feminine" style), and very few mentioned such "masculine" strategies as being aggressive, standing firm, making deals, and trading votes. The women and men of both legislatures were equally likely to consider constituent casework an "extremely important" representational activity, and relatively few legislators adopted "delegate" roles in their policy decision making.[90]

Female Officials Reshape the Policy Agenda

In 1988, CAWP launched a nationwide research project to assess the extent to which female officeholders had changed the nation's policy agendas. A survey of state legislators revealed that in comparison to their male colleagues, female legislators gave higher priority to women's rights policies and to policies related to women's distinctive roles as care-givers in family and society, such as health care, children and the family, education, environment, housing, and the elderly. Women were more active on women's rights legislation, whether or not it was their top priority. They were more feminist and liberal in their attitudes on major public policy issues, such as the ERA, abortion, nuclear power plants, the death penalty, and belief that the private sector could solve economic problems. Democratic women were particularly active in reshaping the policy agenda, but Republican women were more active than men of either party. The types of women most active in reshaping the agenda were feminist, liberal, younger, African-American, and women with close ties to women's organizations. Joining women in reshaping the policy agenda were men who were younger, liberal, and feminist. Female state legislators were also changing the way government worked. Compared to their male colleagues, they were more likely to bring citizens into the governmental process, more likely to opt for government in public view rather than behind closed doors, and more responsive to groups previously denied full access to the policymaking process.[91]

Majorities of both female and male state legislators said the presence of women in public office had made a difference in the extent to which legislators considered how legislation would affect women as a group, in expenditure priorities for the state, and in the number of bills passed dealing with problems faced by women. This was the majority view regardless of party affiliation, region, race, length of service, age, ideology, feminist identification, professionalism of the legislature, the proportion of women serving in the chamber, or whether they were in the upper or lower house. These subjective impressions that women made a policy difference were supported by attitudinal differences between men and women that emerged from the survey. Women's attitudes were more liberal and feminist than men's regardless of similarities in age, seniority, feminist identification, ideology, party affiliation, connections with women's groups, traditionally male occupations, ideology of the district, political party insider status, or legislative leadership positions. Furthermore, male and female attitudes differed regardless of the proportion of women in the legislature or the legislature's level of professionalism. Among women, those who attended women's caucuses or other formal or informal gatherings of female lawmakers were more supportive of feminist and liberal policy views than women who did not attend such meetings. When asked if the increased presence of women in public office had actually changed access to the legislature by different groups, majorities of both male and female legislators agreed that economically disadvantaged groups had greater access because of female legislators. Women and men expressed different views about women's impact on collegial relationships within the legislature: women agreed that they had changed men's behavior on the floor and that men tried to keep women out of leadership positions, but majorities of men disagreed with both statements.[92]

A twelve-state study in 1988 found that, compared to the 1970s, gender differences in legislative activities had nearly disappeared. Women were no less likely to speak from the floor or in committee or to bargain and interact with lobbyists. Men introduced and passed more bills, but women were more successful in passing priority bills. Women brought distinctive policy concerns to the legislative agenda and were more likely to list among their priority bills those affecting women, children, and the family. Many women were in a position to act on these matters because they were more likely than men to serve on committees on health, welfare, and human services. Thus having women in the legislature seemed to make it easier to pass such legislation. There were mixed results on the "token" hypothesis. Contrary to the hypothesis, the proportion of female members was not related to legislators' willingness to give priority to women's issues. Nevertheless, the two states with the lowest percentages of female legislators also had the lowest rate of passing bills concerning women, families, and children. It appeared that having less than 10 percent of women in the legislature was a deterrent to the successful passage of such bills. It also seemed that having either a high percentage of women or a formal caucus helped women pass their priority legislation.[93]

Further evidence of female officials' feminism came from a 1989 study of cabinet appointees in Connecticut, where there were both policy and leadership differences between the sexes. Although only seven of the eighteen women described themselves as feminists, most women related "war stories" of sexism, and they were more supportive than men of feminist issues, such as abortion, child care, gay rights, and family leave. Men and women agreed that the presence of women had made the political agenda more sensitive to children and family issues, had an impact on the extent to which leaders considered the impact of policies on women as a group, changed the ways in which managers conducted themselves in meetings, and increased equality of opportunity in employment for women. Most of the female appointees said the work environment had changed with women's entrance into middle- and upper-range positions in state agencies. There was increased concern for families, children, flexible scheduling, leaves, job sharing, humane working conditions, the expression of emotions, improving worker morale, and helping women advance. When faced with a hypothetical case of budget cutting, women's leadership style was less hierarchical, more consensual, and more open and responsive to subordinates. And most women said that in order to have their contributions taken seriously, women had to work harder, make no mistakes, avoid getting emotional and confrontational, and be more prepared, strategic, aggressive, and persistent.[94]

Feminism showed up among female judges as well. In her 1986 study of judges, Elaine F. Martin compared the views of feminist women, nonfeminist women, feminist men, and nonfeminist men on three matters: perception of the role of female judges, perception of gender bias in the courts, and decisions on five hypothetical cases regarding women's rights. The first two matters were expressed in seven statements: men's view of women is affected positively by the presence of women judges; women have a unique perspective; the bench without women does not reflect the total fabric of society; women judges behave differently; women judges have an ability to bring people together that men do not have; women face special problems in the judicial system; and judges sometimes treat women attorneys, witnesses, or litigants in demeaning, condescending, or unprofessional ways. Feminist women expressed the strongest agreement and nonfeminist men expressed the strongest disagreement, with small differences between feminist men and nonfeminist women. A similar pattern appeared in support for women's rights in the five hypothetical cases, concerning maternity leave, battered women, abortion, divorce, and sexual harassment. Feminist ideology had a stronger influence than did gender, with pro-woman scores in the following rank order: feminist women, feminist men, nonfeminist women, nonfeminist men. There were no statistically significant differences between male and female judges in the maternity leave and sexual harassment cases. Female judges were more supportive of women's rights in the battered women and divorce cases. But nonfeminist female judges were the least supportive of women's rights in the abortion case.[95] In a second study, Martin discovered that judges responded to the same five hypothetical cases in the same pattern.[96]

Martin also asked judges questions about women's changing social roles, the representative role of female judges, and the behavior of female judges. Feminist judges, female and male, were more likely than nonfeminist judges to support continued social change in women's roles and to agree that more female judges were needed on the bench to reflect the total fabric of society. Both feminist and nonfeminist women, however, were more inclined than men to agree with three statements: that women had unique perspectives and life experiences that ought to be represented on the bench by women; that because a female judge had high visibility she had to be more cautious in breaking with precedent; and that female judges behaved differently from male judges. Women were much more likely than men to say that female judges had to be better than male judges to get the same recognition of competence. Women were divided, however, on the question whether female judges were more sensitive to claimants raising issues of sexual discrimination than were male judges. Thus, when asked about general social change and gender in the court system, both gender and feminism were important influences on the attitudes of judges.[97]

Even female civil servants had feminist management styles. In the late 1980s, a survey in Arizona found gender differences in how civil servants said they dealt with power, handled subordinates, and interrelated with others. Both women and men at the middle level saw themselves as process-oriented and task implementers. But mid-level women's "team orientation" was linked to being frank, interpersonal, and task-oriented, whereas for men it was part of aspiring to be "team captain." Among high-level managers, there were gender differences in perceptions of the traits of dominance, intimidation, attractiveness, and affection. Men were more likely to say they could use domination and intimidation to their advantage, and women were more likely to see attractiveness and affection in a positive light.[98]

A Wisconsin study of civil servants explored respondents' behavioral styles and views of the ideal bureaucrat. The conventional Weberian bureaucracy was a masculine organization that undervalued and possibly excluded the feminine, with its hierarchical structure, instrumentally rational modus operandi, preoccupation with control, dysfunctional protection of turf, adherence to rules to ensure equality in the face of competing claims, and professional training developed by men. Mounting evidence that women in bureaucracies were both successful and satisfied with their jobs, however, suggested that the public sector might allow and possibly require styles compatible with behaviors commonly associated with women. In the Wisconsin bureaucracy, the preferred bureaucrat placed equal value on feminine and masculine characteristics. Both women and men crossed gender stereotypes in behavioral styles as well as in their perceptions of good administrators and colleagues, but men adopted more traits of both genders with potential negative connotations. Thus, men had more latitude in style and attended more to hierarchy, competition, opportunism, and other "power games" in bureaucracies. By contrast, women shunned negative masculine and feminine traits while endorsing those most valued by bureaucrats for achieving results. Operating under the assumption of "power to" instead of "power over," women placed more value on efficiently accomplishing tasks and defined success as a job well done.[99]

Indeed, by the 1980s there was some evidence that liberal male legislators were embracing the feminist agenda. One California assemblywoman maintained that "most of those issues that have to do with women are preempted by men."[100] A study of voting in the California Assembly in 1983–84 gave credence to this view. Female assemblymembers were less liberal than their male counterparts; however, women were more supportive of women's rights (Republican women much more so, Democratic women slightly more so than their male counterparts). There was almost a perfect correlation between liberalism and support for women's issues. In the California legislature, liberal men were often in the vanguard on women's issues.[101] In sum, the policy impact studies of the late 1980s found that female officials at the state level were making a difference, both in terms of political style and in terms of policy preferences. And the women's movement had made a difference in the lives of some male officials as well, as evidenced by their adoption of traditionally female political styles and of feminist policy positions.

Female Officials at the Local Level

Compared to other levels of government, at the local level there are fewer salient feminist issues. Local governments are largely concerned with education, land use, infrastructure and public health, and service and safety issues, in most cases without direct policy consequences for women. For example, a study of women on school boards conducted in the mid-1970s suggested that most women did not think there was a distinctive "woman's point of view" on school boards. Respondents' perceived contributions were a mix of masculine and feminine roles, except that men were more likely to mention their business and professional skills and women their public relations capabilities. There were different role perceptions, however, with women more likely to emphasize developing educational policies and philosophies, keeping informed, and representing the public, and men more likely to stress administrative oversight. Men were more often found on finance and physical plant committees, and women on policy, community relations, and special education committees.[102]

In the mid-1970s, Hawaiian state and local officials, both male and female, agreed that women expressed greater concern for people and were willing to work for and listen to constituents.[103] The women were more feminist insofar as they expressed more sympathy for a political role for women; they did not show greater support for feminist policy positions when asked to rank order issues, however. Men and women ranked issues in roughly the same order.[104]

Among city councilmembers in Connecticut, women were somewhat more favorable toward feminist issues, but they did not maintain a higher level of support when those issues competed with others. In this strong-party state, liberalism and party affiliation were better indicators than sex of support for feminist policies. There were no sex differences in support for the women's movement, feminism, or the ERA. Both sexes rejected the idea that women were politically advantaged by feminine charm, diplomacy, idealism, or any other special assets. Women were more sensitive than men to discrimination against women in politics, however, and men were more skeptical of women's pursuit of political careers.[105] Women were less sanguine about the opportunities available to them, less optimistic about their influence, and more likely to see liabilities for women in politics. Men were much less likely to see sex discrimination against women in local government or to see women as excluded from informal contacts. Almost half the men and a quarter of the women felt that men were better suited emotionally for politics. About half of both sexes said women were more sensitive, attached a greater value to human life, and had as their greatest asset feminine charm and diplomacy. Councilwomen said that they served as an example to other women, that they should represent women's interests, and that they ought to provide leadership in women's issues, but not because of a perception of themselves as feminists. The token hypothesis was not borne out in this case study: there was no relationship between perception of women's representational roles and the number of women on the council.[106]

In CAWP's 1977 study of women in public office at all levels of government, 86 percent of the respondents served at the local level. In every office, women devoted more time to their official activity than men, unless they had outside employment, in which case they averaged the same hours as men. Higher proportions of women than men described themselves as giving major emphasis to discovering the public's views, educating the public on issues, helping on individual problems, researching pending issues, and developing policy. Women evaluated their overall effectiveness as highly as men did theirs but women were less confident than men of their financial judgment and technical training.[107]

Female officials at all levels, especially federal judges and state officials, strongly endorsed a more active stance from both government and industry in promoting women's rights. Clear majorities of women in every office endorsed ratification of the ERA and opposed a constitutional ban on abortion, with local female officials the least likely to take the feminist position on these issues. Majorities of female officials favored an extension of social security to homemakers; in this case, female judges were the least supportive group. The only women's issue on which opinion was more evenly divided was government provision of child care. Female judges and local officials had more conservative ideologies than did state-level female officials. Respondents' self-described ideology was strongly related to their position on women's and other issues, with ideology being a better predictor among state legislators than among local councilmembers, who typically achieved office in nonpartisan elections. Higher proportions of women than men professed liberal political philosophies, supported increased activity on the part of government and business on behalf of women's rights, favored ratification of the ERA and homemaker social security, opposed a constitutional ban on abortion, and took a liberal position on busing, criminal penalties, mandatory age retirement, and federal revenue for cities. Women were more supportive of women's issues regardless of ideology, party affiliation, education, district size, or age.[108] The CAWP survey underscored the importance of keeping levels of government analytically distinct when drawing conclusions about the policy preferences and political styles of female officials.

A study of female judges on trial courts, a group of officials that had not been included in the CAWP study, compared two possible explanations of female judicial decision making about women's issues: female judges' personal commitment to feminism versus their structural position as tokens on the bench. It turned out that feminism was much more useful in explaining a judge's views on women's policy questions. Overall, female judges, feminists and nonfeminists alike, were ahead of the public in their support for women's issues.[109]

A 1977 study of city councilmembers in suburban Chicago found that female councilmembers spent more hours at their official duties than their male counterparts did but that this difference disappeared for employed women. Councilmembers agreed that the public saw women as more trustworthy and honest than men. Councilmen enjoyed the negotiating process, whereas councilwomen liked producing a concrete end product. Men and women were equally supportive of changing women's domestic roles, but women were more feminist regarding women working outside the home, women's executive capabilities, and the queen bee syndrome (employed women were less likely than nonemployed women to be queen bees). The two sexes agreed on the major issues facing the city, although nonemployed women were more likely to express an interest in social issues. Outside employment reduced sex differences insofar as it limited the time female officials spent on their official duties and it provided women with professional skills; but employment did not alter women's interest in product over process, their feminist views, or their sense of citizens' trust of them.[110]

One study of current and former female mayors and their male predecessors in five cities closely resembled the case of San Jose. There were few gender differences in perceptions about communities and problems that needed to be addressed. There was an increased acceptance of humanistic concerns that ought to be covered by local government. There were gender differences in leadership styles, however, with female mayors exercising a style that was hands-on, collegial, and involving teamwork. Male mayors' leadership style was more in the command idiom, using staff as implementers and sounding boards and involving more delegation. Both sexes defined a good leader as having a leadership style closely approximating that of female mayors. Four of the female mayors believed that women brought a distinctive dimension to politics, in terms of either style or policy. Female mayors were still self-conscious of themselves as women and felt they had to work twice as hard to prove themselves. One said female officials were less confrontational and more cooperative, with the downside of taking a little longer to put one's foot down and make the final decision. In general, female mayors in these five cities and in San Jose agreed with Texas governor Ann Richards, who said after her first hundred days in office, "The joy of having power is being in a position of distributing it, giving it away, empowering others."[111]

Black female mayors reported that they had a greater commitment to the disadvantaged than their white predecessors did, a commitment that developed from their ties to the black community and from their own personal experiences. It was impossible to sort out the independent effects of race and gender on the impact of these female officials, since often they were the first female mayor and the first black mayor of their towns. And many of these mayors felt uncomfortable acknowledging the effects that race and gender might have had on their actions as elected officials, yet they had accomplished things in their towns that had not been achieved by their male or white predecessors. The economic well-being of the black community came first, followed by a focus on day care, the ERA, and abortion. These women represented towns that had few economic resources and were thus dependent on funds from the federal government and private foundations. They had developed their leadership skills during the civil rights movement and, remembering segregation, took pride in eroding employment discrimination. Black female mayors emphasized that they were accessible to people in the community and that constituents could talk more freely to them than to previous mayors. Many of them had been schoolteachers and community and church activists. One woman made progress in getting water and sewage treatment facilities built for her town through the use of a team of women committed to getting her programs implemented. Another woman succeeded in getting a local sheriff to address the local crime problem by cracking down on the selling of liquor to minors, looking at a cause of the problem instead of just arresting minors for fights and crime. And another black female mayor contrasted her predecessor's attitude—"If it ain't broken, don't fix it"—with her approach—"If it could work better, then improve it"—to illustrate that she saw many more things that needed to be done.[112]

An investigation of city councilmembers found that blacks and women spent more time on constituency service than whites or men did and that there were race and gender differences in perceptions about the importance of various groups in councilmembers' constituencies. Women were more likely than men to say that their constituents cared more about issues than constituent service. Blacks were more likely than whites to say that their constituents were more interested in constituent service than in issues and to agree that they represented a geographical/racial constituency and labor unions/public employees.[113]

In a study of city councilmembers in Dallas-Fort Worth, city managers said women made a difference on city councils in several ways: women brought calm to deliberations, were more accommodating and better listeners, demonstrated more sensitivity and concern for individual city employees, were more down-to-earth and family-oriented, and did not display as much political drive as men did. City managers added, however, that women were known to attack one another at council meetings and could be easily hurt and become bitter. Ironically, and unlike

the case in San Jose, the sole female-majority board in this study was
characterized by bickering and in-fighting. When it came to policy, city
managers thought it was helpful to have a feminine point of view, particularly women's special expertise in human services. Women were assumed to be experts in the arts and on women's issues such as rape and
battered women's shelters but were often patronized when it came to
"male" areas such as the budget. Male and female officials had different
conceptions of the "ideal" local official: for men it was a business leader
whereas for women it was someone who represented a cross-section of
the community. They also had different conceptions of the negative side
of their jobs: men mentioned the loss of time from their businesses and
the lack of community appreciation of their efforts, whereas women
cited family strain, especially the difficulty their husbands had playing a
secondary role at social functions.[114]

One study with surprisingly few similarities to the case of Santa Clara
County focused on seven suburban towns, where council posts were considered volunteer work with little pay. Female and male councilmembers
did not differ in their priorities, positions, tenure, or partisanship. All
were concerned with taxes, development, the quality of life, and (unlike
Santa Clara County) protecting the status quo from "undesirables" moving in. There were also some important differences, however. Although
both sexes said councilwomen were more responsive to constituents,
women saw this as a positive responsiveness and men viewed it as a negative softheartedness. Men thought women asked too many questions,
whereas women saw themselves as better prepared and faulted their
male colleagues for "winging it." Councilwomen adopted a delegate
mode of representation, councilmen a trustee mode. There were more
policy differences between councilmen and councilwomen than was the
case in Santa Clara County. Women emphasized child care, libraries,
women's shelters, motorcycle safety, smaller signs, and redefining "family" in the master plan; men spent more energy on tennis courts, soccer
fields, and a veterans' monument. When presented with two hypothetical cases, both sexes opposed municipal child care and only the councilwomen approved of zoning to allow homeowners to take in boarders
to make money.[115] Although these councilwomen were uncomfortable
with the male model of doing politics, they had not yet developed an alternative model as Santa Clara County officials had done.

In sum, scholarly research about what female officials did in office,
which began in earnest with the advent of the women's movement in the
1970s, found that female officials had distinctive policy preferences and
political styles. Although there were variations by level of government,

geographic area, and historical time period, female officials tended to be more liberal, feminist, and supportive of traditional women's concerns in their policy preferences and to have a distinctive political style: more consensual, approachable, responsive, seeking of information, sensitized to the needs of women and children in the community, knowledgeable about the community, trusted, and critical of politics as usual. With the exception of major policy differences, these differences also characterized officials in Santa Clara County.

Female Officials in Santa Clara County

Because of the favorable political climate and their numerical majorities, female officeholders on the San Jose City Council and the Santa Clara County Board of Supervisors were free from the problems that typically beset token women.[116] Pressures stemming from token status were felt much more acutely by local female officials when they numbered only one or two among their male colleagues. According to Supervisor Rod Diridon, when Geraldine Steinberg first joined the all-male county board in 1974, she was initially dismissed as "just a woman" and not taken seriously. She had to earn the respect of male board members, and eventually she succeeded in "reeducating" them about their traditional expectations about women. This uphill battle to be taken seriously and to reeducate colleagues loomed large in virtually every study discussed in this chapter. It figured into elected women's calculus of their effectiveness and was not a part of male officials' sense of effectiveness.

Freed from the gatekeeping and conformist pressures of tokenism, Santa Clara County women could articulate what was distinctive about them as women. After Mayor Janet Gray Hayes's 1981 public baptism of San Jose as the feminist capital of the nation, the media investigated the appropriateness of the city's new moniker. In an article misleadingly entitled "Female Majorities on Council, Board, Shun Feminist Label," the *San Jose Mercury News* concluded that only one of the new councilmembers, Shirley Lewis, was a ("soft-line") feminist.[117] None of the three female county supervisors was quoted, however, and at least two of them, Susanne Wilson and Zoe Lofgren, did not shun the term "feminist." Councilmember Nancy Ianni remembered that the day after she was elected, she was barraged by phone calls from the media about this issue. "With the first call I was curt—I did not run as a woman, I ran on an antigrowth platform. By the second call I was somewhat philosophical, and by the fifth call I was an expert on the subject! It was not part of my consciousness. It had to be brought to my attention."

Many different meanings of the term "feminist" were tossed around: getting elected because of one's female sex, representing women only, representing honesty and integrity, forming a natural political coalition based on sex, and supporting equal rights and opportunity for women. Though few observers accepted Hayes's "feminist capital" characterization at face value, many suspected that it contained a kernel of truth. Something had to account for the impressive number of elected women, however imperfectly they embodied a feminist consciousness or agenda. The same conditions that favored their election—slow-growth environmentalism, desire for clean government, affluence, risk taking, absence of machine politics, the advent of district elections in 1980, and effective women's organizations—also favored female officials' advocacy of a women's policy agenda and expression of a distinctive political style. In this setting, where male officials were usually as supportive of women's issues as were female officials, female officials typically made two distinctive contributions: framing old issues in a new light as women's issues and articulating their own understanding of power and politics.

In this environment—externally supportive of women's concerns and internally populated by female majorities—male officials often took leadership roles in women's issues and had visible affiliations with women's organizations. Beginning in 1975, for example, Supervisor Rod Diridon convened annual women's congresses of local feminists to assess the policy needs of women. Such efforts resulted in policy improvements for victims of sexual assault, in equal rights for rental housing for families, and in job sharing and flexible hours in county government. The major issues raised at the 1982 congress were abortion rights, child care, child support collection, and comparable worth.[118] In the early 1980s, Councilmember Jerry Estruth was on the advisory board of WOMA, a battered women's shelter, and both he and councilmember (and mayor from 1982 to 1990) Tom McEnery were NWPC members.

An examination of a few key votes on women's issues from the early 1980s showed that male officials were as supportive as female officials when it came to the County Commission on the Status of Women, comparable worth, and funding battered women's shelters. In response to sustained grassroots feminist pressure, an all-male board of supervisors set up the Santa Clara County Commission on the Status of Women in 1973. For nearly a decade, the commission was a powerful antidiscrimination force, handling some five hundred sex discrimination complaints a year. In 1982, however, a female-majority board of supervisors approved budget cuts that severely curtailed the Commission's activities. In that year, county officials were faced with a $57 million deficit, and as Supervisor Rebecca Morgan put it, "We are at the point where we are almost cutting mandated programs. We are morally and legally obliged" to cut the optional ones first.[119] The two male supervisors were as reluctant as the three female supervisors to preside over the demise of the commission.

A second important issue area was comparable worth, also known as pay equity, or equal pay for jobs of equal value to the employer. A comparable worth policy attempts to bring the salaries of female-dominated jobs in line with the salaries of comparable male-dominated jobs. The nation's first strike over this issue was mounted by San Jose municipal employees in 1981.[120] A two-year study that assigned points to city job classifications had found that male-dominated jobs averaged 8 to 15 percent *above* a "trend line" (that is, the average pay for jobs of equal points), whereas female-dominated jobs averaged 2 to 10 points *below* the trend line, some as much as 20 percent. A strike was called when city employees rejected the city's offer to have male jobs currently paid at or above the trend line forgo a raise to fund the pay equity adjustments for female jobs below the trend line. After nine days, a settlement was reached in which the city agreed to provide a $4 million general pay increase and to set aside $1.4 million over two years to raise the pay in sixty-two female-dominated job areas to within 10 percent of the trend line.

What difference did the female majority on the San Jose City Council make in this issue? Mayor Hayes maintained that the city bargained in good faith. She added, "I am proud to be mayor of the city that took the first giant step toward fairness in the workplace for women. This day will go down in history as the day so-called 'women's work' was recognized for its inherent value to society."[121] As for the ten-member city council, it was unanimous in its support of Plan A, which offered a general pay increase over two years but would have put the issue of pay equity on the November ballot for voter approval. Plan B, which was the basis for the final agreement with the union and allocated city monies to redress pay inequities, split the council. The final vote was eight to three with Councilmembers Claude Fletcher, Lu Ryden, and Pat Sausedo opposed. The rest of the women on the council—Shirley Lewis, Blanca Alvarado, and Iola Williams—all voted in favor of the settlement, as did Mayor Hayes and three male members—James Beall, Jerry Estruth, and Tom McEnery. So men on the council actually supported pay equity at least as strongly (3:1) as did their female colleagues (5:2).

A third issue area, county funds for battered women's shelters, had the support of both male and female boardmembers. For example, in 1982 budget considerations, County Executive Sally Reed recommended terminating county funds for two battered women's shelters, but the board of supervisors unanimously added back to the budget both amounts in full.[122]

Although gender differences in policy preferences in Santa Clara County were not as great as those found in most studies of officials elsewhere, such differences were apparent in two areas that were in keeping with other findings: reframing the agenda and having a distinctive approach to power and politics. Supervisor Zoe Lofgren noted that women on the board of supervisors formulated issues as women's issues during board meetings, reminding their male colleagues, for example, that poverty was a women's issue (especially for older women) and so was the effectiveness of the district attorney's Family Support Office. A significant number of officials made one or more of the following observations: women were better at constituency service, more honest, more sensitive and compassionate, more idealistic, more courteous, better listeners, and more understanding. Many female officials described a distinctive female understanding of power. Sally Reed characterized women's sense of power as less authoritarian and more supportive, collaborative, and respectful of intuition. Shirley Lewis described male power as force and domination and women's power as consensus, validation, and cooperation. Lu Ryden described female power as softer and noncompetitive.

With the media spotlight on their majority status, coupled with their workplace proximity to so many other women in public office, female officials in Santa Clara County became increasingly thoughtful about their role as women in politics and their relation to the women's movement. Councilmember Nancy Ianni, for example, began to reflect on women's political activity in a new way:

> I began to realize how proud I was of the women who ran against the men. I owe a lot to those who came before me. They did a good job and made it easier for me. I am not a leader in the women's movement. . . . I am a pragmatic implementer who used to resent the committed ones in the spotlight. But now I recognize that the two are not incompatible. In fact, both are needed. I want to move in the issue direction. Those who give fiery speeches at council meetings, without concrete proposals or doing their homework, are at least raising and publicizing the issue so there is no going back. Maybe the women's movement will produce more women who can have both skills: issue raising and implementation.

Virtually all the female officials described some distinctions between male and female conceptions of power and politics. Though it was possible that such differences would not last if women's political ambitions and career patterns began to resemble those of men, certain patterns indicated that female officials in Santa Clara County would resist the temptation to imitate male politics as usual: (1) the value they placed on household experiences as bona fide preparation for public office and as metaphors for how they saw power and politics, (2) a local tradition in which women networked other women into office, and (3) the persistence through the 1980s of female majorities on both the Santa Clara County Board of Supervisors and the San Jose City Council and the election in 1990 of the second female mayor of San Jose, Susan Hammer, all of which increased many officials' female, even feminist, consciousness.

For four years before Hammer's election, women had outnumbered men on the city council eight to three. Hammer had chaired Mayor Hayes's reelection campaign in 1978. Two years later, when a councilmember resigned with six months left on his term, Hayes rewarded Hammer with the post. In 1982, Hammer was elected to the council seat vacated by newly elected mayor Tom McEnery. Throughout his two terms, McEnery rebuilt downtown San Jose. When she entered the 1990 race, Hammer cited housing as San Jose's top priority, emphasizing the neighborhoods as a corrective to all the attention downtown had received during the McEnery administration. Hammer secured city council approval of the Neighborhood Outreach Program, which allowed neighborhood associations to receive by mail, and at no cost, City Council and Planning Department agendas and the weekly City Calendar.[123] Consistent with female officials' role as agenda shapers, Hammer took credit for leading the way on the issue of child care in San Jose. As a councilmember, she said, "I was the only public official talking about it. ... I established [the city's] first child care task force that met for a year and recommended establishing the office of the child care coordinator." Hammer also initiated policies that exempted day-care providers from the city's business tax and eliminated land use permits for day care at churches, schools, and homes.[124]

Hammer's razor-thin victory was attributed to her support among women, Democrats, Hispanics, Asian-Americans, and blacks.[125] The following spring, Hammer launched her Project Diversity, an effort to draw non-Anglo ethnic groups to the dozens of appointed boards and commissions that advised the city council. In these settings, citizens would learn how government operated, how to win political support for ideas, and how to get things done. Brochures about the project were sent to community centers, libraries, and neighborhood organizations, and Hammer made public service announcements on radio and television.[126]

When asked whether being a woman or a feminist or a mother had influenced her politics, Hammer answered in terms of making San Jose livable for families: her goals were affordable housing, public transportation, open space, child care, and after-school programs. She was described by one supporter as bringing "mom into the mayor's office." As one commentator noted, "Dozens of local women, Hammer included, earned their political spurs together in the 1970s, the heady days of the National Women's Political Caucus. Now, many prominent women feel an almost personal triumph in Hammer's victory."[127] She had been supported by many well-known national and local female officials and activists from NOW, NWPC, and abortion rights groups. And she had been endorsed by the municipal employee union that had secured the 1981 comparable worth settlement; the union also cited her support of child care and parental leave for city employees.[128] Hammer's vision of quality-of-life issues as women's issues bore a striking resemblance to the views of the pioneer women who began appearing on local governing boards in Santa Clara County in the 1970s.

Part Four

*Women and Elite-Mass
Interaction*

7 Agenda Setting

Women Bring New Issues
to Public Attention

FEMALE OFFICIALS were able to reshape agendas in the 1980s because of their relationship with movement "outsiders." Agenda setting is the process through which a problem becomes an issue receiving serious attention from government officials. It involves a relationship between "insiders" (the elite, or government decision makers) and "outsiders" (the mass, including the general public, the attentive public, the media, and interest groups). Agenda setting focuses simultaneously on the activities of elites and masses. Compared to the concepts covered in the previous four chapters—mass mobilization and participation, elite recruitment, and policy preferences and political styles—agenda setting has received much less attention from political scientists, and thus there is less conventional wisdom for feminist scholarship to revise. Nonetheless, feminist research challenged accepted beliefs about agenda setting in several important ways.

Conventional Wisdom about Agenda Setting

In the 1970s, political scientists began to focus on agenda setting as a discrete topic of inquiry. In their 1972 path-breaking book, Roger W. Cobb and Charles D. Elder wanted to know where public policy issues came from. They made a distinction between a systemic agenda (that is, political controversies that fell within the range of legitimate concerns meriting the attention of the polity) and the institutional agenda of lawmakers (that is, the items up for active and serious consideration by

253

authoritative decision makers), arguing that the institutional agenda lagged behind the systemic agenda because of the inertia in political systems. They also distinguished among four issue publics, depicted as concentric circles, each including more people concerned about an issue than the prior one: identification group (those who most closely identified with the issue), attention group (those who were informed and interested in the issue), attentive public (those who were generally informed about and interested in politics, also known as opinion leaders), and general public (those who were less active, interested, and informed about political issues).[1]

This new focus on agenda setting seemed well suited to investigate the policy changes that developed in the wake of the women's movement of the 1960s. After all, many new policies about women were arriving with record speed on the nation's agenda. According to feminist critiques, however, conventional studies failed to link political movements to the insider-outsider picture. In conventional treatments of agenda setting, the population of outsiders typically consisted of interest groups, the media, and experts; movements as such were relegated to the hazy realm of political climate or mood of the times. But in the case of the feminist agenda, the women's movement played an important and observable role in agenda setting. As we have seen, the women's movement was not reducible to women's groups; it also included female and feminist consciousness on the part of individual women, of women as group members, and of female elected officials. Women's relationship to the women's movement more broadly conceived had an important bearing on how women's issues made it onto the public agenda.

An emphasis on groups instead of movements characterized another oft-cited work on agenda setting, John W. Kingdon's 1984 book *Agendas, Alternatives, and Public Policies*.[2] Kingdon studied health and transportation policies of the federal government in the late 1970s. He found that a combination of national mood and elections had a greater influence on agendas than did organized interests, which blocked and adapted measures but were unable to initiate issues on their own. In the case of the feminist policy agenda, however, during the administrations of both liberal Lyndon Johnson and conservative Richard Nixon, the national mood and elections had little bearing on the success of women's agenda setting, thanks in large part to the women's movement. Ironically, the policy successes of the women's movement in the early 1970s, particularly abortion rights and the Equal Rights Amendment, contributed to the emergence of the New Right, and the conservative national mood of the 1980s, along with the elections of Presidents Reagan and Bush, dealt a severe blow to the feminist agenda. Thus, an understanding of the ups and downs of the feminist policy agenda was predicated on an analysis of the women's movement of the 1960s and the antifeminist counter-movement of the 1980s.

Kingdon made a distinction between visible participants (elected officials) and hidden participants (academic specialists, career bureaucrats, and congressional staffers). He found that visible players were more important to agenda setting than were invisible players and participants outside government. Once again, this model did not fit the case of setting a women's policy agenda, which resulted from a reciprocal relationship among the women's movement, women's groups, and female elected officials.

Another part of Kingdon's model that did not fit the case of the feminist policy agenda was the importance of policy entrepreneurs, as opposed to policy innovators. Policy entrepreneurs were defined as people willing to invest their resources for future policies they favored; they were elected officials, civil servants, lobbyists, academics, and journalists. Policy entrepreneurs "softened up the system" to make it amenable to their agenda item by brokering people and ideas in recombinations, or couplings of already familiar elements. By contrast, policy innovators came up with wholly new forms of policies. It was perhaps not surprising that policy innovators played a minor role in the issue areas Kingdon examined, health and transportation in the late 1970s, because these issues had had a relatively long life on the nation's political agenda (even though they were relative newcomers at the federal level of government). But innovators played a major role in formulating the women's policy agenda, in large part because of the novelty of women's issues on the nation's agenda. Before the advent of the women's movement in the 1960s, the condition of women was addressed primarily through family law, the province of state governments. The women's movement produced a seismic shift in public views about women—from family member to individual and (sex) group member—and this shift was reflected in some important innovative public policies that were not recombinations of already familiar elements.

The distinction between a brokered idea and agenda-setting role, on the one hand, and an innovative idea and agenda-setting role, on the other, is reflected in two distinctions developed in this chapter. The first is the distinction between role equity and role change. Agenda items involving role equity, or the same thing for men and women, were brokered by policy entrepreneurs who recombined familiar ideas. Agenda items involving role change, or transformations in conventional views of sex roles, were formed anew by policy innovators who named new problems. The second distinction is among the three types of substantive issues on the feminist agenda. Invisible issues were rendered visible as a problem and given new names by transformational innovators. Equality issues were formulated in familiar accommodationist terms and brokered by policy entrepreneurs. Between these two extremes were issues that were recast from the male model to the female model of experience. Most of the issues on the feminist policy agenda fell into this middle category, and their ascendancy onto the agenda involved both innovation and entrepreneurship, new formulations and familiar ideas, role equity and role change. These distinctions reflect the transformational and accommodationist approaches both within the women's movement and among feminist scholars. And they underscore the centrality of the women's movement in the formulation of the feminist policy agenda.

The Importance of Movement Outsiders in Agenda Setting

Political scientists paid scant attention to the role of mass movements in agenda setting, primarily because conventional policymaking paradigms obscured movements from view. The policy process was typically viewed as involving incremental change, with insiders making small adjustments to existing policies in response to interest group pressure, rather than as involving radical change, with mass movements causing major alterations in policy agendas. But the assumption that policymaking was an incremental process provided no theoretically compelling rationale for why some social movements were capable of producing "policy spirals," such as those generated by the clean air movement and the women's movement in the 1970s. One study of the clean air movement adopted a resource mobilization approach to mass movements, emphasizing political resources, organizations, entrepreneurial elites, and strategic choices. The authors noted the importance of the ability of the status quo to use public opinion as a political resource to oppose the agenda-setting efforts of a mass movement. They found that opponents were not able to use public opinion to counteract the policy spiral set off by the clean air movement, though opponents successfully used public opinion to thwart the efforts of the nuclear freeze movement.[3] In a similar fashion, a women's policy spiral slowed in the 1980s as the backlash against the changing role of women was articulated by the New Right and covered and fueled by the popular media.[4]

Attention to mass movements was important because, historically, feminist issues rose and fell on the public agenda according to the strength of the women's movement. Linda Gordon demonstrated a historical relationship between definitions of the problem of family violence and the strength of feminist influence. Family violence emerged as a social problem in an era of a powerful women's rights movement, the 1870s, and campaigns against child abuse and wife beating lost momentum and support, even disappeared altogether, when feminist influence was in decline. During the 1940s and 1950s, a relative low point for feminist consciousness and feminist organizing, child neglect was redefined as emotional neglect of the child by the mother, rather than as sexual or physical molestation of children. Conversely, wife beating, incest, and child abuse received much more attention with the advent of the current wave of the feminist movement, which empowered women to see their "personal" experiences as social problems in need of political solutions. Clearly, women's group and feminist consciousness, coupled with politicians' perception of the influence of women as a group, had a bearing on agenda setting.[5] Further evidence of a historical relationship between the public agenda and the women's movement came from a longitudinal study of congressional treatment of women's issues from 1900 to 1982, which revealed high levels of congressional action during periods when there was a mobilized women's movement compared to limited activity in nonmovement periods.[6]

Another important reason for considering the women's movement as something broader than women's groups was the fact that the change in women's consciousness spawned by the movement preceded both feminists' attention to the public policy process and the formation of feminist groups to influence governmental decision makers. The women's movement focused on consciousness-raising in the 1960s and public policy in the 1970s. Through consciousness-raising, individual women saw their personal concerns as group concerns, best ameliorated through group action. As we saw in Chapter 3, though feminist consciousness and action were always considered "political," they were not initially directed toward the government. As Ellen Boneparth, editor of the first feminist anthology on women and public policy put it, "By the beginning of the 1970s, feminists came to realize that many of their goals could best be achieved by improving the status of women through public policy. While governmental programs do not provide the solutions to all problems, they do carry with them authority and resources to change behavior, if not attitudes."[7]

The policy focus of the women's movement was documented in a series of books on women and public policy that began to appear in the 1980s. Most of them, however, did not develop the distinction between the politics of getting an issue onto the agenda and the politics of influence

once an issue was on the agenda. Implied but not always developed was
the notion that it took a broad-based movement to get issues articulated
and heard.[8] The exception in this regard was Jo Freeman's 1975 classic
work, *The Politics of Women's Liberation: A Case Study of an Emerging Social
Movement and Its Relation to the Policy Process*. As the subtitle indicated,
Freeman explicitly linked the women's movement to policymaking. She
noted that when the women's movement emerged in the mid-1960s,
there was no national policy on the status of women. Many state laws restricted women's freedoms and opportunities, and those few state laws
providing for equal and fair employment practices were more often ignored than enforced. In 1963, President Kennedy's Commission on the
Status of Women issued its report, which indirectly contributed to the formation of state commissions but did not lead to any specific legislation.
The only federal legislation affecting women at the time, the 1963 Equal
Pay Act and Title VII of the 1964 Civil Rights Act, were "idiosyncratic occurrences." Many civil rights activists and officials were hostile to the addition of sex discrimination to the federal agenda, since women were
competing with minority groups for a share of the slim federal pie.[9]

By 1972, the women's movement had changed things. Most of the demands in NOW's 1968 Bill of Rights had been at least partially attained,
including the two that had caused splits within the organization, legal-
ized abortion and congressional passage of the Equal Rights Amendment. As Freeman put it:

> Federal policy of equal opportunity, if not total equality, was
> clearly emerging in piecemeal fashion, and the legal and ad-
> ministrative tools were being forged with which feminist groups
> could viably work toward equal opportunity. What is striking
> about this new policy is not simply there is still a long way to go,
> but that the notoriously cumbersome governmental apparatus
> has done so much so quickly. . . . It is even more striking when
> one realizes that this new policy is basically redistributive in na-
> ture, although it often uses regulatory techniques, and thus in-
> volves conflict between large classes of people over the redistri-
> bution of social resources from one group to another.
>
> . . . There have been very few case studies of redistributive
> policy decisions; thus there are not really any adequate models
> for analyzing the ones we are concerned with here. I would ar-
> gue that a main reason so few studies have been made of this im-
> portant area is because the development of these major new pol-
> icy areas has often been the result of social movements. Political

scientists have paid little attention to social movements as relevant political phenomena, concentrating primarily on the interest groups into which they occasionally evolve. Thus they have not been able to see the intimate relationship between many new redistributive policies and the emergence of new organized interests in society.[10]

In her analysis of the output of the Ninety-second Congress (1971–72), which passed more women's rights legislation than the sum total of all such legislation passed in U.S. history, Freeman used a model of "an emerging women's policy system" to analyze the relationship between the women's movement and agenda setting. Other feminist scholars adopted similar models of women's policy networks to express the relationship among the women's movement, women's groups, and public officials.

The Emergence of Women's Policy Networks

Freeman described the symbiotic relationship that existed among feminists within governmental institutions, feminists operating in the private sphere, and even feminists opposed to or alienated from the American political system. This symbiosis existed despite the fact that many individuals or groups within these different spheres would consider such a relationship undesirable if they were conscious of its presence. It was maintained by three factors: feminists' sharing of common ideas and symbols, which enabled them to see differences more as a division of labor than as a means of divisiveness; widespread sharing of new ideas and activities by both the feminist and the commercial media, which prevented different segments from becoming totally isolated from one another; and interlocking informal communications networks throughout most of the movement, through which information, ideas, contacts, and some resources were shared.

Drawing on personal interviews and her own experiences in the women's movement, Freeman provided an example of how this informal communications network operated. This example underscored how a methodology of participant observation revealed a role of the women's movement that would be obscured with an exclusive focus on the interest group–elected official relationship.

How this network operates is illustrated by a connection between an obscure radical feminist in California and the White House that occurred in late 1970. Largely as a result of the grand press blitz of that year, the White House received an average of three letters a week from women who wanted to know how they could join a women's liberation group. They were referred to the Women's Bureau who dutifully answered the queries, using chapter lists from NOW and WEAL, a list of primarily East Coast small groups printed in the *Ladies Home Journal* (in their special August 1970 insert on the women's movement agreed to after a hundred feminists held a sit-in in the publisher's office), and *The Mushroom Effect.* The latter was a sixteen-page tabloid directory produced by the efforts of a single woman in Albany, California, and of great value to the Women's Bureau because, unlike the other sources, it was mostly non–East Coast groups. Copies of this directory had been taken by its compiler to a small Minneapolis women's liberation conference in September 1970. Among the people there to whom it was given was a Midwest feminist who was also in occasional contact with Catherine East [a member of the Citizen's Advisory Council on the Status of Women]. As East's office was across the hall from the Women's Bureau, she was aware of their need and acquired a copy of *The Mushroom Effect* for them. Thus the work of a politically alienated feminist on the other side of the country was used to answer the White House's mail.

The traditional perspective on this relationship has seen it as a rather nebulous one-way pattern in which a social movement affects public opinion and that in turn affects policy. Specific influence was exercised through interest groups. While this perspective is not exactly wrong, it is limited. The process is simply much more complicated than that. In general one can say that a social movement provides resources for those within government who are sympathetic to use in the pursuit of common aims. The movement's ability to affect public opinion is just one of those resources. Information on problems, new ideas, skilled help, activities which generate publicity, and lots of warm bodies are some of the other resources.[11]

The women's movement provided many strategic resources for sympathetic government officials. It generated publicity on women's status, which legitimated women's rights as a relevant public concern. It created a climate of expectations that something would be done, especially for issues of educational and employment equality. It created a constituency for "woodwork feminists" in government, who had been concerned with women's issues for years and could now use popular demand to impress those in positions of power with the priority of such issues. It provided grassroots research to feminists within Congress who were sponsoring relevant bills. And it supplied grassroots support: meetings, conferences, and demonstrations. Of course, the provision of resources was a reciprocal relationship. Government officials also provided inside information to feminists about upcoming issues for which public pressure would be of mutual benefit.

A women's policy system emerged in Washington in the early 1970s during efforts to secure congressional passage of the ERA and education legislation. These efforts created a climate in Congress of serious constituent interest in women's rights. Because both issues appealed to the American egalitarian ethic, there was little organized opposition. Freeman noted: "Both the mail and the numerous respectable organizations which backed the ERA helped to dispel the negative impression of the women's liberation movement created by the press. As Martha Griffiths expressed it, 'The ERA created a moral climate for reform. Once it was put through, everything else became logical.' "[12] These legislative efforts also established liaisons between feminist organizations and congressional staff, exposing many of the "woodwork" feminists on Capitol Hill. The incipient policy network made it easier to know who to approach for what kind of support and information for other women's bills.

Freeman's analysis of an emerging women's policy network in Washington in the 1970s was corroborated in several case studies in Irene Tinker's edited volume, *Women in Washington: Advocates for Public Policy*.[13] Each of these cases, written by activist women, documented a relationship among the women's movement, women's groups, and government officials. In addition to the early "equality" issues of the ERA and educational equality (Title IX), a women's policy network was at work in the areas of women's health, domestic violence, flexible work patterns, pregnancy discrimination, government contracts for female-owned businesses, women in the military, women in science, women in development and foreign aid, and federal commissions and conferences on women.

A crucial link in the emerging policy network of the 1970s was, of course, a new breed of women in Congress, whom Irwin N. Gertzog termed "feminist colleagues." They saw themselves as representatives of both their constituents and American women, in whose name they adopted feminist causes. They did not necessarily abjure or dilute their "feminine" behavior, but neither did they go out of their way to please the men with whom they worked. Unlike some "neutral professional" congresswomen who did not mind being addressed as "Congressman," many "feminist colleagues" insisted that they be referred to as "Ms." Some congresswomen who did not arrive in Washington as feminists soon defined themselves as such when they realized that men came to Congress with a presumption of competence but women came with the burden of proof on them to prove their competence. Whereas "neutrals" were more flexible and willing to compromise, "feminists" were more insistent on achieving feminist goals. Social and professional relationships between men and women in the House gradually became less strained. Women increasingly staked out leadership positions on feminist issues, insisting, unlike some of their predecessors, that their identities as women made them better qualified to write laws addressing the needs of women. They devoted large shares of time mobilizing support for the ERA. They evaluated legislative measures from a feminist perspective, asking how bills would effect women. Gertzog observed:

> In the process, they raised the consciousness of male colleagues, politicized issues which had until then been considered private rather than public in character, and began to alter the national agenda. . . . Male members' understanding of their representative responsibilities has also been undergoing change. Congressmen have become less likely to ignore or treat cursorily the women's constituency and they are much less diffident today about identifying with and even dramatizing their support for feminist causes. . . . Congressmen who once treated the women's movement as a source of humor and its goals as insignificant, are now less likely to exchange wise cracks and locker room jokes about matters which women have always taken seriously.[14]

Many studies documented the operations of women's policy networks at the national level of government, but few focused on state and local government. As was the case in Santa Clara County, researchers found that state and local commissions on the status of women were often at the center of women's policy networks.[15] One study of agenda setting in Milwaukee discovered that councilwomen set the agenda in the absence of a formal women's policy network. To the dismay of councilwomen, local women's groups directed their efforts toward state and national issues at the expense of local matters. Even though two-thirds of the women who had served on the Milwaukee City Council between 1966 and 1990 had been leaders on women's issues, they did not benefit from a women's caucus, as their congressional counterparts did. Given their low numbers, partisan differences, and fear of adverse reactions from councilmen, councilwomen formed ad hoc coalitions around issues instead. Their male colleagues overestimated the extent of women's formal caucusing and underestimated women's informal cooperative actions, especially concerning the issues of sexual harassment, day care, sexual assault, minority women, and the environment. Councilwomen raised women's issues, sensitized men to them, and obtained active or passive male support for women's issues. Most councilmembers of both sexes agreed that women made a policy difference in raising women's issues and bringing a different viewpoint to policymaking.[16]

Role Equity and Role Change

Another insight that feminist researchers brought to conventional wisdom on agenda setting was making a distinction between role equity and role change, reflecting the varied goals of the women's movement: equality with men in some instances and a radical rethinking of sex roles in others. Obviously, policies aimed at role change would have a harder time making it onto a policy agenda. An appeal to equality made a policy more palatable than did an appeal to new roles for women. It was no accident that two of the earliest feminist victories in Washington were the role equity issues of the ERA and educational equality.

The distinction between role equity and role change was central to Joyce Gelb and Marian Lief Palley's analysis of major women's policies in the 1970s and 1980s in Washington: Title IX of the 1972 Education Amendments, the 1974 Equal Credit Opportunity Act, the Hyde amendment (first adopted in 1976 to prohibit Medicaid funding of abortions), the 1978 Pregnancy Discrimination Act, and the 1984 Economic Equity Act.[17] These policies fell on a continuum, with equal credit on the equity end and abortion on the change end. The other three policies fell somewhere in the middle. Title IX was on the equity end until it came to certain regulations encompassing role change in college athletics. Similarly, pregnancy discrimination was on the equity end until some provisions ventured into the arena of abortion. And the various measures making up the Economic Equity Act involved both role equity (e.g., child support enforcement and pension reform) and role change (e.g., displaced homemakers' tax credit). The authors defined role equity as the extension of rights currently enjoyed by other groups to women, and role change as an alteration in the dependent role of wife, homemaker, and mother.

Gelb and Palley interviewed participants in the policymaking process in Washington and focused on both political mobilization and interest group development. They argued that feminists in Washington relied on

a generally supportive public in the 1970s, electoral techniques (such as
PACs, direct mail, and the Women's Campaign Fund), and four types of
groups: feminist (NOW, NWPC, WEAL), traditional (League of Women
Voters, AAUW, BPW, General Federation of Women's Clubs, and National Council on Jewish Women), specialized (Center for Women Policy Studies and the ACLU's Reproductive Freedom Project and Women's
Rights Project), and single-issue (National Abortion Rights Action League
and NOW's Project on Equal Education Rights). Although feminists had
fewer resources than their civil rights counterparts did in the 1970s, they
made good use of what they had by being pragmatic professionals who
were compromise-oriented and sought incremental change. Although
women's groups were bureaucratized, they had not become conservative
oligarchies, in which the few ruled in their own interests, nor had they
produced charismatic leaders, comparable to a John Gardner of Common Cause or a Ralph Nader of consumer groups. The notion of sisterhood had carried over to internal democracy within women's groups
and to members' attachment to the movement and ideology over individual leaders. Thus, Gelb and Palley described the women's movement
in Washington as relatively free from the kinds of divisive rivalries that
had consumed the energies of other movements in the 1970s.[18]

Women's groups used various strategies to get issues on the national
agenda. Protest was rarely used, the two notable exceptions being a 1970
protest at a meeting of a Senate Judiciary Committee subcommittee to
get the ERA reported to the full committee and the 1970 Women's Strike
for Equality. Feminists used litigation to force cases for consciousness-
raising purposes; frequently, there was a positive spillover effect even
when feminists lost in court. For example, although the 1976 U.S.
Supreme Court decision in *General Electric v. Gilbert* dealt a blow to opponents of pregnancy discrimination, it provided a catalyst for coalition-
building in Congress, leading ultimately to the enactment of the 1978
Pregnancy Discrimination Act. Women also used litigation to press agencies to enforce women's rights laws.

Gelb and Palley drew several important lessons about the women's
movement's ability to get issues on the agenda and enacted into law.
Movement success was more likely when the policy involved role equity
rather than role change, when the changes sought were incremental
rather than overarching, when there was an image of broad-based popular support, when there were policy networks connecting women in
Congress with aides and research organizations, when there was conventional lobbying by professional experts, when coalitions were formed,
when confrontation was avoided, when feminists could manipulate the

definition of the situation, and when issues were discrete and kept within narrow technical bounds.[19]

The distinction between role equity and role change was an important one for women employed by feminist policy centers; they learned to choose strategies according to the type of issue. The first feminist policy centers appeared in Washington in the early 1970s. The Center for Women Policy Studies (CWPS) was established in 1972 to prepare technically sound proposals for solutions to women's issues, especially in the realm of legal and economic policy. Feminist policy centers were influential in changing government policies on credit discrimination, a role equity issue, and the victimization of women, a role change issue. In the latter case, feminist policy centers got the issues of rape and the battery of women on the federal agenda. Because of the efforts of these centers, a study of rape crisis centers was distributed through the federal Law Enforcement Assistance Administration, and the Office of Domestic Violence was established in the Department of Health, Education and Welfare.[20]

Beginning in the 1970s, public policy analysts began to catalog conditions favorable to placing one's issue on the public agenda: extremity of effects, concentration in one geographic area, visibility of the problem, incremental adjustments to an old issue, evocation of national symbols, and the valence (i.e., high salience and low conflict) character of the issue.[21] Feminist scholarship added to this list the role equity, as opposed to role change, nature of the issue.

The Effect of Countermovements on Agenda Setting

Conventional studies of agenda setting and policymaking agreed that issues were frequently denied access to the agenda or killed during the policymaking process by hostile interests. Since most political science and public policy studies adopted a pluralist model of politics in which interest groups were the major players, conventional studies failed to notice not only the role of movements in getting issues onto the agenda but the related phenomenon of movements' ability to block issues as they made their way through the policymaking process. In the case of feminist policy, it was certainly true that interest groups opposed feminist policies, but the story was more complex than that. Countermovements arose to oppose the policy successes of the feminist movement, and these countermovements were populated by antifeminist women. Conventional models that saw only interest groups missed the import of countermovements and were at a loss to explain why women figured prominently in the campaigns to oppose abortion rights and the Equal Rights Amendment.

In the wake of Ronald Reagan's election in 1980, feminists analyzed of the rise of the New Right and its ability to have its agenda, especially opposition to the ERA and abortion, take precedence over the feminist agenda. The New Right had succeeded in portraying its movement as "profamily" and the women's movement as "antifamily." Analysts pinpointed the 1972 congressional passage of the ERA and the 1973 *Roe v. Wade* decision on abortion as setting off a countermovement in response to these policy victories.

Some analysts put more emphasis on abortion than on the ERA as a causative factor in the emergence of the New Right. Rosalind Pollack Petchesky argued that the New Right's focus on reproductive and sexual issues and on the family gave it ideological legitimacy and organizational coherence. The two themes of the New Right's moral offensive were an antifeminist backlash (against abortion, sexual freedom, and challenges to the patriarchal family) and an anti–social welfare state backlash (against New Deal programs). The organizational base of the countermovement was the church, and its ideological message was the reprivatization of the politics of sexuality and the family and an opposition to the power of the federal government over families (as expressed, for instance, in the proposed Family Protection Act). In Petchesky's view, what accounted for the mass consciousness of the New Right was a reaction to profound changes in U.S. society regarding sexual behavior, a low birthrate, and women's workforce participation.[22]

In a similar vein, Zillah Eisenstein maintained that the 1980 election represented a shift to the right to deradicalize the women's movement by dismantling its reproductive rights and pro-abortion forces. Women's reproductive rights presupposed women's self-determination, which was directly at odds with a patriarchal world view. The Republican party's opposition to abortion and the ERA attacked the liberal feminist section of the women's movement, which embraced the liberal values of freedom of choice, individual self-determination, and equality before the law. Eisenstein linked this assault to the growing radicalization of the demands of liberal feminists, demands that led to efforts to restabilize the family and patriarchy.[23]

Other analysts put equal emphasis on abortion and the ERA as igniting a conflict between the two movements over the family. Pamela J. Conover and Virginia Gray, who studied the roles of these issues in the feminist and New Right movements by interviewing activists at the 1980 White House Conference on Families, developed a model of social movements that went beyond both the collective behavior and the resource mobilization paradigms. Until the 1970s, the collective behavior model, which focused on the emotions and irrationality of the individual who engaged in collective action, was most often used to understand mass movements. The resource mobilization theory developed as a corrective to this view, stating that people became involved in social movements not as a consequence of irrational fears or social isolation but as a result of self-interest, group loyalties, and personal principles. According to Conover and Gray, although there was some appeal to self-interest in both movements, more important were group loyalties and personal principles. Feminists were mobilized on the basis of existing group loyalties to labor unions, civil rights organizations, and leftist student groups and through appeals to the principles of justice and equality. Members of the New Right were mobilized on the basis of their membership in Catholic and fundamentalist Protestant churches and through appeals to the values of traditional family life.[24]

Nevertheless, Conover and Gray faulted the resource mobilization theory for its relative neglect of emotions and feelings. In abandoning the collective behavior paradigm with its emphasis on overly emotional individuals, resource mobilization theorists went too far, downplaying the role of issues in capturing activists' emotions. Issues were key factors in understanding the emotional appeal of both the feminist and the New Right movements. Issues represented the demands of a movement and gave form to the grievances fueling its growth. By defining the substance of an issue, political entrepreneurs established its public meaning. An issue defined in a dry, unemotional fashion by one side in a conflict (e.g., the right to choose) could be turned into a highly emotional issue by the other side simply by the way it was defined or symbolized (e.g., killing babies). In Conover and Gray's view, only a model that included issues and symbolic politics could explain the bitter divisions among women over the ERA and abortion: "The issues of abortion and ERA that the New Right opposes do not concern the principles of equality and independence championed by the women's movement; rather, they are issues of morality, God, and family life. . . . There is no common ground for resolution because the two sides are not talking about the same things."[25]

Other studies of women of the New Right suggested that they were not a monolithic group when it came to issues. Rebecca E. Klatch argued that their class and educational differences led to divergent views on the issue of abortion and to two categories of women: social conservatives and laissez-faire conservatives. Social conservatives were less educated, had a lower socioeconomic status, and were more religious and intolerant than were laissez-faire women. Where social conservatives saw gender roles as divinely ordained and women as supporters of men and others, laissez-faire women saw the sexes as equally rational and autonomous. Social conservatives were active politically as women to defend women's interests as they had been traditionally defined; laissez-faire conservatives were active politically as self-interested members of a market economy. Social conservatives opposed big government for its immorality, secular humanism, and usurpation of male authority in the family; laissez-faire conservatives opposed big government as a threat to economic and political liberty. Social conservatives were primarily concerned with the family and moral decay in their opposition to the ERA, abortion, homosexuality, and busing and in their support for school prayer. Laissez-faire conservatives were concerned with the erosion of political and economic freedoms in their opposition to taxes and the welfare state and in their desire for the United States to maintain its role as world leader. Laissez-faire conservatives often agreed with some feminist views, such as abortion rights, but parted company with feminists' call for changing gender roles and using the state to combat discrimination against women. Klatch argued that the two types of New Right women existed as uneasy partners in a coalition.[26]

One of the most important defining characteristics of the social conservative women of the New Right was their defense of conventional roles for women, from which they derived their status. The theme of the derived status of homemakers was central to Susan E. Marshall's comparison of women who opposed feminism during the antisuffrage movement (1910–18) and during the anti-ERA campaign of the 1970s. In both cases, mandating gender equality was seen by antifeminist women as a threat to their privileged status as homemakers, which excused them from the responsibilities of financial support, political participation, and military service. Sacred symbols of family, God, and country were evoked to defend domestic roles. Feminists were discredited as being selfish, unpatriotic, irreligious, antifamily, antimale, and antifemale. According to the antifeminist view, sex differences were divinely ordained, with men intellectually and physically superior to women. Men were thus better suited to operate in the realms of economics, politics, and the military, and women in the realms of home, childrearing, and morality. Antifeminist homemakers maintained that working mothers neglected their children, resented affirmative action policies that forced employers to hire single women over men with dependents, and argued that the ERA would eliminate the right to be a homemaker and threaten capitalism and limited government. In short, government-mandated equality, whether suffrage or the ERA, was seen as eroding female privilege and adding un-wanted responsibilities. In both time periods, women's perceptions of the privileged status of homemaker varied by social class. Antisuffrage women were wives of the industrial elite in the Northeast, who feared the growing political power of recent immigrants. Anti-ERA women tended to be lower-middle-class women with high school educations who viewed marriage as a form of upward mobility and saw pro-ERA women as elitist and college-educated. And the economic problems of the 1970s, relative to the economic boom of the 1960s, contributed to these women's as-sessment that their economic condition was more likely to be improved through marriage than through their own efforts in the marketplace.[27]

An analysis of strategies used by feminists and antifeminists in influ-encing textbook selection for Texas public schools illustrated how these movements had different ends, organizational principles, styles of lobby-ing, and degrees of success. Although antifeminist women were members of overlapping conservative groups, they presented themselves not as group members but rather as concerned individuals, even though they conceived and executed group strategies. Compared to feminist women, they displayed more experience with and knowledge about the state po-litical system, expended more time per person on the textbook criticism process, and met with greater success. Ironically, antifeminists espoused traditional sex roles yet showed a long-term involvement in public poli-cymaking, and feminists, who were primarily NOW members challenging sexism in the Texas textbooks, presented a much more authoritarian and paranoid image to the public than their antifeminist counterparts did.[28]

Finally, scholarly investigations of the antifeminist movement delved into the role of religion. Interviews with pro- and anti-ERA women in Texas in 1975 found that religious differences between these two groups of women were greater than differences in income and education. Op-ponents were members of conservative religious denominations, whereas proponents either belonged to liberal denominations or were unaffili-ated with a religion.[29] A 1982 analysis of Christian and feminist political action committees demonstrated how they confronted different con-straints in their attempts to mobilize their constituencies to influence the policy agenda. Christian groups often faced apathy, ignorance, and opposition to political activism among their constituents. Though Chris-tian PACs were able to tap into preexisting church networks, they had to compete with churches for members' money and time, and they had to counter charges that they were violating the separation of church and state. Feminist groups typically had apolitical or alienated constituen-cies. Though feminist activists had strong commitments to the cause, they were often politically naive. In addition, the diverse components of the feminist agenda frequently led to fragmentation rather than effective coalitions.[30]

Other analysts maintained that it was a mistake to paint evangelical Protestant women with a single antifeminist brush. Robert Booth Fowler argued that during the 1970s there was a lively debate between feminists and antifeminists within evangelical Protestantism. Evangelical Protestant antifeminist women believed that secular individualism was selfish; that wives should submit to the authority of their husbands; that the Bible was literally true; that the women's movement challenged the biblical basis for motherhood and the family; that equality stemmed from obedience to God, who gave each sex an equally important function (women as caretakers of husband and children, and men as leader of the family); and that women were born to serve others. For their part, evangelical Protestant feminist women argued that women's self-fulfillment was important; that women should serve God, not men; that sex roles should shift from machismo to mutuality; that women should participate in the church; that Jesus treated women as equals; that the Bible contained contradictory messages about the role of women; and that women participated in the early church as equals. During the 1970s, the ideas of evangelical Protestant feminists circulated in underground publications, excluded from a dialogue with mainstream feminists, who tended to see these women as the enemy.[31]

In a similar fashion, Clyde Wilcox argued that evangelical Christians were not a monolithic bloc and that there was room for the mobilization of evangelical women by both feminist and antifeminist organizations. His analysis of data from the 1984 American National Election Study survey revealed that evangelical respondents were divided on feminist issues. Among white evangelical women, one-half supported the ERA, while one-third opposed it; two-thirds favored the distribution of birth control information in public schools, while one-fifth opposed it; one-fourth endorsed abortion on demand, and one-fourth said abortion should never be permitted; and one-fourth approved of government funding for abortion, with one-half opposed to such funding. Overall, 11 percent of the women adopted the feminist position on all four issues, and 5 percent took the antifeminist position on all four issues. As for organizational support, 22 percent of the respondents supported NOW, 17 percent backed the Moral Majority, and 62 percent supported neither. NOW supporters were relatively younger, better educated, employed, wealthy, liberal on women's issues, and less frequent church attenders.[32]

When the analysis of women and religion was extended beyond evangelical Protestantism, it was noted that women had greater attachment to religious beliefs and practices than men did. This attachment held even as women became better educated and entered the workforce. Even female officeholders were more involved in religion than were their male counterparts. Except for Episcopal groups, most religious organizations were populated with women who were not feminists. Thus, at the grassroots level, churches were better able to mobilize women against feminist causes. Until the early 1970s, religious liberals were more likely to be politically involved than were religious conservatives; since the mid-1970s, that pattern has been reversed. The general public was evenly divided between religious conservatives and religious liberals in all denominations. In ANES data from 1976, 1980, and 1984, women who frequently attended church services were more politically active than were less-frequent attenders in 1980 and 1984 but not 1976, evidence that religious participation could have been mobilized into the New Right political participation of the 1980s. In addition, more women than men watched religious television programs at home, and such programs had the effect of mobilizing conservative women.[33]

A Feminist Rethinking of the State

Largely in response to the shock of the antifeminist countermovement, feminists began to rethink the relationship between women and the state. Some who had dismissed the state as a tool of capitalist patriarchy came to see it as a resource for women in their battle against male power at home and in the workplace. Others sought to recapture "the family" from right-wing discourse. And others probed the meaning of women's citizenship in relation to the military state and the social welfare state. Many feminists sought a formulation of the state that was neither Marxist nor liberal but rather based on women's experiences of the state as a benefit provider to interdependent citizens. In her overview of 1980s feminist scholarship on the welfare state, Linda Gordon noted how U.S. research on the topic had lagged behind that of European feminists. She attributed this relative neglect to the comparative weakness of the U.S. social welfare state, its decentralized nature, and the tradition of hostility toward the state on the part of New Left feminists in the United States.[34]

A rethinking of the state from a capitalist patriarchal tool to a resource for women was reflected in socialist feminist analysis of the growing number of female-headed households, initially cast in terms of a shift from the private patriarchy of male households to the public patriarchy of the state. As children were no longer needed for their unskilled labor but instead were valued for their future skilled labor, they became a costly burden that most men wished to avoid, and fathers did not fight to keep their children after divorce. Male-headed families were no longer needed to maintain patriarchy, since the public patriarchy of the state took over women's childbearing and childrearing through policies such as Aid to Families with Dependent Children. Socialist feminists advocated more generous support programs for female-headed households, especially in the areas of welfare benefits, children's allowances, child care, legal assistance, and child support payments, conceding that women's dependence on public patriarchy was preferable to their dependence on private patriarchy, even though ultimately both forms of male power were objectionable.[35]

The social welfare state exercised contradictory emancipatory and control functions in women's lives. Though women's growing workforce participation decreased their dependence on family patriarchy, their disproportionate employment in the human services sector made them especially vulnerable in times of welfare state retrenchment. Female human service providers and welfare recipients constituted over 70 percent of the nation's participants in the social welfare economy. President Reagan's dismantling of the social welfare economy thus had a disproportionate impact on women.[36]

In an attempt to recapture "the family" from right-wing discourse, Irene Diamond argued that women's relation to the social welfare state was best clarified by a feminist analysis of families. Criticizing the inadequacy of the "demographic reductionism" that characterized many accounts of families, she focused instead on the political context within which demographic changes in "the family" had occurred. As social service providers in the federal government became increasingly professionalized, government reports and programs shifted focus from individual opportunity and poverty to familial opportunity and poverty. Social movements had their reasons for focusing on families. Civil rights groups such as the Children's Defense Fund used a familial focus to respond to the national mood of civil rights retrenchment in the 1970s. Ecologists and feminists wanted to emphasize the contextual and relational aspects of human existence. And some leftists and liberals thought a family focus was conducive to comprehensive social planning (as in the Scandinavian model) and to resistance to the unbridled power of professionals and experts. Critics from the New Left challenged what they saw as the scientized, depoliticized, and dehumanized discourse of public policy analysis emanating from social science research institutes. And the New Right criticized the social-expert state as an infringement on the power of the father in the family and attempted to replace state scientific authority with divinely ordained parental authority over family matters. Diamond said that from a feminist perspective, the "state" had become a problematic notion, perhaps an exhausted category.[37]

Research from a comparative perspective found that the state had nowhere been neutral to women and that in order to understand the meaning of the transition from private to public dependence for women, feminists needed to transcend both liberal and Marxist paradigms of the state. The modern welfare state had a double meaning for women, who had gained power as workers, mothers, and citizens but who were subsumed under a new public power hierarchy. As even Scandinavian states were described as social patriarchies, there was a call for more research on welfare states from women's perspective.[38]

While all feminist analysts called for an end to gender-blind research on the welfare state,[39] and most saw both positive and negative features of women's relation to it, some argued that on balance, the welfare state had become a political resource for women, making them more secure and less powerless than they would otherwise be. Frances Fox Piven asserted, "The expansion of social welfare programs has created a far-flung and complex infrastructure of agencies and organizations that are so far proving to be a resource in the defense of the welfare state and may even have larger potential," such as leadership positions for women, the political mobilization of poor women, and cross-class alliances among women as service providers and recipients.[40]

Much of the feminist discussion of women and the state centered on the concept of women's dependence, especially as it shifted from family to state dependence. The concept of dependence also informed feminist considerations of women's citizenship in military and social welfare states: could women be full citizens if they were dependent on a male military for protection and if they were clients dependent on the welfare state? Feminists were ambivalent about pursuing a policy agenda that increased women's dependence, but they were equally ambivalent about accepting male definitions of citizenship based on military prowess and breadwinner status.

On the question of women's citizenship and the military, Judith Hicks Stiehm argued that women were denied full citizenship because they did not have the opportunity to share fully in the state's defining function: the practice of legitimate force. Basic questions about the protection of women had to be answered before women forged a policy agenda. "The policy agenda asks: 'Should women serve in combat?' 'Should women be drafted?' More basic are the questions: 'Should men monopolize legitimate violence?' and 'Does protection necessarily become a racket?' States do many things but the one thing they all do is hold a monopoly on the exercise of legitimate force." Women's status as a "protectee" perpetuated two myths: that women were incapable of taking on the shared risks and responsibilities of citizenship and that the protector's actions were altruistic or directed by the protectee. Much of the thinking that excluded women from combat was not "scientific" but conventional. "When the evidence can so easily dispel a policy justification, one begins to understand that one is not really engaged in disproving but in demythologizing. And demythologizing can be futile if the underlying need for myth continues. If women's physiology does not support a ban on their exemption from combat, is it men's psychology and women's compliance with this psychology that does so?" For Stiehm, protection was ultimately a racket, which women should avoid if they wanted full citizenship. Thus she supported drafting and preparing women for combat.[41]

Others came to different conclusions about women and the military. Many urged women to withdraw from the military state and to devote their energies to the creation of a feminist peace politics and peace education.[42] Sara Ruddick grappled with the dilemma of antimilitarist feminists. As antimilitarists, they opposed the use of weapons of organized violence and sought nonviolent modes of conflict resolution; as feminists, they wanted to eliminate restrictions on women's power. Ruddick agreed with Stiehm that the right to fight was significant for a powerless group; that dividing the protected from the protector was a linchpin of masculinist as well as military ideology; and that the right to participate in organized violence and to share its burdens was, for women, a means to self-respect, full citizenship, and equality with men. Ultimately, however, Ruddick did not trust the U.S. government to wage just wars, and she advocated recruiting women for peace: encouraging women to develop alternative ways of "fighting" and "protecting" through pacifist organizations.[43] Others focused not so much on women's pacifism as on the sources of men's involvement in the making of war. Nancy C. M. Hartsock argued that the key to understanding masculine citizenship was found in masculinity as an ideology: a cultural construction centered on fear and fascination with the problems of death, mortality, and oblivion. On the battlefield, men could attain glory, honor, and immortality in the memory of men. According to Hartsock, before feminists formulated a policy agenda with respect to women and the military, they needed to break the linkage of masculinity with both military capacity and death.[44]

Feminist Policy Analysis

A final feminist challenge to conventional wisdom about agenda set-ting came from researchers who engaged in feminist policy analysis. In the 1990s, they articulated an approach that amounted to a conceptual and methodological alternative to policy analysis as usual. Two re-searchers from the Institute for Women's Policy Research, Roberta Spalter-Roth and Heidi Hartmann, reflected on the concepts and meth-ods they employed in their agenda-setting work *Unnecessary Losses: Costs to Americans of the Lack of Family and Medical Leave.*[45] They gathered empiri-cal evidence for supporters of the Family and Medical Leave Act (FMLA) in order to shift the political debate from a focus on the cost to business of the FMLA to the cost to women and society of not having it. They de-scribed their method as "dual vision": they adopted the dominant para-digm of welfare economics and cost-benefit analysis as objective experts working for policymakers, but they also used a feminist framework that saw the reproduction of gender, race, and class inequities as part of so-cial life and that challenged rigid dichotomies between activists and re-searchers and between social science and social movements. They con-ceded that embracing the contradictions between mainstream and feminist methodologies had its risks.

First, although we were successful at contesting the rhetoric of this particular policy debate, feminist discourse is constrained and often silenced by more powerful mainstream ideologies (and resources). By putting women's rather than families' in-terests at the center, we risk losing the debate. Second, by using sophisticated quantitative methodological techniques, we may make our research less accessible to the advocacy groups with whom we work and the women in whose interests we are work-ing. Time-consuming training is often necessary to make data meaningful and accessible. Third, suppose the data did not turn out to show greater losses for those without some form of parental leave? Given our adherence to the canons of quantita-tive social science research, we would not have "cooked" the data. We might have been able to explore other data sets or other models, but given the time and money constraints of most policy research this would have been unlikely. We surely would have disappointed our constituency, who would probably have been less likely to risk working with us on another research study in the future. Our credibility as a feminist policy research think

tank is based on our embracing the contradictions . . . [of] the
dual vision.[46]

As we saw in the last chapter, Susan E. Clarke and Lyn Kathlene
called for an engendered policy analysis. Based on their extensive studies of Colorado state legislators, they saw a need to develop contextual
research designs and methods; policy criteria that went beyond effi-
ciency and equity to include well-being, respect, and skills; a change orientation to questions of central concern to women; and a clear articulation of the analyst's standpoint.[47] Feminist policy analysts took women's
experiences seriously, marshaled evidence to advance women's policy
concerns, paid attention to the distinctive ways that women framed policy problems, challenged the dichotomy between observer and activist,
and placed gender concerns on equal footing with the more econo-
mistic concerns of conventional policy analysis.

Thus far we have seen how feminist scholarship has challenged conventional understandings of *how* public agendas emerged. We now turn
to a discussion of three types of *substantive* issues on the feminist policy
agenda: previously "invisible" conditions rendered visible and named as
policy problems by feminists (sexual harassment, domestic violence, and
sexual slavery), policies recast by feminists from a model based on male
experience to a model based on female experience (rape, pornography,
abortion, and health care), and policies whereby women sought equality with men (equal pay, credit, and education). The first type of issue reached the policy agenda as a result of transformational feminist
analysis. The third type of issue made its way onto the policy agenda
through accommodationist feminist analysis. And the second type of issue reached the policy agenda thanks to both transformational and
accommodationist feminist analysis.

Invisible Conditions Named Policy Problems by Feminists

In the mid-1970s, transformational feminists reframed previously
"invisible" conditions as problems and secured a place for them on the
policy agenda. Three examples are sexual harassment, domestic violence, and female sexual slavery.

Dorothy McBride Stetson described how feminists "discovered" the
problem of sexual harassment.

One hundred years ago, women workers' vulnerability to male
sexual advances was seen as the result of generalized male sexual

aggression. . . . For the most part, however, such sexual advances were considered not a matter for government interest, but rather a matter of private sexual choice. The women's consciousness-raising groups in the early 1970s brought awareness to feminists of the pervasiveness of these sexual practices at school and work and on the street and their effects on women's status. . . . In 1975, feminists gave the problem a name: sexual harassment . . . What happened next is illustrative of the importance of giving a name to a phenomenon. Once named, the hidden dirty secrets were public, and the evidence mounted. Feminists argued that sexual harassment is sex discrimination against women and is thus prohibited by laws outlawing sex discrimination in employment (Title VII) and in education (Title IX). By naming it, feminists were able to define the issue and retain control of it.[48]

One example of how the women's movement framed this issue for public view and debate was a speak-out on sexual harassment held in May 1975, which drew national media attention to the fact that sexual harassment was a collective and not an individual problem. There were class differences in women's responses to the way the speak-out framed the issue. Women with class and/or educational privilege were the least likely to see sexual harassment as a collective problem for women. Their resistance was expressed in comments to the effect that "together" women could handle harassment, that harassment happened only to women who asked for it, or that the behavior of "one weird guy" did not represent a real problem for women. These women were probably more threatened by the idea that, in spite of their accomplishments, they were still judged as sexual objects. Compared to working-class women, they were more likely to experience milder, verbal forms of harassment. And they had greater job mobility and were more likely to be able to leave the job market entirely.[49]

Feminists not only gave voice to this issue but also exerted a remarkable degree of control over its definition on the public agenda. Legal recognition of sexual harassment as a form of sex discrimination came about in large part thanks to the efforts of feminists such as Catharine MacKinnon, who described her role in the preface to her book *Sexual Harassment of Working Women: A Case of Sex Discrimination*. She began this book in 1974, when no court had held that sexual harassment was sex discrimination; by the time the book was published, in 1979, some courts had agreed with her analysis. She said she rewrote the final manuscript encouraged by the sense that it had "been useful, perhaps even pivotal, in litigation establishing sexual harassment as a legal claim." Her political argument was grounded in the group-based experiences of women (especially her clients) and began with her realization that "many social practices imposed on women because we are women are not considered by the law to be based on our sex. . . . Sexual harassment has been not only legally allowed; it has been legally unthinkable. As I came to analyze it, sexual harassment also appeared neither incidental nor tangential to women's inequality, but a crucial expression of it, a central dynamic in it."[50]

In her attempt to "bring to the law something of the reality of women's lives," MacKinnon used nonconventional methods and evidence, which reflected the consciousness-raising practices of the women's movement.

> To date, there are no "systematic" studies of sexual harassment in the social-scientific sense. So how do I know it exists? Chapter 3 presents evidence from women's observations on their own lives. . . . Personal statements direct from daily life, in which we say more than we know, may be the primary form in which such experiences exist in social space; at this point they may be their only accessible form. I therefore take immediate reflections on lived-through experiences as data.
>
> How valid and generalizable are such data? This issue is particularly important in the sex discrimination context. One woman can bring a legal complaint, but the group-based nature of the *claim* that one's treatment is based on sex requires that the complaint refer to a group-based *experience*. For this purpose, the admittedly selective and necessarily impressionistic evidence from personal life is more than anecdotal or illustrative. Individual experiences of sexual harassment are here seen to derive from a social context: the shared material experience of women as a group, with focus on the world of work. The testimony of individual women, in this context, represents and substantiates a dimension of the social reality of women as a sex. . . . Ultimately, to me, this is also what makes sexual harassment sex discrimination.[51]

In 1986, the U.S. Supreme Court heard its first sexual harassment case, *Meritor Savings Bank v. Vinson,* and ruled in favor of the plaintiff, Michelle Vinson, whom MacKinnon represented as cocounsel.[52] In reflecting on the first decade of sexual harassment court cases, MacKinnon addressed the charge that sexual harassment was a feminist invention. "Sexual harassment, the event, was not invented by feminists; the perpetrators did that with no help from us. Sexual harassment, the legal claim—the idea that the law should see it the way its victims see it—is definitely a feminist invention. Feminists first took women's experience seriously enough to uncover this problem and conceptualize it and pursue it legally."[53] In the *Meritor* case, the Supreme Court reinforced feminist definitions of the issue, covering both quid pro quo and hostile environment types of harassment and sending the message that it was the employer's responsibility to prevent harassment. Subsequent court rulings and other policy initiatives also adhered to feminist definitions of the problem.[54] In 1991, a federal district court judge in Jacksonville, Florida, ruled that posting pictures of nude women in the workplace was a form of sexual harassment. He said women at the Jacksonville Shipyards were "affected by 'sex role spillover,' where the evaluation of women by their coworkers and supervisors takes place in terms of the sexuality of the women and their sexual worth rather than their merit as craft workers. . . . [The judge] ordered the shipyard to institute a comprehensive sexual harassment policy written by the NOW Legal Defense and Education Fund, the New York–based women's advocacy group that brought the case."[55] And in the U.S. Supreme Court's second ruling in a sexual harassment case, it decided in 1993 with surprising speed and unanimity to adopt a broad definition of sexual harassment in the workplace which enabled workers to win suits without having to prove that the offensive behavior left them psychologically damaged or unable to do their jobs.[56]

A second "invisible" condition that feminists defined as a policy problem in the mid-1970s was domestic violence. As noted earlier, in historical periods without a visible women's movement, the problem of domestic violence was privatized as a matter of sin, wickedness, drunkenness, or "marital difficulties" requiring counseling and therapy.[57] The "discovery" of domestic violence in the early 1970s was due to the opening up of debate about sex roles and the family by the women's movement. The slogan "the personal is political . . . rejected the notion that certain subjects were isolated, individual problems or taboo topics."[58] Abused women started identifying themselves on the crisis hotlines and at the advocacy services that had been set up for rape victims. Researchers began to conduct studies about wife abuse and the related problem of child abuse. A 1976 study, cited in congressional hearings on domestic violence, was particularly instrumental in validating that the battering of women was a "real" problem.[59]

Paralleling official studies were women's experiences in grassroots shelter projects. The first battered women's shelter was founded in England in 1971 by Erin Pizzey. Her book about the women who came to the

Chiswick Women's Aid Centre, *Scream Quietly or the Neighbours Will Hear,* had a profound effect on feminists in the United States.[60] In 1976, there were approximately twenty shelters in the United States; within three years, there were about two hundred fifty. Women offered testimony and provided documentation to state legislative committees holding hearings on domestic violence. By 1978, thirty-three states had already passed or were considering domestic violence legislation, covering changes in such areas as civil remedies, criminal statutes, and to a very limited extent, the provision of shelter services.[61]

At the federal level, the first agency to initiate services specifically targeted at domestic violence was the Law Enforcement Assistance Administration (LEAA) within the Department of Justice. In 1978, the LEAA Family Violence Program funded sixteen family violence projects. The availability of federal money and expressed community interest thrust three types of actors into involvement with the issue: battered women clients from the LEAA's Victim/Witness Assistance Program, women's organizations, and grantseekers.[62] Most government action at the federal level was taken in the late 1970s, with a brief life for the Office of Domestic Violence during the Carter administration and some funds for battered women's shelters in 1983.[63] It was difficult to get the issue of domestic violence on the federal agenda, both because it was a role-change issue that challenged male authority and because domestic violence measures in Congress were portrayed by opponents as "antifamily."[64] Meanwhile, at the state and local levels of government, significant policy changes took place throughout the 1980s. Most states amended their assault laws to increase the power of police to remove the batterer from the victim's home. Other reforms included provisions for warrantless arrests, cooling-off periods, restraining orders, and special protection orders; surcharges on marriage licenses to pay for shelters; special training for police; and the admissibility of the battered women syndrome as a defense for women who murdered their batterers.[65]

By 1990, there were more than one thousand shelters nationwide. Some of them had positive relationships with state and local government entities, but some shelters operated on the more radical feminist principle that governments were not serious about the problem of domestic violence. Jean Grossholtz, a political scientist and worker at a battered women's shelter, argued that the state valued keeping the family together more than preventing violence against women and children. The shelter Grossholtz was affiliated with began under government auspices, but soon its collectivist practices were at odds with the bureaucratic and hierarchical operations of government agencies. She asserted that since the shelter did not take the maintenance of the nuclear family or sex-role stereotypes as its goal, it necessarily worked against the ongoing political economy of male violence. Thus it was no wonder that shelters had difficulty finding adequate funding, that they were almost entirely private or voluntary organizations, and that they were castigated as hotbeds of man haters and marriage wreckers. Such accusations were attempts to deny the reality of violence against women, to blame the victim and those who would assist the victim rather than confront the set of power relations that such violence sustained.[66] In this transformational view of women's policy agenda, violence against women was seen as a form of terrorism, which disoriented women in its arbitrariness and kept women conformist and dependent on men for protection.[67]

Another form of violence against women that was given a name and put on the public agenda by feminists in the 1970s was female sexual slavery, brought to the public's attention in the United States by Kathleen Barry's book *Female Sexual Slavery,* published in 1979. In spite of the fact that the United Nations had in 1949 ratified the Convention on the Traffic in Persons and the Exploitation of the Prostitution of Others, when Barry began to research the problem in the mid-1970s, she found that the United Nations, Interpol, and various international human rights organizations had "buried their previous investigations, resolutions and other work on forced prostitution and traffic in women. They accepted the popular misconception that most prostitution is voluntary work and therefore does not constitute a fundamental violation of women's human rights." She defined female sexual slavery as "all situations where women or girls cannot change the immediate conditions of their existence; where regardless of how they got into those conditions they cannot get out; and where they are subject to sexual violence and exploitation." Barry and others pressed the United Nations to include a workshop on female sexual slavery at its 1980 Conference on Women in Copenhagen. In 1983, twenty-five women from around the world formed the International Network against Female Sexual Slavery to organize against the problem at the local, national, and international levels. And at a 1985 UNESCO meeting in Madrid, Barry successfully incorporated into its report the idea that the "commoditization" of women's bodies for sexual exchange was a violation of human dignity. She maintained that the problem of sexual slavery was most effectively addressed by adopting an international human rights perspective that considered the protection of human dignity central to human rights. International human rights agencies were usually more receptive to this analysis than were national and local governments.[68]

Policies Recast from a Male to a Female Model of Experience

In addition to placing new issues on the agenda, feminists recast existing policies from a male to a female model of experience. This reformulation by both accommodationist and transformational feminists took place in many issue areas. Policies on aging had to take into account gender differences in life cycles and society's gender double standard about age.[69] Population policy needed a shift in research focus from household decision making to women's decision making.[70] In the area of criminal justice, feminists challenged conventional views about men's violence against women, methods of adjudicating crime, sanctions for crime, and failure to award women equal credibility with men in court by judges, juries, and attorneys.[71] Attention had to be paid to the differential effects on men and women of divorce and child custody policies.[72] Feminists discussed how poverty had become a women's issue (the "feminization of poverty"), how women's poverty differed from men's, and how meaningful welfare reform was not possible unless the official poverty line was reformulated to include women's child-care expenses.[73] Feminist studies of women and work examined women's unpaid labor at home,[74] job segregation by sex,[75] flexible schedules at the workplace,[76] the limitations of U.S. child-care policies,[77] and male norms of professionalism and the glass ceiling as obstacles to women's career advancement.[78] A shift of focus to the female worker produced new analyses of reproductive risks at the workplace,[79] pregnancy discrimination and leave policies,[80] and family and medical leave policies.[81] In general, feminists traced shifts in presuppositions about women in law and public policy over time: from a view of women as married family members to a view of women as individuals,[82] from assuming the male body was the norm to assuming gendered bodies,[83] from a view of natural, immutable sexual differences to a view of gendered sexual differences that perpetuated male domination,[84] and from a focus on gender difference to a focus on gender disadvantage.[85]

Recasting issues from a male to female model of experience had significant policy consequences when it came to rape, pornography, abortion, and health care. Of course, rape had been recognized as a serious legal offense long before the contemporary women's movement. What was new was an understanding that reflected women's experience.

> Rape has traditionally been defined by male views of male sexuality. To a considerable extent, prohibitions on force against women have functioned to protect men. Historically, rape has

been perceived as a threat to male as well as female interests; it has devalued wives and daughters and jeopardized patrilineal systems of inheritance. But too stringent constraints on male sexuality have been equally threatening to male policymakers. The threat of criminal charges based on female fabrications has dominated the history of rape law. As a result, the offense has been hedged with substantive exceptions and procedural safeguards that leave considerable latitude for aggression.[86]

The women's movement had a profound effect on the reform of rape laws. Susan Brownmiller's *Against Our Will,* published in 1975, was one of the first books to provide a feminist analysis of the problem.[87] As Deborah Rhode noted, "Between the mid-1970s and mid-1980s, the number of reform and victim assistance organizations grew from a few dozen to over fifteen hundred. During the same period, almost every state made some changes in its laws governing rape": criminalizing marital rape, relabeling the crime an assault to emphasize its violent rather than sexual character, redefining consent, eliminating resistance and corroboration requirements, modifying jury instructions, restricting references to the victim's prior sexual activities, and altering penalty structures to increase the likelihood of conviction.[88] Rethinking rape from a woman's experience also meant classifying rape as a form of sexual terrorism insofar as fear of rape limited women's freedom and made them dependent on men.[89]

Pornography was another issue area where feminists substituted women's experiences for those of men. Conventional (male) legal thinking focused on obscenity, which the U.S. Supreme Court deemed outside the zone of constitutionally protected free speech[90] and defined according to a three-part test: "whether an average person applying contemporary community standards would find that the work as a whole appealed to the 'prurient interest'; whether the work depicted sexual conduct in a 'patently offensive way'; and whether the work taken as a whole lacked serious literary, artistic, political, or scientific value. Material falling within that definition could be subject to prohibition."[91] Feminists criticized this formulation on several fronts: obscenity "could encompass sexually explicit material that most feminists would view as erotic, but exclude sexually violent material that they would consider pornographic"; there was no gender-neutral "average person," and men and women were offended in different ways by sexually violent material; there was a deterioration of community standards with the pornography industry's rapid expansion, and some clinical evidence suggested that the more individuals were exposed to pornography, the less likely they were to find it offensive; and given the size of the pornography industry (estimated between $6 and $8 billion in annual gross receipts), anti-obscenity prosecution was minimal in most parts of the country.[92]

Feminists shifted the policy focus from obscenity to pornography: from sexual explicitness to male power, from impurity to violence against women, from offending average tastes to the degradation and debasement of women, from redeeming social value to the harm of the objectification of women, and from prurient interests to the desire to dominate women.[93] Catharine MacKinnon noted that in (male) jurisprudence, the powerful had silenced women by excluding them from definitions of the problem; they had focused on abstract systems such as speech and equality to the exclusion of substantive systems such as real people with social labels attached to them; they defined equality as treating substantive unequals the same; and they downplayed how the marketplace of ideas was dominated by those with money and institutional access to idea formulation. To the extent that a woman was defined in pornographic terms, harm became imperceptible. In the equality-freedom debate, MacKinnon argued that women's equality was incompatible with male freedom to consume pornography. In her view, pornography was a political practice, integral to the attitudes and behaviors of violence and discrimination against women.[94]

The policy consequences of MacKinnon's line of reasoning were local antipornography ordinances. MacKinnon and Andrea Dworkin successfully lobbied city councils in Minneapolis in 1983 and Indianapolis in 1984, in whose ordinances pornography was defined as sex discrimination, a violation of women's civil rights, and the opposite of sex equality. The ordinances stated that those who profited and benefited from pornography's injury would be accountable to those who were injured. The ordinances were enforced through a civil rights commission with an option of direct access to the courts. Four types of injuries were actionable: when victims participated as models; where pornography was forced on people in employment, education, the home, or a public place; when pornography led to assault; and when people trafficked in the production, sale, exhibition, or distribution of pornography. There was the most resistance to the trafficking provision, which MacKinnon attributed to resistance to the notion of group injury in a liberal, individualistic culture.[95]

In 1986, the U.S. Supreme Court affirmed an appellate court invalidation of the Indianapolis ordinance.[96] The appellate court, though accepting the legislation's basic premise that pornography exploited and degraded women, nonetheless held that such material was protected by the First Amendment. The Supreme Court concluded that "depictions of subordination tend to perpetuate subordination. The subordinate status of women in turn leads to affront and lower pay at work, insult and injury at home, battery and rape on the streets." But it went on to say that "this simply demonstrates the power of pornography as speech," which, like other dangerous speech, must be protected by the First Amendment, because "any other answer leaves the government in control of all the institutions of culture, the great censor and director of which thoughts are good for us."[97] Some feminists agreed with the court that governments should not legislate to control pornography. And some adopted the civil libertarian position that both men and women should have access to fantasy through pornography.[98] Nevertheless, the work of MacKinnon and Dworkin had a profound effect on how policymakers viewed pornography: increasingly from the point of view of women's experiences.

Similarly, in the area of abortion policy, feminists shifted the terms of policy debate from individual privacy to women's right to control their reproductive lives and gender equality. Abortion had been framed as a privacy issue, not by women's groups but by the American Civil Liberties Union (ACLU), which in 1965 became the first national organization to support abortion publicly.[99] That same year, an ACLU amicus brief played a key role in *Griswold v. Connecticut,* a U.S. Supreme Court decision that held unconstitutional a Connecticut statute that prohibited couples from using contraceptives and also barred physicians from prescribing them.[100] In this decision, the right to privacy was accepted as a constitutional principle. In its 1973 *Roe v. Wade* decision, the U.S. Supreme Court upheld a woman's right to obtain an abortion, with certain restrictions, on privacy grounds.

According to Linda Gordon, the mid-1960s represented a fourth stage in the birth control movement in the United States. Each stage used a different term for reproductive control. In stage one, during the second half of the nineteenth century, "voluntary motherhood" emphasized choice, freedom, and autonomy and was "a basic plank in the feminist platform, much more universally endorsed than woman suffrage and reaching further to describe and change the total plight of women than any other single issue." During stage two, approximately 1910–20, "birth control" leagues were created by feminists in the socialist movement, a voice not only for autonomy but also "for a revolutionizing of the society and the empowering of the powerless—the working class and the female sex primarily." Stage three produced a new slogan, "planned parenthood," in the 1940s, when the birth control movement "shed not only a feminist orientation but also eschewed any organizational interest in restructuring power in society." The women's liberation movement in the mid-1960s produced a fourth stage, in which birth control once again became a political issue.[101]

Most feminists framed the issues of birth control and abortion in terms of women's right to control their reproductive lives. At its first national conference, in 1967, NOW adopted a Bill of Rights, which included as its last provision "the right of women to control their reproductive lives," calling for access to contraception and abortion.[102] In her study of abortion laws in California, Kristin Luker underscored the importance to agenda setting of framing the issue in terms of rights and control. Abortion in California began as a technical, medical issue in the 1960s and became a women's issue in the 1970s, thanks in large part to the actions of abortion-on-demand activists, who introduced the notion of a woman's right to an abortion. The Society for Humane Abortions (SHA), for example, founded in 1961, used the language of rights, and "by their leafleting, abortion teach-ins, and petitions they accomplished something both subtle and profound: they made the 'unspeakable' speakable and thus cleared the way for public dialogue about women's rights to abortion."[103] SHA activists addressed themselves to "the people," rather than to the professionals courted by the California Committee on Therapeutic Abortion (CCTA), a group advocating the more modest goal of abortion law reform. And SHA activists engaged in civil disobedience, helping women exercise their rights by referring them to illegal abortionists, primarily in Mexico. A process of consciousness-raising affected both those women who wanted reform (CCTA) and those who wanted repeal (SHA) of abortion laws. As the reform women adopted the new claim to a right to abortion, "the two groups became less readily distinguishable from each other; it became more important that the women reformers were *women* than that they were *reformers*. Once exposed to the new definition of the issue, the reform women (in contrast to their male physician peers) became converted to the political goal of repeal."[104] Ultimately, women in the 1970s redefined the experience of abortion from a medical issue into a matter of women's rights for three reasons. First, the medical community became divided over the moral status of abortion. Once it was no longer viewed as simply a technical issue, the field was cleared for new contenders to define the issue. Second, women saw themselves as civil rights crusaders instead of victims of unjust laws. And third, paid work became less of an adjunct to the "real work" of having a family and more of a legitimate activity in its own right. Thus, the right to an abortion to control one's own life became a new "framework of understanding."[105]

Frameworks derived from women's reproductive experiences were heralded as superior to those based on a gender-neutral, individualistic right to privacy. The right to privacy in *Roe v. Wade* isolated and abstracted individuals and threw abortion back into a "private" realm where individuals drew on their own resources to deal with issues. This formulation ignored race and class inequities in ability to obtain abortions, leaving feminists helpless in the face of the Hyde amendment, which outlawed federal funding of abortions. The privacy scheme was detrimental to women insofar as Western political theorists had consistently depicted reproduction as demeaning and tangential to political life, on the "private" side of the public/private split and thus in the prepolitical realm of necessity (not freedom).[106]

A final example of an issue recast from a male to a female model of experience was health care. In its criticism of the male-dominated medical establishment, the women's health movement went through two phases. The first, beginning in the mid-1960s, was largely a self-help movement, focusing on access to contraception and reproductive care at alternative health facilities. The self-help book *Our Bodies, Ourselves,* first published in 1973 and appearing in revised editions into the 1990s, was written by a group of women who met at a women's conference in Boston and wanted to do something about "condescending, paternalistic, judgmental and non-informative" doctors.[107] Feminists redefined women's health in women's terms, instead of taking the male body as the norm. They criticized the male-dominated medical establishment's management and treatment of pregnancy and menopause[108] and called for the demedicalization of childbirth.[109] This first phase in the women's health movement contributed to changes in many of the standard operating procedures in obstetrics and gynecology.

Throughout the 1980s, during the Reagan and Bush era, the battle over abortion overshadowed efforts to address other women's health concerns. The divisiveness of this issue had deterred the Congressional Caucus for Women's Issues (CCWI) from pursuing a women's health policy agenda. Since the caucus's inception in 1977, members had agreed to work only on those issues that united them. Cochairs Patricia Schroeder and Olympia Snowe described how things changed in the late 1980s, setting off a string of events that would give rise to the second phase in the women's health movement:

As the Supreme Court moved in the late 1980s to give states more latitude to restrict access to abortion, escalating the debate in Congress and around the country, we, as caucus cochairs, began to look for a new middle ground that could be embraced by congresswomen on both sides of the abortion divide. There had always been broad support among the congresswomen for reducing the need for abortion. We decided to pursue a new, highly visible research effort aimed at preventing unintended pregnancy through improved contraception.[110]

As they began to put together their health care package, congresswomen were shocked to find that American women had fewer contraceptive options available to them than women in western Europe and that only one major pharmaceutical company was engaged in contraceptive research in 1989, down from thirteen in 1970. They were also struck by a 1985 Public Health Service report, which identified the lack of data on women as an important factor in limiting the understanding of women's health care needs and which recommended that steps be taken to end gender bias in research and clinical practice. In 1986, the National Institutes of Health (NIH) encouraged the research community to include women in clinical trials. The issue of women's health research exploded in 1990, when the General Accounting Office (GAO) told Congress "that three years after establishing a policy to encourage the inclusion of women in research studies, NIH had done little to implement it. . . . It became the 'smoking gun' for the government's neglect of women's health research."[111] The caucus used the GAO report as an opportunity to announce its plan to introduce omnibus legislation on women's health. The Women's Health Equity Act, introduced in Congress in 1990, launched the second phase of the women's health movement. Women were armed with statistics and studies documenting a long history of second-class treatment by the medical establishment, and they called for major changes in the way American health care was researched, financed, and delivered.

Policies for Equality with Men

Accommodationist feminists advanced an agenda for policies seeking equality with men: role equity issues. As noted earlier, such issues encountered less resistance in making their way onto government agendas. If they were transformed into role change issues, much more political effort was required to sustain them. Two examples of the slowing down of role equity issues once they became perceived as role change issues were the Equal Rights Amendment and women in the military.

In Congress, where the ERA succeeded in 1972 with broad majority support, the amendment was perceived as a legal issue and
was discussed in abstract and technical terms. In the ratification
process, where the ERA faltered, the issues dealt with became
broader and the process came to highlight ideological values regarding society and change. Thus the presence of conflict has
represented a bias against the adoption of any new policy: once
conflict arises, differing views are presented; decision makers
seek to avoid taking action; the politics of expediency can no
longer prevail; and potential coalition partners may choose to
stay aloof. Put in somewhat different terms, the group that suc-
ceeds in defining and limiting the parameters of debate may
have a head start on victory.[112]

Similarly, the 1975 bill mandating women's entrance into military acad-
emies passed, as Judith Hicks Stiehm noted, "partly because the terms of
debate centered on equal career opportunity rather than on whether
women should be assigned to combat. Shaping the issue along these
lines represented a victory for the bill's proponents."[113] But to the extent
that the presence of women in the military, particularly in combat, challenged traditional gender expectations and myths about war and the
military, policy victories became more problematic.[114]

Unlike women in the military and the ERA, three policy examples
that remained role equity matters were equal pay, credit, and education.
Interestingly, it was labor unions and not the feminist movement that
put equal pay on the agenda. Unions were concerned that wages for
wartime jobs offered to women in men's absence would become low-
ered. Thus, the flurry of interest in equal pay legislation corresponded
to U.S. involvement in the two world wars.[115] As we saw in the last chapter, however, absent a women's movement, congresswomen such as
Edith Green spent years pushing this bill through Congress. In contrast
to their marginal role in the case of equal pay, feminist activists were indispensable to the success of the 1974 Equal Credit Opportunity Act. Interest in the issue was sparked by a report from the National Commission
on Consumer Finance and subsequent media coverage. Feminist activists
were in the vanguard in advance of mass consciousness, keeping the issue alive for two congressional terms; supplying information, technical
expertise, and policy recommendations to congressmembers; and building on the "policy system" that had been created in the ERA ratification
campaign, made up of lobbyists, volunteers, congressmembers and
their staffs, and administrative policymakers. Women were able to place

the issue of credit reform to eliminate sex discrimination on the political agenda partly because they limited the scope of the issue to role equity.[116]

Finally, equal education for women secured a place on the congressional agenda in large part because of its role equity nature. The initial impetus for Title IX of the 1972 Education Amendments, which outlawed sex discrimination in educational institutions, came not from feminist groups but, as we saw in the last chapter, from Congressmember Green, who advised feminist groups to keep a low profile during the measure's congressional journey. It was not until the implementation of Title IX that opposition took shape as the measure began to be seen less in role equity terms and more in role change terms. Its implementing agency, the Office of Civil Rights (OCR), was lobbied by the male sports establishment, especially the National Collegiate Athletic Association, which wanted to influence OCR rules about men's and women's athletics. Joyce Gelb and Marian Lief Palley observed, "Despite efforts to weaken the athletic regulations from local officials and influential House members, mobilized women's groups quashed the rebellion. Some sixty groups were initial participants in Title IX forays."[117]

Agenda Setting in Santa Clara County

In Santa Clara County, women acted as agenda setters with respect to two transformational policies: domestic violence and comparable worth. The Santa Clara County Commission on the Status of Women was at the center of a policy network that got the issue of domestic violence on Santa Clara County's agenda. The Mid-Peninsula Support Network for Battered Women was founded in 1978 after an assessment conducted by the commission showed an urgent need for battered women's services for the county's affluent northern cities.[118] The county already had two other shelters, the Woman's Alliance (WOMA) in San Jose and La Isla Pacifica in rural Gilroy. Anne Wurr described the situation:

> The battered women who called the commission from North County asking for assistance included women from all walks of life. The upper-middle-class Anglo enclaves of Palo Alto, Stanford, Los Altos, and Los Altos Hills included homes as violent as those in rural South County or urban San Jose. . . . Their abusers included physicians, university professors, ministers, and electronic engineers as well as unemployed men, blue collar workers, and alcoholics. Calls received by the Support Network crisis

line around election time included some from women who
would only give their first name, "Because my husband is running for public office."[119]

When the Support Network was first established, there were no build-
ings immediately available to use as a shelter or money to buy one, so volunteers provided emergency refuge in their own homes.

Even after the residential shelter was opened, the safe homes,
support groups, and legal programs enabled many more battered women to escape their abusers. The goal of the Support
Network Community Education Program was to prevent domestic violence by improving institutional response to victims,
as well as encouraging battered women to call the twenty-four-
hour crisis line or use the resources offered by peer counselors
at the office. The Support Network decided in 1980 that a high
priority for its new community education program would be law
enforcement. The goal was to persuade local police to respond
more effectively to domestic disturbance calls in which there
had been violent assault. Each police department was urged to
adopt specific policy concerning response to battered women,
and then train its officers and ancillary personnel, such as dis-
patchers and receptionists. If an effective policy was developed,
police injuries and callbacks would be reduced, and battered
women would be protected from further assault.[120]

In 1980, a county bar association committee, noting that there were
thirteen different law enforcement agencies in the county, developed a
Proposed Uniform General Order on Domestic Violence to facilitate a
uniform policy for officer training and effective responses for victims
whose home, workplace, and children's schools might be located in
more than one police jurisdiction. Members of the bar association
worked for months in conjunction with shelter workers and family counselors in drafting the document, modeled on general orders in effect in
New York, Oakland, and San Francisco.

Despite initial hostility on the part of most of the police chiefs, eventually many local police departments adopted versions of the general
order. Next, based on feedback from police officers that the district
attorney would not prosecute even when the police had a well-prepared
case, the Support Network turned its attention to training the new crop
of deputy district attorneys, including putting political pressure on

front-runners in the race for district attorney. The Support Network developed a questionnaire on domestic violence prosecution and asked each candidate to respond. Wurr wrote in 1984: "Their replies became the basis for questions asked at candidates' meetings and were used by reporters writing about various issues of the campaign. The eventual winner was reminded of his campaign promises and, although progress is slow, changes are being made in the way domestic violence cases are prosecuted in Santa Clara County."[121]

Women were also agenda setters for comparable worth policy in San Jose, home of the nation's first strike for pay equity by city employees. The strategic location of women as community activists, elected officials, and union members was indispensable to the 1981 strike, settlement, and effective implementation of comparable worth pay adjustments of $1.45 million over two years.[122]

Much like the federal 1963 Equal Pay Act, comparable worth in San Jose was primarily a union issue. A city employee union, the American Federation of State, County and Municipal Employees (AFSCME), saw the issue as a way to swell its ranks. Indeed, more than five hundred city workers signed up with AFSCME in the course of their three-year struggle to obtain pay equity. Nevertheless, comparable worth was also a women's movement issue in three important ways. First, feminist community activists in Santa Clara County had set the agenda for taking women's issues seriously, by providing both moral arguments and political clout. Second, the majority status of female officials on the San Jose City Council gave them a greater freedom of action regarding women's issues than was typically the case for token women on governing boards. And third, women in AFSCME, outraged by gender pay inequities, kept up the pressure on the city council throughout the strike, settlement, and implementation stages. In each of these three settings, women sympathetic to women's issues found that by working with similarly situated women—whether in the community, on the council, or in the union—they could marshal the psychological and political support to bolster their efforts for policy changes.

Comparable worth's appearance on the city's agenda was facilitated by the presence of a female majority on the San Jose City Council. In 1979, the city manager, in an effort to curb the exodus of management-level city employees to greener pastures in Silicon Valley's high-tech firms, had secured city council approval for a job evaluation study. This study assigned points to jobs according to three criteria: knowledge, problem solving, and accountability. Evaluation was based on both internal equity and market considerations; the study did not compare male-

and female-dominated classifications. The report, released in May 1980, recommended adjustments averaging 14 percent. The city council immediately voted these adjustments into effect over a one-year period.[123]

When the union saw the ease with which management raises were approved, it lobbied the city to reopen contract negotiations when the results of a similar nonmanagement study were released.[124] Nonmanagement job classes had been assigned points according to four criteria: knowledge, problem solving, accountability, and working conditions. About one-third of the workers fell more than 15 percent either above or below the trend line, which represented the average pay for jobs of equal points. According to the study's methodology, jobs falling more than 10 percent below the trend line were paid significantly below their value. Male-dominated classes averaged 8 to 15 percent above and female-dominated classes 2 to 10 percent below, with some as much as 25 to 30 percent below. Mixed male-female jobs clustered near the trend line.[125]

The union was anxious to begin talks with the same city council that had authorized the study. Since on January 1 there would be seven new members on the expanded council, it reluctantly agreed to reopen negotiations in December. In January 1981, just as the female majority came on board, collective bargaining talks reached an impasse and a state mediator was called in. Negotiations continued for six months, with activity stepping up as the July 4 contract expiration date neared. Throughout this period, there were rallies and a wildcat strike by librarians, who, along with parks and recreation specialists, had the most to gain from pay equity adjustments and were in the forefront of activity. On June 8, the union received a boost from the U.S. Supreme Court, which in *Gunther v. County of Washington, Oregon* ruled that female prison guards, whose jobs were valued at 95 percent of those of male guards but were paid only 70 percent of male salaries, were victims of sex discrimination because the county ignored the results of its own job evaluation study. Furthermore, the Court held that women had a right to file sex discrimination suits under Title VII of the 1964 Civil Rights Act, which was broader in scope than the 1963 Equal Pay Act because it could be applied to sex-based wage discrimination even when the jobs were not the same.[126] Taking advantage of this ruling, the union filed a sex discrimination complaint against San Jose with the Equal Employment Opportunity Commission, which enforced Title VII of the 1964 Civil Rights Act. The union offered to withdraw the complaint if negotiations were fruitful. The city interpreted the filing of the complaint as an act of bad faith on the union's part, saying it would lose $9.3 million in 1981–82 revenue-sharing funds if charges were upheld.[127] On the eve of the contract expiration date, the two sides were still far apart and a strike was called. It lasted for nine days until agreement was finally reached on July 19, granting pay equity adjustments over two years.

Of the eleven council members, four supported comparable worth from the outset. Three supporters were holdovers from the prior council; the fourth was the only self-described feminist among the 1980 cohort joining the council. Three newcomers, one man and two women, opposed comparable worth. Two of these opponents were conservative Republicans who believed that pay equity meant harmful government intervention in a free market economy; the third felt that the council should not emphasize women's issues over "people's issues," such as the economy, housing, unemployment, and education. Finally, four councilmembers were swing votes who eventually voted to fund comparable worth adjustments. As it turned out, men on the council supported pay equity as strongly (three to one) as did their female colleagues (five to two).[128]

The breakdown of this final eight-to-three vote raises some interesting possibilities. First, some male officials probably perceived a voting bloc of activist women in San Jose. Two male proponents of pay equity were affiliated with women's organizations (NWPC and WOMA). Second, a critical mass of three female proponents provided a counterweight to the three staunch opponents and may have helped attract the two hesitant women. And third, San Jose's female majority captured the attention of local and national media, whose queries caused some women to reflect on the role of women in politics as spokespersons for women's concerns.

Women on the council at the time of the comparable worth decision ranged from liberal Democrats to conservative Republicans and from self-described feminists to antifeminists. Much to the consternation of the union, most of them approached the issue with caution; even Mayor Hayes wanted two years as opposed to four years of benefits on grounds that it was unwise to commit future councils to the policy. Ultimately, however, all but two women were supportive. When formal negotiations broke down, it was the female officials who were contacted informally. The union got political mileage from the fact that the nation's first pay equity strike took place in the feminist capital, and this irony was not lost on the female officials. Thus, women's numbers on the council had a bearing on the outcome of comparable worth in San Jose, both directly (as a critical mass of supporters) and indirectly (as the object of media and union attention).

Once a place was secured for comparable worth on the city's agenda, the next step was the job evaluation process. According to San Jose's personnel services administrator, David Armstrong, the city never would have conducted the nonmanagement study without union pressure to do so. Furthermore, he added, it was a revolutionary idea at the time to have a committee of workers rank the jobs. The committee consisted of five men and five women, among whom Armstrong was the only management representative; the nine slots were spread across a variety of jobs such as librarians, parks and recreation officials, legal secretaries, gardeners, and engineers.

During the strike, female negotiators worried about the female heads of households who had taken great risks to march in the picket lines; they had gone for a week without a paycheck. Nine days of little sleep and great tension also began to take their toll on the energy of the negotiators themselves, but at no point did male union members pressure female negotiators to accept management's offer. Many of the team's men abstained in votes because they felt that this was a women's issue and that women should decide when to stop the strike. The women also had the strong support of the union local's president and of the head city librarian, both men.

The strike settlement raised the prestige of AFSCME in the eyes of the city's other unions, which had been competitive and secretive about their contracts with the city. Many of the older trade unions had disparaged AFSCME as inexperienced and a "women's union" (about half its members were women). Only two city unions—electrical workers and firefighters—supported the comparable worth strike, even though AFSCME had previously honored the others' picket lines. After AFSCME won its settlement, however, the other unions took it seriously.

The final stage of the process was overseeing the implementation of the adjustments over two years and renegotiating the issue in 1983 sessions. AFSCME women oversaw the successful implementation of pay equity benefits, and they kept the issue alive in the 1983 and 1984 bargaining sessions, bolstered by pressure from rank-and-file women to complete pay equity adjustments. As negotiator Linda Dydo said, "The first year there was this huge outcry among women. It was as if you had been denying them the right to vote when they realized how badly they had been cheated out of 27 percent of their wages for all of their life. The rank and file bring it up every year." Women in the union were determined that the issue would not die until their salaries were at or above the trend line. Both the union and the city agreed that good-faith progress toward the trend line was made in the post-strike period.

Female negotiators were careful to address the needs of male AFSCME members as well. One male group, the engineering technicians, feared that pay equity adjustments meant fewer special adjustments or lower cost-of-living increases for them. In the 1983 session, AFSCME obtained a 3 percent special adjustment for these workers.

Finally, union women convinced the city that the issue of comparable worth had come to stay, and they applauded the personnel department's efforts to take a national leadership role on the issue. They particularly commended the efforts of personnel official David Armstrong, who was trusted by the city council as an expert on the topic. He said he fielded numerous inquiries from academics, reporters, and officials from other areas. He coauthored an article assuring public personnel managers that the settlement had not bankrupted the city.[129] And when journalists baited him to reveal the feminist plot behind comparable worth in San Jose, he had this response:

> I bring in some woman and journalists say, "No, we were looking for the real spokeswoman." I respond, "This *is* the real spokeswoman. She has been here twenty-five years and she has made a difference in this organization. She looks you right in the eye, after never having said anything for twenty-five years, and she is livid. She says, 'You'd better square away my pay. We've got this study.'" Women are extremely angry about this issue. It is a gut-level paycheck issue that all women can unify behind because most women have experienced the clerical ranks, or understand what it is.[130]

Union women, both negotiators and the rank and file, were responsible for putting San Jose on the map as the first city to strike successfully for comparable worth adjustments. They were aided by the efforts of women on the city council and female activists in the community, who set the stage for taking women's issues seriously.

Both the undervaluing of women's work and domestic violence were "invisible" conditions rendered visible and named as policy problems by women in Santa Clara County. These cases illustrated the importance of the joint efforts of movement outsiders with government insiders, of the operations of women's policy networks, of the difficulty of working for role change issues, of a rethinking of the state as a benefit provider to interdependent citizens, and of conducting policy analysis that took women's experiences seriously.

8 Political Coalitions

The Hard Work of Sisterhood

IN POLITICAL coalitions, groups come together for common political purposes. The conventional model of coalitions assumes that interest groups are the actors and that they join with other groups out of expediency and self-interest to influence the government. Accommodationist feminists adopted this model of women's coalitions. Transformational feminists, however, argued that this formulation was a truncated view of women's coalitions, focusing on government at the expense of the women's movement.

Conventional Wisdom about Political Coalitions

The conventional approach to political coalitions focuses on office-holding and electoral politics rather than on movement politics. A study of the struggle of blacks and Hispanics for equality in urban politics defined coalitions as joint actions of city councilmembers; another work about black-Latino urban political coalitions measured political competition by the presence of the two groups in elective municipal office.[1] Other studies cast their net more broadly in the direction of movement politics but retained a focus on electoral strategies. One study of blacks in Los Angeles considered movement concerns such as the coalitional perceptions of blacks toward Latinos and Asian-Americans and their views on nonconventional politics, but a major emphasis was their choice of political party.[2] Conventional approaches also assume that political coalitions are composed of interest groups behaving as rational actors who join forces on a short-term basis. A long-range coalition is a convention of groups for a protracted period of time, for example, a political party that coalesces segments of the population with similar goals. A short-range coalition brings participants together for limited purposes and does not assume a broad range of common values. And an ad hoc coalition joins groups for a specific and less permanent purpose.[3]

Most studies of coalition-building concentrate on national politics. Although ad hoc coalitions in Washington are nothing new, they increased in frequency and ease of creation in the 1980s. With so many institutional interests permanently represented in Washington, according to Robert Salisbury, personnel are available to be "assembled in short order under some suitable organizational rubric for the specific and limited purpose of the given legislative campaign. When the campaign is over, 'the interests' remain in their essentially institutionalized forms, ready to be reassembled in different coalitional guises for subsequent battles." There are two spheres of interest group politics in the nation's capital: policymaking and mobilizing. The policymaking sphere devotes "most of its attention to the Washington scene and matters of pragmatic, detailed self-interest, deriving mainly from the impact of public policies upon institutions, public and private. As the total volume of public policy has grown, its differential effects become ever more complex, and all kinds of institutions find that they need more Washington representation to cope." The mobilizing sphere is "based on grass-roots mobilization around issues freighted with moralistic symbols," operating through methods of "electoral pressure and direct action at the local community level." Although many of these groups maintain formal Washington offices, their impact is achieved mainly at the grassroots level.[4]

Accommodationist Feminist Studies of Women's Political Coalitions

Along conventional lines, many studies of women's coalitions looked at interest group behavior in Washington that was pragmatic, self-interested, and short term or ad hoc, aimed at affecting public policy. Probably the most effective women's coalition effort was the one that secured passage of Title IX, as described by Joyce Gelb and Marian Lief Palley:

> Through the use of a highly effective coalition, the Coalition for Women and Girls in Education, they shared information, effectively divided responsibility, and presented a united political front and the image of broad-based political support. The maintenance of this effective single-issue group, which drew on the

resources of mass membership groups, specialized research and legal organizations, and staff and elected officeholders in federal office, gained credibility for feminist interests in education. Feminists gained access to the policy-making process both in Congress and in HEW. In Congress they beat back repeated efforts to weaken Title IX through riders and modified appropriations. At the Office of Civil Rights they were viewed as "the most assertive, viable, and well-organized group," according to one long-time observer.[5]

This coalition started out as an informal lunch group of a few people and expanded to comprise some sixty groups. Participants limited themselves to a single issue—sex discrimination in education—and ironed out their substantive and tactical differences before taking public positions so as to minimize public divisiveness. Participation was flexible: members joined only on those matters with which they agreed. The coalition met biweekly to discuss issues and delineate positions on policy. Power was shared among constituent groups.

Despite the existence of numerous groups of women competing for funding and influence in Washington, Gelb and Palley observed, there was "extensive coalition-building and remarkable unity among feminists. Individuals and groups join together in a variety of contexts linked by loose commitments to feminist ideology, shared symbols of group identity, and the friendships and contacts they have developed." Gelb and Palley placed particular emphasis on feminists' ability to rely on a pre-existing structure of traditional women's groups, whose shared interest in many feminist issues "produced numbers and assistance that would otherwise have been costly and probably unattainable." In addition, they noted that the civil rights movement "served as a model of structure and tactics and provided considerable assistance to the incipient feminist movement as it developed. . . . Feminist successes, in turn, have helped other groups: the Equal Credit Opportunity Act served as a model for minorities and the aged, who lobbied to amend the law to cover their groups as well."[6]

Myra Marx Ferree and Beth B. Hess had a more guarded view of feminists' willingness to form coalitions with groups beyond traditional women's groups. They saw feminists in the mid-1970s as "hesitant to use their influence on issues not having a direct impact on women. In addition, women's organizations were, and are, relatively weak, so that feminists gain more from alliances with more established organizations than the reverse." They continued:

When compared to members of other elites (party, labor, farm, business, media, and minority group leaders), heads of feminist organizations held comparatively radical views of equality, tended to explain poverty in terms of social structural conditions, supported affirmative action for both women and minority group members, and favored greater wage equality for all workers. While most of these goals are held in common with blacks and organized labor, neither the black nor labor leaders saw feminists as particularly helpful allies in their political struggles. Conversely, leaders of feminist organizations saw labor unions and black organizations as potential allies, supported their goals, and felt that these groups should have more political power. But the black and labor leaders did not believe that feminists really shared their goals, that the New Feminist Movement represented all women, that existing feminist organizations had much political influence or deserved more.[7]

Ferree and Hess maintained that differences among feminists accounted for their fragile ties to seemingly natural allies. Those with experiences in the civil rights movement, unions, or the New Left tended to be sympathetic to a socialist analysis in which class and race were important variables. Since they were more likely than other feminists to be women of color or working-class women, they valued links to organized labor and black groups for their own sake as well as for their potential contribution to feminist goals. Radical feminists were deeply concerned with women's distinctive qualities and experiences, particularly those of exploitation and violence, and they sought alliances with peace, disarmament, ecology, and antinuclear groups. And liberal feminists favored coalitions with established civil rights organizations such as the American Civil Liberties Union, with family planning groups such as Planned Parenthood, occasionally making joint cause with blacks, the aged, the disabled, and children's rights advocates. Thus, the women's movement established a broad range of links to other interest groups, but none of these links encompassed the entire movement. Such weak ties to groups had certain negative consequences for the movement, such as the inability to speak with one voice. A positive consequence, however, was "greater flexibility for broad-based feminist organizations such as NOW to maneuver among potential allies and to balance goals and priorities of the many constituencies within the movement. An important aspect of NOW's activities in recent years has been to educate its own members to expand their vision to encompass a variety of feminist perspectives, and to support one another."[8]

One of the most well documented coalitions was the one formed to secure ratification of the Equal Rights Amendment. Unexpected resistance to the ERA led to a high point of feminist coalition-building, from a thirty-group effort in 1973 to a coalition of more than one hundred national groups by 1980. Ironically, during the losing struggle for the amendment, membership gains and financial support reached new peaks, cooperation among women's groups was stronger than ever, and public opinion polls recorded high levels of support for the ERA.[9]

A glimpse into the kinds of concerns faced by women's groups in coalition can be seen in the case of the American Association of University Women's efforts to secure ERA ratification in the Illinois legislature.[10] AAUW had endorsed the ERA in 1971, and it subsequently joined the Illinois ERA Ratification Project, which had been initiated by NOW. The tasks of the project included analyzing the state's political atmosphere, compiling legislators' ERA voting records, targeting specific legislative districts, engaging members in lobbying activities such as letter writing and educational outreach, and supporting pro-ERA candidates in primary and general elections. AAUW was prevented by its rules from endorsing candidates, but it could disseminate information about candidates' issue stands.

AAUW faced several dilemmas in the ERA coalition. The first was retaining group identity in a larger alliance. It set up a pilot project in Chicago to decide how best to serve its own members, spending weeks determining the quantity and quality of resources to contribute to the coalition's unified effort. The second dilemma related to physical resources: money and membership size. AAUW solicited voluntary contributions to the AAUW-ERA Fund to target unratified states, primarily Illinois. AAUW was exceptionally large relative to other voluntary women's organizations: 190,000 members nationally, with nearly 9,000 in Illinois. A third issue was organizational resources. Although the AAUW as an organization provided substantive expertise to the coalitional effort, its broad-based membership did not lend itself to rapid mobilization of organizational resources for political action. A fourth concern was voluntary time. Most AAUW volunteers were unable to devote the full time and attention needed for working within the legislative schedule. There was also the issue of political resources. AAUW's work in Illinois had been pioneering in the areas of marshaling expertise about the state's political process and establishing a reputation for political action. Members from across the country volunteered to travel to Illinois to help with letter writing and lobbying. Finally, there were motivational and intangible resources at stake. The coalition enabled a wide variety of diverse organizations to bring to a central location their "true believers" in the

cause of equal rights. Such motivational resources were vital to successful coalitional efforts. Intangible resources included the prestige and
reputation of the organization. AAUW's participation in the ERA Ratification Project demonstrated its willingness to devote considerable tan-
gible and intangible resources to achieve a political goal.

The foregoing analysis of the AAUW in Illinois centered on group
resources that were mobilized for a political coalition. As we have seen,
resource mobilization theory was the most commonly used approach in
studying social movements and interest group activity. Anne N. Costain's
analysis of the women's lobby in Washington, however, parted company
both with resource mobilization theory and with Gelb and Palley's view
that women's legislative successes resulted from their moderate demands and tactics. Costain attributed the success of the the institutionalized "women's lobby" in Washington to the power of the women's
movement more broadly defined. When she began her research in 1974,
in the wake of congressional passage of major laws dealing with women's
issues, she was fully expecting to find "a dynamic group of women's lobbyists who were reasonably well funded and working cooperatively to
prod the legislature to take action on policies of concern to women.
What I found instead were severely underfunded lobbyists who were frequently divided over issues and split by rivalries among their respective
groups." She searched for the basis for their success:

> I went back through my Washington interviews with women's
> lobbyists, members of Congress, and congressional staff. It be-
> came clear that all, to varying degrees, were responding to the
> size, intensity, and political power of the women's movement.
> From a spokeswoman at the League of Women Voters who mar-
> veled at how psychologically empowering it was for League
> members to work on the Equal Rights Amendment (ERA), to
> movement lobbyists who insisted that all their access and influ-
> ence on Capitol Hill depended upon the mobilizing, organiz-
> ing, and letter writing carried on by movement activists at the
> grass-roots level, to the leader of one women's group who felt
> her organization could now get a hearing because of the "wild-
> eyed" extreme women's groups that made her appear moder-
> ate, it was evident that the movement created the wedge that al-
> lowed Washington groups to gain access to decision makers.[11]

Costain was dissatisfied with resource mobilization theory, with its
emphasis on the acquisition of resources to create advantageous ex-

change relationships with other groups to fulfill goals. Her research had convinced her that the major impact of the women's movement had been largely independent of political resources, strong allies, or very effective political tactics. She was equally uneasy about Gelb and Palley's incrementalist, role equity theory of women's legislative success:

> By asking for equality, women were thought to be both linking their cause to the congressional majority that supported civil rights legislation in the sixties and, at the same time, minimizing their challenge to the status quo. Women's issues were subsumed in the incremental politics of adding "and sex" to new and existing civil rights guarantees. Yet, this incremental and "clever" politics bore little relationship to the messianic, ideological, and often angry politics I had observed in Washington. Lobbyists for most of the women's movement groups described their activity as a kind of crusade to change the world. . . . I believed that the women's movement, with its passion and anger as well as organizations, was the stimulus causing members of Congress to work for, vote for and brag in their campaigns about their support for women's issues.[12]

Instead, Costain adopted a political process approach, which focused on how the structure of political opportunities affected new social movements. According to this theory, much of the policy success of a movement depended on the receptivity of the political process during the time potential supporters of a new movement were psychologically and organizationally ready to challenge the status quo. When the government was strong and committed to repressing a social movement, the movement would usually fail. When the relative balance of power between movement and government was more nearly equal, the movement could acquire leverage within the political system and succeed. For a time, at least, political success bred further success as people rushed to join a winning cause. Costain noted: "As the crumbling New Deal coalition ushered in a period of political uncertainty in the late sixties and early seventies and the potential electoral impact of a women's bloc of votes began to attract attention, strategically placed politicians saw the value of making a serious effort to attract women's support. This allowed the women's movement to gain early legislative victories without possessing many resources or tactical skills."[13] Congress was ready to move on legal equality for women but was not as prepared to move on issues that singled women out for special consideration, such as child care and abortion.

Without downplaying the organizational strength and new political consciousness of women in the late sixties and early seventies, Costain said government willingness to act was a prime determinant of the timing and initial political agenda of the women's movement. The peak of the women's movement and of activity on the ERA occurred in the same year, 1975, as measured by women's events covered in the *New York Times.* Issues of legal equality triumphed over those of women's special needs less as a conscious choice of the women's movement than as the preference of the legislative and executive branches of the federal government. The women's movement, in turn, responded to favorable government action by shifting to a focus on equal rights, with the ERA as the centerpiece. In the early 1980s, the government became unwilling to act on women's issues with the election of a president who was openly antagonistic to most key women's issues and with the defeat of the movement's primary issue, the ERA. The national women's movement began to fade rapidly. Legal equality was the most comfortable response for the federal government to the women's movement, given its recent experience with the civil rights movement. Although government pressure pushed the movement toward the goal of legal equality, Costain rejected the view of some movement critics that the movement shortsightedly undercut women's issues by allowing itself to be attracted unreasonably to the ERA and co-opted by government. Rather, the national movement's increasingly single-minded focus on the ERA was a realistic response to the structure of political opportunity in Washington.[14]

Powerful criticisms of the movement's preoccupation with the ERA came from transformational feminists, however. Their analyses of coalitions went beyond Washington, D.C., interest group politics to local and informal settings, focused on race and class issues, and emphasized emotional coalition efforts within the women's movement itself.

Transformational Feminist Studies of Women's Political Coalitions

Consider Paula Giddings's analysis of NOW's "race/class myopia" in its "misdirected" ERA strategy, which alienated union women at the outset. In 1967, NOW drafted a Bill of Rights for Women to present to parties and candidates for the 1968 election. One article supported the ERA, putting NOW's members from the United Auto Workers (UAW) in an untenable position. They supported the ERA, but their union, and most unions, did not, because it would supersede protective labor laws. Labor women believed that the amendment would benefit professional and upper-class women but would be detrimental to them. The interests of the professional membership of NOW prevailed over those of its union membership. (A 1974 survey of NOW members showed that 66 percent had bachelor's degrees, 30 percent had advanced degrees, and 25 percent were professionally employed. Only 8 percent were clerical workers, despite the fact that clerical workers made up 35 percent of the employed female population, and only 10 percent were women of color.) UAW women were on the verge of changing the union's opposition to the ERA, and they informed NOW that its ERA endorsement was premature. NOW's insistence on the ERA forced UAW women to withdraw their active support for NOW, which at that time was working out of UAW offices and using UAW clerical and mailing services. NOW had to relocate its national offices, creating administrative chaos and the loss of valuable time and energy. NOW's premature support for the amendment also slowed its passage in Congress because of labor opposition. Several unions with significant female constituencies testified against the ERA. In Giddings's words: "That the amendment survived at all was due more to the effort of the UAW women than that of NOW's leadership. A year after the union members withdrew active support, they were prepared to justify the amendment to the labor movement. In turn, large labor unions and the Women's Bureau—headed by a Black woman, Elizabeth Koontz—were able to support it for the first time in their histories."[15]

NOW's response to the Stop ERA campaign was similarly myopic with respect to race and class. Instead of consolidating the constituencies most responsive to the ERA—namely union women and black women—it watered down feminist ideas to make them more palatable to antifeminist women. A 1972 Louis Harris-Virginia Slims poll revealed that 62 percent of black women favored "efforts to strengthen or change women's status in society," compared to only 45 percent of white women; and 67 percent of black women, but only 35 percent of white women, expressed "sympathy with efforts of women's liberation groups."[16]

The case of Aileen Hernandez illustrated women of color's dissatisfaction with NOW. A black woman and NOW founder, she had been a civil rights activist, an organizer for the International Ladies' Garment Workers Union, and a commissioner for the Equal Employment Opportunity Commission. In 1970, she replaced Betty Friedan as NOW president. In a 1979 interview, Hernandez discussed how she and other black women had organized a NOW minority task force to assess minority women's relationship with NOW. Their report made several recommendations, including the need to address issues of concern to minorities, but subsequent action by NOW was sorely lacking: "NOW has been silent on almost any issue that deals with the inequity of society more than the inequity of being female. [NOW] cannot afford the luxury of a single issue focus—even when that issue was as important as the ERA." Hernandez criticized NOW's "totally inappropriate approach" of sponsoring chapters in minority communities rather than dealing with minority issues, which she interpreted as attempting to "indoctrinate minority women" on the ERA rather than attracting them to common issues. At NOW's 1979 national convention, an all-white group of officers was elected for the second straight year, although a black woman who had headed the minority task force was running for a position. Hernandez accused NOW of being "too White and middle-class" and sponsored a resolution saying blacks should quit NOW or refrain from joining the group until it confronted its own racism and that of the larger society. California state senator Diane Watson agreed: "If they don't really go after a mixed group of women, we should not support such an organization, and we should dramatize our non-support."[17]

Giddings's argument about white middle-class feminists' race and class bias was echoed by transformational feminist scholars of women's political coalitions, most of whom were women of color and/or working-class women who wanted to strengthen the movement through a frank discussion of women's race and class differences. We now turn to the four themes that emerged from this scholarship, which distinguished it from accommodationist studies of women's coalitions: emotional conflict, not simply rational calculation; survival, not pure cost/benefit expediency; ethnic/racial identity, not just joining a voluntary group; and an engaged epistemology, not behaviorist conventional wisdom.

Political Coalitions and Emotional Conflict

There were powerful emotional legacies associated with black and white women's relationships. Such legacies also characterized white women's relations with other women of color. These emotions were of central importance in making and breaking coalitions between women of different races, and they ran the gamut from anger to betrayal to frustration at invisibility. Dealing with these emotions often meant conflict and confrontation, denial and guilt. Transformational feminists emphasized that this emotional work was an extremely important part of women's political coalitions.

For some black women, the legacy of anger grew in part from white women's collusion in slavery and lynchings. Black women were much more likely than white women to know the grisly historical details of these two institutions, and they frequently had to educate white feminists about them. For example, an eighty-five-year-old community activist described how she moved from complacency to community involvement:

> We were comfortably fixed in Little Rock: we owned our own home; we built to suit ourselves; and we were comfortably fixed. But the racial situation was pretty bad at the time and something happened that just drove us away immediately— . . . they lynched this boy. . . . They had to pass by our door and my children saw them—the gang, the mob passing my house with this boy in the car just screaming and yelling and having a big picnic on the way to a big bonfire that had been built right in the center of the Black district. . . . They built this fire right at the intersection of two streets and burned him alive—while the women, the white women clapped their hands.[18]

During the 1970s, when many white women were wondering why black women were not rushing to join white-dominated feminist organizations, black feminists were revealing the painful histories of female slaves, which included rape as part of their owners' property rights, forced breeding with selected male slaves, the loss of their children to the auction block, a short life expectancy due to constant pregnancies and grueling long hours of field and house work, the loss of indigenous cultures, and the lack of legal recourse.[19] Black feminists were also uncovering how the lynchings of ten thousand blacks in the three decades following the Civil War were justified on the grounds of protecting white women from rape. These feminists also charged that the white-dominated feminist anti-rape movement failed to take into account this history of the frame-up of black men on rape charges and the fact that white police did not take seriously the rape charges of lower-class and black women.[20]

Another source of anger was some white women's treatment of black female domestic workers. Black feminists pointed out the indignities experienced by domestic workers. Florence Rice, a Harlem activist in tenant and consumer organizations, recounted how the 1930s New York City "Bronx slave market" operated. Black women stood at an assigned spot and waited for white employers to drive up and offer them work for a dollar a day.

> I always remember my domestic days. Some of the women, when
> they didn't want to pay, they'd accuse you of stealing. . . . In
> those days a white woman says something about a black person,
> that was it. . . . This man picked me up and said his wife was ill
> and then when I got there his wife wasn't there and he wanted
> to have an affair. . . . I started crying and he didn't force me and
> I was able to get out. When the maids would get together, they'd
> talk of it. Some of them was very attractive and good-looking.
> They always had to fight off the woman's husband.[21]

White women maintained their privileged position relative to black domestics in many subtle ways. They addressed domestics by their first
names, called them "girls," expected to be addressed as "ma'am," asked
personal questions that they would not ask of members of their own social circle, required uniforms, confined domestics to one area of the
house, and expected them to make themselves invisible when they entered the other areas.

Black women's anger also stemmed from overt acts of racism by white
women. Audre Lorde recounted a childhood subway encounter with a
white woman. When Lorde sat down next to her, the woman jerked her
coat away.

> I look. I do not see whatever terrible thing she is seeing on the
> seat between us—probably a roach. But she has communicated
> her horror to me. It must be something very bad from the way
> she's looking, so I pull my snowsuit closer to me away from it, too.
> When I look up the woman is still staring at me, her nose holes
> and eyes huge. And suddenly I realize there is nothing crawling
> up the seat between us; it is me she does not want her coat to
> touch. The fur brushes past my face as she stands with a shudder
> and holds on to a strap in the speeding train. Born and bred a
> New York City child, I quickly slide over to make room for my
> mother to sit down. No word has been spoken. I'm afraid to say
> anything to my mother because I don't know what I've done. I
> look at the sides of my snowpants, secretly. Is there something on
> them? Something's going on here I do not understand, but I will
> never forget it. Her eyes. The flared nostrils. The hate.[22]

Lorde's response to racism was anger, which she constructively focused against the personal and institutional oppressions that brought

the anger into being. Unexpressed anger was destructive; it lay within people like an undetonated device.

> But anger expressed and translated into action in the service of our vision and our future is a liberating and strengthening act of clarification, for it is in the painful process of this trans-lation that we identify who are our allies with whom we have grave differences, and who are our genuine enemies. Anger is loaded with information and energy. When I speak of women of Color, I do not only mean Black women. The woman of Color who is not Black and who charges me with rendering her invisible by assuming that her struggles with racism are identical with my own has something to tell me that I had better learn from, lest we both waste ourselves fighting the truths between us. If I participate, knowingly or otherwise, in my sister's oppression and she calls me on it, to answer her anger with my own only blankets the substance of our exchange with reaction. It wastes energy. And yes, it is very difficult to stand still and listen to another woman's voice delineate an agony I do not share, or one to which I myself have contributed.[23]

Lorde distinguished between anger and hatred: anger was a grief of distortions between peers, with change as its object; hatred was the fury of those who did not share feminist goals, with death and destruction as its object. Lorde would not hide her anger to spare white women's guilt, because such guilt was a way of avoiding informed action. Most women had not developed tools for facing anger constructively. Consciousness-raising groups in the past, largely white, had dealt with how to express anger at men, but they had not attempted to articulate the differences among women, such as race, color, age, class, and sexual identity.

> If I speak to you in anger, at least I have spoken to you: I have not put a gun to your head and shot you down in the street. . . . The angers between women will not kill us if we can articulate them with precision, if we listen to the content of what is said with at least as much intensity as we defend ourselves against the manner of saying. When we turn from anger we turn from in-sight, saying we will accept only the designs already known, deadly and safely familiar. . . . Anger between peers births

change, not destruction, and the discomfort and sense of loss it often causes is not fatal, but a sign of growth.[24]

Betrayal in the First-Wave Women's Movement

In the case of political coalitions for abolition, white feminists often overlooked the fact that blacks had initiated their own organizations to end slavery before whites became mobilized to the cause. Angela Davis noted that "the first female anti-slavery society was formed by Black women in 1832 in Salem, Massachusetts."[25] Black women were not always welcomed at white Female Anti-Slave Society meetings, as Barbara Omolade described: "There was outright racist exclusion such as the dissolution of the Massachusetts Female Anti-Slave Society at Fall River in 1838 when black women began attending meetings. And there was subtle racist exclusion such as failing to link their early concerns about women's rights with black women organized in anti-slave societies and the underground railroad."[26] White female reformers in the 1830s attacked slavery, not racism. In bell hooks's words: "The basis of their attack was moral reform. That they were not demanding social equality for black people is an indication that they remained committed to white racist supremacy despite their anti-slavery work. . . . It did not help the cause of oppressed black slaves for white women to make synonymous their plight and the plight of the slave. . . . They were not revealing an awareness of or sensitivity to the slave's lot; they were simply appropriating the horror of the slave experience to enhance their own cause."[27] When white feminists described marriage as slavery, it may have provided shock value, but it also implied that slavery was no worse than marriage; for black women, slavery meant whips and chains. There was great potential for alliances between black and white abolitionist women, as exemplified by the antiracist militancy of Prudence Crandall, a white teacher in Canterbury, Connecticut, who risked her life to teach black pupils, and by the promise of unity in the writings of Sarah and Angelina Grimké, who argued that white women could never receive their freedom independently of black people.[28] But this alliance was betrayed by white middle-class women in their quest for suffrage.

At the first formal women's convention to call for women's suffrage, in Seneca Falls in 1848, Elizabeth Cady Stanton introduced a controversial resolution for women's suffrage, and it was seconded by black abolitionist Frederick Douglass, a gifted orator who defended women's right to vote. There were no black women in attendance at Seneca Falls, however. Davis noted: "Nor did the convention's documents make even a passing reference to Black women. In light of the organizers' abolitionist involvement, it would seem puzzling that slave women were entirely disregarded. But this problem is not a new one. The Grimké sisters had previously criticized a number of female anti-slavery societies for ignoring the condition of Black women and for sometimes manifesting blatantly racist prejudices."[29]

At subsequent women's rights conventions, there were often racial tensions. At the 1851 convention in Akron, Ohio, where Sojourner Truth gave her famous "Ain't I a Woman?" speech, several white women hissed and tried to persuade the presiding officer to prevent her from addressing the audience. Although the Equal Rights Association was established in 1866 to bring black and female suffrage into a single campaign, at the first annual meeting of the association in 1867 Stanton argued that it was far more important for white "Saxon race" women to receive the franchise than for black men to gain the vote. At issue was the impending constitutional amendment enfranchising black men and the question whether women's rights advocates would support black suffrage even if women did not receive the vote simultaneously. When the Equal Rights Association voted to support the Fifteenth Amendment, white women felt betrayed. Susan B. Anthony declared, "I will cut off this right arm of mine before I will ever work for or demand the ballot for the Negro and not the woman," and Stanton "made derogatory references to 'Sambo,' and the enfranchisement of 'Africans, Chinese, and all ignorant foreigners the moment they touch our shores.'"[30]

White female suffragists felt betrayed by the Republican party, expecting the franchise in exchange for their pro-Union efforts during the Civil War. Republicans, however, were banking on the black male vote; in turn, many Democratic leaders defended women's suffrage as a calculated measure against their Republican opponents. Stanton and Anthony openly praised and received financial backing from avowedly racist Democratic men who supported female suffrage. At the final meeting of the Equal Rights Association in 1869, Douglass made a last-ditch appeal to the white delegates, attempting to convince them that the vote was a matter of survival for the recently freed slave population, whose oppression was qualitatively and brutally different from the situation of white middle-class women. As Davis observed, "The dissolution of the Equal Rights Association brought to an end the tenuous, though potentially powerful, alliance between Black Liberation and Women's Liberation."[31]

In the last half of the nineteenth century, this alliance was torn asunder as white northern women cast aside black allies in an expedient move to recruit white southern women into the suffrage movement;

simultaneously, the legal system of segregation and the tyranny of the lynch law were established in the South. Ida B. Wells, a Memphis newspaper editor and founder of the first black women's suffrage club, was a friend of Susan B. Anthony's and personally admired most of her suffrage efforts and her individual stance against racism. But she criticized Anthony for failing to make her personal fight against racism a public issue of the suffrage movement. Anthony explained to Wells that she had asked Frederick Douglass not to attend a suffrage association meeting in Atlanta because she did not want anything to get in the way of bringing southern white women into the suffrage association. Anthony also, as Davis described, had "refused to support the efforts of several Black women who wanted to form a branch of the suffrage association. She did not want to awaken the anti-Black hostility of her white Southern members, who might withdraw from the organization if Black women were admitted."[32]

During the last two decades of the suffrage drive, a racial strategy of expediency was articulated by white women at several conventions of the National American Woman Suffrage Association (NAWSA).[33] Educated white women argued that they should have the vote in order to outnumber illiterate black voters in the South. The NAWSA rejected proposed resolutions against southern segregationist laws, for fear of alienating the white southern vote (blacks were effectively disenfranchised in the South at this time). The white supremacist attitudes of the NAWSA did not prevent black women from conducting their own suffrage campaign, as individuals and within black organizations. The National Association of Colored Women (NACW), formed in 1896, had a suffrage department that represented forty thousand black women. By the 1900s, black suffrage clubs had been formed all around the country; their members educated voters, gathered and presented petitions, and worked in political campaigns."[34] By the time the women's suffrage amendment was passed in 1920, black and white women had gone their separate organizational ways. Nancie Caraway noted:

> The suffrage record makes clear why Black women's ample social reform activity at the turn of the century took the form of separate organizations. As new Black feminist histories celebrate, Black female intellectuals in this period sacrificed their middle-class lives to go South, to teach and cajole funds to build schools and clinics for the impoverished former slaves; to write novels as political acts; to tour the country as public speakers and reformers; to agitate for suffrage and women's rights; to

publicize, report on, and resist mob violence by organizing anti-lynching crusades; and to institutionalize mass club networks to honor and redeem their womanhood.[35]

Betrayal in the Second-Wave Women's Movement

Unlike the case in the first wave, there was a mutual sense of betrayal between black and white women in the early years of the second wave of the movement. White women in the civil rights movement were let down when black women opted for a separatist black nationalist strategy; and black women were disappointed by white women's interracial dating. These tensions were illustrated in the case of the Student Nonviolent Coordinating Committee (SNCC), formed in 1960 in the wake of the anti-segregation sit-in movement initiated by black students, and soon joined by white students, across the country.

With parallels to the abolition movement, white women joined SNCC, and many of them participated in the sit-ins, freedom rides, and voter registration drives in the rural South in the summer of 1964, "Freedom Summer." The relationship between the civil right movement and the emerging women's liberation movement looked very different from the perspective of a white woman, Sara Evans, and a black woman, Cynthia Washington, both of whom wrote their recollections of Freedom Summer.

Sara Evans observed that young white southern women in SNCC were treated as housewives, sex objects, nurturers, and political auxiliaries and were eventually banished from the group. They were politically mobilized by their experiences in SNCC. Their decisions to join SNCC usually meant a break with home and childhood friends, isolation, and possible violence and death. They were attracted by the vision of SNCC as a nonviolent "redemptive community" or "beloved community." For the first time, many of them started to see the South through the eyes of poor blacks. In the beginning, blacks and whites agreed that whites should work primarily in the white communities to marshal support for civil rights; eventually, they worked in black communities as well. Violence against the group's efforts escalated when white women became visible in the movement. By October 1964, fifteen people had been killed, four had been wounded, thirty-seven churches had been bombed, and one thousand arrests had been made in Mississippi. Black women, especially Fanny Lou Hamer, served as role models for the white women in SNCC. Both black and white women held important administrative posts in SNCC's Atlanta office, but most women served in a clerical capacity. In 1964, black women in SNCC half-jokingly held a sit-in to protest these conditions. By 1965, the position of white women in SNCC, "especially Southern women whose goals had been shaped by the vision of the 'beloved community,' was in steep decline. Ultimately a growing spirit of Black nationalism, fed by the tensions of large numbers of whites, especially women, entering the movement, forced these women out of SNCC and precipitated the articulation of a new feminism."[36]

Interracial sexual relations became a serious problem for SNCC in the summer of 1964. The struggle against racism "brought together young, naive, sometimes insensitive, rebellious, and idealistic white women with young, angry Black men, some of whom had hardly been allowed to speak to White women before. They sat-in together. If they really believed in equality, why shouldn't they sleep together?"[37] Young black women in the movement felt betrayed by both black men and white women. Two white women who had considerable influence in SNCC were activists Casey Hayden and Mary King. At the tension-filled 1964 Waveland Conference, Hayden circulated her unsigned paper entitled "The Position of Women in SNCC," which criticized the traditional sexual division of labor in SNCC and stirred white women's feminist consciousness. In 1965, Hayden and King wrote a "kind of memo" addressed principally to the black women with whom they had worked and by whom they had been hurt as the civil rights movement shifted from nonviolence to nationalism, from beloved community to Black Power. They spoke of how their experiences in the movement had led them to the conclusion that there was a sex caste system, and they lamented "the lack of community for discussion: Nobody is writing, or organizing, or talking publicly about women, in any way that reflects the problems that various women in the movement come across."[38]

According to Evans, the black women who received this message were on a historical trajectory that was different from that of the white women in the civil rights movement. Black women would fight their battles as women in their own way. For middle-class white women, the memo represented the beginnings of a women's consciousness that would be constructed with the tools provided by the civil rights movement: "a language to name and describe oppression; a deep belief in freedom, equality and community soon to be translated into 'sisterhood'; a willingness to question and challenge any social institution which failed to meet human needs; and the ability to organize. . . . The debate within Students for a Democratic Society (SDS) which started in response to Hayden and King's ideas led, two years later, to the founding of the women's liberation movement."[39]

Cynthia Washington provided another perspective on SNCC's Freedom Summer, during which she, along with other black women, directed her own projects. She reflected on the different approaches of black and white women to community activism and thus different senses of what a women's movement would mean:

> What Casey and other white women seemed to want was an opportunity to prove they could do something other than office work. I assumed that if they could do something else, they'd probably be doing that. I remember driving back to Mississippi in my truck, thinking how crazy they were. I couldn't understand what they wanted. As far as I could see, being a project director wasn't much fun. I didn't realize then that having my own project made a lot of difference in how I was perceived and treated. And I did not see what I was doing as exceptional. The community women I worked with on projects were respected and admired for their strength and endurance. They worked hard in the cotton fields or white folks' houses, raised and supported their children, yet still found time and energy to be involved in struggle for their people. They were typical rather than unusual. Certain differences result from the way in which Black women grow up. We have been raised to function independently. The notion of retiring to housewifery someday is not even a reasonable fantasy. Therefore whether you want to or not, it is necessary to learn to do all of the things required to survive. It seemed to many of us, on the other hand, that white women were demanding a chance to be independent while we needed help and assistance which was not always forthcoming. We definitely started from opposite ends of the spectrum.[40]

Washington said black women's independence took a personal toll that fed into the tension between black and white women. Black women did the same work as men in the field—community organizing and voter registration—usually with men. But when they got back to town where they could relax and go out, the men went out with white women. "Our skills and abilities were recognized and respected, but that seemed to place us in some category other than female. Some years later, I was told by a male SNCC worker that some of the project women had made him feel superfluous. I wish he had told me that at the time because the differences in the way women were treated certainly did add to the tension between Black and white women."[41] According to Evans, many white women in SNCC went out with black men to prove that they were not racists. From Washington's account, it is clear that white women failed to understand such dating relationships from the point of view of black women. It was not surprising that black women were skeptical about a call to sisterhood from women who failed to comprehend the personal pain of their black sisters.

Thus black women felt betrayed by white women's failure to see how their dating and sexual behavior with black men affected black women, and white women felt betrayed when their black sisters ousted them from SNCC and opted for subservience to men in the black nationalist movement. This sense of betrayal was subsequently expressed by black women in more conventional electoral settings as well, for example, in 1972 when NWPC and NOW failed to endorse the presidential candidacy of Shirley Chisholm,[42] and in 1984 when NOW lost an opportunity to join Jesse Jackson's Rainbow Coalition[43] and harmed the possibility of a black-white coalition by stressing the primacy of a female over a black vice-presidential candidate.[44]

Frustration at Invisibility

White women often spoke and acted as if the women's movement was "theirs" and as if women of color were "invited guests." Bell hooks experienced this in her first women's studies class at Stanford University in the early 1970s. What struck hooks as particularly ironic was white women's euphoria at a newly discovered sense of sisterhood—a sisterhood hooks had experienced all her life. She had never known a time when women had *not* been together, helping, protecting, and loving one another deeply. She was also surprised to hear white women tell her they could not be expected to have any knowledge or understanding of the experiences of black women. Despite growing up in the racially segregated South, hooks knew a lot about the lives of white women. And although white women expected black women to provide firsthand accounts of black experiences, white women presumed to be authorities on which black experiences were authentic.

> Frequently, college-educated black women (even those from poor and working class backgrounds) were dismissed as mere imitators . . . as white women were convinced that "real" blackness meant speaking the patois of poor black people, being uneducated, streetwise, and a variety of other stereotypes. If we dared to criticize the movement or to assume responsibility for reshaping feminist ideas and introducing new ideas, our voices

were tuned out, dismissed, silenced. . . . From the time the women's liberation movement began, individual black women went to groups. Many never returned after a first meeting."[45]

Hooks cited the case of a welfare rights activist who received a call from the New York City chapter of NOW asking for a welfare speaker for a conference on urban women: "I was asked that she not be white—she might be 'too articulate'—(i.e., not me), that she not be black, she might be 'too angry.' Perhaps she could be Puerto Rican? She could not say anything political or analytical but confine herself to the subject of 'what the women's movement has done for me.' "[46]

White middle-class feminists often assumed that their race and class were universal, not specifiable. Flaws in this presumed universality were pointed out by black feminists who argued that the real problem was white male patriarchy, not patriarchy; white male supremacy, not male supremacy.[47] Stated differently, white middle-class feminists did not really want equality with men in the abstract; they wanted equality with white middle-class men in particular. As Bev Fisher expressed it:

It is easy to see why the woman who is the wife of a doctor or lawyer may want into the system on equal terms with men. . . . A middle-class woman can hope for the same status, control, comfortable income, and fulfillment she sees the middle-class men around her achieving. But a working class or minority woman most likely can hope only for what she sees her husband or brother doing: hard, dirty work over which he has little control, a job with little or no status, with meager wages, and probably motivated only by the paycheck rather than the work itself.[48]

In her reflections, "On Being White," Marilyn Frye noted that white women's belonging to that group of women from which men of the racially dominant group chose their mates gave them some access to the benefits of the racially dominant male group: material and educational benefits, the false benefit of enjoying secondhand feelings of superiority and supremacy, and

the specious benefit of a certain *hope* (a false hope, as it turns out) which women of subordinated races do not have, namely the hope of becoming actually dominant *with* the white men, as their "equals." This last pseudo-benefit binds us most closely to them in racial solidarity. A liberal white feminism would seek "equality"; we can hardly expect to be heard as saying we want social and economic status equal to that of, say, Chicanos. If what we want is equality with our white brothers, then what we want is, among other things, our own firsthand participation in racial dominance rather than the secondhand ersatz dominance we get as the dominant group's women. No wonder such feminism has no credibility with women of color.[49]

Ironically, though white feminists were familiar with the male habit of false universalization (writing and speaking, and presumably also thinking, that whatever was true of them was true of everybody), many of them failed to see their own false universalization of the white race. Frye commented, "For the most part, it never occurred to us to modify our nouns accordingly; to our minds the people we were writing about were *people*. We don't think of ourselves as *white*."[50]

Adrienne Rich referred to this false white universality as "white solipsism," which was "not a consciously held belief that one race is inherently superior to all others, but a tunnel-vision which simply does not see nonwhite experience or existence as precious or significant, unless in spasmodic, impotent guilt-reflexes, which have little or no long-term, continuing momentum or political usefulness." Guilt allowed white women to remain paralyzed instead of "taking women's condition seriously" and listening to what women of color had to say. "Why, for example, should we feel more alien to the literature and lives of black women than to centuries of the literature and history of white men?"[51]

White women's ignorance about black women's lives was a form of white privilege, as indeed were most white feminist formulations of "the problem of difference." Elizabeth V. Spelman provided several examples of expressions about difference commonly heard in feminist classrooms and at feminist conferences. The claim "Feminist theory must take differences among women into consideration" preserved the relationship between "insiders" who brought in "outsiders," and did nothing to undermine white women's power and authority to control the conditions under which "differences" would be brought up. The statement "We need to hear the many voices of women" raised these questions: "Is hearing from them the same thing as talking with them? Are we really willing to hear anything and everything they might have to say, or only what we don't find too disturbing? Are we prepared to hear what they say, even if it requires learning concepts or whole languages that we don't yet understand?" And the expression "Feminist theory must include more of the experiences of women of different races and classes" pointed to the freedom of the agent in question to take or leave it, as if to say, "I've made a home here, and now I'd like to welcome you in." Welcoming someone into one's own home did not represent an attempt to undermine privilege; it expressed it.[52] Privilege also lurked in feminist writings where gender was accorded a metaphysical space free from race and class. This had the effect of making certain women rather than others paradigmatic examples of "woman"—namely, those women

> who seem to have a gender identity untainted (I use the word advisedly) by racial or class identity, those women referred to in newspapers, magazines, and feminist journals simply as "women," without the qualifier "Black" or "Hispanic" or "Asian American" or "poor." What is in fact a function of the privilege of white middle-class women is being passed off as a metaphysical truth: that is, that we can talk about a woman "as a woman" without explicitly or implicitly alluding to her race or class. I am not saying that we ought never to think about or refer to women "as women" or men "as men." I am only insisting that whenever we do we remember which women and which men we are thinking about.[53]

As Audre Lorde noted, many white and black feminists initially wrote and spoke as if black women were the only women of color, a problem that was soon brought to their attention by other women of color. Sylvia Gonzales wrote in the mid-1970s that Chicanas were stereotyped as passive and invisible by white feminists, who acted as if blacks were the only minority group in the United States. A case in point was the 1975 International Women's Year Conference in Mexico City, where Chicanas felt underrepresented.

> Community groups of activist Chicanas held food fairs, car washes, dances, etc., to finance travel to the conference. But Chicana enthusiasm was quashed by the revelation that the sorrowful position Chicanas occupy within the feminist movement in the United States was to be repeated in Mexico City. . . . Claims of breaking the bonds of prejudice by including a black perspective in the movement are left wanting in light of the continued serious neglect of ethnic minority women such as Chicanas, Puerto Ricans, Asians, and American Indians. This patronization emanates from a lopsided East Coast perspective, where black women are the largest minority and have greater visibility than other minority women. Black women must pay

attention to this. In this case, black women are not oppressors by intent, but because they are less linguistically distinct, communication is more easily established. In addition, the national moral conscience is black-influenced and permeates the eastern liberal mentality to the point where liberal program responses are mainly directed to the black cause.[54]

Along similar lines, Mitsuye Yamada wrote about how Asian Pacific American women were stereotyped as apolitical, passive, sweet, "Oriental" women, who were invited by white feminists to " 'join' them and give them 'input' " but not say anything threatening.

No matter what we say or do, the stereotype still hangs on. I am weary of starting from scratch each time I speak or write, as if there were no history behind us, of hearing that among women of color, Asian women are the least political, or the least oppressed, or the most polite. It is too bad not many people remember that one of the two persons in Seattle who stood up to contest the constitutionality of the Evacuation Order in 1942 was a young Japanese American woman. As individuals and in groups, we Asian Pacific women have been (more intensively than ever in the past few years) active in community affairs and speaking and writing about our activities. . . . And yet, we continue to hear, "Asian women are of course traditionally not attuned to being political," as if most other women are; or that Asian women are too happily bound to their traditional roles as mothers and wives, as if the same cannot be said of a great number of white American women among us.[55]

Political Coalitions as Survival

In addition to underestimating the emotional conflicts of political coalitions, conventional understandings emphasized their expedient nature: groups choose to form coalitions if they are "worth the effort," if they will get a positive return on their investment of resources in a joint political effort. Many women of color described coalitions more as a matter of necessity than of choice, however, since their survival depended on them. Given these high stakes, women of color had to be clear about their terms for joining coalitions with white women.

In her introduction to *Home Girls: A Black Feminist Anthology,* Barbara Smith argued that among all feminists, women of color "felt most viscerally the need for linking struggles" and were the "most capable of forging such coalitions. A commitment to principled coalitions, based not upon expediency, but upon our actual need for each other is a . . . major contribution of Black feminist struggle. Many contributors to *Home Girls* write out of a sense of our ultimate interdependence."[56] Home was where women of color got support for the difficult work of coalitions. Separatist organizations were seen as essential for forging identity and strategy, preparing one to join coalitions. As Barbara Smith and Beverly Smith put it, even though women of color often felt like tokens in the women's movement, separatism was not a viable solution to tokenism. Separatism forged identity and gave strength, but the most effective politics were coalition politics that covered a broad range of issues. One oppressed group could not topple a system by itself; it needed to form principled coalitions around specific issues. Ironically, coalition-building was a more radical strategy than separatism:

> What *I* really feel is radical is trying to make coalitions with people who are different from you. I feel it is radical to be dealing with race and sex and class and sexual identity all at one time. I think *that* is really radical because it has never been done before. . . . We are in a position to challenge the feminist movement as it stands to date and not out of any theoretical commitment. Our analysis of race and class oppression and our commitment to really dealing with those issues, including homophobia, is something we know we have to struggle with to insure our survival. It is organic to our very existence.[57]

People who bore different types of social burdens were best served by a strategy that increased their understanding and effectiveness with respect to all these burdens. Along these lines, Davida J. Alperin opted for what she termed an interactive, rather than a pluralist or a separatist, model of social differences and political action. In the pluralist view, groups competed for benefits and adopted either an assimilationist or a cultural pluralist strategy. The separatist approach posited one form of oppression as the source of other forms and worked to end that basic form (e.g., patriarchy, capitalism, white supremacy). An interactive paradigm posited unfair societal burdens on a variety of groups, with many types of oppression and no single form of domination as the a priori driving force in all contexts. Through consciousness-raising, groups could understand their own and others' oppression. Self-hatred had to be shed in "safe places," with the corresponding need to learn about other disadvantaged groups, since ignoring the oppression that did not touch oneself directly reduced the effectiveness of political action. Oppressed groups needed "separate spaces in which to gain their self-respect, name themselves, and discover their own history"; and they needed "alliances with other groups in order to compare, contrast, and identify the connections among different types of oppression."[58]

Charlotte Bunch also advocated an interactive approach that took into account female diversity as essential for building effective coalitions. This approach pointed out one of the weaknesses of the feminist concept that the personal was political: failure to recognize that personal experiences were shaped by the culture with its prejudices. Feminists had to challenge the limits of their own personal experiences by learning from the diversity of women's lives. The goal for Bunch was for each woman to become a "one-woman coalition," "capable of understanding and raising all issues of oppression and seeing our relationship to them—whites speaking about racism, heterosexuals about homophobia, the able-bodied about disabilities, and so on. Only as we do this will we be able to build lasting coalitions."[59]

Class Differences in the Meaning of Survival

At first, middle-class feminists denied that there were class differences in the meaning of survival. Then working- and lower-class women pointed them out and confusion resulted. Lack of class understanding caused some lower- and working-class women to separate and form groups and alliances among themselves, which had the positive result of their discovery that their survival strengths had gone unnoticed by middle-class movement women. Middle-class women had various defensive responses when confronted with their class privilege, including "How could I be oppressive—I'm just a powerless woman?" denial, guilt, fear, romanticizing and patronizing, confusion, voluntary downward mobility to poverty, and retreat (saying that class issues were divisive to feminism). For purposes of effective coalitions, instead of trying to quiet women for raising class issues, middle-class women had to recognize their privilege and use their skills and privileges to advance women, not themselves individually or their class only. Middle-class feminists "wondered why welfare women weren't beating down their doors," yet they never examined how their behavior reflected their status and alienated lower- and working-class feminists.[60]

To a working-class woman, a middle-class woman's endless analysis and discussion of her feelings was a luxury; out-talking people was often used to exert control, and feelings were excuses for inaction. Another form of middle-class superiority was the mistaken view that a middle-class woman's skills, education, possessions, and position came not from her class privilege but only from her hard work. Less beset by survival imperatives, middle-class women often adopted an attitude of privileged passivity: the sense that everything will work out without having to put up a fight. As Bunch put it, "Because she has made it by following nice middle-class rules of life, she doesn't like for people to be pushy, dogmatic, hostile or intolerant. Material oppression does not bombard her daily, so she has time to move slowly and may resist taking a hard political stand or alienating 'anyone.' She can afford to assume that most people are good and that it is unnecessary to fight or prove oneself to anyone."[61] Some voluntarily downwardly mobile middle-class feminists adopted a "more revolutionary than thou" disdain of working-class feminists' concern about economic security. Or middle-class feminists "helped" working-class women, giving more out of personal graciousness than an obligation to share resources. The hard work of building coalitions across class lines involved the expression of anger and conflict and the sharing of privileges and skills: money, property, access to jobs, and education.

Many women of the working, working poor, and lower classes wrote about how difficult it was for middle-class feminists to understand their lives. Donna Redmund, a clerical worker in a VISTA (Volunteers in Service to America) agency, described her frustration with middle-class feminists' perceptions of hillbillies:

> I really have this thing with these VISTAs, them coming in here with this idea that we're a bunch of poor ignorant hillbillies. I'm proud to be a hillbilly. . . . They come down here and they gonna tell *me* about *poverty?* They tell us they're frustrated, they can't communicate with these people here. *How the hell they gonna communicate with us?* They haven't lived our lives. . . . If being able to work like a horse for a living is being liberated for a woman, I'd just as soon be dependent. When a woman gets up into a high position in one of these corporations that's oppressing people, she's not going to change things. She's gonna be in the same bag the big shot men are. . . .
>
> It might surprise some folks to hear that hillbilly women are in contact with what's happening in the world. A hell of a lot of us do read more than the Sears and Roebuck catalogue. We know about Kate Millet, Germaine Greer, Gloria Steinem, and other middle-class bourgeois who put out more talk than do.

There's some kind of courage and independence in a woman who's had to work hard all her life. . . . When things are not like they should be, you don't sit around and cry . . . or sling around ten-dollar words. You just do whatever has to be done.[62]

Many working-class women had little contact with or felt any support from the women's movement. They felt put down if they wanted to marry and have children; they expressed negative media images of feminists as "bra burners" and "man haters"; and, unlike middle-class women, their sisters, friends, and neighbors did not talk about the kinds of personal issues that became politicized by the women's movement.[63]

In a national study, Barbara Ann Stolz found that most low-income working women either thought the women's movement was irrelevant or expressed ambivalence about it. Only 10 percent strongly supported it, and they tended to be younger women or women who knew movement supporters. Opponents tended to be either older traditional women who felt that women's place was in the home or women who said the movement was not in their interest. In particular, black women spoke of a middle-class white women's movement. One black woman argued that the white women's movement fueled southern white male racism: "It isn't a black women's movement; it's a white movement. This scares the white man, especially in the South, so he takes it out on the black people. He fears that the white woman is getting out of the clutches of her husband, so the white men oppress the black people." Those women who viewed the black male as more oppressed than the black female were more concerned about racism than sexism. "Furthermore," Stolz noted, "they were suspicious of the white women's leadership, sensing these women may co-opt the support and drive of black women, but exclude them from leadership. The women questioned why they should follow white women new to the work force, when black women had more experience."[64]

The most common response about the movement was ambivalence: it was fine at the workplace but not at home. Both white women and women of color expressed a conflict between the need to earn a decent wage and the image of what a woman was. The ambivalence of low-income women stemmed from disagreement with some issue positions of the movement, little personal contact with movement members, suspicion about its leaders, and lack of concrete support from the movement if they differed with family, spouses, friends, or employers. Native American women on the reservation indicated that no one had ever come to speak to them about the movement, the ERA, or how Native American women were affected by the movement; Catholic women opposed abortion; many women thought the Equal Rights Amendment was an amorphous, philosophical idea; and some said the women's movement asked them to take risks based on the privileged and protected world of middle- and upper-middle-class women. The women's movement would be more responsive to the needs of low-income working women if it recognized adequate pay as the primary issue, since the core concern of these women was economic. It was also important to foster respect for their life experiences, everyday concerns, and fears in order to make change less threatening. Personal communication of information about the movement as it related to their everyday lives was more effective than the impersonal mass media, and it was important to work with organizations dealing with a survival focus, such as employment offices, alcoholism treatment centers, thrift shops, clinics, or child-care centers.[65]

Reproductive Rights or Racial Suicide?

Survival for women of color meant racial survival, which was often in conflict with white feminists' agenda of birth control and abortion. For many women of color, birth control and abortion were not simply absolute, individual rights; they were also forms of genocide on the part of whites who wanted fewer black, Native American, and Latino babies.[66]

Angela Davis explained the absence of women of color in the 1970s abortion rights campaign in terms of black women's slave experiences and the racist history of the birth control movement. Self-imposed abortions and reluctant acts of infanticide were common occurrences among slave women, who saw such measures as acts of desperation, not stepping-stones toward freedom. The birth control movement had its origins at the turn of the century, when the white birthrate declined significantly as large farm families became dysfunctional in the context of city life. President Theodore Roosevelt raised the specter of "race suicide," proclaiming that "race purity must be maintained" and admonishing in his State of the Union message well-born white women who engaged in "willful sterility—the one sin for which the penalty is national death, race suicide."[67] The "race suicide" controversy brought to the forefront those issues that most separated middle-class feminists from the working class and the poor. Linda Gordon summarized the controversy:

> This happened in two ways. First, the feminists were increasingly emphasizing birth control as a route to careers and higher education—goals out of the reach of the poor with or without birth

control. In the context of the whole feminist movement, the race-suicide episode was an additional factor identifying feminism almost exclusively with the aspirations of the more privileged women of the society. Second, the pro–birth control feminists began to popularize the idea that poor women had a moral obligation to restrict the size of their families, because large families create a drain on the taxes and charity expenditures of the wealthy and because poor children were less likely to be "superior."[68]

Thus, in Davis's words, "what was demanded as a 'right' for the privileged came to be interpreted as a 'duty' for the poor."[69]

Margaret Sanger's birth control campaign started off in a progressive direction, but by 1919 its eugenic influence had become clear. Sanger defined "the chief issue of birth control" as "more children from the fit, less from the unfit." She approved of the fact that at least twenty-six states had passed compulsory sterilization laws and that thousands of "unfit" persons had already been surgically prevented from reproducing. In 1939, the Birth Control Federation of America launched a "Negro Project" aimed at southern blacks who "still breed carelessly and disastrously, with the result that the increase among Negroes, even more than among whites, is from that portion of the population least fit, and least able to rear children properly." The project called for the recruitment of black ministers to lead local birth control committees, a move approved by Sanger in a letter to a colleague: "We do not want word to get out that we want to exterminate the Negro population and the minister is the man who can straighten out that idea if it ever occurs to any of their more rebellious members." As Davis put it, this phase of the birth control movement advocated for people of color "not the individual right to *birth control,* but rather the racist strategy of *population control.*"[70]

A eugenic policy on the part of the federal government coincided with the contemporary phase of the birth control movement. Within months of the U.S. Supreme Court decision to legalize abortions, the media broke the story of the involuntary sterilization of two black girls in Montgomery, Alabama. Subsequent legal research revealed a pattern of the involuntary sterilization of black women in the South. The U.S. Department of Health, Education and Welfare acknowledged that in 1972 between one hundred thousand and two hundred thousand sterilizations had been funded by the federal government. In 1976, a doctor testified at a Senate hearing that about one-quarter of Native American women of childbearing age had been sterilized. Throughout the 1970s, Native

American, Chicana, Puerto Rican, and black women continued to be sterilized in disproportionate numbers. By the 1970s, more than 35 percent of all Puerto Rican women of childbearing age had been surgically sterilized, as part of a U.S. government program that began in 1939.[71] The federal government had even considered sterilizing Japanese-American women: a 1945 bill to this effect was defeated in Congress by only one vote.[72] It was not until 1974 that the Department of Health, Education and Welfare issued guidelines to prevent involuntary sterilizations.

In contrast with the mostly white reproductive rights movement, the movement against sterilization abuse was made up primarily of women of color. In 1975, eleven Chicanas filed a class action civil rights lawsuit against Los Angeles County Hospital, charging that deceptive tactics were used to get some of them to sign consent forms for sterilization (often when they were in the pain of advanced labor) and that sterilizations were performed on other women without their consent.[73] The Chicana Rights Project of the Mexican-American Legal Defense and Education Fund was instrumental in securing the adoption of informed consent regulations of sterilization procedures by the California Department of Public Health.[74]

During the 1980s, in the wake of antiabortion rulings by the U.S. Supreme Court, many white-dominated feminist organizations devoted an enormous amount of resources to protecting the right to an abortion, and many Latinas questioned their priorities. In Carol Hardy-Fanta's words:

> First, this emphasis on abortion means less attention to Latina issues that have more to do with economic survival. These issues include jobs for Latino men, adequate wages for Latina women who work, sufficient welfare budgets, the availability of day care, and . . . protection against domestic violence. Second, abortion itself is personally and religiously troubling to many Latina women, so that the identification of Anglo feminist organizations with a prochoice position may alienate some Latinas. Finally, even those Latina women who align themselves with the reproductive rights stance of Anglo feminist organizations are angry. They feel that when white women's abortion rights were threatened in the Supreme Court, as during the recent assault on reproductive rights, a huge, well-financed mobilization was initiated. However, the same outpouring of women and money did not take place earlier when poor—and Latina—women's rights were threatened by the loss of Medicaid funding for abortions [in 1976].[75]

Native American women's skepticism about a movement focused on abortion and birth control stemmed in part from bitter memories of genocide and tribal extinction. Many saw population growth as crucial to the survival of their tribe. With a high rate of infant mortality, large numbers of offspring were needed to ensure that several would survive to adulthood. In some cases, Anglo government officials indirectly contributed to high birthrates by altering Native American women's traditional roles. For example, Anglo men refused to deal with Navajo matriarchy and dealt only with Navajo men on all matters where the two cultures touched. As a result, Navajo women lost almost all their important social roles save that of childbearer.[76] The skepticism of Native American women also stemmed from a history of sterilization and contraceptive experimentation abuse and from encounters with professionals who were more interested in the fertility, family planning, and contraceptive behavior in Native American populations than they were in the health care needs of Native American women, who suffered from high rates of alcoholism, suicide, and cervical cancer.[77]

Families as Survival Mechanisms

White middle-class feminists wrote about the family as universally patriarchal, not as the bulwark against racism that Chicanas experienced. They also wrote about the family as isolated in the suburbs and nuclear, not the family of extended kin networks in Appalachia and in many black communities. These kin networks served as "cultures of resistance" in internal colonial situations. In the case of Appalachia, kinship ties were strong, with loyalties to kin taking precedence over civic responsibilities. Families taught children to rebel against certain institutions such as schools; they protected native culture in the face of falsified history and the devaluation of all things hillbilly by the dominant culture; and they instructed family members how to operate biculturally—to act proper in public and hillbilly at home.[78] As for black kin networks, the anthropological and sociological work of Joyce Ladner, Carol Stack, and Nancy Tanner all stressed the importance of black kin-based networks with women as key figures in adopting survival strategies.[79] The basis of family structure and cooperation was an extended cluster of kin related chiefly through children but also through marriage and friendship. This system put a premium on the resourcefulness and flexibility of a range of kin ties that could be activated as the need arose, especially to take care of one another's children.

Bell hooks reflected on the "homeplace" of extended kin:

Historically African-American people believed that the construction of a homeplace, however fragile and tenuous (the slave hut, the wooden shack), had a radical political dimension. Despite the brutal reality of racial apartheid, of domination, one's homeplace was the one site where one could freely confront the issue of humanization, where one could resist. Black women resisted by making homes where all black people could strive to be subjects, not objects, where we could be affirmed in our minds and hearts despite poverty, hardship, and deprivation, where we could restore to ourselves the dignity denied us on the outside in the public world.[80]

Poor women and women of color were of necessity bicultural, living in a home culture that resisted the outside white and/or middle-class culture. Their childhood survival tactics formed their political consciousness and skills, as Aida Hurtado described:

Many children of Color serve as the official translator for their monolingual relatives in disputes with companies and agencies unresponsive to poor, working-class people. Early interaction with the public sphere helps many women of Color to develop a public identity and the political skills to fend off state intervention. . . . In addition, the low-income status of most women of Color means that they must acquire survival skills such as sustaining informal networks of support, practicing alternative forms of health care, and organizing for political and social change. By comparison, the childhoods of many white middle-class feminists were protected by classism and racism. As a consequence, many do not acquire their political consciousness of gender oppression until they become adults. Lacking experience in challenging authorities and white men in particular, white feminists often seem surprised at the harshness with which the power structure responds to threat, and they do not have well-developed defenses to fend off the attacks.[81]

Political Coalitions and Ethnic/Racial Identity

In building political coalitions in the 1970s, most white feminists presupposed that women as a group had a unitary identity and on that basis chose to align with other groups. In their political work, white women were never asked to choose between being a woman and being white.

Women of color, however, saw themselves with a dual identity, and they were often asked by men of color to give political priority to their racial or ethnic identity and by white feminists to put their gender first.

Many of the early writings of feminists of color addressed this dilemma. Some black women resolved it by arguing that their liberation was subsumed under the liberation of their race and that their primary responsibility was to keep the black family together and to support the black male. In their view, there was no need to discuss coalitions with white women, whose relatively trivial complaints made a mockery of the term "oppression."[82] Mae C. King was skeptical of alliances between black and white women. The participation of blacks in prior movements (e.g., Populist, organized labor, and women's suffrage) had not erased their inferior status, she noted. Such alliances were simply instruments that brought about white power realignments. White women had a stake in the racial status quo, and the women's movement was not about to risk alienating white homemakers by focusing on police brutality, prison and welfare reform, and racial quotas. King argued that since race was the basis of black women's oppression, it was strategically unwise to depend on an ally that was an intrinsic part of the oppressive structure.[83]

Elizabeth Almquist disagreed with King's assessment and maintained that there was something for black women in the women's liberation movement, which she said King had defined too narrowly as the desire to work on the part of white homemakers. Almquist said both black and white women would benefit from rooting out sexism and from laws regarding rape, reproductive rights, the ERA, day care, equal pay, and credit. Black women were disadvantaged by high unemployment rates, difficulty in obtaining high-level jobs, and wage discrimination, but in employment and earnings, sex discrimination surpassed race discrimination.[84]

An Identity of Double Jeopardy

Although some women of color debated the relative importance of sex and race disadvantage, most adopted an analysis of what Frances Beal called "double jeopardy," focusing on the simultaneity of race and sex oppression, which Beal and many other feminists of color linked to capitalist oppression. She faulted capitalism for trying to destroy the humanity of blacks by making it impossible for black men to find meaningful employment and giving black women work in white men's kitchens, bestowing on them the role of sole breadwinner and creating turmoil in the black family. Beal stressed the need to eliminate all kinds of oppression, to build more than half an army, and to form coalitions with white women's groups that were anti-imperialist and antiracist.[85]

Such coalitions proved to be a problem when it came to mainstream feminist organizations such as NOW, most of whose members were more interested in reaping capitalism's benefits than in challenging its foundations. A case in point was the August 26, 1970, Liberation Day March commemorating the fiftieth anniversary of the Nineteenth Amendment. Turnout from around the country surpassed organizers' expectations and generated favorable press coverage. It was regarded by white feminists as the first public statement of the potential power of the new feminist movement, but for black feminists in New York, it was an alienating experience, as Paula Giddings described: "Taking part in the demonstration was the Third World Women's Alliance, a Black feminist group that was the only SNCC project still functioning successfully. Led by Frances Beal, the Alliance brandished placards . . . reading 'Hands Off Angela Davis,' . . . and one of the leaders of NOW ran up to us and said angrily, 'Angela Davis has nothing to do with the women's liberation.' 'It has nothing to do with the kind of liberation you're talking about,' retorted Beal, 'but it has everything to do with the kind of liberation we're talking about.' "[86]

At a time when many white feminists thought all rights-conscious women would jump at the chance to join a struggle against men for their rights, many black women were on a different historical trajectory, not struggling against black men for their rights but in fact welcoming the new rights and power accorded them. When Betty Friedan visited a SNCC office to recruit black women to join NOW, she was told that they were not interested in joining the feminist movement but rather wanted to help black men get the rights they had been denied so long.[87]

A double jeopardy perspective meant that neither white women nor men of color could define the identities or politics of women of color. For black feminists, two of the earliest statements of self-definition came from the moderate National Black Feminist Organization (NBFO) and the more radical Combahee River Collective. Both groups grew out of dissatisfaction with other people's definitions of black feminists.

In August 1973, fifteen black feminists held a press conference in New York City announcing themselves as the National Black Feminist Organization. According to Margaret Sloan, they were tired of everyone speaking *for* black women and wanted to speak for themselves in response to antifeminist media coverage on black women. Within a year the NBFO had acquired a headquarters in New York and had expanded to more than two thousand members in ten cities.[88] In 1975, Jo Freeman noted, NBFO membership was "much more heterogeneous than that of any other feminist organization, including women from a wide range of ages and occupations."[89] The NBFO Statement of Purpose challenged both white and black media portrayals of the women's liberation movement as the exclusive property of white middle-class women, with any involvement by black women seen as "selling out" or "dividing the race." It pointed out the lack of examination of the damage to black women caused by the racism that was destroying the black community from without and the sexism destroying it from within.[90]

The Combahee River Collective first started meeting in 1974. Intense consciousness-raising produced a great sense of relief among members of finally having found one another. Because of serious disagreements with NBFO's bourgeois-feminist stance and lack of clear political focus, they decided to become an independent collective. In 1976, they moved beyond consciousness-raising and emotional support to become a study group and to do political work on sterilization abuse, abortion rights, battered women, rape, and health care. They conducted workshops on black feminism on college campuses, at women's conferences, and for high school women. By dealing with the implications of race and class as well as sex, they expanded the feminist principle that the personal is political in their consciousness-raising sessions, going beyond white women's revelations. "Even our black women's style of talking/testifying in black language about what we have experienced has a resonance that is both cultural and political. We have spent a great deal of energy delving into the cultural and experiential nature of our oppression out of necessity because none of these matters have ever been looked at before. No one before has ever examined the multilayered texture of black women's lives."[91]

The need to carve out an identity independent of that offered by other liberation movements was articulated by other women of color as well. When it came to identity formation, Alma M. Garcia said there were four similarities among Chicana, Asian-American, and black feminists: a definition of feminism as a struggle against the multidimensional inequality of race, class, and gender; a challenge to traditional gender roles in cultural nationalist movements; feminist baiting by members of these movements, who described feminism as hostile to racial or ethnic unity, antifamily, individualistic, and focused on white issues; and a desire to forge a relationship with the white women's movement. Chicanas built coalitions with white feminists when their attempts to develop their feminism within the Chicano movement were suppressed. Yet they never felt comfortable in the women's liberation movement and always considered themselves *Chicana primero*. Chicanas found coalitions difficult for several reasons. White women assumed that the women's movement would overcome racial differences among women. White women usually shared a middle-class orientation, whereas Chicana feminists identified with working-class issues such as farmworkers' rights, welfare reform, undocumented workers' rights, and prison rights. And for many Chicanas, white organizations were so exclusionary, patronizing, and/or racist that Chicanas opted for coalitions with white working-class women only or with other women of color only.[92]

Anglo women said they provided a model of sisterhood that would erase differences between women, a simplistic approach to the problem of identity. Consuelo Nieto argued that Anglo women and Chicanas shared a commitment to equality but not a common cultural identity. Only Chicanas could answer the question, What does it mean to be a Chicana?

> The Chicana must demand that dignity and respect within the women's rights movement which allows her to practice feminism within the context of her own culture. The timing and choice must be hers. Her models and those of her daughters will be an Alicia Escalante and a Dolores Huerta. Her approaches to feminism must be drawn from her own world, and not be shadowy replicas drawn from Anglo society. The Chicana will fight for her right to uniqueness; she will not be absorbed. For some it is sufficient to say, "I am woman." For me it must be, "I am Chicana."[93]

Internal Colonialism

Elizabeth Almquist used the internal colonialism model to explain the relationship between the identity of women of color and their participation in feminist organizations. Many peoples of color in the United States were internally colonized insofar as they entered the country involuntarily, had their native cultures destroyed, were subject to racism and control by white bureaucracies, and were confined to unpleasant and low-paying jobs. For women of color, internal colonialism had several results: rural isolation with limited options for transportation, education, media choices, health care, and contraception; urban ghettos and barrios with few economic opportunities; strong attachment to family and ethnic values to save their cultures; a defensive strengthening of the family and self-sacrifice; and the need to work in the face of poverty. In the crucible of identity, racial-ethnic identity temporally and emotionally preceded other identities. Structural barriers between groups of women and the associational and communal ties within groups of women were so strong that they impeded rapid alliances across racial lines. Resource mobilization theory, with its emphasis on organizations more than on participants, neglected the role of ideas and interests for resource-poor women. Women of color accepted feminist beliefs yet gave lower priority to feminist activism than to racial activism. These women could not see themselves just as women; double jeopardy required a double solution.[94]

For some Native American women, the internal colonialism model had a territorial as well as a cultural application. M. Annette Jaimes and Theresa Halsey made a distinction between sovereigntist and civil rights Indian feminists. Native American women activists who most openly identified themselves as feminists

> tended to be among the more assimilated of Indian women activists, generally accepting the colonialist ideology that indigenous nations are now legitimate sub-parts of the U.S. geopolitical corpus rather than separate nations, that Indian people are now a minority within the overall population rather than the citizenry of their own distinct nations. Such Indian women activists are therefore usually more devoted to "civil rights" than to liberation per se. Native American women who are more genuinely sovereigntist in their outlook have proven themselves far more dubious about the potentials offered by feminist politics and alliances.[95]

The sovereigntist agenda focused on the recovery of land and resources, reassertion of self-determining forms of government, and reconstitution of traditional social relations within nations. Sovereigntists called for "an alternative movement of women in North America, one which is mutually respectful of the rights, needs, cultural particularities, and historical divergences of each sector of its membership, and which is therefore free of the adherence to white supremacist hegemony previously marring feminist thinking and practice."[96] Jaimes and Halsey could understand why civil rights–oriented Native American feminists sought to forge coalitions with white feminists, since Native Americans comprised less than 1 percent of the North American population and faced such difficult problems.

The internal colonialism model had sovereignty implications for native Hawaiian women as well. Haunani-Kay Trask argued that in Hawaiian women's struggle for self-determination and sovereignty, their culture was more important than was the notion of women's rights imported with the dominant white (*haole*) culture, which promoted the self-centered and self-motivated values of capitalism.

> Hawaiians hold other cultural values more dear—affection, gen-
> erosity, traditional group activities like fishing and dancing, and,
> perhaps most telling of all, gathering together to share work, play,
> grief, and love. . . . At this point in our struggle, race and culture
> are stronger forces than sex and gender. We will make common
> cause with our own people, and other Native peoples, before we
> make common cause with non-Natives in our lands. I have arrived
> at this political strategy after years of failed alliances with *haole,* in-
> cluding *haole* feminists. In Hawai'i, as in so many parts of the is-
> land Pacific, *haole* feminists have steadfastly refused to support
> our efforts to regain our lands, to protect our civil rights, and to
> achieve self-government. They have defined what is "feminist" as
> that which relates to women—and only to women—e.g., repro-
> ductive rights, women's health problems, employment and edu-
> cational concerns. But to most Native people, women's concerns
> are part of the greater concern for our *lahui,* our nation. . . . *Haole*
> feminists don't see the causal connection between our life condi-
> tions and our status as colonized people.[97]

A Complex Schema of Political Identity

The schema of political identity was more complex for women of color than it was for white middle-class women. In the schema of self, family, race, class, sisterhood, and nation, white middle-class feminists assumed that they could take their race, class, and national identities as givens. The problematic identity questions that remained were those of self, family, and sisterhood, with family often portrayed as an obstacle to self-fulfillment and sisterhood.

The more complex schema of political identity for women of color began with the identity of "self." While white women grappled with sex-ist stereotypes, women of color faced the additional necessity of con-structing a positive sense of self out of the wreckage of racist stereotypes and cultural messages of self-hatred. Black women had to counteract the controlling images of mammy, matriarch, emasculator, Jezebel, and un-wed welfare mother.[98] Latinas fought the stereotypes of *Marianismo* (de-rived from the image of the Virgin Mary as meek, mild, and supportive of men), La Malinche (symbol of the violated mother who gave herself to the Spanish conqueror and thereby emasculated Mexican men and caused the downfall of a people), and *agabachadas* (Anglocized) and *vendidas* (sellouts) who called themselves feminists and were thus anti-*raza*.[99] Native American women countered images of low-status beasts of burden; Malinche, Pocahontas, and Sacajawea (all of whom aided unwillingly in the downfall of their peoples); squaws (this Algonquin term for women came to mean drudge and prostitute); and princesses who died for their white men.[100] And Asian-American women contended with stereotypes of the submissive, subservient, exotic, "Oriental" woman.[101]

Family identity was similarly more complex insofar as the family kept the race together in a racist society. Chicanas wrote of three levels of *la familia:* nuclear, extended, and La Raza.[102] Maxine Baca Zinn coined the term "political familism" to describe cultural and political resistance by family units for liberation.[103] Black women wrote that the centrality of women in African-American extended families reflected both a continuation of West African cultural values and a functional adaptation to race and gender oppression. Biological mothers, or blood mothers, were expected to care for their children, and they were assisted by othermothers: grandmothers, sisters, aunts, or cousins. When many inner-city neighborhoods were plagued by the influx of crack cocaine in the 1980s, the community structure of othermothers, fictive kin, and neighborhood child care came under assault but managed to survive in some communities. This family structure was a revolutionary form of social organization insofar as it challenged the capitalist notion of children as private property, saw the community as responsible for children, and gave othermothers and other nonparents rights in childrearing.[104] Native American women saw their traditional family structures destroyed by European invaders and the federal government. Most Native American women in the cities remained bicultural in orientation to retain their family and tribal identities,

> accepting enough of Anglo culture to get a job, to communicate with employers and with the children's teachers, to establish residence and to vote, and to negotiate the intricacies of federal bureaucracies. [A bicultural orientation] also means rejecting the materialistic values of Anglo culture and retaining an emphasis on native values, such as sharing material goods, being noncompetitive, avoiding manipulation of other people, and not criticizing them. This communal orientation works well in establishing shared bonds with other Native Americans, and it helps to ease the burdens and tensions of life in the often-hostile white city.[105]

The last dimension in the schema of identity, the nation, was a non-issue for white feminists: the nation was simply the territorial United States, the legitimate object of political loyalty and identification. National identity was a problematic notion, however, for Native Americans whose tribal homelands were stolen, for Chicanas whose ancestors had claim to lands in the Southwest, and for Hawaiians whose islands were colonized by the United States. These women devoted considerable political effort to land claims and sovereignty issues and to preserving the cultural manifestations of their national identity: language, customs, dress, religion, art, and ceremonies.

Thus many identities informed women of color's prospects for identifying with a sisterhood that was commonly perceived to have a white middle-class orientation. Some feminists of color, and white feminists as well, argued that the notion of sisterhood ought to be jettisoned altogether.[106] Most analysts resolved the conflict between identities and coalitions by insisting on coalitions based on self-defined group identities. And, for many, the best way to ascertain the relationship between identities and coalitions was an engaged epistemology, not the conventional wisdom of behaviorism.

An Engaged Epistemology

The behaviorist approach did not lend itself to incorporating the self-understandings of the people being studied, and it presupposed that "outside observers" were in a better position than were participants to make valid truth claims about people's politics. By contrast, transformational feminist scholars of political coalitions called for the incorporation of self-understandings into political analyses and sought truth claims from participants.

Patricia Hill Collins observed that her training in the positivist social sciences was inadequate to the task of studying the subjugated political knowledge of black women, who, like other subordinate groups, had developed an epistemological standpoint, with distinctive ways of producing and validating knowledge. In producing the specialized knowledge of black feminist thought, black female intellectuals encountered two distinct epistemologies: one representing elite white male interests and the other expressing Afrocentric feminist concerns. The knowledge claims advanced by black feminist scholars were seen as anomalies by the community of white male elite academicians, who had little familiarity with black women's reality. Collins rejected positivist epistemological criteria that asked "African-American women to objectify ourselves, devalue our emotional life, displace our motivations for furthering knowledge about Black women, and confront in an adversarial relationship those with more social, economic and professional power. It therefore seems unlikely that Black women would use a positivist epistemological stance in rearticulating a Black women's standpoint."[107]

In contrast to a disengaged, subject-object, positivist approach, Collins called for an engaged Afrocentric feminist epistemology that employed both the Afrocentric and the feminist standpoints, using concrete experiences as the criteria for assessing claims about meaning, knowledge, and wisdom. Truth claims were assessed by dialogue: talk between two subjects, not the speech of subject and object. Unlike adversarial debate, dialogue had roots in an African-based oral tradition and in African-American culture. The widespread use of the call-and-response discourse mode among African-Americans illustrated the importance of dialogue. This discourse, in which the speaker's calls or statements were punctuated by responses or expressions from the listener, assumed the active participation of all in the group. As Collins noted, "For ideas to be tested and validated, everyone in the group must participate. To refuse to join in, especially if one really disagrees with what has been said, is seen as 'cheating.' "[108] Moreover, no passive voice construction existed in black English: every sentence assumed the active participation of at least two human beings, the speaker and the listener. Dialogue also figured prominently in the African-American oral tradition of storytelling, which presupposed the importance of the consciousness of the hearer.

Black feminist thought was an alternative both to the ostensibly objective norms of positivist science and to relativism's claim that all groups had equally valid knowledge claims. It allowed African-American women to bring their standpoint to epistemological dialogues concerning the nature of domination, in which each group spoke from its own standpoint, shared its own truth as partial, and centered itself in another group's experience, validating and judging it without the need to adopt it as one's own.

> Everyone has a voice, but everyone must listen and respond to other voices in order to be allowed to remain in the community. . . . Existing power inequities among groups must be addressed. . . . The presence of subjugated knowledges means that groups are not equal in making their standpoints known to themselves and others. "Decentering" the dominant group is essential, and relinquishing privilege of this magnitude is unlikely to occur without struggle.[109]

An engaged epistemology was predicated on the notion that knowledge was advanced by "participation with," not just "observations of." Feminist scholars were urged to meet people on their turf and on their terms, joining the rhythm of their daily lives in order to give greater coherence and articulation to experience as it is lived. Such processes did not fit neatly into the college lecture or a disciplinary field of study. They were more appropriately found over coffee, at kitchen tables, and in unemployment offices.[110] Academic feminists needed to stop spending so much money on women's studies conferences and to redirect those resources toward mass outreach in every state, "with the intention of taking feminism out of the university and into the streets and homes of this society . . . offering women's studies courses at a local community center, YWCA, YMCA, church, etc. . . . The ability to 'translate' ideas to an audience that varies in age, sex, ethnicity, degree of literacy is a skill feminist educators need to develop."[111] Charlotte Bunch described how she went from the "irrelevant theorizing" of the academy, to movement activity as a lesbian feminist, to seeing the need for theory for the survival of feminism. Feminist theory was not objective; it began with the need to end the oppression of women. Like all political theories, it had four parts: description, analysis, vision, and strategy, and this four-part model was a useful way to teach feminist theory. For example, when used to analyze women's magazines, it demystified political theory and showed women how to think and evaluate for themselves.[112]

The advance of knowledge through "participation with" rather than "observation of" was illustrated by Carol Hardy-Fanta's explanation of how she wrote her book, *Latina Politics, Latino Politics*. In the preface, she observed that she had not planned to write a book about Latinas and politics; rather, she had set out with a conventional research agenda: to study Latino political participation, especially whether relatively low voter participation rates among Latinos was best explained by a culture of "political apathy" or by structural obstacles in the sociopolitical system. Her focus changed as she began listening to Latinos in the Boston community and participating in community events. From the first day of interviews and community observations, and consistently throughout more than two years of fieldwork, she noticed a pattern of gender differences in how Latinas and Latinos perceived politics and how their different perceptions informed their way of mobilizing the community. Latinas played a very active role in solving community problems, a finding that challenged the invisibility of Latinas as political actors in the political science literature. Hardy-Fanta noted:

The rationale for using a qualitative, exploratory research design is that such a design has distinct advantages when breaking new ground. First, surveys and other quantitative methods obscure forms of participation that have not been observed before precisely because they measure only previously measured behavior. Second, to understand the role of Latina women in politics requires a research design not biased by gender and culture. Finally, qualitative methods permit the definition of "What is political?" to be determined by Latino community members, not by Anglo or Latino researchers.[113]

Coalition-Building and the National Hispanic Feminist Conference

As described in earlier parts of this book, disparate groups of women in Santa Clara County joined together to achieve common political goals, from instituting district elections in San Jose to securing resources for battered women's shelters. The 1980 National Hispanic Feminist Conference in San Jose provided an interesting case study in coalition-building. The contacts and conflicts across divisions in the Latina community and across Anglo-Latina lines were expressed in the interchange between "elite" women (those with educational and professional credentials) and "community" women (those with service and advocacy group affiliations) in the Latina community, in dialogue between Chicanas and other Latinas, and in encounters between Latinas and Anglo women.

Latina feminism emerged as a response to the failure of Latino men to take seriously the question of women's oppression. Contemporary Latina feminists began delineating their interests and building independent power bases during the civil rights movement of the 1960s and 1970s, a period informed by cultural nationalism and *Chicanismo,* the idea that "Mexicanos living in the United States have the right to—and must for the survival of their group identity—preserve their cultural distinctness."[114] In the 1970s, Chicana feminists "continued undaunted, mostly outside the women's movement, now and then establishing ties and coalitions with it, to develop their own power base for the achievement of Chicana liberation and to provide increased opportunities for Chicanas."[115] This framework of cultural nationalism was crucial to understanding the 1980 National Hispanic Feminist Conference, which was organized by a Chicana, Sylvia Gonzales. Chicana feminists were forging their own route between the Scylla of a white women's liberation movement and the Charybdis of a male-dominated cultural nationalism movement that saw feminism as divisive and assimilationist. Chicana feminists grappled with three important questions: What are the sources of oppressive racial and sexual stereotypes directed against Chicanas? Does feminism threaten Chicano culture? and What is the relationship between the Chicana and white feminist movements?[116]

Throughout the 1970s, similar questions were being raised by other Latinas as well, at meetings of the National Conference of Puerto Rican Women, the National Association of Cuban American Women, and the Inter-American Commission of Women. The 1980 National Hispanic Feminist Conference provided the first opportunity for Latina feminists to come together to compare notes on these problems. Like any national conference, it reflected the agenda of its organizers and underrepresented the views of those who did not hear about it because they were not affiliated with groups receiving conference publicity; those who could not afford to attend; and those who could not arrange for alternative care of dependents. In short, conferences tend to overrepresent the views of people with time, money, and organizational affiliations (particularly those that reimburse for conferences).

These tendencies were borne out by the results of a demographic survey distributed at the conference.[117] Two thousand women from around the nation attended the four-day conference, March 28–31, 1980, in San Jose.[118] About two-thirds of the survey respondents were Chicanas (Mexican-Americans); 15 percent were Latinas of Puerto Rican, Central American, Cuban, South American, or Spanish backgrounds; about 10 percent were Anglos; and about 10 percent cited other backgrounds. Most respondents resided in the West and Southwest and considered themselves bilingual. They were much more highly educated and affluent than Latinas as a whole. Fifty-five percent had a bachelor's degree, 27 percent a master's degree, and 10 percent a doctorate. Only 8 percent had a high school diploma or less. By contrast, nationwide in the 1974–76 period, the median number of years of education for Latina women was 9.7, and Latinas received only 4 percent of the B.A.'s and 1.4 percent of the doctorates granted nationwide to women.[119] As for income, about a third earned up to $10,000 annually; another third between $11,000 and $19,000; 17 percent between $20,000 and $29,000; and 5 percent over $30,000. By contrast, in 1980, the national median income of Hispanic *households* was $13,600.[120] Respondents were also more likely than Latinas as a whole to be single and childless. Thirty-four percent had never been married, and 22 percent were divorced (totaling 56 percent unmarried); 37 percent were currently married. By contrast, in 1975 about 60 percent of all Chicanas were married.[121] Furthermore, 45 percent of the respondents indicated that they had no children. Of the 190 panelists, 36 percent were academics (professors, graduate students, and administrators from forty-three colleges and universities around the country); 28 percent were other professionals (psychologists, social workers, research associates, public affairs directors, political consultants, and teachers); 20 percent represented national or community organizations; and 16 percent worked for federal, state, or local government agencies. The numbers and varied backgrounds of conference participants set the stage for important dialogues.

Dialogue between Elite and Community Women

One important interchange at the conference was between elite women and community women. Although conference organizers maintained that a constructive dialogue between these two groups took place, critics contended that elite women stifled the voices of dissenting activists. An examination of these two positions casts light on the tension between theory and practice in coalitions.

The principal organizer of the meeting was Sylvia Gonzales, who at the time was an associate professor of Mexican-American Graduate Studies at San Jose State University, having received her doctorate in education from the University of Massachusetts in 1974. She was well connected with both federal government agencies and national women's rights groups. A native of Tucson, Arizona, she served on Representative Morris K. Udall's (D-Ariz.) staff (1966–67), worked for the U.S. Civil Rights Commission (1967–68, 1970), was a Robert Kennedy Memorial Fellow in Washington, D.C. (1971–72), and served as executive director of the National Women's Studies Association (Spring 1979) and cochair of NOW's Minority Women's Committee (1980).

In 1978, Gonzales set out to organize the first national conference on Chicana feminist scholarship. She mailed questionnaires to 125 national Hispanic and non-Hispanic women's organizations to determine interest in such a meeting. Within a few weeks, 56 percent of the groups responded, with all but eight indicating an interest in attending. As a result of this preliminary survey, Gonzales expanded the scope of her project from a *Chicana* to a *Hispanic* feminist scholarship conference. Encouraged by the positive responses to her questionnaire, she submitted a proposal to the Women's Educational Equity Act (WEEA) program of the U.S. Office of Education, and in July 1979 WEEA awarded her a $61,000 grant. In her grant proposal, Gonzales described a June 1976 meeting of twenty-three Latinas in Denver, organized under the auspices of the Women's Research Program of the National Institute of

Education (NIE) to develop a research agenda on the educational and occupational needs of Hispanic women. Drawing from the recommendations of this group, Gonzales proposed the following sessions for the conference: Research Literature and the Hispanic Woman, Socialization Process, Education/Bilingual Education, Guidance and Counseling, Political Action for Educational Equity, Feminism, and Higher Education.[122]

These institutional origins of the conference had an important bearing on the tensions that later developed. Since both NIE and WEEA focused on research and education, Gonzales tailored her grant proposal to these ends. For example, the session on political action included the phrase "for educational equity," suggesting a rather limited range of political action. It was also important to remember that the conference agenda was first conceived by professional and academic Latinas. Initially, Gonzales had envisioned a convocation of Latina scholars and researchers, but in response to the wide range of panel proposals mailed to her, she decided on a dialogue between scholars and community women. She wrote in the conference program, "The traditional approach to the presentation of research and formulation of theory . . . results in the exclusion of the very community the theory and research purport to affect. . . . True community change comes from the combination of theory and action. . . . This conference is an attempt to dialogue, researchers and scholars with community women." Although this statement showed flexibility on Gonzales's part, her primary concern was nonetheless with theory. Four months before the conference, she said in a *Los Angeles Times* interview that Hispanic feminists were spinning their wheels and were in need of theory to guide their actions. She noted that Hispanas had not been able to develop theory as easily as Anglo and black women because so few were found in universities. Hispanas needed "to learn how to argue in institutionalized vehicles—the places where change begins. Change filters from the institutions, the think tanks, into action. We need solid research with data. We need to offer economic, social and political reasons for what we want. We need a think-tank kind of conference. We will also include community women to provide the mental tools for action. We're trying to bridge an educational gap that would normally take a generation."[123]

To Gonzales's credit, the funding of the conference marked a historic first: never before had Latinas had access to this amount of money to run their own conference—independent of Hispanic men and Anglo feminists—and to bring together women from various cultural and geographic settings. The conference turned out to be a monumental logistical undertaking: two thousand participants, 190 panelists conducting some one hundred workshops, keynote speakers, general assemblies, banquets, concerts, dances, films, and theatre presentations. A certain amount of bureaucratic rigidity was to be expected in orchestrating an event on this scale.

Some community women, however, found the scope of the conference too ambitious, its structure too rigid, and its attempt to present a united front to the media a premature closure on controversy. In the view of one critic, Che Sandoval, although the program may have looked impressive to government sponsors, it was structured in a way that prevented effective communication among participants.[124] According to Gonzales, the conference was disrupted by ambitious Chicanas jockeying for power in the movement. Some local community leaders had resented being passed over as keynote speakers. And members of Comisión Feminil Mexicana, an advocacy group in Los Angeles, felt left out of planning and leadership roles. In Gonzales's view, they were angered by what they perceived to be the predominant role of the Mexican American Women's National Association, a conference cosponsor: "These women, many long-time activists in the Chicano community and some intensely anti-feminist, sought to establish finally and resolutely their historical position in the Chicana leadership hierarchy at the expense of consensus and group priorities."[125]

Gonzales maintained that she was flexible in the face of this controversy and said the struggle for control of the conference was a healthy part of the emerging Hispanic feminist movement. An ad hoc committee of those who felt excluded from leadership positions was formed to run the final two days of the conference. There were limits to her empowerment of the participants, however. After the general assembly passed three dozen resolutions on the final day of the conference, ad hoc committee members were disappointed that these resolutions were not going to be included in the final report to the federal government or implemented in a concrete plan of action. For her part, Gonzales replied that ad hoc committee members were responsible for taking the resolutions back to their respective cities and that would be as far as the resolutions would go, because the federal grant did not allow political statements or action to come out of the conference. Conference resolutions were published in a *New York Times* article, however, which focused on the theme of disunity.[126]

Despite the controversy, Gonzales was confident that the informal dialogues between scholars and activists at the conference marked an important moment in the mutual education of both sides. Furthermore, some workshops focused specifically on discourse between the two communities. For example, Janie Perez, from a San Jose community center, ran a session entitled "Chicana Professionals: Establishing Working Relationships with Barrio Women." She argued that Chicana professionals owed the existence of their jobs to the efforts of community activists, a debt they should remember as they drifted away from the barrios to higher education and career opportunities. She cautioned Chicana professionals that the barrio was suspicious of anyone who came back having "made it." To be effective in the barrio, professional Chicanas had to spend a lot of time there developing relations of mutual trust and respect, not just studying women's lives.[127]

In retrospect, it was easy to see how certain tensions between elite and community women were bound to play themselves out at the conference. Professional discourse was foreign to the ears of community activists. The agenda of activists conflicted with that of educated professionals. Activists wanting a concrete plan of action did not limit their political demands to educational equity issues, as outlined in the government grant proposal. They wanted to make a statement about various current events and to address the everyday needs of the women they served. By contrast, conference organizers hoped for a research center and an anthology of conference proceedings to impress academic and governmental audiences. Perhaps Gonzales's vision was too ambitious. She admitted as much when she said she was hoping "to bridge an educational gap that would normally take a generation." Perhaps her agenda was lopsided in the direction of academics educating activists, instead of the other way around. And perhaps her efforts to present a united front were premature and overly concerned with looking good to national media and government agencies. Nevertheless, critics and organizers alike agreed that the conference was a historic first step. Both sides came away with a new appreciation of the difficulty of bridging the gap between professionals and activists. As critic Sandoval put it, much of the excitement of the conference "lay in a re-working of differences rather than their settlement," and she considered the event "another beginning."[128]

Dialogue among Latinas

A second important dialogue took place between Chicanas, who constituted about two-thirds of conference participants, and other Latinas. Nationwide, Chicanas were the largest group of Latinas, and their writings were the most numerous in the Latina feminist literature. Conference organizers wanted to provide a forum for the concerns of all Latinas, but conference critics often resented Chicanas' dominant role. Their dialogue brought to light cultural differences and similarities among Latina feminists.

There were important social demographic differences among these groups of Latinas. In 1985, there were about 17 million Hispanics in the United States, about one in fourteen Americans. Chicanos were by far the most populous (10.3 million), followed by Puerto Ricans (2.6 million), Central or South Americans (1.6 million), other Spanish origin (1.4 million), and Cubans (1 million). Not counted in these figures were undocumented workers, mostly Mexicans. Chicanos were concentrated in five southwestern states: Arizona, California, Colorado, New Mexico, and Texas. Puerto Ricans lived primarily in New York City, and Cubans in Florida. A comparison of the unemployment, income, and poverty levels of Chicanos, Puerto Ricans, and Cubans showed that Cubans were relatively the best off, Puerto Ricans the worst off, and Chicanos located in between.[129]

Alongside these differences were important similarities. Latinas shared the Spanish language, the Catholic religious tradition, and a culture of *Marianismo* and *machismo*.[130] They also shared a victimization by racism in America, and they saw the family as a political bulwark against Anglo racism. Compared to the population as a whole, Latinas had larger families, less education, greater poverty, and higher unemployment rates.

It was not surprising that differences among Latinas emerged at the conference, given the numerical dominance of Chicanas and Gonzales's initial interest in a national Chicana conference. The experience of Iliad Estrada, deputy director of the National Puerto Rican Forum, based in New York City, was illustrative of the Chicana focus, if not bias, at the conference. She went to the meeting to "help build a foundation for future cooperation among Chicanas, Cubanas, Puertorriqueñas, and other Latinas." She said her level of expectation was high, since Hispanic feminists had traditionally been relegated to secondary roles by the national feminist movement. She was anxious to publicize the plight of her sisters: "Only 27 percent of Puerto Rican women have found their way into the national labor force, barely half as many as the Mexican-American and Cuban-American communities show. In New York, 62 percent of Puerto Rican families headed by women live in poverty. The public school dropout rate for Puerto Ricans in New York is 80 percent." When Estrada reached the conference site, she was taken aback by a big banner reading, "Welcome to the First Chicana Feminist Conference." She described other unsettling moments: some Puerto Rican workshops were canceled, and one Chicana group categorized Puerto Rican women as "sleek, urban creatures." Nevertheless, when Estrada left the meeting a few days later, she said she did not bother to notice whether the "Chicana Conference" banner was still up: "I was too busy engaging in the Hispanic custom of shared farewell *abrazos*—embraces—with the Chicanas and others I had met and learned to respect. The chaos, the individual agendas, the initial distrust, I concluded, is part of every conference where strangers struggle to change a system. As we departed, we all vowed to keep in touch, to build a network."[131]

Cubanas also came to the conference to make sure their experiences were registered as part of the Hispanic feminist movement. Most Cuban Americans immigrated to the United States in the early 1960s, seeking political asylum. As a result, the median age of Cubans (37.3 years) was the highest of any group in the United States. Elderly Cubans felt lonely and socially isolated, deeply affected by intergenerational conflict and changes in family structure, from extended to nuclear and often to single female-headed (although to a lesser extent than for Anglo and black families). Compared to other Hispanics in Florida's Dade County, Cubans were the most educated, the most likely to speak Spanish in the home, and the most likely to be born outside the United States.[132]

The experiences of urban Cubanas and Puertorriqueñas were contrasted with those of rural Latinas (predominantly Chicanas), the most economically deprived and least educated of all Latinas in the United States. These women were migrant workers, or wives and mothers of migrant workers, who lived in urban centers, their home between harvests. They were urban women with a rural mentality who ended up in ghettos with no skills to enter industrialized society. Although federal funds were available for the education and vocational training of these women, who averaged a third-grade level, such programs often never reached them. Rural Hispanas needed to be trained to become leaders at the migrant community level, to implement community organization projects, to run cooperatives to harvest the fruits of their own labor, and to work in an increasingly complex agricultural milieu and in jobs other than farmwork.[133]

A final difference among Latinas at the conference was international. Female refugees urged conferees to take a stand on oppressive practices in their homelands. The general assembly passed resolutions expressing concern about women in Argentina's Villa Devoto prison and advocating a halt to military aid to El Salvador. In this regard, conferees were clearly expanding the definition of "political action" beyond what Gonzales had originally intended.

In addition to delineating their geographical, economic, educational, and cultural differences, participants spoke of important similarities. The most obvious one was use of the Spanish language. Though the general sessions and most of the workshops were conducted in English, some of the panels were conducted in Spanish. Eighty-two percent of questionnaire respondents considered themselves bilingual.[134] Latinas also had a common set of questions about the family. Because they saw the family as an indispensable line of defense against Anglo racism, they were not about to jettison it as a form of social organization. Some Latinas wanted to use this cornerstone of their culture as the basis for their feminist analyses of social transformation. Representatives from Mi Casa, a resource center for women in Denver, presented a workshop called "La Familia," premised on the idea that "the Hispanic culture is not built around social, political, or educational institutions. The integrating factor of the Hispanic culture is the family, and all other social systems are seen as needing to fit in with or to complement it."

Using the family as a point of departure, in a workshop entitled "The Hispana and the Future of La Raza: Our Children," Latinas asked these questions: "Are we as Hispanics to assimilate, compromise, or retain our unique identity? What are the value conflicts involved in each of these choices? How will these conflicts reflect on our children?" They anticipated conflict along several lines: competition/cooperation, individual/family, bilingual/monolingual, structure/flexibility, family/job, schooling/ job, male role/female role, conformity/diversity, tradition/innovation, and family/society. Their goal was to teach Hispanic children how to function successfully within these conflicts.

Conferees also paid a lot of attention to the psychological concerns of Latinas. Most of the psychology panels focused on counseling Latinas about role and cultural conflicts. Often panelists used distinctively Hispanic terms of analysis, such as "Razalogia," that is, the use of a time line to examine changing environmental demands and self-perceptions, and the theory of internal colonialism, applied not only economically but also psychologically.[135]

Not surprisingly, there were also many panels on education. The conferees were anxious to grapple with the causes and effects of the low educational attainment of Latinas. Participants also shared the realization that Latinas were increasingly joining the workforce, which precipitated cultural strain. As Iliad Estrada noted: "We found areas of common need: for survival's sake, Hispanic women must get into the work force. We identified mutual problems: when women start to work, the result is often divorce."[136]

A final common concern of conferees was the desire to contribute to the development of Hispanic feminist research and an autonomous Hispanic feminist movement. Some conference papers noted how mainstream social science research typically omitted Hispanas as units of analysis altogether. For example, most government data had previously subsumed Hispanas under "nonwhites," making it difficult to generalize about such matters as their family status, employment, income, and education relative to Anglos and others. Panelists promoted Latina scholarship by retrieving the contributions of feminist precursors. Several spoke about revisionist research on Malinche: "Many Chicanas are giving Malinche a second glance as they recognize . . . that the past contains answers to the questions of national character and, especially, answers the question, 'Who are we?' "[137] A feminist precursor whose activity was discussed at the conference was Carmen de Burgos (1867–1932), a Spanish writer, journalist, teacher, and political activist. Her 1927 book *The Modern Woman and Her Rights* traced women's economic and social history and resistance against oppression worldwide, preceding Simone de Beauvoir's classic *The Second Sex* by more than two decades.[138] Puertorriqueñas added their feminist precursors to the archives of Latina feminism, women who "broke out of the traditional female mold in a culture that was resistant to such efforts": Lola Rodriquez de Tío, Ana Roqué de Duprey, Luisa Capetillo, Felisa Rincón de Gautier, and Julia de Burgos.[139]

Dialogue between Latinas and Anglos

A third important interchange at the conference took place between Latinas and Anglos. There was some tension at the meeting between those Latinas who thought the time was ripe for coalition efforts with Anglo women and those who argued that such efforts were premature: they risked being assimilated into or used by Anglo political movements. Marta Cotera described the ideal coalition as "one where groups recognize their respective interests; they operate from independent power bases; and they agree and disagree freely and converge when there is a need to converge."[140]

In the early days of the Hispanic civil rights movement, resisting assimilation by Anglo culture included caution in aligning with the white women's liberation movement. At the 1969 Denver Chicano Youth Conference, a Chicana workshop issued a resolution stating, "It was the consensus of the group that the Chicana woman does not want to be liberated."[141] Cotera interpreted this resolution to mean that Chicanas "were not ready to take a stand on the issue of Anglo feminism."[142] The first national Chicana conference, held in Houston in 1971, was attended by six hundred women; 84 percent of the participants identified distinctions between the problems of Chicanas and those of other women, resulting primarily from racial oppression. The conference issued one of the first proclamations of Chicana feminism, calling for liberated sex lives, free and legal abortions, birth control, equality in marriage, community-run day care, an end to the sexual double standard, and a ban on drug experimentation on Chicanas.[143]

Latina feminists were chary about aligning with Anglo women who did not assume responsibility for educating themselves about their complicity in racist practices. Anglo feminists were charged not only with insensitivity to issues of special concern to Latinas but also with ignorance about Latino culture and the perpetuation of racial stereotypes. Latinas did not see their men as oppressors in the same way that Anglo women portrayed Anglo men. Hispanic men were also victims of racism, and in the power hierarchy it was white men who reaped the most privileges in a racist and sexist social order. Anglo feminists used the term *machismo* pejoratively without realizing that such use stereotyped Latino men and overlooked the fact that, in Chicano culture, this term had a positive meaning of responsibility, bravery, and protection of family members. Furthermore, Anglos typically subsumed Chicana feminism under Black Power or white feminism, when in fact it traced its roots to the heroines of the 1910 Mexican Revolution.

Latinas had lower incomes and were more likely to head family households than were Anglo women. Throughout the 1970s, Latinas' labor force participation grew steadily, and by 1980, they were as likely as Anglo women to work outside the home.[144] Most employed Latinas worked in domestic, service, and factory jobs and were less likely than Anglo women to be found in jobs requiring advanced degrees. Anglo feminists who took education for granted as a stepladder to career advancement were often oblivious to cultural barriers experienced by Latinas: language, a conflict between concern for others and academic competition, and lack of Latina role models.

Given Anglo feminists' assumption that they *were* the women's movement and their ignorance of an autonomous Latina feminist movement, Latinas' hesitation to form coalitions with Anglo feminists was based in two well-founded concerns: first, that such efforts were premature since Latinas were still forging their own terms for joining coalitions, and second, that Latinas would be used by Anglo political organizations, both feminist and partisan. Both concerns were expressed at the 1980 National Hispanic Feminist Conference.

Evidence that coalition efforts might have been premature came from scholars who were still in the process of documenting a feminism informed by a distinctively Hispanic cultural history and familial identity. In her essay "The Problematics of the Chicana Feminist Scholar," Marcela Lucero discussed the differences between bicultural Chicanas and monocultural Anglos. Chicanas embodied not only a Spanish and Indian racial identity but also a history of having been conquered both by Cortes in the sixteenth century and by the United States in 1848, fueling Anglo notions of superiority and Chicano feelings of inferiority. Furthermore, the "dominant majority who had the power and money had no interest in what conquered people were saying . . . —least of all in Spanish."[145] The dilemma of a bicultural identity was described by Nellie Olivencia as stemming from ambivalence about not belonging: *ni aquí, ni allá.* In an attempt to maintain *hispanismo,* Hispanics had created a "rigid, antiquated and stultifying model of what it is to be Latin. Feminists are seen as enemies of *hispanismo* and yet it is within our power not only to be a conveyor of the past, but also to critique the present and revitalize the future through our newly acquired self-identity."[146]

Another indication at the conference that group self-definition took precedence over coalitions with Anglos was the conferees' debate about whether to call themselves Hispanas or Latinas. In the concluding general assembly, delegates voted to refer to themselves as Latinas rather than Hispanics. In an article in the *San Jose Mercury News* a month before the conference, Sue Martinez, who wrote for a local Spanish-language newspaper, criticized the use of the term "Hispanic," which had become a hotly debated issue in the Chicano community. "Hispanic" was a European-sounding "whitewash, omitting any reference to the Indian and African roots that spawned the diverse Latino cultures of this hemisphere," and it "overstated an ignoble Spanish heritage of invaders who tried to destroy the indigenous cultures of the Americas."[147]

Some participants were suspicious of being used by Anglo political organizations. The newly discovered Hispanic voting bloc was of interest in the election year of 1980 to the Democratic party, whose representatives were quite visible at the conference. The potential contribution of the Hispanic vote in California and Texas to President Carter's reelection bid was not lost on Carter's liaison on women's issues, Sarah Weddington, who served on the conference advisory board.[148] In 1980, the ERA needed only a few more states' ratification to become law, and participants were reminded that Hispanas could play an important role in ratification efforts in Illinois, Florida, Missouri, and Virginia.[149] NOW President Eleanor Smeal made a brief appearance at the closing session to urge passage of the amendment. When asked why no Spanish-speaking women were on any NOW committees, she pledged to put them on each of the organization's twenty-seven committees.[150]

In addition to expressing concerns about being used to further the ends of an Anglo-dominated Democratic party or National Organization for Women, opponents of coalitions took issue with the role of Anglos as conference leaders. Gonzales defended her decision to include Anglo women in key posts at the conference as an object lesson to Anglo feminists. She said Hispanic women attempted to be brought into the decision-making process of Anglo-dominated feminist organizations but were typically marginalized in some specialized task force. She explained, "Everyone talks about coalitions, but Anglo feminists can't seem to do it. So we thought we'd show Anglo feminists how to include others so that they get a stake in the success of the conference, not just having Anglos as an adjunct like Anglos do with minority women."[151]

Gonzales, along with many other conference participants, thought the time was ripe for coalition politics. She pointed to the range of non-Hispanic women's organizations that sent representatives to the meeting, including: the National Organization for Women, National Women's Political Caucus, American Association of University Women, Business and Professional Women's Foundation, Coalition of Labor Union Women, National Women's Party, Planned Parenthood, Communication Workers of America, National Council of Churches, Amalgamated Textile Workers Union, Women's Action Alliance, Advocates for Women, and Women's Rights Project. Support for forging coalitions was also expressed in the questionnaire responses. Respondents ranked coalitions as their fourth priority, after developing support networks among Hispanas, fostering Hispanic feminism, and devising political action plans. They also indicated that informal associations with Anglos were an important part of their everyday lives. About two-thirds of the respondents said they had frequent professional contact with both Hispanic and Anglo women in their community, and Anglo women outnumbered Hispanic and Anglo men as role models and mentors for Hispanas. Workplace alliances between Latinas and Anglo women appeared to be a key component of Latinas' professional lives.

Some conference workshops also voiced a need for coalition politics. In a workshop on public policy and Hispanic women, Sandra A. Salazar, from the California Department of Health Services, noted that during the 1970s, Hispanas had devoted their energies to community action, service delivery, feminist support, and civil rights advocacy. Although these actions were beneficial in the short run, they did not address larger, long-term policy issues. With the knowledge gained from various organizational experiences, Hispanas were in a position to assess policy alternatives. By the year 2000, Hispanas would make up the largest group of minority women in the United States, and they had tremendous needs in the areas of education, employment, and housing. As Salazar put it, "The next two decades could prove to be a fruitful period for efforts toward successful coalition-building with other interest groups. The 1960s and 1970s saw progressive fragmentation among constituency groups while the years ahead appear to demand coalition politics."[152]

The hard work of sisterhood at the conference, in Santa Clara County, and across the nation was animated by emotional conflicts and competing claims about identities and what was best for women. It had its rewards, however: the exhilaration of creating concepts that did justice to women's experiences and of engaging in actions that opened up new political possibilities for women, transforming political life in the United States.

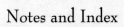

Notes and Index

Notes

PREFACE

1. All direct quotations from local officials, as well as background information about them, are drawn from the following 1982 interviews, unless otherwise specified: Councilmember Blanca Alvarado (26 August), Supervisor Rod Diridon (21 July), Councilmember Nancy Ianni (11 August), Councilmember Shirley Lewis (6 October), Supervisor Zoe Lofgren (12 August), Councilmember Lu Ryden (18 August), Councilmember Pat Sausedo (27 September), and Supervisor Susanne Wilson (22 July). Mayor Janet Gray Hayes was interviewed on 13 July 1984. Direct quotations from activists are from the following interviews: Ann Bender, attorney and former commissioner and chair, Santa Clara County Commission on the Status of Women (8 August 1983); Ellen Boneparth, professor of political science at San Jose State University and NWPC member (6 October 1982); Susan Charles, NWPC chapter president (13 August 1983); Nancy Clifford, San Jose Parks and Recreation Department and business agent for AFSCME District Council 57 (27 July 1984); Patt Curia, San Jose librarian (23 July 1984); Linda Dydo, San Jose librarian (13 July 1984); Kathy Espinoza-Howard, Personnel Division of Hewlett Packard and president of the Chicana Coalition (28 July 1983); Joan Goddard, San Jose librarian (1 August 1984); Sylvia Gonzales, professor of Mexican American Studies at San Jose State University and organizer of the National Hispanic Feminist Conference (13 and 16 August 1983 and 3 April 1986); Sarah Janigian, aide to Supervisor Susanne Wilson and NWPC member (26 July 1983); Anne McCormac, WOMA deputy director (16 August 1983); Pat Miller, president of Family Planning Associates and former commissioner and chair, Santa Clara County Commission on the Status of Women (9 July 1983); Cecilia Preciado-Burciaga, assistant provost at Stanford University (3 August 1983); Fanny Rinn, professor of political science at San Jose State University and NWPC member (24 May 1983); Joyce Sogg, attorney and NOW member (29 August 1983); Myra Strober, professor of education at Stanford and CROW director (16 September 1983); and Robin Yeamans, attorney and NOW member (18 August 1983).

CHAPTER 1

1. Barbara Nelson, "Women and Knowledge in Political Science: Texts, Histories, and Epistemologies," *Women and Politics* 9 (Summer 1989): 5–6.

2. Ibid., pp. 7–9.

3. Martin Gruberg, *Women in American Politics* (Oshkosh, Wis.: Academia Press, 1968).

4. Ibid., p. 26.

5. Debra W. Stewart, *The Women's Movement in Community Politics in the U.S.: The Role of Local Commissions on the Status of Women* (New York: Pergamon, 1980), esp. pp. 5–8; and Esther Peterson, "The Kennedy Commission," in *Women in Washington: Advocates for Public Policy,* ed. Irene Tinker (Beverly Hills, Calif.: Sage, 1983), pp. 21–34.

6. Quoted in Gruberg, *Women in American Politics*, p. 33.

7. Janan Sherman, "Margaret Chase Smith and the Impact of Gender Affinity," in *Gender and Policymaking: Studies of Women in Office*, ed. Debra L. Dodson (New Brunswick, N.J.: Center for the American Woman and Politics, Eagleton Institute, Rutgers University, 1991), pp. 63–72.

8. Gruberg, *Women in American Politics*, pp. 106–7.

9. Sherman, "Margaret Chase Smith."

10. Between 1974 and 1993, only one other revisionist review article appeared in the *American Political Science Review*, with a rejoinder: Virginia Sapiro, "Research Frontier Essay: When Are Interests Interesting? The Problem of Political Representation of Women," *American Political Science Review* 75 (September 1981): 701–16; and Irene Diamond and Nancy Hartsock, "Beyond Interests in Politics: A Comment on Virginia Sapiro's 'When Are Interests Interesting? The Problem of Political Representation of Women,'" *American Political Science Review* 75 (September 1981): 717–21.

11. Wilma Rule Krauss, "Political Implications of Gender Roles: A Review of the Literature," *American Political Science Review* 68 (December 1974): 1706–23.

12. Susan C. Bourque and Jean Grossholtz, "Politics an Unnatural Practice: Political Science Looks at Female Participation," *Politics and Society* 4 (Winter 1974): 225–66.

13. Angus Campbell, Philip E. Converse, Warren E. Miller, and Donald E. Stokes, *The American Voter* (New York: Wiley, 1960), p. 488.

14. Robert Lane, *Political Life* (New York: Free Press, 1965), p. 208.

15. Campbell et al., *American Voter*, p. 492; Lane, *Political Life*.

16. Fred Greenstein, *Children and Politics* (New Haven: Yale University Press, 1965), pp. 114–16.

17. Robert Hess and Judith Torney, *The Development of the Political Attitudes of Children* (Chicago: Aldine, 1967), p. 213.

18. Campbell et al., *American Voter*, p. 490.

19. Greenstein, *Children and Politics*, p. 108.

20. Floyd Hunter, *Community Power Structure* (Chapel Hill: University of North Carolina Press, 1953).

21. Robert Dahl, *Who Governs?* (New Haven: Yale University Press, 1961), p. 169.

22. Robert Presthus, *Men at the Top* (New York: Oxford University Press, 1964), pp. 97, 129.

23. Quoted in Gruberg, *Women in American Politics*, p. 224.

24. Quoted in *Women's Role in Contemporary Society: The Report of the New York City Commission on Human Rights* (New York: Avon, 1972), p. 639.

25. Mary L. Shanley and Victoria Schuck, "In Search of Political Woman," *Social Science Quarterly* 55 (December 1974): 632–44.

26. Ibid., p. 635.

27. Ibid., p. 638.

28. Ibid., p. 640.

29. Ibid., p. 641.

30. Ibid., p. 642; Victoria Schuck, "Women in Political Science: Some Preliminary Observations," *PS: Political Science and Politics* 2 (Fall 1969): 642, 653, Table 1.

31. Ibid., pp. 642–43.

32. This distinction between accommodationist and transformational feminist approaches is developed by Joan Tronto, "Politics and Revision: The Feminist Project to Change the Boundaries of American Political Science," in *Revolutions in Knowledge: Feminism in the Social Sciences*, ed. Sue Rosenberg Zalk and Janice Gordon-Kelter (Boulder, Colo.: Westview, 1991), pp. 91–110.

33. Deborah Tannen, *You Just Don't Understand* (New York: Ballantine, 1990).

34. Thelma McCormack, "Toward a Nonsexist Perspective on Social and Political Change," in *Another Voice: Feminist Perspectives on Social Life and Social Sciences,* ed. Marcia Millman and Rosabeth Moss Kanter (New York: Anchor/Doubleday, 1975), pp. 1–33, quotation from p. 22.

35. Ibid., p. 23.

36. Murray Goot and Elizabeth Reid, *Women and Voting Studies: Mindless Matrons or Sexist Scientism?* (Beverly Hills, Calif.: Sage, 1975).

37. Maurice Duverger, *The Political Role of Women* (Paris: UNESCO, 1955), p. 8.

38. David O. Sears, "Political Behavior," in *The Handbook of Social Psychology,* ed. G. Lindzey and E. Aronson (Reading, Mass.: Addison-Wesley, 1969), pp. 315–458.

39. Philip E. Converse, "Some Priority Variables in Comparative Electoral Research," in *Electoral Behavior: A Comparative Handbook,* ed. Richard Rose (New York: Free Press, 1974), pp. 727–45.

40. Lane, *Political Life,* p. 355.

41. Robert A. Dahl, *A Preface to Democratic Theory* (Chicago: University of Chicago Press, 1956), p. 74; Giovanni Sartori, *Democratic Theory* (New York: Praeger, 1965), p. 18.

42. Goot and Reid, *Women and Voting Studies,* p. 34.

43. Kay Boals, "Review Essay: Political Science," *Signs* 1 (Autumn 1975): 161–74.

44. Jeane J. Kirkpatrick, *Political Woman* (New York: Basic Books, 1974); Susan Tolchin and Martin Tolchin, *Clout: Womanpower and Politics* (New York: Coward, McCann and Geoghegan), 1973.

45. Boals, "Review Essay," p. 168.

46. Jane S. Jaquette, "Introduction," in *Women in Politics,* ed. Jane S. Jaquette (New York: Wiley, 1974), pp. xxviii–xxix, quotations from pp. xxxii, xix.

47. Boals, "Review Essay," pp. 171–72.

48. Jane S. Jaquette, "Review Essay: Political Science," *Signs* 2 (Autumn 1976): 147–64.

49. Maureen Fielder, "The Participation of Women in American Politics" (paper presented at the annual meeting of the American Political Science Association, San Francisco, 1975).

50. Kristi Andersen, "Working Women and Political Participation, 1952–1972," *American Journal of Political Science* 19 (August 1975): 439–53.

51. Jo Freeman, *The Politics of Women's Liberation: A Case Study of an Emerging Social Movement and Its Relation to the Policy Process* (New York: McKay, 1975), pp. 31–32.

52. Jean Bethke Elshtain, "Moral Woman and Immoral Man: A Consideration of the Public-Private Split and Its Political Ramifications," *Politics and Society* 4:4 (1974): 453–73.

53. Jaquette, "Review Essay," pp. 162–63. See Kate Millet, *Sexual Politics* (New York: Avon, 1969).

54. Berenice A. Carroll, "Political Science, Part I: American Politics and Political Behavior," *Signs* 5 (Winter 1979): 289–306.

55. *The Prism of Sex: Essays in the Sociology of Knowledge,* ed. Julia Sherman and Evelyn Beck (Madison: University of Wisconsin Press, 1979).

56. Virginia Sapiro, "Women's Studies and Political Conflict," in *Prism of Sex,* ed. Sherman and Beck, p. 258.

57. Robert Dahl, "The Behavioral Approach in Political Science: Epitaph for a Monument to a Successful Protest," *American Political Science Review* 55 (1961): 763–72.

58. Sapiro, "Women's Studies and Political Conflict" p. 260.

59. Dahl, *Who Governs?* p. 156.

60. Ibid., p. 157.

61. Sapiro, "Women's Studies and Political Conflict," p. 261.

62. Dahl, *Who Governs?* pp. 157–58.

63. Sapiro, "Women's Studies and Political Conflict," pp. 259, 263–64.

64. Jean Bethke Elshtain, "Methodological Sophistication and Conceptual Confusion: A Critique of Mainstream Political Science," in *Prism of Sex,* ed. Sherman and Beck, pp. 229–52.

65. Ibid.

66. Sapiro, "Research Frontier Essay," p. 713.

67. Diamond and Hartsock, "Beyond Interests in Politics," p. 720.

68. Marianne Githens, "The Elusive Paradigm: Gender, Politics, and Political Behavior," in *Political Science: The State of the Discipline,* ed. Ada W. Finifter (Washington, D.C.: American Political Science Association, 1983), pp. 471–99, quotation from pp. 489–90.

69. Gertrude A. Steuernagel and Laurel U. Quinn, "Is Anyone Listening? Political Science and the Response to the Feminist Challenge" (paper presented at the annual meeting of the American Political Science Association, Washington, D.C., 1986), p. 9.

70. Carol Gilligan, *In a Different Voice: Psychological Theory and Women's Development* (Cambridge: Harvard University Press, 1982).

71. Gertrude A. Steuernagel, "Reflections on Women and Political Participation," *Women and Politics* 7 (Winter 1987): 3–13.

72. Virginia Sapiro, *The Political Integration of Women* (Urbana: University of Illinois Press, 1983); Ethel Klein, *Gender Politics: From Consciousness to Mass Politics* (Cambridge: Harvard University Press, 1984); Keith Poole and L. Harmon Zeigler, *Women, Public Opinion, and Politics* (New York: Longman, 1985).

73. These reservations are elaborated on in Linda K. Kerber et al., "On *In a Different Voice:* An Interdisciplinary Forum," *Signs* 11 (Winter 1986): 304–33.

74. Virginia Sapiro, "Reflections on Reflections: Personal Ruminations," *Women and Politics* 7 (Winter 1987): 24–25.

75. Alison M. Jaggar, *Feminist Politics and Human Nature* (Totowa, N.J.: Rowman and Allenheld, 1983), p. 86.

76. Ethel Klein, "A Response to Steuernagel," *Women and Politics* 7 (Winter 1987): 16–17.

77. Ibid., p. 17.

78. Poole and Zeigler, *Women, Public Opinion, and Politics,* p. 4.

79. Harmon Zeigler and Keith Poole, "Comment on Steuernagel's 'Reflections on Women and Political Participation,'" *Women and Politics* 7 (Winter 1987): 30.

80. In a 1990 review essay, Steuernagel continued to express skepticism about the extent to which women and politics research had affected the discipline. See Gertrude A. Steuernagel, "'Men Do Not Do Housework': The Image of Women in Political Science," in *Foundations for a Feminist Restructuring of the Academic Disciplines,* ed. Michele A. Paludi and Gertrude A. Steuernagel (New York: Harrington Park, 1990), pp. 167–83.

81. Martha Ackelsberg and Irene Diamond, "Gender and Political Life: New Directions in Political Science," in *Analyzing Gender: A Handbook of Social Science Research,* ed. Beth B. Hess and Myra Marx Ferree (Newbury Park, Calif.: Sage, 1987), p. 515.

82. See, for example, Sara Ruddick, "Maternal Thinking," *Feminist Studies* 6 (Summer 1980): 342–67; Jane Flax, "Mother-Daughter Relationships: Psychodynamics,' Politics, and Philosophy," in *The Future of Difference,* ed. Hester Eisenstein and Alice Jardine (Boston: Hall, 1980), pp. 20–40; Nancy Chodorow, *The Reproduction of Mothering* (Berkeley: University of California Press, 1978); and Jean Elshtain, "Antigone's Daughters," in *Families, Politics, and Public Policies,* ed. Irene Diamond (New York: Longman, 1983), pp. 300–311.

83. See, for example, Martha A. Ackelsberg, "Women's Collaborative Activities and City Life: Politics and Policy," in *Political Women: Current Roles in State and Local Government,* ed. Janet A. Flammang (Beverly Hills, Calif.: Sage, 1984), pp. 242–59; Mary Dietz, "Citizenship with a Feminist Face," *Political Theory* 13 (February 1985): 19–37; Kathy E. Ferguson, *The Feminist Case against Bureaucracy* (Philadelphia: Temple University Press, 1984); and Flammang, ed., *Political Women.*

84. See, for example, Zillah Eisenstein, *Feminism and Sexual Equality: Crisis in Liberal America* (New York: Monthly Review Press, 1984); Nancy C. M. Hartsock, *Money, Sex, and Power: Toward a Feminist Historical Materialism* (New York: Longman, 1983); and Catharine A. MacKinnon, "Feminism, Marxism, Method, and the State: An Agenda for Theory," *Signs* 7 (Spring 1982): 515–44.

85. See, for example, Ann Bookman and Sandra Morgen, eds., *Women and the Politics of Empowerment* (Philadelphia: Temple University Press, 1988); Temma Kaplan, "Female Consciousness and Collective Action: The Case of Barcelona, 1910–1918," *Signs* 7 (Spring 1982): 545–66; and Ida B. Susser, *Norman Street: Poverty and Politics in an Urban Neighborhood* (New York: Oxford University Press, 1982).

86. See, for example, Helene Silverberg, "What Happened to the Feminist Revolution in Political Science? A Review Essay," *Western Political Quarterly* 43 (December 1990): 887–903.

87. Nelson, "Women and Knowledge in Political Science," p. 21.

88. Ibid., p. 22.

89. Tronto, "Politics and Revision."

90. Ibid.

91. Ibid., p. 105.

CHAPTER 2

1. Daniel J. Elazar, *American Federalism: A View from the States* (New York: Harper and Row, 1984).

2. David C. Saffell, *State and Local Government* (New York: McGraw-Hill 1990), p. 9.

3. John H. Culver and John C. Syer, *Power and Politics in California* (New York: Macmillan, 1988).

4. Philip J. Trounstine and Terry Christensen, *Movers and Shakers: The Study of Community Power* (New York: St. Martin's Press, 1982), pp. 80–85, quotation from p. 83.

5. Quoted in Aileen Kraditor, *The Ideas of the Woman Suffrage Movement, 1890–1920* (Garden City, N.Y.: Anchor Doubleday, 1971), p. 63.

6. Marilyn Gittell and Teresa Shtob, "Changing Women's Roles in Political Volunteerism and Reform of the City," *Signs* 5, supplement (Spring 1980): S67–78.

7. Eleanor Flexner, *Century of Struggle: The Woman's Rights Movement in the United States* (Cambridge: Belknap Press, Harvard University Press, 1975), pp. 230–31.

8. Trounstine and Christensen, *Movers and Shakers,* p. 85.

9. Ibid., pp. 92–93.

10. Ibid., pp. 94–97.

11. Ibid., pp. 99, 100.

12. "Voters Pass on Manager, Three for Council Tuesday," *San Jose Mercury News,* 8 April 1962, p. 40; "Fisher, Shaffer, Pace Win S.J. Council Seats," *San Jose Mercury News,* 9 May 1962, pp. 1–2.

13. "S.J. Mayor's Office Wide Open This Year," *San Jose Mercury News,* 27 October 1974, p. 3F.

14. Lawrence Aragon, "Profile: Susanne Wilson," *Business Journal,* 9 April 1990, p. 12.

15. Quoted in Eric Jansen, "Women in Power," *San Jose Metro*, 10–16 July 1986, p. 8.

16. Interview with Terry Christensen, professor of political science at San Jose State University, 26 August 1982. He referred to Robert Lee from Capital Data Communications, who conducted a poll for Susan Hammer's successful city council campaign against Tony Estremera.

17. For example, in a 1972 Louis Harris poll, respondents gave women a 15 percent edge in response to the question, "When it comes to maintaining honesty and integrity in government, do you feel that women in public office could do a better job than men, a worse job than men, or just as good a job as men in public office?" See Virginia Sapiro, *The Political Integration of Women* (Urbana: University of Illinois Press, 1983), pp. 144–45.

18. Center for the American Woman and Politics (CAWP), *Women in Elective Office, 1980: Mayor and Municipal/Township Councillors* (New Brunswick, N.J.: Rutgers University, n.d.).

19. Thomas R. Dye, *Politics in States and Communities* (Englewood Cliffs, N.J.: Prentice Hall, 1985), pp. 12–13.

20. Kirkpatrick Sale, *Power Shift* (New York: Random House, 1975), p. 13.

21. Trounstine and Christensen, *Movers and Shakers*, pp. 87–88.

22. Steve Johnson, "Military Cutbacks Would Hurt," *San Jose Mercury News*, 14 August 1986, p. 3B.

23. John Markoff, "Silicon Valley's Weapons of the Future," *San Francisco Examiner*, 12 August 1985, pp. 1, 4.

24. Thomas Mahon, *Charged Bodies: People, Power, and Paradox in Silicon Valley* (New York: New American Library, 1985), pp. 23–24.

25. Jansen, "Women in Power," p. 6.

26. Louis Harris and Associates, *The 1972 Virginia Slims American Women's Opinion Poll*, vol. 2 (Chicago: Roper, 1972), p. 18; Ethel Klein, *Gender Politics: From Consciousness to Mass Politics* (Cambridge: Harvard University Press, 1984).

27. Ivan Sharpe, "Is the Future Female?" *Working Woman*, January 1983, pp. 73–77; Everett M. Rogers and Judith K. Larsen, *Silicon Valley Fever: Growth of High Technology Culture* (New York: Basic Books, 1984), p. 169; Bill Soiffer, "Why It's Happening on the Peninsula," *San Francisco Chronicle*, 22 September 1980, p. 6.

28. County Supervisors Association of California, *County Fact Book, 1983* (Sacramento: CSAC, 1983), pp. 53–55; Harold W. Stanley and Richard G. Niemi, *Vital Statistics on American Politics* (Washington, D.C.: Congressional Quarterly Press, 1988), pp. 66–67.

29. "Answer Book for Santa Clara County, 1983 Edition," supplement of the *San Jose Mercury News*, 10 October 1982, p. 17; Stanley and Niemi, *Vital Statistics*, p. 126.

30. *San Francisco Chronicle*, "Biggest Counties in High-Tech," 17 March 1986, p. 19.

31. Rogers and Larsen, *Silicon Valley Fever*, p. 235.

32. Ibid., p. 189.

33. Ibid., pp. 189–90.

34. Ibid., p. 191.

35. Wilma Rule, "Electoral Systems, Contextual Factors, and Women's Opportunity for Election to Parliament in Twenty-three Democracies," *Western Political Quarterly* 40 (September 1987): 477–98; Karen L. Beckwith, "Structural Barriers to Women's Access to Office: The Case of France, Italy, and the United States" (paper presented at the annual meeting of the American Political Science Association, Washington, D.C., September 1984); R. Darcy, Susan Welch, and Janet Clark, *Women, Elections, and Representation* (Lincoln: University of Nebraska Press, 1994), pp. 79, 175–76.

36. Albert K. Karnig and B. Oliver Walter, "Election of Women to City Councils," *Social Science Quarterly* 56 (March 1976): 605–13.

37. Darcy et al., *Women, Elections, and Representation,* p. 169.

38. Ibid., p. 170.

39. Wilma Rule, "Why More Women Are State Legislators: A Research Note," *Western Political Quarterly* 43 (June 1990): 445–46; Wilma Rule, "Does the Electoral System Discriminate against Women?," *PS: Political Science and Politics* (Fall 1986): 866.

40. Susan Welch and Albert Karnig, "Correlates of Female Office Holding in City Politics," *Journal of Politics* 41 (May 1979): 478–91; Darcy et al., *Women, Elections, and Representation,* p. 48.

41. Albert Karnig and Susan Welch, *Black Representation and Urban Policy* (Chicago: University of Chicago Press, 1980); Chandler Davidson, ed., *Minority Vote Dilution* (Washington, D.C.: Howard University Press, 1984).

42. Peggy Heilig and Robert J. Mundt, *Your Voice at City Hall: The Politics, Procedures, and Policies of District Representation* (Albany: State University of New York Press, 1984).

43. Karnig and Welch, *Black Representation.*

44. Albert Karnig and Susan Welch, "Sex and Ethnicity in Municipal Representation," *Social Science Quarterly* 56 (March 1979): 605–13.

45. Susan A. MacManus, "Mixed Electoral Systems: The Newest Reform Structure," *National Civic Review* 74 (November 1985): 484–92; Francine F. Rabinovitz and Edward K. Hamilton, "Alternative Electoral Structures and Responsiveness to Minorities," *National Civic Review* 69 (July 1980): 371–401.

46. The following section is drawn from Janet A. Flammang, "Female Officials in the Feminist Capital: The Case of Santa Clara County," *Western Political Quarterly* 38 (March 1985): 94–118.

47. Trounstine and Christensen, *Movers and Shakers,* p. 105.

48. Philip J. Trounstine, "A New Look: District System Purrs Ahead in Its First Run," *San Jose Mercury News,* 31 October 1980, p. 9D.

49. Interview with Ellen Boneparth, professor of political science at San Jose State University, 6 October 1982.

50. In 1974, San Jose's population was 540,000. The second largest city with a female mayor at that time was Oklahoma City (population 366,000). Chicago's Jane Byrne and San Francisco's Dianne Feinstein did not become mayors until five years later.

51. Philip J. Trounstine, "Reshaped San Jose City Council Takes Oath of Office," *San Jose Mercury News,* 6 January 1981, p. 3B.

CHAPTER 3

1. Rita Mae Kelly, Bernard Ronan, and Margaret A. Cawley, "Liberal Positivistic Epistemology and Research on Women and Politics," *Women and Politics* 7 (Fall 1987): 11–27.

2. Nancy C. M. Hartsock, "The Feminist Standpoint: Developing the Ground for a Specifically Feminist Historical Materialism," in *Feminism and Methodology,* ed. Sandra Harding (Bloomington: Indiana University Press, 1987), pp. 157–80.

3. Marilyn Frye, "The Possibility of Feminist Theory," in *Theoretical Perspectives on Sexual Difference,* ed. Deborah L. Rhode (New Haven: Yale University Press, 1990), pp. 174–84.

4. Sandra Harding, "Introduction: Is There a Feminist Method?" in *Feminism and Methodology,* ed. Harding, pp. 4–5.

5. Ibid., p. 9.

6. Jo Freeman, *The Politics of Women's Liberation: A Case Study of an Emerging Social Movement and Its Relation to the Policy Process* (New York: McKay, 1975). The three articles are reprinted in *Radical Feminism,* ed. Anne Koedt, Ellen Levine, and Anita Rapone (New York: Quadrangle, 1973), pp. 50–59, 127–50, 285–99.

7. Kathie Sarachild, "Consciousness-Raising: A Radical Weapon," in *Feminist Revolution*, ed. Redstockings (New York: Random House, 1978), pp. 144–50.

8. Judith Hole and Ellen Levine, *Rebirth of Feminism* (New York: Quadrangle, 1971), p. 137.

9. "Redstockings Manifesto," in *Sisterhood Is Powerful: An Anthology of Writings from the Women's Liberation Movement*, ed. Robin Morgan (New York: Vintage, 1970), pp. 533–34.

10. Kathie Sarachild, "The Power of History," in *Feminist Revolution*, ed. Redstockings, p. 17.

11. Kathie Sarachild, "Who Are We? The Redstockings Position on Names," in *Feminist Revolution*, ed. Redstockings, pp. 53–55.

12. Ann Popkin, "The Personal Is Political: The Women's Liberation Movement," in *They Should Have Served That Cup of Coffee: Seven Radicals Remember the 60s*, ed. Dick Custer (Boston: South End Press, 1979), p. 213.

13. Aileen S. Kraditor, *The Ideas of the Woman Suffrage Movement, 1890–1920* (Garden City, N.Y.: Anchor Doubleday, 1971); Alice Echols, *Daring to Be Bad: Radical Feminism in America, 1967–1975* (Minneapolis: University of Minnesota Press, 1989); Koedt et al., *Radical Feminism*.

14. Betty Friedan, *The Feminine Mystique* (New York: Norton, 1963).

15. Another early proponent of liberal feminism was Alice Rossi. See her "Equality between the Sexes: An Immodest Proposal," in *The Woman in America*, ed. Robert J. Lifton (Boston: Beacon, 1967), pp. 98–143; and "Women—Terms of Liberation," in *The American Sisterhood*, ed. Wendy Martin (New York: Harper and Row, 1972), pp. 128–43.

16. Zillah Eisenstein, *The Radical Future of Liberal Feminism* (New York: Longman, 1981), p. 4.

17. Echols, *Daring to Be Bad*, pp. 4–5.

18. Catharine A. MacKinnon, "Liberalism and the Death of Feminism," in *The Sexual Liberals and the Attack on Feminism*, ed. Dorchen Leidholdt and Janice G. Raymond (New York: Pergamon, 1990), pp. 3–13.

19. Nancy McWilliams, "Contemporary Feminism, Consciousness-Raising, and Changing Views of the Political," in *Women in Politics*, ed. Jane S. Jaquette (New York: Wiley, 1974), pp. 157–70.

20. San Francisco Redstockings, "Our Politics Begin with Our Feelings," in *Masculine/Feminine*, ed. Betty and Theodore Roszak (New York: Harper and Row, 1969), pp. 285–90.

21. See, for example, Mary Daly, *Gyn/Ecology: The Metaethics of Radical Feminism* (Boston: Beacon, 1978); Marilyn French, *Beyond Power: On Women, Men, and Morals* (New York: Summit, 1985); and Susan Griffin, "The Way of All Ideology," *Signs* 7 (Spring 1982): 641–60.

22. Judith Grant, "I Feel Therefore I Am: A Critique of Female Experience as a Basis for Feminist Epistemology," *Women and Politics* 7 (Fall 1987): 99–114.

23. McWilliams, "Contemporary Feminism," p. 160.

24. Ibid., p. 161. For a recent example of reducing women's politics to the politics of do-goodism, see Michael Kelly, "Hillary Rodham Clinton and the Politics of Virtue," *New York Times Magazine*, 23 May 1993, pp. 22–25, 63–66. Kelly describes Clinton's politics as "the politics of do-goodism, flowing directly from a powerful and continual stream that runs through American history from Harriet Beecher Stowe to Jane Addams to Carry Nation to Dorothy Day" (p. 63).

25. Jean Bethke Elshtain, *Public Man, Private Woman: Women in Social and Political Thought* (Princeton: Princeton University Press, 1981).

26. Ibid., p. 334.

27. Ibid., p. 302.

28. Judith Stacey, *Patriarchy and Socialist Revolution in China* (Berkeley: University of California Press, 1983); and "Can There Be a Feminist Ethnography?" *Women's Studies International Forum* 11:1 (1988): 21–27, quotation from pp. 21–22.

29. Stacey, "Can There Be a Feminist Ethnography?" p. 23.

30. Temma Kaplan, "Female Consciousness and Collective Action: The Case of Barcelona, 1910–1918," *Signs* 7 (Spring 1982): 545–66.

31. Cynthia B. Costello, "Women Workers and Collective Action: A Case Study from the Insurance Industry," in *Women and the Politics of Empowerment,* ed. Ann Bookman and Sandra Morgen (Philadelphia: Temple University Press, 1988), pp. 116–35.

32. Martha A. Ackelsberg, "Communities, Resistance, and Women's Activism: Some Implications for a Democratic Polity," in *Women and the Politics of Empowerment,* ed. Bookman and Morgen, pp. 297–313.

33. See, for example, Blanche Weisen Cook, *Women and Support Networks* (New York: Out and Out Books, 1979); Rosalie Genovese, "A Women's Self-Help Network as a Response to Service Needs in the Suburbs," *Signs* 5, supplement (Spring 1980): S248–56; and Mary P. Ryan, "The Power of Women's Networks: A Case Study of Female Moral Reform," *Feminist Studies* 5 (Spring 1979): 66–86.

34. Ackelsberg, "Communities, Resistance, and Women's Activism," p. 305.

35. Louise A. Tilly and Patricia Gurin, "Women, Politics, and Change," in *Women, Politics, and Change,* ed. Louise A. Tilly and Patricia Gurin (New York: Russell Sage, 1990), pp. 3–32.

36. Maria Lugones and Elizabeth V. Spelman, "Have We Got a Theory for You! Feminist Theory, Cultural Imperialism, and the Demand for 'The Woman's Voice,'" *Women's Studies International Forum* 6:6 (1983): 581.

37. See, for example, Jane Flax, "Contemporary American Families: Decline or Transformation?" in *Families, Politics, and Public Policy,* ed. Irene Diamond (New York: Longman, 1983), pp. 21–40.

38. Susan Moller Okin, *Justice, Gender, and the Family* (New York: Basic Books, 1989).

39. See, for example, Diane Ehrensaft, "When Women and Men Mother," *Socialist Review* 10 (January–February 1980): 37–73; and *Parenting Together: Men and Women Sharing the Care of Their Children* (Champaign: University of Illinois Press, 1990).

40. Jean Bethke Elshtain, "Antigone's Daughters: Reflections on Female Identity and the State," in *Families, Politics, and Public Policy,* ed. Diamond, pp. 300–311.

41. Heidi I. Hartmann, "The Family as the Locus of Gender, Class, and Political Struggle: The Example of Housework," *Signs* 6 (Spring 1981): 366–94.

42. Joan Tronto, "Beyond Gender Difference to a Theory of Care," *Signs* 12 (Summer 1987): 644–63.

43. Sara Ruddick, "Maternal Thinking," *Feminist Studies* 6 (Summer 1980): 342–67; and *Maternal Thinking: Toward a Politics of Peace* (Boston: Beacon, 1989).

44. Carolyn Strange, "Mothers on the March: Maternalism in Women's Protest for Peace in North America and Western Europe, 1900–1958," in *Women and Social Protest,* ed. Guida West and Rhoda Lois Blumberg (New York: Oxford University Press, 1990), pp. 209–24.

45. See, for example, Linda Gordon, "The Struggle for Reproductive Freedom: Three Stages of Feminism," in *Capitalist Patriarchy and the Case for Socialist Feminism,* ed. Zillah R. Eisenstein (New York: Monthly Review Press, 1979), pp. 107–32; and Linda Phelps, "Female Sexual Alienation," in *Women: A Feminist Perspective,* ed. Jo Freeman, 2d ed. (Palo Alto, Calif.: Mayfield, 1979), pp. 18–26.

46. Sara Evans, *Personal Politics: The Roots of Women's Liberation in the Civil Rights Movement and the New Left* (New York: Vintage, 1979).

47. Charlotte Bunch, "Not for Lesbians Only," in Charlotte Bunch, *Passionate Politics: Feminist Theory in Action* (New York: St. Martin's Press, 1987), pp. 174–81.

48. Dorchen Leidholt, "Introduction," in *Sexual Liberals*, ed. Leidholt and Raymond, pp. ix–xvii.

49. Audre Lorde, *Uses of the Erotic: The Erotic as Power* (New York: Out and Out Books, 1978).

50. Patricia Lengermann and Jill Niebrugge-Brantley, "New Feminist Definitions of Power," in *First Annual Women's Policy Research Conference Proceedings* (Washington, D.C.: Institute for Women's Policy Research, 1990), pp.1–6.

51. Elizabeth Janeway, *Powers of the Weak* (New York: Knopf, 1980).

52. Nancy Hartsock, "Political Change: Two Perspectives on Power," *Quest* 1 (Summer 1974): 10–25.

53. Janet A. Flammang, "Feminist Theory: The Question of Power," *Current Perspectives in Social Theory* 4 (1983): 37–83.

54. Nancy C. M. Hartsock, *Money, Sex, and Power: Toward a Feminist Historical Materialism* (New York: Longman, 1983).

55. Sandra Morgen and Ann Bookman, "Rethinking Women and Politics: An Introductory Essay," in *Women and the Politics of Empowerment*, ed. Bookman and Morgen, pp. 3–29.

56. Iva Ellen Deutchman, "The Politics of Empowerment," *Women and Politics* 11 (Summer 1991): 1–18.

57. Jean Bethke Elshtain, "The Feminist Movement and the Question of Equality," *Polity* 7 (Summer 1975): 452–77.

58. Deborah L. Rhode, "Theoretical Perspectives on Sexual Difference," in *Theoretical Perspectives on Sexual Difference*, ed. Deborah L. Rhode (New Haven: Yale University Press, 1990), pp. 1–9.

59. See, for example, Julianne Malveaux, "Gender Difference and Beyond: An Economic Perspective on Diversity and Commonality among Women," in *Theoretical Perspectives on Sexual Difference*, ed. Rhode, pp. 226–38.

60. Carole Pateman, *The Sexual Contract* (Stanford: Stanford University Press, 1988); and *The Disorder of Women: Democracy, Feminism, and Political Theory* (Stanford: Stanford University Press, 1989).

61. Carole Pateman, "Feminism and Democracy," in Pateman, *Disorder of Women*, pp. 210–25.

62. Carole Pateman, "The Patriarchal Welfare State," in Pateman, *Disorder of Women*, pp. 179–209.

63. Mary G. Dietz, "Context Is All: Feminism and Theories of Citizenship," in *Learning about Women: Gender, Politics, and Power*, ed. Jill K. Conway, Susan C. Bourque, and Joan W. Scott (Ann Arbor: University of Michigan Press, 1987), pp. 1–24.

64. Janet Saltzman Chafetz, Anthony Gary Dworkin, and Stephanie Swanson, "Social Change and Social Activism: First-Wave Women's Movements around the World," in *Women and Social Protest*, ed. West and Blumberg, pp. 302–20.

65. Barbara J. Berg, *The Remembered Gate: Origins of American Feminism—the Woman and the City, 1800–1860* (Oxford: Oxford University Press, 1978).

66. Eleanor Flexner, *Century of Struggle: The Woman's Rights Movement in the United States* (Cambridge: Belknap Press, Harvard University Press, 1975).

67. Nancy E. McGlen and Karen O'Connor, "An Analysis of the U.S. Women's Rights Movements: Rights as a Public Good," *Women and Politics* 1 (Spring 1980): 65–85.

68. Frances E. Willard, *Glimpses of Fifty Years: An Autobiography of an American Woman* (1889; rpt. New York: Source Book Press, 1970).

69. Sophonisba P. Breckinridge, *Women in the Twentieth Century: A Study of Their Political, Social, and Economic Activities* (1933; rpt. New York: Arno Press, 1972); Flexner, *Century of Struggle*.

70. See Echols, *Daring to Be Bad*; Evans, *Personal Politics*; Myra Marx Ferree and Beth B. Hess, *Controversy and Coalition: The New Feminist Movement* (Boston: Twayne, 1985); and Hole and Levine, *Rebirth of Feminism*.

71. Ethel Klein, *Gender Politics: From Consciousness to Mass Politics* (Cambridge: Harvard University Press, 1984).

72. Joan Huber, "Toward a Sociotechnological Theory of the Women's Movement," *Social Problems* 23 (April 1976): 371–88.

73. Berg, *Remembered Gate*.

74. Estelle Freedman, "Separatism as Strategy: Female Institution Building and American Feminism, 1870–1930," *Feminist Studies* 5 (Fall 1979): 512–29.

75. Freeman, *Politics of Women's Liberation*.

76. Ibid.

77. Klein, *Gender Politics*, p. 1.

78. Leila J. Rupp and Verta Taylor, *Survival in the Doldrums: The American Women's Rights Movement, 1945 to the 1960s* (New York: Oxford University Press, 1987).

79. Cynthia Harrison, *On Account of Sex: The Politics of Women's Issues, 1945–1968* (Berkeley: University of California Press, 1988).

80. Freeman, *Politics of Women's Liberation*, pp. 54–55. The following discussion of NOW is drawn from pp. 80–86.

81. Ibid., pp. 98–100.

82. Arlene Daniels, "W.E.A.L.: The Growth of a Feminist Organization," in *Women Organizing*, ed. Bernice Cummings and Victoria Schuck (Metuchen, N.J.: Scarecrow Press, 1979), pp. 133–51.

83. Rona F. Feit, "Organizing for Political Power: The National Women's Political Caucus," in *Women Organizing*, ed. Cummings and Schuck, pp. 184–208, quotation from p. 187.

84. Ibid., pp. 202–3.

85. See, for example, Barbara Burrell, "A New Dimension in Political Participation: The Women's Political Caucus," in *A Portrait of Marginality: The Political Behavior of the American Woman*, ed. Marianne Githens and Jewel L. Prestage (New York: McKay, 1977), pp. 241–57.

86. See Freeman, *Politics of Women's Liberation*, for a discussion of BPW; and Ruth C. Clusen, "The League of Women Voters and Political Power," in *Women Organizing*, ed. Cummings and Schuck, pp. 112–32.

87. Anne N. Costain, "Representing Women: The Transition from Social Movement to Interest Group," in *Women, Power, and Policy*, ed. Ellen Boneparth (New York: Pergamon, 1988), pp. 26–47.

88. Anne N. Costain, "The Struggle for a National Women's Lobby: Organizing a Diffuse Interest," *Western Political Quarterly* 33 (December 1980): 476–91.

89. Kay Lehman Schlozman, "Representing Women in Washington: Sisterhood and Pressure Politics," in *Women, Politics, and Change*, ed. Tilly and Gurin, pp. 339–82.

90. Charlotte Bunch, "Woman Power and the Leadership Crisis," in Bunch, *Passionate Politics*, pp. 122–33.

91. Jo Freeman, "The Tyranny of Structurelessness," in *Women in Politics*, ed. Jane Jacquette (New York: Wiley, 1974), pp. 202–14.

92. See, for example, Kathleen P. Iannello, "A Grass-Roots Approach to Change: Anarchist Feminism and Nonhierarchical Organization," in *Women in Politics: Outsiders or Insiders?* ed. Lois Lovelace Duke (Englewood Cliffs, N.J.: Prentice Hall, 1993), pp. 291–300.

93. See, for example, Carol Ehrlich, "The Unhappy Marriage of Marxism and Feminism: Can It Be Saved?" in *Women and Revolution*, ed. Lydia Sargent (Boston: South End Press, 1981), pp. 109–33.

94. Kathy E. Ferguson, *The Feminist Case against Bureaucracy* (Philadelphia: Temple University Press, 1984).

95. Ronald Lawson and Stephen E. Barton, "Sex Roles in Social Movements: A Case Study of the Tenant Movement in New York City," in *Women and Social Protest*, ed. West and Blumberg, pp. 41–56.

96. Lois Lovelace Duke, "Virginia Foster Durr: An Analysis of One Woman's Contributions to the Civil Rights Movement in the South," in *Women in Politics*, ed. Duke, pp. 267–87.

97. Betty Friedan, "How to Get the Women's Movement Moving Again," *New York Times Magazine*, 3 November 1985, pp. 26–28, 66–67, 84–85, 98, 106, 108.

98. Jane J. Mansbridge, "Organizing for the ERA: Cracks in the Facade of Unity," in *Women, Politics, and Change*, ed. Tilly and Gurin, pp. 323–38.

99. Virginia Sapiro, "The Women's Movement, Politics, and Policy in the Reagan Era," in *The New Women's Movements: Feminism and Political Power in Europe and the USA*, ed. Drude Dahlerup (Beverly Hills, Calif.: Sage, 1986), 122–39.

100. See, for example, W. Douglas Costain and Anne N. Costain, "The Political Strategies of Social Movements: A Comparison of the Women's and Environmental Movements," *Congress and the Presidency* 19 (Spring 1992): 1–27; and Verta Taylor, "The Future of Feminism in the 1980s: A Social Movement Analysis," in *Feminist Frontiers*, ed. Laurel Richardson and Verta Taylor (Reading, Mass.: Addison-Wesley, 1983), pp. 434–51.

101. Mary Fainsod Katzenstein, "Comparing the Feminist Movements of the United States and Western Europe: An Overview," in *The Women's Movements of the United States and Western Europe*, ed. Mary Fainsod Katzenstein and Carol McClurg Mueller (Philadelphia: Temple University Press, 1987), pp. 3–20; and "Feminism within American Institutions: Unobtrusive Mobilization in the 1980s," *Signs* 16 (Autumn 1990): 27–54.

102. Judith Stacey, "Sexism by a Subtler Name? Postindustrial Conditions and Postfeminist Consciousness in the Silicon Valley," *Socialist Review* 17 (November–December 1987): 7–30.

103. Deborah Rosenfelt and Judith Stacey, "Second Thoughts on the Second Wave," *Feminist Studies* 13 (Summer 1987): 341–62.

104. Elizabeth Cook, "Measuring Feminist Consciousness," *Women and Politics* 9 (Fall 1989): 71–88.

105. Elizabeth Adell Cook and Clyde Wilcox, "A Rose by Any Other Name: Measuring Support for Organized Feminism Using ANES Feeling Thermometers," *Women and Politics* 12 (Spring 1992): 35–51.

106. Elizabeth Adell Cook, "The Generations of Feminism," in *Women in Politics*, ed. Duke, pp. 57–66.

107. Patricia Gurin, "Women's Gender Consciousness," *Public Opinion Quarterly* 49 (Spring 1985): 143–63.

108. Claudia Wallis, "Onward, Women!" *Time*, 4 December 1989, pp. 80–82, 85–86, 89.

109. Arthur H. Miller, Anne Hildreth, and Grace L. Simmons, "The Mobilization of Gender Group Consciousness," in *The Political Interests of Gender*, ed. Kathleen B. Jones and Anna G. Jonasdottir (London: Sage, 1988), pp. 106–34.

110. This section is taken from Janet A. Flammang, "Filling the Party Vacuum: Women at the Grassroots Level in Local Politics," in *Political Women: Current Roles in State and Local Government*, ed. Janet A. Flammang (Beverly Hills, Calif.: Sage, 1984), pp. 87–113.

111. Sylvia Gonzales, quoted in Janice Mall, "About Women," *Los Angeles Times*, 25 November 1979, pp. 18–19.

112. Sylvia Gonzales, quoted in Robin McKiel, "Historic Hispanic Feminist Conference Establishes Network," *National NOW Times*, May 1980.

113. Interview with Sylvia Gonzales, 16 August 1983.

CHAPTER 4

1. See, for example, Wendy Brown, *Manhood and Politics: A Feminist Reading in Political Theory* (Totowa, N.J.: Rowman and Littlefield, 1988); Jean Bethke Elshtain, *Public Man, Private Woman: Women in Social and Political Thought* (Princeton: Princeton University Press, 1981); Susan Moller Okin, *Women in Western Political Thought* (Princeton: Princeton University Press, 1979); Carole Pateman, *The Disorder of Women: Democracy, Feminism, and Political Theory* (Stanford: Stanford University Press, 1989); and Arlene W. Saxonhouse, *Women in the History of Political Thought: Ancient Greece to Machiavelli* (New York: Praeger, 1985).

2. Louise M. Young, "Women's Place in American Politics: The Historical Perspective," *Journal of Politics* 38 (August 1976): 295–335.

3. Suzanne Lebsock, "Women and American Politics, 1880–1920," in *Women, Politics, and Change*, ed. Louise A. Tilly and Patricia Gurin (New York: Russell Sage, 1990), pp. 35–62.

4. Kristi Andersen, "Women and Citizenship in the 1920s," in *Women, Politics, and Change*, ed. Tilly and Gurin, pp. 177–98, quotation from p. 182.

5. Marguerite J. Fisher, "Women in the Political Parties," *Annals* 251 (1947): 87–93.

6. Susan Ware, "American Women in the 1950s: Nonpartisan Politics and Women's Politicization," in *Women, Politics, and Change*, ed. Tilly and Gurin, pp. 281–99.

7. Hazel Erskine, "The Polls: Women's Role," *Public Opinion Quarterly* 35 (Summer 1971): 276.

8. Rita M. Kelly and Mary Boutillier, *The Making of Political Woman: A Study of Socialization and Role Conflict* (Chicago: Nelson-Hall, 1977).

9. Jeanie R. Stanley, "Life Space and Gender Politics in an East Texas Community," *Women and Politics* 5 (Winter 1985–86): 27–49.

10. Iva Ellen Deutchman, "Socialization to Power: Questions about Women and Politics," *Women and Politics* 5 (Winter 1985–86): 79–91.

11. Rita Mae Kelly and Jayne Burgess, "Gender and the Meaning of Power and Politics," *Women and Politics* 9 (Spring 1989): 47–82.

12. Diane L. Fowlkes, *White Political Women: Paths from Privilege to Empowerment* (Knoxville: University of Tennessee Press, 1992); and "Conceptions of the 'Political': White Activists in Atlanta," in *Political Women: Current Roles in State and Local Government*, ed. Janet A. Flammang (Beverly Hills, Calif.: Sage, 1984), pp. 66–86.

13. Anne Phillips, *Engendering Democracy* (University Park: Pennsylvania State University Press, 1991).

14. Kathleen B. Jones, "Citizenship in a Woman-Friendly Polity," *Signs* 15 (Summer 1990): 781–812, quotation from p. 803.

15. Ibid., p. 807.

16. Nancy C. M. Hartsock, *Money, Sex, and Power: Toward a Feminist Historical Materialism* (New York: Longman, 1983), p. 187.

17. See, for example, Jean Bethke Elshtain, *Women and War* (New York: Basic Books, 1987); Cynthia Enloe, *Bananas, Beaches, and Bases: Making Feminist Sense of International Politics* (Berkeley: University of California Press, 1990); Hartsock, *Money, Sex, and Power,* V. Spike Peterson ed., *Gendered States: Feminist (Re)Visions of International Relations Theory* (Boulder, Colo.: Lynne Rienner, 1992); Sara Ruddick, *Maternal Thinking: Toward a Politics of Peace* (Boston: Beacon, 1989); and Judith Hicks Stiehm, *Arms and the Enlisted Woman* (Philadelphia: Temple University Press, 1989).

18. Wendy Sarvasy, "Beyond the Difference versus Equality Debate: Postsuffrage Feminism, Citizenship, and the Quest for a Feminist Welfare State," *Signs* 17 (Winter 1992): 329–62.

19. Barbara J. Nelson, "The Gender, Race, and Class Origins of Early Welfare Policy and the Welfare State: A Comparison of Workmen's Compensation and Mother's Aid," in *Women, Politics, and Change,* ed. Tilly and Gurin, pp. 413–35; and "Women's Poverty and Women's Citizenship: Some Political Consequences of Economic Marginality," *Signs* 10 (Winter 1984): 209–31.

20. John W. Burgess, quoted in Barbara J. Nelson, "Women and Knowledge in Political Science: Texts, Histories, and Epistemologies," *Women and Politics* 9 (Summer 1989): 7.

21. Manuel Castells, *The City and the Grassroots* (Berkeley: University of California Press, 1983), p. 68.

22. This historical account is drawn from Marilyn Gittell and Teresa Shtob, "Changing Women's Roles in Political Volunteerism and Reform of the City," *Signs* 5, supplement (Spring 1980): S67–78.

23. On the National Association of Colored Women, see Paula Giddings, *When and Where I Enter: The Impact of Black Women on Race and Sex in America* (New York: Morrow, 1984), pp. 135–36.

24. See, for example, Alice Henry, *Women and the Labor Movement* (New York: Macmillan, 1927); Barbara Mayer Wertheimer, *We Were There: The Story of Working Women in America* (New York: Pantheon, 1977); and Philip S. Foner, *Women and the American Labor Movement: From Colonial Times to the Eve of World War I* (New York: Free Press, 1979).

25. Herbert H. Hyman and Charles Wright, "Trends in Voluntary Association Membership of American Adults: Replication Based on Secondary Analysis of National Sample Surveys," *American Sociological Review* 36 (April 1971): 191–206.

26. Norman Fainstein and Susan Fainstein, *Urban Political Movements* (Englewood Cliffs, N.J.: Prentice Hall, 1974); Marilyn Gittell, *Citizen Organization: Citizen Participation in Educational Decisionmaking* (Boston: Institute for Responsive Education, 1979).

27. Quoted in Mary King, *Freedom Song: A Personal Account of the Civil Rights Movement* (New York: Morrow, 1987), pp. 469–70.

28. Charles Payne, "'Men Led, but Women Organized': Movement Participation of Women in the Mississippi Delta," in *Women and Social Protest,* ed. Guida West and Rhoda Lois Blumberg (New York: Oxford University Press, 1990), pp. 156–65.

29. Gittell and Shtob, "Changing Women's Roles," pp. S74–75; Susan Hertz, "The Politics of the Welfare Mothers Movement: A Case Study," *Signs* 2 (Spring 1977): 600–611; Jackie Pope, "Women in the Welfare Rights Struggle: The Brooklyn Welfare Action Council," in *Women and Social Protest,* ed. West and Blumberg, pp. 57–74.

30. Kathleen McCourt, *Working-Class Women and Grass-Roots Politics* (Bloomington: Indiana University Press, 1977).

31. Gittell and Shtob, "Changing Women's Roles," p. S76; Ida Susser, "Working-Class Women, Social Protest, and Changing Ideologies," in *Women and the Politics of Empowerment*, ed. Ann Bookman and Sandra Morgen (Philadelphia: Temple University Press, 1988), pp. 257–71.

32. Gittell and Shtob, "Changing Women's Roles," p. S77.

33. Sandra Perlman Schoenberg, "Some Trends in the Community Participation of Women in Their Neighborhoods," *Signs* 5, supplement (Spring 1980): S261–68.

34. Galen Cranz, "Women in Urban Parks," *Signs* 5, supplement (Spring 1980): S79–95; Dolores Hayden, *The Grand Domestic Revolution: A History of Feminist Designs for American Homes, Neighborhoods, and Cities* (Cambridge: MIT Press, 1981).

35. Martha A. Ackelsberg, "Women's Collaborative Activities and City Life," in *Political Women*, ed. Flammang, pp. 242–59; Ann R. Markusen, "City Spatial Structure, Women's Household Work, and National Urban Policy," *Signs* 5, supplement (Spring 1980): S23–44.

36. Wendy Luttrell, "The Edison School Struggle: The Reshaping of Working-Class Education and Women's Consciousness," in *Women and the Politics of Empowerment*, ed. Bookman and Morgen, pp. 136–56; Lois Saxelby Steinberg, "The Role of Women's Social Networks in the Adoption of Innovations at the Grass-Roots Level," *Signs* 5, supplement (Spring 1980): S257–60.

37. Sandra Morgen, "'It's the Whole Power of the City against Us!' The Development of Political Consciousness in a Women's Health Care Coalition," in *Women and the Politics of Empowerment*, ed. Bookman and Morgen, pp. 97–115.

38. Celene Krauss, "Blue-Collar Women and Toxic Waste Protests: The Process of Politicization," *Second Annual Women's Policy Research Conference Proceedings* (Washington, D.C.: Institute for Women's Policy Research, 1991), pp. 279–83.

39. Sandra Morgen and Ann Bookman, "Rethinking Women and Politics: An Introductory Essay," in *Women and the Politics of Empowerment*, ed. Bookman and Morgen, pp. 3–29.

40. Martha A. Ackelsberg, "Sisters or Comrades? The Politics of Friends and Families," in *Families, Politics, and Public Policies*, ed. Irene Diamond (New York: Longman, 1983), pp. 339–56.

41. Anna G. Jonasdottir, "On the Concept of Interest, Women's Interests, and Limitations of Interest Theory," in *The Political Interests of Gender*, ed. Kathleen B. Jones and Anna G. Jonasdottir (London: Sage, 1988), pp. 33–65.

42. Constance Smith and Ann Freedman, *Voluntary Associations: Perspectives on the Literature* (Cambridge: Harvard University Press, 1972), p. viii.

43. David Sills, "Voluntary Associations: Sociological Aspects," *International Encyclopedia of the Social Sciences* (New York: Macmillan and the Free Press, 1968), 16:372–76.

44. Earl Latham, *The Group Basis of Politics* (Ithaca, N.Y.: Cornell University Press, 1952); David B. Truman, *The Governmental Process* (New York: Knopf, 1951); William Kornhauser, *The Politics of Mass Society* (Glencoe, Ill.: Free Press, 1959).

45. Gabriel A. Almond and Sidney Verba, *The Civic Culture: Political Attitudes and Democracy in Five Nations* (Boston: Little, Brown, 1965).

46. Norman H. Nie, G. Bingham Powell, Jr., and Kenneth Prewitt, "Social Structure and Political Participation: Developmental Relationships, II," *American Political Science Review* 63 (September 1969): 819.

47. Dennis Wayne, "Registration and Voting in a Patriotic Organization," *Journal of Social Psychology* (May 1930): 317–18; Paul S. Lazarsfeld, Bernard Berelson, and Hazel Gaudet, *The People's Choice* (New York: Duell, Sloan, and Pearce, 1944); Bernard A. Berel-

son, Paul F. Lazarsfeld, and William N. McPhee, *Voting* (Chicago: University of Chicago Press, 1954); and William Erbe, "Social Involvement and Political Activity," *American Sociological Review* 24 (April 1964): 198–215.

48. Morris Axelrod, "Urban Structure and Social Participation," *American Sociological Review* 21 (February 1956): 13–19; Robert T. Alford and Harry M. Scoble, "Sources of Local Political Involvement," *American Political Science Review* 62 (December 1968): 1192–1206.

49. Nicholas Babchuk and Alan Booth, "Voluntary Association Membership: A Longitudinal Analysis," *American Sociological Review* 34 (February 1969): 31–45.

50. J. Allen Williams, Nicholas Babchuk, and David R. Johnson, "Voluntary Associations and Minority Status. A Comparative Analysis of Anglo, Black, and Mexican Americans," *American Sociological Review* 38 (October 1973): 637–46.

51. Charles R. Wright and Herbert H. Hyman, "Voluntary Association Memberships of American Adults: Evidence from National Sample Surveys," *American Sociological Review* 23 (June 1958): 284–94; U.S. Department of Labor, Manpower Administration, *Americans Volunteer*, Manpower Automation Research Monograph no. 10 (Washington, D.C.: U.S. Government Printing Office, 1969).

52. Carol Slater, "Class Differences in Definition of Role and Membership in Voluntary Associations among Urban Married Women," *American Journal of Sociology* 65 (May 1960): 616–19.

53. Doris Gold, "Women and Volunteerism," in *Woman in Sexist Society*, ed. Vivian Gornick and Barbara K. Moran, (New York: Basic Books, 1971), pp. 533–54, quotation from p. 535.

54. Arlene Kaplan Daniels, *Invisible Careers: Women Civic Leaders from the Volunteer World* (Chicago: University of Chicago Press, 1988).

55. Florence E. Allen, "Participation of Women in Government," *Annals of the Academy of Political and Social Science* 251 (1947): 94–103, quotation from p. 102.

56. Nancy F. Cott, "Across the Great Divide: Women in Politics before and after 1920," in *Women, Politics, and Change*, ed. Tilly and Gurin, pp. 153–76.

57. Lebsock, "Women and American Politics," p. 57.

58. Naomi Black, *Social Feminism* (Ithaca, N.Y.: Cornell University Press, 1989).

59. David Knoke, "The Mobilization of Members in Women's Organizations," in *Women, Politics, and Change*, ed. Tilly and Gurin, pp. 383–410.

60. Lester W. Milbrath, *Political Participation* (Chicago: Rand McNally, 1966), p. 136.

61. Herbert Tingsten, *Political Behavior: Studies in Election Statistics* (London: P. S. King and Son, 1937), pp. 30–32; Angus Campbell, Philip E. Converse, Warren E. Miller, and Donald E. Stokes, *The American Voter* (New York: Wiley, 1960), chap. 15; William A. Glaser, "The Family and Voting Turnout," *Public Opinion Quarterly* 23 (Winter 1959–60): 563–70.

62. Angus Campbell, Gerald Gurin, and Warren Miller, *The Voter Decides* (Evanston, Ill.: Row Peterson, 1954).

63. Goldie Shabad and Kristi Andersen, "Candidate Evaluation by Men and Women," *Public Opinion Quarterly* 43 (Spring 1979): 18–35.

64. See, for example, Campbell et al., *American Voter*.

65. See, for example, David Easton and Jack Dennis, *Children and the Political System* (New York: McGraw-Hill, 1969); Fred I. Greenstein, *Children and Politics* (New Haven: Yale University Press, 1965); and Robert D. Hess and Judith V. Torney, *The Development of Political Attitudes in Children* (Chicago: Aldine, 1967).

66. M. Kent Jennings, "Gender Roles and Inequalities in Political Participation: Results from an Eight-Nation Study," *Western Political Quarterly* 36 (September 1983): 364–85.

67. Diana Owen and Jack Dennis, "Gender Differences in the Politicization of American Children," *Women and Politics* 8 (Summer 1988): 23–43.

68. Ronald B. Rapoport, "The Sex Gap in Political Persuading: Where the 'Structuring Principle' Works," *American Journal of Political Science* 25 (1981): 32–48; "Sex Differences in Attitude Expression: A Generational Explanation," *Public Opinion Quarterly* 46 (1982): 86–96; and "Like Mother, Like Daughter: Intergenerational Transmission of DK Response Rates," *Public Opinion Quarterly* 49 (1985): 198–208.

69. Nancy Romer, "Is Political Activism Still a 'Masculine' Endeavor?" *Psychology of Women Quarterly* 14 (1990): 229–43.

70. Linda L. M. Bennett and Stephen Earl Bennett, "Enduring Gender Differences in Political Interest," *American Politics Quarterly* 17 (January 1989): 105–22; Stephen Earl Bennett and Linda L. M. Bennett, "Changing Views about Gender Equality in Politics," in *Women in Politics: Outsiders or Insiders?* ed. Lois Lovelace Duke (Englewood Cliffs, N.J.: Prentice Hall, 1993), pp. 46–56; Stephen Earl Bennett and Linda L. M. Bennett, "From Traditional to Modern Conceptions of Gender Equality: Gradual Change and Lingering Doubts," *Western Political Quarterly* 45 (March 1992): 93–111.

71. Anthony M. Orum, Roberta S. Cohen, Sherri Grasmuck, and Amy W. Orum, "Sex, Socialization, and Politics," *American Sociological Review* 39 (1974): 197–209.

72. Roberta S. Sigel and John V. Reynolds, "Generational Differences and the Women's Movement," *Political Science Quarterly* 94 (Winter 1980): 635–48.

73. Claire Knoche Fulenwider, *Feminism and American Politics: A Study of Ideological Influence* (New York: Praeger, 1980); and "Feminist Ideology and the Political Attitudes and Participation of White and Minority Women," *Western Political Quarterly* 34 (March 1981): 17–30.

74. Susan Ann Kay, "Feminist Ideology, Race, and Political Participation: A Second Look," *Western Political Quarterly* 38 (September 1985): 476–84.

75. Arthur Miller, Patricia Gurin, Gerald Gurin, and Oksana Malanchuk, "Group Consciousness and Political Participation," *American Journal of Political Science* 25 (August 1981): 494–511.

76. Virginia Sapiro, *The Political Integration of Women: Roles, Socialization, and Politics* (Urbana: University of Illinois Press, 1983).

77. Ibid.

78. Virginia Sapiro, "What Research on the Political Socialization of Women Can Tell Us about the Political Socialization of People," in *The Impact of Feminist Research in the Academy,* ed. Christie Farnham (Indianapolis: Indiana University Press, 1987), pp.148–73.

79. For a "sex-difference" analysis of the same data Sapiro used in *Political Integration of Women,* see M. Kent Jennings and Richard Niemi, *Generations and Politics* (Princeton: Princeton University Press, 1981).

80. Virginia Sapiro, "If U.S. Senator Baker Were a Woman: An Experimental Study of Candidate Images," *Political Psychology* 3 (Spring–Summer 1981–82): 61–83.

81. See, for example, M. Kent Jennings and Barbara G. Farah, "Ideology, Gender, and Political Action: A Cross-National Study Survey," *British Journal of Political Science* 10 (April 1980): 219–40.

82. Fulenwider, *Feminism and American Politics.*

83. Barbara Agresti Finlay, "Sex Differences in Correlates of Abortion Attitudes among College Students," *Journal of Marriage and the Family* 43 (August 1981): 571–82.

84. Sapiro, "Research on Political Socialization."

85. Cornelia B. Flora and Naomi B. Lynn, "Women and Political Socialization: Considerations of the Impact of Motherhood," in *Women in Politics,* ed. Jane Jaquette (New York: Wiley, 1974), pp. 37–53.

86. Naomi Lynn and Cornelia Butler Flora, "Societal Punishment and Aspects of Female Political Participation: 1972 National Convention Delegates," in *A Portrait of Marginality: The Political Behavior of the American Woman,* ed. Marianne Githens and Jewel L. Prestage (New York: McKay, 1977), pp. 139–49.

87. Nancy E. McGlen, "The Impact of Parenthood on Political Participation," *Western Political Quarterly* 33 (September 1980): 297–313.

88. M. Kent Jennings, "Another Look at the Life Cycle and Political Participation," *American Journal of Political Science* 23 (November 1979): 755–71.

89. Sue Tolleson Rinehart, "Toward Women's Political Resocialization: Patterns of Predisposition in the Learning of Feminist Attitudes," *Women and Politics* 5 (Winter 1985–86): 11–26.

90. Diane L. Fowlkes, "Developing a Theory of Countersocialization: Gender, Race, and Politics in the Lives of Women Activists," *Micropolitics* 3 (Summer 1983): 181–225; "Ambitious Political Woman: Countersocialization and Political Party Context," *Women and Politics* 4 (Winter 1984): 5–32; and *White Political Women.*

91. Alice Rossi, *Feminists in Politics: A Panel Analysis of the First National Women's Conference* (New York: Academic Press, 1982).

92. Morris Levitt, "The Political Role of American Women," *Journal of Human Relations* 15 (1967): 23–35.

93. Kristi Andersen, "Working Women and Political Participation, 1952–1972," *American Journal of Political Science* 19 (August 1975): 439–53.

94. Susan B. Hansen, Linda M. Franz, and Margaret Netemeyer-Mays, "Women's Political Participation and Policy Preferences," *Social Science Quarterly* 56 (March 1976): 576–90.

95. Kent L. Tedin, David W. Brady, and Arnold Vedlitz, "Sex Differences in Political Attitudes and Behavior: The Case for Situational Factors," *Journal of Politics* 39 (May 1977): 448–56.

96. Sandra Baxter and Marjorie Lansing, *Women and Politics: The Visible Majority* (Ann Arbor: University of Michigan Press, 1983).

97. Eileen L. McDonagh, "To Work or Not to Work: The Differential Impact of Achieved and Derived Status upon the Political Participation of Women, 1956–1976," *American Journal of Political Science* 26 (May 1982): 280–97.

98. Kristi Andersen and Elizabeth A. Cook, "Women, Work, and Political Attitudes," *American Journal of Political Science* 29 (August 1985): 606–25.

99. Karen Beckwith, *American Women and Political Participation* (New York: Greenwood, 1986). In a review of Beckwith's book, Kristi Andersen argued that the questions Beckwith wanted to answer could not be addressed by using large national samples with predominantly closed-ended questions designed for other purposes. In order to ascertain how women's own sense of their experiences helped them create a unique understanding of politics, researchers needed to conduct intensive local case studies, in-depth interviews, and experiments. See Andersen's review in *Women and Politics* 8 (Spring 1988): 92–93.

100. See, for example, Naomi B. Lynn, "American Women and the Political Process," in *Women: A Feminist Perspective,* ed. Jo Freeman, 2d ed. (Palo Alto, Calif.: Mayfield, 1979), pp. 404–29; and Margaret A. Conway, *Political Participation in the United States* (Washington, D.C.: Congressional Quarterly Press, 1991).

101. Susan Welch, "Women as Political Animals? A Test of Some Explanations for Male and Female Political Participation Differences," *American Journal of Political Science* 21 (November 1977): 711–30.

102. Cal Clark and Janet Clark, "Models of Gender and Political Participation in the United States," *Women and Politics* 6 (Spring 1986): 5–25.

103. Kathy Bonk, "The Selling of the 'Gender Gap': The Role of Organized Feminism," in *The Politics of the Gender Gap: The Social Construction of Political Influence*, ed. Carol M. Mueller (Newbury Park, Calif.: Sage, 1988), pp. 82–101.

104. Mary Fainsod Katzenstein, "Feminism and the Meaning of the Vote," *Signs* 10 (Autumn 1984): 4–26; Johanna S. R. Mendelson, "The Ballot Box Revolution: The Drive to Register Women," in *Politics of the Gender Gap*, ed. Mueller, pp. 61–80.

105. Kathleen A. Frankovic, "The Ferraro Factor: The Women's Movement, the Polls, and the Press," in *Politics of the Gender Gap*, ed. Mueller, p. 104.

106. Lucy Baruch and Angela Bell, "Gender Gap a Factor in a Majority of Races in 1992," *CAWP News and Notes* 9 (Winter 1993): 7.

107. Henry C. Kenski, "The Gender Factor in a Changing Electorate," in *Politics of the Gender Gap*, ed. Mueller, pp. 38–60.

108. Emily Stoper, "The Gender Gap Concealed and Revealed: 1936–1984," *Journal of Political Science* 17 (Spring 1989): 50–62.

109. Tom W. Smith, "The Polls: Gender and Attitudes toward Violence," *Public Opinion Quarterly* 48 (Spring 1984): 384–96.

110. See, for example, Robert S. Erikson and Norman R. Luttbeg, *American Public Opinion: Its Origins, Content, and Impact* (New York: Wiley, 1973); John E. Mueller, *War, Presidents, and Public Opinion* (New York: Wiley, 1973); and Gerald M. Pomper, *Voter's Choice: Varieties of American Electoral Behavior* (New York: Dodd, Mead, 1975).

111. Alfred Hero, "Public Reaction to Government Policy," in *Measures of Political Attitudes*, ed. John P. Robinson, Jerrold G. Rusk, and Kendra B. Head (Ann Arbor, Mich.: Survey Research Center, Institute for Social Research, 1969), pp. 23–78, p. 54.

112. See, for example, Keith T. Poole and L. Harmon Zeigler, *Women, Public Opinion, and Politics: The Changing Political Attitudes of American Women* (New York: Longman, 1985); and David O. Sears and Leonie Huddy, "On the Origins of Political Disunity among Women," in *Women, Politics, and Change*, ed. Tilly and Gurin, pp. 249–80.

113. Baxter and Lansing, *Women and Politics*, p. 201; Kathleen Frankovic, "Sex and Politics—New Alignments, Old Issues," *PS: Political Science and Politics* 15 (1982): 439–48.

114. Anne N. Costain and Steven Majstorovic, "The Historic Gender Gap" (paper presented at the annual meeting of the Western Political Science Association, Pasadena, 1993).

115. Ethel Klein, "The Gender Gap: Different Issues, Different Answers," *Brookings Review* 3 (Winter 1985): 33–37.

116. Ethel Klein, *Gender Politics: From Consciousness to Mass Politics* (Cambridge: Harvard University Press, 1984).

117. Ibid.; Ethel Klein, "The Diffusion of Consciousness in the United States and Western Europe," in *The Women's Movements of the United States and Western Europe*, ed. Mary Fainsod Katzenstein and Carol McClurg Mueller (Philadelphia: Temple University Press, 1987), pp. 23–43.

118. Robert Y. Shapiro and Harpeet Mahajan, "Gender Differences in Policy Preferences: A Summary of Trends from the 1960s to the 1980s," *Public Opinion Quarterly* 50 (Spring 1986): 42–61.

119. Janet Clark and Cal Clark, "The Gender Gap 1988: Compassion, Pacifism, and Indirect Feminism," in *Women in Politics*, ed. Duke, pp. 32–45.

120. Steven P. Erie and Martin Rein, "Women and the Welfare State," in *Politics of the Gender Gap*, ed. Mueller, pp. 173–91.

121. Susan J. Carroll, "Women's Autonomy and the Gender Gap: 1980 and 1982," in *Politics of the Gender Gap*, ed. Mueller, pp. 236–57.

122. Arthur Miller, "Gender and the Vote: 1984," in *Politics of the Gender Gap,* ed. Mueller, pp. 258–82.

123. Susan Welch and John Hibbing, "Financial Conditions, Gender, and Voting in American Elections," *Journal of Politics* 54 (1992): 197–213.

124. Baxter and Lansing, *Women and Politics,* p. 208.

125. See, for example, Susan Welch, "Support among Women for the Issues of the Women's Movement," *Sociological Quarterly* 16 (Spring 1975): 261–27.

126. Daniel Whirls, "Reinterpreting the Gender Gap," *Public Opinion Quarterly* 50 (Fall 1986): 316–30.

127. Jo Freeman, "Whom You Know versus Whom You Represent: Feminist Influence in the Democratic and Republican Parties," in *Women's Movements,* ed. Katzenstein and Mueller, pp. 215–44, quotation from pp. 231–32.

128. Ibid.

129. Anne N. Costain and W. Douglas Costain, "Strategy and Tactics of the Women's Movement in the United States: The Role of Political Parties," in *Women's Movements,* ed. Katzenstein and Mueller, pp. 196–214.

130. Ibid.

131. Denise L. Baer, "Political Parties: The Missing Variable in Women and Politics Research," *Political Research Quarterly* 46:3 (1993): 547–76.

132. Jeane J. Kirkpatrick, *The New Presidential Elite* (New York: Russell Sage and Twentieth Century Fund, 1976), pp. 380–81.

133. M. Kent Jennings and Norman Thomas, "Men and Women in Party Elites: Social Roles and Political Resources," *Midwest Journal of Political Science* 12 (November 1968): 469–92.

134. Edmond Costantini and Kenneth A. Craik, "Women as Politicians: The Social Background, Personality, and Political Careers of Female Party Leaders," *Journal of Social Issues* 28:2 (1972): 217–36. Their sample included not only delegates to the 1960 and 1964 national party conventions but also congressmembers, state legislators, and party county committee chairs.

135. Kirkpatrick, *New Presidential Elite.*

136. Ibid.

137. Wilma E. McGrath and John W. Soule, "Rocking the Cradle or Rocking the Boat: Women at the 1972 Democratic National Convention," *Social Science Quarterly* 55 (June 1974): 141–50.

138. Virginia Sapiro and Barbara G. Farah, "New Pride and Old Prejudice: Political Ambition and Role Orientations among Female Partisan Elites," *Women and Politics* 1 (Spring 1980): 13–36.

139. M. Kent Jennings and Barbara G. Farah, "Social Roles and Political Resources: An Over-Time Study of Men and Women in Party Elites," *American Journal of Political Science* 25 (August 1981): 462–82.

140. Denise L. Baer and John S. Jackson, "Are Women Really More 'Amateur' in Politics than Men?" *Women and Politics* 5 (Summer–Fall, 1985): 79–92.

141. M. Kent Jennings, "Women in Party Politics," in *Women, Politics, and Change,* ed. Tilly and Gurin, pp. 221–48.

142. Ellen Boneparth, "Women in Campaigns: From Lickin' and Stickin' to Strategy," *American Politics Quarterly* 5 (July 1977): 289–300.

143. Diane Margolis, "The Invisible Hands: Sex Roles and the Division of Labor in Two Local Political Parties," in *Women in Local Politics,* ed. Debra W. Stewart (Metuchen, N.J.: Scarecrow Press, 1980), pp. 22–41.

144. Diane L. Fowlkes, Jerry Perkins, and Sue Tolleson Rinehart, "Gender Roles and Party Roles," *American Political Science Review* 73 (September 1979): 772–80.

145. Harold D. Clarke and Allan Kornberg, "Moving Up the Political Escalator: Women Party Officials in the United States and Canada," *Journal of Politics* 41:2 (1979): 442–77.

146. Anne E. Kelley, William E. Hulbary, and Lewis Bowman, "Gender, Party, and Political Ideology: The Case of Mid-Elite Party Activists in Florida," *Journal of Political Science* 17 (Spring 1989): 6–18.

147. Edmond Costantini and Julie Davis Bell, "Women in Political Parties: Gender Differences in Motives among California Party Activists," in *Political Women*, ed. Flammang, pp. 114–38.

148. Gertrude Bussey and Margaret Tims, *Pioneers for Peace: Women's International League for Peace and Freedom, 1915–1965* (Oxford: Alden Press, 1980).

149. San Jose Branch, Women's International League for Peace and Freedom, "What on Earth Is the WILPF?" (pamphlet, San Jose, Calif., n.d.).

150. The remainder of this chapter is drawn from Janet A. Flammang, "Filling the Party Vacuum: Women at the Grassroots Level in Local Politics," in *Political Women*, ed. Flammang, pp. 102–7.

151. NWPC endorsement and funding procedures are drawn from interviews with Sarah Janigian and Fanny Rinn; NOW endorsement procedures are based on interviews with Joyce Sogg and Robin Yeamans; and Chicana Coalition endorsement procedures are taken from an interview with Kathy Espinoza-Howard.

152. Flammang, "Filling the Party Vacuum," p. 107.

CHAPTER 5

1. Sophonisba P. Breckinridge, *Women in the Twentieth Century: A Study of Their Political, Social, and Economic Activities* (New York: McGraw-Hill, 1933), quotation from p. 327.

2. Ibid.

3. Ibid., pp. 334–35.

4. Martin Gruberg, *Women in American Politics: An Assessment and Sourcebook* (Oshkosh, Wis.: Academia Press, 1968).

5. Kenneth Prewitt, *The Recruitment of Political Leaders: A Study of Citizen-Politicians* (Indianapolis: Bobbs-Merrill, 1970), p. 26.

6. Ibid., pp. 24–25.

7. Center for the American Woman and Politics, *Women in Elective Office 1989* (New Brunswick: National Information Bank on Women in Public Office, Eagleton Institute of Politics, Rutgers University, 1989); Susan Welch and Albert K. Karnig, "Correlates to Female Officeholding in City Politics," *Journal of Politics* 41 (May 1978): 478–91.

8. Jeane J. Kirkpatrick, *Political Woman* (New York: Basic Books, 1974).

9. See, for example, Judith Evans, "USA," in *The Politics of the Second Electorate: Women and Public Participation*, ed. Joni Lovenduski and Jill Hills (London: Routledge and Kegan Paul, 1981), pp. 33–51.

10. Sarah Slavin Schramm, "Women and Representation: Self-Government and Role Change," *Western Political Quarterly* 34 (March 1981): 46–59.

11. Martin Gruberg, "From Nowhere to Where? Women in State and Local Politics," *Social Science Journal* 21 (January 1984): 5–12.

12. Carol Nechemias, "Changes in the Election of Women to U.S. State Legislative Seats," *Legislative Studies Quarterly* 12 (February 1987): 125–42.

13. Susan A. MacManus, "A City's First Female Officeholder: 'Coattails' for the Future Female Officeholders?" *Western Political Quarterly* 34 (March 1981): 88–99.

14. Wilma Rule, "Why Women Don't Run: The Critical Contextual Factors in Women's Legislative Recruitment," *Western Political Quarterly* 34 (March 1981): 60–77.

15. Irene Diamond, *Sex Roles in the State House* (New Haven: Yale University Press, 1977).

16. Woodrow Jones and Albert J. Nelson, "Correlates of Women's Representation in Lower State Legislative Chambers," *Social Behavior and Personality* 9:1 (1981): 9–15.

17. David Hill, "Political Culture and Female Political Representation," *Journal of Politics* 43 (February 1981): 159–68.

18. Jean Bethke Elshtain, "Moral Woman and Immoral Man: A Consideration of the Public-Private Split and Its Political Ramifications," *Politics and Society* 4 (Winter 1974): 453–73.

19. Senator George Vest, quoted in Gruberg, *Women in American Politics*, p. 4.

20. George E. Howard, "Changing Ideals and Status of the Family and the Public Activities of Women," *The Annals*, November 1914, pp. 36–37.

21. Gruberg, *Women in American Politics*, p. 10.

22. Hazel Erskine, "The Polls: Women's Role," *Public Opinion Quarterly* 35 (Summer 1971): 275–90.

23. Frank Colon, "The Elected Woman," *Social Studies* 58 (November 1967): 256–61.

24. Ronald D. Hedlund, Patricia K. Freeman, Keith E. Hamm, and Robert M. Stein, "The Electability of Women Candidates: The Effects of Sex-Role Stereotypes," *Journal of Politics* 41 (May 1979): 513–24.

25. Myra Marx Ferree, "A Woman for President? Changing Responses, 1958–1972," *Public Opinion Quarterly* 38 (Fall 1974): 390–99.

26. Audrey Siess Wells and Eleanor Cutri Smeal, "Women's Attitudes toward Women in Politics: A Survey of Urban Registered Voters and Party Committee Women," in *Women in Politics*, ed. Jane S. Jaquette (New York: Wiley, 1974), pp. 54–72.

27. Susan Welch and Lee Sigelman, "Changes in Public Attitudes towards Women in Politics," *Social Science Quarterly* 63 (June 1982): 312–22.

28. Susan J. Carroll, "Women's Autonomy and the Gender Gap: 1980 and 1982," in *The Politics of the Gender Gap: The Social Construction of Political Influence*, ed. Carol Mueller (Newbury Park, Calif.: Sage, 1988), pp. 250–51.

29. Joseph A. Schlesinger, *Ambition and Politics: Political Careers in the United States* (Chicago: Rand McNally, 1966).

30. See, for example, Kenneth Prewitt and William Nowlin, "Political Ambitions and the Behavior of Incumbent Politicians," *Western Political Quarterly* 22 (June 1969): 98–308.

31. Marcia Lynn Whicker, Malcolm Jewell, and Lois Lovelace Duke, "Women in Congress," in *Women in Politics: Outsiders or Insiders?* ed. Lois Lovelace Duke (Englewood Cliffs, N.J.: Prentice Hall, 1993), pp. 136–51.

32. Jerry Perkins, "Political Ambition among Black and White Women: An Intragender Test of the Socialization Model," *Women and Politics* 6 (Spring 1986): 27–40.

33. Albert K. Karnig and B. Oliver Walter, "Election of Women to City Councils," *Social Science Quarterly* 56 (March 1976): 605–13.

34. Robert A. Bernstein, "Why Are There So Few Women in the House?" *Western Political Quarterly* 39 (March 1986): 155–64.

35. Diane Fowlkes, "Ambitious Political Woman: Countersocialization and Political Party Context," *Women and Politics* 4 (Winter 1984): 5–32.

36. Marianne Githens and Jewel L. Prestage, "Introduction," in *A Portrait of Marginality: The Political Behavior of the American Woman,* ed. Marianne Githens and Jewel L. Prestage (New York: McKay, 1977), pp. 3–10; Marianne Githens, "Women and State Politics: An Assessment," in *Political Women: Current Roles in State and Local Government,* ed. Janet A. Flammang (Beverly Hills, Calif.: Sage, 1984), pp. 41–63.

37. Patrick A. Pierce, "Gender Role and Political Culture: The Electoral Connection," *Women and Politics* 9 (1989): 21–46.

38. Barbara Burt-Way and Rita Mae Kelly, "Gender and Sustaining Political Ambition: A Study of Arizona Elected Officials," *Western Political Quarterly* 45 (March 1992): 11–25.

39. Diane D. Kincaid, "Over His Dead Body: A Positive Perspective on Widows in the U.S. Congress," *Western Political Quarterly* 31 (March 1978): 96–104.

40. Connie Skipitares, "Female Majorities on Council, Board Shun Feminist Label," *San Jose Mercury News,* 6 November 1980, p. 1B.

41. Quotations from officials are taken from the 1982 interviews cited in the Preface, unless otherwise specified.

42. Edward O. Welles, "The Power of the County," *West Magazine* of the *San Jose Mercury News,* 29 January 1984, pp. 10–16, 25–29.

43. Susan J. Carroll and Wendy S. Strimling, *Women's Routes to Elective Office: A Comparison with Men's* (New Brunswick: Center for the American Woman and Politics, Eagleton Institute of Politics, Rutgers University, 1983), p. 7.

44. Philip J. Trounstine and Terry Christensen, *Movers and Shakers: The Study of Community Power* (New York: St. Martin's Press, 1982), p. 116.

45. Faye Boquist, "Women in Politics Discuss Challenges and Frustrations," *San Jose Mercury News,* 27 November 1980, p. 12C.

46. Carroll and Strimling, *Women's Routes,* pp. 14–15, 27.

47. Marcia Lee, "Why Few Women Hold Public Office: Democracy and Sexual Roles," *Political Science Quarterly* 91 (Summer 1976): 297–314; and "Toward Understanding Why Few Women Hold Public Office: Factors Affecting the Participation of Women in Local Politics," in *Portrait of Marginality,* ed. Githens and Prestage, pp. 118–38.

48. Emily Stoper, "Wife and Politician: Role Strain among Women in Public Office," in *Portrait of Marginality,* ed. Githens and Prestage, pp. 320–37.

49. Pat Schroeder, *Champion of the Great American Family* (New York: Random House, 1989), pp. 15, 57.

50. Diane Kincaid Blair and Ann R. Henry, "The Family Factor in State Legislative Turnover," *Legislative Studies Quarterly* 6 (1981): 55–68.

51. Virginia Sapiro, "Public Costs of Private Commitments or Private Costs of Public Commitments? Family Roles versus Political Ambition," *American Journal of Political Science* 26 (May 1982): 265–79.

52. Susan J. Carroll, "The Personal Is Political: The Intersection of Private Lives and Public Roles among Women and Men in Elective and Appointive Office," *Women and Politics* 9 (Summer 1989): 51–67.

53. Melinda Sacks, "From Welfare Mother to Political Powerhouse," *Peninsula Magazine,* June 1989, p. 43.

54. Peggy Lamson, *Few Are Chosen: American Women in Political Life Today* (Boston: Houghton Mifflin, 1968), p. 88.

55. Carroll and Strimling, *Women's Routes,* pp. 25–26.

56. Betty Barnacle, "Call Me 'Madame Mayor' States City's First Lady," *San Jose Mercury News,* 7 November 1974, p. 6.

57. "Janet Gray Hayes, Woman of Achievement," *San Jose Mercury News,* 22 February 1976, p. 65.

58. Boquist, "Women in Politics."

59. Emmy E. Werner, "Women in Congress: 1917–1964," *Western Political Quarterly* 19 (March 1966): 16–30.

60. Charles S. Bullock III and Patricia Lee Findley Heys, "Recruitment of Women for Congress: A Research Note," in *Portrait of Marginality,* ed. Githens and Prestage, pp. 210–20.

61. Joan Hulse Thompson, "Career Convergence: Election of Women and Men to the House of Representatives, 1916–1975," *Women and Politics* 5 (Spring 1985): 69–90.

62. Janet M. Martin, "The Recruitment of Women to Cabinet and Subcabinet Posts," *Western Political Quarterly* 42 (March 1989): 161–72.

63. Susan J. Carroll, "The Recruitment of Women for Cabinet-Level Posts in State Government: A Social Control Perspective," *Social Science Journal* 21 (January 1984): 91–107.

64. Carroll and Strimling, *Women's Routes,* pp. 19–20.

65. Sharyne Merritt, "Winners and Losers: Sex Differences in Municipal Elections," *American Journal of Political Science* 21 (November 1977): 731–43.

66. Sharyne Merritt, "Recruitment of Women to Suburban City Councils: Higgens vs. Chevalier," in *Women in Local Politics,* ed. Debra W. Stewart (Metuchen, N.J.: Scarecrow Press, 1980), pp. 86–105.

67. Lawrence W. Miller, "Political Recruitment and Electoral Success: A Look at Sex Differences in Municipal Elections," *Social Science Journal* 23 (Spring 1986): 75–90.

68. Susan Gluck Mezey, "The Effects of Sex on Recruitment: Connecticut Local Offices," in *Women in Local Politics,* ed. Stewart, pp. 61–85.

69. Carol A. Cassel, "Social Background Characteristics of Nonpartisan City Council Members: A Research Note," *Western Political Quarterly* 38 (September 1985): 495–501.

70. Sara E. Rix, ed., *The American Woman, 1988–89: A Status Report* (New York: Norton, 1988), p. 363.

71. Kirkpatrick, *Political Woman,* p. 61.

72. Susan J. Carroll, *Women as Candidates in American Politics* (Bloomington: Indiana University Press, 1985), p. 70.

73. Kirkpatrick, *Political Woman,* p. 83.

74. Marguerite J. Fisher, "Women in the Political Parties," *The Annals* 251 (1947): 88.

75. Eleanor Roosevelt and Lorena A. Hickok, *Ladies of Courage* (New York: Putnam's Sons, 1954), pp. 15, 38.

76. Barbara Wendell Kerr, "Don't Kid the Women," *Woman's Home Companion,* October 1956, p. 4.

77. Gruberg, *Women in American Politics,* p. 68.

78. Kirkpatrick, *Political Woman,* p. 100.

79. Stewart, ed., *Women in Local Politics.*

80. Quoted in Susan Tolchin and Martin Tolchin, *Clout: Womanpower and Politics,* 2d ed. (New York: Capricorn, 1976), p. 71.

81. Raisa Deber, "'The Fault Dear Brutus': Women as Candidates in Pennsylvania," *Journal of Politics* 44 (May 1982): 463–79.

82. Irwin Gertzog and M. Michele Simard, "Women and 'Hopeless' Congressional Candidacies," *American Politics Quarterly* 9 (October 1981): 449–66; Margery M. Ambrosius and Susan Welch, "Women and Politics at the Grassroots: Women Candidates for State Office in Three States, 1950–1978," *Social Science Journal* 21 (January 1984): 29–42; Nikki R.

Van Hightower, "The Recruitment of Women for Public Office," *American Politics Quarterly* 5 (July 1977): 301–14; Carroll, *Women as Candidates.*

83. Kathy Stanwick, *Political Women Tell What It Takes* (New Brunswick: Center for the American Woman and Politics, Eagleton Institute, Rutgers University), 1983.

84. Carroll and Strimling, *Women's Routes,* pp. 80–81, 39.

85. Jean Graves McDonald and Vicky Howell Pierson, "Female County Leaders and the Perception of Discrimination: A Test of the Male Conspiracy Theory," *Social Science Journal* 21 (January 1984): 13–20.

86. R. Darcy, Susan Welch, and Janet Clark, *Women, Elections, and Representation* (Lincoln: University of Nebraska Press, 1994).

87. Barbara Burrell, "John Bailey's Legacy: Political Parties and Women's Candidacies for Public Office," in *Women in Politics,* ed. Duke, pp. 123–34.

88. Marian Bergeson, remarks at the annual conference of California Elected Women's Association for Education and Research, Sacramento, 30 March 1989.

89. Richard Zeiger and Sherry Bebitch Jeffe, "Women in Politics," *California Journal* 19 (January 1988): 9.

90. Carroll, *Women as Candidates,* p. 169.

91. Dale Lane, "Many Non-Partisan Local Races Awash in Partisanship," *San Jose Mercury News,* 8 November 1984, p.11B.

92. Sacks, "From Welfare Mother," p. 43.

93. Bill Strobel, "Small-Town Girl Now a Big-Time Councilwoman," *San Jose Mercury News,* 1 August 1980, p. 1B.

94. See, for example, Kristi Andersen and Stuart J. Thorson, "Congressional Turnover and the Election of Women," *Western Political Quarterly* 37 (March 1984): 143–56; and Carroll, *Women as Candidates.*

95. Darcy et al., *Women, Elections, and Representation,* pp. 176–77.

96. Diamond, *Sex Roles in the State House;* Beverly Blair Cook, "Political Culture and Selection of Women Judges in Trial Courts," in *Women in Local Politics,* ed. Stewart, pp. 42–60.

97. David Hill, "Political Culture and Female Political Representation," *Journal of Politics* 43 (February 1981): 159–68.

98. Carol Nechemias, "Geographic Mobility and Women's Access to State Legislatures," *Western Political Quarterly* 38 (March 1985): 119–31.

99. Darcy et al., *Women, Elections, and Representation,* pp. 53–54.

100. Albert K. Karnig and B. Oliver Walter, "Election of Women to City Councils," *Social Science Quarterly* 56 (March 1976): 605–13; Susan Welch, Margery M. Ambrosius, Janet Clark, and Robert Darcy, "The Effect of Candidate Gender on Electoral Outcomes in State Legislative Races: A Research Note," *Western Political Quarterly* 38 (September 1985): 464–75.

101. Darcy et al., *Women, Elections, and Representation,* pp. 67–70.

102. Diane L. Fowlkes, "Women in Georgia Electoral Politics: 1970–1980," *Social Science Journal* 21 (January 1984): 43–55.

103. Beverly B. Cook, "Women on the State Bench: Correlates of Access," in *Political Women,* ed. Flammang, pp. 191–218.

104. Rule, "Why Women Don't Run."

105. Wilma Rule, "Why More Women Are State Legislators: A Research Note," *Western Political Quarterly* 43 (June 1990): 437–48.

106. Ruth B. Mandel, *In the Running: The New Woman Candidate* (New Haven: Ticknor and Fields, 1981); Carroll, *Women as Candidates,* pp. 50–55.

107. Carroll, *Women as Candidates,* pp. 50–51.

108. Gerald L. Ingalls and Theodore S. Arrington, "The Role of Gender in Local Campaign Financing: The Case of Charlotte, North Carolina," *Women and Politics* 11 (Summer 1991): 61–90.

109. Barbara Burrell, "The Presence of Women Candidates and the Role of Gender in Campaigns for the State Legislature in an Urban Setting: The Case of Massachusetts," *Women and Politics* 10 (Fall 1990): 85–102.

110. Barbara Burrell, "Women's and Men's Campaigns for the U.S. House of Representatives, 1972–1982: A Finance Gap?" *American Politics Quarterly* 13 (1985): 251–72; Robert Darcy, Margaret Brewer, and Judy Clay, "Women in the Oklahoma Political System: State Legislative Elections," *Social Science Journal* 21 (January 1984): 67–78; Carole Jean Uhlaner and Kay Lehman Scholzman, "Candidate Gender and Congressional Campaign Receipts," *Journal of Politics* 48 (February 1986): 30–50; Barbara Burrell, "The Political Opportunity of Women Candidates for the U.S. House of Representatives in 1984," *Women and Politics* 8 (Spring 1988): 51–68.

111. Center for the American Woman and Politics, *CAWP News & Notes* 9 (Winter 1993): 10–23.

112. Mandel, *In the Running*, p. 100.

113. Eric Jansen, "Women in Power," *San Jose Metro*, 10–16 July 1986, pp. 8, 9, 6, 9, 6.

114. Ibid., p. 8.

115. Bert Robinson, "San Jose's Incumbents Have Cash Advantage," *San Jose Mercury News*, 2 June 1986, pp. 1A, 14A.

116. "Money, Mailers, Endorsements and Energy Fueled McKenna Win," *San Jose Mercury News*, 8 November 1984, p. 1B.

117. Robinson, "San Jose's Incumbents"; David A. Sylvester, "Growth Is Again the Issue in San Jose," *San Francisco Chronicle*, 8 May 1990, p. A9.

118. Robinson, "San Jose's Incumbents."

119. Carroll and Strimling, *Women's Routes*, pp. 32–36.

120. Darcy et al., *Women, Elections, and Representation*, p. 156.

121. Ibid., p. 157.

122. Susan J. Carroll and Barbara Geiger-Parker, *Women Appointed to the Carter Administration: A Comparison with Men* (New Brunswick: Center for the American Woman and Politics, Eagleton Institute of Politics, Rutgers University, 1983), pp. viii–ix.

123. Kathy Stanwick, *Getting Women Appointed: New Jersey's Bipartisan Coalition* (New Brunswick: Center for the American Woman and Politics, Eagleton Institute of Politics, Rutgers University, 1984), pp. 7–8, 27–29.

124. Kate Karpilow, "The California Board and Commission Outreach Project," in CEWAER, *Moving In, Moving Up*, Spring 1990, p. 3.

125. Carroll and Strimling, *Women's Routes*, p. 9.

126. Denise Antolini, "Women in Local Government: An Overview," in *Political Women*, ed. Flammang, pp. 23–40.

127. Welles, "Power of the County," p. 27.

128. Ruth B. Mandel, "The Political Woman," in *The American Woman, 1988–89: A Status Report*, ed. Sara E. Rix (New York: Norton, 1988), pp. 78–122.

129. Irene Diamond, "Exploring the Relationship between Female Candidacies and the Women's Movement," in *Women Organizing*, ed. Bernice Cummings and Victoria Schuck (Metuchen, N.J.: Scarecrow Press, 1979), pp. 241–52.

130. Carol Mueller, "Feminism and the New Women in Public Office," *Women and Politics* 2 (Fall 1982): 7–21; and "Collective Consciousness, Identity Transformation, and the Rise of Women in Public Office in the United States," in *The Women's Movements of the United*

States and Western Europe, ed. Mary Fainsod Katzenstein and Carol McClurg Mueller (Philadelphia: Temple University Press, 1987), pp. 89–108.

131. Susan J. Carroll, "Women Candidates and Support for Feminist Concerns: The Closet Feminist Syndrome," *Western Political Quarterly* 37 (June 1984): 307–23.

132. Thomas J. Volgy, John E. Schwartz, and Hildy Gottlieb, "Female Representation and the Quest for Resources: Feminist Activism and Electoral Success," *Social Science Quarterly* 67 (March 1986): 156–68.

133. *CAWP News & Notes* 9 (Winter 1993): 10–21.

134. The following discussion of the CAWP survey is drawn from Carroll and Strimling, *Women's Routes*.

135. Louis Harris 1972 Virginia Slims poll, cited in Virginia Sapiro, *The Political Integration of Women: Roles, Socialization, and Politics* (Urbana: University of Illinois Press, 1984), p. 145.

136. Laura K. McFadden, "Offering More Than Women's Issues," *Newsday*, 19 August 1990, p. 13.

137. Quoted in Kirkpatrick, *Political Woman*, p. 87.

138. Robert Darcy and Sarah Slavin Schramm, "When Women Run against Men," *Public Opinion Quarterly* 41 (Spring 1977): 1–12; Cal Clark and Janet Clark, "The Growth of Women's Candidacies for Nontraditional Political Offices in New Mexico," *Social Science Journal* 21 (January 1984): 57–66; John F. Zipp and Eric Plutzer, "Gender Differences in Voting for Female Candidates: Evidence from the 1982 Election," *Public Opinion Quarterly* 49 (Summer 1985): 179–97.

139. Susan Gluck Mezey, "Does Sex Make a Difference? A Case Study of Women in Politics," *Western Political Quarterly* 31 (December 1978): 492–501.

140. Mandel, *In the Running*, p. 22.

141. Mary Houghton, "Prospects Bright for Women Candidates, NWPC Poll Says," *Women's Political Times* 10 (January–February 1985): 1, 8.

142. One such poll was conducted by Robert Lee for Capital Data Communications, and other polls were mentioned by people I interviewed, not for attribution.

CHAPTER 6

1. Hope Chamberlin, *A Minority of Members: Women in the U.S. Congress* (New York: Mentor, 1974); Martin Gruberg, *Women in American Politics* (Oshkosh, Wis.: Academia Press, 1968); Marilyn Johnson and Susan Carroll, "Statistical Report: Profile of Women Holding Office, 1977," in Center for the American Woman and Politics, *Women in Public Office: A Biographical Directory and Statistical Analysis* (Metuchen, N.J.: Scarecrow Press, 1978); R. Darcy, Susan Welch, and Janet Clark, *Women, Elections, and Representation* (Lincoln: University of Nebraska Press, 1994).

2. Gruberg, *Women in American Politics*, pp. 277–78.

3. Chamberlin, *Minority of Members*, p. 6.

4. Frieda L. Gehlen, "Legislative Role Performance of Female Legislators," *Sex Roles* 3:1 (1977): 11–18.

5. Irene Diamond, *Sex Roles in the State House* (New Haven: Yale University Press, 1977).

6. Emmy E. Werner and Louise M. Bachtold, "Personality Characteristics of Women in American Politics, in *Women in Politics*, ed. Jane S. Jaquette (New York: Wiley, 1974), pp. 75–84.

7. Shelah Gilbert Leader, "The Policy Impact of Elected Women Officials," in *The Impact of the Electoral Process*, ed. Louis Maisel and Joseph Cooper (Beverly Hills, Calif.: Sage, 1977), pp. 265–84.

8. Kathleen A. Frankovic, "Sex and Voting in the U.S. House of Representatives: 1961–1975," *American Politics Quarterly* 5 (July 1977): 315–30.

9. Johnson and Carroll, "Statistical Report."

10. Susan Welch, "Are Women More Liberal than Men in the U.S. Congress?" *Legislative Studies Quarterly* 10 (February 1985): 125–34.

11. Susan J. Carroll and Barbara Geiger-Parker, *Women Appointed to the Carter Administration: A Comparison with Men* (New Brunswick: Center for the American Woman and Politics, Eagleton Institute, Rutgers University, 1983).

12. Nancy McGlen and Meredith Reid Sarkees, "The Unseen Influence of Women in the State and Defense Departments," in *Gender and Policymaking: Studies of Women in Office*, ed. Debra L. Dodson (New Brunswick: Center for the American Woman and Politics, Eagleton Institute, Rutgers University, 1991), pp. 81–92.

13. John C. Wahlke, Heinz Eulau, William Buchanan, and Leroy C. Ferguson, *The Legislative System: Explorations in Legislative Behavior* (New York: Wiley, 1962).

14. Jeane J. Kirkpatrick, *Political Woman* (New York: Basic Books, 1974), p. 155.

15. Ibid., p. 43.

16. Ibid., p. 159.

17. Ibid., p. 157.

18. Quoted in ibid.

19. Marianne Githens, "Spectators, Agitators, or Lawmakers: Women in State Legislatures," in *A Portrait of Marginality: The Political Behavior of the American Woman*, ed. Marianne Githens and Jewel L. Prestage (New York: McKay, 1977), pp. 196–209.

20. Joan Hulse Thompson, "Role Perceptions of Women in the Ninety-fourth Congress, 1975–1976," *Political Science Quarterly* 95 (Spring 1980): 71–81.

21. James D. Barber, *The Lawmakers* (New Haven: Yale University Press, 1965).

22. Werner and Bachtold, "Personality Characteristics."

23. Githens, "Spectators, Agitators, or Lawmakers," p. 206.

24. Kirkpatrick, *Political Woman*, pp. 170–216, quotation from p. 176.

25. Quoted in ibid., p. 214.

26. Hanna Pitkin, *The Concept of Representation* (Berkeley: University of California Press, 1967).

27. Kirkpatrick, *Political Woman*, pp. 142–47.

28. Ibid., pp. 143–44.

29. Ibid., pp. 106, 109.

30. Irwin Gertzog, *Congressional Women: Their Recruitment, Treatment, and Behavior* (New York: Praeger, 1984), pp. 51–75, quotation from p. 54.

31. Ibid., p. 55.

32. Ibid., p. 57.

33. Ibid., pp. 60–62, quotation from pp. 61–62.

34. Frieda L. Gehlen, "Women in Congress," *Trans-Action* 6 (October 1969): 36–40.

35. Ibid., p. 40.

36. Thompson, "Role Perceptions of Women."

37. Emmy Werner, "Women in State Legislatures," *Western Political Quarterly* 21 (March 1968): 40–50.

38. Marianne Githens and Jewel L. Prestage, "Styles and Priorities of Marginality: Women State Legislators," in *Race, Sex, and Policy Problems*, ed. Marian Lief Palley and Michael B. Preston (Lexington, Mass.: Lexington Books, 1979), pp. 221–35.

39. Gehlen, "Legislative Role Performance."

40. Jeanie R. Stanley and Diane D. Blair, "Gender Differences in Legislative Effectiveness: The Impact of the Legislative Environment," in *Gender and Policymaking*, ed. Dodson, pp. 115–29.

41. Marianne Githens, "Women and State Politics: An Assessment," in *Political Women: Current Roles in State and Local Government*, ed. Janet A. Flammang (Beverly Hills, Calif.: Sage, 1984), pp. 41–63, quotation from p. 54.

42. Githens, "Spectators, Agitators, or Lawmakers."

43. Karen Van Wagner and Cheryl Swanson, "From Machiavelli to Ms.: Differences in Male-Female Power Styles," *Public Administration Review* 39 (January–February 1979): 66–72.

44. Gertzog, *Congressional Women*, pp. 167–79, quotations from pp. 177–78, 179.

45. Kirkpatrick, *Political Woman*, p. 120–21.

46. Marcia Manning Lee, "The Participation of Women in Suburban Politics: A Study of the Influence of Women as Compared to Men in Suburban Governmental Decision-Making" (Ph.D. dissertation, Tufts University, 1973).

47. Diamond, *Sex Roles in the State House*, p. 47.

48. Johnson and Carroll, "Statistical Report."

49. Lyn Kathlene, "Uncovering the Political Impacts of Gender: An Exploratory Study," *Western Political Quarterly* 42 (June 1989): 397–421.

50. Nancy Chodorow, "Family Structure and Feminine Personality," in *Women, Culture, and Society*, ed. Michelle Zimbalist Rosaldo and Louise Lamphere (Stanford: Stanford University Press, 1974), pp. 43–66; Carol Gilligan, *In a Different Voice: Psychological Theory and Women's Development* (Cambridge: Harvard University Press, 1982); Nel Noddings, *Caring: A Feminine Approach to Ethics and Moral Education* (Berkeley: University of California Press, 1984).

51. Kathlene, "Political Impacts of Gender."

52. Ibid.

53. Lyn Kathlene, "Power and Influence in State Legislative Policymaking: The Interaction of Gender and Position in Committee Hearing Debates" (paper presented at the annual meeting of the American Political Science Association, Chicago, 1992).

54. Lyn Kathlene, Susan E. Clarke, and Barbara A. Fox, "Ways Women Politicians Are Making a Difference," in *Gender and Policymaking*, ed. Dodson, pp. 31–38.

55. Susan E. Clarke and Lyn Kathlene, "Women as Political Actors and Policy Analysts" (paper presented at the annual meeting of the Association for Public Policy Analysis and Management, Denver, 1992).

56. Gertzog, *Congressional Women*.

57. Ibid., pp. 117–18.

58. Quoted in Chamberlin, *Minority of Members*, p. 264.

59. Gertzog, *Congressional Women*, pp. 165–66.

60. Joyce Gelb and Marian Lief Palley, *Women and Public Policies* (Princeton: Princeton University Press, 1987), p. 99.

61. Gertzog, *Congressional Women*, pp. 163–67, 181–83.

62. Jo Freeman, *The Politics of Women's Liberation: A Case Study of an Emerging Social Movement and Its Relation to the Policy Process* (New York: McKay, 1975), p. 236.

63. Kirkpatrick, *Political Woman*, pp. 164–67.

64. Gehlen, "Women in Congress."

65. Frieda L. Gehlen, "Women Members of Congress: A Distinctive Role," in *Portrait of Marginality*, ed. Githens and Prestage, pp. 304–19.

66. Gehlen, "Legislative Role Performance."

67. Gertzog, *Congressional Women*, p. 142.

68. Ibid., p. 143.

69. Quoted in Peggy Lamson, *Few Are Chosen: American Women in Political Life Today* (Boston: Houghton Mifflin, 1968), p. 107.

70. Quoted in Gertzog, *Congressional Women*, p. 159.

71. Geraldine Ferraro, "Women as Candidates," *Harvard Political Review* 7 (1979): 21–24.

72. Gertzog, *Congressional Women*, p. 161.

73. Johnson and Carroll, "Statistical Report," pp. 1A–68A.

74. Carroll and Geiger-Parker, *Women Appointed*, pp. 72–73.

75. Joanne V. Hawks and Carolyn Ellis Staton, "On the Eve of Transition: Women in Southern Legislatures, 1946–1968," in *Women in Politics: Outsiders or Insiders?* ed. Lois Lovelace Duke (Englewood Cliffs, N.J.: Prentice Hall, 1993), pp. 97–106.

76. Werner, "Women in State Legislatures."

77. Diamond, *Sex Roles in the State House.*

78. Jewel L. Prestage, "Black Women State Legislators: A Profile," in *Portrait of Marginality*, ed. Githens and Prestage, pp. 401–18.

79. Leader, "Policy Impact of Elected Women Officials."

80. Johnson and Carroll, "Statistical Report," pp. 33A–37A.

81. Joyce Lilie, Roger Handberg, Jr., and Wanda Lowrey, "Women State Legislators and the ERA: Dimensions of Support and Opposition," *Women and Politics* 2 (Spring–Summer 1982): 23–38.

82. David B. Hill, "Women State Legislators and Party Voting on the ERA," *Social Science Quarterly* 64 (June 1983): 318–26.

83. Carol Mueller, "Women's Organizational Strategies in State Legislatures," in *Political Women*, ed. Flammang, pp. 156–76.

84. Ibid., pp. 170–71.

85. Center for the American Woman and Politics (CAWP), "Women in Elective Office 1990," fact sheet (New Brunswick: National Information Bank on Women in Public Office, Eagleton Institute of Politics, Rutgers University, 1990).

86. Rosabeth M. Kanter, "Some Effects of Proportions on Group Life: Skewed Sex Ratios and Response to Token Women," *American Journal of Sociology* 82 (March 1977): 965–90.

87. Michelle A. Saint-Germain, "Does Their Difference Make a Difference? The Impact of Women in Public Policy in the Arizona Legislature," *Social Science Quarterly* 70 (December 1989): 956–68.

88. Beth Ann Reingold, "Representing Women: Gender Differences among Arizona and California State Legislators" (Ph.D. dissertation, University of California at Berkeley, 1992), pp. 162–63.

89. Ibid., pp. 163–65, quotation from pp. 164–65.

90. Ibid., pp. 474–91.

91. Susan J. Carroll, Debra L. Dodson, and Ruth B. Mandel, *The Impact of Women in Public Office: An Overview* (New Brunswick: Center for the American Woman and Politics, Eagleton Institute, Rutgers University, 1991).

92. Debra L. Dodson and Susan J. Carroll, *Reshaping the Agenda: Women in State Legislatures* (New Brunswick: Center for the American Woman and Politics, Eagleton Institute, Rutgers University, 1991), p. 11.

93. Susan Welch and Sue Thomas, "Do Women in Public Office Make a Difference?" in *Gender and Policymaking*, ed. Dodson, pp. 13–19; see also Sue Thomas and Susan Welch,

"The Impact of Gender on Activities and Priorities of State Legislators," *Western Political Quarterly* 44 (June 1991): 445–56.

94. Catherine M. Havens and Lynne M. Healy, "Cabinet Level Appointees in Connecticut: Women Making a Difference," in *Gender and Policymaking*, ed. Dodson, pp. 21–30.

95. Elaine F. Martin, "Differences in Men and Women Judges: Perspectives on Gender," *Journal of Political Science* 17 (Spring 1989): 74–85.

96. Elaine Martin, "Judicial Gender and Judicial Choices," in *Gender and Policymaking*, ed. Dodson, pp. 49–61.

97. Ibid.

98. Rita Mae Kelly, Mary M. Hale, and Jayne Burgess, "Gender and Managerial/Leadership Styles: A Comparison of Arizona Public Administrators," *Women and Politics* 11 (Summer 1991): 19–40.

99. Georgia Duerst-Lahti and Cathy Marie Johnson, "Gender and Style in Bureaucracy," *Women and Politics* 10 (Winter 1990): 67–120.

100. Mueller, "Women's Organizational Strategies," pp. 171–72.

101. Sue Thomas, "Voting Patterns in the California Assembly: The Role of Gender," *Women and Politics* 9 (Winter 1989): 43–56.

102. Judy H. Bers, "Local Political Elites: Men and Women on Boards of Education," *Western Political Quarterly* 31 (September 1978): 381–91.

103. Susan Gluck Mezey, "Does Sex Make a Difference? A Case Study of Women in Politics," *Western Political Quarterly* 31 (December 1978): 492–501.

104. Susan Gluck Mezey, "Women and Representation: The Case of Hawaii," *Journal of Politics* 40 (May 1978): 369–85.

105. Susan Gluck Mezey, "Support for Women's Rights Policy: An Analysis of Local Politicians," *American Politics Quarterly* 6 (October 1978): 485–97.

106. Susan Gluck Mezey, "Perceptions of Women's Roles on Local Councils in Connecticut," in *Women in Local Politics*, ed. Debra W. Stewart (Metuchen, N.J.: Scarecrow Press, 1980), pp. 177–97.

107. Johnson and Carroll, "Statistical Report."

108. Ibid.

109. Beverly Blair Cook, "Women Judges and Public Policy in Sex Integration," in *Women in Local Politics*, ed. Stewart, pp. 130–48.

110. Sharyne Merritt, "Sex Differences in Role Behavior and Policy Orientations of Suburban Officeholders: The Effect of Women's Employment," in *Women in Local Politics*, ed. Stewart, pp. 115–29.

111. Sue Tolleson Rinehart, "Do Women Leaders Make a Difference? Substance, Style, and Perceptions," in *Gender and Policymaking*, ed. Dodson, pp. 93–102, quotation from p. 102.

112. Jeanette Jennings, "Black Women Mayors: Reflections on Race and Gender," in *Gender and Policymaking*, ed. Dodson, pp. 73–79.

113. Sue Thomas, "The Effects of Race and Gender on Constituency Service," *Western Political Quarterly* 45 (March 1992): 169–80.

114. Sandra Shew Campbell and Barbara A. Presnall, "Assessment of Male and Female Leadership in Local Government" (paper presented at the annual meeting of the American Political Science Association, San Francisco, 1990).

115. Susan Abrams Beck, "Rethinking Municipal Governance: Gender Distinctions on Local Councils," in *Gender and Policymaking*, ed. Dodson, pp. 103–13.

116. The material from this section is taken from Janet A. Flammang, "Female Officials in the Feminist Capital: The Case of Santa Clara County," *Western Political Quarterly* 38 (March 1985): 105–14.

117. Connie Skipitares, "Female Majorities on Council, Board Shun Feminist Label," *San Jose Mercury News,* 6 November 1980, p. 1B.

118. Minutes provided by Supervisor Diridon's office; Joe Stell, "Diridon Lends Sympathetic Ear as Women's Congress Meets," *San Jose Mercury News,* 10 March 1982, p. 11.

119. Quoted in Lynn Meyerson, "Women's Panel May Die in Budget Cuts," *San Jose Mercury News,* 20 June 1982, p. 2B.

120. This account is drawn from John H. Bunzel, "To Each According to Her Worth?" *Public Interest* 67 (Spring 1982): 77–93; Mike McGuire, "A New Way to Equal Pay: Women Win in San Jose," *Dollars and Sense* (April 1982): 12–14; and Philip J. Trounstine and Gary Swan, "Job Comparison Study: How It Was Done," *San Jose Mercury News,* 8 July 1981, p. 1A.

121. Quoted in Philip J. Trounstine, "City Workers Ratify Contract for $5.4 Million to End Strike," *San Jose Mercury News,* 15 July 1981, p. 1A.

122. Dorothy Ellenberg, fact sheet on Budget Advocacy Campaign, Coalition for Effective Human Services, San Jose, 6 July 1982.

123. "City Council Approves Hammer's Neighborhood Outreach Program," *El Observador,* 11 April 1990.

124. Maline Hazle, "Child Care Gains a Starring Role in Mayor's Race," *San Jose Mercury News,* 25 March 1990, pp. 1B–2B.

125. Larry N. Gerston, "Where Hammer Won Support," *San Jose Mercury News,* 11 November 1990, pp. 1C, 3C.

126. "Drawing on Diversity," editorial, *San Jose Mercury News,* 4 March 1991, p. 6B.

127. Fran Smith, "What's a Mayor to Do?" *West Magazine, San Jose Mercury News,* 13 January 1991, p. 12.

128. "Local 101 Endorses Susan Hammer for Mayor," *Union News, AFSCME Local 101,* Spring 1990, p. 1.

CHAPTER 7

1. Roger W. Cobb and Charles D. Elder, *Participation in American Politics: The Dynamics of Agenda-Building* (Boston: Allyn and Bacon, 1972).

2. John W. Kingdon, *Agendas, Alternatives, and Public Policies* (New York: Harper Collins, 1984).

3. L. Marvin Overby and Sarah J. Ritchie, "Mobilized Masses and Strategic Opponents: A Resource Mobilization Analysis of the Clean Air and Nuclear Freeze Movements," *Western Political Quarterly* 44 (June 1991): 329–52.

4. Susan Faludi, *Backlash: The Undeclared War against American Women* (New York: Crown, 1991).

5. Linda Gordon, *Heroes of Their Own Lives: The Politics and History of Family Violence* (New York: Viking, 1988).

6. Anne N. Costain and W. Douglas Costain, "Movements and Gatekeepers: Congressional Responses to Women's Movement Issues, 1900–1982," *Congress and the Presidency* 12 (Spring 1985): 21–42.

7. Ellen Boneparth, "A Framework for Policy Analysis," in *Women, Power, and Policy,* ed. Ellen Boneparth (New York: Pergamon, 1982), p. 1.

8. Martha A. Ackelsberg, "Feminist Analyses of Public Policy," *Comparative Politics* (July 1992): 477–93.

9. Jo Freeman, *The Politics of Women's Liberation: A Case Study of an Emerging Social Movement and Its Relation to the Policy Process* (New York: McKay, 1975).

10. Ibid., pp. 171–72.

11. Ibid., pp. 231–32.

12. Ibid., p. 222.

13. Irene Tinker, ed., *Women in Washington: Advocates for Public Policy* (Beverly Hills, Calif.: Sage, 1983).

14. Irwin N. Gertzog, *Congressional Women: Their Recruitment, Treatment, and Behavior* (New York: Praeger, 1984), pp. 248–50.

15. Debra W. Stewart, "Commissions on the Status of Women and Building a Local Policy Agenda," in *Women in Local Politics,* ed. Debra W. Stewart (Metuchen, N.J.: Scarecrow Press, 1980), pp. 198–214; Rina Rosenberg, "Representing Women at the State and Local Level: Commissions on the Status of Women," in *Women, Power, and Policy,* ed. Boneparth, pp. 38–46.

16. Janet K. Boles, "Advancing the Women's Agenda within Local Legislatures: The Role of Female Elected Officials," in *Gender and Policymaking: Studies of Women in Office,* ed. Debra L. Dodson (New Brunswick: Center for the American Woman and Politics, Eagleton Institute, Rutgers University, 1991), pp. 39–48.

17. Joyce Gelb and Marian Lief Palley, *Women and Public Policies* (Princeton: Princeton University Press, 1987).

18. Ibid.

19. Ibid.

20. Jane Roberts Chapman, "Policy Centers: An Essential Resource," in *Women in Washington,* ed. Tinker, pp. 177–90.

21. See, for example, Barbara Nelson, *Making an Issue of Child Abuse: Political Agenda Setting for Social Problems* (Chicago: University of Chicago Press, 1984); and B. Guy Peters, *American Public Policy: Promise and Performance* (Chatham, N.J.: Chatham House, 1986).

22. Rosalind Pollack Petchesky, "Antiabortion, Antifeminism, and the Rise of the New Right," *Feminist Studies* 7 (Summer 1981): 206–46.

23. Zillah Eisenstein, "Antifeminism in the Politics and Election of 1980," *Feminist Studies* 7 (Summer 1981): 187–205.

24. Pamela J. Conover and Virginia Gray, *Feminism and the New Right: Conflict over the American Family* (New York: Praeger, 1983).

25. Ibid., p. 199.

26. Rebecca E. Klatch, *Women of the New Right* (Philadelphia: Temple University Press, 1987); and "The Two Worlds of Women of the New Right," in *Women, Politics, and Change,* ed. Louise A. Tilly and Patricia Gurin (New York: Russell Sage, 1990), pp. 529–52.

27. Susan E. Marshall, "Keep Us on the Pedestal: Women against Feminism in Twentieth-Century America," in *Women: A Feminist Perspective,* ed. Jo Freeman, 3d ed. (Palo Alto, Calif.: Mayfield, 1984), pp. 568–81.

28. Bonnie Cook Freeman, "Antifeminists and Women's Liberation: A Case Study of a Paradox," *Women and Politics* 3 (Spring 1983): 21–38.

29. Kent L. Tedin, "Religious Preference and Pro/Anti Activism on the Equal Rights Amendment," *Pacific Sociological Review* 21 (January 1978): 55–66.

30. Margaret Ann Latus, "What Every Feminist Should Know about Mobilization Tactics of the Christian Right in Elections" (paper presented at the annual meeting of the American Political Science Association, Denver, 1982).

31. Robert Booth Fowler, "The Feminist and Antifeminist Debate within Evangelical Protestantism," *Women and Politics* 5 (Summer–Fall 1985): 7–39.

32. Clyde Wilcox, "Feminism and Anti-feminism among White Evangelical Women," *Western Political Quarterly* 42 (March 1989): 147–60.

33. Robert Wuthnow and William Lehrman, "Religion: Inhibitor or Facilitator of Political Involvement among Women?" in *Women, Politics, and Change*, ed. Tilly and Gurin, pp. 300–322.

34. Linda Gordon, "The New Feminist Scholarship on the Welfare State," in *Women, the State, and Welfare*, ed. Linda Gordon (Madison: University of Wisconsin Press, 1990), pp. 9–35.

35. Carol Brown, "Mothers, Fathers, and Children: From Private to Public Patriarchy," in *Women and Revolution*, ed. Lydia Sargent (Boston: South End Press, 1981), pp. 239–67.

36. Steven P. Erie, Martin Rein, and Barbara Wiget, "Women and the Reagan Revolution: Thermidor for the Social Welfare Economy," in *Families, Politics, and Public Policy*, ed. Irene Diamond (New York: Longman, 1983), pp. 94–119.

37. Irene Diamond, "Introduction," in *Families, Politics, and Public Policy*, ed. Diamond, pp. 1–17.

38. Birte Siim, "Towards a Feminist Rethinking of the Welfare State," in *The Political Interests of Gender*, ed. Kathleen B. Jones and Anna G. Jonasdottir (London: Sage, 1988), pp. 160–86.

39. See, for example, the chapters in *Women, the State, and Welfare*, ed. Gordon.

40. Frances Fox Piven, "Ideology and the State: Women, Power, and the Welfare State," in *Women, the State, and Welfare*, ed. Gordon, p. 260.

41. Judith Hicks Stiehm, "Women, Men, and Military Service: Is Protection Necessarily a Racket?" in *Women, Power, and Policy*, ed. Boneparth, pp. 282–93, quotations from pp. 282, 292.

42. See, for example, Birgit Brock-Utne, *Educating for Peace: A Feminist Perspective* (New York: Pergamon, 1985); Birgit Brock-Utne, *Feminist Perspectives on Peace and Peace Education* (New York: Pergamon, 1989); and Adrienne Harris and Ynestra King, eds., *Rocking the Ship of State: Toward a Feminist Peace Politics* (Boulder, Colo.: Westview, 1989).

43. Sara Ruddick, "Pacifying the Forces: Drafting Women in the Interests of Peace," *Signs* 8 (Spring 1983): 471–89.

44. Nancy C. M. Hartsock, "Masculinity, Heroism, and the Making of War," in *Rocking the Ship of State*, ed. Harris and King, pp. 133–49.

45. Roberta M. Spalter-Roth and Heidi Hartmann, *Unnecessary Losses: Costs to Americans of the Lack of Family and Medical Leave* (Washington, D.C.: Institute for Women's Policy Research, 1990).

46. Roberta Spalter-Roth and Heidi Hartmann, "Science and Politics: The 'Dual Vision' of Feminist Policy Research—The Example of Family and Medical Leave," in *First Annual Women's Policy Research Conference Proceedings* (Washington, D.C.: Institute for Women's Policy Research, 1990), p. 110.

47. Susan E. Clarke and Lyn Kathlene, "Women as Political Actors and Policy Analysts" (paper presented at the annual meeting of the Association for Public Policy Analysis and Management, Denver, 1992).

48. Dorothy McBride Stetson, *Women's Rights in the U.S.A.: Policy Debates and Gender Roles* (Pacific Grove, Calif.: Brooks-Cole, 1991), pp. 222–23.

49. Dierdre Silverman, "Sexual Harassment: Working Women's Dilemma," in *Building Feminist Theory: Essays from "Quest, A Feminist Quarterly,"* ed. Charlotte Bunch (New York: Longman, 1981), pp. 84–93.

50. Catharine A. MacKinnon, *Sexual Harassment of Working Women: A Case of Sex Discrimination* (New Haven: Yale University Press, 1979), p. xi.

51. Ibid., pp. xii–xiii.

52. *Meritor Savings Bank, FSB v. Vinson,* 106 S.Ct. 2399 (1986).

53. Catharine A. MacKinnon, "Sexual Harassment: Its First Decade in Court," in *Feminism Unmodified: Discourses on Life and Law,* ed. Catharine A. MacKinnon (Cambridge: Harvard University Press, 1987), p. 103.

54. Susan Ehrlich Martin, "Sexual Harassment: The Link Joining Gender Stratification, Sexuality, and Women's Economic Status," in *Women: A Feminist Perspective,* ed. Jo Freeman, 4th ed., (Mountain View, Calif.: Mayfield, 1989), pp. 57–75.

55. Tamar Lewin, "Nude Pictures Are Ruled Sexual Harassment," *New York Times,* 23 January 1991.

56. Linda Greenhouse, "Court, 9–0, Makes Sex Harassment Easier to Prove," *New York Times,* 10 November 1993, pp. A1, A15. The case was *Teresa Harris v. Forklift Systems, Inc.,* No. 92–1168.

57. Gordon, *Heroes of Their Own Lives.* See also Elizabeth Pleck, *Domestic Tyranny: The Making of Social Policy against Family Violence from Colonial Times to the Present* (New York: Oxford University Press, 1987).

58. Sandra Wexler, "Battered Women and Public Policy," in *Women, Power, and Policy,* ed. Boneparth, pp. 184–204.

59. Data from this 1976 National Violence Survey were cited in hearings conducted by a subcommittee of the House Committee on Science and Technology and published in *Research into Violent Behavior: Domestic Violence Hearings* (Washington, D.C.: U.S. Government Printing Office, 1978), pp. 72–77.

60. Erin Pizzey, *Scream Quietly or the Neighbours Will Hear* (Harmondsworth, England: Penguin, 1974).

61. Wexler, "Battered Women and Public Policy," pp. 188–89.

62. Ibid., pp. 194–96.

63. Stetson, *Women's Rights in the U.S.A.,* p. 248.

64. Joyce Gelb, "The Politics of Wife Abuse," in *Families, Politics, and Public Policy,* ed. Diamond, pp. 250–62.

65. Stetson, *Women's Rights in the U.S.A.,* p. 248.

66. Jean Grossholtz, "Battered Women's Shelters and the Political Economy of Sexual Violence," in *Families, Politics, and Public Policy,* ed. Diamond, pp. 59–69.

67. Carole J. Sheffield, "Sexual Terrorism," in *Women,* ed. Freeman, 3d ed., pp. 3–19.

68. Kathleen Barry, *Female Sexual Slavery* (New York: New York University Press, 1979); and "Female Sexual Slavery: The Problem, Policies and Cause for Feminist Action," in *Women, Power, and Policy,* ed. Ellen Boneparth and Emily Stoper, 2d ed. (New York: Pergamon, 1988), pp. 282–96, quotations from pp. 283–84.

69. Inge Powell Bell, "The Double Standard: Age," in *Women,* ed. Freeman, 3d ed., pp. 256–63; Laura Olson Katz, "Older Women: Longevity, Dependency, and Public Policy," in *Women, Biology, and Public Policy,* ed. Virginia Sapiro (Beverly Hills, Calif.: Sage, 1985), pp. 157–75.

70. Jane Jaquette and Kathleen Staudt, "Women as 'At Risk' Reproducers: Biology, Science, and Population in U.S. Foreign Policy," in *Women, Biology, and Public Policy,* ed. Sapiro, pp. 235–68; Jane S. Jaquette and Kathleen A. Staudt, "Politics, Population, and Gender: A Feminist Analysis of U.S. Population Policy in the Third World," in *Political Interests of Gender,* ed. Jones and Jonasdottir, pp. 214–33.

71. Kathryn Daly, "New Feminist Definitions of Justice," in *First Annual Women's Policy Research Conference Proceedings,* pp. 7–12; Victor F. D'Lugin, "On Credibility: Differential Treatment of Women and Men in the Law," in *Women in Politics: Outsiders or Insiders?* ed. Lois Lovelace Duke (Englewood Cliffs, N.J.: Prentice Hall, 1993), pp. 185–97.

72. Emily Stoper and Ellen Boneparth, "Divorce and the Transition to the Single-Parent Family," in *Women, Power, and Policy*, ed. Boneparth and Stoper, 2d ed., pp. 206–18; Lenore J. Weitzman, *The Divorce Revolution* (New York: Free Press, 1985).

73. Mary Jo Bane, "Politics and Policies of the Feminization of Poverty," in *The Politics of Social Policy in the United States*, ed. Margaret Weir, Ann Shola Orloff, and Theda Skocpol (Princeton: Princeton University Press, 1988), pp. 381–96; Diana M. Pearce, "The Feminization of Poverty: Update," in *First Annual Women's Policy Research Conference Proceedings*, pp. 147–52.

74. Margaret Benston, "The Political Economy of Women's Liberation," *Monthly Review* 21 (September 1969): 13–27; Myra Marx Ferree, "Housework: Rethinking Costs and Benefits," in *Families, Politics, and Public Policy*, ed. Diamond, pp. 148–67.

75. Barbara Deckard and Howard Sherman, "Monopoly Power and Sex Discrimination," *Politics and Society* 4:4 (1974): 475–82; Heidi Hartmann, "Capitalism, Patriarchy, and Job Segregation by Sex," *Signs* 1 (Spring 1976): 137–69.

76. Kathleen Christensen and Halina Maslanka, "Flexible Schedules in U.S. Businesses," in *Second Annual Women's Policy Research Conference Proceedings* (Washington, D.C.: Institute for Women's Policy Research, 1991), pp. 201–5; Emily Stoper, "Alternative Work Patterns and the Double Life," in *Women, Power, and Policy*, ed. Boneparth and Stoper, 2d ed., pp. 93–112.

77. Sheila B. Kamerman and Alfred J. Kahn, "Child Care and Privatization under Reagan," in *Privatization and the Welfare State*, ed. Sheila B. Kamerman and Alfred J. Kahn (Princeton: Princeton University Press, 1989), pp. 235–59; Jill Norgren, "In Search of a National Child-Care Policy," in *Women, Power, and Policy*, ed. Boneparth and Stoper, 2d ed., pp. 168–89.

78. Diane W. Franklin and Joan L. Sweeney, "Women and Corporate Power," in *Women, Power, and Politics*, ed. Boneparth and Stoper, 2d ed., pp. 48–65.

79. Maureen Paul, Cynthia Daniels, and Robert Rosofsky, "Health, Equality, and Reproductive Risks at the Workplace," in *Second Annual Women's Policy Research Conference Proceedings*, pp. 76–80; Louise A. Williams, "Toxic Exposure in the Workplace: Balancing Job Opportunity with Reproductive Health," in *Women, Power, and Policy*, ed. Boneparth and Stoper, 2d ed., pp. 113–30.

80. Roberta M. Spalter-Roth, Claudia Withers, and Sheila R. Gibbs, "Ten-Year Legal and Economic Impact of the Pregnancy Discrimination Act of 1978," in *Second Annual Women's Policy Research Conference Proceedings*, pp. 229–37; Lise Vogel, "Debating Difference: Pregnancy, Feminism, and the Workplace," *Feminist Studies* 16 (Spring 1990): 9–32.

81. Suzanne E. England and Beatrice T. Naulleau, "Women, Work, and Eldercare: The Family and Medical Leave Debate," *Women and Politics* 11 (Summer 1991): 91–107; Joan Hulse Thompson, "The Family and Medical Leave Act: A Policy for Families," in *Women in Politics*, ed. Duke, pp. 212–26.

82. Jo Freeman, "Women, Law, and Public Policy," in *Women*, ed. Freeman, 3d ed., pp. 381–401; Jo Freeman, "From Protection to Equal Opportunity: The Revolution in Women's Legal Status," in *Women, Politics, and Change*, ed. Tilly and Gurin, pp. 457–81.

83. Zillah R. Eisenstein, *The Female Body and the Law* (Berkeley: University of California Press, 1988).

84. Catharine A. MacKinnon, "Legal Perspectives on Sexual Difference," in *Theoretical Perspectives on Sexual Difference*, ed. Deborah L. Rhode (New Haven: Yale University Press, 1990), pp. 213–25; Deborah L. Rhode, "Definitions of Difference," in *Theoretical Perspectives on Sexual Difference*, ed. Rhode, pp. 197–212.

85. Deborah L. Rhode, *Justice and Gender: Sex Discrimination and the Law* (Cambridge: Harvard University Press, 1989).

86. Ibid., pp. 244–45.

87. Susan Brownmiller, *Against Our Will: Men, Women, and Rape* (New York: Simon and Schuster, 1975).

88. Rhode, *Justice and Gender,* p. 251.

89. Dianne Herman, "The Rape Culture," in *Women,* ed, Freeman, 2d ed., pp. 41–63.

90. *Roth v. United States* (1956).

91. *Miller v. California* (1973); Rhode, *Justice and Gender,* p. 265.

92. Rhode, *Justice and Gender,* pp. 265–66.

93. Sue Bessmer, "Antiobscenity: A Comparison of the Legal and Feminist Perspectives," in *Women, Power, and Policy,* ed. Boneparth, pp. 167–83.

94. Catharine A. MacKinnon, "Francis Biddle's Sister: Pornography, Civil Rights, and Speech," in *Feminism Unmodified,* ed. MacKinnon, pp. 163–97.

95. Ibid.

96. *American Booksellers Association v. Hudnut,* 771 F.2d 323 (7th Cir. 1985).

97. *New York Times,* 25 February 1986, pp. 1, 12.

98. See, for example, the discussion of Feminists Against Censorship Task Force (FACT) in Alida Brill, "Freedom, Fantasy, Foes, and Feminism: The Debate around Pornography," in *Women, Politics, and Change,* ed. Tilly and Gurin, pp. 503–28.

99. Nadean Bishop, "Abortion: The Controversial Choice," in *Women,* ed. Freeman, 4th ed., p. 45.

100. Melvin L. Wulf, "On the Origins of Privacy," *The Nation,* 27 May 1991, pp. 700, 702–4.

101. Linda Gordon, *Woman's Body, Woman's Right: A Social History of Birth Control in America* (New York: Penguin, 1977), pp. xv–xviii.

102. "NOW (National Organization for Women) Bill of Rights," in *Sisterhood Is Powerful: An Anthology of Writings from the Women's Liberation Movement,* ed. Robin Morgan (New York: Vintage, 1970), pp. 512–14.

103. Kristin Luker, *Abortion and the Politics of Motherhood* (Berkeley: University of California Press, 1984), p. 97.

104. Ibid., p. 101.

105. Ibid., pp. 108–21.

106. Wendy Brown, "Reproductive Freedom and the Right to Privacy," in *Families, Politics, and Public Policy,* ed. Diamond, pp. 322–38.

107. The Boston Women's Health Book Collective, *Our Bodies, Ourselves: A Book By and For Women,* 2d ed. (New York: Simon and Schuster, 1979), p. 11.

108. Barbara Ehrenrich and Dierdre English, *For Her Own Good: One Hundred Fifty Years of the Experts' Advice to Women* (New York: Anchor Doubleday, 1978); Barbara Katz Rothman, "Women, Health, and Medicine," in *Women,* ed. Freeman, 2d ed., pp. 27–40.

109. Barbara Katz Rothman, "Childbirth Management and Medical Monopoly," in *Women, Biology, and Public Policy,* ed. Sapiro, pp. 117–35.

110. Patricia Schroeder and Olympia Snowe, "The Politics of Women's Health," in *The American Woman, 1994–95: Where We Stand, Women and Health,* ed. Cynthia Costello and Anne J. Stone (New York: Norton, 1994), p. 92.

111. Ibid., p. 95.

112. Gelb and Palley, *Women and Public Policies,* pp. 10–11. For alternative explanations for the defeat of the ERA, see Mary Frances Berry, *Why the ERA Failed: Politics, Women's Rights, and the Amending Process of the Constitution* (Bloomington: Indiana University Press, 1986); Val Burris, "Who Opposed the ERA? An Analysis of the Social Basis of Antifeminism," *Social Science Quarterly* 64 (June 1983): 305–17; Elinor Langer, "Why Big Business Is

Trying to Defeat the ERA," *Ms.* 4 (May 1976): 64–66, 100–108; and Jane Mansbridge, *Why We Lost the ERA* (Chicago: University of Chicago Press, 1986).

113. Judith Hicks Stiehm, *Bring Me Men and Women: Mandated Change at the U.S. Air Force Academy* (Berkeley: University of California Press, 1981), p. 4.

114. Judith Hicks Stiehm, *Arms and the Enlisted Woman* (Philadelphia: Temple University Press, 1989).

115. Freeman, *Politics of Women's Liberation,* pp. 175–76.

116. Gelb and Palley, *Women and Public Policies,* pp. 61–64.

117. Ibid., p. 100.

118. This account of the Mid-Peninsula Support Network is drawn from Anne Wurr, "Community Responses to Violence against Women: The Case of a Battered Women's Shelter," in *Political Women: Current Roles in State and Local Government,* ed. Janet A. Flammang (Beverly Hills, Calif.: Sage, 1984), pp. 221–41.

119. Ibid., p. 222.

120. Ibid., p. 223.

121. Ibid., pp. 230–31.

122. The following account is taken from Janet A. Flammang, "Women Made a Difference: Comparable Worth in San Jose," in *The Women's Movements of the United States and Western Europe,* ed. Mary Fainsod Katzenstein and Carol McClurg Mueller (Philadelphia: Temple University Press, 1987), pp. 290–309. The primary sources for this account were interviews conducted between 1982 and 1985 with elected officials and the following union members: Nancy Clifford, San Jose City Parks and Recreation Department and business agent for AFSCME District Council 57 (27 July 1984); Patt Curia, San Jose librarian (23 July 1984); Linda Dydo, San Jose librarian (13 July 1984); and Joan Goddard, San Jose librarian (1 August 1984). Also interviewed was David R. Armstrong, personnel services administrator, city of San Jose (11 July and 30 August 1984).

123. "'Comparable Worth' Strike Averted in San Jose," *California Public Employees Relations* 49 (June 1981): 16–18.

124. Ibid.

125. Hay Associates, *City of San Jose Study of Non-Management Classes* (San Francisco, 1980).

126. John H. Bunzel, "To Each According to Her Worth?" *Public Interest* 67 (Spring 1982): 77–93; Wendy Kahn and Joy Ann Grune, "Pay Equity: Beyond Equal Pay for Equal Work," in *Women, Power, and Policy,* ed. Boneparth, pp. 75–89.

127. Philip J. Trounstine, "San Jose Braces for Strike," *San Jose Mercury News,* 3 July 1981, pp. 1B, 5B.

128. Philip J. Trounstine, "City Workers Ratify Contract for $5.4 Million to End Strike," *San Jose Mercury News,* 15 July 1981, p. 1A.

129. Robert L. Farnquist, David R. Armstrong, and Russell P. Strausbaugh, "Pandora's Worth: The San Jose Experience," *Public Personnel Management Journal* 12 (Winter 1983): 358–68.

130. Interview with David Armstrong, 11 July 1984.

CHAPTER 8

1. Rufus P. Browning, Dale Rogers Marshall, and David H. Tabb, *Protest Is Not Enough: The Struggle of Blacks and Hispanics for Equality in Urban Politics* (Berkeley: University of California Press, 1984), p. 25; Paula D. McClain and Albert Karnig, "Black and Hispanic Socio-Economic and Political Competition," *American Political Science Review* 84 (June 1990): 535–45.

2. Byran O. Jackson, Elisabeth R. Gerber, and Bruce E. Cain, "Coalitional Prospects in a Multi-Racial Society: African-American Attitudes toward Other Minority Groups," *Political Research Quarterly* 47 (June 1994): 277–94.

3. Andrew M. Greeley, *Building Coalitions: American Politics in the 1970s* (New York: New Viewpoints, 1974), pp. 130–32.

4. Robert H. Salisbury, "Interest Groups: Toward a New Understanding," in *Interest Group Politics*, ed. Allan J. Cigler and Burdett A. Loomis (Washington, D.C.: Congressional Quarterly Press, 1983), pp. 368–69, 366.

5. Joyce Gelb and Marian Lief Palley, *Women and Public Policies* (Princeton: Princeton University Press, 1987), pp. 125–26.

6. Ibid., p. 57.

7. Myra Marx Ferree and Beth B. Hess, *Controversy and Coalition: The New Feminist Movement* (Boston: Twayne, 1985), p. 120.

8. Ibid., p. 121.

9. Ibid., pp. 128–29.

10. The following account is drawn from Nancy Douglas Joyner, "Coalition Politics: A Case Study of an Organization's Approach to a Single Issue," *Women and Politics* 2 (Spring–Summer 1982): 57–70.

11. Anne N. Costain, *Inviting Women's Rebellion: A Political Process Interpretation of the Women's Movement* (Baltimore: Johns Hopkins University Press, 1992), pp. xi, xii–xiii.

12. Ibid., pp. xiv–xv.

13. Ibid., p. xv.

14. Ibid., p. 138.

15. Paula Giddings, *When and Where I Enter: The Impact of Black Women on Race and Sex in America* (New York: Morrow, 1984), p. 342.

16. Ibid., p. 345.

17. "Ex-President of NOW Calls Group 'Racist,'" *San Diego Union*, 21 October 1979.

18. Mrs. White, quoted in Cheryl Townsend Gilkes, "'Holding Back the Ocean with a Broom': Black Women and Community Work," in *The Black Woman*, ed. La Frances Rogers-Rose (Beverly Hills, Calif.: Sage, 1980), p. 227.

19. Angela Davis, "Reflections on the Black Woman's Role in the Community of Slaves," *Black Scholar* 3 (December 1971): 2–15; bell hooks, *Ain't I a Woman: Black Women and Feminism* (Boston: South End Press, 1981); E. Frances White, "Listening to the Voices of Black Feminism," *Radical America* 18 (March–June 1984): 7–25.

20. Angela Davis, "Rape, Racism, and the Capitalist Setting," *Black Scholar* 9 (April 1978): 24–30.

21. Florence Rice, "It Takes a While to Realize That It Is Discrimination," in *Black Women in White America: A Documentary History*, ed. Gerda Lerner (New York: Vintage, 1972), p. 275.

22. Audre Lorde, "Eye to Eye: Black Women, Hatred, and Anger," in Audre Lorde, *Sister Outsider* (Trumansburg, N.Y.: Crossing Press, 1984), pp. 147–48.

23. Audre Lorde, "The Uses of Anger: Women Responding to Racism," in Lorde, *Sister Outsider*, pp. 127–28.

24. Ibid., pp. 130–31.

25. Angela Y. Davis, *Women, Race, and Class* (New York: Random House, 1981), p. 34.

26. Barbara Omolade, "Black Women and Feminism," in *The Future of Difference*, ed. Hester Eisenstein and Alice Jardine (Boston: Hall, 1980), p. 252.

27. Hooks, *Ain't I a Woman*, pp. 125–26.

28. Davis, *Women, Race, and Class*, pp. 44–45.

29. Ibid., p. 57.

30. Ibid., pp. 62–76, quotation from p. 76.

31. Ibid., pp. 82–84, quotation from p. 84.

32. Ibid., pp. 111–12.

33. Aileen S. Kraditor, *The Ideas of the Woman Suffrage Movement* (New York: Anchor Doubleday, 1971), p. 143.

34. Giddings, *When and Where I Enter,* p. 129.

35. Nancie Caraway, *Segregated Sisterhood: Racism and the Politics of American Feminism* (Knoxville: University of Tennessee Press, 1991), p. 157.

36. Sara Evans, "Women's Consciousness and the Southern Black Movement," in *Reweaving the Web of Life: Feminism and Nonviolence,* ed. Pam McAllister, (Philadelphia: New Society, 1982), pp. 115–27, quotation from p. 122.

37. Ibid., p. 123.

38. Ibid., p. 126.

39. Ibid., pp. 126–27.

40. Cynthia Washington, "We Started from Opposite Ends of the Spectrum," in *Reweaving the Web of Life,* ed. McAllister p. 113.

41. Ibid.

42. Giddings, *When and Where I Enter,* pp. 337–40.

43. Nancie Caraway, "'We Are Somebody?' Feminism, Racism, and the Rainbow Coalition" (paper presented at the annual meeting of the American Political Science Association, Washington, D.C., 1986).

44. Toni-Michelle C. Travis, "Women as an Emerging Power Bloc: Ethnic and Racial Considerations," in *Ethnicity and Women,* ed. Winston A. Van Horne (Madison: University of Wisconsin System American Ethnic Studies Coordinating Committee, 1986), pp. 79–112.

45. Bell hooks, *Feminist Theory: From Margin to Center* (Boston: South End Press, 1984), pp. 11–12.

46. Ibid., p. 54.

47. Gloria Joseph, "The Incompatible Ménage à Trois: Marxism, Feminism, and Racism," in *Women and Revolution,* ed. Lydia Sargent (Boston: South End Press, 1981), p. 98; Mae C. King, "Oppression and Power: The Unique Status of the Black Woman in the American Political System," *Social Science Quarterly* 56 (June 1975): 122.

48. Bev Fisher, "Race and Class: Beyond Personal Politics," *Quest* 3:4 (1977): 10.

49. Marilyn Frye, "On Being White: Toward a Feminist Understanding of Race and Race Supremacy," in Marilyn Frye, *The Politics of Reality: Essays in Feminist Theory* (Trumansburg, N.Y.: Crossing Press, 1983), pp. 124–25.

50. Ibid., p. 117.

51. Adrienne Rich, "Disloyal to Civilization: Feminism, Racism, Gynephobia," in Adrienne Rich, *On Lies, Secrets, and Silence: Selected Prose, 1966–1978* (New York: Norton, 1979), pp. 306–7.

52. Elizabeth V. Spelman, *Inessential Woman: Problems of Exclusion in Feminist Thought* (Boston: Beacon, 1988), pp. 162–63.

53. Ibid., p. 186.

54. Sylvia Gonzales, "The White Feminist Movement: The Chicana Perspective," *Social Science Journal* 14 (April 1977): 71–72.

55. Mitsuye Yamada, "Asian Pacific American Women and Feminism," in *This Bridge Called My Back: Writings by Radical Women of Color,* ed. Cherrie Moraga and Gloria Anzaldua (Watertown, Mass.: Persephone Press, 1981), pp. 71–72.

56. Barbara Smith, "Introduction," in *Home Girls: A Black Feminist Anthology,* ed. Barbara Smith (New York: Kitchen Table Press, 1983), p. xxxiii.

57. Barbara Smith and Beverly Smith, "Across the Kitchen Table: A Sister-to-Sister Dialogue," in *This Bridge Called My Back,* ed. Moraga and Anzaldua, pp. 126–27.

58. Davida J. Alperin, "Social Diversity and the Necessity of Alliances: A Developing Feminist Perspective," in *Bridges of Power: Women's Multicultural Alliances*, ed. Lisa Albrecht and Rose M. Brewer (Philadelphia: New Society, 1990), pp. 23–33, quotation from p. 31.

59. Charlotte Bunch, "Making Common Cause: Diversity and Coalitions," in Charlotte Bunch, *Passionate Politics: Feminist Theory in Action* (New York: St. Martin's Press, 1987), pp. 149–57, quotation from p. 156.

60. Charlotte Bunch, "Class and Feminism," in Bunch, *Passionate Politics*, p. 98.

61. Ibid., p. 99.

62. Donna Redmund, "I'm Proud to Be a Hillbilly," in *Hillbilly Women*, ed. Kathy Kahn (New York: Doubleday, 1973); reprinted in *The Women Say, the Men Say*, ed. Evelyn Shapiro and Barry M. Shapiro (New York: Dell, 1979), pp. 215–16.

63. Lillian Breslow Rubin, *Worlds of Pain: Life in the Working Class Family* (New York: Basic Books, 1976).

64. Barbara Ann Stolz, *Still Struggling: America's Low Income Working Women Confront the 1980s* (Lexington, Mass.: Heath, 1985), p. 178.

65. Ibid., pp. 185–86.

66. Irene I. Blea, *La Chicana and the Intersection of Race, Class, and Gender* (New York: Praeger, 1992).

67. Davis, *Women, Race, and Class*, p. 209.

68. Linda Gordon, *Woman's Body, Woman's Right: Birth Control in America* (New York: Penguin, 1976), pp. 157–58.

69. Davis, *Women, Race, and Class*, p. 210.

70. Ibid., pp. 213–15, quotation from p. 215.

71. Ibid., pp. 216–19.

72. Committee to Stop Forced Sterilization, Los Angeles, quoted in *Women Say*, ed. Shapiro and Shapiro, p. 158.

73. "Eleven Women File Suit on Sterilization," *Los Angeles Times*, 19 June 1975, sec. 2, p. 1.

74. Theresa Aragon de Valdez, "Organizing as a Political Tool for the Chicana," *Frontiers* 5 (Summer 1980): 9.

75. Carol Hardy-Fanta, *Latina Politics, Latino Politics: Gender, Culture, and Political Participation in Boston* (Philadelphia: Temple University Press, 1993), pp. 157–58.

76. Shirley Hill Witt, "Native American Women Today: Sexism and the Indian Woman," in *Women Say*, ed. Shapiro and Shapiro, pp. 171–72.

77. Rayna Green, "Native American Women: Review Essay," *Signs* 6 (Winter 1980): 261.

78. Mina Davis Caulfield, "Imperialism, the Family, and Cultures of Resistance," in *Women Say*, ed. Shapiro and Shapiro, pp. 192–95.

79. Joyce Ladner, *Tomorrow's Tomorrow: The Black Woman* (Garden City, N.Y.: Doubleday, 1971); Carol Stack, *All Our Kin: Strategies for Survival in a Black Community* (New York: Harper and Row, 1974); Nancy Tanner, "Matrifocality in Indonesia and Africa and among Black Americans," in *Woman, Culture, and Society*, ed. Michelle Zimbalist Rosaldo and Louise Lamphere (Stanford: Stanford University Press, 1974), pp. 129–56.

80. Bell hooks, *Yearning: Race, Gender, and Cultural Politics* (Boston: South End Press, 1990), p. 42.

81. Aida Hurtado, "Relating to Privilege: Seduction and Rejection in the Subordination of White Women and Women of Color," *Signs* 14 (Summer 1989): 852.

82. Linda La Rue, "The Black Movement and Women's Liberation," *Black Scholar* 1 (May 1970): 36–42.

83. King, "Oppression and Power."

84. Elizabeth Almquist, "Untangling the Effects of Race and Sex: The Disadvantaged Status of Black Women," *Social Science Quarterly* 5 (June 1975): 129–42.

85. Frances M. Beal, "Double Jeopardy: To Be Black and Female," in *Sisterhood Is Powerful,* ed. Robin Morgan (New York: Vintage, 1970), pp. 340–53.

86. Quoted in Giddings, *When and Where I Enter,* p. 305.

87. Betty Friedan, *It Changed My Life: Writings on the Women's Movement* (New York: Random House, 1975), p. 96.

88. Margaret Sloan, "Black Feminism: A New Mandate," *Ms.* 2 (May 1974): 97–100.

89. Jo Freeman, *The Politics of Women's Liberation: A Case Sudy of an Emerging Social Movement and Its Relation to the Policy Process* (New York: McKay, 1975), p. 156.

90. Sloan, "Black Feminism."

91. Combahee River Collective, "A Black Feminist Statement," in *Capitalist Patriarchy and the Case for Socialist Feminism,* ed. Zillah Eisenstein (New York: Monthly Review Press, 1979), pp. 362–72, quotation from p. 366.

92. Alma M. Garcia, "The Development of Chicana Feminist Discourse, 1970–1980," *Gender and Society* 3 (June 1989): 217–38.

93. Consuelo Nieto, "The Chicana and the Women's Rights Movement: A Perspective," *Civil Rights Digest* 6:3 (1974): 42.

94. Elizabeth M. Almquist, "Further Consequences of Double Jeopardy: The Reluctant Participation of Racial-Ethnic Women in Feminist Organizations," in *Ethnicity and Women,* ed. Winston A. Van Horne, (Madison: University of Wisconsin Press, 1986), pp. 113–34; and "Race and Ethnicity in the Lives of Minority Women," in *Women: A Feminist Perspective,* ed. Jo Freeman, 3d ed. (Palo Alto, Calif.: Mayfield, 1984), pp. 423–53.

95. M. Annette Jaimes and Theresa Halsey, "American Indian Women: At the Center of Indigenous Resistance in Contemporary North America" in *The State of Native America,* ed. M. Annette Jaimes (Boston: South End Press, 1992), pp. 331–32.

96. Ibid., pp. 335–36.

97. Haunani-Kay Trask, "Pacific Island Women and White Feminism," in Haunani-Kay Trask, *From a Native Daughter: Colonialism and Sovereignty in Hawai'i* (Monroe, Maine: Common Courage Press, 1993), pp. 263–66.

98. Patricia Hill Collins, *Black Feminist Thought: Knowledge, Consciousness, and the Politics of Empowerment* (New York: Routledge, 1991); Mae C. King, "The Politics of Sexual Stereotypes," *Black Scholar* (March–April 1973): 12–23; and Pauli Murray, "The Liberation of Black Women," in *Voices of the New Feminism,* ed. Mary Lou Thompson (Boston: Beacon, 1970), pp. 87–102.

99. Martha P. Cotera, *The Chicana Feminist* (Austin, Tex.: Information Systems Development, 1977); Sylvia Gonzales, "La Chicana: Malinche or Virgin?" *Nuestro* (June–July 1979): 41–43; and Alfredo Mirande and Evangelina Enriquez, *La Chicana: The Mexican American Woman* (Chicago: University of Chicago Press, 1979).

100. Gretchen M. Bataille and Kathleen Mullen Sands, *American Indian Women: Telling Their Lives* (Lincoln: University of Nebraska Press, 1984); Green, "Native American Women"; Witt, "Native American Women Today."

101. Asian Women United of California, eds., *Making Waves: An Anthology of Writings by and about Asian American Women* (Boston: Beacon, 1989); Esther Ngan-Ling Chow, "The Development of Feminist Consciousness among Asian American Women," *Gender and Society* 1 (September 1987): 284–99; Mitusye Yamada, "Invisibility as an Unnatural Disaster: Reflections of an Asian American Woman," in *This Bridge Called My Back,* ed. Moraga and Anzaldua, pp. 35–40.

102. Cecilia de Burciaga, Viola Gonzales, and Ruth A. Hepburn, "The Chicana as Feminist," in *Beyond Sex Roles*, ed. Alice Sargent (St. Paul, Minn.: West, 1977), pp. 266–73.

103. Maxine Baca Zinn, "Political Familism: Toward Sex Role Equality in Chicano Families," *Aztlán* 6:1 (1975): 13–26.

104. Collins, *Black Feminist Thought*, pp. 119–20, 122–23.

105. Elizabeth M. Almquist, "The Experiences of Minority Women in the United States: Intersections of Race, Gender, and Class," in *Women: A Feminist Perspective*, ed. Jo Freeman, 4th ed. (Mountain View, Calif.: Mayfield, 1989), p. 418.

106. Caraway, *Segregated Sisterhood*, p. 195; Bonnie Thorton Dill, "Race, Class, and Gender: Prospects for an All-Inclusive Sisterhood," *Feminist Studies* 9 (Spring 1983): 131–50; Elizabeth Fox-Genovese, "The Personal Is Not Political Enough," *Marxist Perspectives* (Winter 1979–80): 94–113; Fox-Genovese, *Feminism without Illusions: A Critique of Individualism* (Chapel Hill: University of North Carolina Press, 1991).

107. Collins, *Black Feminist Thought*, pp. 205–6.

108. Ibid., p. 213.

109. Ibid., pp. 236–37.

110. Michele Russell, "An Open Letter to the Academy," *Quest* 3 (Spring 1977): 70–80.

111. Hooks, *Feminist Theory*, pp. 110–11.

112. Charlotte Bunch, "Not by Degrees: Feminist Theory and Education," in Bunch, *Passionate Politics*, pp. 240–53.

113. Hardy-Fanta, *Latina Politics*, pp. xi–xii.

114. Terry Mason, "Symbolic Strategies for Change: A Discussion of the Chicana Women's Movement," in *Twice a Minority: Mexican-American Women*, ed. Margarita B. Melville (St. Louis, Mo.: Mosby, 1980), p. 96.

115. Marta Cotera, "Feminism: The Chicana and Anglo Versions, a Historical Analysis," in *Twice a Minority*, ed. Melville, p. 228.

116. Garcia, "Chicana Feminist Discourse."

117. Sylvia Gonzales, "Analysis of Demographic Data and Sex Role Inventories of Participants in the National Hispanic Feminist Conference," in *Hispanic Women: A Feminist Anthology*, ed. Sylvia Alicia Gonzales (unpublished manuscript, 1984), pp. 220–28. Although the response rate to the questionnaire was only 15 percent, Gonzales considered the survey an accurate reflection of women at the conference.

118. Most press reports put the number at one thousand, but this figure reflected pre-registration. Actual attendance was double this amount, according to Gonzales (personal interview, 3 April 1986). Only a few men attended.

119. Maria Eugenia Matute-Bianchi, "A Chicana in Academe," *Women's Studies Quarterly* 10 (Spring 1982): 14–17.

120. Bureau of the Census, *Statistical Abstract of the United States, 1982–83* (Washington, D.C.: U.S. Government Printing Office, 1982), p. 429.

121. Elizabeth Waldman, "Profile of the Chicana: A Statistical Fact Sheet," in *Mexican American Women: Struggles Past and Present*, ed. Magdalena Mora and Adelaida R. Del Castillo (Los Angeles: University of California at Los Angeles Chicano Studies Research Center Publications, 1980), pp. 195–204.

122. Unless otherwise indicated, information about the conference is drawn from files containing conference correspondence and documents, given to me by Sylvia Gonzales.

123. Janice Mall, "San Jose to Host Hispanic Feminists," *Los Angeles Times*, 25 November 1979, part 9, p. 18.

124. Che Sandoval, "Hispanic Feminist Conference Meets," *La Razón Mestiza/Union Wage* (June 1980): 4–6.

125. Sylvia Gonzales, "The Latina Feminist: Where We've Been, Where We're Going" (unpublished manuscript, 1981), p. 5.

126. Pamela G. Hollie, "Hispanic Group Sets Priorities for the 1980's," *New York Times,* 1 April 1980; Connie Skipitares, "Latina Women End San Jose Conference," *San Jose Mercury News,* 1 April 1980, pp. 1B, 3B.

127. Janie Perez, "Chicana Professionals: Establishing Working Relationships with Barrio Women" (paper presented at the National Hispanic Feminist Conference, San Jose, March 1980).

128. Sandoval, "Hispanic Feminist Conference Meets."

129. Alma Garcia, "Latinas in the United States," fact sheet (Department of Sociology, Santa Clara University, 1986).

130. Elizabeth McTaggart Almquist, "Race and Ethnicity in the Lives of Minority Women," in *Women,* ed. Freeman, 3d. ed., pp. 423–53.

131. Iliad Estrada, "Hispanic Feminists Meet—It's a Trip," *La Luz* 8 (August–September 1980): 35.

132. Dorita Marina and Silvia Unzueta, "Cuban American Women: A Dade County Overview," in *Hispanic Women,* ed. Gonzales, pp. 201–8.

133. Norma Varisco de Garcia, "Rural Hispanic Women," in *Hispanic Women,* ed. Gonzales, pp. 123–33.

134. Gonzales, "Analysis of Demographic Data."

135. For an elaboration of this theory, see Mario Barrera, *Race and Class in the Southwest: A Theory of Racial Inequality* (Notre Dame, Ind.: University of Notre Dame Press, 1979).

136. Estrada, "Hispanic Feminists Meet."

137. Nancy Sternbach, "Malinche's Moment: Redefinition of the Woman, the Myth, and the Symbol," in *Hispanic Women,* ed. Gonzales, p. 8.

138. Elizabeth Starcevic, "Carmen de Burgos: Feminist Precursor," in *Hispanic Women,* ed. Gonzales, pp. 13–21.

139. Annette Oliveria, "Transforming the Feminine Reality: The Lives of Five Puertorriqueñas," in *Hispanic Women,* ed. Gonzales, p. 184.

140. Cotera, "Feminism," p. 233.

141. Enriqueta Longeaux y Vasquez, "The Mexican American Woman," in *Sisterhood Is Powerful,* ed. Robin Morgan (New York: Vintage, 1970), p. 379.

142. Cotera, "Feminism," pp. 228–29.

143. Mirta Vidal, *Women: New Voice of La Raza* (New York: Pathfinder Press, 1971).

144. Rosemary Santana Cooney, "Changing Labor Force Participation of Mexican American Wives: A Comparison with Anglos and Blacks," *Social Science Quarterly* 56:2 (1975): 252–61; Patricia Zavella, "The Impact of 'Sun Belt Industrialization' on Chicanas," *Frontiers* 8:1 (1984): 21–27.

145. Marcela Lucero, "The Problematics of the Chicana Feminist Scholar," in *Hispanic Women,* ed. Gonzales, pp. 68–69.

146. Nellie Olivencia, "The Hispanic Woman as Separatist and Integrationist" (paper presented at the National Hispanic Feminist Conference, San Jose, March 1980), p. 3.

147. Sue Martinez, "All of a Sudden, They're Calling Us 'Hispanic-Americans,'" *San Jose Mercury News,* 25 February 1980, p. 7B.

148. Philip J. Trounstine, "Take a Stand, Hispanic Women Advised as S.J. Conference Opens," *San Jose Mercury News,* 29 March 1980, pp. 1B, 6B.

149. Ibid.

150. Skipitares, "Latina Women."

151. Sylvia Gonzales, interview with the author, 3 April 1986.

152. Sandra A. Salazar, "Public Policy and Hispanic Women: The Need for a National Agenda" (workshop proposal for the National Hispanic Feminist Conference, San Jose, 1980), p. 1.

Index

abolition movement, 78–80, 98, 310; World Anti-slavery Convention (1840), 80

abortion: abortion activism, 63, 286, 332; and the American Civil Liberties Union, 285; and antifeminism, 265–70; arguments about, 66; and candidate endorsement guidelines, 84; and Congress, 303; and congresswomen, 287–88; and feminism, 90; Hyde amendment and, 263, 287, 327; and the New Right, 265–70; and NOW, 82–83, 87, 258, 286; and privacy, 285, 287; public opinion about, 91, 120, 128, 129, 130–31; and race, 325–28; as redefined by the women's movement, 285–87; restrictions on access to, 287; and *Roe v. Wade*, 285, 287; in Santa Clara County, 94, 141; and the women's movement, 254; and women's PACs, 190

Abzug, Bella, 9, 17, 165, 175, 211, 215, 222, 226

accommodationist approach, x, 7, 13, 16, 24, 25, 32, 70, 89, 96, 114, 115, 124, 131, 157, 197, 256, 276, 282, 288, 297–98, 306; definition of, x, 13

Ackelsberg, Martha, 31

Addams, Jane, 39, 68, 141, 364n. 24

affirmative action, 152, 268; in Santa Clara County, 141

age: differences in, among women, 76; and support for women in politics, 156; and the women's movement, 80, 83, 91, 128

agenda setting, 253–96 (Chapter 7); by congresswomen, 260–62; definition of, 253–54; and equality issues, 256, 261, 276, 288–90; favorable conditions for, 265; and female models of experience, 256, 276, 282–88; by female officials in Santa Clara County, 248, 249; by female state legislators, 234; and feminist policy centers, 265; by insider/outsider coalitions, 253–63; and invisible issues, 256, 276–81, 290–96; by local female officials, 262–63; and the media, 256; and the New Right, 256; policy entrepreneurs and, 255–56, 267; policy innovators and, 255–56; and policy spirals, 256; role change and, 255–56, 263–65, 288–90, 290–96; role equity and, 255–56, 263–65, 288–90, 302–3; in Santa Clara County, 246, 290–96; strategies of women for, 264–65; and women's policy networks, 259–63; women's movement and, 253–59, 264–65. *See also* women's policy agenda

Aid to Families with Dependent Children, 105, 112, 272; public opinion about, 126

Allen, Florence E., 112–13

Almquist, Elizabeth McTaggart, 330, 333–34

Alperin, Davida J., 321–22

Alvarado, Blanca, 51, 161, 166, 172, 178, 194–95, 247

ambition, 10; of congressmembers, 157–59; of convention delegates, 135–37; definitions of, 157; of local party activists, 139–40; of men, 157; of widows in Congress, 159; of women, 156–60, 193; of women in local government, 157–58, 169–70; and the women's movement, 189–90

American Association of University Women, 80, 85, 264; and the ERA, 301–2; and female officials, 191; in Santa Clara County, 47, 352

American Civil Liberties Union (ACLU), 264, 285, 300

403

American Federation of State, County
and Municipal Employees (AFSCME),
47, 181, 292–96
American National Election Studies
(ANES), 18, 89–91, 117–19, 121,
123–24, 126, 129, 165, 270–71
American Political Science Association
(APSA), 4, 12, 63; Committee on the
Status of Women, 12
American Political Science Review, xi, 4, 7,
11, 20, 358n. 10
Andersen, Kristi, 115, 374n. 99
Anthony, Susan B., 39, 78, 79, 311–12
antifeminism, 73, 87–91; and abortion,
266–70; and agenda setting, 265–
71; and the ERA, 266–70; and family,
266–70; of female officials, 160,
220; of Reagan administration, 53,
87–88; and textbook selection,
269; and women's policy agenda,
265–71
antiwar movement, 11, 63, 64, 73, 79
appointees, female, 81, 85, 184–85; backgrounds of, 169; conservatism of, 198;
and family responsibilities, 165–66;
feminism of, 227, 236; and interest
groups, 168–69; liberalism of, 198; occupational backgrounds of, 168, 169;
public service vs. careerism, 227; by
type of post, 152–53, 168–69; and
women's organizations, 227
Armstrong, David, 295–96
Asian (Pacific)-American women: and
coalitions, 297; Japanese-American
women, 327; and racist stereotypes,
336; and white women, 320; and
women of color, 320, 332
attorneys, female: in Santa Clara County,
94; in the women's movement, 82, 84,
87
autonomy: of individuals, 3, 26, 65, 103;
of women, 130

Baer, Denise L., 134
Barber, James D., 202–3
Barry, Kathleen, 281
battered-women's shelters: funding for,
281; history of, 279–81; and mobilization, 92, 95, 332; opposition to,
280–81; in Santa Clara County, 47,
91–92, 247–48, 290–92
Beal, Frances M., 330–31
Beall, James, 247
Bechtel, Betsy, 42, 177, 182, 183, 184

Beckwith, Karen L., 123, 374n. 99
behaviorism, 9–11, 13, 15–16, 17, 19,
20–21, 23, 26, 28, 34, 58, 97, 116, 140,
337
belief systems, constraint in, 120, 127; for
women, 129
Bender, Ann, 93–94
Bergeson, Marian, 177
blacks, 61, 64, 67; and the black nationalist movement, 11, 88, 313–16; and
coalitions, 297, 299–300; and the ERA,
81; group consciousness of, 90; political participation of, 119; in Santa
Clara County, 46–47, 51, 53; and voluntary organizations, 107, 111
black women: and abortion, 332; and
anti-slavery societies, 310; and battered women, 332; and birth control,
325–27; and black candidates, 316;
and the civil rights movement,
313–16; and cultures of resistance,
328–29; as domestic workers, 307–8;
and double jeopardy, 330–33; and
dual identity, 329–30; and families,
328–29, 336; female officials and coalitions, 229; feminism of, 117–18, 305,
331–32, 337–38; and health care, 332;
and homeplace, 328–29; and interracial dating, 313–16; and involuntary
sterilization, 326–27, 332; and kinship
networks, 328–29, 336; and lynchings,
306–7, 312; as mayors, 242–43; political participation of, 117–18, 123; and
racism of white women, 306–7,
308–10; and racist stereotypes, 335;
and rape, 332; and slavery, 98, 306–7,
325; and suffrage clubs, 312; and the
underground railroad, 310; and voluntary organizations, 107–8, 111; and
white feminists, 316–19; and women
of color, 319–20, 332; and women's
and feminist organizations, 191; and
the women's movement, 229, 324
Boals, Kay, 16–18
Boneparth, Ellen, 138, 257
Bourque, Susan C., 7, 9
Boyer, Elizabeth, 82, 84
Breckinridge, Sophonisba P., 149–52
Briody, Lynn, 44
Brownmiller, Susan, 283
Bunch, Charlotte, 322–23, 339
Burgess, John W., 4, 106
Burke, Yvonne Brathwaite, 211
Burrell, Barbara, 176

Bush, George, 254, 287
Business and Professional Women
(BPW), 6–7, 80, 85, 87, 264; and the
ERA, 6, 87; and female officials, 191;
and feminism, 223; in Santa Clara
County, 47, 91, 352
Byrne, Jayne, 363n. 50

California: abortion laws in, 286; feminist
agenda in, 239; legislature, 53, 233–35;
men in, 233–35, 239; political culture
of, 37; women in, 177, 233–35, 239
California Elected Women's Association
for Education and Research
(CEWAER), 186, 188
candidates, female, 36, 49, 85; and appearing "hard" and "soft," 160–61; and campaign funds, 179, 181–84; and electoral
structures, 179–80; and family obligations, 164–67; and fear of sex discrimination, 162; and feminism, 189–90; and
feminist organizations, 189–92; and incumbency, 178–79; and lack of self-confidence, 162; and the media, 164; occupational backgrounds of, 167–73; and
old boys' networks, 179, 182–84; and
political culture, 159, 178–80; and political opportunity structure, 178–80; and
political parties, 174–78; and role
strain, 159; self-concepts of, 154–64;
and sex discrimination, 189; social bias
and, 154–64; as supporter vs. decision
maker, 161–62; and supportive spouses,
165–66; and timing of bid for public office, 158; and voluntarism, 169–70; and
the women's movement, 180, 188–92,
223; and women's organizations,
188–92. *See also* ambition
Capital Data Communications, 383n. 142
capital punishment, support for, 126, 129
Caraway, Nancie, 312–13
care: ethic of, 26, 72–73, 92; politics of,
31, 68, 106, 110
caretakers: men and women as, 102;
women as, 31, 72–73, 78–79
Carroll, Berenice A., 20, 26
Carroll, Susan J., 130, 169, 171, 181, 190
Carter, Jimmy, 128, 132, 161, 185, 198,
232, 280, 351
Castells, Manuel, 106
caucuses, of women: as candidates, 189;
as officials, 222, 230–31, 233; as professionals, 88. *See also* Congressional
Caucus for Women's Issues

Center for the American Woman and Politics (CAWP), 16, 151–52, 235
Center for Research on Women
(CROW), 94–95
Center for Women Policy Studies, 264,
265
charities, and women, 38, 78, 106, 108
Charles, Susan, 143
Chicana Coalition, 47, 52, 91, 94, 141;
candidate endorsement procedures
of, 143–44
Chicanas, 51–52, 177, 319–20, 326–27,
332–33, 335–36, 337, 340–41, 345–51
child care, 71, 82, 83, 84, 91, 101, 106,
226, 330; and Congress, 303; in local
politics, 263; in Santa Clara County,
94, 249
child custody policies, women and, 282
childrearing, 24, 59; and community, 31,
70, 121; and countersocialization, 122;
and feminism, 68–69; and men, 72;
and political participation, 7, 121,
123, 124; and survival, 129; and the
women's movement, 79
children, politics of, 8, 15, 17; and feminism, 117; and parents, 116–17; sex
differences in, 116–17
Children's Defense Fund, 272; and coalitions, 300
Chisholm, Shirley, 17, 211, 222, 316
Chodorow, Nancy, 217
Christensen, Terry, 38, 40, 362n. 16
citizenship, 76–77, 92, 96–100, 102,
103–4, 105, 120, 271–74
civic life, 7, 105–6; definition of, 105; duties (responsibilities) of, 11, 36, 137,
155, 208; and kinship, 328
Civil Rights Act (1964), 6, 19, 82, 220,
258, 277, 293
civil rights movement, 11, 19, 67, 73, 79,
80, 103, 258, 264; and black female
mayors, 243; and electoral structures,
50; and families, 272; and interracial
dating, 313–16; and race, 313–16; in
Santa Clara County, 47; and women's
community organizing, 107; and the
women's movement, 64, 267, 299–300,
303, 304, 313–16
Clarke, Susan E., 219–20, 270
class, 13, 14; and biculturalism, 329; and
birth control, 325–28; and coalitions,
304–53; differences in, among women,
67, 76, 77–78, 79, 84, 107, 108, 121,
123, 127, 300, 322–25, 333; and elec-

class (*continued*)
 tions, 38; and the ERA, 304–6; and feminism, 19; and gender consciousness, 88; and the gender gap, 130; and NOW, 304–6; and political culture, 36–37; in Santa Clara County, 93; in Silicon Valley, 45–46; women as a, 63, 65; and the women's movement, 324–25

clean government (politics), 36–42, 65; and female officials, 41, 192–95; in Santa Clara County, 194–95

Clinton, Bill, 232

Clinton, Hillary Rodham, 364n. 24

coalitions, political, x, 20, 297–353 (Chapter 8); and betrayal, 310–16; on city councils, 50, 297; definition of, 297–98; and emotional conflict, 306–20; and the ERA, 87, 125, 301–2, 304–6; of feminists and traditional women's groups, 299; and health care, 109; and the National Hispanic Feminist Conference, 340–53; in Santa Clara County, 340–53; as survival, 320–29; and Title IX, 298–99; of women's groups, 85, 113

Cobb, Roger W., 253

Collins, Patricia Hill, 337–38

colonialism, internal, 328, 333–35, 348

Combahee River Collective, 331–32

commissions on the status of women, 5–6, 80–81, 82, 93, 258, 262

communication: communication networks, 77, 79–80, 119; in conversations, 13; styles of, 20

community, 4, 24, 26, 30–31, 32, 33, 70–71, 74, 76, 78, 79, 96, 101, 102–4, 105–10; of mothers, 119; of women, x, 15, 34, 68, 80, 92, 99, 106–9

comparable worth, 247, 292–96

compassion, of women, 128–31, 160

Congress: women's issues and, 133, 220–27, 287–88, 303–4, 327; and the women's movement, 257, 259, 303–4

Congressional Caucus for Women's Issues, 133, 211, 221–22, 226–27, 287–88

congresswomen, 11, 19, 49; and abortion, 287–88; as amateurs, 209; and the Civil Rights Act of 1964, 220, 224; and committee assignments, 224–25; as committee chairs, 211, 221; and constituent casework, 211, 224; and contraception, 287–88; and education legislation, 221–23; and the Equal Pay Act, 220–21,

226, 289; and the ERA, 220–24; female consciousness of, 220–27; feminism of, 198, 209, 211–12, 215, 220–27, 261–62; legislative roles of, 201–2, 212; legislative success of, 211, 212–16; liberalism of, 197–98, 212; and male colleagues, 208–12, 221, 262; as mavericks, 209; media and, 209–10; as neutral professionals, 261–62; occupational backgrounds of, 168; in party leadership positions, 210, 211, 221; and political parties, 158, 168; as representing women as a group, 211–12, 225–26; as sponsors of bills, 224–26; and supportive spouses, 167; and Title IX, 221, 226; and traditional women's concerns, 224–25; volunteer backgrounds of, 168; as widows, 159, 168; and women's health, 287–88; and the women's movement, 260–62; and women's organizations, 221, 223. *See also* ambition, of congressmembers; Congressional Caucus for Women's Issues

connections (connectedness), politics of, 26, 69, 70, 101

Conover, Pamela J., 266–67

consciousness. *See* female consciousness; feminism; gender: gender consciousness; group consciousness; political consciousness

consciousness raising, ix, 18, 64, 87, 102, 332; consciousness-raising groups, x, 20, 63, 66–67, 68, 83, 86, 88, 98, 121; and differences among women, 309, 321–22; and epistemology, 60, 278; and group consciousness, 62; litigation as, 264; in Santa Clara County, 94; and sexual harassment, 277; and women's policy agenda, 257

conservatism: and preservation of life, 70; public opinion and, 114, 254; in Santa Clara County, 48; and temperance, 79; of women, 14–15, 73, 82, 119, 126–30

constituents: public officials' views of, 173, 200–201, 219, 234, 243; in Santa Clara County, 248; service to, 50, 193–95, 200–201, 234–35, 240, 241, 243, 244

context, 23, 25, 26, 27, 32, 33, 34, 69

contraception, 285; and congresswomen, 288; experimentation abuse and, 328; and *Griswold v. Connecticut*, 285; and NOW, 286

convention delegates, 17, 18–19, 84, 101–2, 114, 121, 132, 134, 135–37
Cook, Elizabeth Adell, 89–90
corruption, 8, 36–37, 99, 101, 126, 193–95
Costain, Anne N., 133–34, 302–4
Costain, W. Douglas, 133–34
Costantini, Edmond, 376n. 134
Cotera, Marta, 349
Craik, Kenneth A., 376n. 134
Crandall, Prudence, 310
criminal justice policies, women and, 282
Cuban-American women, 346, 347
culture, 7, 13–15, 36–44, 59; and bicultural-ism, 328–29; of can-do risk taking, 36, 42–44; and differences among women, 67, 332; and female officials, 44, 49, 153, 179; and gender, 26–28, 59, 75; in-dividualistic political, 36, 179, 180; and lesbians, 73; male and female, 13–15, 26, 72; of male public office, 207–12; men's political, 113; moralistic political, 36–37, 41, 49, 153, 179, 180, 230; politi-cal, in Santa Clara County, 36–44; of poverty, 14; of resistance, 328–29, 336; and sexuality, 73; traditional political, 36–37, 49, 153, 179, 180, 230; women's political, 14, 80, 97, 113, 216–20

Dahl, Robert, 21–22
Davis, Angela, 310–12, 325–26, 331
Day, Dorothy, 364n. 24
de Beauvoir, Simone, 68, 349
de Burgos, Carmen, 349
defense spending, support for, 127, 129
democracy, 9, 11, 15, 32, 33, 61, 76–77, 79; and voluntary organizations, 110–11
Democratic party, 6; feminist positions of, 132; issue positions of, 126; and Lati-nos, 351; male defection from, 131; and the New Deal, 107; and NOW, 125; political culture of, 132; in Santa Clara County, 45; structure of, 132; women's identification with, 125; and the women's movement, 84, 88; and women's suffrage, 98;
demonstrations, 84, 95, 261; of AFDC mothers, 107; and civil disobedience for abortions, 286; for the ERA, 87; in Santa Clara County, 95; sit-ins, 260, 313–14; speak-outs, 277; teach-ins, 286; zap actions, 64. *See also* protests
dependence, of women: economic, 9, 78, 130; and support for women in poli-tics, 156

Diamond, Irene, 24, 31, 204–7, 216, 228–29, 230, 272–73
differences: between men and women, 74–75, 87, 92; and models of social burdens, 321–22; among women, 75–76,
Diridon, Rod, 171–72, 183, 245, 246
divorce, 71, 348; policies and women, 282; and the women's movement, 79, 87, 127–28
Dobyns, Winifred Starr, 98
do-goodism, of women, 9, 68, 106, 173, 364n. 24
domestic violence, x, 91, 257, 261, 265, 279–81, 290–92. *See also* violence against women
domestic workers: race and, 307–8; work-ers' compensation for, 112
Douglass, Frederick, 310–12
Duverger, Maurice, 15
Dworkin, Andrea, 284–85
Dydo, Linda, 295

Eagle Forum, 88
East, Catherine, 260
Economic and Social Opportunities (ESO), 92
Economic Equity Act (1984), 263
education: equal opportunity in, 82–84, 98, 127, 222, 290; and feminism, 44, 65, 123; and political participation, 36, 119–20, 122–24; and role expan-sion, 108; support for education pro-grams, 129; and support for women in public office, 156; of women, 79, 82; and the women's movement, 78, 84, 91, 128
education policy: 221–22, 290; and sexual harassment, 277; Title IX of the Edu-cation Amendments (1972), 19, 221, 260–61, 263, 290; and women's coali-tions, 290
Egeland, Leona, 53, 178, 187
Eisenhower, Dwight D., 8, 81
Eisenstein, Zillah, 65, 266
Elazar, Daniel J., 36
Elder, Charles D., 253
elections: at-large, 36, 38, 48–53, 179; class aspects of, 170; district, 36, 38, 41, 48–53, 179; and female candi-dates, 158, 179; general, 179; initia-tive, 37–38, 98; and men of color, 40–41; mixed, 50; multimember dis-trict, 48–53; nonpartisan, 37–38, 179;

elections (*continued*)
  primaries, 37–38; recall, 37–38, 40,
  98; referendum, 37–39, 98; single-
  member district, 48–53. *See also* presidential elections
elite politics, x, 8, 11, 22, 29, 36; elite-
  mass distinction, 4, 35–36
Elshtain, Jean Bethke, 19, 20, 23, 69, 104,
  154
EMILY's List, 182, 190
emotions (feelings): and citizenship, 103;
  and equality, 74; and group consciousness, 92; and movements, 267; and
  politics, 8, 67
employment: contracts of, 76; discrimination and, 82–83; equal opportunity in,
  82–84, 260; and feminism, 123; and
  low-income women, 127; and political
  participation, 119, 122–24. *See also* labor force participation of women
environmental protection, 61–62; local
  female officials and, 263; public opinion of, 29, 127, 129; in Santa Clara
  County, 39–42, 144–45; and working-
  class women, 108–9
epistemology, 24, 32; black women's epistomological standpoint, 337–38; conventional, 3, 4, 58; empiricism and,
  32, 61; engaged, 337–40; feminist, 3,
  58–61; feminist epistomological standpoint, 59–60, 104; objectivity and subjectivity and, 58–61; paradigms and,
  58–61, 66, 75; positivism and, 4–5, 21,
  32, 58–60, 337–38. *See also* methodology
Equal Credit Opportunity Act (1974), 263,
  265, 299, 330; feminists and, 289–90
equal pay, 6, 91, 112, 128, 289, 330; and
  the gender gap, 130; and unions, 289
equality, 22, 27, 66, 71, 78, 79, 80, 81, 86,
  90, 92, 104; definitions of, 74–75; and
  difference debate, 74–75, 104; and
  feminism, 127, 267; government role
  in securing, 129; of opportunity, 258;
  and pornography, 284; socioeconomic, 19; and white women, 317–18;
  and women of color, 317–18
Equal Pay Act (1963), 258, 292; congresswomen and, 220–21, 226, 289; and
  pay equity, 293
Equal Rights Amendment (ERA), 6–7, 19,
  66, 81–84, 87–88, 104, 124–25, 127–28,
  254, 261–63; and antifeminism, 265–70;
  and class, 304–6, 325; and ERAmerica,

87; female officials and, 220; and the
  New Right, 265–70; and NOW, 258,
  351; and political parties, 131–32; and
  protests, 264; and race, 304–6, 330; as
  role equity and role change issue,
  288–89; in Santa Clara County, 92, 94,
  192; and the women's movement, 304;
  women's opinions about, 131–32;
  women's opposition to, 160, 265–70
Escalante, Alicia, 333
Espinoza-Howard, Kathy, 141
Estrada, Illiad, 346–47, 348
Estruth, Jerry, 50, 178, 246, 247
ethnicity, 13; and differences among
  women, 76; and political culture, 36;
  in Santa Clara County, 46, 47, 51
Evans, Sara, 313–16
explanation, 3, 7, 10, 14, 32, 61, 69; scientific vs. semantic, 59

families, 20, 21, 32, 33, 34, 70, 71–72, 78,
  92, 97, 100, 101; and community role,
  109; and the New Right, 266–70; and
  political participation, 105, 116,
  119–22; and race, 328–29; and the
  state, 10, 271–73; and survival, 129,
  328–29; White House Conference on
  Families, 266–67; and women of color,
  336
Family and Medical Leave Act (FMLA),
  275, 282
family leave, 275, 282; maternity, 82, 91,
  282; parental, 71
Family Protection Act, 266
Farenthold, Frances, 17
farmworkers, 61–62; rights of, 333
Feinstein, Dianne, 160, 363n. 50
Feit, Rona, 84
female consciousness, 70, 109, 220–50
female officials. *See* women in public office
feminism, 6, 18, 29; anarchist, 86; of civil
  servants, 238–39; and class, 19; closet,
  190, 220; of congressmembers,
  260–62; cultural, 65, 67; and the Democratic party, 132–34; and education,
  44; of female candidates, 189–90; of
  female officials, 16–17, 53, 220–50;
  group consciousness and, 127–28; as
  an ideological climate, 131; ideology
  and, 127–28; of judges, 237–38, 241;
  lesbian, 73; liberal, 64–66, 68, 74–75,
  86, 266, 300, 317–18; and male liberals, 239; and marriage, 30; Marxist, 68;

men's definition of, 27, 29, 127–28; and mothers, 72–73; and New Right women, 268; and nonconventionality, 78–79; and political participation, 18–19; postfeminism, 89; psychoanalytic, 68; public support for, 29, 89–91, 127–28; radical, 63–66, 68, 70, 73, 74–75, 77, 83, 84, 86, 259–60, 280–81, 300; and the Republican party, 132–34; of Santa Clara County female officials, 187–88, 192, 245–46, 250; self-interest and, 127–28; self-understandings of, ix, 224; and sexual harassment, 278–79; social, 113; socialist, 64, 74–75, 271–73, 285, 300; and textbook selection, 269; unobtrusive mobilization of, 88; in Washington, D.C., 263–65; women's definition of, 27, 29, 127–28; and women's policy networks, 259–61; women's support for, 90–91, 117–18, 127–31; "woodwork feminists," 19, 222, 260–61. *See also* antifeminism

feminist theory, ix, xi, 60, 62
Ferguson, Miriam "Ma," 153
Ferraro, Geraldine, 125, 226
Ferree, Myra Marx, 299–300
Firestone, Shulamith, 63
Fisher, Bev, 317
Fletcher, Claude, 177, 247
Fletcher, Ellen, 42
Flora, Cornelia B., 121
Ford, Gerald, 132
Fowler, Robert Booth, 270
Fowlkes, Diane L., 102
Frankovic, Kathleen A., 125, 375
freedom, 20, 66, 76, 79, 268; and pornography, 284
Freeman, Jo, 62, 83, 86, 132, 222–23, 258–61, 331–32
Friedan, Betty, 5, 65, 80, 82, 84, 87, 99, 186, 305, 331
friendship: men's politics of, 113; women's politics of, 27, 70, 71, 103, 109
Frye, Marilyn, 317–18
Fulenwider, Claire Knoche, 117–18
Fund for the Feminist Majority, 190

Garcia, Alma, xiii, 332–33
Gehlen, Frieda L., 210–11, 224–25
Gelb, Joyce, 263–65, 290, 298–99, 302–3
gender: definition of, 26–27, 91; and domination, 60; gender consciousness, 27, 59, 88–91; gender neutrality, 66; political observers and, 3, 16, 23, 34; political subjects and, 27, 31–32, 68; and sex, 26–28, 59, 75, 120

gender gap, x, 32, 96, 124–31, 134, 176, 224
General Federation of Women's Clubs, 38, 99, 106, 264
generational differences, of women: and opinions, 117; and political participation, 124
Gertzog, Irwin, 209–10, 215, 225–27, 261–62
Giddings, Paula, 304–6, 331
Gilligan, Carol, 26–28, 72, 217
Githens, Marianne, 25, 201, 202–3, 214
Gold, Doris, 111–12
Gonzales, Sylvia, 95, 319–20, 340, 342–47, 352, 399nn. 117, 118
Goot, Murray, 15–16
Gordon, Linda, 257, 271, 285–86, 325–26
Grasso, Ella, 153, 222
Gray, Virginia, 266–67
Green, Edith, 221–23, 289, 290
Griffiths, Hicks, 167
Griffiths, Martha, 167, 175, 221, 261
Grimké, Angelina, 78, 310, 311
Grimké, Sarah, 78, 310, 311
Grossholtz, Jean, 7, 9, 280–81
group consciousness, ix; and caretaking, 72; definition of, 127; and mobilization, 57; and political participation, 118–19; in Santa Clara County, 92–95; and support for women in public office, 156; and survival, 129; of women, 62–77, 90, 278; and the women's movement, 66, 127–28, 314; and women's policy agenda, 257
groups: cross-pressures of, 14–15; and deprivation, 77–79; domination and subordination of, 30–31, 60, 74, 76, 285, 317–18, 329, 337–38; membership of, 14, 36; women acting as, 77–91. *See also* interest groups
Gruberg, Martin, 5, 7, 149, 151
gun control, support for, 126, 129
Gurin, Patricia, 90

Hamann, Anthony P. "Dutch," 40–41
Hamer, Fanny Lou, 313
Hammer, Susan, 173, 178, 183, 184, 187, 249–50
Hansen, Julia Butler, 222
Hardy-Fanta, Carol, 327, 339–40

Harris, Louis, and Associates, 362n. 17
Hartmann, Heidi, 275
Hartsock, Nancy C. M., 24, 104, 274
Hayden, Casey, 314
Hayes, Janet Gray, 41, 42, 44, 53, 163, 167, 173, 178, 186–87, 192, 245–47, 249, 294
health care, 287–88; and Medicare and Medicaid, 105; support for health care programs, 129; and women in Santa Clara County, 141; women's, 91, 104, 109, 261, 332; women's centers for, 86, 106, 287
Hearst, Mrs. William Randolph, 39
Heckler, John, 167
Heckler, Margaret, 167, 175, 211, 222
Hernandez, Aileen, 305–6
Hess, Beth B., 299–300
Hispanics. *See* Latinas; Latinos
Hole, Judith, 63
Holtzman, Elizabeth, 211, 222
homemakers, 27, 79; antifeminism of, 268–69; antisuffragism of, 268–69; and definitions of politics, 249; displaced, 226; female officials as, 41; and the gender gap, 130; and leadership, 86; and life space, 100; and neighborhood politics, 162–63; political participation of, 18, 119–20, 122–24; responsibilities as, 65, 71, 72, 95, 102; and shared parenting, 71, 95; and survival, 129; and the women's movement, 83, 84
honesty, and female officials, 41–42, 192–95; in Santa Clara County, 194–95, 248
hooks, bell, 310, 316–17, 328–29
Hoover, Herbert, 99
House Committee on Science and Technology, 391n. 59
housing, 82, 101, 105, 108
Huerta, Dolores, 333
Hurtado, Aida, 329
husband-wife decisions, 7, 9, 15, 100, 114–15; in Santa Clara County, 194

Ianni, Nancy, 42, 51, 52, 142, 163–64, 172, 173, 183, 186, 192, 245, 248
identity: dual, 329–30; family, 336; national, 13, 97, 334–35, 337; political, 335–37; social vs. individual, 28; vicarious, 5
ideology, 28–29, 30, 75, 77, 83. *See also* conservatism; feminism; liberalism; socialism

income: and feminism, 44; income redistribution, support for, 129; and political participation, 36, 122–24
incumbency and the election of women, 176, 178–79, 181
independence, of women, 91; economic, 65, 78, 130; from men, 130; psychological, 130; and support for women in politics, 156
individualism, 3, 23, 24, 28, 30, 31, 32, 33, 68, 70, 76, 102–3, 105
insider/outsider coalition, xi, 4, 5, 35, 57, 134, 206–7, 221, 302–3; and agenda setting, 253–63; in Santa Clara County, 246
Institute for Women's Policy Research, 275
institutionalism, 9–11, 33, 58, 97–98
interest groups, xi, 4, 10, 19, 22, 24, 77, 96, 98, 101, 110–11; and coalitions, 297–304; and community, 30–31; and mobilization, 57, 88; and movements, 57, 259–60, 263, 265–66; in Santa Clara County, 46–48; women as, 84, 125, 132; and the women's movement, 57, 62, 88
interests: children's, 113; definition of, 109–10; men's self-interest, 22, 129; representation of, 206–7, 233–34, 240; self-interest, 23; women's group interest, 22, 24, 109–10, 113, 127; women's self-interest, 20, 70, 128–31
interpretation, 3, 14, 23, 59
involuntary sterilization, 326–28, 332

Jaggar, Alison M., 27–28
Janigian, Sarah, 142, 188, 192
Jaquette, Jane, 17–20
job programs: for women, 82; support for, 129
Johnson, Lyndon B., 107, 152, 254
Jonasdottir, Anna G., 109–10
Jones, Kathleen, 103
juries, women and, 97, 104, 112
justice, 71, 79, 97; and feminism, 127, 267

Kanter, Rosabeth M., 232
Kathlene, Lyn, 216–20, 270
Katzenstein, Mary Fainsod, 88–89
Kay, Susan Ann, 118
Kelley, Florence, 39
Kelly, Michael, 364n. 24
Kennedy, Ted, 132
Kennedy, John F., 5–6, 80–81, 107, 115, 178, 258

Keys, Martha, 211
King, Mae C., 330
King, Mary, 314
Kingdon, John W., 254–55
kinship networks, 88–89, 102, 107, 328–29
Kirkpatrick, Jeane J., 16, 135–36, 152, 171, 174, 199–204, 208, 216, 223
Klatch, Rebecca E., 267–68
Klein, Ethel, 26–30, 127–29
Krauss, Wilma Rule, 7

labor force participation of women, 6, 71; and the election of women, 180; and the New Right, 266; and political integration, 26; and political participation, 18–19; and women's independence, 272; and the women's movement, 77–79, 127
Ladner, Joyce, 328
Lamson, Peggy, 167
Larsen, Judith K., 45
Latinas, 327, 335–36, 339–53. *See also* Chicanas; Puerto Rican women; undocumented workers
Latinos: and coalitions, 297; and the Democratic party, 350–51; and political participation, 339–40; in Santa Clara County, 47, 50, 51; as a voting bloc, 351
leaders, 116; bureaucratic, 214; charismatic, 14, 214, 264; cult of, 64; men as, 22, 86; styles of, 20; transactional, 87; transforming, 87; women as, 84, 86–87, 237, 242; in women's movement, 80, 83, 84, 86, 264
League of Women Voters, 10, 80, 81, 85, 108, 112, 113, 264; and the ERA, 87, 302; and female officials, 41, 191; as nonpartisan, 99, 174–75; and recruitment of women, 150, 174–75; in Santa Clara County, 46, 91, 142, 145, 173, 186, 192
Lebsock, Suzanne, 98, 113
Lee, Robert, 383n. 142
legislative roles: advertiser, 202; benchwarmer, 159; broker, 198–200; charismatic agitator, 214; delegate, 17, 200–202, 235, 244; female public service, 198–207, 228, 231; housewife benchwarmer, 204–7, 230; innovator, 212, 218–19; inventor, 198–200, 202, 212; lawmaker, 202, 205; leader, 203; male careerism, 198–207, 228, 231; moralizer, 203; passive women's rights

advocate, 204–7; personalizer, 203; politico, 201–2; problem solver, 202, 212, 218; reluctant, 202; ritualist, 198–200, 202; spectator, 202–3, 205; traditional civic worker, 204–7, 230; trustee (tribune), 17, 200–202, 229, 244; women's rights advocate, 204–7
lesbians, 15, 73; and civil rights, 73, 84; and homophobia, 321; and New Right women, 268; and NOW, 84, 87
Levine, Ellen, 63
Lewis, Shirley, 51, 52, 162, 163, 166, 167, 172, 178, 188, 192, 194, 245, 247, 248
liberalism: and citizenship, 76–77; and equality, 74–75; of female officials, 16–17; and feminism, 29, 91; male defection from, 131; public opinion and, 114, in Santa Clara County, 48; sexual, 38; and women, 126–29, 131; in the women's movement, 83, 84
liberty, 4; and feminism, 127; positive and negative, 76
life: and the gender gap, 130; life cycles, 120–21; life spaces, 100–101; preservation of, 70, 71, 72
local officials, female, 150, 239–45, 262–63
Lofgren, Zoe, 41, 166, 172, 178, 188, 192, 194, 245, 248
Lorde, Audre, 308–10, 319
Loucheim, Katie, 9
Lucero, Marcela, 351
Lugones, Maria, 71
Luker, Kristin, 286
Lynn, Naomi B., 121

MacKinnon, Catharine A., 66, 277–79, 284–85
Mahajan, Harpeet, 128–29
Mandel, Ruth, 181–82
Margolis, Diane, 138
marriage: and the gender gap, 130; marriage contract, 76; and political participation, 119–21, 124; and support for feminism, 30; and the women's movement, 77, 79, 128
Marshall, Susan E., 268
Martin, Elaine F., 237–38
Martinez, Sue, 351
maternal thinking, 68, 72, 104, 109
McCloskey, Pete, 93, 144
McCormac, Anne, 92
McCormack, Thelma, 14
McCourt, Kathleen, 108

McEnery, Tom, 50, 178, 184, 246, 247, 249
McGovern, George, 135, 223
McKenna, Dianne, 173, 177, 184
McWilliams, Nancy, 67, 68
meaning, 13, 23, 29, 61, 97, 102; act and action, 58–59; and community, 92; imposed and non-imposed, 3, 4, 16, 17, 23, 34, 59, 69; social, 75
media: female officials and, 196–97, 228; feminist, 84; images of women in, 83, 95, 103; and political parties, 134; and the women's movement, 65, 81–82, 86, 87–88, 95, 126, 133, 135, 223–24, 259–61, 277, 331, 332
mentors, female, 152; of female appointees, 227; in Santa Clara County, 186–88
methodology, 10, 27–28, 31; of "add women," 60; contextual gender analysis, 216–17, 223; engendered (feminist) policy analysis, 219–20, 275–76, 290–96; ethnographic, 13, 69–70, 88–89; and evidence, 60–62; historical, 96–98, 223; intensive interviews, ix, 3,16, 28, 89, 96, 121, 136, 151, 152, 218, 263, 266, 269, 302; linguistic analysis, 217–18; "methodological individualism," 32, 34; participant observation, 3, 69–70, 259, 339; participation with, 339; personal statements, 278; qualitative, 4, 5, 9, 13, 96–98, 181, 340; quantitative, 3, 13, 181, 340; small group studies, 20; survey research 3, 15–16, 27-30, 34, 59, 89, 96–97, 114, 120, 128, 156, 223–24, 340; transcript analysis, 218. *See also* epistemology
Mexican-American Legal Defense and Education Fund, 327
Mexican American Political Association (MAPA), 47, 51, 161
Mid-Peninsula Support Network for Battered Women, 290–92
Mikulski, Barbara, 211, 222, 226
Milbrath, Lester, 114–15
military, women in, 88, 261, 273–74, 288–89
Miller, Arthur H., 130
Miller, Pat, 93, 141, 144, 145
Millet, Kate, 20, 323
Mink, John, 167
Mink, Patsy, 167, 211, 222, 226
Molina, Gloria, 177

Mondale, Walter, 125, 134
moral reform societies, 38–39, 42, 106
moralism, of women, 8, 9, 17, 19, 64, 68, 72
morality and politics, 4, 10, 11, 19, 23, 27, 33–34, 36, 64, 68, 71, 76, 154; and the ERA, 87; and an ethical policy, 68; and New Right women, 267–68
Morgan, Rebecca, 172, 177, 184, 188, 247
mothers, 27, 61; and AFDC, 107; and feminism, 68, 72; and mothering, 31; and peace, 72, 104; and political integration, 26; and political participation, 101, 119–21; surrogate, 76; working, 71, 78
Mott, Lucretia, 78, 80
movements: collective behavior theory of, 267; and countermovements, 265–70; and insider/outsider coalitions, 35–36; and interest groups, 57; policy spirals and, 256; political process theory of, 303–4; and redistributive policies, 258–59; resource mobilization theory of, 256, 260–61, 267, 302–3, 334; rivalries in, 264; social vs. political, xi, 4, 5, 19, 28, 32, 34, 35, 36, 57, 62; strength of, 88
Mueller, Carol McClurg, 189–90

Nadler, Judy, 182
Nation, Carry, 364n. 24
National Abortion Rights Action League (NARAL), 264; PAC of, 181
National American Woman Suffrage Association (NAWSA), 312
National Association for the Advancement of Colored People (NAACP), 82
National Association of Colored Women (NACW), 106, 312
National Black Feminist Organization (NBFO), 331–32
National Council of Jewish Women, 106, 264
National Federation of Republican Women, 176
National Hispanic Feminist Conference, 95, 340–53, 399nn. 117, 118
National Organization for Women (NOW), 6–7, 49, 65, 80–85, 260, 264; and abortion, 82–83, 87, 258, 286; and Bill of Rights for Women, 82, 258, 286, 304; candidate endorsement guidelines of, 88, 143–44; and class, 304–6; and coalitions, 300; and con-

traception, 286; and the Democratic party, 125, 134; and the ERA, 87–88, 124–25, 258, 301, 304–6, 351–52; and female candidates, 180, 189; and female officials, 191; and a female vice-presidential candidate, 316; and the gender gap, 124; leadership in, 87; and the Legal Defense and Education Fund, 279; and lobbying, 134; membership in, 190; PAC of, 190; and Project on Equal Education Rights, 264; and race, 304–6, 317, 331, 352; radical women's groups and, 223; and the Rainbow Coalition, 316; and the Republican party, 134; in Santa Clara County, 47, 91, 92, 93, 142, 192, 250, 352; and sexual harassment, 279; and Shirley Chisholm, 316; and textbook selection, 269; and union women, 304–6; and volunteering, 108
National Violence Survey (1976), 391n. 59
National Welfare Rights Organization, 107–8
National Woman's Party, 81
national women's conference (1977), 122
National Women's Education Fund (NWEF), 189
National Women's Political Caucus (NWPC), 82, 84–86, 88, 194, 264; candidate endorsement guidelines of, 84, 143–44; and the Coalition for Women's Appointments, 185; and female candidates, 189, 191; and female officials, 191; and the 1972 party conventions, 132; PAC of, 190; and political parties, 132; in Santa Clara County, 47, 53, 142, 192, 246, 250, 294, 352; and Shirley Chisholm, 316
Native American women, 324–25, 326–28, 334, 336, 337
native Hawaiian women, 334–35, 337
nature, human, 8, 23, 28; women's 8–9, 11, 15
Nechemias, Carol, 153
neighborhoods, 78; civic duty in, 36, 42; and female officials, 41, 42, 51, 52; and leadership, 86; and networks, 70; in Santa Clara County, 48, 50; and survival, 129; women's politics in, 107, 108
Nelson, Barbara J., 4, 31–32
networks, women's, 49, 88; in Congress, 182; of female candidates, 182; old boys', 86, 207–16; professional, 87; in

Santa Clara County, 94, 95, 141–43, 186–88, 249, 290–96. *See also* communication: communication networks; kinship networks; women's policy networks
New Deal, 107, 210, 266
New Frontier, 81, 107
New Left movement, 11, 65, 67, 79, 80; and the women's movement, 267, 300, 314
New Right movement, 88, 254, 265–70
Nieto, Consuelo, 333
Nixon, Richard M., 6, 111, 254
Noddings, Nel, 217
nuclear power, support for, 129

obligation, political, 68, 102–3
Okar, Mary Rose, 211
older women, 83, 87; public policy and, 282; in Santa Clara County, 93
Olivencia, Nellie, 351
Omolade, Barbara, 310

pacifism, of women, 26, 126–27, 128–31, 274
Palley, Marian Lief, 263–65, 290, 298–99, 302–3
Parent Teachers Association (PTA), 22; and female officials, 41, 175
patriarchy, 24, 69, 71, 73, 76
pay equity (comparable worth) in San Jose, 247, 292–96
peace groups: in Santa Clara County, 47; of women, 72, 86, 274
pensions for women, 92, 93
Perez, Janie, 345
personal is political, ix, 18, 20, 62, 63, 65, 67, 83, 92, 102, 103, 262; and class, 332; and domestic violence, 279; and prejudice, 322; and race, 332
personalization of government, 8, 9, 15, 17, 115–16
Petchesky, Rosalind Pollack, 266
Pitkin, Hanna, 207
Piven, Frances Fox, 273
Pizzey, Erin, 279
Planned Parenthood: and coalitions, 300, 352; in Santa Clara County, 94, 352
pluralist theory, 21–22, 110–11, 208, 265
police: police brutality, 330; and women, 101
policy preferences of women in public office, 150, 197, 198, 203, 219, 228, 229–31, 235, 236, 241, 242, 243, 244

political action committees (PACs): and
women, 181; of women, 134, 182, 189,
190, 264, 269–70
political consciousness, 4, 28, 33, 59, 70;
of working-class women, 108
political culture. *See under* culture
political efficacy, 114; and community organizing, 103; of mothers, 119, 121;
sex differences in, 8, 123; of working-
class women, 108
political integration, women and, 26,
119–21
political machines, 36–39; League of
Women Voters and, 112–13; women
and, 38–39, 108
political mobilization, x, 7; definition of,
57; unobtrusive, 88; of women, 57–95
(Chapter 3), 263
political opportunity structure, 178–80
political participation, x, 7, 16, 17, 18, 28;
definition of, 96; and electoral structure, 50; and feminism, 18–19; of
homemakers, 19; and labor force participation, 18–19; of mothers, 27; sex
differences in, 7; and suffragists, 19; of
wives, 27; of women, 29, 36, 96–145
(Chapter 4)
political parties, xi, 4, 6–7, 45, 49; and
ambition of local activists, 139–40,
157; and antiparty measures, 37, 42,
131; as cue-givers, 134; and definitions of politics, 101–2; and the ERA,
131; gender division of labor in,
138–40; loyalty to, 11, 88, 113, 128;
identification with, 28, 45, 114; and
the media, 134; and motivations of
local activists, 139–40; national committee, members of, 134, 174; and
NWPC, 85; and political mobilization, 57; as programmatic, 134; and
the recruitment of women, 134, 158;
reforms of, 84, 134, 176; and sacrificial lambs, 175–77; in Santa Clara
County, 138, 177–78; sex discrimination in, 138, 175–76; volunteers for,
114, 124, 138–40; and women, 15, 73,
81, 96–99, 131–40, 174–78; and the
women's movement, 57, 88, 133–34;
and women's suffrage, 98. *See also*
convention delegates
political recruitment, x; definition of, 149;
of men, 22; of women, 33, 49, 149–95
(Chapter 5); by women in Santa Clara
County, 142–43; of women in Santa

Clara County, 160–64, 166–67, 172–
73, 177–78, 182–84, 186–88, 192,
194–95
political science, 7, 10, 105–6; and advocacy, 21; gender bias in, 3–34, 58–62,
96–100, 114–16, 151, 198; history of,
3–34; normative, 11; and resistance to
change, ix, 12, 17, 21; as a science,
10–11, 15, 33, 58–60; women in,
12–13, 16, 62–63; and the women's
movement, 3, 5, 15
political stability, 4, 9, 17, 18, 19, 20, 33,
59, 120
political style of women in public office,
86, 196–250 (Chapter 6), 245; bureaucratic styles, 238–39; on city councils,
243–44; distinctive work environment,
237; facilitation vs. control, 219; management styles, 238; in Santa Clara
County, 248
politics: definitions of, xi, 5, 9, 10, 12, 17,
18, 19, 21, 31, 33, 62, 68, 70–71,
101–2, 120, 154; of everyday life, xi,
17, 18, 20, 66, 68, 69, 71, 88, 100, 102,
129, 162, 278; irrational and rational,
14; irregular and regular, 10–11; marketplace vs. moralistic, 207–8; and
protopolitics, 70–71; in Santa Clara
County, 248–50; sex differences in definitions of, 8, 101–3; as social housekeeping, 38–39; and use of force, 154.
See also morality and politics
Poole, Keith, 26, 29–30
population policy, women and, 282
pornography, 66, 73, 87, 103, 129, 283–85
poverty, 78; and antipoverty programs,
107, 126–27; feminization of, x, 105,
106, 282, 323; and the gender gap,
130; opposition to, 11, 38, 84, 87; in
Silicon Valley, 45–46
power, 74, 92; competition for, 30; as empowerment, 4, 33, 34, 74, 242; the
erotic as, 73–74; female public officials' definition of, 197; and gender
relations, 62, 68; partisan differences
in definitions of, 101–2; and political
participation, 101; power to vs. power
over, 4, 33, 74, 104, 239; sex differences in definitions of, 101–2, 110; of
the state, 33–34; and women in Santa
Clara County, 94, 248–49
Pregnancy Discrimination Act (1978),
263–64
presidential elections: of 1928, 99; of

1952, 8, 115; of 1956, 115; of 1960, 6, 115; of 1964, 5, 6; of 1968, 82; of 1972, 117–19, 128; of 1976, 115, 117–19, 128; of 1980, 45, 105, 116–17, 118, 124–25, 128, 266, 351; of 1984, 125
Prewitt, Kenneth, 151
prison reform, women and, 330, 333
professionals: and the election of women, 180; and mobilization, 121; men as, 78; women as, 80, 107–8, 130
Progressives, 4, 21, 79, 98, 107–8; in Santa Clara County, 36–42; and women, 98
prostitution, 38, 76, 83, 106; and female sexual slavery, 281
protective labor laws, 6, 104, 112; and the ERA, 304; and the 1964 Civil Rights Act, 131
protests, 88, 114, 119, 132, 264. *See also* demonstrations
psychology, 20, 21; developmental, 27; identity, 5; object relations theory of, 31; psyche, 20; self-actualization, 65; subconscious, 5
public opinion, 114; of equality for women, 130; of equal sex roles, 89–91; of feminism, 89–91, 131; of motherhood and public office, 136; sex differences in, 29, 100, 126–28; of a woman as president, 17, 48, 155–56; of women as a group, 89–91; of women in Congress, 48; of women in public office, 155–56, 194; of women's emotional suitability for public office, 136, 156; of women's honesty, 192–94; of women's issues, 89–91, 128–31; of the women's movement, 89–91, 131; of women's trustworthiness, 192–94
public opinion polls, ix, 126; male bias in, 17, 99–100; about women's issues, 18, 90–91, 136. *See also* American National Election Studies (ANES)
public-private distinction, x, 4, 18–20, 21, 24, 30, 31, 33, 154–55; and abortion, 287; and interdependence, 68, 70, 92, 102, 113, 120, 154–55
Puerto Rican women (Puertorriqueñas), 326–27, 335, 346–47, 349

Quinn, Laurel U., 25–26

race, 13, 37; and community, 31; and differences among women, 67, 76, 117–18, 123, 304–53; and discrimination, 6, 243, 330; and electoral struc-
ture, 49–50; and the ERA, 304–6; and gender consciousness, 88; and interest groups in Santa Clara County, 47, 50; and NOW, 304–6; public opinion about, 126; and quotas, 330; in Silicon Valley, 46–47, 50–51; and voting, 50. *See also* Asian (Pacific)-American women; black women; Latinas; white women
racism, 11, 84, 308–10, 332
Rankin, Jeannette, 196–97, 226
rape, 83, 91, 103, 265, 282–83, 307, 330, 332
Ray, Dixy Lee, 153
Reagan, Ronald, 53, 86–88, 90, 124–25, 130, 132, 177, 198, 254, 266, 272, 287
Redmund, Donna, 323–24
Redstockings, 63–64, 67
Reed, Sally, 161, 188, 247, 248
Reid, Elizabeth, 15–16
Reingold, Beth Ann, 233–35
religion, 13, 14, 15, 29, 38, 61, 101, 106, 111; and antifeminism, 269–71; Catholic women, 88; and Christian PACs, 269–70; and the civil rights movement, 107; and the ERA, 269; and female officials, 188; and feminism, 270, 271; and the general public, 271; and liberalism, 269, 271; and the New Right, 266, 267, 271; and political culture, 36; and support for women in politics, 156; and survival, 129; women and, 92, 98, 106, 107, 108, 270–71; and the women's movement, 83
representation. *See* legislative roles; women in public office: and representing women
reproduction: artificial, 74; politics of, 21, 25, 61, 68, 76, 86, 103, 110
reproductive rights, 122, 132, 285–86, 325–28, 330. *See also* abortion
Republican party, 6, 45, 52, 88, 98, 126, 132, 133, 266
Rhode, Deborah, 283
Rice, Florence, 307–8
Rich, Adrienne, 318
Richards, Ann, 160, 242
rights, 4, 9, 10, 26, 64, 76, 87, 97, 103; and equality, 74; natural, 78; property, 79. *See also* reproductive rights
Rogers, Barbara, 42
Rogers, Edith Nourse, 220
Rogers, Everett, 45

Roosevelt, Eleanor, 107, 152, 174
Roosevelt, Franklin, 81, 155, 174, 210
Roosevelt, Theodore, 325
Rosenfelt, Deborah, 89
Ross, Nellie Taloe, 153
Rossi, Alice, 364n. 15
Ruddick, Sara, 104, 274
Rule, Wilma, 48–49
Ryden, Lu, 51, 52, 160, 162, 167, 172,
  177, 186, 247, 248

Saint-Germain, Michelle A., 232–34
Salazar, Sandra A., 352–53
Salisbury, Robert, 298
Sandoval, Che, 344, 345
Sanger, Margaret, 68, 326
San Jose, 35; history of, 37–53
San Jose City Council: female majority
  on, 36; and gay rights, 144–45; history
  of female members of, 53
Santa Clara County: development in,
  39–42, 52, 173, 183–84; as a feminist
  capital, ix-xii, 35, 53, 91–95, 245–46,
  249, 294; history of, 36–53; homeowners' associations in, 40, 42, 50, 51, 173;
  political culture of, 36–43
Santa Clara County Board of Supervisors:
  and abortion, 141; female majority on,
  53; and gay rights, 144–45, history of
  female members of, 53
Santa Clara County Commission on the
  Status of Women, 91, 92–94, 141,
  142–43, 246–47; and domestic violence, 290
Sapiro, Virginia, 20–24, 26–28, 30,
  119–121, 373n. 79
Sausedo, Pat, 42, 51, 162, 172, 173, 247
Schlesinger, Joseph A., 157
school(s): boards, 42; textbook selection
  for, 269; women and, 101, 108, 109, 121
Schroeder, Patricia, 17, 164–65, 175, 182,
  211, 222, 287–88
Schuck, Victoria, 9–12
separate spheres, 4, 6, 8, 11, 15, 77–79, 155
settlement houses, 3, 39, 42, 79, 106–7;
  Hull House, 39
sex discrimination, 22, 29, 86, 332; and
  Civil Rights Act (1964), 6, 82, 258; in
  employment, 91, 92, 330; and pregnancy, 261, 263–64; public opinion
  about, 131; in Santa Clara County,
  92–94; by voters, 48
sexism, 24, 64, 68, 84; of men as normal,
  3, 7, 17, 72, 97, 198

sex roles, 7–8, 18, 27–28, 59, 65; egalitarian, 124; traditional, 124
sex-role socialization, 5, 7, 20, 25, 75; and
  campaign fundraising, 181; and countersocialization, 122, 129, 158; and political ambition, 158; and political participation, 116–19, 120, 124; and
  resocialization, 121–22
sexual division of labor, 24, 28, 59, 70, 75,
  77
sexual harassment, x, 92, 103, 270,
  276–79; local female officials and, 263;
  as sex discrimination, 277–79
sexuality, 21, 25, 34, 61, 73, 92, 97, 103
sexual orientation (preference), 67, 76,
  122, 321. *See also* lesbians
Shabad, Goldie, 115
Shaffer, Virginia, 40–41, 173, 187
Shanley, Mary, 9–12
Shapiro, Robert Y., 128–29
Silicon Valley, 40, 42–47, 69, 88–89
Sloan, Margaret, 331
Smeal, Eleanor, 124–25, 190, 351–52
Smith, Al, 99
Smith, Barbara, 320–21
Smith, Beverly, 321
Smith, Margaret Chase, 5, 6, 220
Snowe, Olympia, 287–88
socialism, 81, 98, 107
Social Security, women and, 6, 105
socioeconomic status and political partici-
  pation, 116, 118–19, 122–24, 126
sociology of knowledge, ix, xii, 20–23
Sogg, Joyce, 143
Southern Christian Leadership Confer-
  ence, 107
Spalter-Roth, Roberta, 275
Speier, Jackie, 177
Spellman, Gladys, 211
Spelman, Elizabeth V., 71, 318–19
Stabile, Judy, 173, 178, 183, 192
Stacey, Judith, 69–70, 88–89
Stack, Carol, 328
Stanford, Mrs. Leland, 39
Stanton, Elizabeth Cady, 78, 80, 310–11
state, 4, 15, 96; and family, 10, 71, 271–73;
  loyalty to, 97; military, 4, 96, 103–5,
  271, 273–74; skepticism about, 104;
  state-building, 3, 4; and use of force,
  33, 106, 154; women and, 271–74. *See
  also* welfare state
state legislators, female, 11, 16–17, 152;
  and authorship of legislation, 150,
  218–19, 229, 233, 234; backgrounds of,

149–50, 199; black, 229; and clean government, 228; and coalitions, 219; as committee chairs, 199–200, 219, 228; and committee deliberations, 216, 218, 229, 236; committee membership of, 150, 204, 212, 236; and community needs, 228; and definitions of politics, 207–8; and the ERA, 223, 229–31; and family responsibilities, 150, 165–66, 203–4; and female constituents, 233–35; and female suffrage, 149; feminism of, 205–7, 233, 235; homemaking backgrounds of, 171, 227–28; and interest groups, 228; legislative roles of, 199–201, 202–7, 218–19; legislative strategies of, 234; legislative success of, 212–16, 218, 233, 236; liberalism of, 197, 235; and male colleagues, 16–17, 150, 206, 208–9, 212, 228, 236; occupational backgrounds, 199; and party leadership positions, 212, 219, 228, 236; and political parties, 150, 228, 230; as problem-solvers, 199–200; proportions of, 232–35, 236; and representing women, 206–7, 233–34; and sex discrimination, 150; and staff, 213; and supportive spouses, 165–66; and timing of bid for public office; 165, 206; and voluntarism, 199, 204; and women's caucuses, 206–7, 213, 230–31, 233, 236; and the women's movement, 223, 233; and women's organizations, 149–50, 205–7; and women's traditional concerns, 228–29, 233, 235, 236. *See also* media: female officials and; policy preferences of women in public office
Steinberg, Geraldine, 53, 172, 188, 245
Steinhem, Gloria, 17, 86, 186, 323
Stetson, Dorothy McBride, 276–77
Steuernagel, Gertrude A., 25–30, 360n. 80
Stewart, Debra W., 174–75
Stiehm, Judith Hicks, 104, 273–74, 289
Stolz, Barbara Ann, 324–25
Stone, Lucy, 78
Stowe, Harriet Beecher, 364n. 24
Strober, Myra, 94
Student Non-violent Coordinating Committee (SNCC), 64, 67, 313–16, 331
Sullivan, Leonor, 175, 222

Tannen, Deborah, 13
Tanner, Nancy, 328
temperance movement, 3, 78–79

Third World Women's Alliance, 331
Thompson, Joan Hulse, 201–2
Tinker, Irene, 261
Tolchin, Martin, 16
Tolchin, Susan, 16
transformational approach, 13, 16, 17, 18, 25, 31–34, 96, 101, 103, 110, 114, 157, 158, 172, 197, 198, 216, 256, 275–76, 281, 282, 297, 304, 306; definition of, x, 13; need for, x, 33–34
Trask, Haunani-Kay, 334–35
Tronto, Joan, 32, 72
Trounstine, Philip J., 38, 40
Truth, Sojourner, 78, 311
trust: citizenship and, 103; female officials and, 42, 192–95; in Santa Clara County, 194–95; voting and, 116; women and, 119; women's organizations and, 113

understanding, 3, 7, 14, 21, 23, 71, 75
undocumented workers, 346; rights of, 333; in Santa Clara County, 46; women as, 347
unemployment: and black women, 330; public opinion about, 126; unemployment benefits, 105
unions, 111: and coalitions, 300; and the Equal Pay Act, 289; and the ERA, 6, 81, 304–6; as a movement, 88; and protective labor laws, 6; in Santa Clara County, 46–47, 50; women in, 82, 106, 107, 267; women in the Coalition of Labor Union Women, 352; women in the United Auto Workers, 304–5
United Nations: Conference on Women (1980), 281; and female sexual slavery, 281
United States Supreme Court, decisions about women's issues: *American Booksellers Association v. Hudnut* (1985), 284–85; *General Electric v. Gilbert,* 264; *Griswold v. Connecticut* (1965), 285; *Gunther v. County of Washington, Oregon* (1981), 293; *Meritor Savings Bank v. Vinson,* 278–79; *Miller v. California* (1973), 283; *Roe v. Wade,* 266, 285, 287, 326; *Roth v. United States* (1956), 283; upholding state restrictions on access to abortion, 287, 327

Van Buren, Martin, 98
violence, 26, 74, 84; women's opinions about, 126, 128–29. *See also* pacifism

violence against women, 27, 60, 66, 263, 265, 279–81, 283–85. *See also* domestic violence; rape

voluntarism (volunteerism), of women, 4, 10, 31, 32, 41, 78, 80, 87, 108, 111–13, 117, 137, 169–70, 173

voluntary associations, 110–14; class and, 78, 111; definition of, 110; and democracies, 110–11; female officials and, 199; first-wave women and, 80; membership in, 107; race and, 111; women and, 4, 31, 34, 87, 96, 111, 113, 121, 124, 125

voting, 114; registration for, 45, 51, 107, 112, 114, 125, 313; restrictions to, 37; turnout for, 37, 45, 98, 114, 115, 119, 122; and voluntary organizations, 111; Voting Rights Act (1965), 49; women and, xi, 6, 7, 11, 14, 97, 113, 115, 124, 125, 132, 155

Wallace, Lurleen, 153

war, 3, 8; and citizenship, 103–4, 273–74; just, 274; Korean, 8; and masculinity, 274; opposition to, 11, 72, 274; and women, 72–73, 97, 126–27; World War I, 6, 141

Washington, Cynthia, 314–16

Waters, Maxine, 193–94

Watson, Diane, 306

Weddington, Sarah, 351

welfare, 76, 105; sex differences in welfare benefits, 104; support for welfare programs, 129; welfare reform, 282, 330, 333; women and, 101, 104

welfare state, 4, 5, 32, 76, 96, 103, 104–5, 130, 140–41, 268, 271–74

Wells, Ida B., 312

white women, 78; and feminism, 117–18, 331; and political identity, 335–37; and political participation, 117–18; and privilege, 11, 317–19

Wilcox, Clyde, 90, 270

Willard, Frances, 38

Williams, Iola, 42, 50, 53, 163, 166, 167, 172, 187, 188, 247

Willis, Ellen, 63

Wilson, Kathy, 88

Wilson, Susanne, 41, 42, 44, 53, 141–42, 173, 182, 187–88, 192, 195, 245

WISH List, 190

Wollstonecraft, Mary, 102

Woman's Alliance (WOMA), 92, 246, 290, 294

women and politics, as an academic field of study, xi, 12, 32

women in public office: and citizen involvement, 235; and consciousness raising, 206; and contextualism vs. instrumentalism, 217–20; and credit for legislation, 215–16; critical mass of, 218; and definitions of politics, 207–8; and definitions of power, 197; and electoral structure, 48–53; female consciousness of, 220; feminism of, 197, 205–6, 233, 235–39, 245; as governors, 153; historical patterns in number of, 152–53; and homemaking skills, 162–64; and homework, 213, 216, 244; and honesty, 242; and legislative success, 197, 212–16, 231, 233; liberalism of, 197–98, 235, 245; majorities of, 36, 53, 218, 244, 249, 292–93; male careerism vs. female public service, 197–207, 227; in national legislatures, 48; number of, x, xi, 11, 42, 53, 84, 151, 152, 196, 204, 232; and open governmental processes, 235; and parenting skills, 162–64; and party leadership positions, 219, 236; as policy experts, 199–200, 204; and political culture, 153; power styles of, 215; and preparation, 213, 216, 237; and prestige of office, 152, 153; as problem solvers, 197, 202–4, 208; proportion of, 231–35, 240, 292–93; and representing women, 206–7, 233–34, 240; and responsiveness to new groups, 235–36; and role conflict, 206; as role models, 203, 214, 240; in Santa Clara County, 245; sisters vs. queen bees, 186, 232, 242; as soft, 209; and staff, 213; in state legislatures, 48–49; and supportive spouses, 165–66, 167; as tokens, 232–34, 236, 240; as trustworthy, 242; and volunteer skills, 162–64; voter preference for, 193–95; and women's caucuses, 207, 213, 236; and women's traditional concerns, 224–25, 233, 245; as working hard, 212, 213, 216, 237, 240–42. *See also* appointees, female; congresswomen; legislative roles; local officials, female; media, female officials and; policy preferences of women in public office; political style of women in public office; state legislators, female

women of color, 71, 107–8, 111, 263, 300, 304–53

Women's Bureau, 260; and the ERA, 305
Women's Campaign Fund, 88, 189, 190, 264
Women's Caucus for Political Science, APSA's, 12, 63
Women's Christian Temperance Union (WCTU), 38, 78, 99, 106, 150
Women's Equity Action League (WEAL), 81–82, 84–85, 223, 260, 264
Women's Health Equity Act (1990), 288
Women's International League for Peace and Freedom (WILPF), 47, 140–41
women's movement: and agenda setting, 253–59, 264–65; and birth control, 325–28; bureaucracy in, 86, 264; and coalitions, 264–65, 299–304; as democratic, 77; and elected officials, 17, 49, 51, 248; and fertility patterns, 127; first- wave, 64–65, 74–76, 77–80, 104; and interest groups, 57–58; and lobbying, 264–65, 302–4; as moral and political climate, 19, 190, 260–61; as the Nylon Revolution, 136; and period between waves, 81; and policymaking, 18–19; as political, ix, x, 3, 62, 77; and political elites, 132; and political parties, 57, 58, 133–34; and political science, 3, 12; pro-woman line of, 63, 65; radicals vs. moderates, 85, 133, 188–89, 223, 302; second-wave, xii, 5, 6, 7, 11, 13, 28, 62–66, 74–75, 77–91, 133–34; and the study of politics, ix-xii; and subgovernments (iron triangles), 134; and support for women in public office, 155–56; and survival issues, 325; and the tyranny of structurelessness, 86; of the United States compared to Europe, 57, 133–34; and the value of women's unpaid work, 162; and the White House, 259–60; women's opposition to, 223; and women's policy networks, 259–65; and women's studies, ix, 60;

women's support for, 89–91, 119. *See also* media: and the women's movement
women's organizations, 77–87, 188–92, 264
women's policy agenda, xi, 7, 19, 91, 109, 237, 253, 254–63
women's policy networks, 19, 259–63, 289–90
women's rights conventions, 80, 310–11
Women's Strike for Equality (1970), 81, 83, 264, 331
women's studies, 31; concepts of, ix, 53; courses in, 65; and female political scientists, 16, 23; as ideological, 30; journals in, 16; and women's movement, ix, 88
women's suffrage, 3, 4, 5, 9, 10, 15, 19, 37, 39, 58, 74–75, 78–79, 81, 154; and political parties, 98, 311; and race, 310–13, 330; and voluntary motherhood, 285
work, 76, 79; and flexible schedules, 71, 261, 282; and glass ceiling, 282; and leadership, 86; nonmarket, 75, 162, 282; pregnancy and, 282; productive, 19; reproductive risks at, 282; and role expansion, 108; sex segregation of, 70, 282; women's 19, 60. *See also* family leave
Wright, Fanny, 79, 98
Wurr, Anne, 290–92

Yamada, Mitsuye, 320
Year of the Woman, in 1975, 135; in 1992, 232
Young, Andrew, 107
Young, Louise M., 97–98
Young Women's Christian Association (YWCA), 41, 188

Zeigler, L. Harmon, 26, 29–30
Zinn, Maxine Baca, 336

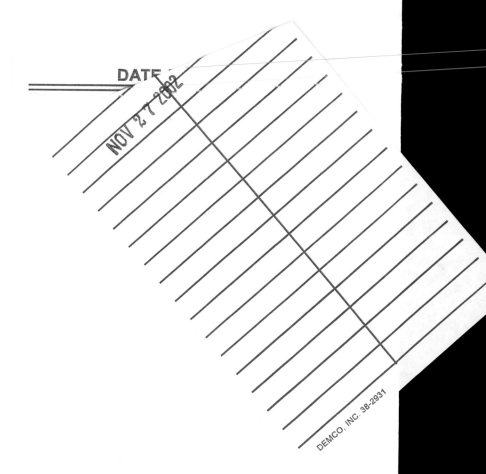